PHYSICS OF SEMICONDUCTOR DEVICES

Physics of Semiconductor Devices

Dilip K Roy

Universities Press

Universities Press (India) Private Limited

Registered Office
3-6-747/1/A & 3-6-754/1, Himayatnagar,
Hyderabad 500 029 (A.P.), India
e-mail: info@universitiespress.com

Distributed by
Orient Blackswan Private Limited

Registered Office
3-6-752, Himayatnagar, Hyderabad 500 029 (A.P.), India

Other Offices
Bangalore / Bhopal / Bhubaneshwar / Chennai
Ernakulam / Guwahati / Hyderabad / Jaipur / Kolkata
Lucknow / Mumbai / New Delhi / Patna

First Published 1992
Reprinted 1999, 2000, 2001, 2002
Second edition 2004
Reprinted 2008, 2009, 2011, 2013

ISBN: 978 81 7371 494 8

Typeset by
Krishtel eMaging Solutions, Chennai 600 017

Printed in India at
Orion Printers Private Limited
Hyderabad 500 004

Published by
Universities Press (India) Private Limited
3-6-747/1/A & 3-6-754/1, Himayatnagar
Hyderabad 500 029 (A.P), India

Contents

Preface to the second edition

The warm response received by the first edition of this book has encouraged the author to present this revised edition. The basic outline of the book and its underlying philosophy however remain unchanged. The principal changes in this edition are the rewriting of several sections of various chapters. The discussions on "quantum mechanical tunnelling" have been updated. Most of the problems in the last edition have been retained and a large number of problems have been added both as solved examples and as unsolved exercises. Appendices containing material on amorphous semiconductors and technology of semiconductors and devices have been added. I have sought to incorporate all pedagogical improvements suggested by students and teachers who have used this text. This revision, I hope, will make this book more useful to the students and teachers concerned.

DILIP KUMAR ROY

Gurgaon
April, 2004

Preface

This book is intended as an introduction to the physics of semiconductors and devices for advanced undergraduate and postgraduate students of physics, electronics and electrical engineering. The main prerequisite for studying the material in this book is an elementary knowledge of solid state physics, quantum mechanics and electronics. The emphasis here is on the essential physical principles involved. The theoretical and mathematical approaches have therefore been kept as simple and intuitive as possible.

The contents are organized in a logical sequence. First, a detailed account of the physics of semiconductors and of *pn* junctions is presented. The reader is next introduced to transistors and their basic applications. Schottky barriers, the metal-insulator-semiconductor and related devices are dealt with thereafter. Finally, the new theory on quantum mechanical tunnelling and its applications to semiconductor tunnel devices is presented.

The ideas on tunnelling have been developed on the basis of the principles of quantum measurement and observations. Two research monographs written by me, titled 'Tunnelling and Negative Resistance Phenomena in Semiconductors' and 'Quantum Mechanical Tunnelling and its Applications' have already appeared. They have been published by Pergamon Press, Oxford, and World Scientific Publishing Co., Singapore in 1977 and 1986 respectively. This book differs from the rest in the field in its treatment of tunnel devices.

Every chapter begins with a brief introduction. Subsequent sections present the physical and mathematical analyses of various devices. A large number of solved examples are included in each chapter to illustrate the methods of solution. The exercises, on the other hand, are designed to test the student's knowledge of the topics dealt with in that chapter. In an introductory text of this nature, it was not thought necessary to give a comprehensive and up-to-date list of references. However, a list of references has been appended at the end of each chapter to guide the interested reader to greater depths of knowledge.

An outline for the reader

We shall now present a brief survey of the material covered. Chapter 1 introduces the reader to the physics of semiconductor materials. This includes discussions on energy bands, mobility and diffusivity of carriers, intrinsic and impurity doped semiconductors, lifetime of carriers and the mechanism of their recombinations, dielectric relaxation, the Gunn effect and superlattice devices.

Chapter 2 discusses *pn* junctions. Abrupt and linearly graded varieties are analyzed and expressions for built-in-potential, depletion-layer width, maximum junction field intensity, space-charge layer capacitance, etc. are derived. It has been shown how, by employing different diode characteristics, it is possible to arrive at a number of their applications, such as in solar cells, IMPATT devices, semiconductor lasers, etc.

Chapter 3 develops the physics of transistors and their equivalent circuits. Low and high-frequency transistors as well as their switching behaviours are presented here. Related devices such as FET, UJT, thyristor, etc. are also analyzed in detail.

Chapter 4 summarizes the physics of Schottky barriers and the metal-insulator-semiconductor junctions. Their applications to the design of MOSFET, MESFET, MIS solar cells, etc. are considered.

Chapter 5 analyzes quantum mechanical tunnelling on the ideas of quantum measurement and observations and applies it to derive the *I-V* characteristics of tunnel devices.

To the instructor

The book contains sufficient material for a one-semester course (of about 50 lecture hours). The introduction of Chapters 1 to 5 is very simple and straightforward. Proper understanding of Chapter 5, however, demands a good knowledge of quantum mechanics. For a qualitative knowledge of the physics of tunnel devices one need not, however, understand the mathematical theory of tunnel effect in depth. The contents of this chapter therefore need to be handled very carefully and according to the requirements of the students concerned.

DILIP K. ROY

Acknowledgements

I wish to express my appreciation for the help rendered by a number of individuals in the preparation of this book. My ideas on quantum mechanical tunnelling and semiconductor devices were shaped over a number of years while teaching M.Sc and M.Tech students at I.I.T., Delhi. Some of the original contributions presented in this book originated over a number of years as a result of research collaboration with my doctoral students at I.I.T., Delhi. It has been a real pleasure working with the editors at Universities Press throughout the preparation of the manuscript. They provided the required motivation for the improvement of the quality and presentation at various stages. Last but not least, I wish to thank my family members for their moral support and understanding. I will consider my efforts amply rewarded if this book is found useful to those for whom it is intended.

DILIP K. ROY

List of symbols

Symbol	Description and unit
a	Acceleration (m/s^2), lattice constant (Å), impurity gradient (m^{-4}), FET channel width (m)
a_B	Bohr radius (Å)
A	Junction area (m^2), Gain (dB), Richardson's constant ($A/°K^2$), a constant
A^*	Richardson's constant
b	Lattice constant (Å), FET channel width (m)
B	Magnetic flux density (T), a constant
c	Velocity of light (m/s)
C	Capacitance (F), a constant
d	Spacing (m)
D	Diffusion coefficient (m^2/s), a constant
E	Energy (eV)
E_c	Conduction band edge (eV)
E_v	Valence band edge (eV)
E_F	Fermi energy level (eV)
E_G	Energy gap (eV)
ε	Electric field intensity (V/m)
f_B	Bloch frequency (Hz)
f	Fraction, flux ($m^{-2} \cdot s^{-1}$), frequency (Hz), Fermi-function
$f(E), f_{t0}$	Fermi-Dirac distribution function
F	Electric force
f_m	Maximum frequency of oscillation (Hz)
FF	Fill factor
g_0	Generation rate ($m^{-3} \cdot s^{-1}$)
g	Reciprocal lattice vector (m^{-1})
g_m	Transconductance (ohm^{-1})
G	Basic reciprocal lattice vector (m^{-1}), conductance
h	Planck's constant ($\hbar = h/2\pi$) ($J \cdot s$)
H	Hamiltonian operator
i	$(-1)^{1/2}$
I	Current (A), intensity ($m^{-2} \cdot s^{-1}$)
I_d	Drain current
J	Current density (A/m^2)

J_{01}, J_{02}	Current density coefficients (A · m)
$\boldsymbol{k}, \boldsymbol{k}_0$	Wave vectors (m^{-1})
k	Boltzmann constant (J/°K)
l	Spacing (m)
L	Length (m), inductance (Henry)
L_d	Characteristic Debye length (m)
m	A number, electron mass (kg)
m^*	Electron effective mass (kg)
M	Mass (kg), carrier multiplication rate (s^{-1}), matrix element
n	Density of free electrons (m^{-3})
n_i	Intrinsic carrier density (m^{-3})
N	Doping concentration (m^{-3})
N_d	Donor concentration (m^{-3})
N_a	Acceptor concentration (m^{-3})
N_c	Effective density of states in the conduction band (m^{-3}
N_i	Impurity density
N_v	Effective density of states in the valence band (m^{-3})
p	Hole density (m^{-3})
P	Electric power (V · A), momentum (kg · m s^{-1}), probability
q	Electronic charge (Coul)
Q	Electric charge (Coul)
R	Radius (m), resistance (ohm), recombination rate ($m^{-3} \cdot s^{-1}$), reflection coefficient
R_L	Load resistance (ohm)
R_H	Hall coefficient ($m^3 \cdot coul^{-1}$)
r_H	Impurity Bohr radius (Å)
S	Standard deviation $= j\omega$, where $j = (-1)^{1/2}$
t	Thickness (m), time (s)
T	Absolute temperature (°K), time part of the wave function
$T_{ll}, T_{lr}, T_{rl}, T_{rr}$	Transition matrix elements (eV-m)
u_ν	Electromagnetic energy density function ($J \cdot m^{-3} \cdot s^{-1}$)
v, v_x, v_{ox}	Thermal velocity of carriers (m/s)
v, v_d, v_i, v_j	Electron velocity (m/s)
V_c	Contact potential (V)
V_0	Height of a potential barrier (eV)
$V(r)$	Electron potential energy (eV)
V_g	Gate potential (V)
V_{bi}	Built-in potential (V)

V_B	Breakdown voltage (V)
V_d	Drain voltage (V)
W	Depletion layer width (m)
$W_{11}, W_{12}, W_{21}, W_{22}$	Matrix elements (eV)
x	Distance (m)
Y	Admittance (ohm^{-1})
Z	Impedance (ohm), tunnelling probability
α	Absorption coefficient (m^{-1}), carrier multiplication rate (m^{-1}), common-base current gain, constant
α^*	Collector multiplication factor
β	q/kT (V^{-1}), common-emitter current gain, a constant
β^*	Transport factor
δ, δ_0	Distance (m)
ϵ_0	Permittivity of vacuum (F/m)
ϵ_s	Semiconductor permittivity (F/m)
ϵ_i	Insulator permittivity (F/m)
$\epsilon_s/\epsilon_o = \epsilon_{s0}$	Dielectric constant
ϕ_0	Neutral level
γ	Phase difference (radians), emitter efficiency
λ	Wavelength (Å), screening constant (m^{-1})
μ	Refractive index, carrier mobility ($m^2 \cdot V \cdot s^{-1}$), amplification factor
μ_0	Permeability of vacuum (H/m)
μ_n, μ_p	Electron and hole mobilities respectively
ν	Frequency (Hz)
η	Efficiency of a solar cell, intrinsic stand-off ratio
ω	Angular frequency (rad/s)
Ω	Volume of the electrode (m^3)
ρ	Resistivity (ohm-m), charge density
$\rho\,(E)$	Density of states function (m^{-3} J^{-1})
σ	Angular frequency (rad/s), electrical conductivity (ohm^{-1}-m^{-1})
σ_a	Capture cross-section (m^2)
τ_n, τ_p	Electron and hole lifetimes (s)
τ, τ_i	Electron tunnelling times (s)
ϕ	Fermi potential, phase difference (rad)
ϕ_1, ϕ_2, ϕ_3	Line voltages (V)
ϕ_m, ϕ_s	Metal and semiconductor work functions (eV)
$\phi_{Bn}, \phi_{Bp}, \phi_{Bi}$	Potential barrier heights (V)
ψ	Wave function, Electrostatic potential (V)
ψ_s	Surface potential (V)
χ	Penetration constant

1 Semiconductor physics

This chapter presents a brief introduction to the physics of semiconductor materials. Semiconductors belong to a class of solids whose resistivity is intermediate to those of metals and insulators. Semiconductors are known to possess resistivities ranging from 10^{-3} ohm cm to 10^{8} ohm cm. Elemental semiconductors viz., Germanium (Ge) and Silicon (Si) are found in column IV of the periodic table. Compound semiconductors may be realized by combining elements of groups III & V (e.g., GaAs) and also elements of groups II and VI (e.g., ZnS) of the periodic table. The energy gaps of Ge, Si and GaAs at 0 K are 0.74, 1.17 and 1.52 eV respectively. Electrical conduction in semiconductors arises due to the presence of a continuum of allowed energy levels in them in the form of bands. Normally, electrons, cannot acquire energies as large as the energy gaps of semiconductors from externally applied electric fields, to be field-ionized from the valence band directly into the conductance band. But, even under room temperature conditions (~ 300 K), some of the valence electrons do acquire enough thermal energies to break their bonds, be ionized thermally and move freely in the conduction band. The resulting vacancy so created in the valence structure may be identified with a positive electronic charge and is called a hole. Electrons may also be excited from the valence to the conduction band by optical means. Both electrons and holes move in response to an applied electric field and a concentration gradient. Resulting motions of carriers can then be explained in terms of drift and diffusion phenomena respectively.

Semiconductors, in their natural crystalline forms are known as intrinsic semiconductors. If traces of certain known chemical impurities ($\sim$1 part in a billion) are introduced in them, they give rise to energy levels lying within the energy gaps, closer to the band edges. These impurities are able to control the semiconductor's conductivity over wide limits. Such a variability in their electrical conductivity makes semiconductors natural choices for electronic device investigations. It is also interesting to note that the particular nature of the temperature dependence of the semiconductor's conductivity can be used to distinguish it from metals.

Carriers in semiconductors are constantly in the process of generation and recombination. Hence, they have an average or mean life which is called the carrier lifetime. The carrier recombination process is generally mediated by deep level energy states within the energy gap which are called traps. The physics of carrier recombination through trap levels, as worked out by Shockley and his co-workers, is presented in this chapter. In the early days of semiconductor research, Ge was widely used to produce diodes and transistors. Nowadays, Si is mostly used for rectifiers, transistors and integrated circuits. However, compound semiconductors (e.g., GaAs) are employed for high speed and light emitting devices. Fluorescent materials, such as those used in television screens are usually II–VI compound semiconductors (e.g., ZnS). Photodetectors are usually made up of InSb, CdSe, PbTe, HgCdTe etc. Important devices like Gunn diodes and those based on quantum wells are also made up of binary, ternary and quaternary III–V semiconducting alloys. The operations of Gunn and superlattice devices, which are dependent on the bulk properties of semiconductors are also discussed in this chapter.

1.1 Energy bands

(a) A qualitative analysis

X-ray diffraction studies convincingly reveal that most of the naturally occurring solids are crystalline in nature and that they consist of an array of atoms formed by a regular repetition of a basic structural unit in space. The electronic energy levels of individual atoms of the solids then no longer represent the energy levels of electrons inside the crystal. Once a crystal is formed, it is found that the energy levels of the inner-shell electrons of atoms are not affected appreciably, but those of the outer-shell ones are, because they are shared by more than one atom of the crystal. The new and modified set of energy levels of the outer-shell electrons may however be calculated by using techniques based on wave mechanics. As a result of such an attempt, we find that the coupling among the outer-shell electrons of atoms results in a band of closely spaced electronic energy levels. Before undertaking such an analysis, we first present a qualitative description of the formation of energy bands in a semiconductor crystal. Let us consider a Si or a Ge crystal. The outer subshell of the atom of such an element is chemically known to contain $2s$ and $2p$-electrons. Imagine such a crystal to be formed of N atoms such that it is possible to vary the interatomic spacing between any two of them. When the atoms are situated very far apart, the electrostatic interaction among them is quite small. In such a case, the electronic energy levels of isolated atoms inside the crystal may be regarded to merge with one another. The electronic energy levels of the crystal will then be the same as those of the isolated atoms. Hence, if the inner-shell electrons of the atoms are completely ignored, there are $2N$ electrons completely filling $2N$ s-levels and another $2N$ electrons partially filling $6N$ p-levels above them. This has been illustrated in Fig. 1.1(a). Now, if the interatomic spacing of our imaginary crystal is gradually reduced, the forces exerted by atoms on electrons bound to the adjacent nuclei are no longer negligible. In that case, the electronic wave functions of individual atoms overlap one another and the crystal becomes a single electronic unit which must obey Pauli's exclusion principle. As a result, the $2N$ electronic states originally belonging to the same energy level must now spread out in the energy space in order to accommodate the $2N$ electrons, so that Pauli's exclusion principle continues to be obeyed. The separation between the consecutive energy levels of the group so formed will however be very small since N is usually around 10^{29} m^{-3}. Such a group of closely spaced energy levels is called an energy band which is indicated by the shaded regions in Fig. 1.1(a). The $2N$ states in the lower band are completely filled with $2N$ s-electrons. The upper band of $6N$ states are however partially filled with $2N$ p-electrons. It may now be noticed in Fig. 1.1(a) that there is an energy gap between the two groups of levels which first decreases with decrease in the atomic spacing. When the interatomic distance becomes too small, the bands may eventually overlap one another as shown in Fig. 1.1(b). In that case, the $6N$ upper states merge with the $2N$ lower ones giving rise to a total of $8N$ allowed states. But, owing to the scarcity of electrons, only half of these energy levels viz., $4N$ of them which are the lowermost ones, will be occupied at 0 K. Each atom of the crystal may then be presumed to contribute four electrons to the lower band. These electrons are capable of moving inside the crystal under suitable circumstances. They can no

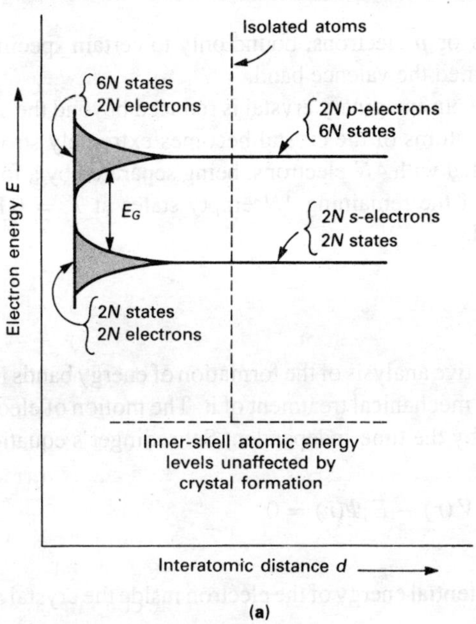

Figure 1.1 *Formation of energy bands in a semiconductor crystal: (a) electron energy E vs interatomic spacing d (for $d >$ lattice spacing)*

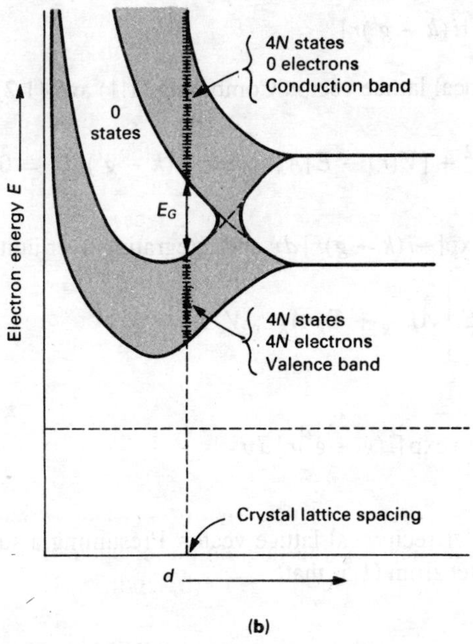

Figure 1.1 *continued (b) electron energy E vs interatomic spacing d ($d \sim a$)*

longer be treated either as s or p electrons, bound only to certain specific atoms. The band in which these electrons reside is termed the valence band.

When the atomic distance in our imaginary crystal is reduced beyond the stage when bands overlap, the interaction among different atoms of the crystal becomes extremely strong. As shown in Fig. 1.1(b), we find the valence band filled with $4N$ electrons, being separated by a forbidden energy gap E_G from an empty band consisting of the remaining $4N$ empty states at $T = 0\,\mathrm{K}$. The upper vacant band is termed the conduction band.

(b) Quantitative analysis

Having presented the qualitative analysis of the formation of energy bands in crystals, we next proceed to undertake a simplified wave mechanical treatment of it. The motion of electrons inside a semiconductor crystal may be represented by the time-independent Schrodinger's equation viz.,

$$-\left(\frac{\hbar^2}{2m}\right)\nabla^2\Psi(r) + [V(r) - E]\Psi(r) = 0 \tag{1.1}$$

where $V(r)$ measures the potential energy of the electron inside the crystal and ∇^2 denotes the Laplacian in the polar form given by

$$\nabla^2 = \left(\frac{1}{r^2}\right)\left(\frac{\partial}{\partial r}\right)\left(\frac{r^2\partial}{\partial r}\right) + \left[\frac{1}{(r^2\sin\theta)}\right]\left(\frac{\partial}{\partial\theta}\right)\left[\sin\theta\left(\frac{\partial}{\partial\theta}\right)\right] + \left[\frac{1}{(r^2\sin^2\theta)}\left(\frac{\partial^2}{\partial\phi^2}\right)\right]$$

The electronic wave function satisfying (1.1) may however be expressed in the Bloch form viz.,

$$\Psi(r) = \Sigma_{g'} A_{\boldsymbol{k}-g'} \exp[i(\boldsymbol{k} - g')r] \tag{1.2}$$

where g' denotes the reciprocal lattice vector. Combining (1.1) and (1.2), we get

$$\Sigma_{g'}\left[\left(\frac{\hbar^2}{2m}\right)(k - g')^2 + [V(r) - E]A_{\boldsymbol{k}-g'}\exp[i(\boldsymbol{k} - g')r]\right] = 0 \tag{1.3}$$

Now, multiplying (1.3) by $\exp[-i(\boldsymbol{k} - g)r]\,dv$ and integrating over unit cell volume Ω, we get

$$\left[\left(\frac{\hbar^2}{2m}\right)(k - g)^2 - E\right]A_{\boldsymbol{k}-g} + \Sigma_{g'} A_{\boldsymbol{k}-g'} V_{g-g'} = 0 \tag{1.4}$$

where

$$V_{g-g'} = \left(\frac{1}{\Omega}\right)\int_{\text{cell}} V(r)\exp[i(g - g')r]\,dv \tag{1.5}$$

g in (1.5) denotes a particular reciprocal lattice vector. Presuming a suitable mathematical form for $V(r)$, it is not difficult to infer from (1.5) that

$$V_{g-g'} \propto \left[\frac{1}{(g - g')^2}\right] \tag{1.6}$$

Thus $V_{g-g'}$ is expected to be smaller for larger values of $(g - g')$.

The boundaries of the first Brillouin zone are located at $\pm(G/2)$ where G measures the basic reciprocal lattice vector. If we now shift our origin of the wave vector to the zone boundary $+(G/2)$, the new wave vector $\boldsymbol{k}_0$ may be expressed as

$$\boldsymbol{k}_0 = \boldsymbol{k} - \left(\frac{G}{2}\right) \tag{1.7}$$

With this new wave vector, (1.4) reduces to

$$[E^0_{k_0+(G/2)-g} - E'(k_0)]A_{k_0+(G/2)-g} + \Sigma_{g'} A_{k_0+(G/2)-g'} V_{g-g'} = 0 \tag{1.8}$$

where E^0 represents the free electron energy corresponding to a particular wave vector while $E'(k_0)$ measures the energy as a function of the new wave vector. Since $V_{g-g'}$ decreases very sharply with increasing g', we will simply consider $(g - g') = \pm G$. We would therefore first set $g = 0$ and $g' = G$, and next $g = G$ and $g' = 0$ in (1.8). We then get the following two equations

$$[E^0_{k_0+(G/2)} - E'(k_0)]A_{k_0+(G/2)} + A_{k_0-(G/2)} V_{-G} = 0 \tag{1.9}$$

and

$$[E^0_{k_0-(G/2)} - E'(k_0)]A_{k_0-(G/2)} + A_{k_0+(G/2)} V_{G} = 0 \tag{1.10}$$

The higher terms in (1.9) and (1.10) obtained as a result of Bragg scatterings by larger reciprocal vectors have been ignored. The above pair of equations, therefore, considers the interactions between the two adjoining bands centered around the zone boundary. Eliminating the constants from the above pair of equations, we get the following determinant

$$\begin{vmatrix} E^0_{k_0+(G/2)} - E'(k_0)] & V_{-G} \\ V_G & [E^0_{k_0-(G/2)} - E'(k_0) \end{vmatrix} = 0 \tag{1.11}$$

It follows from (1.5) that $V_{-G} = V_{G*}$, the complex conjugate of V_G. Expanding (1.11) we then get

$$E'^2(k_0) - E'(k_0)[E^0_{k_0+(G/2)} + E^0_{k_0-(G/2)}] + E^0_{k_0+(G/2)} E^0_{k_0-(G/2)} = |V_G|^2 \tag{1.12}$$

The solution to this quadratic equation follows to be

$$E'(k_0) = \left(\frac{1}{2}\right)[E^0_{k_0+(G/2)} + E^0_{k_0-(G/2)}] \pm \left(\frac{1}{2}\right)[E^0_{k_0+(G/2)} - E^0_{k_0-(G/2)}]^2 + 4|V_G|^2]^{1/2} \tag{1.13}$$

Restricting ourselves to smaller wave vector values (i.e. $k_0 \ll G/2$), (1.13) reduces to

$$E'(k_0) = E^0\left(\frac{G}{2}\right) \pm \left(\frac{1}{2}\right)\left[\left\{4\left(\frac{\hbar^2 k_0}{2m}\right)\left(\frac{G}{2}\right)\right\}^2 + 4|V_G|^2\right]^{1/2}$$

$$E(\boldsymbol{k}_0) = E'(\boldsymbol{k}_0) - E^0\left(\frac{G}{2}\right) = \pm(s^2 k_0^2 + |V_G|^2)^{1/2} \tag{1.14}$$

where

$$s = \left(\frac{\hbar^2 G}{2m}\right) \tag{1.15}$$

Since $\boldsymbol{k}_0$ is small, we may expand (1.14) binomially and ignore higher powers to obtain

$$E(\boldsymbol{k}_0) = \pm|V_G|\left[1 + \left(\frac{s^2 k_0^2}{2}|V_G|^2\right)\right]^{1/2} \tag{1.16}$$

Thus $E(\boldsymbol{k}_0)$ as a function of $\boldsymbol{k}_0$ is given by (1.16) and plotted in Fig. 1.2. Such an energy band representation is particularly suitable for semiconductors and is well-known as the two-band model. The uppermost band may be identified with the conduction band and the lowermost one with the valence band of a semiconductor.

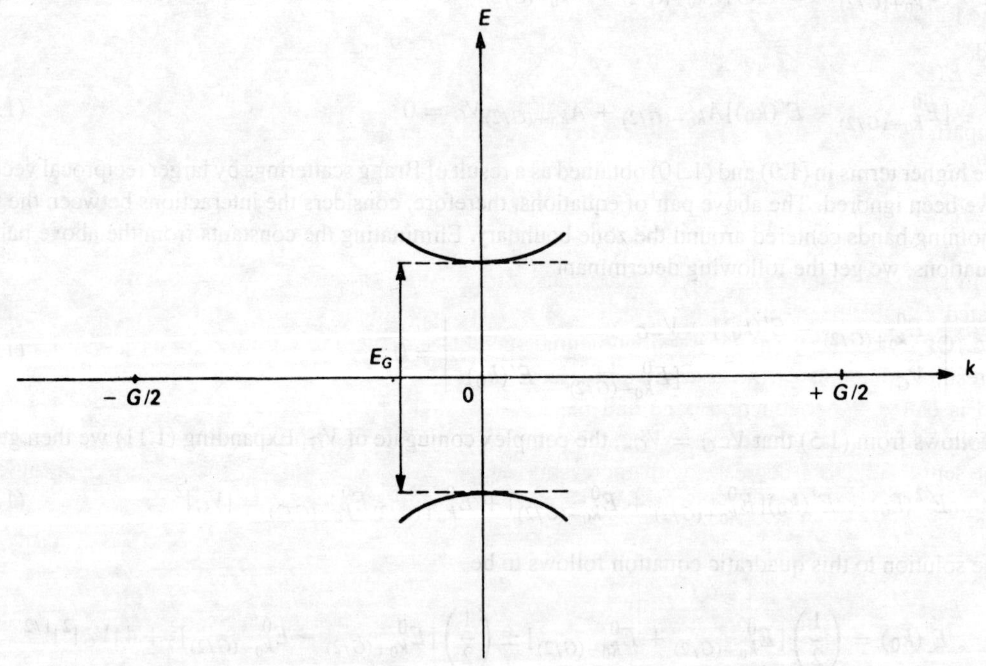

Figure 1.2 *The two-band model*

This two-band model of semiconductors may also be understood from the following simple physical considerations: The electrons in the conduction band may be considered as free electrons and assigned a constant and a positive effective mass m^*, near the band minimum and, therefore, their E–$\boldsymbol{k}$ relation may be expressed as

$$E = \left(\frac{\hbar^2 k_0^2}{2m^*}\right)$$

The electrons in the valence band, on the other hand, are bound ones and therefore their total energy is negative. In spite of their having negative energy, they are able to move in the valence band. This is accounted for by assuming that their kinetic energy is negative due to their effective mass in the valence band being negative and the E–$\boldsymbol{k}$ relation of electrons in the valence band may be represented by the following relation

$$E = -\left(\frac{\hbar^2 k_0^2}{2m^*}\right)$$

Both the above two relations are symmetrical about the $\boldsymbol{k}$-axis with the minimum energy difference between the two bands being the energy gap E_G of the crystal. This is what is known as the two-band representation of the energy band model of semiconductors.
Equation (1.14) is analogous to relativistic Dirac equation for free electrons which is expressed below in the following form for the sake of comparison

$$E(\boldsymbol{k}_0) = \pm(\hbar^2 c^2 \boldsymbol{k}_0^2 + m_0^2 c^4)^{1/2} \tag{1.17}$$

Comparing (1.14) with (1.17), one infers that

$$\hbar c \rightarrow s \text{ and } m_0 c^2 \rightarrow \left(\frac{E_G}{2}\right) \tag{1.18}$$

But in real semiconductors, in the general case, the nature of the E–$\boldsymbol{k}$ relation is far more complicated and has been studied by a variety of numerical methods viz., (i) the orthogonalized plane wave (OPW) method, (ii) the pseudopotential method and (iii) the k.p method. Figure 1.3 shows the results of studies of the energy band structures of Ge, Si and GaAs. Conventionally, the upper band is called the conduction band and the lower one, the valence band. The separation between the two bands is called the energy gap. Experimental measurements indicate that the band gaps of most semiconductors decrease with increasing temperatures according to the following empirical relation

$$E_G(T) = E_G(0) - \left[\frac{\alpha T^2}{(T+\beta)}\right] \tag{1.19}$$

where α and β are the two appropriate constants whose values are given in Table 1.1
For some semiconductors e.g., PbS, (dE_G/dT) is found to be positive. Around room temperatures, the energy gaps of Ge and GaAs increases with pressure and that of Si decreases.
The band structure of GaAs has a minimum in the conduction band and a maximum in the valence band for the same $\boldsymbol{k}(=0)$ value. Thus an electron making the smallest energy transition in GaAs can do so without any change in its wave vector. Such a semiconductor is termed 'direct'. But, similar transitions in Ge and Si require some change in the $\boldsymbol{k}$ value also and therefore these semiconductors are termed 'indirect'.

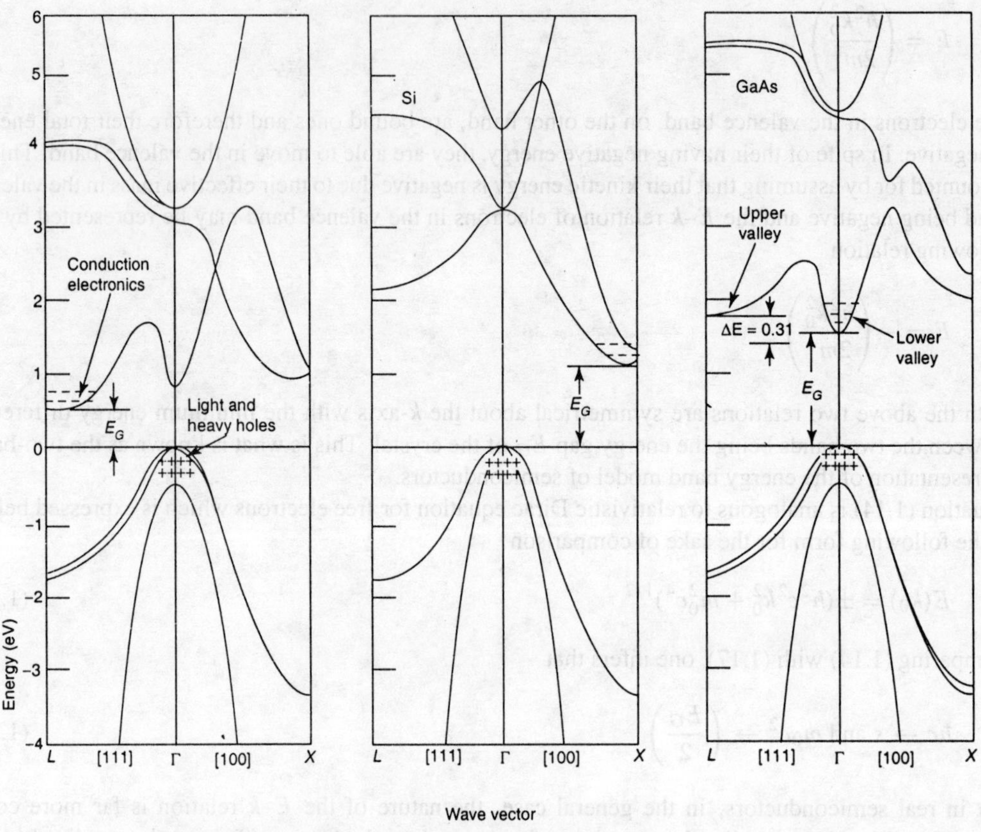

***Figure 1.3** Energy band structures of Ge, Si and GaAs where E_G is the energy band gap.*

Table 1. 1 *The constants α and β*

Material	$E_G(0)$ eV	α (eV/K)10^{-4}	β (K)
Ge	0.7437	4.774	235
Si	1.1700	4.730	636
GaAs	1.5190	5.405	204

As the compositions of the III–V ternary and quaternary alloys are varied, their band structures are found to change. Figures 1.4(a) and (b) illustrate the band structures of GaAs and AlAs. Figure 1.4(c) illustrates the way the band structures change with the composition x in the ternary semiconducting alloy $Al_xGa_{1-x}As$. It may be seen from Fig. 1.4(c) that in an alloy with an Al composition above 38%, the indirect conduction band minimum becomes the lowest lying conduction band. Therefore, AlGaAs is a direct band gap semiconductor for an Al composition of up to 38% and is an indirect band gap semiconductor for higher compositions. The variation of the energy band structure of the ternary alloy $GaAs_{1-x}P_x$ is also similar to that of $Al_xGa_{1-x}As$, as shown in Fig. 1.4. On the other hand, GaAsP is a direct gap semiconductor for As concentrations up to 55%. For higher concentrations, it turns into an indirect band semiconductor.

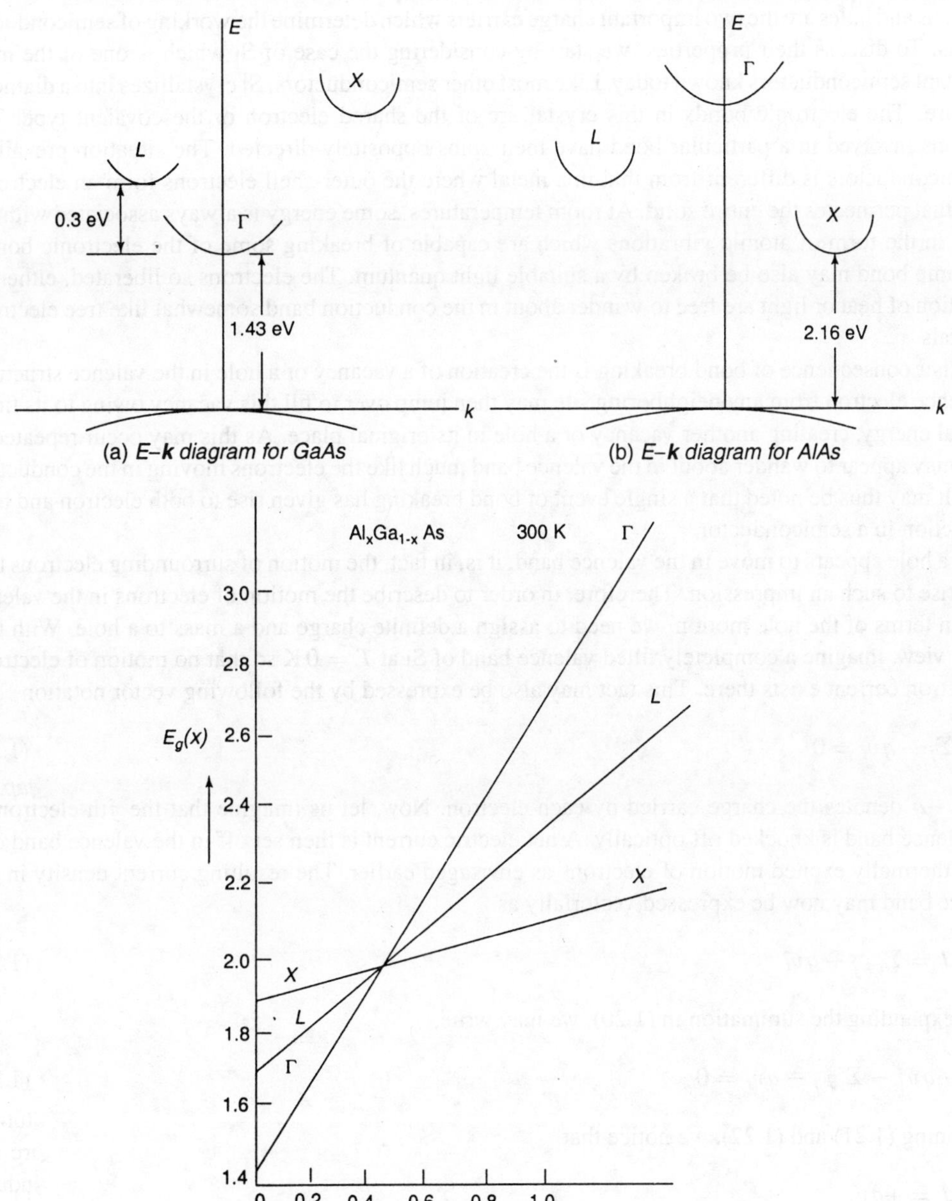

Figure 1.4 *Energy band diagrams of GaAs and AlAs*

1.2 Electrons and holes

Electrons and holes are the two important charge carriers which determine the working of semiconductor devices. To discuss their properties, we start by considering the case of Si which is one of the most important semiconductors known today. Like most other semiconductors, Si crystallizes into a diamond structure. The electronic bonds in this crystal are of the shared electron or the covalent type. The electrons involved in a particular bond have their spins oppositely directed. The situation prevailing in semiconductors is different from that in a metal where the outer-shell electrons form an electronic cloud that permeates the entire solid. At room temperatures, some energy is always associated with the lattice in the form of atomic vibrations which are capable of breaking some of the electronic bonds. The same bond may also be broken by a suitable light quantum. The electrons so liberated, either by the action of heat or light are free to wander about in the conduction band somewhat like free electrons in metals.

The other consequence of bond breaking is the creation of a vacancy or a hole in the valence structure. A valence electron from any neighboring site may then jump over to fill this vacancy owing to its finite thermal energy, creating another vacancy or a hole in its original place. As this may occur repeatedly, holes may appear to wander about in the valence band much like the electrons moving in the conduction band. It may thus be noted that a single event of bond breaking has given rise to both electron and hole conduction in a semiconductor.

When a hole appears to move in the valence band, it is, in fact, the motion of surrounding electrons that gives rise to such an impression. Therefore, in order to describe the motion of electrons in the valence band in terms of the hole motion, we need to assign a definite charge and a mass to a hole. With this end in view, imagine a completely filled valence band of Si at $T = 0\,\mathrm{K}$ so that no motion of electrons or electron current exists there. This fact may also be expressed by the following vector notation

$$\Sigma_i - qv_i = 0 \tag{1.20}$$

where $-q$ denotes the charge carried by each electron. Now, let us imagine that the jth electron in the valence band is knocked off optically. A net electric current is then set off in the valence band due to the thermally excited motion of electrons as envisaged earlier. The resulting current density in the valence band may now be expressed vectorially as

$$J = \Sigma_{i \neq j} - qv_i \tag{1.21}$$

Next, expanding the summation in (1.20), we may write,

$$-qv_j - \Sigma_{i \neq j} - qv_i = 0 \tag{1.22}$$

Combining (1.21) and (1.22), we notice that

$$J = +qv_j \tag{1.23}$$

Thus, according to (1.23), the resulting current density in the valence band which is produced due to the removal of the jth electron by an optical means may be expressed in terms of the motion of a single positive charge $+q$ associated with the vacancy (site of the jth electron). Hence, if the valence electrons are all presumed absent, the net current density produced by them when its jth member has been knocked out may be described in terms of the motion of the vacancy now imagined carrying a positive charge $+q$, which is called a hole.

Next, in order to identify its mass, the physical significance of the electron effective mass m^* used in semiconductor physics needs to be explained. An electron in a metal may be considered to move almost freely because the electrostatic influences of the neighboring positive ions on it can be regarded to be nearly screened out by other surrounding mobile electrons. The situation is, however, different in a semiconductor. In this case, as the electrons undergo a thermal motion, they continue to experience finite internal forces due to the neighboring positive nuclei. Their effects cannot be regarded as screened out as in metals because the free electron density in semiconductors is much lower compared to that of metals. Hence, if an external electric field is applied to a semiconductor, the motion of an electron in it may be described by an equation of the following type

$$F_{\text{ext}} + F_{\text{int}} = mf \tag{1.24}$$

where m denotes the free electron mass and f represents its resulting acceleration inside the semiconductor crystal under the influence of the external force F_{ext}. F_{int} denotes the internal crystalline forces that the electron experiences in course of its motion. It is not an easy task to evaluate its magnitude. Thus, one fails to represent the motion of the said electron by the conventional formula expressing a proportionality between the applied force and the resulting acceleration (Newton's second law of motion). To overcome this difficulty, a parameter termed effective mass (m^*) of carriers in semiconductors has been introduced to take care of the effects of the internal crystalline forces. With its help, the electronic motion in a semiconductor can be represented in the following standard form

$$F_{\text{ext}} = m^* f \tag{1.25}$$

This constant m^* may therefore be regarded as the equivalent mass of the electron with which it may be regarded as moving inside the semiconductor crystal freely when the internal crystalline forces on it can be ignored. In that case, we may express the E–k relation of electrons in a semiconductor sample as

$$E = \left(\frac{\hbar^2 k^2}{2m^*}\right) \tag{1.26}$$

Differentiating (1.26) twice with respect to $\boldsymbol{k}$, we find

$$m^* = \left[\frac{\hbar^2}{\left(\dfrac{\partial^2 E}{\partial k^2}\right)}\right] \tag{1.27}$$

Equation (1.27) suggests that if the E–$\boldsymbol{k}$ relation of electrons in semiconductors is known a priori (as given by Fig. 1.3), their effective masses at any $\boldsymbol{k}$-value may easily be derived from it. Since $(\partial^2 E/\partial k^2)$ is negative in the valence band, m^* for electrons in the valence band is negative.

We are now in a position to identify the mass of a hole. For this purpose, we once again start with a completely full valence band at $T = 0\,\text{K}$. Since there cannot be any motion in it, we must have for the net momentum

$$\Sigma_i - m_i^* v_i = 0 \tag{1.28}$$

When the jth electron is knocked off optically, a thermal motion of electrons results in the valence band, as before. The net electronic momentum in the valence band may then be expressed vectorially as

$$P = \Sigma_{i \neq j} - m_i^* v_i \tag{1.29}$$

Rewriting (1.28) in the expanded form, we get

$$\Sigma_{i \neq j} - m_i^* v_i - m_j^* v_j = 0 \tag{1.30}$$

Combining (1.29) and (1.30), we find

$$P = +m_j^* v_j \tag{1.31}$$

Thus, according to (1.31), the net momentum in the valence band due to all the electrons but the jth one can be generated by imagining a mass $+m_j^*$ to be assigned to the vacancy representing a hole when all the valence electrons are considered absent.
Thus it is clear that holes may be likened to real particles possessing a charge $+q$ and a mass $+m^*$ in the valence band for the purpose of replacing the motion of the surrounding electrons. The magnitudes of the carrier effective masses in Ge, Si and GaAs are given in Table 1.2.

Table 1.2 *Carrier effective masses*

Effective mass	Ge	Si	GaAs
m_n^*	$0.55\ m_0$	$1.1\ m_0$	$0.067\ m_0$
m_p^*	$0.37\ m_0$	$0.56\ m_0$	$0.48\ m_0$

(m_0 denotes the free electron mass)

The phenomenon of bond breaking of electrons by light or heat is called carrier generation. The reverse process by which an electron-hole pair is annihilated is called carrier recombination. In a semiconductor at a definite temperature, a dynamic balance exists between these two processes and a constant density of carriers is always maintained in the respective bands. The minimum energy absorbed during carrier generation or emitted during carrier recombination in an ideal semiconductor crystal is its energy gap.

1.3 Mobility and diffusivity

The charge carriers in semiconductors at room temperatures possess thermal energies which are distributed among carriers according to the Maxwell–Boltzman statistics. When a cloud of such carriers is subjected to either an external electric field or a concentration gradient, it starts moving in an appropriate direction as directed by the driving agency. The motion of carriers in response to an electric field is described in terms of drift, while that in a concentration gradient is caused by diffusion. We will first describe these phenomena independently and then try to correlate them.

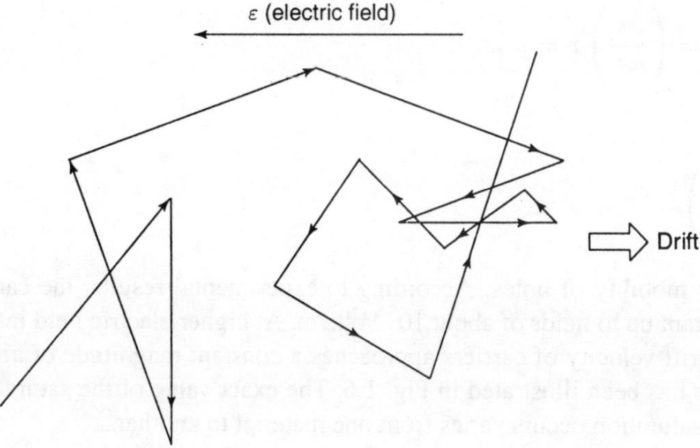

Figure 1.5 *The thermal motion of an electron in a semiconductor. Each vector 0 represents the thermal velocity after every lattice scattering*

1.3.1 Mobility

In semiconductors, the thermal motion of carriers is impeded by lattice vibrations, impurities and crystal defects. At reasonably higher temperatures, carriers are scattered randomly by lattice vibrations, while at lower temperatures, the Coulomb interactions between carriers and impurity ions is the dominant scattering mechanism. Figure 1.5 illustrates the random thermal motion of an electron in a solid as a result of the different types of scatterings encountered by it. When an electric field is applied to a semiconductor crystal, carriers are accelerated in appropriate directions till they are scattered by crystal defects, impurities or lattice vibrations. The special feature about this interaction is that the velocity of carriers after each encounter becomes essentially random once again and their accelerations in the electric field start afresh. Thus, for moderate field intensities, carriers never go far out of the thermal equilibrium. By that, it is implied that in spite of the presence of the electric field, the carrier energy remains essentially thermal. Considering, as an example, the random interruption of the hole thermal motion by lattice vibrations or crystal defects in the presence of an applied electric field ε, it may be described in terms of the drift of holes along the electric field direction with an average drift velocity v_d. To understand it, we write the velocity of holes in a sample of p-type Si after an instant t seconds from the start of their motion in an electric field of intensity ε by using the equation of motion as

$$v(t) = v(0) + \left(\frac{q\varepsilon}{m_p^*}\right) t \tag{1.32}$$

where $v(0)$ measures the velocity of holes at $t = 0$. Averaging (1.32) over a very large number of collisions, we get

$$\langle v(t) \rangle = \langle v(0) \rangle + \left(\frac{q\varepsilon}{m_p^*}\right) \langle t \rangle \tag{1.33}$$

As the initial velocity is essentially random after every collision, it is not difficult to conclude that $v(0) = 0$ when the averaging is carried out. Defining $t = \tau$ as the mean free time between successive collisions, we obtain from (1.33),

$$v_d = \langle v(t) \rangle = \left(\frac{q\varepsilon}{m_p^*} \right) \tau = \mu_p \varepsilon \tag{1.34}$$

where

$$\mu_p = \left(\frac{q\tau}{m_p^*} \right) \tag{1.35}$$

is termed the drift mobility of holes. According to experimental results, the carrier mobilities in Si remain fairly constant up to fields of about 10^5 Volts/m. At higher electric field intensities the mobility declines and the drift velocity of carriers approaches a constant magnitude of about 10^5 m/s at room temperatures. This has been illustrated in Fig. 1.6. The exact value of the saturation velocity and the field at which the saturation occurs varies from one material to another.

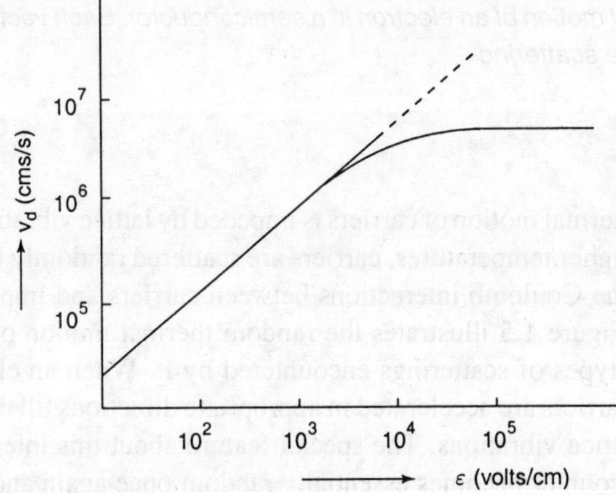

Figure 1.6 *Drift velocity (v_d) vs electric field (ε) in a normal semiconductor crystal*

By definition, the current density produced by a group of holes is their number passing through a unit area in unit time and is given by

$$J_p = qpv_d = qp\mu_p\varepsilon = \sigma_p\varepsilon \tag{1.36}$$

where

$$\sigma_p = qp\mu_p \tag{1.37}$$

represents the conductivity of the Si sample due to holes. Similarly, for electrons

$$\sigma_n = qn\mu_n \tag{1.38}$$

where n and μ_n denote the electron density and mobility respectively. As holes and electrons drift opposite each other in an electric field, they produce a current in the same direction because they carry opposite charges. As such, the total electronic conductivity of the semiconductor sample follows to be

$$\sigma = \sigma_p + \sigma_n = qp\mu_p + qn\mu_n \tag{1.39}$$

The total electric current density J produced in the sample, as given by Ohm's law, is

$$J = \sigma \varepsilon \tag{1.40}$$

The dependence of the carrier mobility upon temperature is also of interest. To study this we express (1.35) as follows

$$\mu_p = \left(\frac{q\tau}{m_p^*}\right) = \frac{ql}{(m_p^* \langle v \rangle)} = \frac{ql\langle v \rangle}{(m_p^* \langle v \rangle^2)} = \frac{ql\langle v \rangle}{3kT} \tag{1.41}$$

where $l = \langle v \rangle \tau$ denotes the mean free path between successive collisions and k denotes the Boltzmann constant. In deriving (1.41), we also presumed that $1/2\ m_p^* \langle v \rangle^2 = (3/2)kT$ — a result that follows from the kinetic theory of gases. Presuming the mean free path to be proportional to the average energy per degree of freedom, we may express it as

$$l = \left[\frac{\text{const}}{kT}\right] \tag{1.42}$$

Combining (1.41) and (1.42) and substituting for $\langle v \rangle$, we obtain

$$\mu_{pl} = \frac{\text{const}}{T^{3/2}} \tag{1.43}$$

where μ_{pl} denotes the drift mobility when the lattice vibrations are responsible for carrier scatterings. The lattice mobility has been experimentally observed to decrease with increase in T.

To account for the effects due to impurity scatterings on the drift mobility, we use Rutherford's law of alpha particle scattering by heavy nuclei, according to which

$$l = \frac{\text{const}\langle v \rangle^4}{N_i} \tag{1.44}$$

where N_i denotes the impurity density. Combining (1.41) with (1.44) and substituting for $\langle v \rangle$, one obtains

$$\mu_{pi} = \frac{\text{const}\, T^{3/2}}{N_i} \tag{1.45}$$

where μ_{pi} denotes the drift mobility as a result of the impurity scattering. μ_{pi} is predicted to increase with decrease in N_i and increase in T. Equations (1.43) and (1.45) are approximately plotted in Fig. 1.7. The combined influences of lattice and impurity scatterings give rise to a maximum mobility somewhat below the room temperature.

When both types of scatterings are equally important and take place at rates ν_l and ν_i respectively, the net rate of impurity scattering would be given by

$$\nu = \nu_l + \nu_i \tag{1.46}$$

If $\tau = (\nu)^{-1}$, $\tau_l = (\nu_l)^{-1}$ and $\tau_i = (\nu_l)^{-1}$, we have combining (1.41) and (1.46)

$$(\mu)^{-1} = (\mu_l)^{-1} + (\mu_i)^{-1} \tag{1.47}$$

where μ denotes the effective mobility as a result of lattice and impurity scatterings.

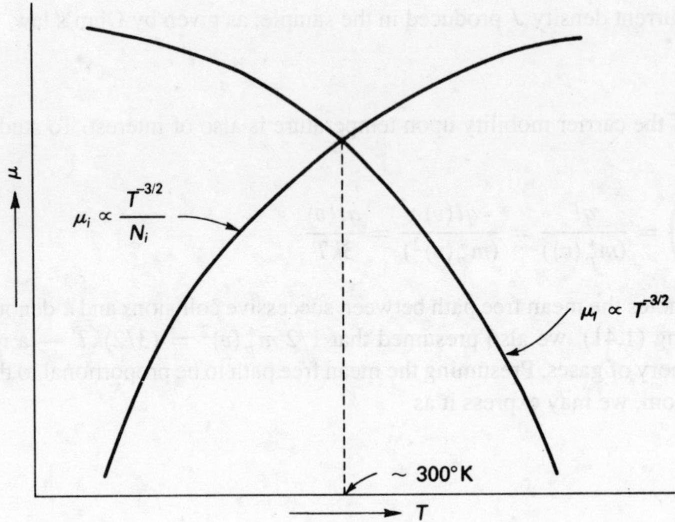

Figure 1.7 *Dependence of drift mobilities on temperature*

1.3.2 Diffusivity

If, however, the motion of the cloud of carriers is initiated by a concentration gradient instead of an electric field, as discussed above, its motion would equally be affected by lattice vibrations, impurities and crystal defects. The resulting carrier motion is termed diffusion. To discuss it, let us consider a point inside a semiconductor sample where the equilibrium electron density is n. Since the carrier motion in thermal equilibrium is entirely random, it may be presumed on the basis of the principle of equipartition of energy, that half of them would be moving towards the right and the remaining half towards the left. If, therefore, a uniform carrier density exists inside the semiconductor sample, the net number of particles moving per unit area in each direction would be zero. But, when a concentration gradient exists, there would result a net flow of carriers inside the sample along the direction of decreasing concentration. To determine the number of carriers moving through unit area in unit time, let us consider two planes A' and A'' on both sides of A, where the carrier density is n. The situation is depicted in Fig. 1.8. The different sections are separated from each other by a distance equal to the mean free path l of carriers so that the carriers are not expected to collide with one another unless they cross these sections. Before collision they maintain their equilibrium electron concentrations. Now, if n_1 and n_2 are the carrier densities at A' and A'' respectively, the number of particles crossing unit area of A in unit time from the right (i.e. flux) is $1/2\, n_1\langle v\rangle$ and that from the left is $1/2\, n_2\langle v\rangle$. Since $n_1 > n_2$, the net flux towards the right would be $1/2\,(n_1 - n_2)v$. Referring to Fig. 1.8, we may express

$$n_1 = n - \left(\frac{dn}{dx}\right) l$$

and (1.48)

$$n_2 = n + \left(\frac{dn}{dx}\right) l$$

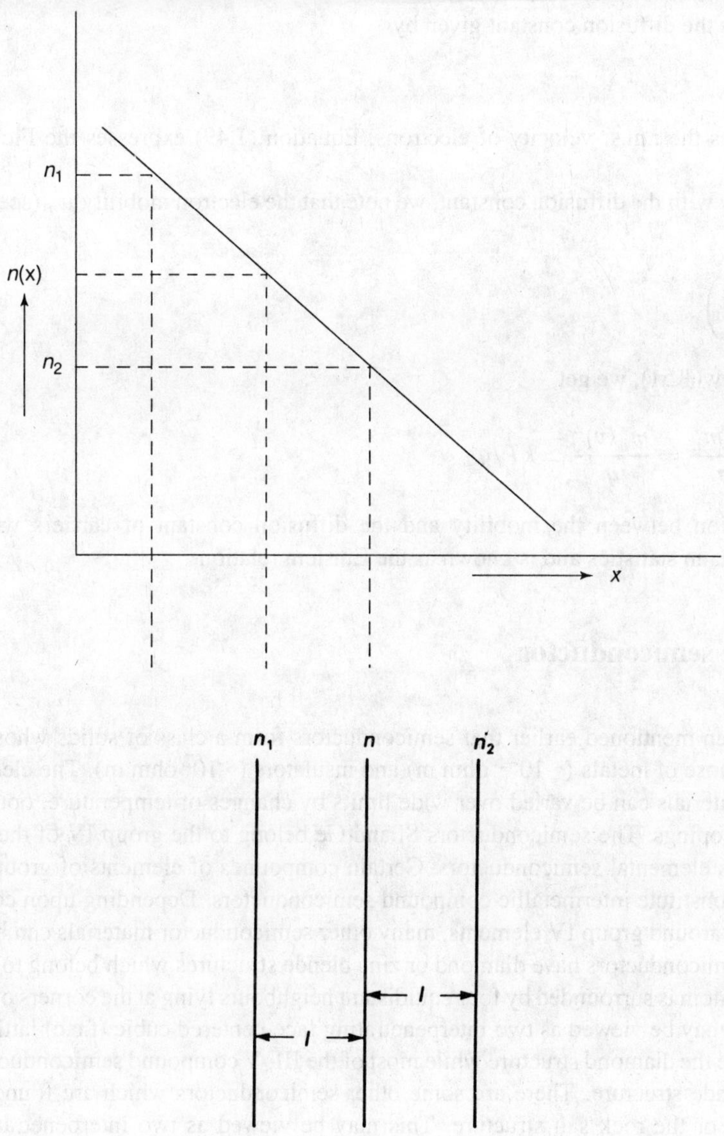

Figure 1.8 *Three successive planes separated by a carrier mean free path*

where we have presumed dn/dx to be negative. Hence, the net flux of particles from right to left would be

$$f = \frac{1}{2}(n_1 - n_2)\langle v \rangle = -l\langle v \rangle \left(\frac{dn}{dx}\right) = -D_n \left(\frac{dn}{dx}\right) \tag{1.49}$$

where D_n defines the diffusion constant given by

$$D_n = l\langle v \rangle \tag{1.50}$$

where $\langle v \rangle$ denotes the r.m.s. velocity of electrons. Equation (1.49) expresses the Fick's first law of diffusion.

To relate mobility with the diffusion constant, we note that the electron mobility μ_n (see (1.41)) should be expressed as

$$\mu_n = \left(\frac{q\tau}{m_n^*} \right) \tag{1.51}$$

Dividing (1.50) by (1.51), we get

$$\frac{D_n}{\mu_n} = \frac{l\langle v \rangle m_n^*}{q\tau} = \frac{m_n^* \langle v \rangle^2}{q} \simeq kT/q \tag{1.52}$$

This is the relation between the mobility and the diffusion constant of carriers when they obey Maxwell–Boltzmann statistics and is known as the Einstein relation.

1.4 Intrinsic semiconductor

It has already been mentioned earlier that semiconductors form a class of solids whose resistivity is intermediate to those of metals ($\sim 10^{-5}$ ohm m) and insulators ($\sim 10^{2}$ ohm m). The electrical conductivity of these materials can be varied over wide limits by changes of temperature, optical irradiation and by suitable dopings. The semiconductors Si and Ge belong to the group IV of the periodic table and are known as elemental semiconductors. Certain compounds of elements of groups III & V and groups II & VI constitute intermetallic compound semiconductors. Depending upon combinations of various elements around group IV elements, many other semiconductor materials can be realized.

Many of these semiconductors have diamond or zinc blende structures which belong to the tetrahedral phases where an atom is surrounded by four equidistant neighbours lying at the corners of a tetrahedron. These structures may be viewed as two interpenetrating face-centered cubic (f.c.c) lattices. Ge and Si are known to have the diamond structure while most of the III–V compound semiconductors crystallize into the zinc blende structure. There are some other semiconductors which are found to crystallize into the wurtzite or the rock salt structure. This may be viewed as two interpenetrating hexagonal close-packed lattices. In the rock salt structure one atom has six nearest neighbours. Ge and Si cleave along the $\langle 111 \rangle$ planes while GaAs prefer to cleave along the $\langle 110 \rangle$ planes.

A semiconductor in its natural crystalline form without any impurity content is called an intrinsic semiconductor. Electron-hole pairs are generated within it by the thermal vibrations of the lattice. The recombination process takes away one electron-hole pair out of the sample. A condition of detailed balance exists in a crystal at thermal equilibrium when the two rates are equal and opposite.

To derive expressions for the carrier densities in an intrinsic semiconductor sample, the latter is regarded to behave as a potential well for mobile carriers. The electrons in the conduction band are then surrounded by potential barriers as in a potential box whose heights are equal to semiconductor work functions. As the magnitude of the semiconductor work functions are usually larger than the electron energies in the conduction band, we may presume the potential well to be of infinite depth. To compute the density of electrons in the conduction band, we must therefore know the expression for the density of states function in it.

Density of states function It has already been discussed above that the conduction band of a semiconductor material can be regarded as a three dimensional potential well of infinite depth. In that case, the spreads or uncertainties of three Cartesian co-ordinates of a particular electron viz., Δx, Δy, and Δz within the well must be of the order of the well widths viz., L_x, L_y and L_z in the X, Y and Z directions respectively. But, according to the principles of quantum mechanics, the uncertainties in the position Δx and the momentum Δp_x of a particular electron must be related as

$$\Delta x \Delta p_x \approx h \tag{1.53}$$

where $h = 6.626 \times 10^{-34}$ Js is the Planck's constant. Similar relations may very well be written down for Y and Z directions. Hence, if Δx, Δy and Δz are maximized to L_x, L_y and L_z respectively, the minimum momentum uncertainty product for an electron follows to be

$$\Delta p_x \Delta p_y \Delta p_z = \left(\frac{h^3}{V}\right) \tag{1.54}$$

where V denotes the volume of the semiconductor material in question. Now, if there is a group of electrons having their momenta lying between p and $p+dp$ in the same volume V with their Cartesian components p_x, p_y and p_z respectively, the total number of allowed states in this range would be given by

$$N(p)dp = \frac{2(dp_x dp_y dp_z)}{\left[\left(\frac{h^3}{V}\right)\right]} \tag{1.55}$$

The total number of electronic states in (1.55) is doubled owing to the two possible spin orientations of every electron. Switching over to the Cartesian polar co-ordinates, (1.55) reduces to

$$N(p)dp = \left(\frac{2V}{h^3}\right) 4\pi p^2 dp \tag{1.56}$$

where $p^2 = 2m_n^* E$ and m_n^* denotes the electron effective mass in the semiconductor conduction band. Substituting for p in (1.56), the density of states in the energy range E and $E + dE$ is given by

$$\rho(E)dE = 4\pi \left(\frac{2m_n^*}{h^2}\right)^{3/2} E^{1/2} dE \tag{1.57}$$

If the electron energy E is measured from E_c (the conduction band edge) upwards, (1.57) should be revised to

$$\rho(E)dE = 4\pi \left(\frac{2m_n^*}{h^2}\right)^{3/2} (E - E_c)^{1/2} dE \tag{1.58}$$

Fermi–Dirac distribution function In the deliberation above, we have derived an expression for the number of electronic states per unit volume in the energy range E and $E + dE$ in a semiconductor sample. But their occupancy by electrons is determined by the Fermi–Dirac distribution function which is based upon their indistinguishability, their wave nature and the Pauli's exclusion principle. According to it, the probability of an electron to occupy a level of an energy E at a temperature T is given by

$$f(E) = \left[1 + \exp\left\{\frac{(E - E_F)}{kT}\right\}\right]^{-1} \tag{1.59}$$

where k is the Boltzman constant ($= 8.62 \times 10^{-5}$ eV/K $= 1.38 \times 10^{-23}$ J/K). The quantity E_F is called the Fermi level and it is an important quantity in the analysis of the behaviour of carriers in semiconductors. It may be seen from (1.59) that at $E = E_F$, the occupation probability reduces to 1/2. Thus, an energy state at the Fermi energy enjoys a 50% chance of being occupied by an electron. A closer examination of (1.59) reveals that at $T = 0$ K, every available energy state up to E_F is filled with electrons, and all states above E_F are empty. At higher temperatures, there is a finite probability of some states above E_F to be occupied and there is a corresponding probability $[1 - f(E)]$ that states below E_F are empty. The Fermi function given by (1.59) is symmetrical about $E = E_F$ at all temperatures. For an intrinsic semiconductor, an electron-hole pair is formed due to the breaking of a particular covalent bond in the crystal. As such, the electron concentration in the conduction band must be equal to the hole concentration in the valence band. Therefore, the Fermi level in an intrinsic material must lie at the center of the energy gap. For example, for Si at room temperatures $n_i = p_i = 10^{10}/\text{cm}^3$ whereas the densities of available states at E_c and E_v are of the order of $10^{19}/\text{cm}^3$. Therefore, the probability of occupancy $f(E)$ of an electron state in the conduction band and the probability of occupancy $[1 - f(E)]$ of hole states in the valence band have to be quite small. A small change in $f(E)$ may therefore cause significant changes in the respective carrier densities.

In an n-type material, there is a higher concentration of electrons in the conduction band compared to the hole concentrations in the valence band. Thus, for an n-type material E_F must lie above its intrinsic position in the energy scale. If E_F moves closer to the conduction band edge E_c, the electron density increases. Therefore, $(E_c - E_F)$ gives a measure of n. For a p-type material, on the other hand, the Fermi level must lie near the valence band edge so that the $[1 - f(E)]$ tail below E_v is larger than the $f(E)$ tail above E_c. Hence, $(E_F - E_v)$ determines the extent of doping of the p-type material.

Electron and hole concentrations at equilibrium To obtain an expression for the electron density in an intrinsic semiconductor, we have to multiply the electronic density of states given by (1.58) with the Fermi probability function (1.59). Hence

$$n = \int_{E_c}^{\infty} \rho_c(E - E_c) f(E)\, dE \tag{1.60}$$

Under room temperature conditions, we may presume $(E - E_F) \gg kT$. In such a case, the Fermi function may be simplified as

$$f(E) \cong \left[-\exp\left\{\frac{(E - E_F)}{kT}\right\}\right] \tag{1.61}$$

which is equivalent to the Maxwell–Boltzmann distribution function. Combining (1.58), (1.60) and (1.61), we get

$$n = 4\pi\left(\frac{2m_n^*}{h^2}\right)^{3/2}\left[-\exp\left\{\frac{(E_c-E_F)}{kT}\right\}\right]\int_{E_c}^{\infty}(E-E_c)^{1/2}\left[-\exp\left\{\frac{(E-E_c)}{kT}\right\}\right]dE \tag{1.62}$$

The integral in (1.62) can be evaluated by setting $x = (E - E_c)/kT$. One then obtains

$$n = N_c\left[-\exp\left\{\frac{(E_c-E_F)}{kT}\right\}\right] \tag{1.63}$$

where

$$N_c = 2\left[\frac{2\pi m_n^* kT}{h^2}\right]^{3/2} \tag{1.64}$$

is known as the effective density of states in the conduction band. By an analogous procedure, one may compute the hole density in the valence band as

$$p = \int_{-\infty}^{E_v}\rho_v(E_v-E)[1-f(E)]\,dE = 4\pi\left(\frac{2m_p^*}{h^2}\right)^{3/2}\left[-\exp\left\{\frac{(E_F-E_v)}{kT}\right\}\right]x$$

$$\int_{-\infty}^{E_v}(E_v-E)^{1/2}\left[-\exp\left\{\frac{(E_v-E)}{kT}\right\}\right]dE \tag{1.65}$$

where $x = \dfrac{E-E_c}{kT}$. Upon integration, one obtains

$$p = N_v\left[-\exp\left\{\frac{(E_F-E_v)}{kT}\right\}\right] \tag{1.66}$$

where

$$N_v = 2\left[\frac{2\pi m_p^* kT}{h^2}\right]^{3/2} \tag{1.67}$$

is the effective density of states in the valence band. For intrinsic samples $n = p = n_i$ (intrinsic carrier density). Therefore, equating (1.63) to (1.66), we get

$$E_F = \left[\frac{(E_c+E_v)}{2}\right] + \left(\frac{3}{4}\right)kT\ln\left(\frac{m_p^*}{m_n^*}\right) \tag{1.68}$$

As electron and hole effective masses are different, E_F in an intrinsic specimen does not lie exactly at the energy gap centre. This is shown in Fig. 1.9. Forming the product of (1.63) and (1.66), we get upon simplification

$$n_i = (N_c N_v)^{1/2} \exp\left(\frac{-E_G}{2kT}\right) \tag{1.69}$$

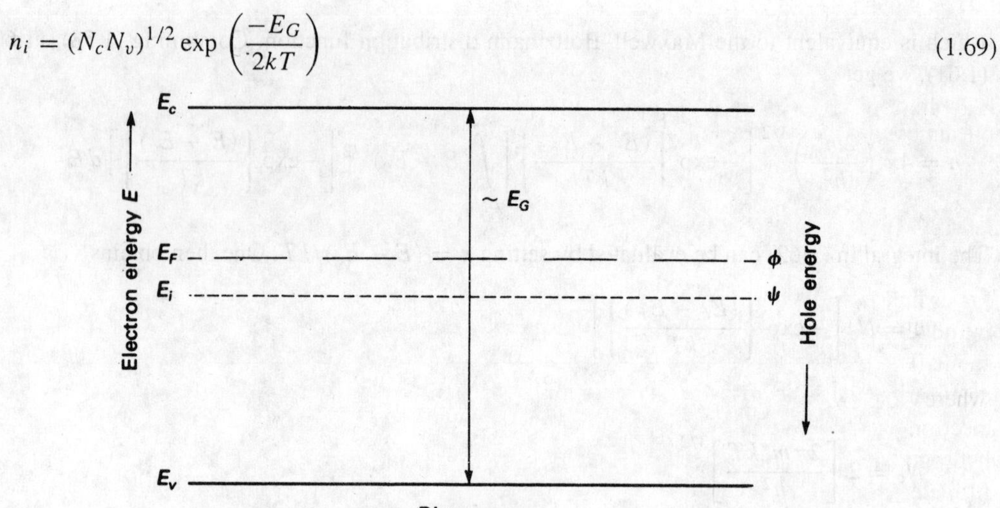

Figure 1.9 Energy (E) vs distance (x) diagram for an intrinsic semiconductor

Since $(N_c N_v)^{1/2}$ precedes an exponential factor and N_c differs from N_v because $m_p^* \neq m_n^*$, for many practical cases, we may presume $(N_c N_v)^{1/2} \approx N_c \approx N_v$
Sometimes, it becomes necessary to express the carrier densities in terms of electrostatic potentials instead of carrier energies. To derive such expressions, we define the Fermi potential by $\varphi = -(E_F/q)$ and the crystal potential by $\Psi = (-E_i/q)$ (see Fig. 1.9) where E_i represents the energy gap centre. Then one may write,

$$(E_c - E_F) = \left[\left(\frac{E_G}{2}\right) - q(\Psi - \varphi)\right]$$

and (1.70)

$$(E_F - E_v) = \left[\left(\frac{E_G}{2}\right) - q(\varphi - \Psi)\right]$$

Using the above expressions in (1.63) and (1.66), one obtains

$$n = n_i \exp\left[\left(\frac{q}{kT}\right)(\Psi - \varphi)\right] \tag{1.71}$$

and

$$p = n_i \exp\left[\left(\frac{q}{kT}\right)(\varphi - \Psi)\right] \tag{1.72}$$

1.5 Doped semiconductors

The electronic and optical properties of semiconductors are strongly affected by chemical impurities. One appropriate impurity atom per ten million of host atoms of the crystal can convert a Si sample from a poor conductor to a good conductor of electricity. The process of adding controlled amounts of chemical impurities to a semiconductor sample is termed doping. Owing to an excessively large separation between the impurity atoms in a sample of a normally doped semiconductor, they may be presumed to remain almost electrically isolated from one another.

1.5.1 Donor doping

Let us first consider the column V elements e.g., Phosphorus (P), Arsenic (As) and Antimony (Sb) to be introduced to Si and Ge as chemical impurities. These elements have five electrons in their outermost shells. Therefore, when they occupy substitutional positions within the Si lattice (say), four of their five electrons are consumed in the formation of covalent bonds like other Si atoms of the crystal. The fifth electron which is loosely bound to the impurity atom may be likened to an electron bound to an ordinary hydrogen nucleus. Therefore, by extending Bohr's theory to such a problem, the binding energy of the fifth electron may be calculated in the usual manner. But while doing so one must take into account the roles played by the mobile electrons present within the semiconductor crystal in partially screening out the electrostatic influence between the nucleus and the electron bound to it. It has been observed experimentally that the binding energy of the fifth electron vanishes when the impurity densities are about $10^{16} - 10^{17}/\text{cm}^3$ in Si under room temperature conditions.
At intermediate doping densities, the binding energies of the electrons to the impurity atoms is finite but is very small ($\sim$0.01 eV). Therefore, the energy states introduced by the column V impurity atoms may be designated by short lines just below the conduction band edge of the semiconductor energy band diagram. The energy difference between E_c and the states introduced by the impurity atoms then measures the ionization energy of the electrons bound to the impurity atoms. This is a small fraction of the average thermal energy associated with the lattice under room temperature conditions (viz., 0.259 eV at 300 K). Consequently, there is every probability of the fifth electron being dislodged to the conduction band. The impurity energy levels are filled by electrons at 0 K. At about 50–100 K virtually all the electrons are donated to the conduction band. As such, these impurity states are called donor levels and the column V impurities (viz., P, As, and Sb) in Ge and Si are called donor impurities. A material doped with donor impurities will have electron concentrations considerably larger than its hole concentrations and is called an n-type semiconductor. A donor impurity, after it contributes the electron to the conduction band becomes a positive donor ion. A charge $+q$ then gets permanently lodged in the semiconductor lattice.
In an n-type semiconductor, holes may continue to exist simultaneously in the valence band because of the breaking of bonds by atomic vibrations. But owing to the increased supply of electrons provided by donors, the density of holes must fall off. To establish a relationship between the electron and the hole densities in an n-type semiconductor under equilibrium conditions, let us first consider an intrinsic sample of Si. Under room temperature conditions, the electron and the hole populations in it are built up by the thermal generation of carriers. At any stage during the carrier build up one may then write

$$\left(\frac{dn}{dt}\right) = \left(\frac{dp}{dt}\right) = g_0 - r_0 np = g_0 - r_0 n_i^2$$

where g_0 and $(r_0 np)$ respectively denote the rates of generation and recombination of carriers respectively. Therefore, at equilibrium when $(dn/dt) = 0 = (dp/dt)$, one must have

$$g_0 = r_0 n_i^2 \tag{1.73}$$

as $n = p = n_i$ for an intrinsic material. When the same semiconductor sample is doped with donor impurities, the electron and hole concentration respectively change to n_n and p_n (say). Then on the basis of the above rate equation, it is not difficult to arrive at the following relation

$$g_0 - r_0 n_n p_n = 0$$

or

$$g_0 = r_0 n_i^2 = r_0 n_n p_n$$

i.e.

$$n_n p_n = n_i^2 \tag{1.74}$$

Equation (1.74) is the required relation between the electron and hole densities in an n-type semiconductor. If the electron density builds up due to the supply of electrons from donors, the hole density must fall off in accordance with the above equation. In an n-type semiconductor, electrons are the majority carriers while the holes are the minority ones. The states introduced by donor atoms are localized in space because impurity atoms are immobilized inside the semiconductor lattice. Since the donor states are almost all ionized under room temperature conditions, the Fermi level in donor doped samples must lie below these states in the semiconductor energy level diagram (Fig. 1.10).

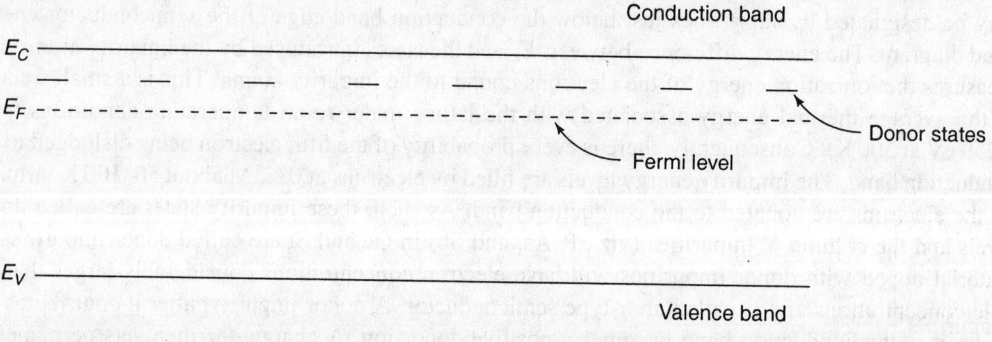

Figure 1.10 *Locations of donor states and the Fermi level in an n-type semiconductor*

For III–V compound semiconductors, the column VI impurities serve as donors. For example, S, Se and Te are the donors to GaAs. These elements occupy As sites and they donate the extra electrons to the conduction band for the necessary n-type conductivity of the semiconductor.

1.5.2 Acceptor doping

Next, let us suppose that the atoms from column III of the periodic table are substituted for the Si atoms in the lattice. These atoms are short of one electron in their outermost orbits to complete their covalent bondings with the neighboring Si atoms. Because of a very strong affinity existing between electrons of opposite spins, an electron from a neighboring Si atom may jump over to the impurity atom to fill the vacancy, creating another in its place. The impurity atom would then start behaving as a negatively charged ion because of the extra electron bound to it. As the extra electron was drawn from the valence band, a positively charged hole will be released there. Thus, the column III impurity atoms when introduced inside a Si lattice is capable of increasing the hole density in the valence band by accepting electrons from it. Since, the electrons are excited from the valence band to the acceptor states, the latter must be localized above the valence band edge in the energy level diagram of the semiconductor. As most of the acceptor states are almost occupied by electrons under room temperature conditions, the Fermi level in an acceptor doped specimen must be situated above the acceptor states (Fig. 1.11). With the increase in the hole density due to the introduction of acceptor impurities in a semiconductor, its hole density must drop off in accordance with the relation $n_p p_p = n_i^2$, for reasons already discussed earlier. The acceptor doped semiconductor is termed as a p-type semiconductor, because the dominant charge carriers in them are the positively charged holes. Holes are the majority carriers in a p-type specimen while the electrons are the minority ones in it. The acceptor levels must be all empty at $T = 0\,\text{K}$. Around 50–100 K, enough lattice thermal energy is available to ionize electrons from the valence band into the acceptor levels leaving behind holes in the valence band. In Si, acceptor levels lie about 0.03–0.06 eV above E_v.

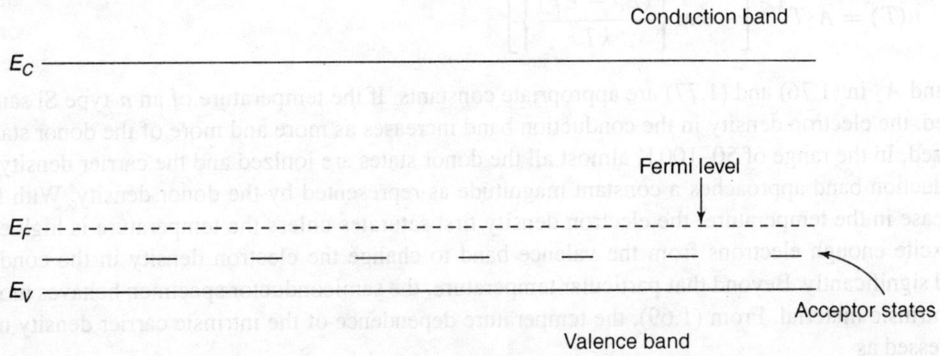

Figure 1.11 *Locations of acceptor states and the Fermi level in a p-type semiconductor*

Impurities from group II (viz., Be, Zn and Cd) substitute group III atoms in III–V compound semiconductors to serve as acceptors. A more ambiguous case arises when a III–V compound semiconductor material is doped with Si or Ge which are from group IV of the periodic table. These impurities are termed amphoteric, meaning that they can serve either as donors or acceptors depending upon whether they occupy group III or group V sublattice of the III–V compound semiconductor crystal.

When a semiconductor is doped with both types of impurities, its resulting conductivity is determined by the impurity which has a larger concentration. The Fermi level would then reside either above or below the energy gap centre depending on whether the material is n- or p-type. If the impurities are such as to cancel each other's contribution, the specimen is termed a compensated intrinsic semiconductor. But, in this case, due to the presence of a larger concentration of impurities, the motion of free carriers would be adversely affected by the impurity scattering phenomenon. There are certain other elements e.g., Au, Cu, Ag etc. with which a semiconductor sample is often doped. These elements are known to introduce states throughout the energy gap of the concerned semiconductor. They are however not used to control the electrical conductivity of the material but to monitor carrier lifetime within the sample.

1.6 Temperature dependence of the semiconductor conductivity

A semiconductor specimen can be distinguished from a metal if data of the temperature dependence of its conductivity are analyzed. To explain this statement, we will study the variation of the semiconductor conductivity as a function of the temperature. For this purpose, we select an n-type specimen whose conductivity may be expressed as

$$\sigma_n(T) = q\mu_n(T)n(T) \tag{1.75}$$

Now, by virtue of (1.43), we may immediately write

$$\mu_n(T) = \frac{A_1}{T^{3/2}} \tag{1.76}$$

presuming that the carriers are being scattered only by lattice vibrations.

But from (1.63) and (1.64), we may now write

$$n(T) = A_2 T^{3/2}\left[-\exp\left\{\frac{(E_c - E_F)}{kT}\right\}\right] \tag{1.77}$$

A_1 and A_2 in (1.76) and (1.77) are appropriate constants. If the temperature of an n-type Si sample is raised, the electron density in the conduction band increases as more and more of the donor states are ionized. In the range of 50–100 K almost all the donor states are ionized and the carrier density in the conduction band approaches a constant magnitude as represented by the donor density. With further increase in the temperature, the electron density first saturates unless the temperature is high enough to excite enough electrons from the valence band to change the electron density in the conduction band significantly. Beyond that particular temperature, the semiconductor specimen behaves more like an intrinsic material. From (1.69), the temperature dependence of the intrinsic carrier density may be expressed as

$$n_i(T) = 2\left[\frac{2\pi kT}{h^2}\right]^{3/2}(m_n^* m_p^*)^{3/4}\exp\left(\frac{-E_G}{2kT}\right) \tag{1.78}$$

Therefore, the plot of $\ln(n_i)$ against $(T)^{-1}$ must be linear. Also, at lower temperatures, the plot of $\ln(n)$ against $(T)^{-1}$ must also be nearly linear (1.77). The combined variation of $\ln(n)$ as a function of $(T)^{-1}$ is shown in Fig. 1.12. Next, to obtain an expression for the semiconductor conductivity, we combine (1.75), (1.76) and (1.77) to obtain

$$\sigma_n(T) = A\exp\left[\frac{(E_c - E_F)}{kT}\right] \tag{1.79}$$

where $A = A_1A_2$. In a doped semiconductor sample the temperature dependence of E_F is also to be considered. If such a variation is first ignored, the variation of $\ln(n)$ with $(T)^{-1}$ would be linear up to about 60 K. With a further rise in temperature, as has already been mentioned earlier, the supply of electrons from the donor states is exhausted and the electron density levels off at $n \cong N_d$. At this stage, (1.75) predicts the electronic conductivity to be given by

$$\sigma(T) = q\left[\frac{A_1}{T^{3/2}}\right]N_d \tag{1.80}$$

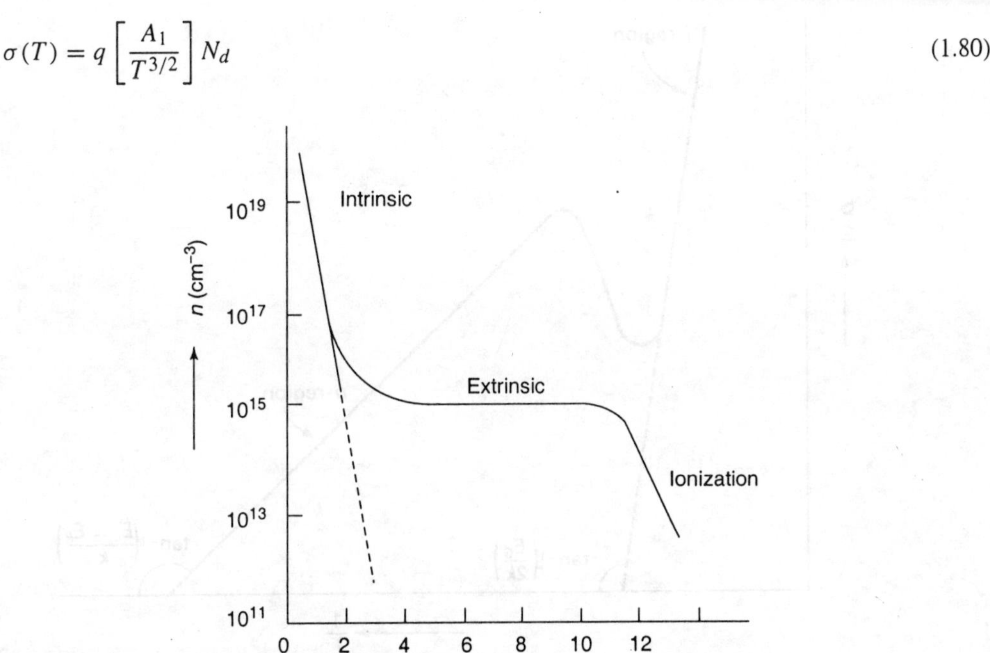

Figure 1.12 *Carrier concentration vs inverse absolute temperature for Si doped with* 10^{15} *donors/cm*^{3}

Thus, when the carrier density has stopped increasing further, $\sigma(T)$ must drop off with increase in T as represented by (1.80). However, when the temperature of the semiconductor is increased sufficiently so as to excite enough electrons from the valence to the conduction band (so as to exceed N_d cm^{-3}), the semiconductor specimen starts behaving more like an intrinsic material. The intrinsic semiconductor conductivity may now be expressed as

$$\sigma_i = q[\mu_n(T) + \mu_p(T)]\,2\left[\frac{2\pi kT}{h^2}\right]^{3/2}(m_n^* m_p^*)^{3/4}\exp\left(\frac{-E_G}{2kT}\right) \tag{1.81}$$

In such a case, $\ln(\sigma_i)$ will vary linearly as a function of $(T)^{-1}$. The composite variation of $\ln(\sigma)$ as a function of $(T)^{-1}$ has been depicted in Fig. 1.13. Such a characteristic dependence is a special one for semiconductors and distinguishes them from metals, whose conductivity is known to decrease monotonically with the rise in temperature.

1.7 Carrier lifetime

When the carrier densities in a semiconductor sample are altered by some external means, once the disturbing influence is arrested they tend to regain back their original magnitudes as quickly as possible. The characteristic time required by the carriers to regain their original magnitudes when the disturbances subside is termed the carrier lifetime. We will now discuss the lifetimes associated with

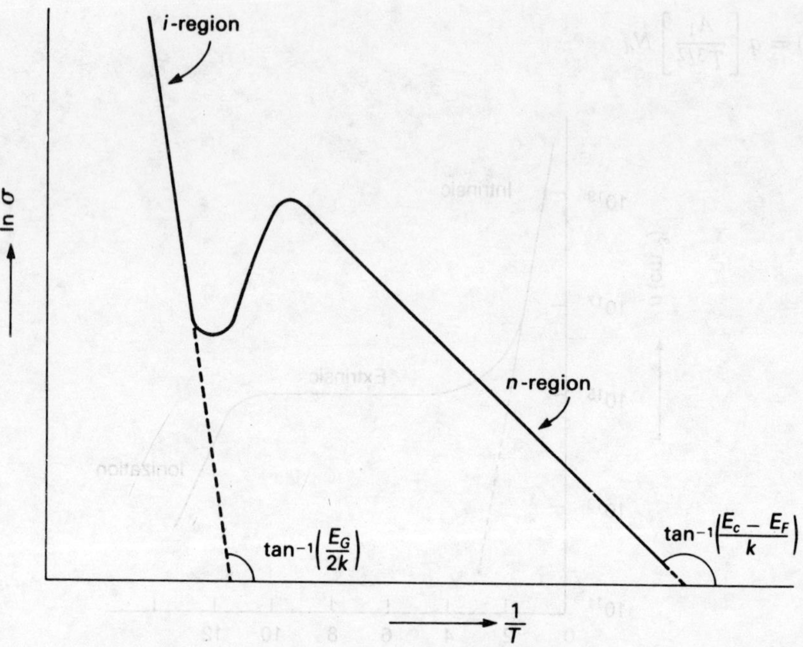

Figure 1.13 *Variation of* $\ln(\sigma)$ *vs* T^{-1}

the (i) carrier recombination and (ii) dielectric relaxation processes. These two phenomena are known to play important roles in the working of semiconductor devices.

1.7.1 Recombination lifetime

In the subsequent analysis, we will only refer to the direct recombination of carriers across the energy gap. Let n_n and p_n denote the thermal equilibrium densities of electrons and holes in an n-type Si sample. When it is irradiated by a steady source of ultraviolet radiation, the respective carrier densities builds up to n_0 and p_0 before they stabilize. Since electrons and holes are always produced in pairs, we must have

$$(p_0 - p_n) = (n_0 - n_n) \tag{1.82}$$

Now, let the source of radiation be turned off abruptly so that the carrier generation is suddenly put off. Then, the excess carriers, represented by (1.82), start recombining. The recombination rate of carriers is proportional to the instantaneous densities of electrons and holes. We may then represent the rate of carrier decay by recombination at any time t by the following relation

$$-\left(\frac{dn}{dt}\right) = -\left(\frac{dp}{dt}\right) = r_0 np - g_0 \tag{1.83}$$

where r_0 is the coefficient of recombination and g_0 denotes the temperature-dependent carrier generation rate. Expressing (1.83) in a differential form, we get

$$\frac{-d(\delta n)}{dt} = \frac{-d(\delta p)}{dt} = r_0 n \delta p + r_0 p \delta n = r_0 np\left[\left(\frac{\delta p}{p}\right) + \left(\frac{\delta n}{n}\right)\right] \tag{1.84}$$

where δn and δp may be taken to represent the magnitudes of the decrements in the electron and the hole densities respectively at any time t during the recombination process. For an n-type specimen, one may presume the fractional decrease in the electron density to be negligible compared to the corresponding fractional decrease in the hole density i.e., $(\delta n/n) \ll (\delta p/p)$. Under this approximation (1.84) simplifies to

$$\frac{-d(\delta p)}{dt} = r_0 n_n \delta p \tag{1.85}$$

where we have assumed $n_n \cong n$. Integrating (1.85) from the instant the light is switched off to any arbitrary instant t, we find

$$\int_{\delta p_0}^{\delta p} \frac{d(\delta p)}{(\delta p)} = -r_0 n_n \int_0^t dt$$

Integrating, we get

$$\delta p = \delta p_0 \exp\left(\frac{-t}{\tau_p}\right) \tag{1.86}$$

where $\delta p = (p - p_n)$ and $\delta p_0 = (p_0 - p_n)$ and

$$\tau_p = (r_0 n_n)^{-1} = \frac{n_i^2}{(g_0 n_n)} = \left(\frac{p_n}{g_0}\right) \tag{1.87}$$

In deriving (1.87), we assumed $r_0 = (g_0/n_i^2)$. Now, the constant τ_p is defined as the minority carrier lifetime for holes. Similarly, the decay equation for electrons in a p-type sample may be expressed as

$$(n - n_p) = (n_0 - n_p) \exp\left(\frac{-t}{\tau_n}\right) \tag{1.88}$$

where

$$\tau_n = (r_0 p_p)^{-1} = \frac{n_i^2}{(g_0 p_p)} = \left(\frac{n_p}{g_0}\right) \tag{1.89}$$

denotes the minority carrier lifetime for electrons in a p-type sample. From (1.86) and (1.88), we may conclude that for smaller deviations from the condition of thermal equilibrium, the excess carriers decay exponentially with time. The decay constant is called the recombination lifetime or the carrier lifetime (τ_p or τ_n). Figure 1.14 shows the decay curve of the photoexcited carriers. It is however easy to realize that the dependence shown for minority carriers must be equally valid for majority carriers, as well. Since it is easier to observe the decay of minority carriers by experimental means, it is customary to refer to the minority carrier lifetimes only. The latter may now be defined in the following three ways:

(i) From (1.86) and (1.88), we see that the recombination lifetime is the time required by the excess carriers to decay to $(e)^{-1}$ of its original value.

(ii) We also find from (1.86) that $(dp/dt)_{t=0} = -(\delta p_0/\tau_p)$. Hence, the intercept of the tangent drawn to the decay curve (Fig. 1.14) at $t = 0$ cuts the time axis at $t = \tau_p$. This result may, therefore, be taken to provide another definition to the carrier lifetime.

(iii) From Fig. 1.14 we also notice that the excess carriers of a density $\delta p = (p - p_n)$ at any time t may be taken to live for a time dt only. Then the average life t_{av} of excess carriers may be calculated as

$$t_{av} = \int_0^\infty \frac{(p - p_n)dt]}{(p_0 - p_n)} = \int_0^\infty \exp\left(\frac{-t}{\tau_p}\right) dt = \tau_p \qquad (1.90)$$

Thus, the excess carriers, on an average, live for a time τ_p which incidentally is the minority carrier lifetime. An n-type Si bar can be injected with an excess of electrons (Fig. 1.15) or holes (Fig. 1.16)

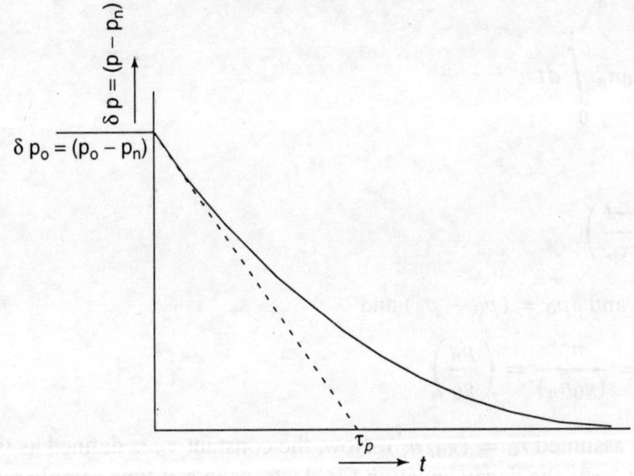

Figure 1.14 *Decay curve of photoexcited carriers*

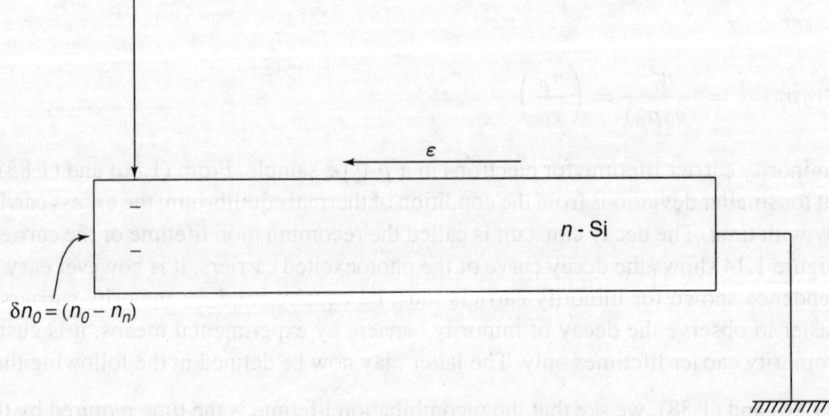

Figure 1.15 *Injection of excess electron density at one end of an n-type Si bar*

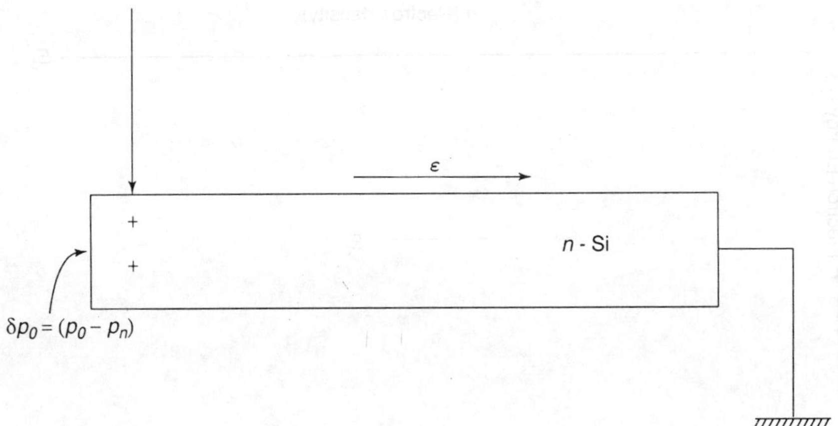

Figure 1.16 Injection of excess hole density at one end of an n-type Si bar

1.7.2 Dielectric relaxation time

Let us next consider the situation where the initial disturbance can alter the concentration of only a particular kind of carrier in a semiconductor sample. In an n-type Si bar having a thermal equilibrium density n_n of electrons, let some electrons be injected at one end from an external source so that the local electron density there increases to n_0. Owing to the increment in the electron density there, by $\delta n_0 = (n_0 - n_n)$, the following sequence of events sets in:

(i) Due to the presence of excess charges at that end of the bar, an electric field is set up within it which travels down its length with the speed of light.

(ii) As a result, the conduction electrons in the bar undergo a net displacement in an appropriate direction producing an electric current due to drift which eventually expels the excess electrons injected into the bar and restores the electrical neutrality.

The characteristic time required for the expulsion of excess electrons is called the dielectric relaxation time. An expression for it may now be derived as discussed below. The electric field intensity generated within the bar due to the introduction of excess carriers of a density $\rho = -q(n_0 - n_n)$ is given by Gauss's law of electrostatics as

$$\text{div}\ \varepsilon = \left(\frac{\rho}{\kappa\varepsilon_0}\right) \tag{1.91}$$

where κ denotes the dielectric constant of the semiconductor and $\varepsilon_0 = 8.854 \times 10^{-12}$ F/m, is the permittivity of free space. The current density J that results within the sample due to the establishment of the electric intensity ε is given by the equation of continuity as

$$\text{div}\ J + \left(\frac{\partial}{\partial t}\right)\rho = 0 \tag{1.92}$$

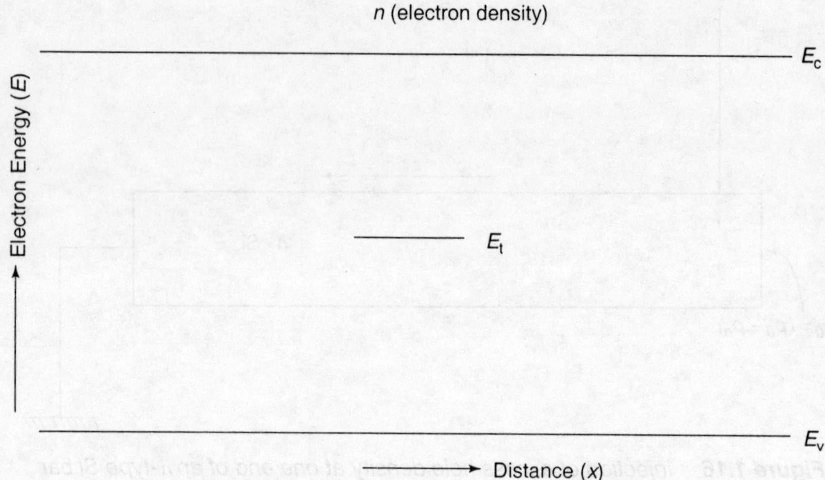

Figure 1.17 *Recombination of carriers through trap levels*

The resulting current density J and the electric intensity ε are related to one another by Ohm's law as

$$J = \sigma \varepsilon \tag{1.93}$$

Now to obtain an expression for the time rate of decay of excess carriers, we relate (1.91), (1.92) and (1.93) suitably to get

$$\left(\frac{\partial}{\partial t}\right) \rho = -\left(\frac{\sigma \rho}{\kappa \varepsilon_0}\right)$$

Integrating the above equation, we get

$$\rho = \rho_0 \exp\left(\frac{-\sigma t}{\kappa \varepsilon_0}\right)$$

or

$$(n - n_n) = (n_0 - n_n) \exp\left(\frac{-t}{\tau_d}\right) \tag{1.94}$$

where

$$\tau_d = \left(\frac{\kappa \varepsilon_0}{\sigma}\right) \tag{1.95}$$

is known as the dielectric relaxation time. For a Si sample of resistivity 1 ohm cm, this τ_d works out to be around 10^{-12} s. With increase in σ, this time may even become shorter. For metals, therefore, it may be quite small to measure. For insulators, on the other hand, this may be as high as minutes, hours or even days.

However, instead of electrons, if holes are injected at one end of the n-type bar of our previous example, the situations would be a little different. In this case, the electrical neutrality would be restored as quickly as before, with the characteristic time τ_d. As a result, the same number of electrons as that of injected holes would be drawn inside the bar from outside for the restoration of the electrical neutrality with the same characteristic dielectric relaxation time. The excess electrons and holes present inside the bar then begin to decay with a far longer recombination lifetime, as discussed earlier. In a reasonably good semiconductor sample, the recombination lifetime is found to lie somewhere in the range of milliseconds to microseconds.

1.8 Recombination of electrons and holes through traps: Shockley–Read–Hall theory

In the last section, we discussed the mechanism of direct recombination of electrons in the conduction band with holes in the valence band across the energy gap. But in semiconductors, the recombination of carriers takes place mostly through energy levels, known as traps, which are located somewhere near the energy gap centre. We now present below an account of such a theory of recombination, as developed by Shockley and his co-workers.
Let n denote the instantaneous free electron density in the conduction band and f_t denote the fraction of trap levels at an energy E_t occupied by electrons. The time rate of capture of electrons by the trap levels may then be expressed as

$$R_c = C_n n(1 - f_t) \tag{1.96}$$

where C_n is a constant that measures the rate of capture per electron when all the trap levels are empty. On the other hand, the rate of emission of electrons from the trap levels may be expressed as

$$R_e = C'_n f_t \tag{1.97}$$

where C'_n denotes the rate of emission per electron. At thermal equilibrium $R_c = R_e$. Therefore, it follows that

$$C'_n = C_n n_0 \left[\frac{(1 - f_{t0})}{f_{t0}}\right] \tag{1.98}$$

where n_0 is the equilibrium electron density and f_{t0} is the corresponding Fermi probability function. Since, f_{t0} is given by the Fermi–Dirac statistics, it is easy to notice that

$$\left[\frac{(1 - f_{t0})}{f_{t0}}\right] = \exp\left[\frac{(E_t - E_F)}{kT}\right] \tag{1.99}$$

Under non-equilibrium conditions, the net rate of electron capture would be given by

$$R_n = R_c - R_e = C_n n(1 - f_t) - C'_n f_t \tag{1.100}$$

Combining (1.98), (1.99) and (1.100), we find

$$R_n = C_n n(1 - f_t) - C_n n_0 f_t \exp\left[\frac{(E_t - E_F)}{kT}\right] \tag{1.101}$$

We may now express (1.101) as

$$R_n = C_n[n(1 - f_t) - n_1 f_t] \tag{1.102}$$

where

$$n_1 = n_0 \exp\left[\frac{(E_t - E_F)}{kT}\right] \tag{1.103}$$

Thus n_1 measures the electron density in the conduction band when the trap level E_t coincides with E_F. The net rate of hole capture by the trap levels may also be calculated similarly and expressed as

$$R_p = C_p[pf_t - p_1(1 - f_t)] \tag{1.104}$$

where

$$p_1 = p_0 \exp\left[\frac{(E_F - E_t)}{kT}\right] \tag{1.105}$$

measures the hole density in the valence band when the Fermi level coincides with the trap level. Carrier recombination begins whenever there is a departure from the condition of thermal equilibrium. Since, electron-hole recombination occurs in pairs, we must have the net rate of recombination R given by

$$R = R_n = R_p \tag{1.106}$$

Therefore, equating (1.102) and (1.104), we get

$$f_t = \frac{[(nC_n + p_1 C_p)]}{[C_n(n + n_1) + C_p(p + p_1)]} \tag{1.107}$$

Substituting for f_t in (1.102), the net rate of electron-hole recombination may be obtained in the following form:

$$R = \frac{[np - n_i^2]}{[(n + n_1)\tau_{p0} + (p + p_1)\tau_{n0}]} \tag{1.108}$$

where $\tau_{p0} = (C_p)^{-1}$ and $\tau_{n0} = (C_n)^{-1}$ denote the carrier lifetimes in strongly doped n and p materials respectively. Equation (1.108) gives the carrier recombination rate in a lightly doped semiconductor specimen. When the specimen becomes heavily doped, the effect of trap levels in determining the recombination rate becomes insignificant.

1.9 Optical properties of semiconductors

The optical behaviour displayed by materials can be thought of merely as a special case of the response of a solid to the application of an external electric field. The electric field in an electromagnetic wave can exert forces on and its energy can be absorbed either by electrons or the atomic nuclei present inside the material, since both carry electrostatic charges. As the frequency of the incident wave is raised and it approaches the natural frequency of the lattice, the amplitude of the induced nuclear motion rises and the corresponding energy absorbed by it also increases, reaching a maximum at the resonant or the natural frequency. Beyond this stage, the induced motion and its frequency decreases. The science which studies the absorbed or emitted radiation as a function of wavelength is called 'spectroscopy'. This is a powerful tool in investigating the properties of solids, liquids and gases.

The seeming paradox that metals can both absorb and reflect electromagnetic waves strongly is no contradiction. This is because an accelerated electronic charge radiates electromagnetic waves. Most of the incident energy is, therefore, reradiated and a part of it is also able to penetrate the surface. A fraction of the absorbed energy of the electrons is then quickly transferred to the lattice by collision. Strong absorption and reflection of electromagnetic waves persist in solids as the frequency of electromagnetic waves is raised through infrared, visible and near ultraviolet portions of the electromagnetic spectrum until in the far ultraviolet portion, around 100 nm, a piece of a metal becomes significantly more transparent. It is only at high frequencies, above 10^{16} Hz, that electrons are unable to follow the variations in the magnitudes of the electromagnetic signal intensity due to their inertia. Consequently, they are then unable to emit or absorb the incident radiation significantly.

Because the free carrier concentration in semiconductors is relatively smaller compared to metals, the free carrier absorption in them is also relatively weaker. Significant absorption in them is observed to occur only for $h\nu \geq E_G$, the semiconductor energy gap.

(i) Optical absorption An important technique for measuring the energy gap of semiconductors is the absorption of incident photons by the material as a photon of energy $h\nu \geq E_G$ can only be absorbed by a semiconductor material. We would expect the ratio of the transmitted to the incident light on a semiconductor specimen to depend upon the photon wavelength (λ) and the thickness of the sample. As a light beam passes through a sample, its intensity $I(x)$ at a distance x below the surface can be calculated by presuming that the decrease in intensity there is proportional to $I(x)$ and the thickness 'dx' of the material traversed. That is,

$$-dI(x) \propto I(x)dx$$

or

$$-dI(x) = \alpha I(x)dx$$

Integrating, we find

$$I(x) = I_0 \exp(-\alpha x) \tag{1.109}$$

where α is a constant called the absorption coefficient of the material and this has a unit of m^{-1}. This coefficient varies with the photon wavelength and the semiconductor material.

(ii) Photoluminescence If carriers are excited by photon absorption, the radiation resulting from the recombination of the excited carriers is called 'photoluminescence'. Many semiconductors, especially compound semiconductors with direct energy gaps are well-suited for light emissions. Direct recombination is a very fast process and takes about 10^{-8} s or less. This fast luminescence process is often

referred to as 'fluorescence'. In some materials emission continues for a few seconds after the source of excitation is turned off. This slower process is termed 'phosphorescence' and materials giving out such emissions are known as 'phosphors'. The colour of the light emitted by a phosphor depends primarily on the impurities present.
One of the common examples of photoluminescence is found in the fluorescent lamp. Such a light source essentially consists of a glass tube filled with a mixture of argon and mercury gases at a low pressure with a fluorescent coating inside the tube. When an electric discharge is initiated between the electrodes in the tube, the excited atoms of the gas emit photons, largely in the visible and the UV regions of the electromagnetic spectrum. The emitted light is next absorbed by the luminescent coating within the tube and visible photons are re-emitted by it. The colour of the emitted light may be adjusted by a proper selection of the fluorescent material.

(iii) Cathodoluminescence This refers to the phenomenon of light emission when a material is bombarded by a high energy electron beam. The most common example of excitation of luminescent materials by energetic electrons and subsequent emission of light is found in a cathode ray tube. The basic principle involved is the selective excitation of a phosphorescent screen by a beam of energetic electrons within a vacuum tube.

(iv) Electroluminescence If carriers are excited to a state by the injection of a suitable electric current so that they are capable of emitting light, the consequent phenomenon is called, 'electroluminescence'. In light emitting diodes (LEDs) and semiconductor lasers, an electric current causes the injection of minority carriers within the depletion layer resulting in the emission of recombination radiation.

(v) Photoconductive devices There are a number of materials whose resistances undergo a change when exposed to a radiation. This property has been exploited usefully in the design of devices to measure illumination levels of incident lights. Many systems use a light beam directed to a photoconductor whose obstruction by an external object generates an electric signal thereby detecting the presence of a foreign object. Such systems are useful in the design of burglar's alarms, moving object counters and many other useful applications. Light detectors are also used in optical signalling systems.where a light beam carries the information. Before selecting a photoconducting material for a particular application, one must be aware of its sensitivity to a given wavelength range and the response time. Most of the usual semiconductors are sensitive to photons with energies equal to their band gaps. CdS ($E_G = 2.42\,\text{eV}$) is the most useful one in the visible range whereas Ge ($E_G = 0.67\,\text{eV}$) and InSb ($E_G = 0.18\,\text{eV}$) are useful in the infrared portions of the spectrum. Some photoconductors respond to excitations of carriers from the impurity levels to the conduction band and, therefore, they are sensitive to photons of energies less than the energy gap of the material.
The optical sensitivity of a photoconductor can be evaluated by examining the steady state carrier density generated by the optical generation rate g_{op} because they are given by

$$\delta n = g_{op}\tau_n \quad \text{and} \quad \delta p = g_{op}\tau_p \tag{1.110}$$

and the change in the photoconductivity is given by

$$\Delta\sigma = q g_{op}(\tau_n\mu_n + \tau_p\mu_p) \tag{1.111}$$

Therefore, for a better optical response, higher carrier mobilities associated with very long carrier lifetimes are desired.

1.10 Gunn effect

Ohm's law is obeyed by most homogeneous semiconductors over a wide range of current density J and electric intensity ε. Such a situation persists as long as the carriers in semiconductors remain in thermal equilibrium. The situation becomes quite interesting when the velocities acquired by the carriers moving in electric fields of increasing intensities are unable to increase any further due to their frequent collisions with the vibrating lattice. The J–V characteristic of the semiconductor specimen deviates from its usual linear behaviour and then tends to saturate or become sublinear (Fig. 1.6). For some semiconductors like GaAs and InP, a portion of the v_d vs.ε plot then displays a negative conductance region which is usually unstable.

Such a negative conductance region in a GaAs crystal arises due to the partial transfer of electrons from the Γ-conduction band to the X-point satellite valley of the E–$\boldsymbol{k}$ curve. A simplified energy band diagram of GaAs crystal is shown in Fig. 1.18. At normal electric field intensities no electron is excited to the X-point satellite valley. Electrons acquire enough thermal energy to be excited to the X-point satellite valley at a field of about 10^5 Volts/m. As the rate of carrier transfer by the thermal vibrations of the atoms of the crystal from the Γ-conduction band to the X-point satellite valley and vice versa is proportional to the densities of states in respective bands, an electron enjoys a better chance of being retained in the upper valley because of the very large density of states there relative to that in the lower band ($\sim$70 : 1). After the transfer of carriers to the X-point satellite valley, their effective masses are enhanced significantly because of the modifications of their E–k relation. Some of the transferred electrons may also revert back to their original Γ-conduction band states after releasing their excess

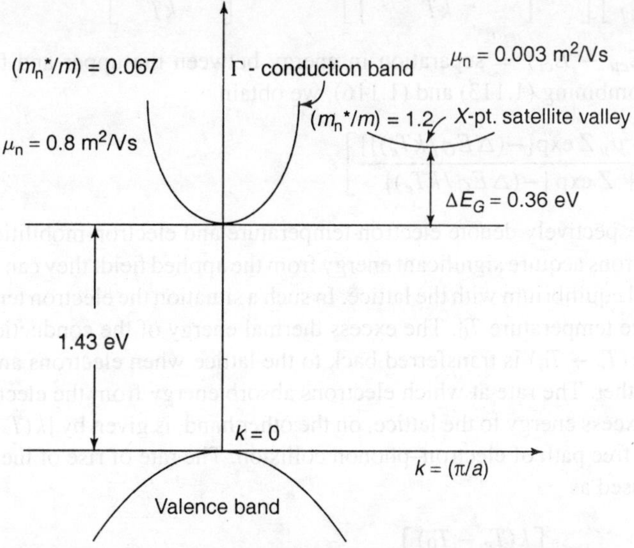

Figure 1.18 *A simplified energy band diagram for GaAs*

energy to phonons. Thus, at reasonably high electric field intensities, a dynamic equilibrium between carrier excitation to the X-point satellite valley and their subsequent reversion to the Γ-conduction band is realized with a significant proportion of electrons being present in both bands.

If (n_l, v_l) and (n_u, v_u) respectively are the electron densities and drift velocities in the lower and upper valleys (Fig. 1.18) of the semiconductor, the average drift velocity of carriers may be expressed as

$$v_d = \left[\frac{(n_l v_l + n_u v_u)}{(n_l + n_u)}\right] \tag{1.112}$$

Expressing $v_l = \mu_l \varepsilon$ and $v_u = \mu_u \varepsilon$, we get from (1.112),

$$v_d = \left[\frac{\left\{\mu_l + \left(\frac{n_u}{n_l}\right)\mu_u\right\}}{\left\{1 + \left(\frac{n_u}{n_l}\right)\right\}}\right]\varepsilon \tag{1.113}$$

Using (1.63), we may write

$$n_u = N_{cu}\left[\exp\left\{-\frac{(E_{cu} - E_F)}{kT}\right\}\right] \tag{1.114}$$

and

$$n_l = N_{cl}\left[\exp\left\{-\frac{(E_{cl} - E_F)}{kT}\right\}\right] \tag{1.115}$$

Dividing (1.114) by (1.115), we find

$$\left[\frac{n_u}{n_l}\right] = \left[\frac{N_{cu}}{N_{cl}}\right]\left[\exp\left\{-\frac{(E_{cu} - E_{cl})}{kT}\right\}\right] = Z\exp\left[-\frac{(\Delta E_G)}{kT}\right] \tag{1.116}$$

where $\Delta E_G = (E_{cu} - E_{cl})$ = separation in energy between the upper and the lower valleys and $Z = [N_{cu}/N_{cl}]$. Combining (1.113) and (1.116), we obtain

$$v_d = \left[\frac{[\mu_l + \mu_u Z\exp\{-(\Delta E_G/kT_e)\}]}{[1 + Z\exp\{-(\Delta E_G/kT_e)\}]}\right]\varepsilon \tag{1.117}$$

where T_e, μ_l, μ_u respectively denote electron temperature and electron mobilities at lower and upper valleys. When electrons acquire significant energy from the applied field, they can no longer be regarded to remain in thermal equilibrium with the lattice. In such a situation the electron temperature T_e is higher relative to the lattice temperature T_0. The excess thermal energy of the conduction electrons over that of the lattice viz., $k(T_e - T_0)$ is transferred back to the lattice when electrons and phonons happen to collide with each other. The rate at which electrons absorb energy from the electric field is $q\varepsilon v_d$. The rate of transfer of excess energy to the lattice, on the other hand, is given by $[k(T_e - T_0)/(l/v_d)]$ where l denotes the mean free path of electron–phonon collision. The rate of rise of the electron temperature may then be expressed as

$$C\left(\frac{dT_e}{dt}\right) = q\varepsilon v_d - \left[\frac{k(T_e - T_0)}{(l/v_d)}\right] \tag{1.118}$$

where C denotes the specific heat per electron. At equilibrium when the electron temperature attains a steady value i.e., $(dT_e/dt) = 0$, one must have

$$T_e = T_0 + \left(\frac{ql}{k}\right)\varepsilon \tag{1.119}$$

Thus, T_e and T_0 are related by (1.119). For lower electric field intensities i.e., $\varepsilon \ll (k/ql)$, $T_e \cong T_0$, and in (1.117), we may presume $\Delta E_G \gg kT_e$. In such a case, the second terms in the numerator and the denominator of (1.117) are negligible compared to the first one. We then find $v_d = \mu_l\varepsilon$. On the other hand, for larger electric field intensities i.e., $\varepsilon \gg (k/ql)$, when $T_e \gg T_0$, we have $\Delta E_G \ll kT_e$ and the second terms in the numerator and the denominator of (1.117) dominate over the first one and we then find, $v_d = \mu_u\varepsilon$. However, when $\Delta E_G \cong kT_e$, both the terms in the numerator and the denominator of (1.117) are comparable to one another and the denominator may exceed unity. The effective mobility of the sample then lies between μ_l and μ_u. The slope of the v_d vs.ε curve has been shown in Fig. 1.19. This is determined by the following three factors: (i) the ratio of the density of states Z, (ii) the mobility ratio (μ_u/μ_l) and (iii) the lattice temperature T_0. The requirements to obtain the negative mobility region in the v_d vs.ε curve of a two valley semiconductor may now be summarized as follows:

i) the higher energy satellite valley must have an appreciably larger electron effective mass than the main conduction band. The negative mobility region cannot be identified unless $\mu_l > 50\ \mu_u$;
ii) the energy difference ΔE_G between the main conduction band and the satellite valley must be greater than the thermal energy of the lattice i.e., $\Delta E_G > kT_0$; otherwise, carriers may be excited thermally from the lower to the upper band; and finally,
iii) $\Delta E_G \ll E_G$, otherwise, carriers would be field-ionized directly from the valence to the conduction band along with their ionization to the satellite valley. This would ultimately wipe out the negative mobility region from the v_d vs.ε characteristic altogether.

At lower electric field intensities across a GaAs sample, electrons reside in the lower valley where the mobility μ_l is constant and high. At higher electric field intensities, on the other hand, when the carriers are excited to the upper valley, the mobility μ_u is low but is once again constant. Between these two regions lies the portion of the negative slope of the v_d vs.ε curve where we find the negative differential mobility $\mu^* = -(dv_d/d\varepsilon)$. Such a possible drop in the mobility was predicted by Ridley, Hilsum and Watkins several years before Gunn actually demonstrated this effect in GaAs in 1963. As such, this phenomenon associated with the negative differential mobility is often termed the Ridley-Hilsum-Watkins (RHW) mechanism. Clearly, this depends upon the bulk properties of the semiconductor. The effect has been exploited successfully to design a solid state source for microwaves.

To understand the working of such an oscillator, we must remember that any departure from the space-charge neutrality of an n-type semiconductor due to the presence of some extra electrons introduced in it by some external means is restored almost instantaneously (Equation (1.94)). When μ or σ happens to be negative this equation predicts a remarkable result. Any space-charge fluctuation then has a tendency to build up instead of decaying. A space-charge may initially be presumed to be nucleated at the site of any doping inhomogeniety or a crystal imperfection when the electric field across the sample corresponds to the point C of Fig. 1.19. A tiny space-charge developed within a GaAs sample then grows into a dipole layer and at the same time it maintains its steady drift from the vicinity of the cathode to the anode under the influence of an external electric field. The variation of the potential difference V, the electric field intensity ε, the charge density ρ, the displacement current density $(\partial\varepsilon/\partial t)$ and the total current density J as functions of x (position coordinate) measured along the length of the bar in

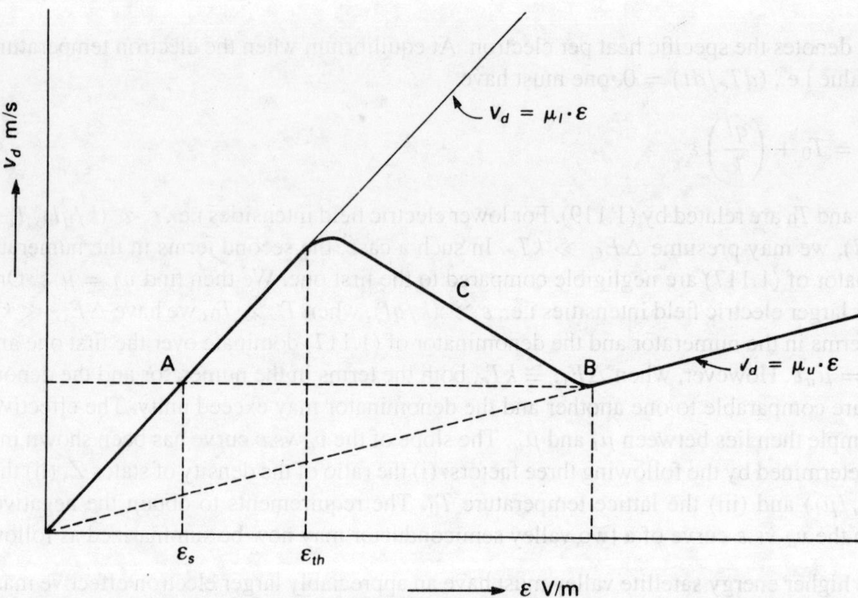

Figure 1.19 *Velocity (v_d) vs electric field (ε) characteristics of electrons in GaAs*

the steady state condition are shown in Fig. 1.20. When the electric field falls in the negative mobility region, corresponding to C of Fig. 1.19, the electron density at a point within the semiconductor then grows with time according to (1.94). This causes the electric field intensity within the region occupied by electrons to increase. But, according to Fig. 1.19, the accumulated electrons then start moving very slowly. But, since the applied electric field intensity is held constant and is maintained at ε_{th}, the field outside the electron space-charge must drop below ε_{th} where the electron drift velocity, according to Fig. 1.19, must be higher. This causes electrons outside the accumulation layer to drift with greater velocities producing an electron depletion layer adjacent to the accumulation layer. Such accumulation and depletion layers continue to grow until the electric field inside the dipole layer stabilizes at B while that outside, at A (Fig. 1.19). The drift velocities at A and B being the same (v_s), the space-charge layer thereafter drifts down the rest of the bar without any further growth. Once the pulse of electrons which has developed inside the bar is released at the output, the situation inside the bar reverts back to the case corresponding to the ε_{th} applied across the specimen in the beginning. As this electric field lies in the negative mobility region, a space-charge would once again be nucleated as before and it would grow as it drifts down the bar. Further growth of the space-charge layer is arrested when the field inside and outside it once again stabilizes and the developed charge pulse is delivered at the output. The process described above would be repeated over and over again as long as the external electric field lies in the negative mobility region. Due to a very small dielectric relaxation time, the frequency of such an oscillator is expected to be in the microwave range.

During the initial growth of the domain, an increasing fraction of the applied voltage appears across it, at the expense of the electric field in the rest of the bar. As a result, it is unlikely that more than one domain will be present in the bar at a time. After the formation of one domain, the electric field in the rest of the bar quickly drops below the threshold value required for the onset of the negative differential conductivity. In our earlier discussions we assumed that the domain finds sufficient time to grow to its full size before it finally drifts out of the bar. Proper limits on the electron density n_0 and

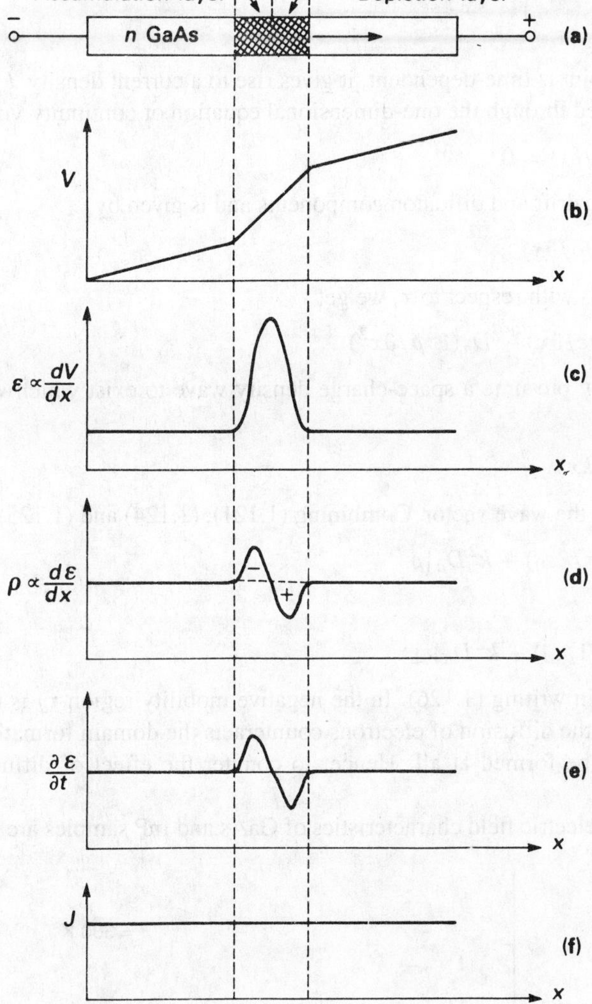

Figure 1.20 *Motion of a domain in a GaAs bar: (a) domain; (b) voltage variation across the bar; (c) electric field profile; (d) charge density variation with distance; (e) variation of displacement current density with distance and (f) total current density profile*

the sample length L have to be clearly specified for this purpose by requiring that (L/v_d) be greater than the magnitude of the dielectric relaxation time τ_d in the negative mobility region. That is,

$$\left(\frac{L}{v_d}\right) \geq |\tau_d| = \left[\frac{\kappa\varepsilon_0}{q\mu^* n_0}\right] \quad \text{or} \quad Ln_0 \geq \left|\frac{\kappa\varepsilon_0 v_d}{q\mu^*}\right| \sim 10^{12}\ \text{cm}^{-2} \tag{1.120}$$

where we use (1.94).

During the drift of domains, electrons constituting it, also have a tendency to diffuse. Such an effect may prevent or impede the domain formation. We may quantify the effect of diffusion in the following manner: The electric field intensity within the domain on the Gauss's law of electrostatics is given by

$$(\partial\varepsilon/\partial x) - (\rho/\kappa\varepsilon_0) = 0 \tag{1.121}$$

Since, ρ at a given point is time-dependent, it gives rise to a current density J inside the bar. J and ρ are known to be related through the one-dimensional equation of continuity viz.,

$$(\partial J/\partial x) + (\partial \rho/\partial t) = 0 \tag{1.122}$$

But J consists of both drift and diffusion components and is given by

$$J = \sigma\varepsilon - D_n(\partial \rho/\partial x) \tag{1.123}$$

Differentiating (1.123) with respect to x, we get

$$(\partial J/\partial x) = \sigma(\partial \varepsilon/\partial x) - D_n(\partial^2 \rho/\partial x^2) \tag{1.124}$$

Along the bar we may presume a space-charge density wave to exist which will have the following form

$$\rho = \rho_0 \exp(-j\boldsymbol{k}x) \tag{1.125}$$

where $\boldsymbol{k} = (2\pi/\lambda)$, is the wave vector. Combining (1.121), (1.124) and (1.125), we find

$$(\partial \rho/\partial t) = -[(\sigma/\kappa\varepsilon_0) + \boldsymbol{k}^2 D_n]\rho$$

Integrating, we find

$$\rho = \rho_0 \exp[-\{(1/\tau_d) + \boldsymbol{k}^2 D_n\}t] \tag{1.126}$$

We have used (1.94) in writing (1.126). In the negative mobility region τ_d is negative and therefore, according to (1.126), the diffusion of electrons counteracts the domain formation. If $\boldsymbol{k}^2 D_n > (1/\tau_d)$, the domain may not be formed at all. Hence, to counter the effect of diffusion, one must ensure $(\boldsymbol{k}^2 D_n) \ll (1/\tau_d)$.

The drift velocity vs. electric field characteristics of GaAs and InP samples are shown in the Fig. 1.21.

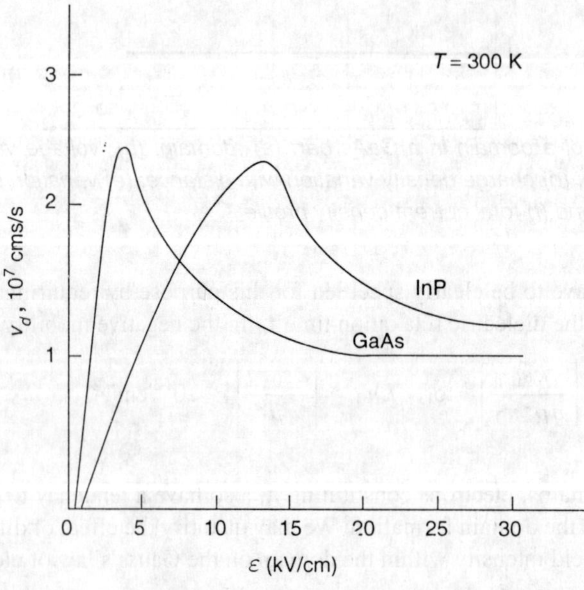

Figure 1.21 *Drift velocity (v_d) vs. electric field (ε) characteristic of electrons in GaAs and InP.*

Modes of operations of Gunn diodes The drift of stable domains as observed by Gunn is attainable in a circuit containing a Gunn diode, a resistance and a source of d.c. power. But such a mode is hardly employed for a practical conversion of d.c. power into microwaves. Negative conductivity devices are normally employed with resonant circuits such as a high Q microwave cavity. Since the applied voltage in such cases varies with time, the device behaviour is expected to depend on both the frequency and the amplitude of the signal applied to the Gunn diode. We discuss below some of the important modes of operation of a Gunn diode.

When the field applied to a Gunn diode exceeds ε_{th}, a negative conductance exists within it till a stable domain is nucleated. Thereafter, the domain moves with a constant velocity ($v_d = v_s$) down the bar both in its high and low field regions. Domains drift down the bar until they reach the anode or till its low field value drops below ε_s required to maintain a steady v_s. For a steady bias above ε_{th}, stable Gunn domains are formed which drift towards the anode. This is the so called resistive mode of operation, already discussed. The current wave forms received at the output, in this case, consist of a series of spikes appearing at a frequency of (v_s/L). This mode is depicted in Fig. 1.22(a). As already mentioned, a Gunn diode in this mode is hardly employed for the conversion of d.c. power into microwaves.

An a.c. transit time mode of operation can be realized easily if a Gunn diode is used in conjunction with a resonant circuit whose time period of oscillation is chosen to be equal to the carrier transit time down the bar. Presuming that during the transit of the domain, the field never drops below ε_s, a domain (or a dipole layer) can be formed and be propagated during each a.c. cycle (Fig. 1.22(b)). In this mode, the d.c. to microwave conversion efficiency can be as low as 10%.

To increase the conversion efficiency, the domain should be collected early in the negative half cycle and the formation of the next domain should be delayed. For example, if the transit time is so chosen that the domain is collected while $\varepsilon < \varepsilon_{th}$ (Fig. 1.22(c)), a new domain cannot be formed unless the effective field rises above ε_{th}, once again. The efficiency of this delayed domain mode is better than the simple transit time mode.

If the bias drops below ε_s during the negative half cycle and the domain is collected soon thereafter, the efficiency of the device can be increased up to 20%. If the bias drops below ε_s during the negative half cycle (Fig. 1.22(d)), the domain collapses before it is able to reach the anode. In this quenched domain mode, the a.c. period of oscillation has to be less than the domain transit time.

One of the most efficient modes of Gunn diode operation does not involve the formation of any domain at all. In this so called limited space-charge accumulation (LSA) mode, the a.c. frequency of the associated resonant circuit is chosen to be so high compared to the transit time frequency that the domains have an insufficient time to be formed when the field is above the threshold. As such, the sample is effectively maintained in its negative conductance state during a larger fraction of the voltage cycle (Fig. 1.22(e)). This mode of operation can be easily realized by imposing an a.c. microwave field upon the d.c. field biasing the sample in the negative conductivity region. Such an a.c. field may be derived easily from the associated resonant circuit. The frequency of the a.c. field must be high enough to prevent any domain formation when the field remains above the threshold value. The d.c. and the a.c. field magnitudes are so chosen that during the negative half cycle the effective field over the GaAs sample drops below the sustaining field ε_s, so that a domain which might have been formed would soon be quenched. The negative conductance offered by the GaAs sample may then be used to compensate for the finite losses in the resonant cavities where microwave oscillations could be sustained indefinitely. Gunn diodes are unquestionably one of the most important sources of microwave power known today. Portable radar sets could be developed because of their discovery.

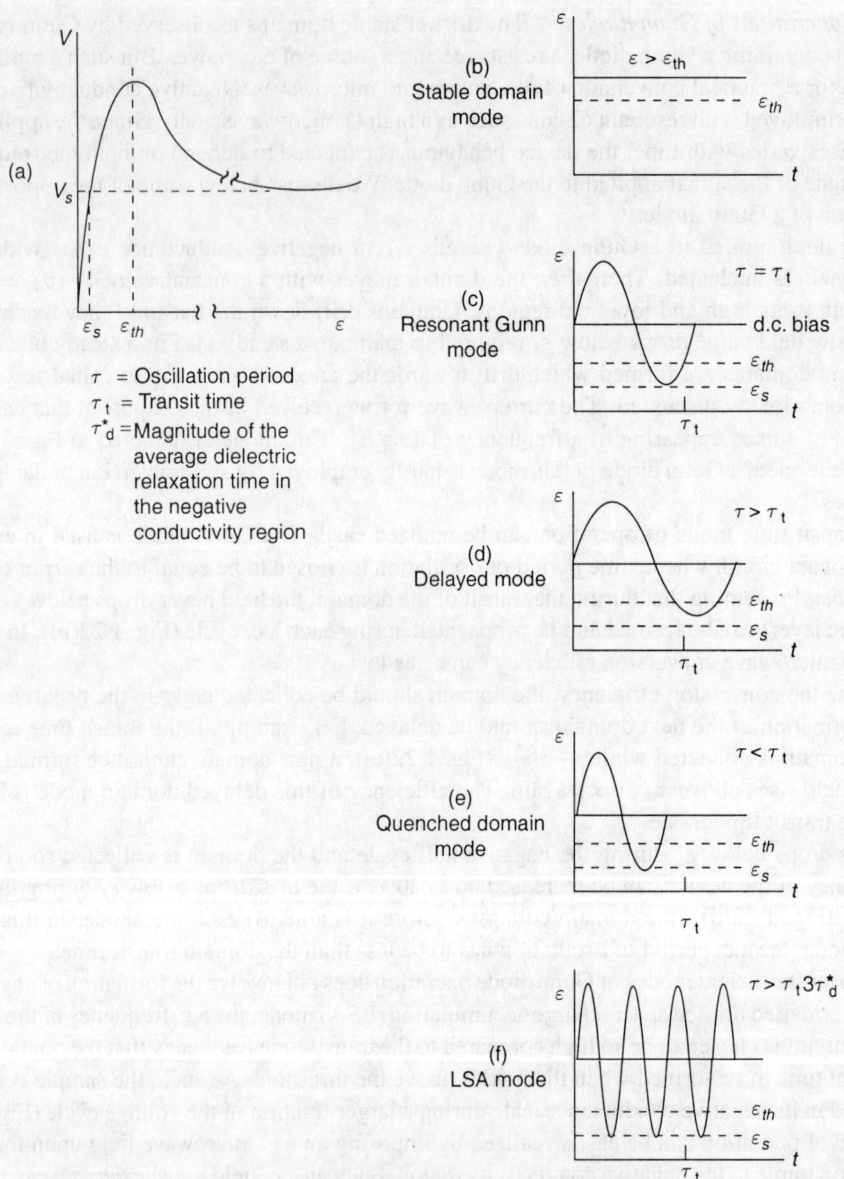

Figure 1.22 *Modes of operation: (a) velocity-field characteristic for n-type GaAs, with threshold and sustaining fields for domains indicated; (b) d.c. biasing for stable domain propagation; (c) bias at the transit time frequency for resonant Gunn mode; (d) delayed or inhibited mode; (e) quenched domain mode; (f) LSA mode.*

There are other modes of operations of Gunn diodes, as well, including the amplification mode where the negative conductance is once again employed without any domain formation. In samples which are subcritically doped ($n_0 L \ll 10^{12}/\text{cm}^2$), there are a very few carriers to form a domain within a transit time. Therefore, in such cases, amplification of the applied signals near the transit time frequency can be realized.

1.11 Low dimensional quantum phenomena

Low dimensional quantum phenomena which have been made possible due to recent advances in semiconductor technology (e.g., the developments of molecular beam epitaxy and metal organic chemical vapour deposition) are currently becoming important. This is due to the novel electrical, optical and thermal properties of the low dimensional semiconductors. Such new features have been possible due to the modifications in the density of states functions of the electrons brought about by the changes in the dimensionality of the crystal. The carriers confined to the normal semiconductors move in their quantized energy levels, which for all practical purposes are taken to form an energy continuum. Additional quantization to the motion of carriers is possible by imposing upon the crystal, a certain specified geometry. The quantization which is realized this way is known as the 'size quantization'. The effect of the additional quantization is to modify the behaviour of some of the electron transport coefficients of solids. This is so, because the latter is determined by the free carrier density as well as the scattering rate of carriers from one particular state to another. Both of them are controlled by the electron density of states which is modified as a result of the size quantization. Consequently, electrical, thermal and optical properties would be strongly dependent upon the dimensionality of electronic motion within the solid. Now, we are going to analyze theoretically how it is possible to realize two dimensional, one dimensional and zero dimensional motions of electrons in semiconductors.

Density of states The uncertainty relation expressed by (1.53) may equally be put as,

$$\Delta x \Delta k_x \cong 2\pi \tag{1.127}$$

since $p = hk_x$. The electron energy band diagram of three dimensional semiconductors is modelled on the basis of the free electron theory of Sommerfeld in which the positive potentials of the nuclei are considered to be screened out by the free electrons. Then, according to (1.54),

$$\Delta k_x \Delta k_y \Delta k_z \cong \left[\frac{(2\pi)^3}{V}\right] \tag{1.128}$$

where $V = L_x L_y L_z$ measures the volume of the potential well. The volume of the $\boldsymbol{k}$-space, as given by (1.128) measures the minimum volume required to accommodate an electron. The number of available quantum states in a volume element dk^3 of the $\boldsymbol{k}$-space is then given by

$$dN = V\left(\frac{dk}{2\pi}\right)^3 \tag{1.129}$$

Changing over to polar co-ordinates, the number of states available within the spherical shells of radii $(\boldsymbol{k} + d\boldsymbol{k})$ and $\boldsymbol{k}$ is given by

$$dN = \frac{2V[4\pi k^2 dk]}{(2\pi)^3} = \frac{4V[k^2 dk]}{(2\pi)^2} \tag{1.130}$$

where the factor of 2 takes into account the effect of spin degeneracy. Substituting for $\boldsymbol{k}$ in terms of E in (1.130), one obtains for the 3D density of states function $\rho(E)dE$ the following relation

$$\rho(E)dE = \left[\frac{1}{(2\pi)^2}\right]\left[\frac{2m^*}{h^2}\right]^{3/2} E^{1/2} dE \tag{1.131}$$

which is identical to (1.57). The carrier density at $T = 0\,\mathrm{K}$ can then be obtained as

$$n = \int_0^{\boldsymbol{k}_F} \rho(\boldsymbol{k}) d\boldsymbol{k} = \int_0^{\boldsymbol{k}_F} \frac{(4k^2 dk)}{4\pi^2} = \left(\frac{k_F^3}{3\pi^2}\right) \tag{1.132}$$

where $\boldsymbol{k}_F$ is the Fermi wave vector. The electron waves within the potential well (assumed infinitely high) form nodes at its walls. For example, along the Z-axis, the length L_z must satisfy the condition $L_z = (n_z\lambda/2)$. As a result, the electron energy in that direction would be given by

$$E_z = \left(\frac{p^2}{2m^*}\right) = \left(\frac{h^2}{2m^*\lambda^2}\right) = \left(\frac{n_z^2 h^2}{8m^* L_z^2}\right) \tag{1.133}$$

where n_z is any integer. Thus, if we make one of the sides of the 3D potential well L_z, small enough so that the first quantized state in the Z-direction lies above the crystal Fermi energy E_F, no electron would be available for motion along the Z-axis. In other words, all electrons within the solid would lie on a circular disc in the XY plane with radius $\boldsymbol{k}_F$. Thus, the motion of electrons in the crystal has now become two dimensional. The number of available states in the area $d\boldsymbol{k}^2$ of the $\boldsymbol{k}$-space would then be given by (see (1.129))

$$dN = L_x L_y \left(\frac{dk}{2\pi}\right)^2 \tag{1.134}$$

Changing over to polar co-ordinates, the number of available states lying within a circular ring of area $\pi\boldsymbol{k}d\boldsymbol{k}$ is

$$dN = 2L_x L_y \left(\frac{kdk}{2\pi}\right) \tag{1.135}$$

where the factor of 2 takes into account the effect of spin degeneracy. The two dimensional density of states is then given by

$$\rho(E)dE = \left(\frac{m^*}{\pi h^2}\right) dE \tag{1.136}$$

The $2D$ carrier density may then be obtained as

$$n = \int_0^{E_F} \rho(E)\, dE = \int_0^{k_F} (kdk)/\pi = \left(\frac{k_F^2}{2\pi}\right) \tag{1.137}$$

Next, if L_y and L_z are both so small that E_F lies below the first quantized states in both the Y and Z directions, no electron would be available for conduction in those directions. The electronic motion then becomes one dimensional, taking place only along the X-axis. In such a case, the number of states within a length dk would be

$$dN = 2L_x\left(\frac{2dk}{2\pi}\right) \tag{1.138}$$

The factor of 2 within the parenthesis accounts for states along the $+k$ and $-k$ directions. The other factor of 2 takes into account the effect of spin degeneracy. The one dimensional density of states is then expressible as

$$\rho(E)dE = \left(\frac{2}{h}\right)\left(\frac{2m^*}{E}\right)^{1/2} dE \tag{1.139}$$

The carrier density may then be obtained as

$$n = \int_0^{E_F} \rho(E)\,dE = \int_0^{k_F} \frac{(4dk)}{2\pi} = \left(\frac{2}{\pi}\right) k_F \tag{1.140}$$

Extending our above arguments, if now our solid crystal is so designed that L_x, L_y and L_z are so small that the crystal Fermi energy lies above the first quantized states along the X, Y and Z directions, no electron can exist inside the crystal. Such a structure has therefore been termed zero dimensional in nature. 3D, 2D, 1D and 0D semiconductors along with their density of states vs. E plots have been shown in Fig. 1.23. We now summarize below the important results of our calculations. The quantized energy levels in various cases are

$$\begin{aligned}
E &= \left(\frac{h^2}{2m^*}\right)[k_x^2 + k_y^2 + k_z^2] \quad \text{(Bulk semiconductor)}\\
E &= \left(\frac{h^2}{2m^*}\right)[k_x^2 + k_y^2] + \left(\frac{n_z^2 h^2}{8m^* L_z^2}\right) \quad \text{(Quantum well)}\\
E &= \left(\frac{h^2}{2m^*}\right)[k_x^2] + \left(\frac{h^2}{8m^*}\right)\left[\left(\frac{n_y^2}{L_y^2}\right) + \left(\frac{n_z^2}{L_z^2}\right)\right] \quad \text{(Quantum wire)}\\
E &= \left(\frac{h^2}{8m^*}\right)\left[\left(\frac{n_x^2}{L_x^2}\right) + \left(\frac{n_y^2}{L_y^2}\right) + \left(\frac{n_z^2}{L_z^2}\right)\right] \quad \text{(Quantum dot)}
\end{aligned} \tag{1.141}$$

The respective density of states functions are as under

$$\begin{aligned}
\rho(E) &= 4\pi\left(\frac{2m^*}{h^2}\right)^{3/2} E^{1/2} \quad \text{(Bulk semiconductor)}\\
\rho(E) &= \frac{(4\pi m^*)}{(h^2 L_z)}\Sigma H(E - E_z); \quad H(E) = 0 \text{ for } E < E_z \quad \text{(Quantum well)}\\
&\qquad \& H(E) = 1 \text{ for } E > E_z
\end{aligned} \tag{1.142}$$

$$\rho(E) = \left[\frac{2(2m^*)^{1/2}}{(hL_yL_z)}\right]\Sigma[E - E_{yz}]^{-1/2} \quad \text{(Quantum wire)}$$

$$\rho(E) = \left[\frac{2}{(L_xL_yL_z)}\right]\Sigma\delta(E - E_{x,y,z});\ \delta(0) = 1;\ \text{otherwise } 0 \text{ (Quantum dot)}$$

From our earlier arguments, it may now be derived that the motion of electrons in a solid would change to $2D$ from $3D$ if $E \leq E_z$ (1.133). That is,

$$\left(\frac{h^2k_F^2}{2m^*}\right) \leq \left[\frac{h^2}{8m^*L_z^2}\right]$$

or

$$L_z \leq \left(\frac{\pi}{k_F}\right) \leq [3\pi^2 n]^{1/3} \leq \left(\frac{\pi}{3n}\right)^{1/3} \tag{1.143}$$

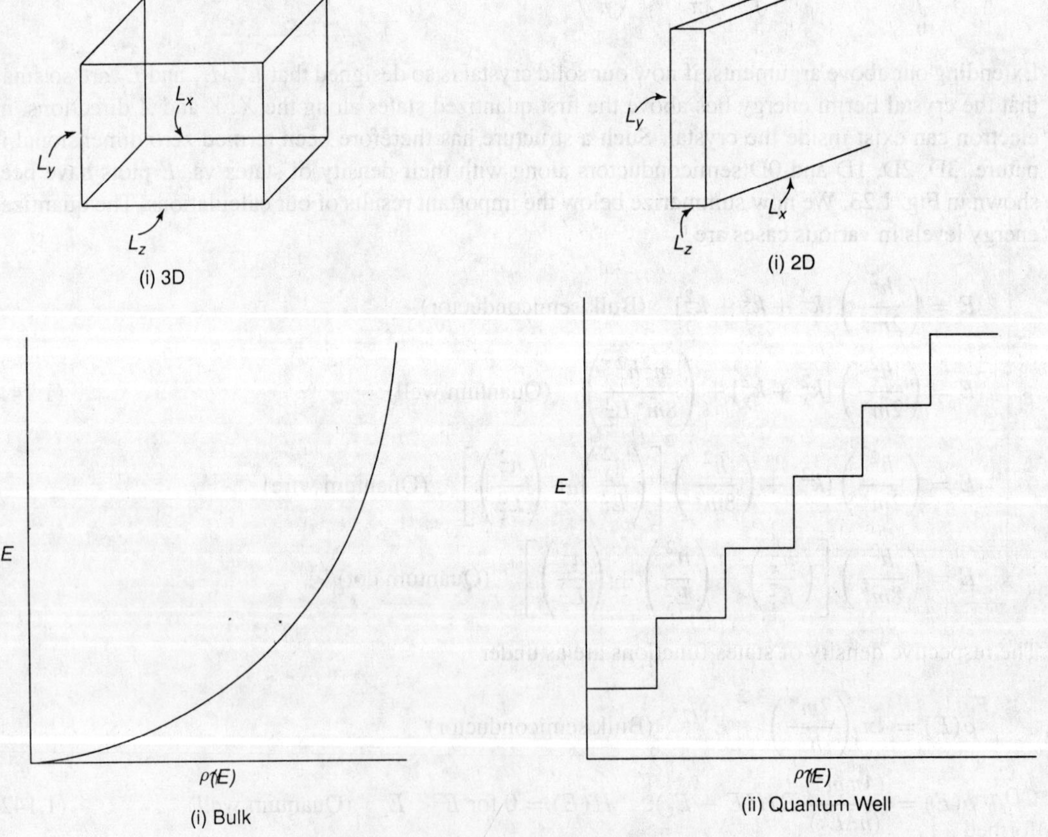

Figure 1.23 *3D, 2D, 1D and 0D conductors along with their $\rho(E)$ vs E plots*

But the average separation of electrons in a crystal of density n is $\sim(n)^{-1/3}$. Thus to observe the change in dimensionality of the electronic motion, L_z must be smaller than the average separation between the electrons in a solid. In metals, the electron density being very high ($\sim 10^{23}$ cm^{-3}), the separation between two neighboring electrons would only be a few angstroms. A metallic layer of this thickness is difficult to grow in practice. Therefore, in order to observe the change in the dimensionality, a system with a metallic behaviour at a lower carrier concentration is desired. Doped semiconductors solve this problem. Due to the interaction of electrons with the periodic lattice, the curvature of the E–k diagram changes significantly, giving rise to a lower electron effective mass m^*. When the separation between the dopant impurities is of the order of $[h/m^*q^2]$ (impurity Bohr radius), the semiconductor is known to make a transition to the metallic behaviour. As m^* for semiconductors is very low, it is possible to grow a semiconductor sample with an average thickness of about 20 nm where electrons have a metallic character. It is for this reason that semiconductors are found to exhibit low dimensional transport properties.

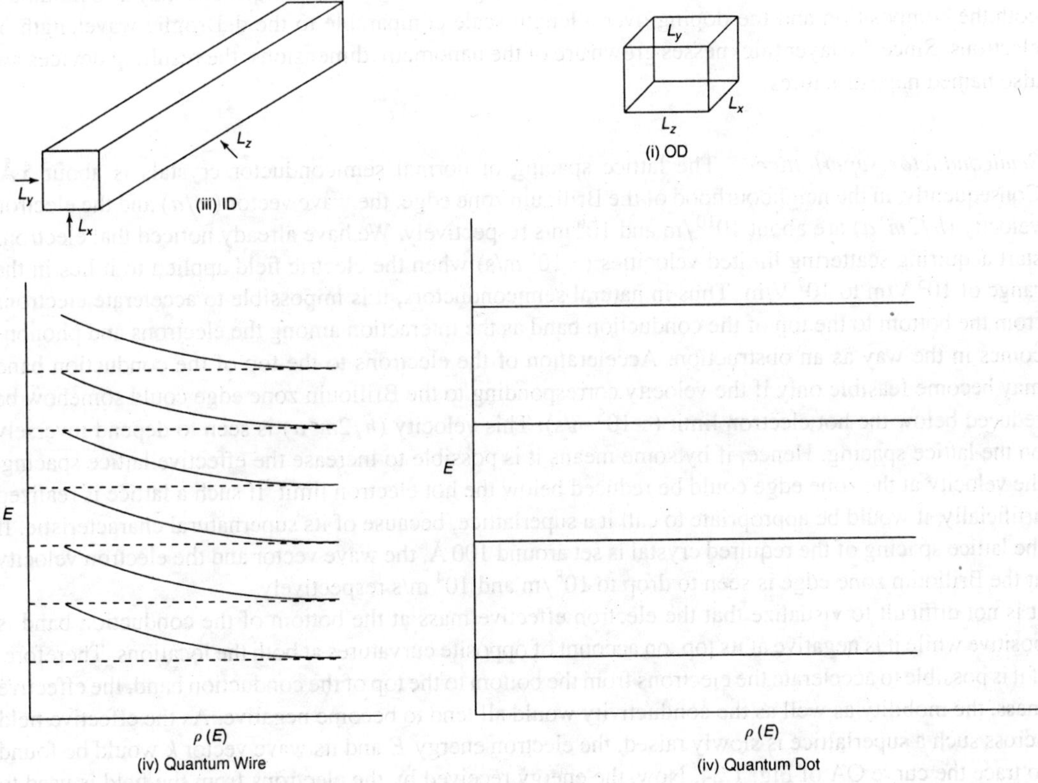

***Figure 1.23** continued (b) $3D, 2D, 1D$ and $0D$ conductors along with their $\rho(E)$ vs. E plots*

2D transport in semiconductors Most of the low dimensional physics experiments have been performed on devices containing a $2D$ electron gas (2DEG). This is a system where an electron gas is confined to a region separated by parallel planes spaced a distance L_z apart where $L_z < (\lambda_F/2)$

where λ_F measures the Fermi wavelength (1.143). This is accomplished by confining electrons at the interface between a layer of Si and a thin layer of SiO_2 by means of a positive voltage on the metallic gate electrode deposited on top of the SiO_2 layer. Electrons are then able to propagate parallel to the interface while their flow normal to the SiO_2 layer is obstructed.
To form a 2DEG in a GaAs sample, a completely different scheme is used which relies on the fact that the atomic separation of GaAs (5.653 Å) is almost identical to the AlAs(5.660 Å) crystàl although the energy gaps of the two materials are different. A whole range of materials having different energy gaps can be generated by replacing a fraction x of Ga atoms in GaAs by Al atoms to produce $Al_xGa_{1-x}As$. The material band gap is then given by the following empirical relation

$$E_G = (1.424 + 1.247x)\ \text{eV} \tag{1.144}$$

at room temperatures. The growth of $Al_xGa_{1-x}As$ is made possible by the Molecular beam epitaxy (MBE) technique, where a layer as thin as 2.5 Å can be grown. By this technique one may also modulate both the composition and the doping over a length scale comparable to the deBroglie wavelength of electrons. Since the layer thicknesses grown are of the nanometre dimensions, the resulting devices are also named nanostructures.

Semiconductor superlattice The lattice spacing of normal semiconductor crystals is about 5 Å. Consequently, in the neighbourhood of the Brillouin zone edge, the wave vector (π/a) and the electron velocity $(h/2m^*a)$ are about 10^{10}/m and 10^6 m/s respectively. We have already noticed that electrons start acquiring scattering limited velocities ($\sim 10^5$ m/s) when the electric field applied to it lies in the range of 10^5 V/m to 10^7 V/m. Thus in natural semiconductors, it is impossible to accelerate electrons from the bottom to the top of the conduction band as the interaction among the electrons and phonons comes in the way as an obstruction. Acceleration of the electrons to the top of the conduction band may become feasible only if the velocity corresponding to the Brillouin zone edge could somehow be reduced below the hot electron limit ($\sim 10^5$ m/s). This velocity $(h/2m^*a)$ is seen to depend inversely on the lattice spacing. Hence, if by some means it is possible to increase the effective lattice spacing, the velocity at the zone edge could be reduced below the hot electron limit. If such a lattice is realized artificially, it would be appropriate to call it a superlattice, because of its supernatural characteristic. If the lattice spacing of the required crystal is set around 100 Å, the wave vector and the electron velocity at the Brillouin zone edge is seen to drop to 10^8/m and 10^4 m/s respectively.
It is not difficult to visualize that the electron effective mass at the bottom of the conduction band is positive while it is negative at its top, on account of opposite curvatures at both the locations. Therefore, if it is possible to accelerate the electrons from the bottom to the top of the conduction band, the effective mass, the mobility as well as the conductivity would all tend to become negative. As the effective field across such a superlattice is slowly raised, the electron energy E and its wave vector k would be found to trace the curve OA of Fig. 1.24. Now, the energy received by the electrons from the field is used to increase its velocity as the chances of electron-lattice interaction has become smaller due to increased lattice spacing. At A, electrons suffer Bragg scattering and they switch their positions to B where the new wave vector is $(-\pi/a)$. The electron then starts tracing the curve BO under the influence of the applied electric field. The sample conductance, once again, changes from negative to positive as the wave vector crosses the point O of the E–k curve. Thus, in a superlattice, it is possible to realize high frequency oscillations of a current just by applying a d.c electric field of strength ε. The equation of

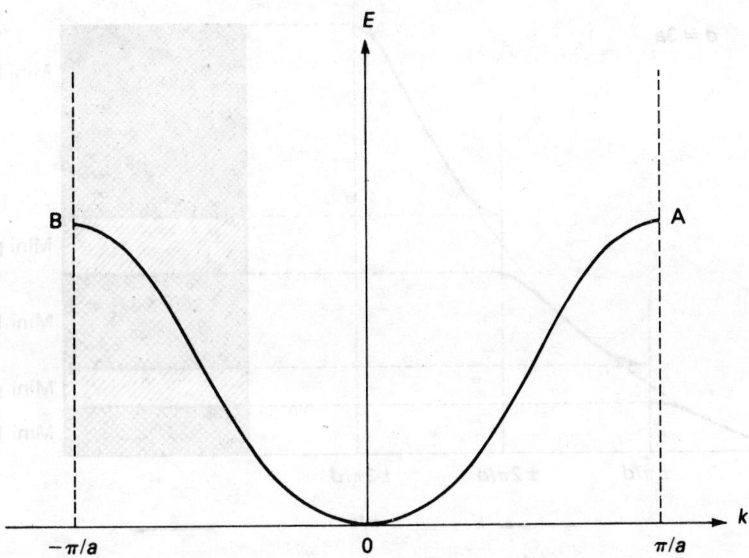

Figure 1.24 *First Brillouin zone*

motion of an electron from Newton's second law of motion, when decelerations due to electron-lattice interactions are almost absent is given by

$$h\left(\frac{dk}{dt}\right) = q\varepsilon \tag{1.145}$$

Integrating the above equation over the new Brillouin zone of the superlattice of spacing d, we get,

$$f_B = (\tau_B)^{-1} = \left(\frac{q\varepsilon d}{h}\right) \tag{1.146}$$

where f_B denotes the Bloch frequency of oscillation. For a superlattice of d = 100 Å and $\varepsilon = 10^5$ V/m, the Bloch frequency works out to be 10^{12} Hz.

A practical superlattice may be realized by growing alternate layers of semiconductors of different compositions but with matched lattices. As it has been mentioned earlier, such a pair of semiconductors is formed of GaAs and AlAs. The resulting superlattice is shown in Fig. 1.25. This behaves somewhat like a one-dimensional crystal.

Let us next presume that $Al_xGa_{1-x}As$ layers are doped with donor impurities introducing states just below the conduction band edge of $Al_xGa_{1-x}As$. The donated electrons from $Al_xGa_{1-x}As$ then migrate into the lower energy and undoped GaAs quantum wells. The electrical conductivity of GaAs, normal to the superlattice axis, especially at lower temperatures would be exceedingly high owing to the increased mobility in that direction as there would only be a few scattering centres. Such a practice of doping a superlattice to produce increased conduction perpendicular to the superlattice axis is known as 'modulation doping'.

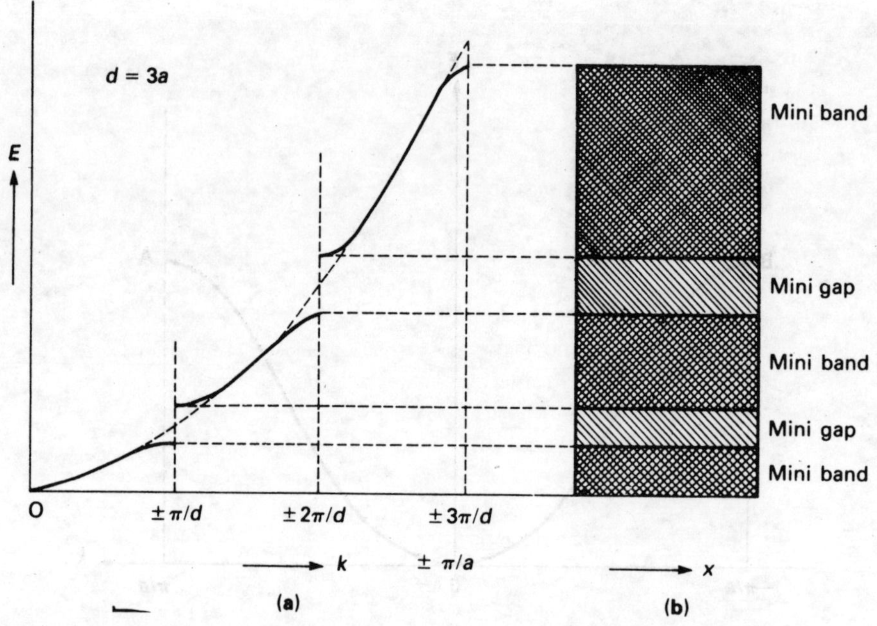

Figure 1.25 *Energy spectrum of a superlattice: (a) E–k diagram; (b) E–x diagram*

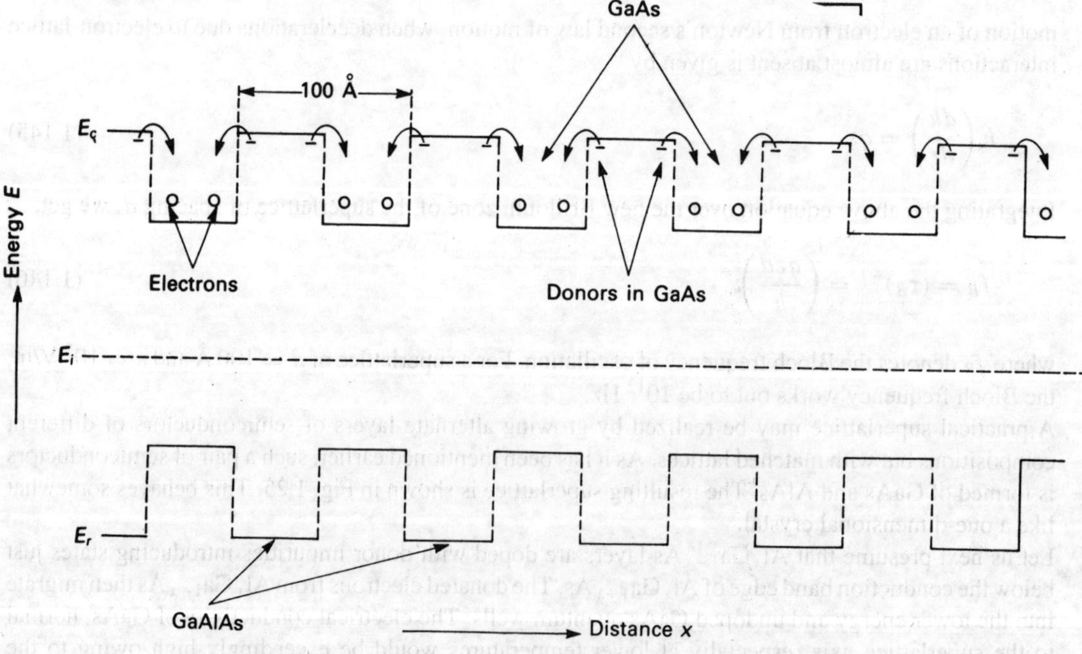

Figure 1.25 *continued (c) Modulation doping of superlattices*

Electrons and holes in quantum wells We have discussed about discrete energy levels in the band gap region arising out of doping of a semiconductor and a continuum of allowed states in its conduction and valence bands. A third possibility is the formation of discrete energy levels for electrons and holes as a result of their quantum mechanical confinements by potential energy barriers in semiconductors. Figure 1.26 shows the spatial variations in the conduction and valence bands for a multilayered structure in which a very thin layer of GaAs is sandwiched between two layers, of $Al_xGa_{1-x}As$, which has a wider band gap than GaAs. It is interesting to point out here that the consequence of confining electrons and holes in a very thin layer, is to make them behave like particles confined within a potential well. Therefore, instead of having a continuum of states which is normally available in the conduction band, electrons in the narrow gap material are restricted only to the discrete quantum states of the potential well. Similarly, states in the valence band available to holes are also restricted to discrete levels of the hole quantum well in the valence band. From a practical device point of view, the formation of discrete quantum states in a GaAs layer changes the energy of photons which are emitted as a result of electron-hole recombination between conduction and valence bands. An electron in a discrete conduction band state E_e within a well can make a transition to an empty discrete valence band state in the GaAs quantum well, such as, E_h, giving up a photon of an energy $E_G + E_e + E_h$ which is larger than the band gap of GaAs (E_G). Light emitters have been designed of such quantum wells because it helps to raise the energy of the photon emission from the infrared region (corresponding to E_G), which is typical of GaAs, to the red portion of the spectrum.

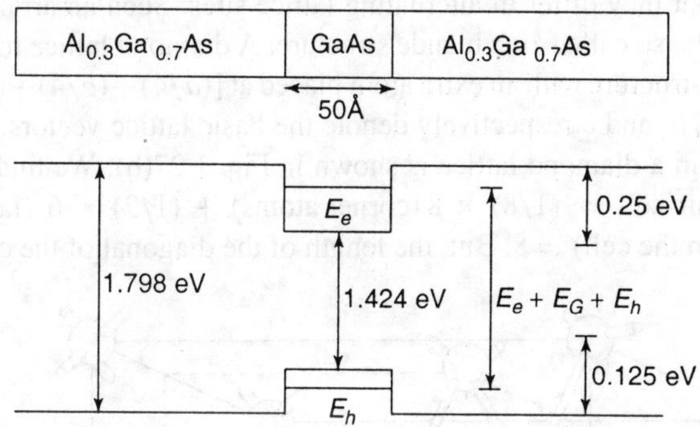

Figure 1.26 *The formation of discrete states inside a potential well*

Solved Examples

1.1 Show that the maximum fraction of the unit cell volume space in a diamond lattice, which may be considered to be occupied by hard spheres placed in regular lattice positions, is 0.34. Also, calculate the density of Silicon. (At.wt of Si $= 28.1$, mass of a pròton $= 1.66 \times 10^{-27}$ kg, and lattice constant of Si $= 5.43$ Å).

Solution

The basic structure of many important semiconductors like Ge and Si is of the diamond type (Fig. 1.27(a)). The atoms of group III–V compound semiconductors are arranged in a basic diamond structure but they differ in alternating lattice sites. Such an arrangement of atoms in a lattice gives rise to the so called zinc blende structure. A diamond lattice may also be viewed as a face-centered cubic structure with an extra atom placed at $[(a/4)+(b/4)+(c/4)]$ from each of the f.c.c atoms,where a, b, and c respectively denote the basic lattice vectors. The two-dimensional plan view of atoms in a diamond lattice is shown in Fig. 1.27(b). We find the number of atoms contained in the unit cell $= (1/8) \times 8$ (corner atoms) $+ (1/2) \times 6$ (face-centered atoms) $+$ 4 (atoms fully within the cell) $= 8$. But, the length of the diagonal of the cube $= [(a)^2 + (a)^2 +$

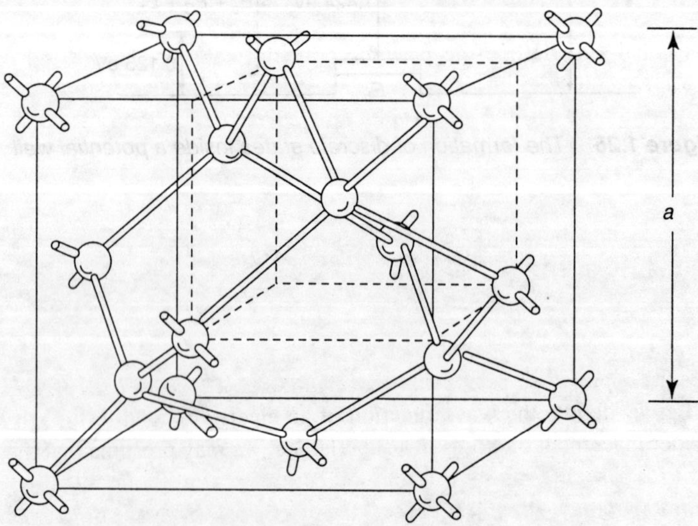

Figure 1.27 *(a) Basic diamond lattice structure*

$(a)^2]^{1/2} = \sqrt{3}a$. Therefore, the nearest neighbour distances between the centres of atoms = $(\sqrt{3}a/4)$. Next, assuming the spheres to be hard, the radii of each sphere would be $(\sqrt{3}a/8)$. Hence, the volume of each spherical atom would be = $(4/3)\pi(\sqrt{3}a/8)^3 = (\sqrt{3}\pi a^3/128)$. Hence, the maximum fraction of the unit cell volume filled = [(no. of spheres in a unit cell) × (volume of a sphere)/total volume of the cell] = $[8 \times (\sqrt{3}\pi a^3/128)/a^3] = (\sqrt{3}\pi/16) = 0.34$.

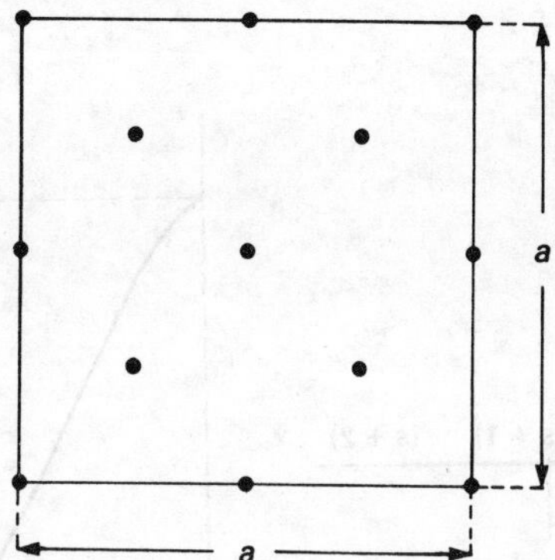

Figure 1.27 *continued (b) Two-dimensional plan view of diamond lattice atoms*

The density of Si may be expressed as $\rho(\text{Si})$ = [total mass of atoms in a unit cell/total volume of the unit cell]. Therefore,

$$\rho(\text{Si}) = \left[\frac{8 \times 28.1 \times 166 \times 10^{-24}}{(5.43 \times 10^{-8})^3}\right] = 2.33 \text{ gm/cc}$$

1.2 In a one-dimensional superlattice the periodic potential energy is expressed as $V(x) = V_0 \cos(2\pi x/d)$ where d denotes the superlattice period. Derive expressions for the following: (i) the width of a miniband, (ii) the group velocity of electrons in a miniband, (iii) their effective masses and (iv) the width of a minigap.

Solution

In a one-dimensional superlattice, the atomic positions may be expressed as,

$$x = sd \tag{1}$$

where d denotes the superlattice period and s is any integer (e.g. $s = 0, \pm1, \pm2, \pm3, \pm4 \ldots\ldots$) (Fig. 1.28(a)). Let Ψ_s denote the wave function of an electron bound to the sth site. Owing to the relatively wider placement of atoms in a superlattice, we may presume that the electron wave function bound to a particular atom will only be perturbed slightly due to the presence of the neighboring atoms. We may, therefore, express the electronic wave functions bound to $(s-1)$th and $(s+1)$th atoms as Taylor's expansions of the wave function bound to the sth site. Hence, we may write,

$$\Psi_{s+1} = \Psi_s + \left(\frac{\partial \Psi_s}{\partial x}\right)\bigg|_{\hat{s}.} d + \left(\frac{\partial^2 \Psi_s}{\partial x^2}\right)\bigg|_{s.} \left(\frac{d^2}{2!}\right) \tag{2}$$

and

$$\Psi_{s-1} = \Psi_s - \left(\frac{\partial \Psi_s}{\partial x}\right)\bigg|_{\hat{s}.} d + \left(\frac{\partial^2 \Psi_s}{\partial x^2}\right)\bigg|_{s.} \left(\frac{d^2}{2!}\right) \tag{3}$$

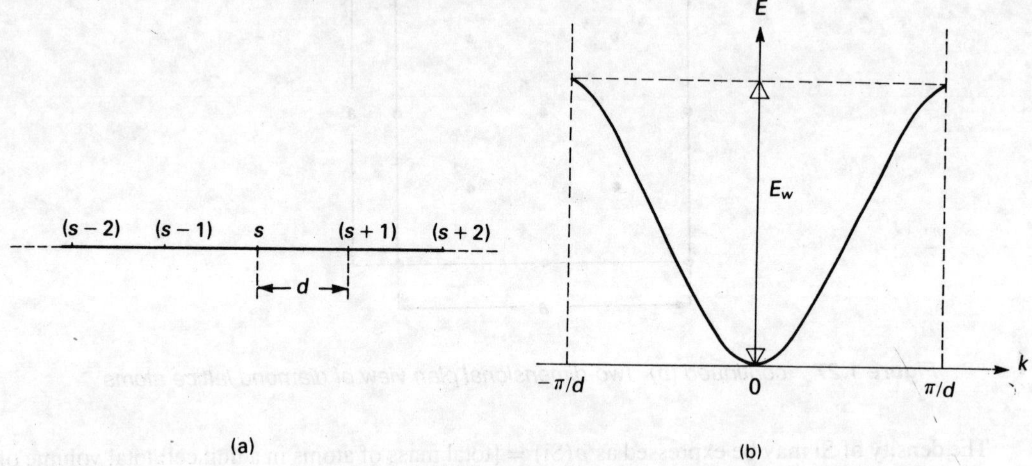

Figure 1.28 *A one-dimensional lattice of spacing d; (b) E–k diagram of the superlattice*

where we have ignored higher order terms because of very small variation of $(\partial \Psi_s/\partial x)$ with x. If atoms are placed extremely wide apart, $\Psi_{s+1} = \Psi_s$. Combining (2) and (3), we find

$$\left(\frac{\partial^2 \Psi_s}{\partial x^2}\right) = \left[\frac{(\Psi_{s+1} + \Psi_{s-1} - 2\Psi_s)}{d^2}\right] \tag{4}$$

Now, on the basis of the effective mass approximations, the electronic motion in the superlattice direction may be represented by the Schrodinger's time-independent wave equation viz.,

$$-\left(\frac{\hbar^2}{2m^*}\right)\left(\frac{\partial^2 \Psi_s}{\partial x^2}\right) = E\Psi_s \tag{5}$$

where E measures the electron energy. Combining (4) and (5), we find

$$\Psi_{s+1} + \Psi_{s-1} - 2\Psi_s + \left(\frac{2m^* E d^2}{\hbar^2}\right)\Psi_s = 0 \tag{6}$$

But, Ψ_s must be a wave function of the Bloch type which may be expressed as

$$\Psi_s = \Sigma_k C(k) \exp(iksd) \tag{7}$$

where $\boldsymbol{k}$ denotes the electron wave vector. Combining (6) and (7), we find

$$\Sigma_k C(\boldsymbol{k}) \exp(i\boldsymbol{k}sd)\left[\exp(i\boldsymbol{k}d) + \exp(-i\boldsymbol{k}d) - 2 + \left(\frac{2m^* Ed^2}{\hbar^2}\right)\right] = 0 \tag{8}$$

Since, each term in the above series must be a positive quantity, we must have

$$\left[\exp(i\boldsymbol{k}d) + \exp(-i\boldsymbol{k}d) - 2 + \left(\frac{2m^* Ed^2}{\hbar^2}\right)\right] = 0$$

or

$$\left[\exp\left(\frac{i\boldsymbol{k}d}{2}\right) - \exp\left(\frac{-i\boldsymbol{k}d}{2}\right)\right]^2 + \left(\frac{2m^* Ed^2}{\hbar^2}\right) = 0$$

or

$$E = E_W \sin^2\left(\frac{\boldsymbol{k}d}{2}\right) \tag{9}$$

where

$$E_W = \left(\frac{2\hbar^2}{m^* d^2}\right) \tag{10}$$

Equation (9) gives the E–$\boldsymbol{k}$ relation of a one-dimensional superlattice. We see that $E = 0$ for $\boldsymbol{k} = 0$ and $E = E_W$ for $\boldsymbol{k} = \pm(\pi/d)$ which denote the Brillouin zone edge of the E–$\boldsymbol{k}$ curve of the superlattice (Fig. 1.28).

The width of the superlattice miniband is given by (10). From (9), we observe that

$$\left(\frac{dE}{dk}\right) = E_W\left(\frac{d}{2}\right)\sin(\boldsymbol{k}d) = \left(\frac{\hbar^2}{m^* d}\right)\sin(\boldsymbol{k}d)$$

Therefore, the group velocity v_g of electrons is given by

$$v_g = \left(\frac{i}{h}\right)\left(\frac{dE}{dk}\right) = \left(\frac{\hbar}{m^* d}\right)\sin(\boldsymbol{k}d) \tag{11}$$

so that it is zero both at $\boldsymbol{k} = 0$ and $\boldsymbol{k} = \pm(\pi/d)$. Next, the electron effective mass in the superlattice direction may be expressed as $m_s^* = [\hbar^2/(\partial^2 E/\partial \boldsymbol{k}^2)]$. From (9), we find

$$\left(\frac{\partial^2 E}{\partial \boldsymbol{k}^2}\right) = \left(\frac{\hbar^2}{m^*}\right)\cos(\boldsymbol{k}d)$$

Therefore,

$$m_s^* = \left[\frac{m^*}{\cos(\boldsymbol{k}d)}\right] \tag{12}$$

so that $m_s^* = m^*$ for $\boldsymbol{k} = 0$ and $m_s^* = -m^*$ for $\boldsymbol{k} = \pm(\pi/d)$.

To calculate the width of the minigap of the superlattice, let us presume an electron of wave function exp $(-iGx/2)$ to be undergoing Bragg scattering by the reciprocal lattice vector G. After scattering, the wave function would be of the type exp $(iGx/2)$. The interference of the two waves may give either a cosine or a sine wave depending upon whether they interfere in the same or opposite phases. The normal versions of such wave functions are expressed as

$$\Psi_+ = \left(\frac{2}{d}\right)^{1/2} \cos\left(\frac{Gx}{2}\right) \tag{13}$$

and

$$\Psi_- = \left(\frac{2}{d}\right)^{1/2} \sin\left(\frac{Gx}{2}\right) \tag{14}$$

The scattering potential of the superlattice is however given by

$$V(x) = V_0 \cos(Gx) \tag{15}$$

The energy differences between the two groups expressed in (14) may then be expressed as

$$\Delta E = \int_0^d [|\Psi_+|^2 - |\Psi_-|^2] V(x) dx \tag{16}$$

Combining (13), (14), (15) and (16), we find

$$\Delta E = \left(\frac{2}{d}\right) \int_0^d \left[\cos^2\left(\frac{Gx}{2}\right) - \sin^2\left(\frac{Gx}{2}\right)\right] V_0 \cos(Gx)\, dx$$

$$= \left(\frac{2V_0}{d}\right) \int_0^d \cos^2(Gx)\, dx = V_0 \tag{17}$$

Thus, the width of the minigap of the superlattice is given by the amplitude of the oscillating superlattice potential energy.

1.3 The $E - k$ relation of a particular semiconductor is given by $E = Ak^2 + Bk^3$ where A and B are positive constants.

(a) Find the wave vectors for which the electron group velocity is zero.

(b) Determine the electron effective masses and the phase velocities of electron waves for those wave vector values.

Solution

(a) The E–k relation of electrons in the given semiconductor specimen is

$$E = Ak^2 + Bk^3 \tag{1}$$

Differentiating E with respect to k, we get

$$\left(\frac{dE}{dk}\right) = 2k\left[A + \left(\frac{3}{2}\right)Bk\right] \tag{2}$$

The group velocity of electrons is given by $v_g = (1/\hbar)(dE/dk)$. From (2), we therefore, derive that $v_g = 0$ if $\boldsymbol{k} = 0$ and $\boldsymbol{k} = -(2A/3B)$.

(b) The electron effective mass is given by $m^* = [\hbar^2/(\partial^2 E/\partial \boldsymbol{k}^2)]$. To determine m^*, we therefore, need to differentiate (2) once more with respect to k, to get

$$\left(\frac{d^2E}{dk^2}\right) = 2A + 6Bk \tag{3}$$

(i) If $\boldsymbol{k} = 0$, $(d^2E/dk^2) = 2A$. Therefore, $m^* = [\hbar^2 2A]$
(ii) If $\boldsymbol{k} = -(2A/3B)$, $(d^2E/dk^2) = -2A$ and $m^* = -[\hbar^2/2A]$

Thus, $\boldsymbol{k} = 0$ refers to the conduction band minimum while $\boldsymbol{k} = -(2A/3B)$ refers to the top of the valence band.
Finally, the phase velocity of the electron wave is defined to be $v_{\text{ph}} = (\omega/\boldsymbol{k}) = (E/h\boldsymbol{k}) = (Ak^2 + Bk^3)/h\boldsymbol{k} = [(Ak + Bk^2)/\hbar]$. Hence, (i) if $k = 0$, $v_{\text{ph}} = 0$ and (ii) if $\boldsymbol{k} = -(2A/3B)$, $v_{\text{ph}} = -[2A^2/9B\hbar]$

1.4 The impurity ionization energy of Arsenic (As) atoms in Si varies with the doping density N_d according to the following relation

$$E_i = E_{i0}\left[1 - \left(\frac{N_d}{N_{cr}}\right)^{1/3}\right]$$

where $E_{i0} = 0.013\,\text{eV}$ and $N_{cr} = 2 \times 10^{17}/\text{cm}^3$ at 300 K. Calculate the average distance between Arsenic atoms when $E_i = 0$. Express this distance in terms of the impurity Bohr radius. ($m^* = 0.01$ m where m = free electron mass).

Solution

Obviously, $E_i = 0$ when $N_d = N_{cr} = 2 \times 10^{17}/\text{cm}^3$. If Arsenic atoms are situated at an average distance of 'd' apart, the number of Arsenic atoms associated with the volume d^3 is 1. Hence, the concentration N_d of Arsenic atoms when $E_i = 0$ would be given by

$$N_d = N_{cr} = (d)^{-3}$$

or

$$d = (N_{cr})^{-1/3} = (2 \times 10^{17})^{-1/3}$$
$$= 1.71 \times 10^{-6}\,\text{cm} = 171\,\text{Å}$$

The impurity Bohr radius, on the other hand, is given by

$$a_B = \left(\frac{4\pi\varepsilon_0 h^2}{m^* q^2}\right) = \left[4 \times 3.14 \times 8.85 \times 10^{-12} \times \frac{(1.05 \times 10^{-34})^2}{0.01} \times 9 \times 10^{-31} \times (1.6 \times 10^{-19})^2\right]$$

or

$$a_B = 759.86 \times 10^{-11}\ \text{m} = 75.986\ \text{Å}$$

Therefore, $(d/a_B) = (171/75.986) = 2.25$. Thus, when the impurity atoms are separated by nearly twice the impurity Bohr radius, they may be regarded to have completely ionized.

1.5 A bar of n-type Si with a cross-sectional area of 1 mm × 1 mm and a length of 1 cm is connected to a 2 V battery supply and is carrying a current of 2 mA at 300 K.

(a) Calculate the thermal equilibrium electron and hole densities in the bar.
(b) Calculate the dopant concentration presuming that the only donors with an energy level of 0.148 eV below the conduction band are present.
(c) Determine the temperature at which the bar becomes intrinsic.

Solution

(a) The resistance R of the bar is given by

$$R = \rho\left(\frac{L}{A}\right) = \rho\left[\frac{10^{-2}}{10^{-3} \times 10^{-3}}\right] = 10^4\,\rho \tag{1}$$

Also,

$$R = \left(\frac{V}{I}\right) = \frac{2}{(2 \times 10^{-3})} = 10^3\ \text{ohms} \tag{2}$$

Comparing (1) and (2), we find

$$\left(\frac{1}{\rho}\right) = q(\mu_n n + \mu_p p) = 10 \tag{3}$$

Since the sample is n-type, $n \gg p$.Therefore, $q\mu_n n = 10$ (4)
Taking $\mu_n = 1350\ \text{cm}^2/\text{Vs} = 0.135\ \text{m}^2/\text{Vs}$, we get from (4),

$$n = \frac{10}{(1.5 \times 10^{-19} \times 0.135)} = 4.63 \times 10^{20}/\text{m}^3$$

But,

$$p = \left(\frac{n_i^2}{n}\right) = \frac{(1.5 \times 10^{16})^2}{4.63 \times 10^{20}} = 4.86 \times 10^{11}/\text{m}^3$$

Hence,

$$n = 4.63 \times 10^{14}/\text{cm}^3 \text{ and } p = 4.86 \times 10^5/\text{cm}^3$$

(b) The electron density is given by

$$n = N_C \exp\left[\frac{-(E_C - E_F)}{kT}\right] \tag{5}$$

where for Si,

$$N_C = 2\,[2\pi m_n^* kT/h^2]^{3/2} = 2.8 \times 10^{19}/\text{cm}^3.$$

Therefore, from (5),

$$(E_C - E_F) = kT \ln\left(\frac{N_C}{n}\right) = 0.026 \ln[2.8 \times 10^{19}/4.63 \times 10^{14}]$$

$$= 0.286\,\text{eV}$$

But, it is given that

$$(E_C - E_d) = 0.148\,\text{eV}.$$

We may now write,

$$(E_d - E_F) = (E_C - E_F) - (E_C - E_d)$$

$$= (0.286 - 0.148) = 0.138\,\text{eV}$$

Therefore, the number of electrons in the donor states is

$$n_d = \frac{N_d}{\left[1 + \exp\left\{\dfrac{(E_d - E_F)}{kT}\right\}\right]} = \frac{N_d}{\left\{1 + \exp\left(\dfrac{0.138}{0.026}\right)\right\}} = \frac{N_d}{\{1 + \exp(5.318)\}}$$

But

$$N_d = n + n_d \text{ or } n = N_d/\{1 + \exp(-5.318)\} = 4.63 \times 10^{20}.$$

Solving for N_d, one finds,

$$N_d = 4.65 \times 10^{20}/\text{m}^3.$$

(c) The semiconductor specimen becomes intrinsic at a temperature T when $n_i(T) = N_d$, That is,

$$(N_C N_V)^{1/2} \exp\left[-\left(\frac{E_G}{2kT}\right)\right] = N_d, \text{ or } N_C \exp\left[-(E_G 2kT)\right] \cong N_d$$

Taking $E_G = 1.12\,\text{eV}$ and $k = 1.38 \times 10^{-23}$ J/K and solving for T, one obtains, $T = 606.8$ K or $t = 333.8°$ C. Therefore the bar becomes intrinsic at a temperature of 333.8° C.

1.6 Calculate the Fermi level position in Si doped with 10^{15} Phosphorus atoms/cm^3 at room temperature assuming complete ionization. From the calculated Fermi level position, check the assumption of complete ionization of carriers. Given that $N_C = 2.8 \times 10^{19}/\text{cm}^3$, and $(E_C - E_d) = 0.148$ eV.

Solution

Since,

$$n \cong N_d = N_C \exp[-(E_C - E_F)/kT]$$

it follows that

$$(E_C - E_F) = 0.266 \text{ eV}$$

taking $kT = 0.026$ eV at 300 K. Therefore,

$$\begin{aligned}(E_d - E_F) &= (E_C - E_F) - (E_C - E_d)\\ &= (0.266 - 0.148) \text{ eV}\\ &= 0.118 \text{ eV}.\end{aligned}$$

Hence, the number of electrons in the donor states is

$$n_d = \frac{N_d}{\left[1 + \exp\left\{\dfrac{(E_d - E_F)}{kT}\right\}\right]} = 1.05 \times 10^{13}/\text{cm}^3$$

Hence, the fraction of the donor atoms ionized $= [1 - (n_d/N_d)] = [1 - 0.01] = 0.99$. Therefore, 99% of the donor atoms are ionized.

1.7 In a semiconductor specimen, donor and acceptor levels are placed 0.3 eV apart. If 80% of acceptors are ionized at 300 K, evaluate the fraction of ionized donors. If the donor level is $2\,kT$ below the conduction band edge, determine the Fermi level position in the semiconductor.

Solution

The density of electrons in the acceptor states is given by

$$n_a = \frac{N_a}{\left[1 + \exp\left\{\dfrac{(E_a - E_F)}{kT}\right\}\right]} \tag{1}$$

where N_a = density of acceptors, E_a = acceptor ionization energy and E_F = Fermi energy level. Therefore, the fraction of acceptors ionized is

$$f = \left(\frac{n_a}{N_a}\right) = \frac{1}{\left[1 + \exp\left\{\dfrac{(E_a - E_F)}{kT}\right\}\right]} \tag{2}$$

Since, it is given that $f = 0.8$, it follows from (2) that

$$(E_a - E_F) = -1.386\,kT$$

Now,

$$\begin{aligned}(E_d - E_a) &= (E_d - E_F) - (E_F - E_a)\\ &= 0.3\,\text{eV}\\ &= (0.3/0.26)\,kT\\ &= 11.538\,kT \text{ (at 300 K)}\end{aligned}$$

Hence,

$$\begin{aligned}(E_d - E_F) &= (11.538 - 1.386)\,kT\\ &= 10.152\,kT\end{aligned}$$

Now the density of electrons in the donor states is

$$n_d = \frac{N_d}{\left[1 + \exp\left\{\dfrac{(E_d - E_F)}{kT}\right\}\right]} = \frac{N_d}{[1 + \exp(10.152)]}$$

or

$$\begin{aligned}\left[1 - \left(\frac{n_d}{N_d}\right)\right] &= \frac{1}{[1 + \exp(-10.152)]}\\ &= 0.9999\end{aligned}$$

Therefore, the percentage of donor atoms ionized is 99.99 %.
It is given that

$$(E_c - E_d) = 2kT$$

Therefore,

$$\begin{aligned}(E_C - E_F) + (E_F - E_d) &= (E_c - E_d)\\ &= 2kT\end{aligned}$$

Therefore,

$$\begin{aligned}(E_C - E_F) &= (2 + 10.152)kT\\ &= 12.152\,kT = 12.152 \times 0.026\\ &= 0.31592 \text{ at 300 K}\end{aligned}$$

The Fermi level is thus situated 0.316 eV below the conduction band edge.

1.8 Consider a donor level at an energy E_d below the conduction band edge of a semiconductor. Assume that the semiconductor is doped with N_d donors per m^3 and that the hole density p in it is negligibly small compared to n. Prove that

$$\left[\frac{n^2}{(N_d - n)}\right] = N_C \exp\left(\frac{-E_d}{kT}\right)$$

Solution

As the valence band contribution to the electron density in the semiconductor is negligibly small, the major fraction of it must come from the donor states only. The un-ionized donor concentration can be written as

$$(N_d - n) = \frac{N_d}{\left[1 + \exp\left\{\frac{(E'_d - E_F)}{kT}\right\}\right]} \quad (1)$$

where E'_d = ionization energy of the donor states. Simplifying (1), we find

$$\exp\left[\frac{(E'_d - E_F)}{kT}\right] = \left[\frac{n}{(N_d - n)}\right] \quad (2)$$

Multiplying both sides of (2) by n, we find

$$\left[\frac{n^2}{(N_d - n)}\right] = n \exp\left[\frac{(E'_d - E_F)}{kT}\right] = N_C \exp\left[\frac{-(E_C - E_F)}{kT}\right] \exp\left[\frac{(E'_d - E_F)}{kT}\right]$$

$$= N_C \exp\left[\frac{(E'_d - E_C)}{kT}\right] = N_C \exp\left[-\left(\frac{E_d}{kT}\right)\right]$$

since it is given that, $E_d = (E_C - E'_d)$. Hence proved.

1.9 Imagine that a positively charged donor ion is immersed within an electron gas of an n-type semiconductor. Show that its electrical influence decays beyond a distance L_d (Debye length) from the ion which is given by

$$L_d = \left[\frac{(\kappa \varepsilon_0 k T)}{(q^2 n_n)}\right]^{1/2}$$

where the symbols used have their usual significance.

Solution

The thermal equilibrium value of the electron concentration n_n in an n-type semiconductor and its equilibrium electrostatic and Fermi potentials viz. Ψ and φ respectively are known to be related as

$$n_n = n_i \exp\left[\left(\frac{q}{kT}\right)(\Psi - \varphi)\right] \quad (1)$$

The introduction of a positive ion within the electron gas modifies the electron density around it. The change in the electron density may be written by taking the differential of (1) as

$$\delta n_n = \left(\frac{qn_n}{kT}\right)\delta\Psi \tag{2}$$

where $\delta\Psi$ measures the perturbation in the electrostatic potential caused by the introduction of the positive ion. This δn_n and $\delta\Psi$ are also related to each other through the Poisson's equation, as mentioned below

$$\left(\frac{d^2}{dr^2}\right)(\delta\Psi) = -\left(\frac{\rho}{\kappa\varepsilon_0}\right) = -\frac{(-q\delta n_n)}{\kappa\varepsilon_0} = \left[\frac{(q^2 n_n)}{(\kappa\varepsilon_0 kT)}\right]\delta\Psi$$

where we made use of (2). We may rewrite it as

$$\left(\frac{d^2}{dr^2}\right)(\delta\Psi) = \frac{\delta\Psi}{(L_d)^2} \tag{3}$$

where

$$L_d = \left[\frac{(\kappa\varepsilon_0 kT)}{(q^2 n_n)}\right]^{1/2} \tag{4}$$

The solution of (3) may now be written as

$$\delta\Psi(r) = A\exp\left[-\left(\frac{r}{L_d}\right)\right] \tag{5}$$

where A is a constant. To estimate its value, we observe that as $r \to 0$,

$$\delta\Psi(r) = \frac{q}{(4\pi\kappa\varepsilon_0 r)} \tag{6}$$

as given by the Coulomb's law of electrostatics. Combining (5) and (6), therefore, we find

$$\delta\Psi(r) = \left[\frac{q}{(4\pi\kappa\varepsilon_0 r)}\right]\exp\left[-\left(\frac{r}{L_d}\right)\right] \tag{7}$$

where $+q$ denotes the charge carried by the positive ion. The expression for L_d, given in (4), is valid for a non-degenerate electron gas which obeys Maxwell–Boltzman statistics. For a degenerate electron gas (as in a metal), we may write

$$\delta|E_F| = q\delta\Psi = \delta\left[\left(\frac{h^2}{2m}\right)\left(\frac{3n}{8\pi}\right)^{2/3}\right]$$

Therefore,

$$\delta n = \left[\frac{4mq}{h^2}\right](3\pi^2 n)^{1/3}\delta\Psi \tag{8}$$

The Poisson's equation for this case then reduces to (3), where

$$\left(\frac{1}{L_d}\right) = \left(\frac{2q}{h}\right)\left(\frac{m}{\kappa\varepsilon_0}\right)^{1/2} (3\pi^2 n)^{1/6} \tag{9}$$

The above expression may also be written as

$$\lambda = \left(\frac{1}{L_d}\right) = \left(\frac{mq^2}{\pi\kappa\varepsilon_0\hbar^2}\right)^{1/2}\left(\frac{3n}{\pi}\right)^{1/6} \tag{10}$$

where L_d measures the Debye length for a degenerate electron gas. It is seen to be independent of temperature. But for a non-degenerate electron gas it is seen to be temperature dependent. (see equation 4).

1.10 An intrinsic Germanium sample is used as a thermistor. Calculate the ratio of the sample conductivities when the temperature is increased from 27° C to 100° C.

Solution

In Ge, $\mu_n \cong 2\mu_p$. Therefore, neglecting the hole contribution to the conductivity, the latter may be written as

$$\sigma(T) = q\mu_n(T)n_i(T) \tag{1}$$

But the lattice mobility μ_n is temperature dependent as expressed by

$$\mu_n(T) = \frac{A_1}{T^{3/2}} \tag{2}$$

The intrinsic carrier density, on the other hand, is given by

$$n_i(T) = A_2(T)^{3/2}\exp\left(\frac{-E_G}{2kT}\right) \tag{3}$$

Combining (1), (2), (3), we find

$$\sigma(T) = A\exp\left(\frac{-E_G}{2kT}\right) \tag{4}$$

The ratio of the conductivities of a Ge sample at two temperatures T_1 and T_2 may therefore be written as

$$\left[\frac{\sigma_1(T_1)}{\sigma_2(T_2)}\right] = \exp\left[-\left(\frac{E_G}{2k}\right)\left\{\left(\frac{1}{T_1}\right)-\left(\frac{1}{T_2}\right)\right\}\right]$$

or

$$\ln\left[\frac{\sigma_1(T_1)}{\sigma_2(T_2)}\right] = \left(\frac{E_G}{2k}\right)\left\{\left(\frac{1}{T_2}\right)-\left(\frac{1}{T_1}\right)\right\} \tag{5}$$

Next, taking $T_2 = 27 + 273 = 300\,\text{K}$, $T_1 = 100 + 273 = 373\,\text{K}$, $E_G = 0.67\,\text{eV}$ and $k = 1.38 \times 10^{-23}$ J/K, we get, $[\sigma_1(T_1)/\sigma_2(T_2)] = 12.49$. Thus, on heating the sample from 27° C to 100° C, the sample conductivity increases by about 12.5 times.

1.11 Obtain the condition for the observation of the negative differential conductivity effect in an n-type GaAs crystal.

Solution

The electrical conductivity σ of an n-type GaAs crystal is the sum of the electrical conductivities σ_l in the Γ-conduction band and σ_u in the upper X-point satellite valley. We may, therefore, write

$$\sigma = \sigma_l + \sigma_u = (q\mu_l n_l + q\mu_u n_u) \tag{1}$$

The current density J produced by an electrical intensity ε is then given by

$$J = \sigma\varepsilon \tag{2}$$

Differentiating (2) with respect to ε, we find

$$\left(\frac{dJ}{d\varepsilon}\right) = \sigma + \varepsilon\left(\frac{d\sigma}{d\varepsilon}\right) \tag{3}$$

We now have to derive the condition for which $(dJ/d\varepsilon)$ is negative. Combining (1) and (3) and simplifying, we find

$$\left(\frac{dJ}{d\varepsilon}\right) = q\left[n_l\left(\frac{d\mu_l}{d\varepsilon}\right) + n_u\left(\frac{d\mu_u}{d\varepsilon}\right) + \mu_l\left(\frac{dn_l}{d\varepsilon}\right) + \mu_u(dn_u/d\varepsilon)\right]\varepsilon + q(\mu_l n_l + \mu_u n_u) \tag{4}$$

Presuming that the electron density in the conduction band is constant, we may write

$$n_u + n_l = n \tag{5}$$

Therefore,

$$\left(\frac{dn_u}{d\varepsilon}\right) = -\left(\frac{dn_l}{d\varepsilon}\right) \tag{6}$$

Using (6) in (4), we find

$$\left(\frac{dJ}{d\varepsilon}\right) = q(\mu_l - \mu_u)\left(\frac{dn_l}{d\varepsilon}\right)\varepsilon + q\varepsilon\left[n_l\left(\frac{d\mu_l}{d\varepsilon}\right) + n_u\left(\frac{d\mu_u}{d\varepsilon}\right)\right] + q(\mu_l n_l + \mu_u n_u) \tag{7}$$

To get the required negative differential conductivity effect $(dJ/d\varepsilon)$ must be negative. It, therefore, follows from (7) that the required condition is

$$\left[\left\{(\mu_l - \mu_u)\left(\frac{dn_l}{d\varepsilon}\right) + n_l\left(\frac{d\mu_l}{d\varepsilon}\right) + n_u\left(\frac{d\mu_u}{d\varepsilon}\right)\right\}\frac{\varepsilon}{(\mu_l n_l + \mu_u n_u)}\right] < -1 \tag{8}$$

This is the required criterion for the observation of the negative differential conductivity effect.

1.12 Show that for a semiconductor specimen, the ratio of maximum to intrinsic resistivities is given by

$$\frac{\rho_{\max}}{\rho_i} = \left[\frac{(\mu_n + \mu_p)}{2(\mu_n \mu_p)^{1/2}}\right]$$

where the symbols have their usual meanings. Assuming $\mu_n = 3\mu_p$, solve for the doping levels which results in $\rho_{\max}$.

Solution

The intrinsic resistivity of a semiconductor sample is given by

$$\left(\frac{1}{\rho_i}\right) = \sigma_i = qn_i(\mu_n + \mu_p) \tag{1}$$

But the resistivity of any other doping level may be expressed as

$$\left(\frac{1}{\rho}\right) = \sigma = q(n\mu_n + p\mu_p) \tag{2}$$

Since, $np = n_i^2$, we may express (2) as

$$\left(\frac{1}{\rho}\right) = \sigma = q\left[n\mu_n + \mu_p\left(\frac{n_i^2}{n}\right)\right] \tag{3}$$

To obtain an expression for $\rho_{\max}$ or $\sigma_{\min}$, we must differentiate σ in (3) with respect to n and equate $(d\sigma/dn) = 0$. That is

$$\left(\frac{d\sigma}{dn}\right) = q\left[\mu_n - \mu_p\left(\frac{n_i^2}{n^2}\right)\right] = 0 \tag{4}$$

or

$$\mu_n = \mu_p\left(\frac{n_i^2}{n^2}\right) \tag{5}$$

Differentiating (4) once again with respect to n, we find

$$\left(\frac{d\sigma}{dn}\right) = 2\mu_p\left(\frac{n_i^2}{n^3}\right) \tag{6}$$

Combining (5) and (6), we find

$$\left(\frac{d^2\sigma}{dn^2}\right) = 2n_i\mu_n\left(\frac{\mu_n}{\mu_p}\right)^{1/2} \tag{7}$$

which is always a positive quantity. This confirms that for μ_n given by (5), σ in (2) would be a minimum. From (5), we find

$$n = n_i \left(\frac{\mu_p}{\mu_n}\right)^{1/2} \tag{8}$$

Since $np = n_i^2$,

$$p = n_i \left(\frac{\mu_n}{\mu_p}\right)^{1/2} \tag{9}$$

Dividing (1) by (9), we find

$$\left(\frac{\rho_{max}}{\rho_i}\right) = \left[\frac{(\mu_n + \mu_p)}{2(\mu_n \mu_p)^{1/2}}\right] \tag{10}$$

If $\mu_n = 3\mu_p$, $n = (n_i/\sqrt{3})$ and $p = \sqrt{3}n_i$. Since we find $p > n$, the semiconductor of maximum resistivity must be doped with acceptors.

1.13 A 0.01 m bar of n-type Ge ($m_n^* = 0.45$ m) with an electron mobility of 0.39 m^2/Vs is connected to a power supply of 50 V.

(i) How long will the electrons take to drift down the full length of the bar ?
(ii) On an average, how many collisions will an electron suffer during one transit ?
(iii) What is the total energy received by the electrons from the field and lost to the lattice ?
(iv) What is the mean free path of an electron-lattice collision? ($m_n^* = 0.45$ m)

Solution

(i) The electric field, $\varepsilon = (V/L) = (50/0.01) = 5 \times 10^3$ V/m. Therefore, the drift velocity, $v_d = \mu_n \varepsilon = 0.39 \times 5 \times 10^3 = 1.95 \times 10^3$ m/second. The drift time t_d is given by

$$t_d = \left(\frac{L}{v_d}\right) = \frac{0.01}{1.95} \times 10^3 = 5 \text{ microsecond}$$

(ii) Since, the mobility is given by $\mu_n = (q\tau/m_n^*)$, one finds, $\tau = [(m_n^* \mu_n)/q]$. Therefore, the number of collisions made during one transit is given by

$$N = \left(\frac{t_d}{\tau}\right) = \left(\frac{q t_d}{m_n^* \mu_n}\right) = \frac{(5 \times 10^{-6} \times 1.6 \times 10^{-19})}{(0.45 \times 9 \times 10^{-31} \times 0.39)}$$
$$= 5.06 \times 10^6$$

(iii) The energy gained from the electric field = 50 eV. Since, the applied field does not disturb the thermal equilibrium of carriers in the semiconductor, the same energy must be delivered to the lattice.

(iv) The mean free path of the electron-lattice collision is given by, $l = \langle v \rangle_{rms}$. $\tau = (3kT/m_n^*)^{1/2}[(m_n^* \mu_n)/q] = (3kTm_n^*)^{1/2}(\mu_n/q)$. Therefore, substituting the values of the appropriate parameters, we get

$$l = (3 \times 0.026 \times 1.6 \times 10^{-19} \times 0.45 \times 9 \times 10^{-31})^{1/2} \times 0.39/(1.6 \times 10^{-19})$$
$$= 0.173 \mu \text{ m}$$

1.14 Show that the carrier lifetime in an intrinsic semiconductor specimen varies with the trapping level E_t as

$$\tau = \tau_0 \left[1 + \cosh \left\{ \frac{(E_t - E_i)}{kT} \right\} \right]$$

where E_i corresponds to the energy gap center and τ_0 measures the lifetime in a srongly doped p- or n-semiconductor.

Solution

The recombination rate through the deep level traps, as given by Shockley–Read–Hall statistics (SRH) is given by

$$R = \frac{(np - n_i^2)}{[(n + n_1)\tau_{p0} + (p + p_1)\tau_{n0}]} \tag{1}$$

where $n_1 = n_0 \exp[(E_t - E_F)/kT]$ and $p_1 = p_0 \exp[(E_F - E_t)/kT]$. As the specimen is intrinsic, $n_0 = p_0 = n_i$, and $E_F \cong E_i$. Also, $n = n_i + \delta n$ and $p = n_i + \delta p$. Making use of these relations in (1), we find

$$R = \frac{[(n_i + \delta n)(n_i + \delta p) - n_i^2]}{n_i \left\{ \exp \dfrac{(E_t - E_i)}{kT} + \exp \dfrac{(E_i - E_t)}{kT} \right\} + 2n_i \tau_0}$$

where $\tau_{p0} = \tau_{n0} = \tau_0$. Therefore,

$$R = \frac{[n_i^2 + 2n_i \delta n - n_i^2]}{\left[1 + \cosh \left\{ \dfrac{(E_i - E_t)}{kT} \right\} \right] \tau_0} = (\delta n / \tau) \text{ (say)} \tag{2}$$

From (2), the expression for the carrier lifetime is given by

$$\tau = \tau_0 \left[1 + \cosh \left\{ \frac{(E_t - E_i)}{kT} \right\} \right] \tag{3}$$

This, therefore, is the expression for the carrier lifetime as a function of the trapping energy level in an intrinsic semiconductor sample. If $(E_t - E_i)$ increases, τ also increases. If E_t approaches E_i, the lifetime is the shortest and is equal to $2\tau_0$ where τ_0 is the lifetime in a strongly doped n- or p-material. One may thus conclude that deep level traps behave as the most efficient recombination centres.

1.15 An n-type Si has 2×10^{16} Arsenic atoms per cc., 2×10^{15} bulk recombination centres per cm^2. Calculate the bulk minority carrier lifetime, the diffusion length and the surface recombination velocity under low level injection. If the sample is illuminated with light which creates 10^{17} electron-hole pairs per cm^3 per second, what is the hole concentration at the surface ?

$[\sigma_p = 5 \times 10^{-15}\ \text{cm}^{-2}; \sigma_s = 2 \times 10^{-16}\ \text{cm}^{-2}]$

Solution

The bulk minority carrier lifetime τ_p in an n-type semiconductor may be expressed as

$$\tau_p = (\sigma_p v_{th} N_t)^{-1} \tag{1}$$

where σ_p = capture cross-section for holes; $v_{th} = v_{rms} = (3kT/m_n^*)$ and N_t = conc. of trap centres. Therefore,

$$v_{th} = \left[\frac{(3 \times 0.026 \times 1.6 \times 10^{-19})}{0.49 \times 9.1 \times 10^{-31}}\right]^{1/2} = 1.67 \times 10^5 \text{ m/s}$$

Next, from (1), we derive

$$\tau_p = (5 \times 10^{-19} \times 1.67 \times 10^5 \times 2 \times 10^{21})^{-1} = 6 \times 10^{-9} \text{ s}$$

The diffusion constant D_P for holes in Si is $D_P = (kT/q)\mu_p = 0.026 \times 0.15 = 0.0039 \text{ m}^2/\text{Vs} = 39 \text{ cm}^2/\text{s}$. Therefore, the diffusion length $= (D_P \tau_p)^{1/2} = (39 \times 6 \times 10^{-9})^{1/2} = 4.84\mu\text{ m} = L_p$. The surface recombination velocity S_P, is given by

$$S_P = (\sigma_p v_{th} N_{st}) = 2 \times 10^{-20} \times 1.67 \times 10^5 \times 10^{14} = 0.334 \text{ m/s} = 33.4 \text{ m/s}$$

The minority hole density upon irradiation at any distance x from the surface is given by

$$p_n(x) = p_{n0} + \tau_p G \left[1 - \left\{\tau_p S_P \exp\frac{(-x/L_p)}{(L_p + \tau_p S_P)}\right\}\right]$$

Therefore at $x = 0$,

$$p_n(0) = \left(\frac{n_i^2}{N_d}\right) + \tau_p G \left[1 - \left\{\frac{\tau_p S_P}{(L_p + \tau_p S_P)}\right\}\right] = \left(\frac{n_i^2}{N_d}\right) + \left\{\frac{G \tau_p L_P}{(L_p + \tau_p S_P)}\right\}$$

For Si, $n_i = 1.45 \times 10^{16} \text{ m}^{-3}$. Therefore,

$$p_n(0) = \left[\frac{(1.45 \times 10^{16})^2}{(2 \times 10^{22})}\right]$$

$$+ \left[\frac{(10^{23} \times 6 \times 10^{-9} \times 4.84 \times 10^{-6})}{(4.84 \times 10^{-6} + 2 \times 10^{-9})}\right]$$

$$= 1.05 \times 10^{10} + 6 \times 10^{14} \cong 6 \times 10^{14} = 6 \times 10^8/\text{cm}^3$$

1.16 To a Germanium sample of length L and cross-sectional area A, a constant voltage V is applied. A source of radiation generates g_0 electron-hole pairs per m^3 per second. Presuming $\mu_n > \mu_p$, show that the optically induced change in current is given by $\Delta I = [qALg_0\tau_n/t_d]$ where t_d measures the transit time of electrons drifting down the bar.

Solution

If Δn measures the increment in the electron density due to optical irradiation, the change in current ΔI may be expressed as

$$\Delta I = Aqv\Delta n \tag{1}$$

where v denotes the drift velocity of electrons. Owing to the lower hole mobility, the contribution of holes in increasing the current may be ignored. We know that the recombination law for electrons is

$$(n - n_p) = (n_0 - n_p)\exp\left(\frac{-t}{\tau_n}\right) \tag{2}$$

Differentiating (2) with respect to t, we get at t = 0,

$$\left(\frac{dn}{dt}\right)_{t=0} = -\left[\frac{(n_0 - n_p)}{\tau_n}\right] = -\left(\frac{\Delta n}{\tau_n}\right) = -g_0 \tag{3}$$

at equilibrium. It, therefore follows from (3),

$$\Delta n = g_0\tau_n \tag{4}$$

Now, writing $v = (L/t_d)$ and combining (1) and (4), we find

$$\Delta I = \left[\frac{qALg_0\tau_n}{t_d}\right] \tag{5}$$

Hence proved.

1.17 In an n-type semiconductor, g_0 electron-hole pairs are generated per s, by a strong source of radiation. The holes are trapped immediately and free electrons disappear by recombination with the trapped holes. If the light is switched on at $t = t_0$, show that

$$n = \left(\frac{g_0}{r_0}\right)^{1/2} \tanh[(g_0r_0)^{1/2}(t - t_0)]$$

When the light is switched off at $t = t_1$, show that

$$n = \frac{\left(\frac{g_0}{r_0}\right)^{1/2}}{[1 + (g_0r_0)^{1/2}(t - t_1)]}$$

Solution

When the n-type semiconductor is irradiated by a strong source of radiation, the carrier population initially builds up. The growth rates of the carrier densities may be expressed as

$$\left(\frac{dn}{dt}\right) = \left(\frac{dp}{dt}\right) = [g_0 - r_0 np] \tag{1}$$

Since the light source is very strong, the generated carrier densities may be considered to be significantly high relative to their thermal equilibrium densities. We may, therefore, regard n and p to be the excess electron and hole densities generated by the irradiation process only and write $n = p$. Rewriting (1) under this assumption and integrating it, we find

$$\int \left[\frac{dn}{(g_0 - r_0 n^2)}\right] = \int dt + \text{ const.} \tag{2}$$

To evaluate (2), we make the following substitution: $n = (g_0/r_0)^{1/2} \tanh x$, so that $(g_0 - r_0 n^2) = g_0 \operatorname{sech}^2 x$ and $dn = (g_0/r_0)^{1/2} \operatorname{sec h}^2 x dx$. Making these substitutions in (2), we find

$$\int \left[\frac{dx}{(g_0 r_0)^{1/2}}\right] = \int dt + \text{const. so that } x = (g_0 r_0)^{1/2} t + \text{const.}$$

But, according to our assumption,

$$\left(\frac{r_0}{g_0}\right)^{1/2} n = \tanh x = \tanh[(g_0 r_0)^{1/2} t + \text{const.}] \tag{3}$$

It is however presumed that $n = 0$ at $t = t_0$, i.e. when the light was switched on. Imposing this condition in (3), we find const. $= -(g_0 r_0)^{1/2} t_0$. Substitituting for the constant in (3), we find

$$n = \left(\frac{g_0}{r_0}\right)^{1/2} \tanh[(g_0 r_0)^{1/2} (t - t_0)] \tag{4}$$

When t approaches a very large value n, the carrier density expression reduces to

$$n = \left(\frac{g_0}{r_0}\right)^{1/2} \tag{5}$$

Now, if the source of light is switched off at $t = t_1$, carriers begin to decay by recombination. The corresponding decay rate may be derived from (1) as

$$-\left(\frac{dn}{dt}\right) = r_0 n^2 \tag{6}$$

Integrating (5) within appropriate limits, we get

$$-\int_{(g_0/r_0)^{1/2}}^{n} \left(\frac{dn}{n^2}\right) = \int_{t_1}^{t} r_0 dt \tag{7}$$

Integrating, we find

$$n = \frac{\left(\frac{g_0}{r_0}\right)^{1/2}}{[1 + (g_0 r_0)^{1/2} (t - t_1)]} \tag{8}$$

Hence proved.

1.18 A 0.5 μm thick sample of GaAs at 300 K has an area of 1 cm^2. The sample is uniformly illuminated with a monochromatic light of $h\nu = 2.1$ eV. The absorption coefficient α at this wavelength is 4×10^4 cm^{-1}. The power incident on the sample is 12 mW.

(a) Calculate the power absorbed by the sample;
(b) determine how much power is dissipated by the excess electrons to the lattice before recombination; and
(c) determine the number of photons/second falling on the sample and the number of photons emitted per second by electron-hole recombination.

Solution

I_0 = incident light intensity = energy crossing per unit area in unit time = $(12 \times 10^{-3}/10^{-4}) =$ 120 J/m^2.
α = absorption coefficient = 4×10^4 cm^{-1} = 4×10^6 m^{-1}.
Therefore, the transmitted intensity $= I(W) = I_0 \exp(-\alpha W) = 120 \exp[-4 \times 10^6 \times 0.5 \times 10^{-6}] = 16.24$ J/m^2
Loss in intensity $= 120 - 16.24 = 103.76$ J/m^2. Therefore, the power absorbed by the sample $= 103.76 \times 10^{-4}$ J/s $= 10.376$ mW
Excess energy possessed by an electron excited across the energy gap $= (2.1 - 1.43)$ eV $=$ 0.67 eV. This excess energy has to be delivered to the lattice before the electron is able to participate in the recombination process.
The fraction of power dissipated by electrons $= (0.67/2.1) \times 12 = 3.83$ mW
The number of photons/second falling on the sample $= (12 \times 10^{-3}/2.1 \times 1.6 \times 10^{-19}) =$ 3.57×10^{16}
Number of photons emitted by the sample/second $= (10.38 - 3.83) \times 10^{-3}/(1.43 \times 1.6 \times 10^{-19}) =$ 2.86×10^{16}

1.19 A homogeneous and intrinsic semiconductor bar is illuminated by a beam of radiation that generates G_L cm^{-3} s^{-1}. Assuming low level carrier injection, calculate:

(a) the excess carrier density as a function of time;
(b) the steady state electron and hole densities. Show that the induced photoconductivity is given by $\Delta\sigma = q(\mu_n + \mu_p)\tau_n$.

Solution

(a) The rate of the population build up in the semiconductor bar as a function of time is represented by the following equation:

$$\left(\frac{dn}{dt}\right) = \left(\frac{dp}{dt}\right) = G_L - rnp \tag{1}$$

where $n = n_i + \Delta n$ and $p = n_i + \Delta n$, such that $\Delta n \ll n_i$ (low level injection). Since $n = p$, equation (1) may be rewritten as

$$\int \left[\frac{dn}{(G_L - rn^2)}\right] = \int dt + \text{const.} \tag{2}$$

To evaluate (1), we substitute $n = (G_L/r)^{1/2} \tanh x$. Equation (2) then integrates to

$$x = (G_L r)^{1/2} t + \text{const.}$$

$$\tanh x = \tanh[(G_L r)^{1/2} t] + \text{const.}$$

$$\left[\left(\frac{r}{G_L}\right)^{1/2} n\right] = \tanh[(G_L r)^{1/2} t] + \text{const.}$$

at

$$t = 0, n = n_i; \text{ therefore const } = \left[\left(\frac{r}{G_L}\right)^{1/2} n_i\right]$$

Hence,

$$\left[\left(\frac{r}{G_L}\right)^{1/2} (n - n_i)\right] = \left[\left(\frac{r}{G_L}\right)^{1/2} \Delta n\right] = \tanh[(G_L r)^{1/2} t]$$

or

$$\Delta n = \Delta p = \left(\frac{G_L}{r}\right)^{1/2} \tanh\,[(G_L r)^{1/2} t] \tag{3}$$

Equation (3) thus expresses the excess electron and hole densities as a function of time.

(b) To calculate the steady state electron and hole densities, we note that at $t = \infty$, $\tanh\,[(G_L r)^{1/2} t] = 1$. Therefore, the steady state electron and hole densities are given by

$$\Delta n_0 = \Delta p_0 = \left(\frac{G_L}{r}\right)^{1/2}$$

Therefore,

$$n_0 = p_0 = \left(\frac{G_L}{r}\right)^{1/2} + n_i \tag{4}$$

To calculate the induced photoconductivity, we notice that the carrier recombination law can be represented as

$$\left(\frac{dn}{dt}\right) = \frac{-[n(t) \; - \; n_i]}{\tau_n} \tag{5}$$

which in the steady state becomes

$$\left(\frac{dn}{dt}\right) = \frac{-[n_0 - n_i]}{\tau_n = -G_L}$$

or

$$\Delta n_0 = \Delta p_0 = G_L \tau_n \tag{6}$$

Hence, the induced photoconductivity $= \Delta\sigma_p = q(\mu_n + \mu_p)\Delta n_0 = q(\mu_n + \mu_p)G_L \tau_n$. (7)

1.20 A Silicon sample is doped with 10^{15} donors/cm^3. Calculate the excess electron and hole densities required to increase the sample conductivity by 15%. What carrier generation rate is required to maintain this excess concentration? Assume $\mu_n = 0.3\mu_p$, $\tau_p = 10^{-6}$ s and $T = 300$ K.

Solution

The sample conductivity is given by

$$\sigma = q\,(n\mu_n + p\mu_p) = q\left[n\mu_n + \left(\frac{n_i^2}{n}\right)\mu_p\right] \tag{1}$$

Differentiating (1) with respect to n, we get

$$\Delta\sigma = q\left[\Delta n\mu_n - \left(\frac{n_i^2}{n^2}\right)\mu_p\Delta n\right] = q\Delta n\mu_n\left[1 - 0.3\left(\frac{n_i^2}{n^2}\right)\right] \tag{2}$$

Equation (1) may also be expressed as

$$\sigma = qn\mu_n\left[1 + 0.3\left(\frac{n_i^2}{n^2}\right)\right] \tag{3}$$

Dividing (2) by (3), we find

$$\left(\frac{\Delta\sigma}{\sigma}\right) = \left(\frac{\Delta n}{n}\right)\frac{\left[1 - 0.3\left(\frac{n_i^2}{n^2}\right)\right]}{\left[1 + 0.3\left(\frac{n_i^2}{n^2}\right)\right]} \tag{4}$$

But in Si, $n_i = 1.5 \times 10^{10}\ \text{cm}^{-3} \ll n(= 10^{15}/\text{cm}^3)$. In such a case, (4) simplifies to

$$\left(\frac{\Delta\sigma}{\sigma}\right) = \left(\frac{\Delta n}{n}\right) = \left(\frac{15}{100}\right)$$

or

$$\Delta n = \left(\frac{15}{100}\right) \times n = 0.15 \times 10^{15}/\text{cm}^3$$

Therefore, the excess carrier densities required to be generated are given by

$$\Delta n = \Delta p$$
$$= 1.5 \times 10^{14}/\text{cm}^3$$

Carrier generation rate required to maintain this excess concentration is given by

$$G = \left(\frac{\Delta p}{\tau_p}\right) = \left(\frac{1.5 \times 10^{14}}{10^{-6}}\right) = 1.5 \times 10^{20}\ \text{per cm}^3\ \text{per s}$$

1.21 A photoconductor with dimensions $L = 6\,\text{mm}$, $W = 2\,\text{mm}$ and $D = 1\,\text{mm}$ is placed under a uniform radiation. The absorption of light increases the current by 2.83 mA. A voltage of 10V is applied across the device. When the radiation is suddenly turned off, the electric current initially falls at a rate of 23.6 A/s. Let $\mu_n = 3600\,\text{cm}^2/\text{Vs}$ and $\mu_p = 1700\,\text{cm}^2/\text{Vs}$. Find the equilibrium densities of electron-hole pairs generated under irradiation, minority carrier lifetime and the excess density of electrons and holes remaining, 10 ms after the radiation is turned off.

Solution

From Ohm's law, we write

$$I = \frac{V}{R} = GV = \sigma\left(\frac{A}{L}\right)V$$

Therefore,

$$\Delta I = \left(\frac{AV}{L}\right)\Delta\sigma = \left(\frac{AV}{L}\right)q(\mu_n + \mu_p)\Delta n$$

or

$$\Delta n = \left(\frac{L\Delta I}{AV}\right)\left[\frac{1}{q(\mu_n + \mu_p)}\right] = \Delta p \tag{1}$$

Substituting appropriate values in (10), we get

$$\Delta n = \Delta p = \left[\frac{(6\times10^{-3})(2.83\times10^{-3})}{(2\times10^{-3})(1\times10^{-3})}\right]\left[\frac{1}{1.6\times10^{-19}(0.36+0.17)}\right]$$

or $\Delta n = \Delta p = 10^{20}/\text{m}^3$ = equilibrium densities of electron-hole pairs generated.
Also,

$$\left(\frac{\Delta I}{\Delta t}\right) = \left(\frac{AV}{L}\right)q(\mu_n + \mu_p)\left(\frac{\Delta n}{\Delta t}\right)$$

or

$$\left(\frac{dn}{dt}\right) = \frac{\left(\frac{dI}{dt}\right)}{\left[\left(\frac{AV}{L}\right)q(\mu_n + \mu_p)\right]}$$

$$= \frac{(-23.6)}{\left[\left(\frac{2\times10^{-6}}{6\times10^{-3}}\right)\times 10\right][1.6\times10^{-19}(0.36+0.17)]}$$

or

$$\left(\frac{dn}{dt}\right) = -\,8.35\times10^{22}/\text{m}^3\,\text{s}$$

But, we know that

$$\tau_n = \frac{-\Delta n}{\left(\dfrac{dn}{dt}\right)} = \left(\frac{10^{20}}{8.35 \times 10^{22}}\right) = 1.2 \times 10^{-3}\ \text{s} = \text{minority carrier lifetime}$$

Therefore, the excess density of carriers left after 1 ms $= \Delta n \exp(-t/\tau_n) = 10^{20} \exp(-8.33) = 2.4 \times 10^{16}/\text{m}^3$.

1.22 Four equidistant pointed metallic probes spaced a distance d apart touch the surface of a flat and thick semiconductor specimen away from its periphery. A current I flowing between the outer pair of probes develops a floating potential V between the inner ones. Express the electrical conductivity σ of the sample as a function of V and I.

Solution

The constant current density wave form generated by the current entering at A will be hemispherical in shape since the sample is infinitely thick. The current density $J(r)$ at a distance r from A is then given by (Fig. 1.29),

$$J(r) = \sigma\varepsilon(r) = \left[\frac{I}{(2\pi r^2)}\right] \tag{1}$$

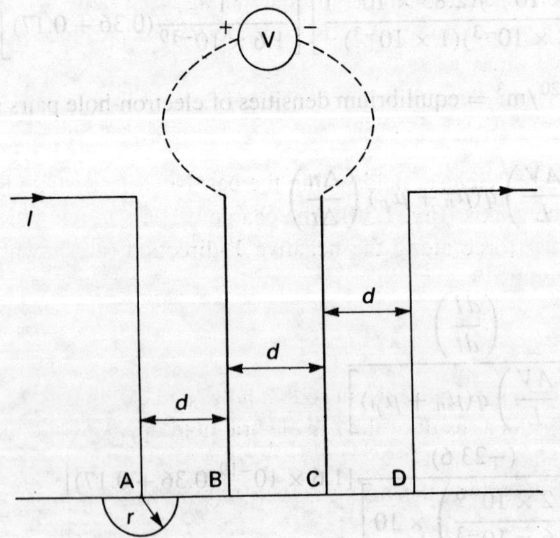

Figure 1.29 Four probe apparatus

where $(2\pi r^2)$ measures the surface area of the hemisphere of radius r. Since B would be at a higher potential than C due to the current entering at A, we may write

$$V_{\mathrm{BC,A}} = -\int_{2d}^{d} \varepsilon(r)\,dr \tag{2}$$

Combining (1) and (2), we find

$$V_{\mathrm{BC,A}} = -\left(\frac{I}{2\pi\sigma}\right)\int_{2d}^{d}\left[\frac{dr}{r^2}\right] = \left(\frac{I}{2\pi\sigma}\right)\left[\left(\frac{1}{d}\right)-\left(\frac{1}{2d}\right)\right] = \left(\frac{I}{4\pi\sigma d}\right) \tag{3}$$

The effect of the current entering at A would be the same as that of the current leaving at D. Therefore, the net p.d. developed between the inner pair of probes may be obtained by doubling (3). We then get

$$V = 2V_{\mathrm{BC,A}} = \left(\frac{I}{2\pi\sigma d}\right) \text{ or } \sigma = \left(\frac{1}{2\pi d}\right)\left(\frac{I}{V}\right) \tag{4}$$

Equation (4) gives the required relation. This is used to estimate the electrical conductivity of a sample by the four probe apparatus.

1.23 Obtain an expression for the Hall coefficient of an intrinsic semiconductor sample.

Solution

To an intrinsic semiconductor sample oriented along the X-axis, a bias is so applied that a net current density J_x flows along the X-axis. Considering the presence of both holes and electrons within the sample, we may write

$$J_x = q(n\mu_n + p\mu_p)\varepsilon_x \tag{1}$$

where ε_x is the applied electric field within the bar. Next, let a static magnetic flux density B_z be applied along the z-axis (Fig. 1.30). The charge carriers moving along the X-axis will then experience a Lorentz force along the negative Y-direction (as shown). The magnitude of the Lorentz field is given by

$$\varepsilon'_y = -v_x B_z \tag{2}$$

This Hall field generates its own current so that holes and electrons start piling up over the B and A faces respectively. As a result of this, an electric field opposing the Lorentz field is generated. This is termed the Hall field.

The net current flowing along the Y-axis is then given by

$$J_y = qp\mu_p(\varepsilon_y - \varepsilon'_y) + qn\mu_n(\varepsilon_y - \varepsilon'_y) \tag{3}$$

Substituting for the magnitude of ε'_y from (2), we get

$$J_y = qp\mu_p(\varepsilon_y - v_{xp}B_z) + qn\mu_n(\varepsilon_y - v_{xn}B_z) \tag{4}$$

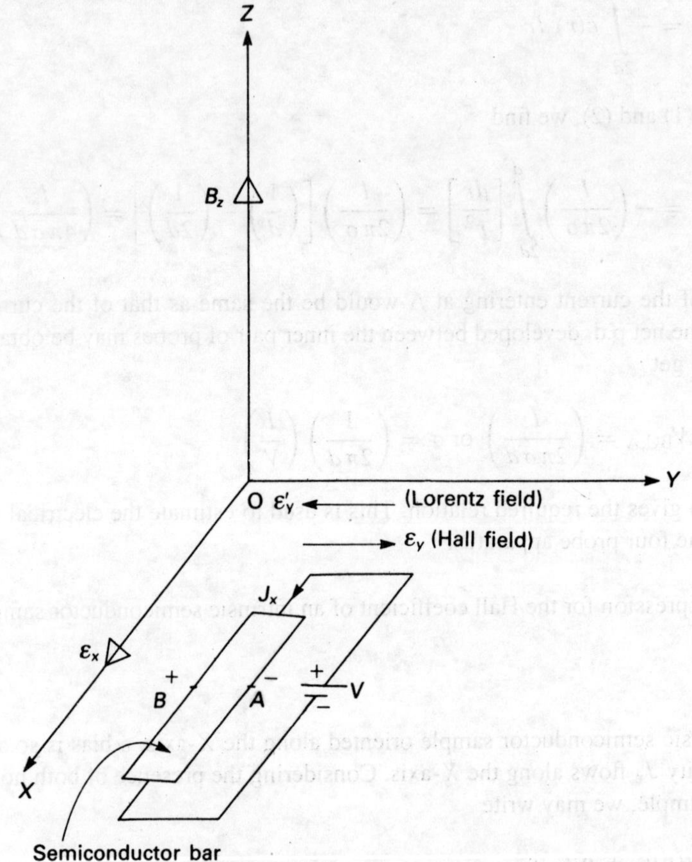

Figure 1.30 *Field orientations in the Hall effect experiment*

where v_{xp} and v_{xn} respectively denote the drift velocities of holes and electrons respectively. But since, $v_{xp} = \mu_p \varepsilon_x$ and $v_{xn} = -\mu_n \varepsilon_x$, equation (4) simplifies to

$$J_y = qp\mu_p(\varepsilon_y - \mu_p \varepsilon_x B_z) + qn\mu_n(\varepsilon_y + \mu_n \varepsilon_x B_z) \tag{5}$$

where μ_n and μ_p respectively denote the mobilities of the electrons and holes. To calculate the Hall field we set $J_y = 0$ to get

$$\varepsilon_y = \left[\frac{(p\mu_p^2 - n\mu_n^2)}{(n\mu_n + p\mu_p)}\right] \varepsilon_x B_z \tag{6}$$

Substituting for ε_x from (1) in (6), we get

$$\varepsilon_y = \left[\frac{(p\mu_p^2 - n\mu_n^2)}{(n\mu_n + p\mu_p)^2}\right] J_x B_z \tag{7}$$

Writing

$$R_H = \left[\frac{(p\mu_p^2 - n\mu_n^2)}{(n\mu_n + p\mu_p)^2}\right] \tag{8}$$

equation (7) simplifies to

$$\varepsilon_y = R_H J_x B_z \tag{9}$$

The equation (9) defines the Hall effect. The constant R_H is defined as the Hall coeffcient. Putting $n = p = n_i$ in (8), we find

$$R_H = \left(\frac{1}{qn_i}\right)\left[\frac{(\mu_p - \mu_n)}{(\mu_n + \mu_p)}\right] \tag{10}$$

which gives the Hall coefficient of an intrinsic semiconductor sample. For $n \gg p$ (n-type sample), $R_H = -(1/qn)$. Similarly, for $p \gg n$, $R_H = (1/qp)$. Thus, R_H gives both the magnitude and the sign of the charge carriers.

1.24 Analyze the motion of electrons in a p-type semiconductor sample at a very low temperature under a crossed electric and a magnetic field so that the effects of electron-phonon interaction could be suppressed.

Solution

Let us imagine a hole at rest at the origin O of a right-handed co-ordinate system. An electric field ε_x and a magnetic field B_z are applied in the directions as shown (Fig. 1.31). After a certain instant of time when the hole acquires a finite velocity under the influence of ε_x, its equations of motion become

$$\left(\frac{dv_x}{dt}\right) = \left(\frac{q\varepsilon_x}{m^*}\right) + \left[\frac{(qv_yB_z)}{m^*}\right] = a + \omega_c v_y \tag{1}$$

$$\left(\frac{dv_y}{dt}\right) = -\left[\frac{(qv_xB_z)}{m^*}\right] = -\omega_c v_x \tag{2}$$

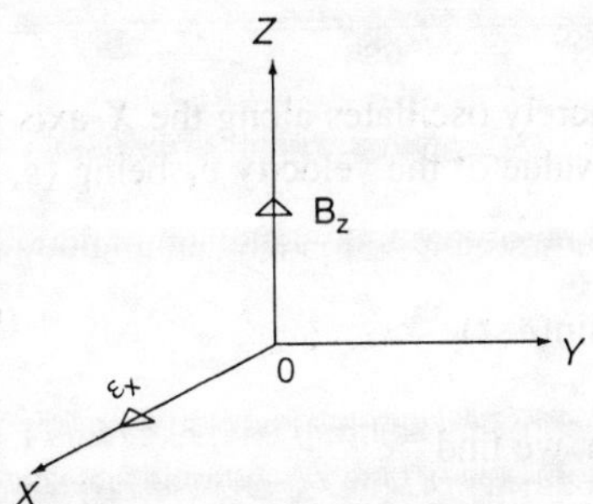

Figure 1.31 *A right-handed co-ordinate system with the electric field ε_x applied along X-axis and B_z along Z-axis*

and

$$\left(\frac{dv_z}{dt}\right) = 0 \tag{3}$$

where q only denotes the magnitude of the hole charge, $a = (q\varepsilon_x/m^*)$ and $\omega_c = [(qB_z)/m^*]$. Differentiating (1) with respect to t, we find

$$\left(\frac{d^2v_x}{dt^2}\right) = \left[\frac{(qB_z)}{m^*}\right]\left(\frac{dv_y}{dt}\right) = \omega_c\left(\frac{dv_y}{dt}\right) \tag{4}$$

Combining (2) and (4), we find,

$$\left(\frac{d^2v_x}{dt^2}\right) = -\left[\frac{(qB_z)}{m^*}\right]^2 v_x = -\omega_c^2 v_x \tag{5}$$

Equation (5) represents an S.H.M and its solution may be expressed as

$$v_x = A\sin(\omega_c t) \tag{6}$$

To evaluate A, we differentiate (6) to find

$$\left(\frac{dv_x}{dt}\right) = A\omega_c\cos(\omega_c t)$$

But at $t = 0$, since $v_y = 0$, we find from (1)

$$\left(\frac{dv_x}{dt}\right) = \left(\frac{q\varepsilon_x}{m^*}\right) = A\omega_c$$

or

$$A = \left(\frac{q\varepsilon_x}{m^*\omega_c}\right) = \left(\frac{\varepsilon_x}{B_z}\right)$$

Substituting for A in (6), we find

$$v_x = \left(\frac{\varepsilon_x}{B_z}\right)\sin(\omega_c t) \tag{7}$$

According to (7), the hole merely oscillates along the X-axis with a cyclotron frequency $\omega_c = [(qB_z)/m^*]$. The maximum value of the velocity v_x being (ε_x/B_z). Combining (2) and (7), we find

$$\left(\frac{dv_y}{dt}\right) = \omega_c(\varepsilon_x/B_z)\sin(\omega_c t)$$

Integrating the above relation, we find

$$v_y = -\omega_c\left(\frac{\varepsilon_x}{B_z}\right)\left[\frac{\cos(\omega_c t)}{\omega_c}\right] + B$$

Since $v_y = 0$ at $t = 0$, $B = (\varepsilon_x/B_z)$. Therefore,

$$v_y = \left(\frac{\varepsilon_x}{B_z}\right)[1 - \cos(\omega_c t)] \tag{8}$$

Thus, along the Y-axis, the hole propagates with a steady velocity (ε_x/B_z), on top of which an oscillating component $(\varepsilon_x/B_z)\cos(\omega_c t)$ has been superimposed.

When a high magnetic field is applied to a semiconductor maintained at 4.2 K, a phenomenon known as cyclotron resonance is observed. Additionally, if a two-dimensional carrier gas is used, one observes the Quantum Hall effect (QHE).

We have just seen that for vanishingly low values of ε_x, carriers describe circles in the XY plane with a cyclotron frequency

$$\omega_c = \left[\frac{(qB_z)}{m^*}\right] \tag{9}$$

whose radii are given by

$$R = \left[\frac{m^* v}{qB_z}\right] = \left(\frac{v}{\omega_c}\right) \tag{10}$$

Thus, higher the magnetic field, smaller are the radii of circles. v denotes the velocity with which holes describe the circles. When the carrier-phonon scattering is negligible such that the mean free path is longer than the circular path, the quantized energy states are separated distinctly. The energy of holes moving in the Nth Landau level is then given by

$$E_N = \left(N + \frac{1}{2}\right)\hbar\omega_c \tag{11}$$

where N is an integer. In a cyclotron resonance experiment, an electromagnetic signal close to ω_c is superimposed on the sample. When it exactly matches ω_c, excitation between the levels occur and there is a very strong resonance absorption. Having measured ω_c for resonance, one may use (9) to estimate m^*.

We have noticed that with vanishingly small values of ε_x, holes describe circles in the clockwise sense. Increasing ε_x, one observes a spiral movement of holes in the Y-direction. The centre of the loop moves with a velocity (equation 8)

$$v_y = \left(\frac{\varepsilon_x}{B_z}\right) \tag{12}$$

and the Hall conductivity $\sigma_{yx} = (1/\rho_{yx})$ is given by

$$\sigma_{yx} = \left(\frac{J_y}{\varepsilon_x}\right) = \left(\frac{qpv_y}{\varepsilon_x}\right) = \left(\frac{qp}{\varepsilon_x}\right)\left(\frac{\varepsilon_x}{B_z}\right) = \left(\frac{qp}{B_z}\right) \tag{13}$$

where p denotes the hole density within the semiconductor. Since the average velocity along the X-axis is zero, the longitudinal current $J_x = 0$. Hence $\sigma_{xx} = 0$. The situation however changes if one allows the build up of the Hall voltage in an open circuit condition (letting $J_y = 0$). As a result of (12), $\varepsilon_x = 0$ or $\rho_{xx} = (\varepsilon_x/J_x) = 0$. In such a case, we have

$$\sigma_{xy} = \left(\frac{J_x}{\varepsilon_y}\right) = \left(\frac{qpv_x}{\varepsilon_y}\right) = \left(\frac{qp}{\varepsilon_y}\right)\left(\frac{-\varepsilon_y}{B_z}\right) = -\left(\frac{qp}{B_z}\right) \tag{14}$$

In deriving (14), we used, $\varepsilon_y = -v_x B_z$. By comparing (13) and (14), we find that $\sigma_{yx} = -\sigma_{xy}$. Thus, if a current I_x is passed through the semiconductor along the X-axis, the resistive voltage V_y appearing across the sample along X and Y axes may be measured. Hence, the resistivities ρ_{xx} and ρ_{xy} can be determined. If the sample happens to be a two-dimensional one (so that only a motion along the XY plane is possible) ρ_{xx} and ρ_{xy} will now have dimensions of resistances only. In particular, ρ_{xy} is the ratio of the electric field $\varepsilon_y = (V_y/Y)$, across the sample of width Y to the current per unit length (I_x/Y). In other words, (V_y/I_x) is independent of the width Y. As the thickness along the Z-axis in a two dimensional system cannot be ascertained exactly, it is convenient to change the units of p, σ and R_H to $(\text{cm})^{-2}$, $(\text{ohm})^{-1}$ and $(\text{cm})^2/\text{C}$ respectively. If N denotes the total number of Landau levels filled with holes, we may then write

$$p = N\rho(E_\perp)dE_\perp = N\left[\frac{2m^*}{2\pi\hbar^2}\right]\left(\frac{1}{2}\hbar\,\omega_c\right)$$

where $E_\perp$ denotes electron energy levels perpendicular to the magnetic field. Or

$$p = \left(\frac{NqB_z}{h}\right) \tag{15}$$

Combining (14) and (15), we find

$$\sigma_{xy} = N\left(\frac{q^2}{h}\right) \tag{16}$$

It is important to note that the measured quantity σ_{xy} is a multiple of (q^2/h). This is independent of the sample size, applied fields or the material itself. This effect is known as the Quantum Hall effect (QHE).

Substituting for h and q, one finds $\rho_0 = (h/q^2) = 25812.807$ ohms $\cong 25813$ ohms. Figure 1.32 shows the remarkable way in which ρ_{xx} and ρ_{xy} are found to vary with the magnetic field strength B_z. The Hall resistance ρ_{xy} rises in steps instead of a linear variation (which is observed only for low B_z). The energy dissipating component ρ_{xx} is effectively zero except when ρ_{xy} is changing from one step to the next. Most remarkably, each step of ρ_{xy} is given with a great accuracy (to better than 1 part in 10^7) by the expression

$$\rho_{xy} = (h/Nq^2) \tag{17}$$

Such an extraordinary phenomenon thus provides a very precise and convenient resistance standard.

At still lower temperatures and at very high magnetic fields, at which these experiments are usually carried out, $kT \ll h\omega_c$ so that there is a negligible thermal excitation from one Landau level to another. The values of ρ_{xy} at which steps appear exactly N Landau levels are filled. The conductivity component σ_{xx} will then vanish because there is then an energy gap of $h\omega_c$ between the filled states in the Nth and the $(N+1)$ th levels. Because of this gap, holes can neither gain energy from the applied field nor lose energy by collisions, so that $\sigma_{xx} = 0$. If σ_{xx} vanishes while σ_{xy} remains finite, ρ_{xx} also disappears (as already explained). Sometime later, it was discovered that in carefully prepared samples, steps for ρ_{xy} also appeared for fractional values of N such as $1/3, 2/3, 4/3, 5/3, 2/5, 3/5, 4/5, 2/7, \ldots\ldots$ Under such extreme conditions of a very low temperature and a very high magnetic field, the carriers are considered to have liquefied. Because, their uncertainties in positions tends to be very near zero, the uncertainties in their momenta tend to be increasingly larger. This causes the carrier gas to have liquid like properties.

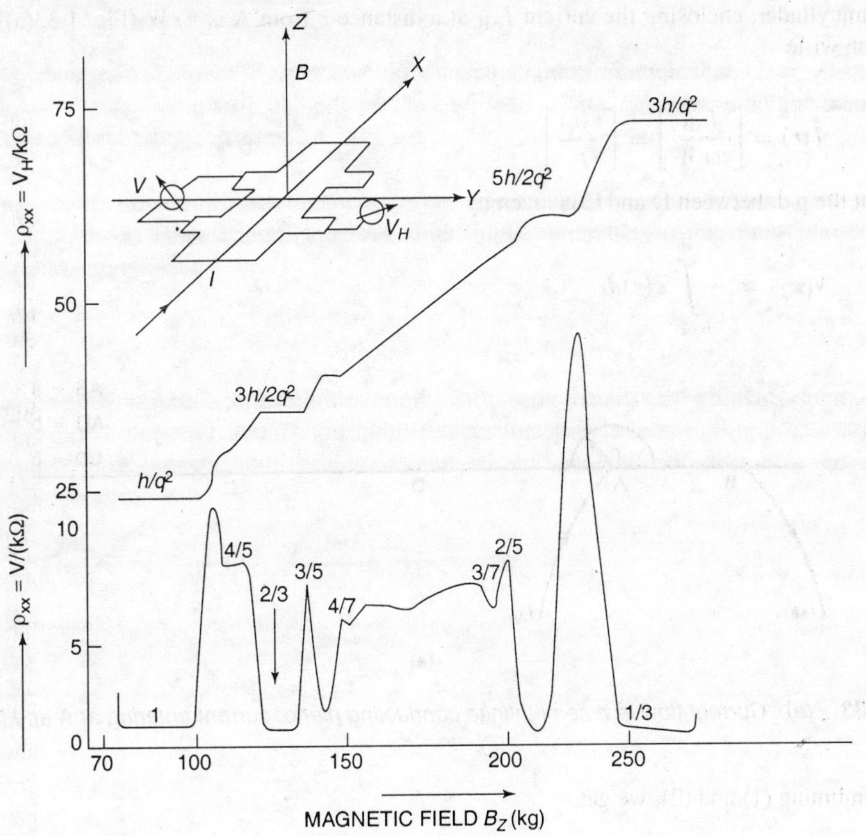

Figure 1.32 *Quantum hall effect at a temperature of 90 mK.*

1.25 Four metallic contacts (A, B, C, D) exist at the boundary of a flat, thin and a plane semiconductor sample. First, a current I_{AB} is passed between A and B and the resulting floating potential V_{CD} developed, is measured between C and D. Next, a current I_{BC} is passed between B and C and the corresponding floating potential between D and A (viz. V_{DA}) is measured. Show that

$$\exp\left[-\left(\pi R_{AB,CD}\frac{W}{\rho}\right)\right]+\exp\left[-\left(\pi R_{BC,DA}\frac{W}{\rho}\right)\right]=1$$

where $R_{AB,CD} = (V_{CD}/I_{AB})$, $R_{BC,DA} = (V_{DA}/I_{BC})$, W = width of the semiconductor sample and ρ = semiconductor resistivity.

Solution

Since, the semiconductor sample is thin and of width W, the current density wave form generated by the current entering at A would be semicylindrical in nature. The surface area of the semicylinder, enclosing the current I_{AB} at a distance r from A is $\pi r W$ (Fig. 1.33(a)). We may then write

$$J(r) = \left[\frac{I_{AB}}{\pi r W}\right] = \left[\frac{\varepsilon(r)}{\rho}\right] \tag{1}$$

But the p.d. between D and C is given by

$$V_{DC,A} = -\int_{b+c}^{b} \varepsilon(r)dr \tag{2}$$

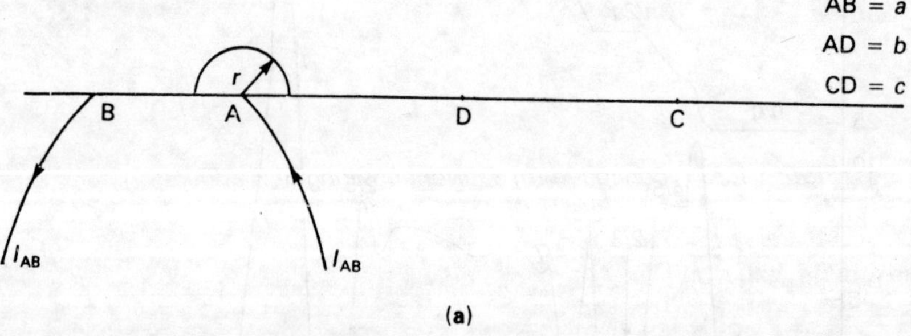

Figure 1.33 *(a) Current flow in a semi-infinite conducting plane: current entering at A and leaving at B*

Combining (1) and (2), we get,

$$V_{DC,A} = -\left[\frac{\rho I_{AB}}{\pi W}\right]\int_{b+c}^{b}\left(\frac{dr}{r}\right) = \left[\frac{\rho I_{AB}}{\pi W}\right]\ln\left[\frac{(b+c)}{b}\right] \tag{3}$$

Similarly, if the current I enters at B instead of A, the p.d. between D and C would be given by

$$V_{DC,B} = -\left[\frac{\rho I_{AB}}{\pi W}\right]\int_{(a+b+c)}^{(a+b)}\left(\frac{dr}{r}\right) = \left[\frac{\rho I_{AB}}{\pi W}\right]\ln\left[\frac{(a+b+c)}{(a+b)}\right] \tag{4}$$

Since the current is entering at A and leaving at B, the p.d. between D and C would be given by

$$V_{DC} = V_{DC,A} - V_{DC,B} = \left[\frac{\rho I_{AB}}{\pi W}\right] \ln\left[\frac{(a+b)(b+c)}{b(a+b+c)}\right] \tag{5}$$

Therefore,

$$R_{AB,CD} = \left(\frac{V_{DC}}{I_{AB}}\right) = \left[\frac{\rho}{\pi W}\right] \ln\left[\frac{(a+b)(b+c)}{b(a+b+c)}\right] \tag{6}$$

Next, let us presume that the current is passed between B and C and the floating potential is measured between A and D (Fig. 1.33(b)). The p.d. between A and D due to the current entering at B is given by

$$V_{AD,B} = -\left[\frac{\rho I_{BC}}{\pi W}\right] \int_{(a+b)}^{a} \left(\frac{dr}{r}\right) = \left[\frac{\rho I_{BC}}{\pi W}\right] \ln\left[\frac{(a+b)}{a}\right] \tag{7}$$

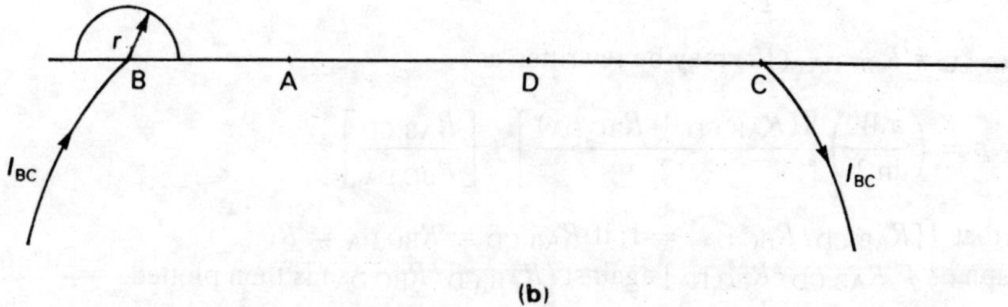

Figure 1.33 continued (b) Current entering at B and leaving at C

Similarly, if I_{BC} enters at C, we have

$$V_{AD,C} = -\left[\frac{\rho I_{BC}}{\pi W}\right] \int_{(b+c)}^{c} \left(\frac{dr}{r}\right) = \left[\frac{\rho I_{BC}}{\pi W}\right] \ln\left[\frac{(b+c)}{c}\right] \tag{8}$$

Since I_{BC} leaves C, the net p.d. between A and D is

$$V_{AD} = V_{AD,B} + V_{AD,C} = \left[\frac{\rho I_{BC}}{\pi W}\right] \ln\left[\frac{(a+b)(b+c)}{ca}\right]$$

Therefore,

$$R_{BC,DA} = \left(\frac{V_{AD}}{I_{BC}}\right) = \left[\frac{\rho}{\pi W}\right] \ln\left[\frac{(a+b)(b+c)}{ca}\right] \tag{9}$$

Exponentiating both sides of (6) and (9), and then adding, we find

$$\exp\left[-\left(\pi R_{AB,CD}\frac{W}{\rho}\right)\right] + \exp\left[-\left(\pi R_{BC,DA}\frac{W}{\rho}\right)\right] = 1 \tag{10}$$

Van der Pauw's method of measurement of resistivity is based on (10). It has also been proved to be independent of the sample shape. To simplify the evaluation of the resistivity using (10), let us choose A,B,C and D such that $R_{AB,CD} = R_{BC,DA} = R$(say). In that case, (10) simplifies to

$$2\exp\left[-\left(\frac{\pi RW}{\rho}\right)\right] = 1 \text{ or } \exp\left[\left(\frac{\pi RW}{\rho}\right)\right] = 2 \tag{11}$$

Taking the logarithm of (11), we get

$$\rho = \left(\frac{\pi W}{\ln 2}\right) R \tag{12}$$

Now if we define the average resistivity R_{av} as

$$R_{av} = \frac{[R_{AB,CD} + R_{BC,DA}]}{2} \tag{13}$$

If $R_{AB,CD} \neq R_{BC,DA}$, (12) may be rewritten as

$$\rho = \left(\frac{\pi W}{\ln 2}\right)\left[\frac{(R_{AB,CD} + R_{BC,DA})}{2}\right] f\left[\frac{R_{AB,CD}}{R_{BC,DA}}\right] \tag{14}$$

such that $f[R_{AB,CD}/R_{BC,DA}] = 1$, if $R_{AB,CD} = R_{BC,DA} = R$.
A graph of $f[R_{AB,CD}/R_{BC,DA}]$ against $(R_{AB,CD}/R_{BC,DA})$ is then plotted.

1.26 An n-type Ge sample is used in the Haynes–Shockley experiment. The length of the sample is 1 cm and the two probes are separated by 0.95 cm. The battery voltage is 2 V. A pulse arrives at the second electrode 0.25 ms after injection at the first; the width of the pulse Δt is 117 microseconds. Calculate the hole mobility and the diffusion constant.

Solution

It is obvious from Fig. 1.34 that

$$\mu_p = \left(\frac{v_d}{\varepsilon}\right) = \frac{\left(\frac{L}{t_d}\right)}{\left(\frac{E_0}{L_0}\right)} = \frac{\left(\frac{0.95}{0.35 \times 10^{-3}}\right)}{\left(\frac{2}{1}\right)} = 1900\,\text{cm}^2/\text{Vs}$$

The diffusion equation which injected holes satisfy is

$$\frac{\partial}{\partial t[\delta p(x,t)]} = \frac{D_p \partial^2}{\partial x^2[\delta p(x,t)]} \tag{1}$$

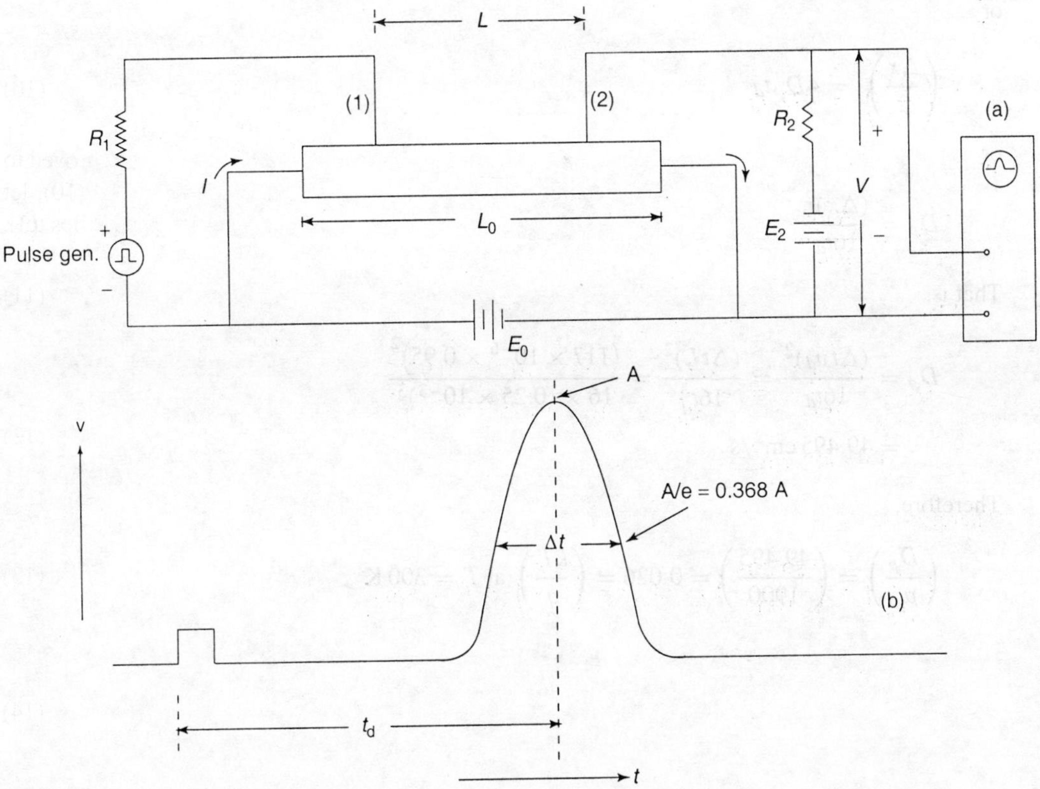

Figure 1.34 *The Haynes–Shockley experiment: (a)the schematic circuit, (b) a typical trace on the oscilloscope screen*

The solution to this equation is

$$\delta p(x,t) = \left[\frac{\Delta P}{2(\pi D_p t)^{1/2}}\right]\exp\left[-\left(\frac{x^2}{4D_p t}\right)\right] \tag{2}$$

where ΔP is the number of holes per unit area created over a negligibly small distance at $t = 0$. The factor in the bracket indicates the peak value of the hole pulse at $x = 0$. Equation (2) clearly suggests that this value decreases with time and the exponential factor predicts the spread of the pulse in the positive and the negative X-axis. If we denote this peak value of the hole pulse by δp_0 at any time t_d,we may use (2) to calculate D_p from the value of δp at some point x. The most convenient check is the point $(\Delta x/2)$ where δp is down by $(1/e)$ of the peak value δp_0. At this point, we may write

$$\left(\frac{1}{e}\right)\delta p_0 = \delta p_0 \exp\left[\frac{-\left(\dfrac{\Delta x}{2}\right)^2}{4D_p t_d}\right]$$

or

$$\left(\frac{\Delta x}{2}\right)^2 = 4D_p t_d$$

or

$$D_p = \frac{(\Delta x)^2}{16t_d} \tag{3}$$

That is,

$$D_p = \frac{(\Delta t v_d)^2}{16t_d} = \frac{(\Delta t L)^2}{16t_d^3} = \frac{\left(117 \times 10^{-6} \times 0.95\right)^2}{16 \times (0.25 \times 10^{-3})^3}$$

$$= 49.495\,\text{cm}^2/\text{s}$$

Therefore,

$$\left(\frac{D_p}{\mu_p}\right) = \left(\frac{49.495}{1900}\right) = 0.026 = \left(\frac{kT}{q}\right) \text{ at } T = 300\,\text{K}$$

Exercises

1.1 Draw a unit cube of a GaAs crystal in which corner atoms are Ga. Taking one Ga atom as the origin, write down the co-ordinates of the four nearest atoms and the next nearest Arsenic atoms. Also, write down the co-ordinates of the nearest Ga atoms.

[(a/2,a/2,0), (a/2,0,a/2), (0,a/2, a/2), (a/4,a/4,a/4); (a/4,a/4,a/4), (3a/4,3a/4,a/4), (3a/4,3a/4,3a/4), (a/4,3a/4,3a/4); (a/2,a/2,0), (a/2,0,a/2), (0,a/2,a/2)]

1.2 Calculate the specific gravity of a GaAs crystal. At.wt. of Ga = 69.7, At.wt of As = 74.9, mass of a proton = 1.66×10^{-34} kg, and lattice spacing of GaAs = 5.65Å. [5.32]

1.3 The density of a GaP crystal at 300 K is 4.13 gm/c.c. and its molecular wt. is 100.7. Calculate its lattice spacing. How will this be affected if the crystal is cooled down to the liquid nitrogen temperature? (At.wt of Ga = 69.72 and At.wt. of P = 30.98) [5.45Å]

1.4 A one dimensional crystal has a lattice constant of 2.5 Å. Determine the electron momentum and the energy at which the first Bragg reflection occurs. [1.32×10^{-24} kgm/s ; 4.56 eV]

1.5 Calculate the width of the conduction band of Si. The lattice spacing of Si crystal is 5.43A and $m_n^* = 1.1$ m, where m = 9.11×10^{-31} kg. [1.16 eV]

1.6 A hypothetical semiconductor crystal has a conduction band that can be described by

$$E_{cb} = E_1 - E_2 \cos{(ka)}$$

and a valence band that can be described by

$$E_{vb} = E_3 - E_4 \sin^2\left(\frac{ka}{2}\right)$$

where $E_3 = (E_1 - E_2)$ and $-(\pi/a) \leq k \leq (\pi/a)$.

a) Sketch the variation of the energy of the two bands as a function of k over a Brillouin zone. b) What are the band widths of the conduction and valence bands? c) What is the band gap of the material? d) What is the effective mass of the electrons at the bottom of the conduction band? $[2E_2, E_4; (E_1 - E_2 - E_3); h^2/a^2E_2)]$

1.7 Derive an expression for the electron effective mass of carriers in semiconductors on the basis of the two-band model. $[m^* = 2E_G m^2 a^2/h^2]$

1.8 A Si crystal ($\rho = 2.53$ gms/c.c in the molten state) is to be pulled from the melt and doped with Phosphorus (segregation coefficient = 0.35). How many grams of P should be added to 1 kg of Si to obtain a donor concentration of 10^{16} /cm^3 during initial growth? [0.585mgm]

1.9 Phosphorus in Si has a donor level of 0.045 eV below E_c. It is observed that the ionization energy of P disappears at a dopant concentration of 2×10^{17}/c.c. Calculate the average separation between the impurity atoms at this stage. $[d \cong 2\, a_B]$

1.10 Derive an expression for the shift in the Fermi energy level with changes in the doping concentration of a semiconductor sample. $[\Delta E_F = k(\Delta n/n)]$

1.11 Show that the effective density of states N_C represents the density of states in an energy strip 1.21 kT wide near the conduction band edge.

1.12 Show that for an exponential impurity distribution the built-in electric field in a semiconductor is nearly constant. Calculate the magnitude of the electric field for $N = N_0 \exp(-x/x_0)$ at room temperature with $x_0 = 0.4$ micrometers. $[6.5 \times 10^4\, V/m]$

1.13 Show that the probability of occupancy of the state of energy E above E_F by an electron in a semiconductor is the same as the probability of occupancy of the state of energy E below E_F by a hole.

1.14 An intrinsic semiconductor sample has a resistance of 10 ohms at 364 K and 100 ohms at 333 K. Presuming that such a change is entirely caused by the temperature variation of n_i, calculate the band gap energy of the semiconductor. [1.55 eV]

1.15 A 300 ohm resistor is connected in series with a piece of intrinsic Ge bar. Near 300 K the value of the resistance changes by 1% $(\mathrm{K})^{-1}$. Calculate what would be the resistance of the sample to ensure that the resistance of the combination remains invariant when the temperature is changed by a few degree centigrade around 300 K. Ignore the temperature dependencies of the carrier mobilities. [69.85 ohms]

1.16 Discuss the possibility of observing the negative differential conductivity effect in a bulk semiconductor crystal.

1.17 Assuming the carrier mobilities to be independent of doping concentrations, calculate the maximum possible resistivities of Si and GaAs crystals at 300 K. Compare these values with the corresponding intrinsic resistivities.

[3.6×10^5 ohm cm, 1.58; 9.47×10^8 ohm cm, 2.41]

1.18 An electric field of 1000 V/cm is applied across an n-type Ge crystal at 300 K. Calculate the (a) thermal and (b) drift velocities of electrons. (Given: $m_n^* = 0.037$ m, and $\mu_n = 0.39\,\mathrm{m^2/Vs}$)

[6.12×10^5 m/s; 390 m/s]

1.19 Calculate the mean free time of collision of an electron, with the lattice, having a mobility of $0.39\,\mathrm{m^2/Vs}$. Also, calculate the mean free path between successive collisions. Assume $m_n^* =$ 0.037 m. [8×10^{-14} s; 490Å]

1.20 The mobility of electrons in a Ge crystal is $3900\,\mathrm{cm^2/Vs}$ at room temperature. Using $m^* = 0.12$ m, find the value of the relaxation time τ. At what frequency will the electric field and the current be $(\pi/4)$ out of phase? [2.6×10^{-13} s; 4.8×10^{11} Hz]

1.21 The hole diffusion coefficient in a Si sample is $12\,\mathrm{cm^2/s}$. Determine the mean free path and the carrier drift velocity in a field of 200 V/cm. Also calculate the energy gained by the carrier in a free path. Assume T = 300 K. [276.66 Å, 923 m/s, 0.013 eV]

1.22 A Si bar of length 0.02 m and cross-sectional area $10^{-4}\,\mathrm{m^2}$ is doped to a concentration of $10^{21}/\mathrm{m^3}$. The resistance of the bar at room temperature is 10 ohm. What is the electron mobility?

[$1250\,\mathrm{cm^2/Vs}$]

1.23 Minority holes are injected into a homogeneous n-type semiconductor sample at one point. An electric field of 50 V/cm is applied across the sample and the field displaces the minority carriers by a distance of 1 cm in 100 microsec. Find the drift velocity and the diffusivity of the minority carriers. [100 m/s; $5.2 \times 10^{-4}\,\mathrm{m^2/s}$]

1.24 A square-shaped Si crystal has a side of 0.037 cm. Its thickness is 10^{-4} cm. It has excess hole density linearly distributed over the entire thickness from its maximum value of 9.92×10^{15} holes/cm^3 at one surface to zero at the other. Calculate the diffusion current flowing across the semiconductor sample. [7.34×10^{-5} A]

1.25 An n-type ($N_d = 10^{21}/\text{m}^3$) Si bar has a cross-section of 10^{-6} m^2 and a length of 0.01m. The minority carrier lifetime is 100μ s. Calculate the resistance of the bar a) in the dark and b) under an illumination that generates 10^{17} electron-hole pairs/cm^3/s uniformly throughout the sample ($\mu_n = 0.15\,\text{m}^2/\text{Vs}$). [416.67 ohms, 412.54 ohms]

1.26 A 0.25 μ m thick single crystal Si is illuminated with a monochromatic light of $h\nu = 3$ eV. The incident power is 10 mW. Find the total energy absorbed by the semiconductor per s, the rate of excess thermal energy dissipated to the lattice and the number of photons given off per s by recombination via intrinsic transitions. (The absorption coeff. of Si = 4×10^4 cm^{-1}) [6.32 mW, 3.96 mW, 1.32×10^{16}]

1.27 Consider an n-type GaAs crystal with an electron density of 10^{16} cm^{-3}. (a) Assuming that each of the absorbed photon produces one electron-hole pair in the sample, calculate the densities of excess electrons and holes within the sample in the steady state. (b) Calculate the induced photoconductivity of the sample. (c) Also, determine whether this is the case of low or high injection. [1.4×10^{20}/cm^3, 1.99×10^7 (ohm m)$^{-1}$; high level injection]

1.28 A GaAs sample is illuminated with light having a wavelength of 0.6μ m. The incident power is 15 mW. If one-third of the incident power is reflected and another third exits from the other end of the sample, what is the thickness of the sample? Also, calculate the thermal energy dissipated to the lattice per second ($\alpha = 5 \times 10^4$ cm^{-1}). [13.86μ m, 5 mW]

1.29 A 0.46 μ m thick sample of GaAs is illuminated with a monochromatic light of $h\nu = 2$ eV. The absorption coefficient α is 5×10^4 cm^{-1}. The power incident on the sample is 10 mW. (a) Find the total energy absorbed by the sample per second (b) Find the rate of the excess thermal energy given up by the electrons to the lattice before recombination. (c) Find the number of photons per second given off from recombination events, assuming perfect quantum efficiency. [9 mW, 2.565 mW, 2.81×10^{16}/s]

1.30 A 100 mW laser beam with a wavelength $\lambda = 6328$Å is focussed onto an InP sample 100 μ m thick. The absorption coefficient at this wavelength is 10^5 cm^{-1}. Find the number of photons emitted per second by radiative recombination in InP, assuming perfect quantum efficiency. What power is delivered to the sample as heat? E_G (InP) = 1.35 eV. [31.9×10^{16}; 31 mW]

1.31 Consider an intrinsic bar of GaAs at 77 K with $\mu_n = 10^5\ \text{cm}^2/\text{Vs}$ and $\mu_p = 10^4\ \text{cm}^2/\text{Vs}$ (a) Using absorption coefficient to be $10\ \text{cm}^{-1}$ for the sample, calculate its conductivity immediately following an impulse of light with an energy density of $1\ \text{J/cm}^2$. Assume that each absorbed photon generates one electron-hole pair and that the product $\alpha W \gg 1$; (b) assuming a continuous radiation with an intensity of $10\ \text{W/cm}^2$, what is the steady state sample conductivity if the electron-hole recombination lifetime is 10^{-7} s, $h\nu = 2$ eV., and $W = 1$ cm.

[$55 \times 10^3\ (\text{ohm cm})^{-1}$; $550\ (\text{ohm cm})^{-1}$]

1.32 A p-type Ge sample with a resistivity of 40 ohm cm at 300 K is uniformly illuminated with light that generates 10^{13} electron-hole pairs/cm^3/s. Calculate the resistivity of the sample caused by light. If the light is switched off at $t = 0$, calculate the time required for the excess conductivity to drop to 10% of its value at $t = 0$. Assume $\tau_n = 10^{-6}$ s.

[−0.15 ohm cm; 2.3 μ.s]

1.33 A sample of n-type Si has a dark resistivity of 10^3 ohm cm at 300 K. The sample is illuminated uniformly to generate 10^{21} electron-hole pairs/cm^3/s. The hole lifetime in the sample is 1 μ s. Calculate the sample resistivity and the percentage change in the conductivity after illumination owing to both the majority and minority carriers.

[2.93×10^4 ohm cm; 2.93×10^4]

1.34 A photoconducting bar of n-CdSe is 0.5 cm long, 0.2 cm wide and 0.02 cm thick. The material has a $E_G = 1.7$ eV, $\mu_n = 400\ \text{cm}^2/\text{Vs}$ and a negligible hole mobility. One of the largest area faces of the bar is illuminated uniformly with a 0.45 μ m wavelength light with an incident power of 1 mW/cm^2. Assuming unit quantum efficiency and $\tau_n = 10^{-3}$ s calculate the photocurrent when 5 V is applied across the bar.

[0.47μ A]

1.35 Four equidistant and spring-loaded pointed metallic probes are centrally positioned on the surface of a flat and a very thin semiconducting specimen. A current flowing between the outer pair of probes develops a floating potential V between the inner pairs. Express the elctrical conductivity of the specimen as a function of V and I.

[$\sigma = (\ln 2/\pi W)(I/V)$]

1.36 A four point probe (with a probe spacing of 0.5 mm) is used to measure the resistivity of a p-type Si sample. Find its resistivity if its thickness is 50μ m. The constant current is 1 mA and the measured voltage between the inner two probes is 10 mV.

[0.227 ohm cm]

1.37 The four point probe readings for a very large and a very thick n-type Si sample are $V = 10$ mV and $I = 1$ mA. The spacing between collinear probes is 1 mm. Determine the resistivity and the dopant concentration of the sample. ($\mu_n = 0.39\ \text{m}^2/\text{Vs}$)

[6.28 ohm cm; $2.55 \times 10^{14}/\text{cm}^3$]

1.38 Consider a p-type Si sample of an arbitrary shape. The sample is 0.15 mm thick with four contacts A, B, C and D at its periphery. If $(V_{CD}/I_{AB}) = 20$ ohms, and $(V_{BC}/I_{AD}) = 100$ ohms, determine the resistivity and the sheet resistance of the sample.

[3.35 ohm cm; 22.33×10^3 ohms]

1.39 In the Haynes–Shockley experiment, the supply voltage is varied to control the drift time t_d. It was noticed that the peak heights of the hole pulses under the collector terminals were 20 mV and 80 mV respectively for drift times of 200μ s and 50μ s respectively. Calculate the lifetime of holes.

[108.2μ s]

References

[1] Allen, L.C.,1955, Interpolation Scheme for Energy bands in Solids, *Phys. Rev.*, **98**, 993.

[2] Dekker, A.J.,1957, *Solid State Physics*, Prentice Hall Inc., Englewood Cliff, N.J.

[3] Dingle, R.L., Stormer, H.L., Gossard, A.C.,and Weigmann,W.,1978, Electron Mobilities in Modulation Doped Semiconductor Heterojunction Superlattices, *Appl.Phys. lett*, **33**, 65.

[4] Dunlap, W.C.,1957, *An Introduction to Semiconductors*, Wiley, New York

[5] Grove, A.S.,1967, *Physics and Technology of Semiconductor Devices*, Wiley, New York.

[6] Gunn, J.B.,1964, Microwave Oscillations of Current in III–V Compound Semiconductors, *IBM.J. Res. & Dev.*, **8**, 141.

[7] Hilsum,C.,1978, Historical Background of Hot Electron Physics, *Solid State Electronics*, **21**, 5.

[8] Kittel, C.,1991, *Introduction to Solid State Physics*, Wiley, New York.

[9] Kroemer,H.,1964, Theory of Gunn Effect, *Proc.IEEE*, **52**, 1736.

[10] Moll, J.L.,1964, *Physics of Semiconductors*, McGraw Hill, New York.

[11] Moss,T.S.,(ed.,) 1980, *Handbook of Semiconductors, Vols,1–4*, North Holland, Amsterdam.

[12] Ridley,B.K., and Watkins,T.B.,1961,The Possibility of Negative Resistance Effects in Semiconductors, *Proc. Phys. Soc., Lond*, **78**, 293.

[13] Ruch,J.G.,and Kino, G.S.,1967, Measurement of Velocity-Field Characteristics of *GaAs, Appl. Phys. Lett.*, **10**, 40.

[14] Sah, C.T., Noyce, R.N., and Shockley, W.,1957, Carrier generation and Recombination in *pn* Junctions and *pn* Junction Characteristics, *Proc. IRE*, **45**, 1228.

[15] Shockley, W.,1950, *Electrons and Holes in Semiconductors*, Van Nostrand, Princeton, N.J.

[16] Smith, R.A., 1979, *Semiconductors*, 2nd ed., Cambridge University Press, London.

[17] Streetman, B.G.,1991, *Solid State Electronic Devices*, Prentice Hall Inc.,Englewood Cliffs, New Jersey.

[18] Sze, S.M.,1983, *Physics of Semiconductor Devices*, Wiley, New York.

[19] Van der Pauw, L.J.,1958, A Method of Measuring Specific Resistivity and Hall Effect of a Disc of Arbitrary Shape, *Phillips Res. Reports*, **13**, 1.

[20] Ziman, J.M.,1964, *Principles of the Theory of Solids*, Cambridge University Press, London.

2 Physics of *pn* junctions

The *pn* homo-and heterojunctions are the two essential ingredients of semiconductor devices. We will discuss here the physics of their operation. The existence of donor and acceptor ions on both sides of a *pn* junction gives rise to a potential barrier for the motion of electrons and holes across it. The dependencies of barrier heights and widths on the applied biases play a crucial role in the function of the resulting semiconductor devices. To analyze their behaviour we will first study the properties of one-dimensional abrupt and linearly graded homojunctions and derive expressions for barrier heights, depletion layer widths, field intensities, space-charge layer capacitances, etc. The operations of *pn* junction devices under d.c., a.c., and pulsed conditions will be considered next. The essential principles of semiconductor heterojunctions will also be discussed.

A *pn* junction is known to perform various circuit functions. Because of its asymmetrical I–V characteristic, it is capable of rectifying low-frequency alternating signals. Zener diodes with sharp breakdown characteristics have been employed for voltage control applications. Because of the non-ohmic (or non-linear) nature of its I–V curve, a *pn* diode are also used as a variable resistor (varistor). Since the depletion layer capacitance of such *pn* junctions can be made to vary as a function of the applied reverse voltage, these diodes are also used as variable capacitors (varactors). Again, if the terminals of such junctions are left open and are irradiated by an external source of light, carriers are generated inside the junction. Depending on the polarity of the carriers they are collected at the appropriate ends of the depletion layer. This causes an open-circuit voltage to develop across the *pn* junction. The voltage can be employed suitably to convert solar energy into useful electricity in the form of a solar cell. If a *pn* diode is made up of a III–V compound semiconductor material and is forward biased, light is given off by the junction due to the electron-hole recombination inside it. Such junctions are called light-emitting diodes (LEDs). On meeting other additional requirements, these diodes can also release coherent electromagnetic radiations and behave as semiconductor lasers. Also, in a reverse biased *pn* junction, carriers may be generated by the impact ionization process. The reverse current, in such a case, is found to lag behind the externally applied a.c.signal because of a finite time lag inherent in the impact ionization process. By proper adjustments of the device parameters, the phase lag between the current and the voltage can be made to be exactly π radians. The device will then be found to exhibit a negative conductance behaviour and can be used successfully for the conversion of d.c. power into microwaves. When used in this way, the device is known as an IMPATT (impact ionization by avalanche and transit time) diode. The chapter finally concludes with a description of some other applications of *pn* junctions and their subsequent use in electronic circuitry.

2.1 *pn* homojunctions

Let a p-type semiconductor contain N_a atoms per unit volume. To such a specimen, a uniform density N_d of donors per unit volume is next introduced to produce a sharp metallurgical pn junction (Fig. 2.1(a)). Its n-side then has a rich supply of electrons while its p-side acts as a reservoir of holes.Due to the very large density gradients of electrons and holes existing across such a junction, the carriers tend to diffuse over to the other side, following Fick's first law of diffusion (1.49). This process then leads to the uncovering of donor and acceptor atoms of their electrons and holes respectively near the junction interface and their subsequent diffusion to the other side of the junction. Consequently, we are left with ionized donor and acceptor atoms on both sides of the junction which give rise to an electric field. This electric field motivates electrons and holes to drift opposite to their directions of diffusion. Equilibrium is established when the two types of currents cancel one another, i.e., when

$$j_n(x) = q\mu_n(x)\varepsilon(x) + qD_n\left[\frac{dn(x)}{dx}\right] = 0$$

or

$$\varepsilon(x) = -\left[\frac{kT}{qn(x)}\right]\left[\frac{dn(x)}{dx}\right] \tag{2.1}$$

A similar equation also follows, if we set $j_p(x) = 0$. Equation (2.1) clearly suggests that $\varepsilon(x)$ would be a maximum at the junction ($x = 0$) because of the maximum carrier density gradient there. This field is expected to fade out gradually as one moves away from the junction on both sides of it towards the bulk due to decreasing concentration gradients. To simplify the resulting mathematical analysis, assume that the electric field drops suddenly to zero at $x = -x_n$ and at $x = x_p$ instead of an expected gradual decay. Such imaginary boundaries are called transition layers because as one crosses them, there is a sudden change from the condition of complete ionization within the depletion layer to a case of complete neutrality in the bulk regions and vice versa. The fully ionized region lying between the two transition layers at $x = -x_n$ and at $x = x_p$ is called the depletion layer as it is considered

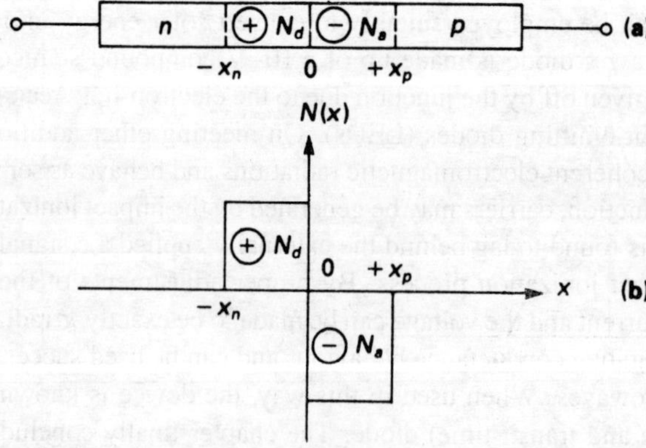

Figure 2.1 *An abrupt pn junction: (a) the pn junction configuration; (b) the space-charge on either side of the pn junction*

fully depleted of free carriers. Now, the expressions for the electric field, the electrostatic potential and the transition layer widths may be derived by solving the one-dimensional Poisson's equations in the appropriate regions of the depletion layer. The procedure is discussed below.

The one-dimensional Poisson's equation on the *n*-side (Fig. 2.1(b)) of the depletion layer may be written as

$$\frac{d^2\Psi_n}{dx^2} = -\frac{\rho}{\kappa\varepsilon_0} = -\frac{qN_d}{\kappa\varepsilon_0} \tag{2.2}$$

where κ denotes the semiconductor dielectric constant and ε_0 is the permittivity of the free space = 8.854×10^{-12} F/m. The one-dimensional Poisson's equation is used as the doping in the semiconductor is considered one-dimensional. Integration of (2.2) yields

$$\frac{d\Psi_n(x)}{dx} = -\left(\frac{qN_d}{\kappa\varepsilon_0}\right)(x + x_n) \tag{2.3}$$

where it is assumed that at $x = -x_n$, $d\Psi_n/dx = -\varepsilon(x) = 0$. Setting $\varepsilon_m = -d\Psi_n/dx$ at $x = 0$, we get

$$\varepsilon_m = \frac{qN_d\,x_n}{\kappa\varepsilon_0} \tag{2.4}$$

Fig. 2.1(c) describes the variation of the electric field intensity across the depletion layer of a *pn* junction. Integrating (2.3) once again and defining $\Psi_n = 0$ at $x = 0$, the variation of the electrostatic potential on the *n*-side of the depletion layer is given by

$$\Psi_n(x) = -\frac{qN_d}{\kappa\varepsilon_0}\left[\left(\frac{x^2}{2}\right) + x\,x_n\right] \tag{2.5}$$

According to (2.5), $\Psi_n(x)$ varies with x parabolically on the *n*-side of the depletion layer (Fig. 2.1(d)). The potential attains a maximum value Ψ_{n0} at $x = -x_n$, given by

$$\Psi_{n0} = \frac{qN_d\,x_n^2}{2\kappa\varepsilon_0} \tag{2.6}$$

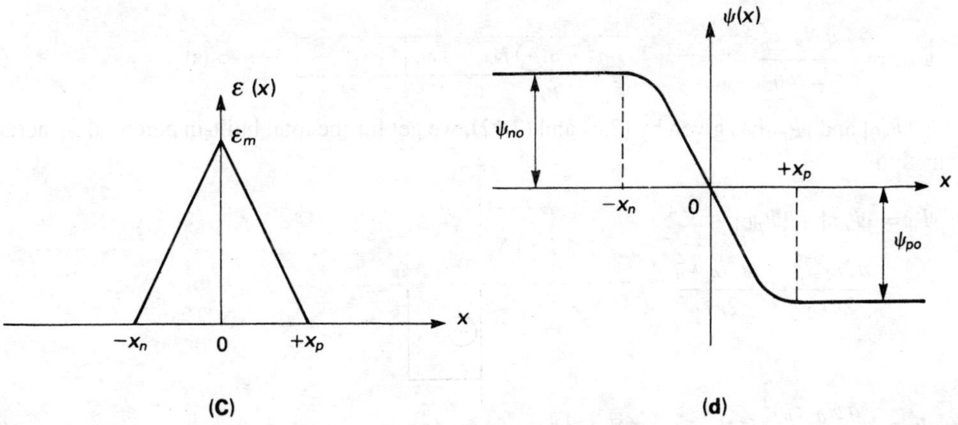

Figure 2.1 *continued (c) the electric field variation across the depletion layer; (d) the variation of electrostatic potential across the junction*

A similar set of equations also follows by solving Poisson's equation in the depletion layer on the p-side of the junction, which is given by

$$\frac{d^2\Psi_p}{dx^2} = \frac{qN_a}{\kappa\varepsilon_0} \tag{2.7}$$

Integrating (2.7), we find

$$\frac{d\Psi_p(x)}{dx} = \left(\frac{qN_a}{\kappa\varepsilon_0}\right)(x - x_p) \tag{2.8}$$

where x_p is the width of the transition layer on the p-side. Setting $x = 0$ in (2.8), we obtain

$$\varepsilon_m = \frac{qN_a\, x_p}{\kappa\varepsilon_0} \tag{2.9}$$

Since the normal component of the electric field intensity must be continuous across a homojunction, it follows from (2.4) and (2.9) that

$$N_d\, x_n = N_a\, x_p \tag{2.10}$$

Equation (2.10) also states that the number of ionized impurity atoms existing on both sides of a *pn* junction per unit area must be equal to one another. The condition (2.10) can be written from the charge neutrality considerations also. Integrating (2.8) once again and taking $\Psi_p = 0$ at $x = 0$, as before, we get

$$\Psi_p(x) = \frac{qN_a}{\kappa\varepsilon_0}\left[\left(\frac{x^2}{2}\right) - x\,x_p\right] \tag{2.11}$$

Equation (2.11) establishes the parabolic nature of the potential variation on the p-side of the junction, as well. The maximum electrostatic potential Ψ_{p0} developed on the p-side may be obtained by setting $x = x_p$ in (2.11), when we get

$$\Psi_{p0} = -\frac{qN_a\, x_p^2}{2\kappa\varepsilon_0} \tag{2.12}$$

Adding $|\Psi_{n0}|$ and $|\Psi_{p0}|$ as given by (2.6) and (2.12), we get for the total built-in potential Ψ_0 across the *pn* junction

$$\Psi_0 = |\Psi_{n0}| + |\Psi_{p0}|$$

$$= \frac{qN_d\, x_n^2}{2\kappa\varepsilon_0} + \frac{qN_a\, x_p^2}{2\kappa\varepsilon_0}$$

i.e.

$$\Psi_0 = \frac{(qN_a\, x_p)^2}{2\kappa\varepsilon_0}[(N_a)^{-1} + (N_d)^{-1}] \tag{2.13}$$

Since from (2.10), $N_d\, x_n = N_a\, x_p$. From (2.13), it therefore follows that

$$x_p = \left[\left(\frac{2\kappa\varepsilon_0}{q}\right)\left(\frac{N_d}{N_a}\right)\left\{\frac{\Psi_0}{N_a + N_d}\right\}\right]^{1/2} \tag{2.14}$$

Writing $(N_d x_n)^2 = (N_a x_p)^2$ in (2.13), we obtain

$$x_n = \left[\left(\frac{2\kappa\varepsilon_0}{q}\right)\left(\frac{N_a}{N_d}\right)\left\{\frac{\Psi_0}{N_a + N_d}\right\}\right]^{1/2} \tag{2.15}$$

The total width of the depletion layer may now be expressed as

$$W = |x_n| + |x_p| = \left(\frac{2\kappa\varepsilon_0\Psi_0}{qn^*}\right)^{1/2} \tag{2.16}$$

where n^* is the reduced doping density defined as

$$(n^*)^{-1} = (N_a)^{-1} + (N_d)^{-1} \tag{2.17}$$

Thus, it follows from (2.14), (2.15) and (2.16) that in order to estimate x_n, x_p and W, we must know Ψ_0 in addition to N_a and N_d. We must, therefore, seek an independent expression for Ψ_0, if possible in terms of N_a and N_d. Such a relation may be obtained by using (1.71) and (1.72) in the following manner:

$$N_d \cong n \cong n_i \, \exp\left[\frac{q}{kT}(\Psi_{n0} - \varphi)\right] \tag{2.18}$$

and

$$N_a \cong p \cong n_i \, \exp\left[\frac{q}{kT}(\varphi - \Psi_{p0})\right] \tag{2.19}$$

In writing (2.18) and (2.19), we presumed that there was complete ionization of impurity states. Also, the Fermi potential φ was presumed to remain invariant throughout the junction. By multipling (2.18) and (2.19) and remembering that Ψ_{p0} is negative (Fig. 2.1(d)), we get

$$\Psi_0 = \left(\frac{kT}{q}\right) \ln\left[\frac{N_d N_a}{n_i^2}\right] \tag{2.20}$$

Thus if N_a and N_d in a *pn* homojunction are known, we may determine Ψ_0, x_n, x_p and W.

Now due to the presence of the electric field within the depletion layer, the *pn* junction must possess a capacitance. It is evident from (2.20) that the presence of ionized charges controls Ψ_0. If a change dQ_n of charge per unit area on the *n*-side of the junction alters the junction potential by $d\Psi_0$, the differential junction capacitance per unit area is expressed as

$$C_j = \frac{dQ_n}{d\Psi_0} \tag{2.21}$$

But the total positive charge on the *n*-side of the junction is $Q_n = qN_d x_n$ (per unit area). We must therefore have

$$dQ_n = qN_d dx_n \tag{2.22}$$

Differentiating (2.15), we get

$$dx_n = \left(\frac{x_n}{2\Psi_0}\right) d\Psi_0 \tag{2.23}$$

Combining (2.22) and (2.23), we find

$$C_j = \frac{dQ_n}{d\Psi_0} = \frac{qN_d x_n}{2\Psi_0} \tag{2.24}$$

Substituting for x_n from (2.15) in (2.24), we get

$$C_j = \left(\frac{\kappa\varepsilon_0 q n^*}{2\Psi_0}\right)^{1/2} \tag{2.25}$$

Next combining (2.16) with (2.25), we get

$$C_j = \frac{\kappa\varepsilon_0}{W} \tag{2.26}$$

Reverse biasing the *pn* junction by a voltage V, the effective built-in junction potential increases to $(\Psi_0 + V)$. Equation (2.25) then modifies to

$$(C_j)^{-2} = \frac{2}{\kappa\varepsilon_0 q n^*}(\Psi_0 + V) \tag{2.27}$$

The plot of $(C_j)^{-2}$ against V is shown in Fig. 2.2. Experimentally measured points are found to lie on a straight line. The results confirm the validity of the depletion layer approximation, which was presumed in deriving the above relations. The intercept of the straight line on the V-axis is a direct measure of the built-in junction potential Ψ_0. The gradient of the line with the V-axis gives a measure of n^*. Thus having determined Ψ_0 and n^* from the experimental graph, one may solve for N_a and N_d on both sides of the *pn* junction.

We may also analyze the above problem for a linearly graded *pn* junction where the impurity density variation across the *pn* is represented as

$$N(x) = -ax \tag{2.28}$$

where a denotes the impurity gradient. Solving the Poisson's equation in this case, as before, we get

$$W = 2\,x_n = 2\,x_p = 2\left(\frac{3\kappa\varepsilon_0\Psi_0}{2qa}\right)^{1/3} \tag{2.29}$$

$$\Psi_0 = \frac{2kT}{q}\ \ln\left(\frac{aW}{2n_i}\right) \tag{2.30}$$

and

$$C_j = \frac{qax_n^2}{3\Psi_0} = \frac{\kappa\varepsilon_0}{W} \tag{2.31}$$

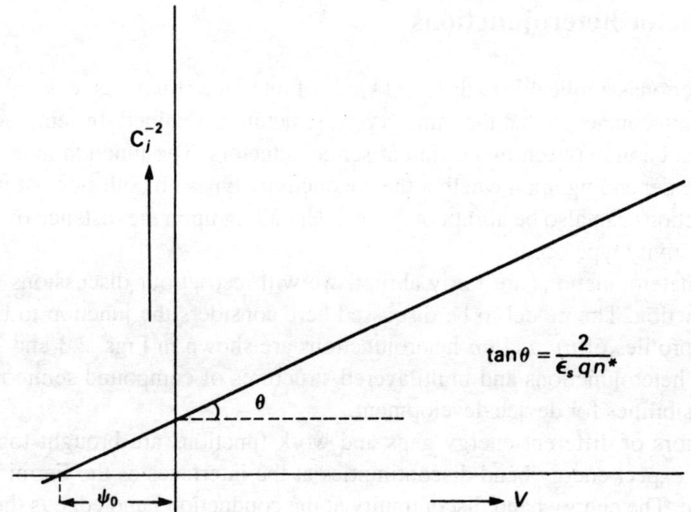

Figure 2.2 C_j^{-2} vs V curve for an abrupt *pn* junction

For a reverse biased *pn* junction (2.31) modifies to

$$(C_j)^{-3} = \frac{12}{qa\kappa^2\varepsilon_0^2}(\Psi_0 + V) \tag{2.32}$$

Thus, for a linearly graded *pn* junction $(C_j)^{-3}$ vs V curve would be a straight line. From the intercept of the line on the V-axis, we may similarly estimate Ψ_0. The slope of the line, on the other hand, gives the impurity gradient a.

If the doping across the depletion layer is made to vary as

$$N(x) = ax^m \tag{2.33}$$

the depletion layer capacitance should be dependent on voltage as

$$C_j = C_0(\Psi_0 + V)^{-s} \tag{2.34}$$

For a one-sided *pn* junction, the profile of the lighter doping is given by equation (2.33). It can be shown that

$$s = \frac{1}{(m+2)}$$

For a one-sided step profile, if $m = 0, s = 1/2$. For a linearly graded *pn* junction, $m = 1$ and $s = 1/3$. If $m < 0$, the junction is said to be hyperabrupt. Specific cases of interests are $m = -1, -(3/2), -(5/3)\ldots$ when $s = 1, 2, 3, \ldots$ respectively. In that case, the variation of C_j may be controlled sensitively by the variation of V.

2.2 Semiconductor heterojunctions

The term heterojunction is applicable to different kinds of interface structures realized by bringing two dissimilar materials in contact so that the same crystal structure is retained. In semiconductor physics, the term means a junction between two different semiconductors. The junction is respectively called isotype or anisotype depending upon whether the conductivity types on both sides of it are the same or opposite. Such junctions can also be abrupt or graded depending upon the distance over which a given transition of conductivity type occur.

Since most of the heterojunctions are fairly abrupt, we will restrict our discussions only to the case of abrupt heterojunction. The model to be discussed here considers the junction to be ideal in every respect. The band profiles of *np* and *nn* heterojunctions are shown in Figs. 2.3 and 2.4 respectively. The availability of heterojunctions and multilayered structures of compound semiconductors open a broad range of possibilities for device development.

When semiconductors of different energy gaps and work functions are brought together to form a heterojunction, we expect energy band discontinuities at the interfaces as the Fermi levels line up at thermal equilibrium. The energy band discontinuity at the conduction band edge is then given by

$$\Delta E_c = (E_{\text{vac}} - E_{c1}) - (E_{\text{vac}} - E_{c2}) = \chi_1 - \chi_2 \tag{2.35}$$

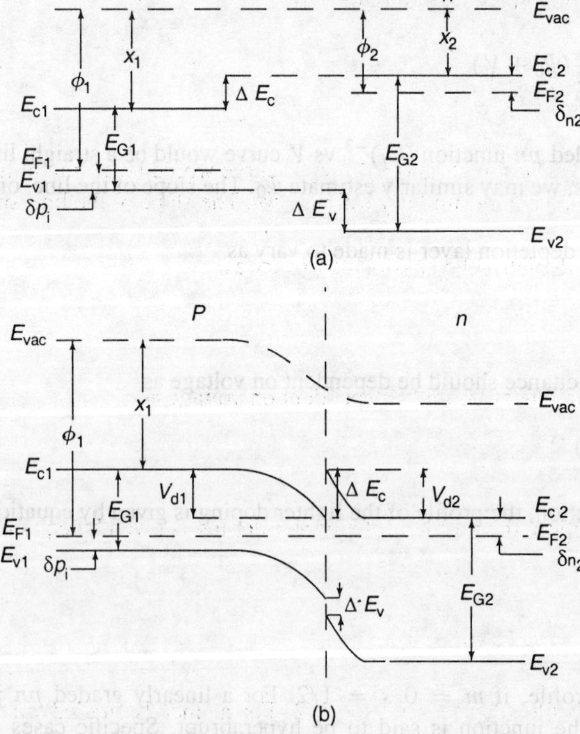

Figure 2.3 *The energy band diagram of a pn (anisotype) heterojunction: (a) the energy diagram before contact, (b) the energy diagram after contact*

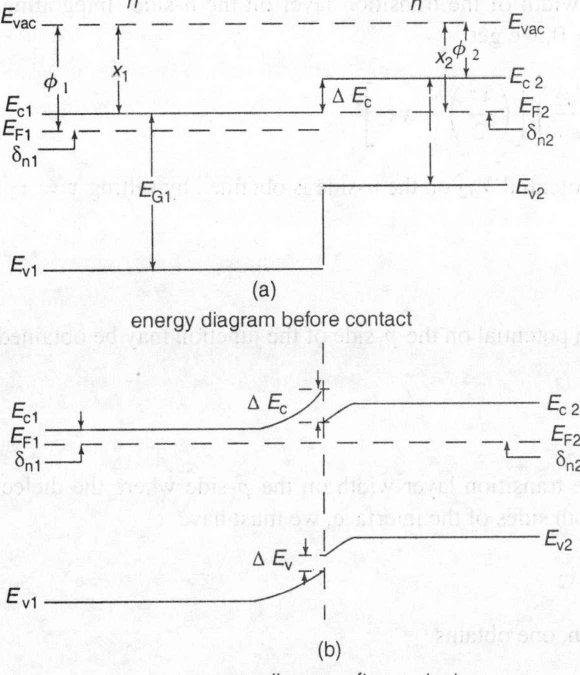

Figure 2.4 *The energy band diagram of an nn (isotype) heterojunction*

Similarly, the discontinuity at the valence band edge is

$$\Delta E_v = (E_{G2} + \chi_2) - (E_{G1} + \chi_1) = (E_{G2} - E_{G1}) + (\chi_2 - \chi_1) \tag{2.36}$$

Combining (2.35) and (2.36), we get

$$\Delta E_c + \Delta E_v = E_{G2} - E_{G1} \tag{2.37}$$

Thus, the sum of the energy band discontinuities is independent of the semiconductor work functions. Space-charge layers are formed on both sides of the interface, as a result of the diffusion of carriers across the heterojunction, which ultimately bring Fermi levels on both sides into alignment. To derive expressions for various junction parameters, we write the one-dimensional Poisson's equation on the n-side of the junction as

$$\frac{d^2\Psi_n}{dx^2} = -\frac{qN_{d2}}{\kappa_2\varepsilon_0} \tag{2.38}$$

where N_{d2} measures the donor density on the n-side, κ_2 denotes the dielectric constant of the second semiconductor and Ψ_n represents the electrostatic potential at a distance x from the interface on the n-side. Integrating (2.38) and remembering that $(d\Psi_n/dx) = 0$ at $x = x_2$, we get

$$\frac{d\Psi_n}{dx} = -\left(\frac{qN_{d2}}{\kappa_2\varepsilon_0}\right)(x - x_2) \tag{2.39}$$

where x_2 denotes the width of the transition layer on the n-side. Integrating (2.39) once again and defining $\Psi_n = 0$ at $x = 0$, we get

$$\Psi_n(x) = -\left(\frac{qN_{d2}}{\kappa_2\varepsilon_0}\right)\left[\left(\frac{x^2}{2}\right) - xx_2\right] \tag{2.40}$$

The built-in junction potential V_{d2} on the n-side is obtained by setting $x = x_2$ and is given by

$$V_{d2} = \frac{qN_{d2}\,x_2^2}{2\kappa_2\varepsilon_0} \tag{2.41}$$

Similarly, the diffusion potential on the p-side of the junction may be obtained as

$$V_{d1} = \frac{qN_{a1}\,x_1^2}{2\kappa_1\varepsilon_0} \tag{2.42}$$

where x_1 measures the transition layer width on the p-side where the dielectric constant is κ_1. For charge neutrality on both sides of the interface, we must have

$$qN_{a1}x_1 = qN_{d2}x_2 \tag{2.43}$$

Imposing this condition, one obtains

$$x_1 = \left[\frac{2\kappa_1\kappa_2\varepsilon_0\,N_{d2}(V_{d1} + V_{d2})}{qN_{a1}(\kappa_1 N_{a1} + \kappa_2\,N_{d2})}\right]^{1/2} \tag{2.44}$$

and

$$x_2 = \left[\frac{2\kappa_1\kappa_2\varepsilon_0\,N_{a1}(V_{d1} + V_{d2})}{qN_{d2}(\kappa_1 N_{a1} + \kappa_2\,N_{d2})}\right]^{1/2} \tag{2.45}$$

Adding (2.44) and (2.45), we get

$$W = x_1 + x_2 = \left[\frac{2\kappa_1\kappa_2\varepsilon_0\,V_d(N_{a1} + N_{d2})}{qn^*(\kappa_1 N_{a1} + \kappa_2\,N_{d2})}\right]^{1/2} \tag{2.46}$$

where

$$V_d = V_{d1} + V_{d2} \quad \text{and} \quad n^* = \frac{N_{a1}N_{d2}}{N_{a1} + N_{d2}} \tag{2.47}$$

Owing to the presence of space-charge layers on both sides of the interface, a capacitance gets associated with the *pn* junction. Now, if a change dV_d in the diffusion potential is able to produce a change dQ in the charge content per unit area on one side of the depletion layer, the transition layer capacitance per unit area is defined as

$$C_j = \frac{dQ}{dV_d} \tag{2.48}$$

But owing to the change in the depletion layer width by dx_2, the change in the charge density per unit area is given by

$$dQ = qN_{d2}dx_2 \tag{2.49}$$

But from (2.45) it follows that

$$\frac{dx_2}{dV_d} = \frac{x_2}{2V_d} \tag{2.50}$$

Combining (2.48), (2.49) and (2.50), we get

$$C_j = \left(\frac{q\kappa_1\kappa_2\varepsilon_0 N_{a1} N_{d2}}{2(\kappa_1 N_{a1} + \kappa_2 N_{d2})}\right)^{1/2} \tag{2.51}$$

Next, multiplying (2.46) by (2.51), we get

$$C_j = \frac{\left(\frac{\kappa_1\kappa_2\varepsilon_0}{W}\right) N_{a1} + N_{d2}}{\kappa_1 N_{a1} + \kappa_2 N_{d2}} \tag{2.52}$$

Now since the normal component has to be continuous across the interface, one must have

$$\kappa_1\varepsilon_1 = \kappa_2\varepsilon_2 \tag{2.53}$$

or

$$\frac{\kappa_1 V_{d1}}{\kappa_2 V_{d2}} = \frac{x_1}{x_2} \tag{2.54}$$

Combining (2.43) with (2.54), we find

$$\frac{\kappa_1 V_{d1}}{\kappa_2 V_{d2}} = \frac{N_{d2}}{N_{a1}} \tag{2.55}$$

The ratio $[V_{d1}/V_{d2}]$ may be estimated by using (2.55). However, if the experimental values of the energy band offsets ΔE_c and ΔE_v are known, one may proceed to draw an approximate energy band diagram of the heterojunction as follows:

i) Align the Fermi levels of the two semiconductors without the bands being connected. Space for transition layers should be earmarked.
ii) The heterojunction interface should be located near the heavily doped side. Thereafter, at the interfacial layer, ΔE_c and ΔE_v are marked out by a pair of points, which are separated by appropriate gaps.
iii) Finally, the conduction and the valence band edges on both sides of the interface are connected to the respective points to obtain the energy band diagram.

The above mentioned steps are illustrated by means of a diagram in Fig. 2.5. It is easy to notice that in a heterojunction, the potential barriers for electrons and holes are different and the flow of only one type of carrier can be suppressed relative to the other. Such an effect may improve the injection efficiency for the emitter-base junction of a bipolar transistor.

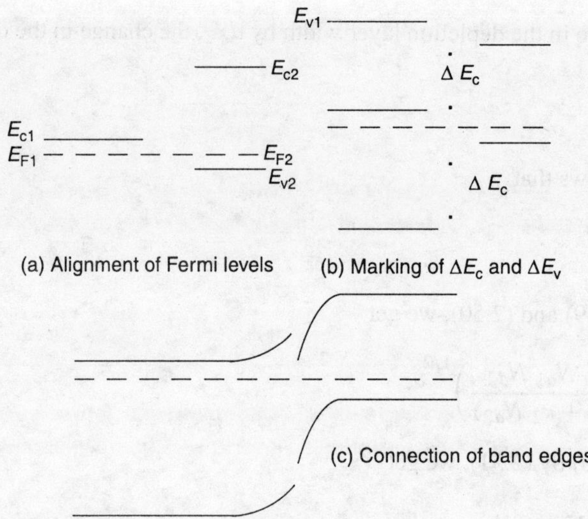

Figure 2.5 *Drawing of a heterojunction energy band diagram*

2.3 *pn* Diode equation

The energy–distance diagram of a *pn* homojunction under unbiased condition may be derived easily from Fig. 2.1(d). The latter must be inverted about the energy axis because normally the variation of the electron energy (instead of the electrostatic potential) is plotted as a function of distance in a *pn* junction. This is shown in Fig. 2.6. The flow of carriers from each side of the junction must be detail-balanced under equilibrium. When a forward bias of V volts is applied across a *pn* junction, most of the applied voltage would be available over the high resistance depletion layer. As the externally applied electric field opposes the built-in electric field, the junction potential is reduced from Ψ_0 to $(\Psi_0 - V)$. Therefore to redraw the energy band diagram for the forward biased condition, the portion of the diagram on the right of $+x_p$ has to be moved down by qV relative to that on the left-hand side in the energy scale. Such a process also shifts the equilibrium Fermi energy on both sides of the junction by qV because the applied bias will not affect the equilibrium carrier densities on the n and p sides. The equality of drift and diffusion currents flowing across the junction at equilibrium is disturbed with the application of the forward bias. Since the effective field now becomes smaller, the diffusion current grows stronger. The net electron current density flowing across the junction in this case is given by

$$j_n(x) = q\mu_n(x)n(x) + qD_n[dn(x)dx] \tag{2.56}$$

But from (1.71) it follows that

$$n(x) = n_i \exp\left[\left(\frac{q}{kT}\right)\{\Psi_n(x) - \varphi_n(x)\}\right] \tag{2.57}$$

Substituting for $n(x)$ from (2.57) in (2.56), we get

$$j_n(x) = -q\mu_n(x)n(x)\left[\frac{d\varphi_n(x)}{dx}\right] \tag{2.58}$$

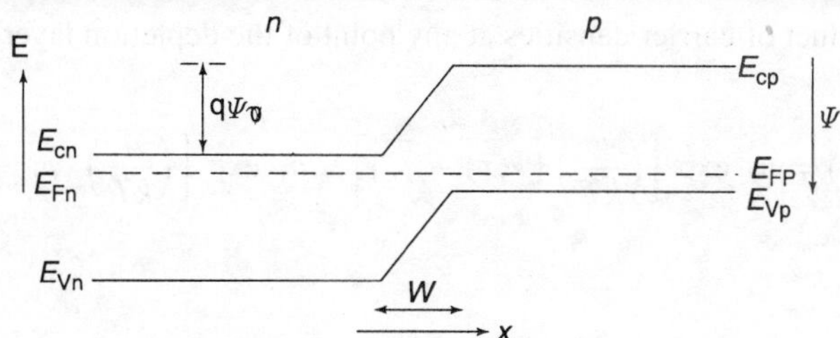

Figure 2.6 *The energy-distance diagram of a pn homojunction in the unbiased condition*

According to (2.58), if $j_n(x) \neq 0$, the Fermi level through the depletion layer must be position dependent. However, if any carrier recombination through the depletion layer is ignored, we must have

$$j_n(+x_p) = j_n(-x_n). \tag{2.59}$$

Combining (2.58) and (2.59), it follows that

$$n(-x_n)\left[\frac{d\varphi_n(x)}{dx}\right]_{-x_n} = n(+x_p)\left[\frac{d\varphi_n(x)}{dx}\right]_{+x_p} \tag{2.60}$$

It is not difficult to observe that $n(-x_n) \gg n(+x_p)$. It therefore follows from (2.60) that

$$\left[\frac{d\varphi_n(x)}{dx}\right]_{-x_n} \ll \left[\frac{d\varphi_n(x)}{dx}\right]_{+x_p} \tag{2.61}$$

Equation (2.61) states that the variation of $\varphi_n(x)$ with x in the neighbourhood of $x = -x_n$ is negligibly small compared to its variation near $x = +x_p$. The electron current density given by (2.58) when flowing over to the p-side disturbs the thermal equilibrium there. By that we mean that the carrier densities on the p-side can no longer be represented by the equilibrium Fermi level φ_p because now the electron density on the p-side is more than what it was at thermal equilibrium. As the electric charge neutrality on the p-side is now disturbed due to the injection of excess electrons, excess holes (equal in number to the injected electrons) are then drawn inwards from the external source of supply for the maintenance of charge neutrality (as required by the dielectric relaxation principle). These excess carriers then recombine in the normal fashion. The injected electrons meet the excess holes beyond $x = +x_p$ and thereafter their number gradually fades out with distance. To represent the perturbed carrier densities in the vicinity of $+x_p$, a new Fermi potential φ_n (called quasi Fermi level) has to be defined. As the carrier densities approach thermal equilibrium values, because of carrier recombination as one moves towards the bulk of the semiconductor from $x = +x_p$, the quasi Fermi level φ_n ultimately merges with its thermal equilibrium counterpart φ_p. Exactly parallel arguments are applicable for injected holes from the p to the n-side of the junction at $x = -x_n$, where the quasi Fermi level φ_p is introduced to represent the perturbed hole densities. Since, the variation of φ_n at $x = -x_n$ has been found to be small relative to that at $x = +x_p$, it is regarded to be almost invariant throughout the depletion layer. Crossing $x = +x_p$, it varies rapidly with x, ultimately merging with the equilibrium Fermi level on the p-side. Similar arguments apply equally well to the variation of φ_p on the n-side of the junction. The energy-distance diagram of a forward biased pn junction is given in

Fig. 2.7. Now, the product of carrier densities at any point of the depletion layer may be expressed as (1.71) and (1.72),

$$n(x)p(x) = n(x) = n_i \ \exp\left[\left(\frac{q}{kT}\right)\{\Psi(x) - \varphi_n\}\right] \times n_i \ \exp\left[\left(\frac{q}{kT}\right)\{\varphi_p - \Psi(x)\}\right]$$

or

$$n(x)p(x) = n_i^2 \ \exp\left[\left(\frac{q}{kT}\right)(\varphi_p - \varphi_n)\right] = n_i^2 \ \exp\left(\frac{qV}{kT}\right) \tag{2.62}$$

According to (2.62), the product of electron and hole densities at any point of the depletion layer must be independent of x. But when the electrons are injected to the p-layer across $x = +x_p$, the local charge neutrality there gets disturbed. The local hole density p_p must increase by the same amount as that of the injected electrons at x_p which is $n(+x_p)$. Therefore,

$$p(+x_p) = p_p + n(x_p) \tag{2.63}$$

From (2.62) and (2.63), we may now write

$$n(x_p) = \left[\frac{n_i^2}{p(+x_p)}\right] \exp\left(\frac{qV}{kT}\right)$$

$$= \left[\frac{n_i^2}{p_p + n(+x_p)}\right] \exp\left(\frac{qV}{kT}\right) \tag{2.64}$$

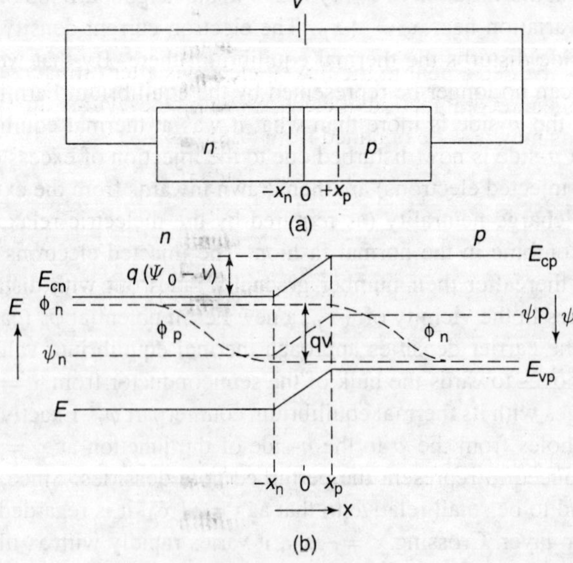

Figure 2.7 *(a) A forward biased pn diode (b) the energy-distance of a forward biased pn junction*

If we now presume that the injected electron density is a small fraction of p_p, (2.64) simplifies to

$$n(+x_p) = \frac{n_i^2}{n_n} \exp\left(\frac{qV}{kT}\right)$$

i.e.

$$n(+x_p) = n_p \exp\left(\frac{qV}{kT}\right) \tag{2.65}$$

where n_p denotes the thermal equilibrium electron density on the p-side. Thus, as a result of applying a forward bias, the minority carrier densities on each side of the *pn* junction increases by a factor of $\exp(qV/kT)$ at the respective transition layer boundaries viz.,$+x_p$ and $-x_n$. As a result of this, the injected electrons at $x = +x_p$ starts diffusing towards the bulk p-region in accordance with the Fick's first law of diffusion viz.,

$$f(x) = -D_n\left[\frac{dn(x)}{dx}\right] \tag{2.66}$$

The flux $f(x)$ (number of electrons entering per unit area and per unit time) decays with x due to carrier recombination. The flux density $f(x+dx)$ at $(x+dx)$ may be obtained from Taylor's theorem as

$$f(x+dx) = f(x) + f'(x)dx + \ldots = f(x) + \frac{\partial}{\partial x}\left\{\frac{-D_n dn(x)}{dx}\right\} dx$$

Therefore,

$$f(x+dx) - f(x) = -D_n\left[\frac{d^2n(x)}{dx^2}\right] dx \tag{2.67}$$

The above equation gives the decrement in the flux of electrons after diffusing through a volume dx. Such a decay is caused by the recombination of electrons with holes within the volume dx. The rate of recombination of electrons may now be obtained from (1.88) as

$$\frac{dn}{dt} = -\left[\frac{n - n_p}{\tau_n}\right] \tag{2.68}$$

on per unit volume basis. If there is no other cause for the decay of electrons, we have from (2.67) and (2.68)

$$D_n\left[\frac{d^2n(x)}{dx^2}\right] - \left[\frac{n(x) - n_p}{\tau_n}\right] = 0 \tag{2.69}$$

The above equation may also be written as

$$\left[\frac{d^2n(x)}{dx^2}\right] - \left[\frac{n(x) - n_p}{L_n^2}\right] = 0 \tag{2.70}$$

where $L_n^2 = D_n \tau_n$. The solution of (2.70) for a long *pn* diode may be expressed as

$$n(x) - n_p = [n(+x_p) - n_p] \exp\left(\frac{-x}{L_n}\right) \tag{2.71}$$

remembering that $n(x) = n(+x_p)$ at the transition layer boundary on the p-side which is presumed to be the new origin ($x = 0$) for the measurement of the distance co-ordinates. Combining (2.65) with (2.71), we find

$$n(x) - n_p = n_p\left[\exp\left(\frac{qV}{kT}\right) - 1\right] \exp\left(\frac{-x}{L_n}\right) \tag{2.72}$$

Equation (2.72) represents the electron density distribution, which is set up in the p-region. Owing to this, a diffusion current density due to electrons is produced beyond $x = +x_p$ which is given by

$$j_n(+x_p) = -qD_n\left[\frac{dn(x)}{dx}\right] = q\left(\frac{D_n n_p}{L_n}\right)\left[\exp\left(\frac{qV}{kT}\right) - 1\right] \tag{2.73}$$

Similarly, the hole current density at $x = -x_n$ may be obtained as

$$j_p(-x_n) = -qD_p\left[\frac{dp(x)}{dx}\right] = q\left(\frac{D_p p_n}{L_p}\right)\left[\exp\left(\frac{qV}{kT}\right) - 1\right] \tag{2.74}$$

Although holes and electrons diffuse opposite to one another, they produce a current density only in one direction because they carry equal and opposite charges. Since, no carrier is presumed to be lost by recombination within the depletion layer, the net current density crossing the *pn* junction is given by

$$j = j_n(+x_p) + j_p(-x_n) = q\left[\left(\frac{D_p p_n}{L_p}\right) + \left(\frac{D_n n_p}{L_n}\right)\right]\left[\exp\left(\frac{qV}{kT}\right) - 1\right] \tag{2.75}$$

The current flowing in the external diode terminals would be the same as given by (2.75) because of the dielectric relaxation process which has already been discussed earlier. This equation represents the ideal *pn* diode terminal I–V characteristic. The experimental and the theoretical I–V characteristics are compared in Fig. 2.8. The various anomalies between the theory and the experiment will now be analyzed.

Reverse biased case

According to the idealized theory, the reverse current of a *pn* diode must saturate at I_s which is given by

$$I_s = Aq\left[\left(\frac{D_p p_n}{L_p}\right) + \left(\frac{D_n n_p}{L_n}\right)\right] \tag{2.76}$$

where A denotes the junction area. But experimentally, the reverse current is never found to saturate.

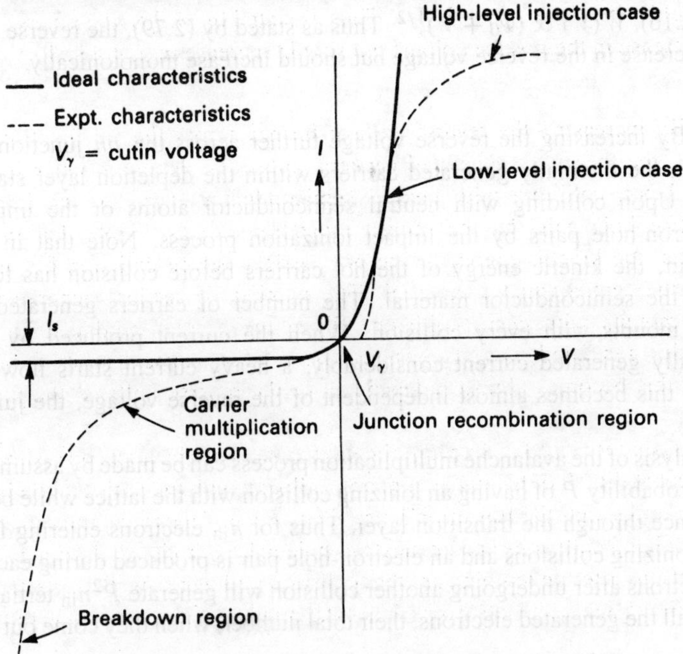

Figure 2.8 *The I–V characteristic of a pn junction*

(i) Generation current The reverse current continues to increase with the rise in the reverse voltage and beyond a particular value of it, the reverse current rises abruptly, leading to the junction breakdown. Such a departure from the normal behaviour may be due to several causes. A finite leakage current may flow over the diode surface. But a more important contribution to the reverse current is due to carriers which are thermally generated within the depletion layer. This component increases with the reverse voltage because of the widening of the depletion layer with increasing bias level. The thermally generated carriers are swept away by the junction field causing the reverse current to increase. This generation current may be computed by employing Shockley–Read–Hall (SRH) statistics in the following manner (1.108). In the reverse biased case and within the depletion layer we may presume $np < n_i^2$ (2.62) and $n_1 \sim p_1 \sim n_i$. In that case, the carrier generation rate which is the inverse of the recombination rate (1.108) may be expressed as

$$g_o = -R = \frac{n_i}{2\tau_i} \tag{2.77}$$

where $\tau_i = \tau_{po} = \tau_{no}$. The net current density produced by the thermally generated carriers may then be expressed as

$$j_{\text{gen}} = 2qg_oW = \frac{qn_iW}{\tau_i} \tag{2.78}$$

The factor of 2 takes care of both electron and hole generations. The reverse current density may then be expressed as

$$j = j_s + j_{\text{gen}} = q\left[\left(\frac{D_p p_n}{L_p}\right) + \left(\frac{D_n n_p}{L_n}\right)\right] + \left[\frac{qn_iW(V)}{\tau_i}\right] \tag{2.79}$$

But according to (2.16), $W(V) \propto (\Psi_0 + V)^{1/2}$. Thus as stated by (2.79), the reverse current must not saturate with the increase in the reverse voltage but should increase monotonically.

(ii) Breakdown By increasing the reverse voltage further across the *pn* junction, which has not been heavily doped, the thermally generated carriers within the depletion layer start gaining more and more energy. Upon colliding with neutral semiconductor atoms or the impurity ions they then generate electron-hole pairs by the impact ionization process. Note that in order to excite an electron-hole pair, the kinetic energy of the hot carriers before collision has to be larger than the energy gap of the semiconductor material. The number of carriers generated by the impact ionization process mounts with every collision. When the current produced by such a process exceeds the thermally generated current considerably, a heavy current starts flowing through the *pn* junction. When this becomes almost independent of the reverse voltage, the junction is said to breakdown.

An approximate analysis of the avalanche multiplication process can be made by assuming that a carrier of each type has a probability P of having an ionizing collision with the lattice while being accelerated over a certain distance through the transition layer. Thus for n_{in} electrons entering from the p-side, there will be Pn_{in} ionizing collisions and an electron-hole pair is produced during each collision. The Pn_{in} secondary electrons after undergoing another collision will generate P^2n_{in} tertiary electron-hole pairs. Summing up all the generated electrons, their total number, when they come out of the depletion layer, would be

$$n_{\text{out}} = n_{\text{in}}(1 + P + P^2 + \ldots) \tag{2.80}$$

assuming no loss of carriers by recombination. The factor of electron multiplication is then given by

$$M_n = \frac{n_{\text{out}}}{n_{\text{in}}} = 1 + P + P^2 + P^3 + \ldots = (1 - P)^{-1} \tag{2.81}$$

assuming that $P < 1$. As this ionization probability approaches unity, the carrier multiplication factor M_n rises without limit. The ionization probability P depends upon the magnitude of the reverse voltage applied to the junction. Measurements of carrier multiplication M in junctions near breakdown have lead to an empirical relation for M_n as

$$M_n = \left[1 - \left(\frac{V}{V_{br}}\right)^s\right]^{-1} \tag{2.81a}$$

where the exponent s varies from 3 to 6, depending on the type of semiconductor material used for the *pn* junction.

To set a criterion for the junction breakdown by the avalanche multiplication process, we define the electron ionization rate as

$$\alpha_n = \left(\frac{1}{n}\right)\left(\frac{dn}{dx}\right) \tag{2.82}$$

where α_n measures the fractional increase in the electron density per unit distance travelled within the depletion layer. Similarly, α_p may also be defined. For simplicity, we may presume $\alpha_n = \alpha_p = \alpha$.

Now, if I_{ni} is the electron current entering the depletion layer, the current emerging out will be more due to impact ionization within, which is say I_{no}. In that case, we have from (2.81) (Fig. 2.9),

$$M_n = \frac{n_{out}}{n_{in}} = \frac{I_{no}}{I_{ni}} \quad \text{or} \quad \frac{1}{M_n} = \frac{I_{ni}}{I_{no}}$$

or

$$1 - \left(\frac{1}{M_n}\right) = 1 - \left(\frac{I_{ni}}{I_{no}}\right) = \frac{I_{no} - I_{ni}}{I_{no}}$$

i.e.

$$1 - \left(\frac{1}{M_n}\right) = \frac{\Delta I_n}{I_{no}} = \frac{\Delta n}{n_{out}} = P \tag{2.83}$$

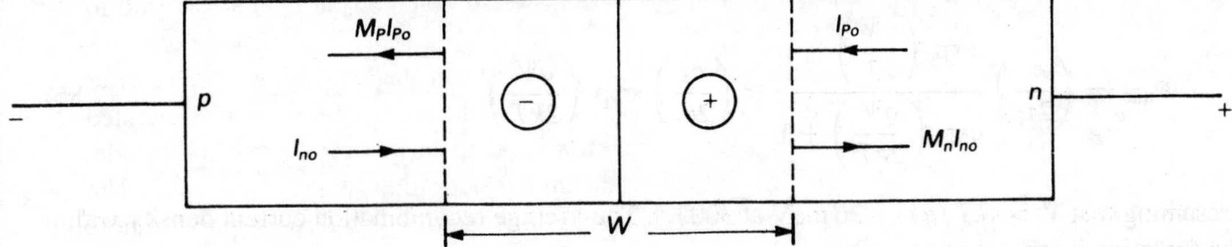

Figure 2.9 Carrier multiplication within the depletion layer

where ΔI_n and Δn respectively measure the increments in the electron current and the electron density. The breakdown sets in when $\Delta n \to n_{out}$ or $\Delta I_n \to I_{no}$. In such a case, $M_n \to \infty$. Using (2.82), the breakdown condition may be rewritten as

$$\frac{\Delta I_n}{I_{no}} = \frac{\Delta n}{n_{out}} = \int_0^W \alpha_n dx = 1 \tag{2.84}$$

A similar expression may also be written for holes. The mechanism of breakdown of *pn* junctions above 12 V is found to be caused by carrier multiplication due to impact ionization process (more popularly known as the avalanche multiplication process).

But *pn* junctions which are doped relatively heavily ($\sim 10^{16}$ cm^{-3}) are found to break down at smaller voltages. Owing to larger doping concentrations, the depletion layer widths of such junctions become very narrow (of the order of electron wavelengths) so that quantum mechanical tunnelling of carriers through the depletion layer becomes possible. As this mechanism of breakdown was initially proposed by Zener, diodes breaking down by quantum mechanical tunnelling are called Zener diodes. The breakdown of Zener diodes is relatively sharp compared to avalanche diodes. Therefore, they are put to voltage control applications.

Forward biased case

While deriving the ideal diode equation (2.75), carrier generation within the depletion layer was ignored. But a fraction of injected carriers would always be lost due to recombination within it when carrier capture through trap levels play a dominant role.

(i) Recombination current Presuming $E_i = E_t$ in (1.108), the recombination rate through trap levels may be expressed as

$$R = \frac{n_i^2\left[\exp\left(\frac{qV}{kT}\right) - 1\right]}{n_i\left[\exp\left\{\frac{q(\Psi - \varphi_n)}{kT}\right\} + \exp\left\{\frac{q(\varphi_p - \Psi)}{kT}\right\} + 2\right]\tau_i} \tag{2.85}$$

where it was presumed that $\tau_{po} = \tau_{no} = \tau_i$. The recombination rate is seen to be dependent on the electrostatic potential Ψ which varies through the depletion layer. R in (2.85) is a maximum if the denominator is a minimum. It is easy to notice that the denominator is a minimum for $\Psi = [(\varphi_p + \varphi_n)/2]$. Using this value in (2.85), one finds

$$R_{\max} = \left(\frac{n_i}{2\tau_i}\right)\frac{\exp\left(\frac{qV}{kT}\right) - 1}{\exp\left(\frac{qV}{2kT}\right) + 1} \approx \left(\frac{n_i}{2\tau_i}\right)\exp\left(\frac{qV}{2kT}\right) \tag{2.86}$$

presuming that $V > (kT/q)$ ($\sim$26 meV at 300 K). The average recombination current density within the depletion layer is then given by

$$j_{\text{rec}} = 2qR_{\text{av}}W = 2q\left(\frac{R_{\max}}{2}\right)W = qR_{\max}W$$

where R_{av} denotes the average recombination rate within the depletion layer. The factor of 2 takes care of both electrons and holes. Using (2.86) in the above equation, we get

$$j_{\text{rec}} = \left[\frac{qn_iW(V)}{2\tau_i}\right]\exp\left(\frac{qV}{2kT}\right) \tag{2.87}$$

The diffusion current density given by (2.75) may also be expressed as

$$j_{\text{diff}} = q\left[\left(\frac{D_p}{N_dL_p}\right) + \left(\frac{D_n}{N_aL_n}\right)\right]n_i^2\left[\exp\left(\frac{qV}{kT}\right) - 1\right] \tag{2.88}$$

For Ge diodes, n_i is relatively high compared to that of Si. It may be seen that $j_{\text{rec}} \propto n_i$ while $j_{\text{diff}} \propto n_i^2$. Therefore if a forward bias across a *pn* diode is gradually raised, j_{diff} becomes comparable to j_{rec} at a smaller bias for Ge junctions than for Si units. Unless j_{diff} exceeds j_{rec}, the carriers injected into the depletion layer will be lost by recombination and no current would be detected to flow across the external terminals. The point in the voltage axis of the I–V curve where the current starts rising is denoted by V_γ (cut-in voltage). For Ge and Si units this is recorded to be 0.2 V and 0.6 V respectively. The forward I–V characteristic of *pn* diodes can be fitted by the following empirical relationship:

$$j_F = j_s\exp\left(\frac{qV}{nkT}\right) \tag{2.89}$$

where n is found to lie between 1 and 2. We may see in Fig. 2.5 that for intermediate voltage ranges, the idealized diode theory agrees with experiment. But when the applied voltage is increased, the current is observed to fall short of theoretically predicted values. This effect may partially be attributed to finite potential drops over bulk n and p regions which in the simpler analysis were presumed to be zero. But the most important reason for the observed current drop is the injected minority carrier density becoming comparable to the majority carrier densitiy on both sides of the pn junction at high forward bias levels. We will now consider such a case.

(ii) High level injection case To analyze this problem in a simplified manner, we will consider a p^+n diode whose p-side is doped relatively heavy compared to that of the n-side. By doing so, we will be able to consider the hole flow only, as the electron component of the current would be too small (Fig. 2.10). Following (2.72), the hole distribution over the body of the n-layer may be represented as

$$p(x) - p_n = p_n \left[\exp\left(\frac{qV}{kT}\right) - 1 \right] \exp\left(\frac{-x}{L_p}\right) \tag{2.90}$$

This has been plotted. Due to the injection of excess holes into the n-layer, its electrical neutrality is disturbed. To restore it, a parallel density gradient for electrons has to be established almost at the same time, so that at every point of space, we must have

$$p(x) - p_n = n(x) - n_p \tag{2.91}$$

But the injected hole density gradient is permanently locked over the n-layer by the applied forward bias while there is nothing to hold the electron density gradient in place. Consequently, the electrons

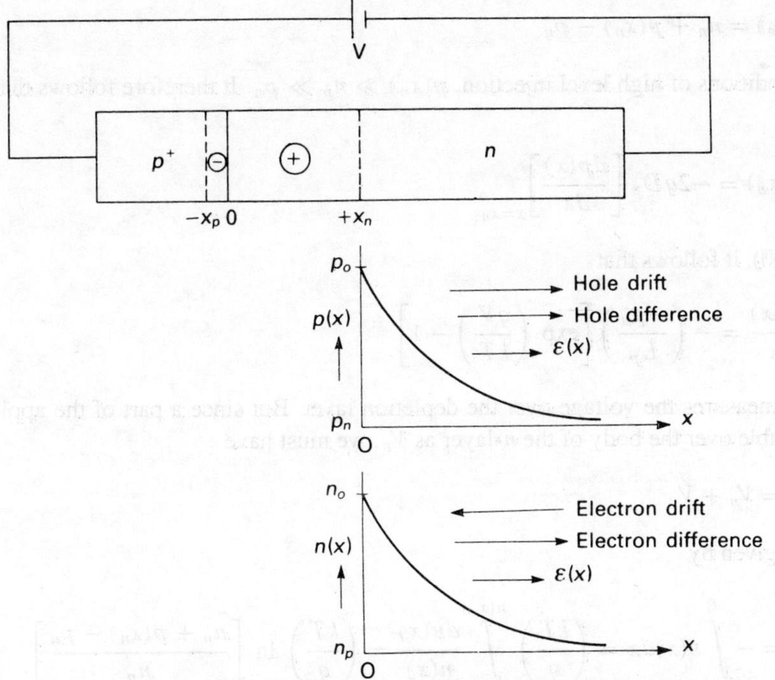

Figure 2.10 *A highly forward-biased p^+n junction*

tend to diffuse away exposing counterbalancing hole charges. Their very attempt generates an electric field which tends to hold back the diffusing electrons. But such an electric field enhances the hole flow. In order to compute the resulting hole current density we must determine the electric field intensity $\varepsilon(x)$ by requiring that $j_n(x) = 0$. That is

$$j_n(x) = 0 = q\mu_n n(x)\varepsilon(x) + qD_n\left[\frac{dn(x)}{dx}\right]$$

or

$$\varepsilon(x) = -\left(\frac{kT}{q}\right)\left[\frac{1}{n(x)}\right]\left[\frac{dn(x)}{dx}\right] \tag{2.92}$$

The resulting net hole current density may now be expressed as

$$j_p(x) = q\mu_p p(x)\varepsilon(x) - qD_p\left[\frac{dp(x)}{dx}\right] \tag{2.93}$$

Since $[dn(x)/dx] \approx [dp(x)/dx]$ for space-charge neutrality, we have combining (2.92) and (2.93),

$$j_p(x) = -qD_p\left[1 + \frac{p(x)}{n(x)}\right]\left[\frac{dp(x)}{dx}\right] \tag{2.94}$$

But for the maintenance of electrical neutrality at $x = +x_n$, we find that

$$n(x_n) = n_n + p(x_n) - p_n \tag{2.95}$$

Under conditions of high level injection, $p(x_n) \gg n_n \gg p_n$. It therefore follows that $n(x_n) \approx p(x_n)$. Hence

$$j_p(x_n) = -2qD_p\left[\frac{dp(x)}{dx}\right]_{x=x_n} \tag{2.96}$$

From (2.90), it follows that

$$\frac{dp(x)}{dx} = -\left(\frac{-p_n}{L_p}\right)\left[\exp\left(\frac{qV}{kT}\right) - 1\right] \tag{2.97}$$

where V measures the voltage over the depletion layer. But since a part of the applied voltage V_0 is also available over the body of the n-layer as V_n, we must have

$$V_0 = V_n + V \tag{2.98}$$

But V_n is given by

$$V_n = -\int_{\infty}^{0}\varepsilon(x)dx = \left(\frac{kT}{q}\right)\int_{n_n}^{n(x_n)}\frac{dn(x)}{n(x)} = \left(\frac{kT}{q}\right)\ln\left[\frac{n_n + p(x_n) - p_n}{n_n}\right]$$

Under conditions of high level injection the above equation reduces to

$$V_n = \left(\frac{kT}{q}\right) \ln \left[\frac{p(x_n)}{n_n}\right] \tag{2.99}$$

But we know that $p(x_n) = p_n \exp(qV/kT)$. Hence, it follows from (2.99) that

$$V_n = \left(\frac{kT}{q}\right) \ln \left[\frac{p_n \exp\left(\frac{qV}{kT}\right)}{\frac{n_i^2}{p_n}}\right] = \left(\frac{kT}{q}\right) \ln \left[\left(\frac{p_n}{n_i}\right)^2 \exp\left(\frac{qV}{kT}\right)\right]$$

or

$$V_n = \left(\frac{2kT}{q}\right)\left[\ln\left(\frac{p_n}{n_i}\right)\right] + V \tag{2.100}$$

Combining (2.99) and (2.100), we find

$$V_n = \left[\left(\frac{V_0}{2}\right) - \left(\frac{kT}{q}\right) \ln \left(\frac{p_n}{n_i}\right)\right] \tag{2.101}$$

Using (2.96), the diode current under high level injection conditions is given by

$$j_p(x_n) = -2D_p \left[\frac{dp(x)}{dx}\right]_{x=x_n} = \left[\frac{2qD_p p_n}{L_p}\right] \exp\left[\frac{q}{kT}\left\{\left(\frac{V_0}{2}\right) - \left(\frac{kT}{q}\right) \ln \left(\frac{p_n}{n_i}\right)\right\}\right]$$

i.e.

$$j_p(x_n) \cong \left[\frac{2qD_p n_i}{L_p}\right] \exp\left(\frac{qV_0}{2kT}\right) \tag{2.102}$$

Thus, according to (2.102), the slope of the ln j_p vs. V_0 characteristic is halved relative to the low injection case.

(iii) Diffusion capacitance We have just noticed that electron and hole densities co-exist in the neutral n-region of a p^+n junction under the forward biased condition and there is an electric field given by (2.92). Owing to the existence of this field in the bulk n-region, a capacitance gets associated with the pn diode. The number of holes stored per unit cross-sectional area of the n-layer may then be expressed as

$$\frac{Q_p}{q} = \int_0^\infty [p(x) - p_n]\, dx = p_n \left[\exp\left(\frac{qV}{kT}\right) - 1\right] \int_0^\infty \exp\left(\frac{-x}{L_p}\right) dx$$

where we have used (2.90). Integrating the above relation, we find

$$Q_p = qp_n L_p \left[\exp\left(\frac{qV}{kT}\right) - 1\right] \tag{2.103}$$

Equation (2.103) measures the number of holes stored per unit area of the n-layer. Now, if we bring about a change dQ_p in the stored hole charge by changing the applied forward bias by dV, the diffusion capacitance due to the stored holes on the n-side is given by

$$C_p = \left(\frac{dQ_p}{dV}\right) = \left(\frac{q^2 p_n L_p}{kT}\right) \exp\left(\frac{qV}{kT}\right) \tag{2.104}$$

The diffusion (or storage) capacitance per unit area due to electrons on the p-side is similarly given by

$$C_n = \frac{dQ_n}{dV} = \left(\frac{q^2 n_p L_n}{kT}\right) \exp\left(\frac{qV}{kT}\right) \tag{2.105}$$

Therefore, when the forward voltage of V volts across a pn diode is changed by dV, the changes in the electron and the hole stored charges on both side of the pn junction are given by dQ_n and dQ_p respectively. Therefore, the two capacitors C_n and C_p behave as if they are connected in parallel to each other. Hence, the total diffusion capacitance per unit area of the junction is given by

$$C = C_n + C_p = \left(\frac{q^2}{kT}\right)(p_n L_p + n_p L_n) \exp\left(\frac{qV}{kT}\right) \tag{2.106}$$

Equation (2.106) may also be written in the following differential forms:

$$C = \frac{q}{kT}\left[q\left(\frac{D_p p_n}{L_p}\right)\left(\frac{L_p^2}{D_p}\right) + q\left(\frac{D_n n_p}{L_n}\right)\left(\frac{L_n^2}{D_n}\right)\right] \exp\left(\frac{qV}{kT}\right) \tag{2.107}$$

or

$$C = \frac{q}{kT}[j_{p0}\tau_p + j_{n0}\tau_n] \exp\left(\frac{qV}{kT}\right) \tag{2.108}$$

where j_{p0} and j_{n0} denote the hole and the electron saturation current densities respectively in a pn junction.

2.4 A.C. behaviour of *pn* diodes

Let us now consider a pn diode which has both d.c. and a.c. biases (Fig. 2.11) superimposed upon each other. Since the widths of the depletion layers of the pn junctions are bias dependent, their transition layer boundaries are expected to oscillate with time about the d.c. magnitudes. However, if the d.c. bias magnitudes is sufficiently larger than the a.c. bias amplitude (i.e. $V_0 > V_a$), the oscillations of the type mentioned above may be insignificant and the transition layer boundaries can be regarded to remain stationary at their d.c. values. The injected hole density at $x = x_n$ will then consist of d.c. and a.c. components and may be expressed as

$$\begin{aligned} p(x_n) &= p_s + p(t) \\ &= p_s + p_a \exp(j\omega t) \end{aligned}$$

$$= p_n \exp\left(\frac{q}{kT}\right)[V_0 + V(t)]$$

$$= p_n \exp\left(\frac{qV_0}{kT}\right) \exp\left[\frac{qV(t)}{kT}\right]$$

or

$$p(x_n) = p_n \exp\left(\frac{qV_0}{kT}\right)\left[\frac{1 + qV(t)}{kT}\right] \tag{2.109}$$

where we have expanded the exponential involving $V(t)$ and ignored higher powers since $|V(t)| < (kT/q)$. We may now isolate the d.c. and a.c. components in (2.109) as

$$p_s = p_n \exp\left(\frac{qV_0}{kT}\right) \tag{2.110}$$

and

$$p(t) = \left(\frac{qp_s}{kT}\right) V(t) \tag{2.111}$$

Similarly, on the p-side we may derive

$$n_s = n_p \exp\left(\frac{qV_0}{kT}\right) \tag{2.112}$$

and

$$n(t) = \left(\frac{qn_s}{kT}\right) V(t) \tag{2.113}$$

Now to derive an expression for the alternating current crossing the pn junction, we have to set up the a.c. diffusion equations for electrons and holes. By inspecting (2.69), we obtain

$$D_p\left[\frac{\partial^2 p(x,t)}{\partial x^2}\right] - \left[\frac{p(x,t) - p_n}{\tau_p}\right] = \frac{\partial[p(x,t)]}{\partial t} \tag{2.114}$$

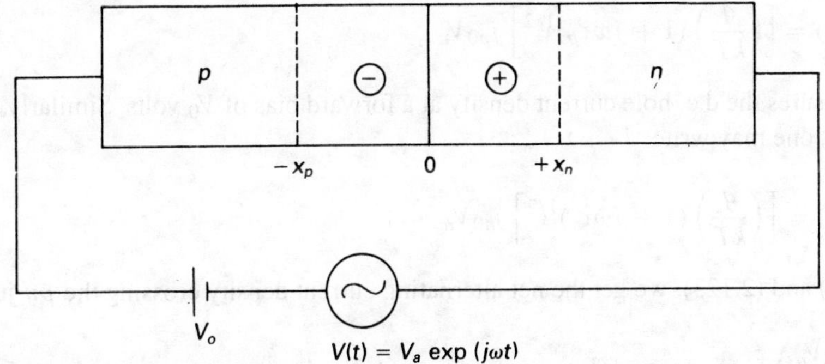

Figure 2.11 a.c. behaviour of pn diodes

In the d.c. case, the right-hand side of (2.114) is known to reduce to zero. The holes injected on the n-side have already been presumed to have the following form:

$$p(x,t) = p_s(x) + p_a(x)\exp(j\omega t) \tag{2.115}$$

Equation (2.115) must therefore be a solution of (2.114). Substituting for $p(x,t)$ in (2.114), we get

$$\left[\frac{\partial^2 p_s}{\partial x^2}\right] - \left[\frac{p_s - p_n}{L_p^2}\right] = \left[\frac{\partial^2 p_a}{\partial x^2}\right] - \left[\left(\frac{1+j\omega\tau_p}{L_p^2}\right) p_a\right] \exp(j\omega t) = 0 \tag{2.116}$$

Writing the space and time parts of the above equation separately, we get

$$\left[\frac{\partial^2 p_s}{\partial x^2}\right] - \left[\frac{p_s - p_n}{L_p^2}\right] = 0 \tag{2.117}$$

$$\left[\frac{\partial^2 p_a}{\partial x^2}\right] - C_p^2 p_a = 0 \tag{2.118}$$

where

$$C_p^2 = \frac{1+j\omega\tau_p}{L_p^2} \tag{2.119}$$

The solution of (2.118) for a long pn diode may now be written as

$$p_a(x) = p_a \exp(-C_p x) \tag{2.120}$$

The alternating component of the hole current density at $x = x_n$ then follows to be

$$j_{pa}(+x_n) = -qD_p\left[\frac{\partial p_a}{\partial x}\right]_{x=x_n} = qD_p p_a C_p \tag{2.121}$$

Restoring the values of different parameters in (2.121), we get

$$j_{pa}(+x_n) = \left[\left(\frac{q}{kT}\right)(1+j\omega\tau_p)^{1/2}\right] j_{p0} V_a \tag{2.122}$$

where j_{p0} measures the d.c. hole current density at a forward bias of V_0 volts. Similarly, on the p-side of the junction, one may write

$$j_{na}(-x_p) = \left[\left(\frac{q}{kT}\right)(1+j\omega\tau_n)^{1/2}\right] j_{n0} V_a \tag{2.123}$$

Adding (2.122) and (2.123), we get the net alternating current density crossing the pn junction as

$$j_a = \left(\frac{qV_a}{kT}\right)\left[(1+j\omega\tau_p)^{1/2} j_{p0} + (1+j\omega\tau_n)^{1/2} j_{n0}\right] \tag{2.124}$$

The a.c. diode admittance under low frequencies ($\omega\tau_p < 1$) may then be expressed as

$$Y = \frac{j_a A}{V_a} = \left(\frac{q}{kT}\right)\left[\left\{\frac{1 + j\omega\tau_p}{2}\right\} I_{p0} + \left\{\frac{1 + j\omega\tau_n}{2}\right\} I_{n0}\right] \tag{2.125}$$

where I_{p0} and I_{n0} denote the hole and the electron currents crossing the junction respectively. We may now express (2.125) as

$$Y = G + j\omega C \tag{2.126}$$

where

$$G = \frac{q I_0}{kT} \tag{2.127}$$

and

$$C = \frac{C_{\text{diff}}}{2} = \frac{q}{2kT}[\tau_p I_{p0} + \tau_n I_{n0}] \tag{2.128}$$

where C_{diff} represents the total diffusion capacitance (2.108).

2.5 Transient response of a *pn* diode

The transient behaviour of *pn* junctions differs from its static behaviour because under transient conditions there is a change in the stored charge distributions. Since a finite time is required to build up or deplete a given charge distribution, the latter would inevitably lag behind the current.

For a proper solution of the transient problem, we must use the time-dependent continuity equation which is developed below.

Let us consider an infinitesimal length Δx of a semiconductor sample having a cross-sectional area A in the YZ plane. The hole current density leaving the volume element $J_p(x + \Delta x, t)$ can be larger or smaller than the current density $J_p(x, t)$ entering the volume, depending on whether generation or recombination of carriers is taking place within it. The net increase in the hole density per unit time $\partial p(x, t)/\partial t$ within the volume is the difference of the hole flux entering and leaving the volume, minus the carrier recombination rate within it. That is,

$$\frac{\partial p(x,t)}{\partial t} = \frac{Jp(x) - Jp(x + \Delta x)}{q\Delta x} - \frac{\delta p(x,t)}{\tau_p}$$

As Δx approaches zero, the above expression may also be written in the following form:

$$-\left[\frac{\partial J_p(x,t)}{\partial x}\right] = q\left[\frac{\partial p(x,t)}{\partial t}\right] + q\left[\frac{\delta p(x,t)}{\tau_p}\right] \tag{2.129}$$

To obtain an expression for the instantaneous current density we have to integrate both sides of (2.129) at time t, to obtain

$$J_p(0) - J_p(x) = q\int_0^x \left[\frac{\partial p(x,t)}{\partial t} + \frac{\delta p(x,t)}{\tau_p}\right] dx$$

For injection into a long n-region from a p^+ region, we can take the current at $x_n = 0$ to be the hole current J_p and at infinity to be zero. In that case, the net instantaneous current is

$$i(t) = \frac{qA}{\tau_p}\int_0^\infty \delta p(x,t)\,dx + qA\frac{\partial}{\partial t}\int_0^\infty \delta p(x,t)\,dx$$

where $\delta p(x,t)$ now denotes the excess hole density stored in the n-region of a cross-sectional area A. Integrating the above expression, we find

$$i(t) = \left[\frac{Q_p(t)}{\tau_p}\right] + \left[\frac{dQ_p(t)}{dt}\right] \tag{2.130}$$

where $Q_p(t)$ denotes the total hole charge stored in the n-region. The above result indicates that the diode current (which is approximately equal to the hole current injected across the p^+n junction) is determined by the two charge storage effects: (i) the usual recombination term $[Q_p(t)/\tau_p]$ and (ii) a charge build up (or depletion) term $[dQ_p(t)/dt]$, which takes into account the time dependence of the excess charge carriers. In the steady state, the latter component is zero.

The minority hole charge stored in the neutral n-region of a forward biased long p^+n junction, in the steady state, is obtained in equation (2.103) as

$$Q_p = Aqp_nL_p\left[\exp\left(\frac{qV}{kT}\right) - 1\right] \tag{2.131}$$

But the diode forward current in that condition is given by

$$I_F = Aq\left(\frac{D_p p_n}{L_p}\right)\left[\exp\left(\frac{qV}{kT}\right) - 1\right] \tag{2.132}$$

Dividing (2.131) by (2.132), we get

$$I_F = \frac{Q_p}{\tau_p} \tag{2.133}$$

thus confirming (2.130). We can now solve for stored charge as a function of time for a given current transient. For example, the step off transient (Fig. 2.12(a)) in which the current is suddenly switched off at $t = 0$, leaves the diode with a stored charge within its body. Since the excess holes in the n-region must die out by recombination with a matching electron population, some time is needed for $Q_p(t)$ to reduce to zero. Using (2.130), we get for $t > 0$,

$$\frac{Q_p(t)}{\tau_p} + \frac{dQ_p(t)}{dt} = 0 \tag{2.134}$$

Solving this differential equation and remembering that $Q_p(t) = I_F\tau_p$ at $t = 0$, we get

$$Q_p(t) = I_F\tau_p \exp\left(\frac{-t}{\tau_p}\right) \tag{2.135}$$

As expected, the stored charges die out exponentially with time from its initial value $I_F \tau_p$, with a time constant equal to the hole lifetime τ_p in the n-type material (Fig. 2.12(b)). Combining (2.131) with (2.135) we get the following expression for the time-dependent diode voltage

$$V(t) = \left(\frac{kT}{q}\right) \ln \left[1 + \left[\frac{I_F \tau_p}{A q p_n L_p}\right] \exp\left(\frac{-t}{\tau_p}\right)\right] \tag{2.136}$$

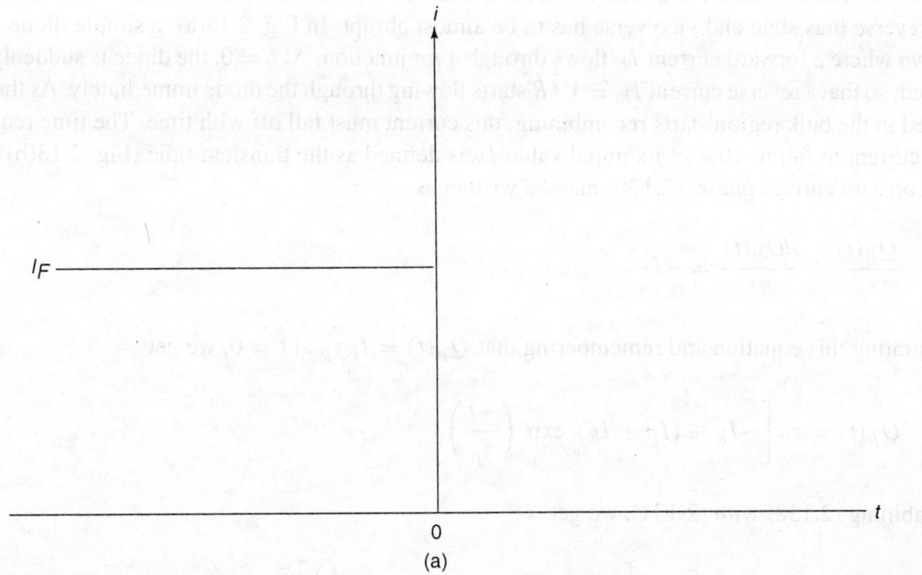

(a)

Figure 2.12 The effects of a step off transient on a p^+n diode: (a) the current flowing through the diode

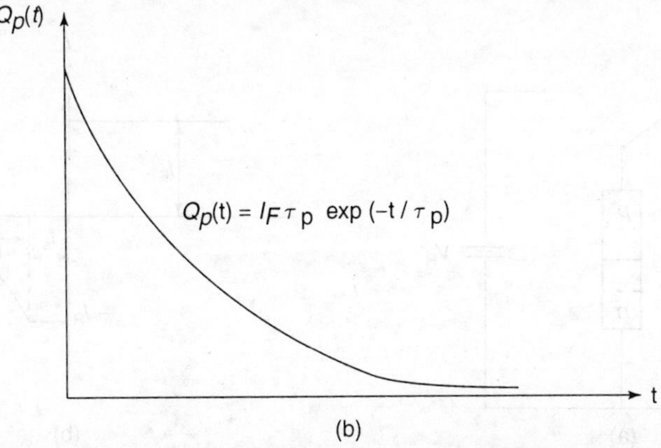

(b)

Figure 2.12 continued (b) the decay of stored charges in the n-region

This analysis clearly indicates that the voltage across a *pn* junction does not subside instantaneously when the current flowing across it is turned off. This is because of the fact that the stored charges live for a finite time τ_p only.

Problems associated with stored charges may be solved by designing a p^+n junction with a very narrow n-region. If the n-region is shorter than the hole diffusion length, very little charge would be stored in the bulk n-region. Therefore, in such a case, very little time would be required to switch both the diode current and the voltage to the off state simultaneously. The switching process can also be made faster by purposely adding recombination centres e.g., Au and Ag in Si to curtail carrier lifetimes or to increase the recombination rates. For switching applications of *pn* junctions, the transition from its forward to the reverse bias state and vice versa has to be almost abrupt. In Fig. 2.13(a), a simple diode circuit is shown where a forward current I_F flows through a *pn* junction. At $t = 0$, the diode is suddenly reverse biased, so that a reverse current $I_R \cong V/R$ starts flowing through the diode immediately. As the carriers stored in the bulk region starts recombining, this current must fall off with time. The time required for this current to fall to 10% of its initial value I_R is defined as the transient time (Fig. 2.13(b)). During the constant current phase, (2.130) may be written as

$$\frac{Q_p(t)}{\tau_p} + \frac{dQ_p(t)}{dt} = -I_R \tag{2.137}$$

Integrating this equation and remembering that $Q_p(t) = I_F\tau_p$ at $t = 0$, we get

$$Q_p(t) = \tau_p \left[-I_R + (I_F + I_R) \exp\left(\frac{-t}{\tau_p}\right) \right] \tag{2.138}$$

Combining (2.138) with (2.131), we get

$$V(t) = \left(\frac{kT}{q}\right) \ln \left[\frac{1 + \left[-I_R + (I_F + I_R) \exp\left(\frac{-t}{\tau_p}\right) \right]}{I_R} \right] \tag{2.139}$$

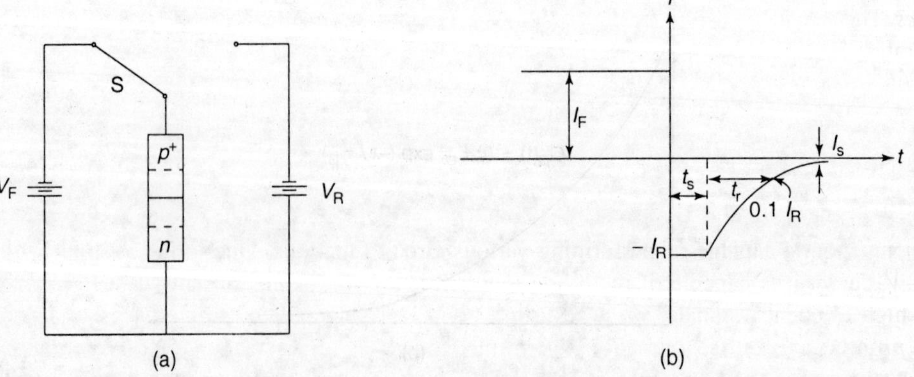

Figure 2.13 *The transient behaviour of a pn junction: (a) the basic circuit, (b) the transient response*

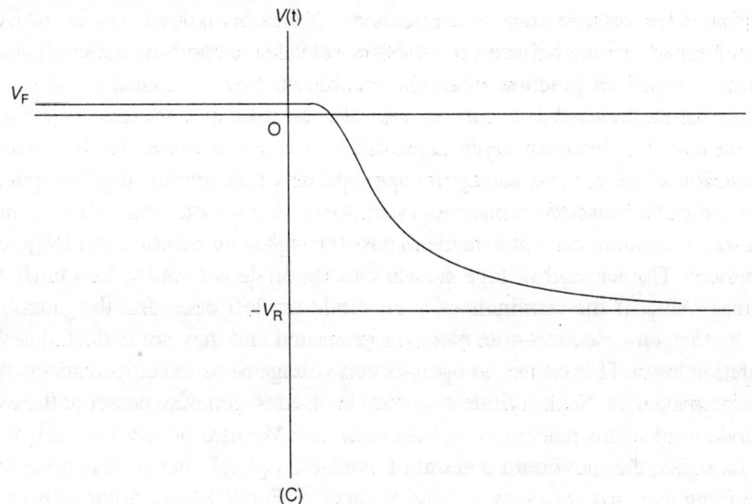

Figure 2.13 continued (c) the junction voltage as a function of time

The variation of $V(t)$ with t has been shown in Fig. 2.13(c). The diode voltage would continue to remain finite and positive as long as the minority holes are stored in the n-region. An expression for the storage time may now be obtained by requiring that $V(t_s) = 0$. This yields

$$t_s = \tau_p \ \ln \left[1 + \left(\frac{I_F}{I_R} \right) \right] \tag{2.140}$$

The above equation clearly suggests that the storage time t_s is of the order of the carrier lifetime τ_p. After all the excess charges stored in the neutral regions recombine, the charges stored in the depletion layer capacitance start decaying with a characteristic time constant t_r, at the end of which the diode reverse voltage $-V_R$ is restored. The time t_r may be reduced by curtailing the diode RC time constant. The total time, $(t_s + t_r)$ (Fig. 2.12(b)) measures the total transient time needed to recover the reversed biased state of the diode after which it is switched off. Diodes possessing lower recovery times are called *fast (or step) recovery diodes* while those having longer recovery times are called *charge storage diodes*. The former are useful for high speed switching while the latter are well known for their harmonic generation applications.

2.6 Solar cells

A pn junction is capable of performing various circuit functions. Due to the asymmetric nature of its I–V curve, it is capable of rectifying low frequency alternating currents. But in order to rectify very high frequency signals, we need to use point contact rectifiers (to be discussed later) or short base pn diodes (discussed already). The former is capable of rectifying very high frequency signals because its operation is independent of the conventional recombination phenomena between electrons and holes, which are relatively slow processes. Due to very sharp breakdown characteristics, Zener diodes are employed for voltage control applications. Zener breakdown is caused by the quantum mechanical tunnelling of carriers between conduction and valence bands of the semiconductor forming the relatively heavy doped *pn* junction when the breakdown field is around 10^8 V/m. A *pn* junction, because of its non-linear forward I-V curves, may also be used as a variable resistor (varistor). We have already seen that the depletion layer capacitance of a *pn* junction can be designed to vary as some desired function of the reverse voltage by appropriately tailoring the diode impurity profile. The resulting diodes are called variable capacitors (varactors). A *pn* diode may also be made to act as a temperature sensor. A constant current is made to pass through a *pn* junction and its junction voltage is constantly monitored. The forward voltage drop across the diode is found to be a fairly linear function of the temperature. Also, if the terminals of a *pn* diode are left open and the junction is irradiated externally (e.g. by the sun), electron-hole pairs are generated and they are collected at the appropriate ends of the depletion layer. This causes an open-circuit voltage to be developed across the *pn* junction under suitable circumstances. Such a diode may then be used to generate power at the expense of solar energy. A *pn* diode used in this manner is called a solar cell. We next proceed to analyze the physics of such a device. To utilize the maximum amount of available optical energy, it is necessary to design a solar cell with a large junction area located near its surface (Fig. 2.14(a)). Solar cells are usually made of Si, InP, GaAs, CdSe and CdTe. The planar junction is either formed by diffusion or ion implantation and the surface of the device is coated with an appropriate antireflection coating to reduce reflection and surface recombination. Many compromises need to be made in the design of solar cells, such as, the junction depth d thickness of the p-region and the mean optical penetration depth which must be less than L_p in the top n-type material to allow holes generated near the surface to diffuse to the junction before they are able to recombine. Similarly, the thickness of the p-region must also be such that electrons generated in this region can diffuse to the junction before any recombination takes place. This requirement implies a proper match among the electron diffusion length L_n, the $(1/\alpha)$ (for Si, $\alpha \sim 10^5\ \text{cm}^{-1}$). To secure a larger photovoltage, it is necessary to have a *pn* junction of a large built-in junction potential. This, therefore, requires diode doping levels to be higher. But heavier doping levels reduce carrier lifetimes. For a better performance of solar cells, longer carrier lifetimes are desirable. It is also important that the device series resistance must be kept small so that the generated power is not unduly lost as ohmic or heat losses. Since the area of the device is made larger, the resistance offered by the p-region of the device can be kept quite small. However, contacts to the thin n-region

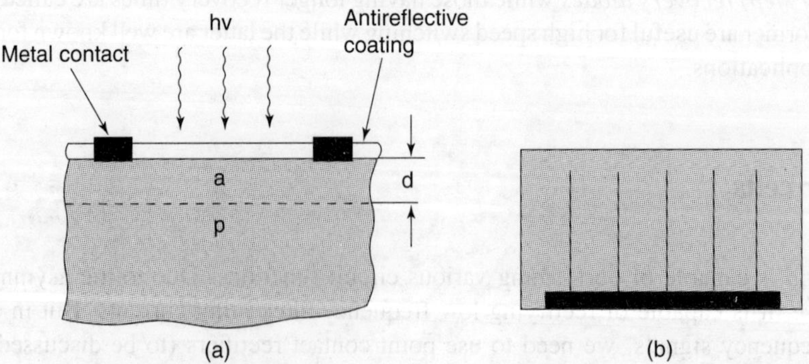

Figure 2.14 *The configuration of a solar cell: (a) the enlarged view of a planar junction, (b) the top view showing metal contact "fingers"*

(over the p-region) require special design. If the contact is made only at the edges, the current must flow along the thin n-region giving rise to a high series resistance effect. To minimize it, the contact must be distributed over the surface of the n material by means of contact fingers (Fig. 2.14(b)). These narrow contact fingers reduce the series resistance wi..out appreciably interfering with the incoming radiation.

If P measures the incident light power on the surface of the device and R, the reflection coefficient, the power absorbed by the material would be $P(1-R)$. The rate of electron-hole pair generation by a photon of energy $h\nu$ would then be $[\eta' P(1-R)/h\nu]$ where η' measures the probability of electron-hole pair generation. Let us consider a suitable pn junction forward biased to V volts (Fig. 2.15). The current flowing through the diode may then be expressed by the well-known formula

$$I = I_s\left[\exp\left(\frac{qV}{kT}\right) - 1\right]$$

Now, in the presence of an external source of radiation, the electron-hole pairs are generated within the depletion layer, as already discussed. Owing to the existence of the built-in field across the pn junction, the generated carriers produce a current I_L opposite to I. Therefore, the pn diode I–V characteristic in the presence of an external source of radiation may be expressed as

$$I = I_s\left[\exp\left(\frac{qV}{kT}\right) - 1\right] - I_L \tag{2.141}$$

Since $I = -I_L$, at $V = 0$, I_L is called the short-circuit current. Evidently, it will depend on the incident power P_{in}, the frequency ν of the radiation, the efficiency η' of electron-hole pair generation and the reflection coefficient R of the semiconductor surface. The expression for the open-circuit voltage V_{oc} may now be derived from (2.141) by requiring that $V = V_{\text{oc}}$, if $I = 0$. We then get

$$V_{\text{oc}} = \left(\frac{kT}{q}\right) \ln\left[1 + \left(\frac{I_L}{I_s}\right)\right] \tag{2.142}$$

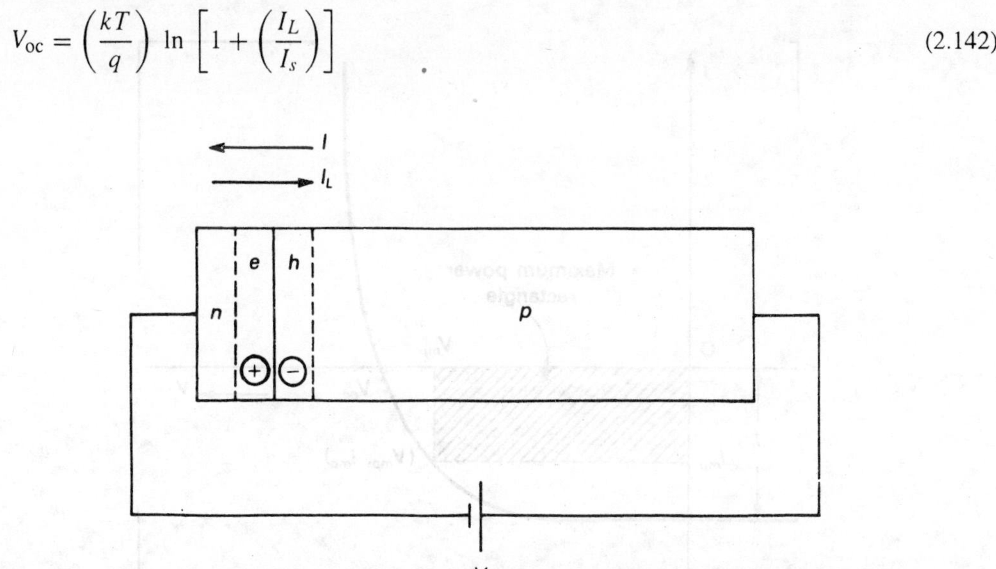

Figure 2.15 *A forward biased pn junction solar cell*

For weaker light intensities $(I_L/I_s) \ll 1$. In that case, (2.142) simplifies to

$$V_{oc} = \left(\frac{kT}{q}\right)\left(\frac{I_L}{I_s}\right) \tag{2.143}$$

Since $V_{oc} \propto I_L$, the device is then said to operate in the linear mode. For higher light intensities $(I_L/I_s) \gg 1$. Equation (2.142) then simplifies to

$$V_{oc} = \left(\frac{kT}{q}\right) \ln\left(\frac{I_L}{I_s}\right) \tag{2.144}$$

The device then operates in the logarithmic mode. Equation (2.141) is plotted in Fig. 2.16. The device is clearly seen to possess a negative conductance in the fourth quadrant. Therefore, if the operating point of the device is selected in this quadrant, it could be used to deliver power to an external load. It may then act as the source or a converter of solar energy into useful electricity. But the same diode if operated in the other three quadrants would behave as a simple resistor acting as a sink of power. The output power delivered by a solar cell to an external load may now be expressed as

$$P = IV = I_s V[\exp(\beta V) - 1] - I_L V \tag{2.145}$$

where $\beta = (q/kT)$. The maximum power condition may be obtained by setting $dP/dV = 0$. One then obtains

$$\exp(\beta V_m) = \frac{1 + \left(\dfrac{I_L}{I_s}\right)}{1 + \beta V_m}$$

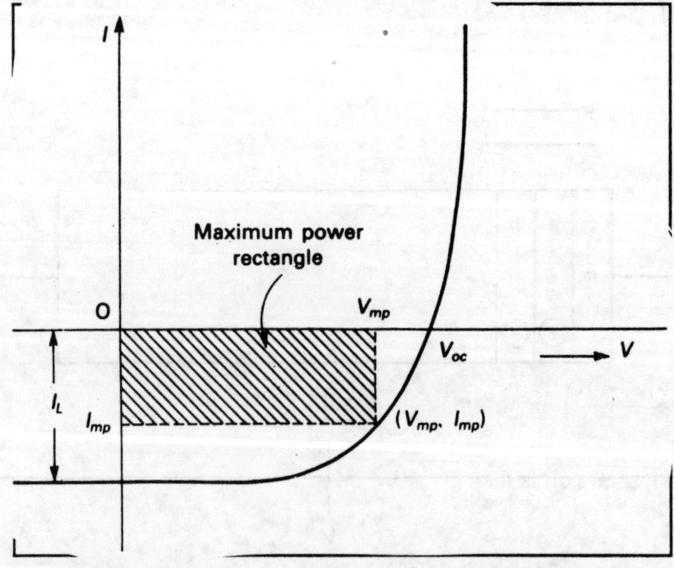

Figure 2.16 *The I–V characteristics of a solar cell*

or

$$V_m = \left(\frac{1}{\beta}\right) \ln \frac{1 + \left(\frac{I_L}{I_s}\right)}{(1 + \beta V_m)}$$

or

$$V_m \cong V_{oc} - \left(\frac{1}{\beta}\right) \ln (1 + \beta V_m) \tag{2.146}$$

where V_m denotes the maximum power voltage. It can be obtained by solving the transcendental equation (2.146). The current I_m, corresponding to the maximum power, is obtained by putting V for V_m in (2.141). One then gets

$$I_m = I_s \exp (\beta V_m) - I_s \left[1 + \left(\frac{I_L}{I_s}\right)\right] \tag{2.147}$$

Combining (2.146) and (2.147), we obtain

$$I_m = -\beta I_s V_m \exp (\beta V_m) = \frac{-\beta I_s V_m \left[1 + \left(\frac{I_L}{I_s}\right)\right]}{(1 + \beta V_m)} = -\beta V_m \frac{(I_s + I_L)}{(1 + \beta V_m)}$$

or

$$I_m = \frac{-I_L}{[1 + (\beta V_m)^{-1}]} \text{ (since } I_s \ll I_L)$$

or

$$I_m = -I_L[1 - (\beta V_m)^{-1}] \text{ (since } \beta V_m > 1) \tag{2.148}$$

The maximum power expression then follows to be

$$P_m = V_m I_m = \beta I_s V_m^2 \exp (\beta V_m)$$

Substituting for exp (βV_m) from (2.146) in the above relation, one obtains

$$P_m = \frac{\beta I_s V_m^2 \left[1 + \left(\frac{I_L}{I_s}\right)\right]}{1 + \beta V_m} = \left[V_{oc} - \left(\frac{1}{\beta}\right) \ln (1 + \beta V_m)\right] I_L[1 - (\beta V_m)^{-1}]$$

or

$$P_m = I_L \left[V_{oc} - \left(\frac{1}{\beta}\right) \ln (1 + \beta V_m) - \left(\frac{1}{\beta}\right)\right] \tag{2.149}$$

The efficiency of the solar cell is then given by

$$\eta = \frac{P_m}{P_{in}} \tag{2.150}$$

where P_{in} denotes the incident power of the sun falling upon the solar cell. This is about 1.35 kW/m^2 on a normal sunny day. For Si and GaAs diodes, the cell efficiency lies between 10% to 15%. Another figure of merit of the solar cell is represented by its fill factor (FF) defined as

$$FF = \frac{V_m I_m}{V_{oc} I_{sc}} \tag{2.151}$$

so that

$$P_m = (V_{\text{oc}} I_{sc})(FF)$$

Therefore, if the solar cell I–V curve in the fourth quadrant approaches a rectangle of sides $V_m = V_{\text{oc}}$ and $I_m = I_{sc}$, the FF approaches unity. Practical solar cells have fill factors lying between 0.6 to 0.8, V_{oc} between 0.5 to 1.0 V, J_{sc} between 10 to 40 mA/cm^2 and conversion efficiencies between 5 and 25%. Both the short-circuit current I_{sc} and the efficiency η are found to increase with the increase in the input light intensity. Lower conversion efficiencies are recorded due to the following factors:

(i) Optical energy losses due to reflection and shadowing by metal contacts,
(ii) loss of generated carriers at the surface and in the bulk due to recombination effects,
(iii) unused portion of the spectrum defined by $h\nu < E_G$, and
(iv) waste of excess energy (above $h\nu > E_G$).

A solar cell may also be fabricated of a *np* heterojunction formed of two semiconductors having energy gaps E_{G1} and E_{G2} such that $E_{G1} > E_{G2}$. An incident beam of light of energy less than E_{G1} but greater than E_{G2} will pass through the first semiconductor and will be absorbed in the second. Technically, the first semiconductor in such a case behaves as a window. The heterojunction solar cell has the following advantages over the homojunction variety :

(i) enhanced short wavelength response if $E_{G1} > E_{G2}$,
(ii) lower series resistance if the first semiconductor is heavily doped,
(iii) higher radiation tolerance if the first semiconductor is a thicker one.

Solar cells have found unique applications, especially in two areas. The first is for generating power for remote and rural areas and the other is for satellites and space vehicles. Other applications include providing power to marine navigational lights, calculators, exposure meters in photographic equipments etc. In applications where a higher voltage becomes necessary, a larger number of solar cells are connected in series. They may be connected in parallel if larger currents are required. For optimum power output, solar cells may also be connected in series and parallel combinations.

2.7 Light emitting diodes (LEDs)

Light emitting diodes are popular light sources in solid state electronic circuitry and their operation is based on junction electroluminescence which converts electrical energy to light output. Previously, LEDs were made of direct band-gap semiconductors. But nowadays commercial LEDs are also fabricated of indirect gap materials. LEDs are a special type of *pn* junction which produces junction electroluminescence. There are two basic configurations of the device viz.,: (i) surface emitting and

(ii) edge emitting structures. In the former, light is emitted perpendicular to the junction plane and in the latter, parallel to the junction. In the edge emitting structure, emitted light is more directional in nature. Heterostructures are often employed for optical and carrier confinements. The II–VI and III–V compound semiconductors offer direct energy band-gaps from the infrared through the visible to the ultraviolet regions of the electromagnetic spectrum. There are also materials where transitions via impurity levels play a dominant role in the emission of light. Diode lamps are useful for many applications where incandescent lamps or the gas discharge tubes are found unsuitable: The important features of the diode lamps are: (i) they operate well when cold; (ii) they require minimum power for their operation; (iii) their switching speed is very high; (iv) because of their small sizes they are easily integrated in low power electronic circuitry; and (v) their operating life is quite long.

(i) LED materials

The requirements of a material of which an LED is to be fabricated are as follows: (i) It must have an energy gap of appropriate width to emit radiation in a desired wavelength range; (ii) both p and n type forms of the semiconductor material must be available; and (iii) efficient radiative pathways must be present. Common semiconductor materials, mostly II–VI and III–V compounds, with the range of their emitted wavelengths and their sensitivities to the human eye are given in Fig. 2.17. Although, most II–VI compound semiconductors are of the direct band-gap types, they cannot be used to fabricate LEDs because of the technical problem of making *pn* junctions out of them. The active films are usually grown by liquid phase or vapour phase epitaxy on substrates that have a close lattice comparable with the active layers. Commonly used substrates are GaAs, GaP and InP. Commercially, LEDs are produced both as single elements and as monolithic arrays.

Commercial LED materials

(a) Gallium arsenide (GaAs) This is a direct band-gap semiconductor with $E_G = 1.43\,\text{eV}(\lambda = 860\,\text{nm})$. *pn* Junctions can be readily fabricated from them and they have very high luminous efficiencies. One way of making *pn* junctions out of them is to diffuse Zn into pulled crystals of n-type GaAs. The radiation is given off due to band-to-band transitions and is subject to heavy reabsorption after emission.

(b) Gallium phosphide (GaP) This is an indirect band-gap material with a band-gap of 2.26 eV ($\lambda = 549\mu\,\text{m}$). No band-to-band transition leading to the emission of light is observed in it. Group V elements e.g., N and Bi are commonly used as doping elements to assist in the radiative recombination process. Since these elements have the same valency as the atoms they replace, e.g, (P) in GaP, they do not form donor or acceptor states. The states introduced by these elements in the energy gap of the material act as recombination centres. They are known as "isoelectronic traps".

(c) Gallium arsenide phosphide ($GaAs_{1-x}P_x$) This is an interesting material because it changes from the direct band-gap type (for $x < 0.45$) to the indirect band-gap type (for $x > 0.45$). At the change over point, the direct energy gap is 2.1 eV. Using *pn* diodes of $GaAs_{0.6}P_{0.4}$, red emission due to band-to-band transition has been recorded. Doping this material with Nitrogen, yellow and orange emissions have also been observed with the following compositions: Ga $As_{0.15}$ $P_{0.8}$: N (yellow) and Ga $As_{0.35}$ $P_{0.65}$: N (orange).

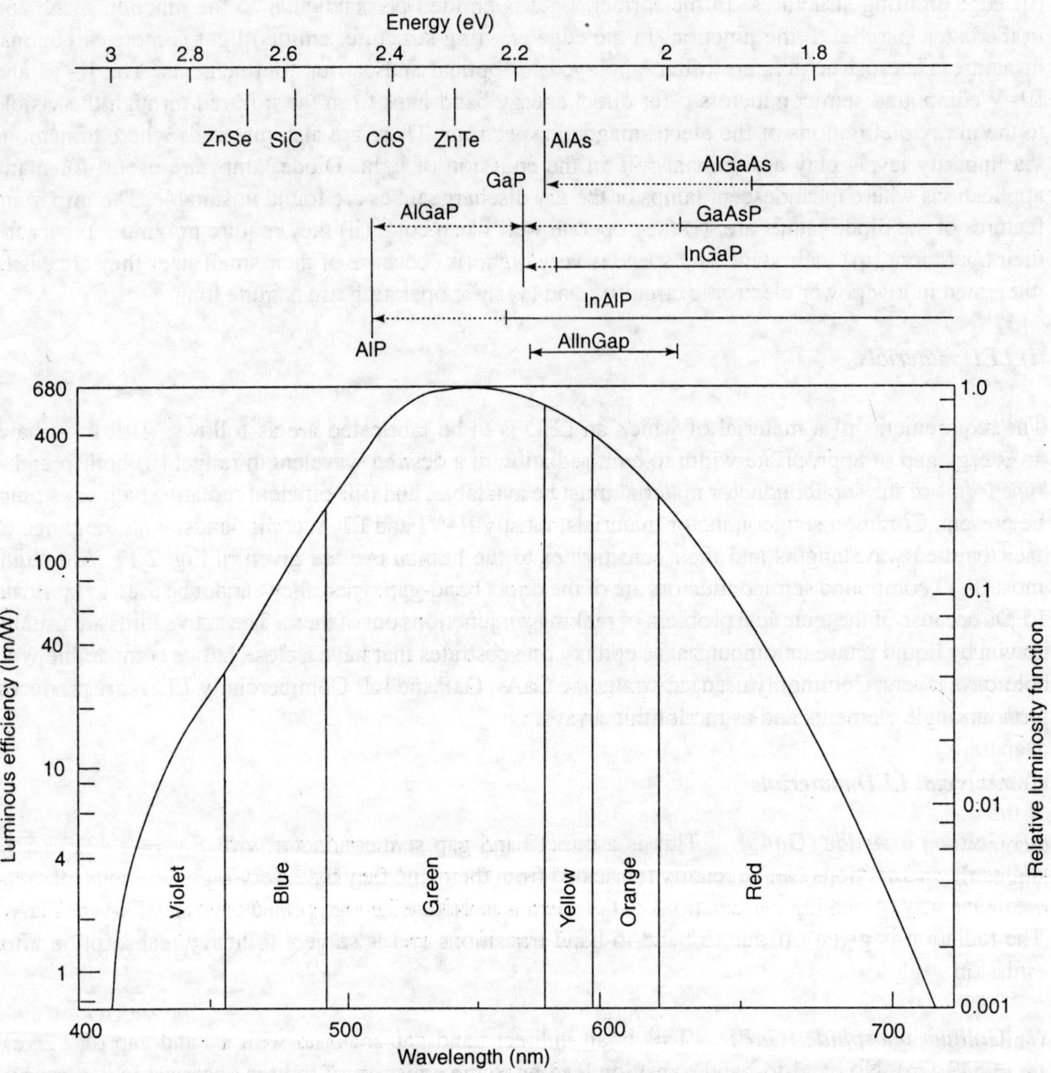

Figure 2.17 *Common LED materials and their corresponding emitted wavelengths and the luminous efficiencies of the human eye*

(d) Gallium aluminium arsenide ($Ga_xAl_{1-x}As$) This is a relatively new material used to fabricate highly efficient red and near infrared LEDs. A heterojunction is formed between *n*-type $Ga_{0.3}$ $Al_{0.7}$ As and *p*-type $Ga_{0.6}$ $Al_{0.4}$ As. The *n*-layer is the surface layer from where electrons are injected into the *p*-material. Radiative recombination via acceptor levels gives rise to emission of radiation at 650 nm. This radiation is able to cross the surface *n*-layer as the latter has a wider energy gap. The emission efficiencies of these LEDs are superior to those made of GaAsP.

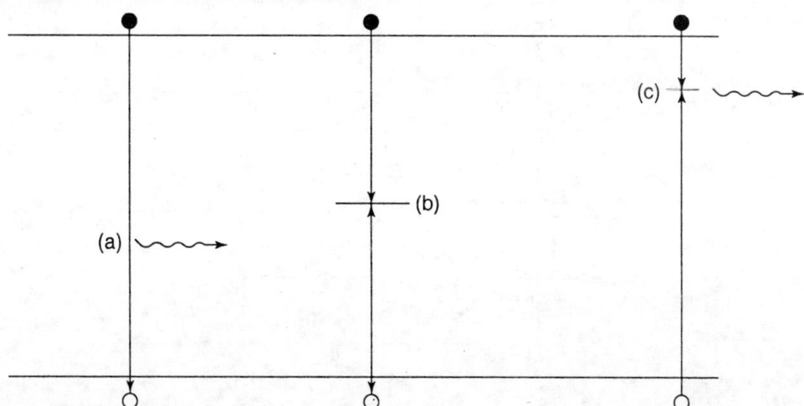

Figure 2.18 *The major recombination processes outside the space-charge layer. (a) Band-to-band radiative recombination, (b) Non-radiative recombination through deep level traps, (c) Recombination through isoelectronic traps which could either be radiative or non radiative*

(ii) Theoretical considerations

To produce a light output from an LED, it must be operated in the forward biased mode. The current flowing through the junction consists of the following three types: (a) electron diffusion current, (b) hole diffusion current and (c) space-charge recombination current. The latter is known to be more pronounced at lower biases and at lower temperatures. This current flows via recombination through deep trap levels which are usually non-radiative. The injected minority carriers to the neutral regions on both sides of the junction cause a corresponding enhancement of majority carrier population because of the dielectric relaxation mechanism. Both types of carriers in the respective neutral regions then recombine according to the conventional recombination law, emitting radiation within a diffusion length of the pn junction. The wavelength of the emitted radiation may then be derived from the relation $E_G = h\nu$ which leads to the following simplified relation:

$$\lambda(\mu m) = \frac{1.24}{E_G(eV)} \tag{2.152}$$

While designing an LED, it is preferred that light be emitted from the p-side of the junction. There are two main reasons for this: (a) Because of higher electron mobility, injection efficiency of electrons is higher than that of holes. (b) The energy gap narrowing effect due to heavier dopings being more pronounced on the p-side than on the n-side, the chances of the emitted light being reabsorbed by the n-side is smaller.

The different mechanisms of recombination outside the space-charge layer are shown in Fig. 2.18. Process A is due to band-to-band recombination which is radiative (Fig. 2.19(a)). Process B represents the non-radiative recombination through the deep trap levels and C represents recombination through the isoelectronic traps that could either be radiative or non-radiative (Fig. 2.19(c)). For lower injection levels, we have already seen that the radiative recombination rate R_r is proportional to both electron and hole densities, and is given by

$$R_r = r_0 np = r_0 \Delta np \tag{2.153}$$

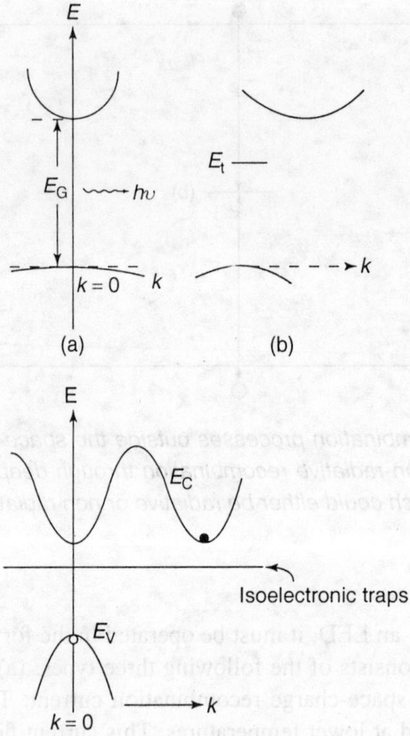

Figure 2.19 *The energy band diagrams: (a) direct semiconductor, (b) indirect semiconductor, (c) E–k relationship of an indirect energy gap material with isoelectronic traps*

where Δn denotes the injected electron density on the p-side which has an acceptor density of N_a and r_0 denotes the recombination coefficient which is a function of temperature and the band structure of the semiconductor concerned. The band-to-band recombination process A can be characterized by a radiative lifetime τ_r, given by

$$\tau_r = \frac{\Delta n}{R} = \frac{\Delta n}{r_0 \Delta n N_a} = \frac{1}{r_0 N_a} \tag{2.154}$$

Thus in order to reduce this time, the acceptor density has to be reasonably higher. The non-radiative lifetime associated with process B is however given by

$$\tau_{nr} = \frac{1}{\sigma \upsilon_{th} N_t} \tag{2.155}$$

where σ denotes the capture cross-sectional area; N_t, the density of trap centres and υ_{th}, the thermal velocity of carriers. The recombination process C is applicable only to indirect semiconductors. The competition between A and B determines the so called radiative efficiency η_{rad}, given by

$$\eta_{\text{rad}} = \frac{R_r}{R_r + R_{nr}} = \frac{\tau}{\tau_r} \tag{2.156}$$

where the total lifetime τ, is given by

$$(\tau)^{-1} = (\tau_r)^{-1} + (\tau_{nr})^{-1} \tag{2.157}$$

To improve the radiative recombination in LEDs made with indirect band semiconductors, isoelectronic centres are introduced in their energy gaps. These impurities replace one element of the compound semiconductor and are neutral dopants. Examples are N in ZnO and GaP. The function of an isoelectronic trap is, first to capture an electron from the conduction band, and then to look for a hole in the valence band with which the captured electron may eventually recombine, thereby releasing a photon. Isoelectronic impurities being highly localized in space have a very wide spectrum in momentum space, by virtue of the Heisenberg's uncertainty relation (Fig. 2.19(c)). Therefore, they can very easily account for the conservation of momentum required to be obeyed during the transition of electrons from the conduction to valence bands of indirect semiconductors (Fig. 2.19(b)).
Another feature which is worth mentioning in connection with an LED is its brightness. Human eyes have different sensitivities for different colours (Fig. 2.17). An LED must be designed for optimum visibility, especially for display applications. Maximum visibility is observed for a wavelength of 555 nm which lies in the central portion of the green spectrum.
Typically, an LED is biased with a voltage slightly below the energy gap of the material of which it is built and the current passing through the junction is about 1 mA. The emitted light output has a spectral width of about 20–50 nm. The cutoff frequency of an LED may now be representedas,

$$f_c = (2\pi\tau)^{-1} \tag{2.158}$$

That is, if the junction voltage is modulated at this frequency, the light output would be diminished to half its d.c. value.

(iii) Applications

An LED is a practical light source for modern electronic applications. Compared to an incandescent lamp, it consumes less power and is more reliable. It has a relatively long life, a simpler drive circuit, lesser temperature sensitivity and better capabilities for analog modulation. The major applications of an LED can be classified into the following three categories:

Display LEDs have been extremely popular as light sources — numeric and alpha numeric displays in watches, calculators, audio and video equipments etc. A serious contender for this application is an LCD (liquid crystal display) which has even lower power consumption, although it can never be used in total darkness.

Fibre-optic communication An LED can act as a light source in optical fibre communication (Fig. 2.20)

Light source An LED can be a light source in a source-detector package forming an opto-isolator. (Fig. 2.21)

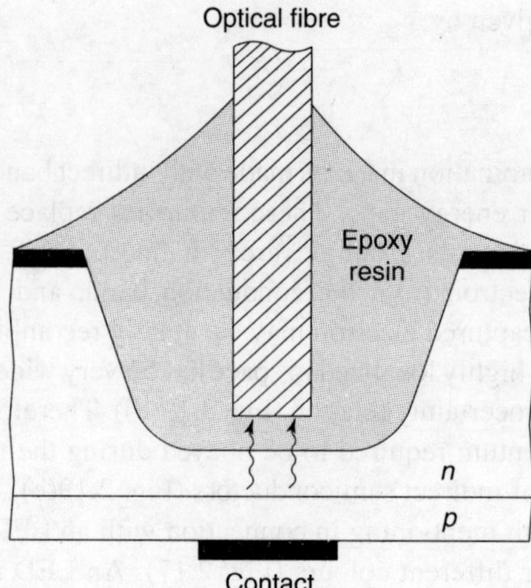

Figure 2.20 *A package showing the interfacing of the optical fibre and the LED*

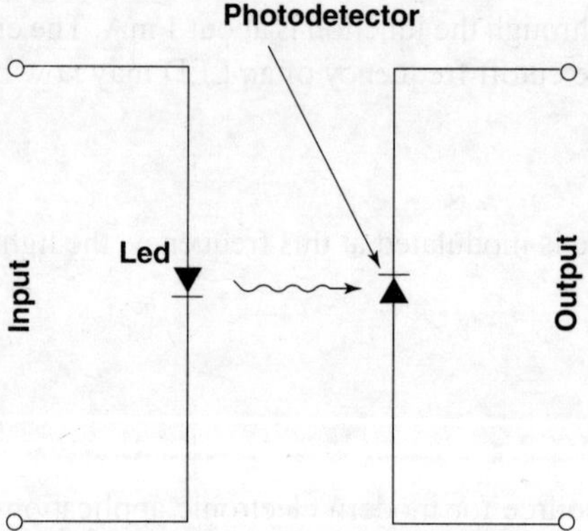

Figure 2.21 *An opto-isolator provides isolation between the input and the output*

LED drive circuitry The electrical characteristics of LEDs are essentially those of rectifying diodes. Typical operating currents are between 20 mA and 100 mA, while forward voltages in them may vary from 1.2 V (GaAs) and 2 V (GaP). The circuit shown in Fig. 2.22 is used for the continuous operation of the LED. If the light output is desired to be modulated, the circuit shown in Fig. 2.23 is used. Typical LED mountings are shown in Fig. 2.24.

2.8 Laser diodes

Light emitted from *pn* junction LEDs are incoherent. But the emitted radiation may be made coherent by fulfilling some additional requirements. Diodes then function as semiconductor!lasers. To achieve this laser action, the semiconductors employed have to be necessarily of the direct band-gap type, so that

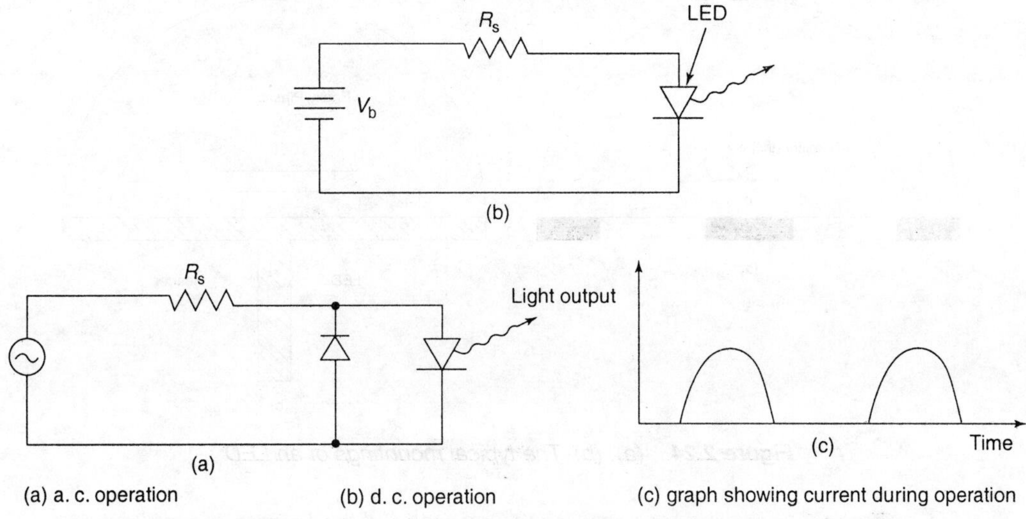

(a) a. c. operation (b) d. c. operation (c) graph showing current during operation

Figure 2.22 *The circuit for continuous operation of an LED*

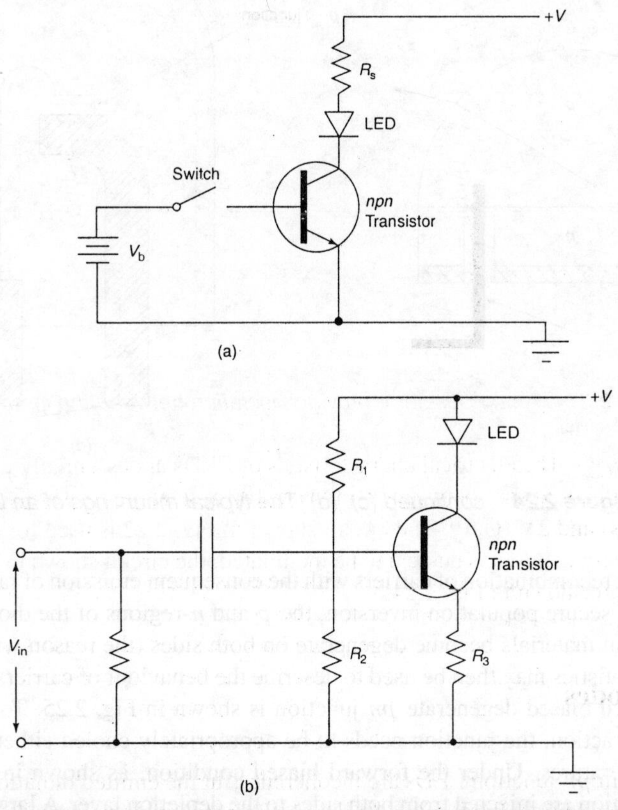

Figure 2.23 *Circuit for the light output modulation*

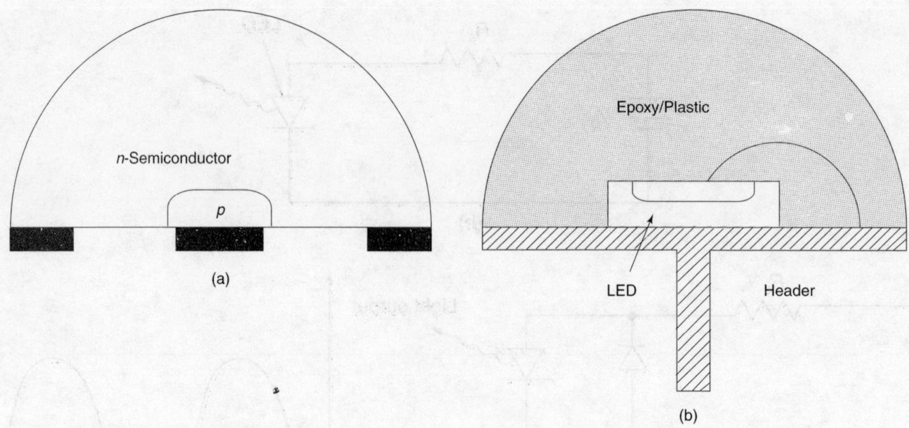

Figure 2.24 *(a), (b) The typical mountings of an LED*

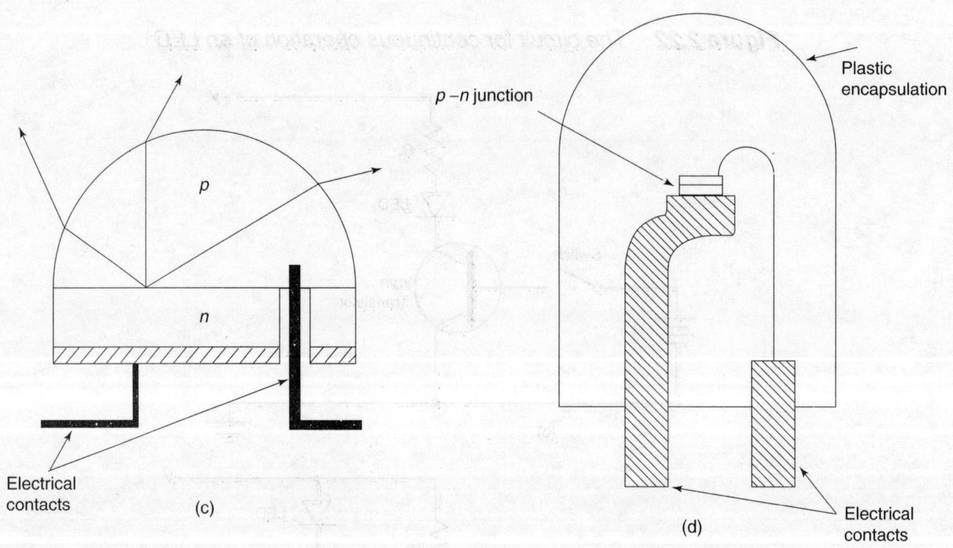

Figure 2.24 *continued (c), (d) The typical mountings of an LED*

the chances of direct recombination of carriers with the consequent emission of radiation becomes quite significant. Next, to secure population inversion, the p and n-regions of the diode have to be slightly heavily doped so that materials become degenerate on both sides (the reason will be explained later). The Fermi–Dirac statistics may then be used to describe the behaviour of carriers. The energy-distance diagram of a forward biased degenerate pn junction is shown in Fig. 2.25. To minimize chances of electron-lattice interaction, the junction needs to be appropriately cooled either to liquid nitrogen or liquid helium temperatures. Under the forward biased condition, as shown in Fig. 2.25, carriers in considerable proportion are injected from both sides to the depletion layer. A large number of electrons are available on the n-side just above the vacant states on the p-side of the pn junction, fulfilling the required condition of population inversion necessary for the laser light emission. Light is expected to be emitted due to the electron-hole recombination in this region.

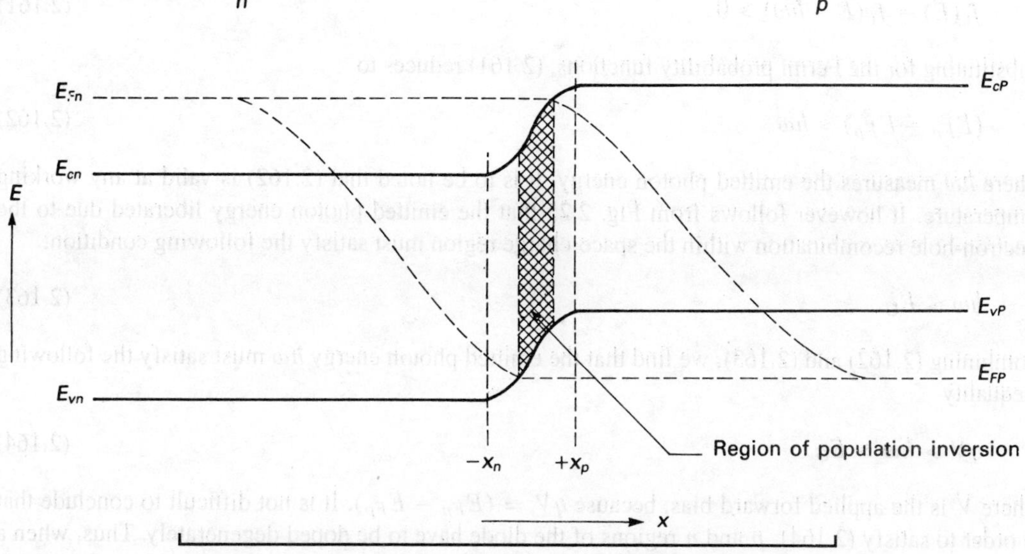

Figure 2.25 *Energy–distance diagram of a laser diode*

A laser diode (injection laser) is basically a vertical *pn* junction with a special design for optical reflection from its vertical walls. This is realized by growing a heavily doped *p*-layer over a heavily doped *n*-type substrate by any of the following techniques: (i) liquid phase epitaxy (LPE), (ii) vapour phase epitaxy (VPE), (iii) molecular beam epitaxy (MBE) and (iv) metal organic chemical vapour deposition (MOCVD) techniques. But, LPE is the most common technique for fabricating commercial laser diodes. Ion implantation or diffusion is also used at times, to grow heavily doped *p*-layers.

The structural requirements for a semiconductor laser is an optical resonator called a Fabry–Perot etalon. The resonator consists of two vertical walls perfectly perpendicular to the junction and having a mirror-like smoothness with optimum reflectivity. This can be achieved by etching, polishing or most commonly by cleaving.

Considering transitions of electrons from a group of levels around an energy level E in the conduction band to a group of levels around $(E - \hbar\omega)$ in the valence band (Fig. 2.25), the transition rate using Fermi's golden rule may be expressed as

$$dW_{\text{em}} \propto |M|^2 \rho_c(E) f_c(E) \rho_v(E - \hbar\omega)[1 - f_v(E - \hbar\omega)]\, dE \tag{2.159}$$

where $\rho_c(E)$ and $\rho_v(E - \hbar\omega)$ respectively denote the density of states functions in the conduction and valence bands, $f_c(E)$ and $f_v(E - \hbar\omega)$ denote the Fermi probability functions in respective bands and $|M|^2$ measures the square of the matrix element either for emission or absorption. Similarly, the absorption rate from a group of levels at $(E - \hbar\omega)$ in the valence band to the group of states at E in the conduction band is given by

$$dW_{\text{abs}} \propto |M|^2 \rho_v(E - \hbar\omega) f_v(E - \hbar\omega) \rho_c(E)[1 - f_c(E)]\, dE \tag{2.160}$$

For the emission rate to exceed absorption rate, we must have $dW_{em} > dW_{abs}$ From (2.159) and (2.160), we then find

$$f_c(E) - f_v(E - \hbar\omega) > 0 \tag{2.161}$$

Substituting for the Fermi probability functions, (2.161) reduces to

$$(E_{Fn} - E_{Fp}) > \hbar\omega \tag{2.162}$$

where $\hbar\omega$ measures the emitted photon energy. It is to be noted that (2.162) is valid at any working temperature. It however follows from Fig. 2.25 that the emitted photon energy liberated due to the electron-hole recombination within the space-charge region must satisfy the following condition:

$$\hbar\omega > E_G \tag{2.163}$$

Combining (2.162) and (2.163), we find that the emitted photon energy $\hbar\omega$ must satisfy the following inequality

$$qV > \hbar\omega > E_G \tag{2.164}$$

where V is the applied forward bias, because $qV = (E_{Fn} - E_{Fp})$. It is not difficult to conclude that in order to satisfy (2.164), p and n regions of the diode have to be doped degenerately. Thus, when a degenerately doped pn junction, made up of a direct band-gap material is forward biased (by a voltage more than the semiconductor energy gap), a few photons are first emitted within the depletion layer spontaneously. These then lead to the stimulated emissions of other coherent photons of the same frequency. The vertical diode surfaces, normal to the direction of the propagation of light act as the reflectors of light. The other pair of surfaces parallel to the direction of the propagation of light is roughened so that no light may be emitted through them at all. Due to multiple reflections of photons from the diode surfaces, the density of electromagnetic radiation within the cavity builds up with time. The frequency (or the energy) distribution among the emitted photons is given by Bose–Einstein statistics. From among the emitted photons, we can always identify a group at a definite frequency containing a maximum number of photons. The photons belonging to that particular group would ultimately flourish within the electromagnetic cavity, as they give rise to subsequent photon emissions by stimulation. In due course of time, such a process makes the emitted radiation monochromatic and coherent. Light, in this case, is emitted due to the injection of current and hence is a junction electroluminescence.

Figure 2.26 displays the variation of light intensity as a function of the diode current. There is a characteristic knee in each curve which may be identified with the threshold current density (J_{th}) required for lasing. Below this current density, spontaneously emitted photons are mostly absorbed. At and above J_{th}, photons are emitted in sufficient numbers to overcome their absorption losses. They are then capable of giving rise to stimulated emissions and the diode then behaves as a semiconductor laser. Below J_{th}, the diode behaves as an LED. The threshold current density also increases exponentially with the rise in temperature [$J_{th} \propto \exp(T/T_0)$].

Fig. 2.27 shows the variation of light intensity as a function of wavelength for different input currents (pumping levels) in a laser diode. Below J_{th}, the spectrum produced due to the spontaneous emission (as in an LED) has a band width of 200–500 Å (Fig. 2.27(a)). For a current level higher than J_{th}, discrete lines appear in the emission spectrum with a much reduced width of about a few angstroms

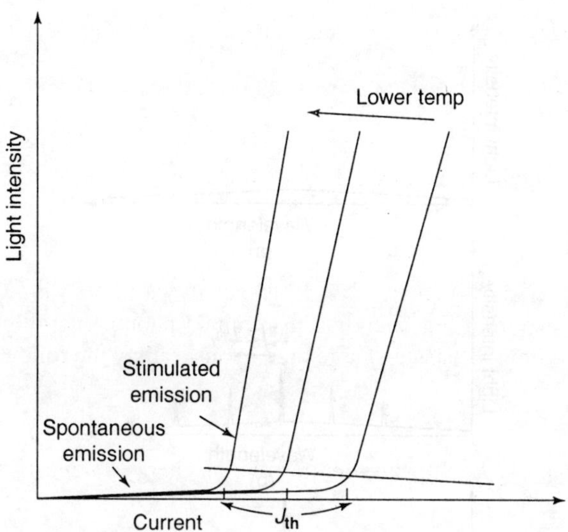

Figure 2.26 *Emitted light intensity as a function of the diode current*

only. Multiple modes appear because the reflected light wavelength within the resonant cavity of a length L must satisfy the condition $L = (n\lambda_s/2)$, where λ_s measures the wavelength of the radiation within the semiconductor and n is an integer. For two consecutive modes of wavelengths λ_s and λ_s', one must have (Fig. 2.27(b)),

$$L = \frac{n\lambda_s}{2} = (n-1)\left(\frac{\lambda_s'}{2}\right) \tag{2.165}$$

The wavelengths λ in air and λ_s in the semiconductor are related by

$$\lambda_s = \frac{\lambda}{n_r} \tag{2.166}$$

The quantity n_r measures the refractive index of the semiconductor. Combining (2.165) and (2.166) and presuming $\lambda_s \cong \lambda_s'$, we find that the wavelength difference $\Delta\lambda$ in air for two consecutive modes is given by

$$\Delta\lambda = \frac{\lambda^2}{2Ln_r} \tag{2.167}$$

The multiple lines are called the longitudinal modes because they are determined by the longitudinal length parallel to the direction of the light output. With increase in the diode current density, the number of modes gradually decreases as the central mode absorbs more and more of the energy (Fig. 2.27(c)). The important features of a beam of light from a semiconductor laser are:(a) a high directionality, (b) a very narrow spectrum, (very nearly monochromatic), (c) coherence, (d) a high power density and (e) a high switching speed. A semiconductor laser is attractive for its small size, high efficiency and low voltage operation. It can be operated in a continuous mode for low power applications and

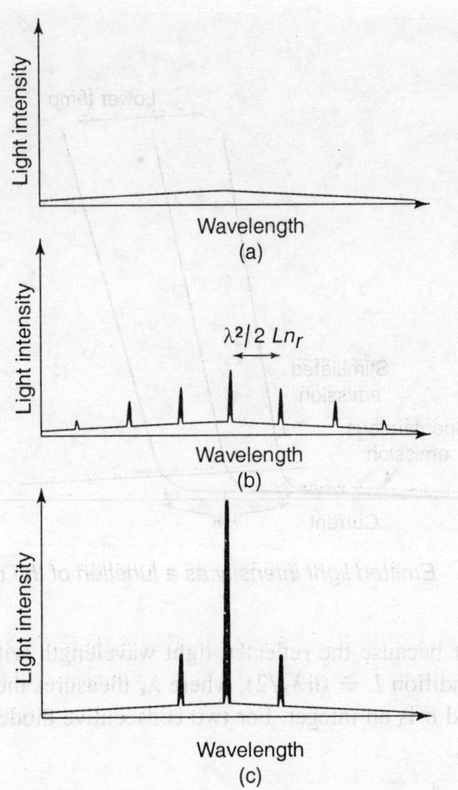

Figure 2.27 *Variation of light intensity as a function of wavelength*

in a pulsed mode for high power applications. It is indispensable for optical fibre communications in the wavelength range of 1.3 to 1.5μ m where the absorption of light in fibres is the least. But, a homojunction laser, which we have used as an example to discuss its operating principles, is unsuitable for most of the applications described above. To remove its inherent drawbacks, heterojunction lasers are put into use instead.

Calculation of threshold current density In a gas, containing an assembly of atoms at room temperature, the population of electrons in higher quantized states gradually decreases following Maxwell–Boltzman statistics. Such an electron population is said to be 'normal'. The electron population is said to be 'inverted', if the opposite is true. Let us consider a pair of discrete states at energy levels E_1 and E_2 of a particular atom, such that, $(E_1 - E_2) = h\nu$. Let the electron densities in those discrete states be n_1 and n_2 respectively. Now, if A_{12} measures the probability of spontaneous emission per electron and per unit time, the spontaneous emission rate of electrons from level 1 to 2, is given by $A_{12}n_1$. If the gas containing such atoms is placed in an electromagnetic field of density $u_\nu d\nu$, corresponding to a particular frequency ν, stimulated transitions of electrons from level 1 to 2 or vice versa may also occur. Presuming that the stimulated transition rate is proportional to $u_\nu d\nu$ (the energy density) and n_1, the former may be expressed as $B_{12}u_\nu d\nu n_1$, where B_{12} measures the probability of stimulated emission per electron per unit time and per unit energy density. Stimulated absorption of energy by electrons present in level 2 will also occur raising them to level 1 at a rate $B_{21}u_\nu d\nu n_2$ where B_{21} denotes the stimulated absorption rate per electron and per unit energy density. For dynamic equilibrium, we must have

$$A_{12}n_1 + B_{12}u_\nu d\nu n_1 = B_{21}u_\nu d\nu n_2 \tag{2.168}$$

Solving for $u_\nu d\nu$, one finds

$$u_\nu d\nu = \frac{A_{12}}{B_{21}\exp\left(\frac{h\nu}{kT}\right) - B_{12}} \tag{2.169}$$

where it is presumed that

$$\frac{n_2}{n_1} = \frac{\exp\left(\frac{-E_2}{kT}\right)}{\exp\left(\frac{-E_1}{kT}\right)} = \exp\left(\frac{h\nu}{kT}\right) \tag{2.170}$$

But according to Planck's theory of black body radiation, the radiation density within a black body cavity is given by

$$u_\nu d\nu = \left(\frac{8\pi\nu^2}{c^3}\right)\left[\frac{h\nu}{\exp\left(\frac{h\nu}{kT}\right) - 1}\right] d\nu \tag{2.171}$$

Comparing (2.169) with (2.171), we immediately notice that

$$B_{12} = B_{21}$$

and

$$\frac{A_{12}}{B_{12}} = \left(\frac{8\pi h\nu^3}{c^3}\right) d\nu \tag{2.172}$$

The above ratio is about 10^{-5} J m^3 at optical frequencies.

In a semiconductor laser diode, as the radiation of a frequency ν propagates through the depletion layer where there is a population inversion ($n_1 > n_2$), the radiation density is expected to build up due to the stimulated emission process. If I_ν measures the intensity of radiation of a frequency ν, then according to its definition (energy crossing unit area per unit time), we must have

$$I_\nu = \left(\frac{c}{n_r}\right)(u_\nu d\nu) \tag{2.173}$$

where c denotes the velocity of light in vacuum and n_r is the refractive index of the semiconductor. But the net stimulated transition rate of electrons per unit area over a distance dx of the depletion layer multiplied by the released photon energy must give the increase in intensity dI_ν, of the radiation field. Therefore, we must have

$$dI_\nu = (n_1 - n_2)B_{12}(u_\nu d\nu)dx(h\nu) \tag{2.174}$$

Substituting for B_{12} and $u_\nu d\nu$ in (2.174), we find

$$dI_\nu = (n_1 - n_2)\left[\frac{\left(\frac{c}{n_r}\right)^3}{8\pi h\nu^3 d\nu}\right] A_{12}\frac{I_V}{\left(\frac{c}{n_r}\right)} dx(h\nu) \tag{2.175}$$

If τ_{spon} denotes the time for spontaneous transition of electrons, we must have, $A_{12} = (\tau_{\text{spon}})^{-1}$. If the junction is maintained at $T = 0\,\text{K}$, and $n_1 \gg n_2$, (2.175) may be written in the following simplified form:

$$g_\nu = \frac{\left[\frac{dI_\nu}{dx}\right]}{I_\nu} = \frac{c^2 n_1}{8\pi\nu^2 n_r^2 \tau_{\text{spon}} d\nu} \tag{2.176}$$

Equation (2.176) measures the fractional increase in the optical intensity per unit distance travelled within the depletion layer and is defined as the gain coefficient of the semiconductor laser. (n_1/τ_{spon}) in (2.176) may be taken as a measure of the number of radiative transitions per unit volume and per unit time in the active region of the depletion layer. Now, if J measures the recombination current density flowing through the semiconductor laser diode whose depletion layer width is W, the number of electrons crossing unit area of the junction in unit time and undergoing recombination with holes (or the recombination rate) within a volume W (as the cross-section is presumed to be unity) would be $[J/2qW]$. The factor of 2 takes care of the contributions of both electrons and holes in producing the recombination current. If η measures the probability of photon emission by electron-hole recombination, then the number of photons emitted per unit volume and per unit time would be

$$\frac{n_1}{\tau_{\text{spon}}} = \frac{\eta J}{2qW} \tag{2.177}$$

Combining (2.176) and (2.177), we find

$$g_\nu = \frac{\eta J c^2}{16\pi q\nu^2 n_r^2 W d\nu} \tag{2.178}$$

Having obtained an expression for the gain coefficient, we next proceed to establish the criterion for the net gain within the diode cavity to be able to counteract the effects of losses within it. Only then will the diode start functioning as a laser diode (or a light amplifier). The radiation within the depletion layer at O, as shown in Fig. 2.28, starts travelling towards the diode surface where it undergoes a reflection. After two consecutive reflections within the electromagnetic cavity if the angle of incidence of the light is very small, it may be seen to reach O once again, some light may also be lost at the diode surface during reflection. Now, if I_0 denotes the intensity at O, α denotes the absorption coefficient of

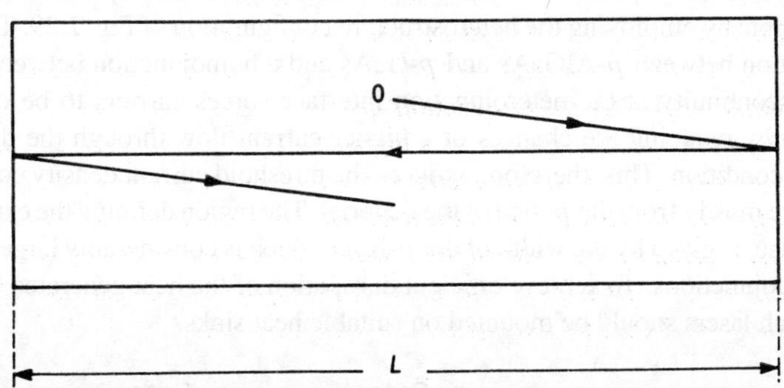

Figure 2.28 *The Fabry–Perot cavity of a laser diode*

the semiconductor material and R denotes the reflection coefficient at the end faces, the intensity of radiation after a round trip is given by

$$I = I_0 R^2 \exp\left[(g_\nu - \alpha)2L\right] \tag{2.179}$$

The diode will start lasing if $I = I_0$. Equation (2.179) then simplifies to

$$g_\nu = \alpha + \left(\frac{1}{L}\right) \ln \left(\frac{1}{R}\right) \tag{2.180}$$

Combining (2.178) and (2.180), the threshold current density required for the diode to lase at $T = 0\,\mathrm{K}$ is given by

$$J_{\text{th}} = \left[\frac{16\pi q \nu^2 n_r^2 W d\nu}{\eta c^2}\right]\left[\alpha + \left(\frac{1}{L}\right) \ln \left(\frac{1}{R}\right)\right] \tag{2.181}$$

Substituting for appropriate parameters, one finds from (2.181), $J_{\text{th}} \sim 10^6\ \mathrm{A/m^2}$. Around room temperatures, however, it is several times higher. This is so, because at higher temperatures a larger fraction of the carrier energy is required in exciting lattice vibrations and then the chances of light emission by electron-hole recombination becomes too small. The junction laser of the type discussed above may be operated continuously at liquid He temperatures. Owing to the considerable amounts of heat liberated, they cannot operate continuously under room temperature conditions. Pulsed operation under suitable circumstances is then suggested. When the junction current density is less than J_{th}, the absorption of light dominates over emission. It may be seen from (2.178) that the gain coefficient of the laser is inversely proportional to the square of the frequency of the emitted light. Therefore, from the theoretical point of view, it is difficult to fabricate very high frequency lasers.

Heterojunction lasers

The primary problem with the operation of the homojunction laser is the need to reduce their threshold current density magnitudes beyond a certain limit so that they may be operated conveniently under room temperature conditions. With this end in view, several different heterojunction laser configurations have been developed. These configurations are discussed below.

(i) A single heterojunction (SH) laser Continuous room temperature operation of semiconductor laser diodes is possible by employing the heterostructure configuration of Fig. 2.29. This consists of an isotype heterojunction between *p*-AlGaAs and *p*-GaAs and a homojunction between *p* and *n*-GaAs. The band edge discontinuity at the heterojunction interface forces carriers to be confined within a potential well thereby reducing the chances of a higher current flow through the diode terminals in the forward biased condition. This, therefore, reduces the threshold current density considerably. Light emission takes place mostly from the *p*-side of the material. The region defining the extent of population inversion, in this case, is given by the width of the *p*-layer which is considerably large compared to that found in usual homojunctions. To achieve efficient dissipation of the heat generated by the passage of higher currents, such lasers should be mounted on suitable heat sinks.

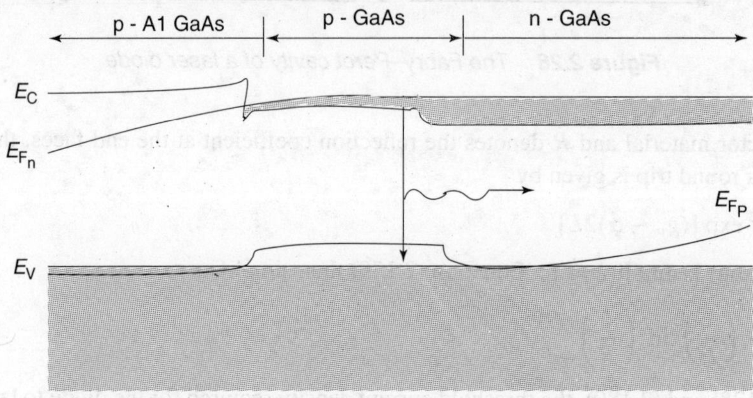

Figure 2.29 *A single heterojunction (SH) laser diode*

(ii) Double heterojunction (DH) laser Such a structure is realized by forming two heterojunctions between *p*-AlGaAs & *p*-GaAs (isotype) and between *p*-GaAs & *n*-AlGaAs (anisotype), as shown in Fig. 2.30. This laser, not only provides better optical and carrier confinements but there is also a better injection efficiency for electrons across the anisotype heterojunction.

(iii) Quantum well laser When the width of the middle layer of the DH laser becomes extremely thin (~100Å), it turns into a quantum well laser diode with quantized energy levels formed within it. The advantages of such a quantum well laser are the reduction in the threshold current density (due to the reduced number of the electronic states to be filled) for the diode operation, greater frequency tuning ranges (because of the effective change in the energy gap of the semiconductor) and greater quantum efficiency (due to better overlapping between electron and hole states). The only disadvantage is that the region of the optical confinement is extremely narrow. Multiple quantum well (MQW) lasers are often employed to enlarge the optical cavity. When the barrier and well widths of such MQW lasers become smaller than the carrier mean free path, it turns into a superlattice laser.

(iv) Large optical cavity (LOC) laser In a standard DH laser, the optical intensity within the potential well is very high. This at times may even damage the reflecting surfaces. To overcome this difficulty, the width of the optical cavity is made wider by forming two separate heterojunctions on both sides

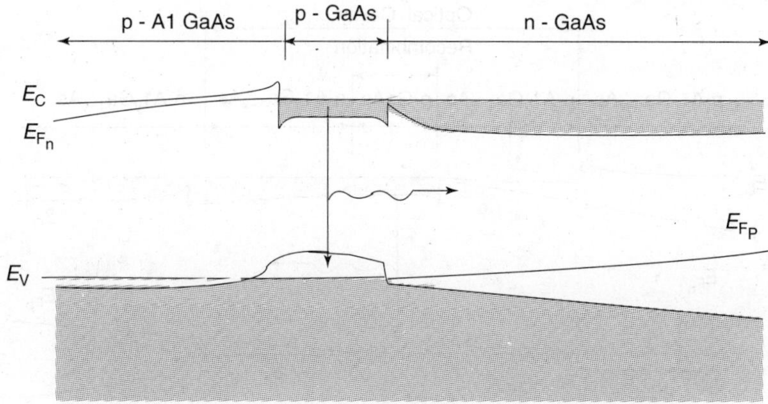

Figure 2.30 *A double heterojunction (DH) laser diode*

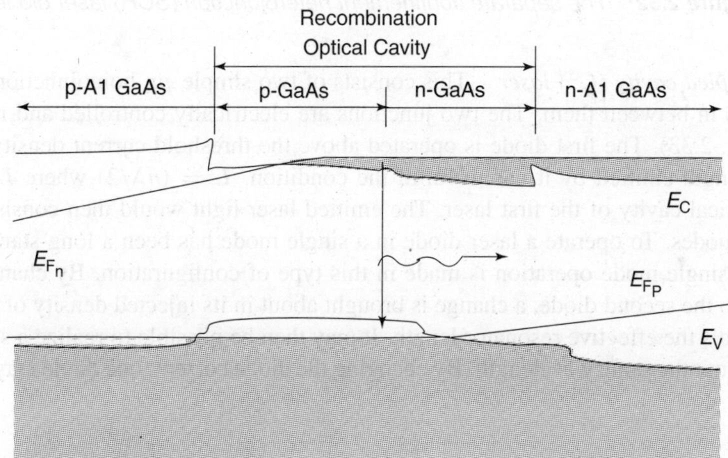

Figure 2.31 *A large optical cavity (LOC) laser diode*

of the homojunction which generates light, as shown in Fig. 2.31. The change in the refractive index at the GaAs-AlGaAs interfaces confines the generated light within the optical cavity formed by the heterojunctions.

(v) Separate confinement heterojunction (SCH) and Graded-index SCH laser The SCH laser has four heterojunctions: the inner two define the region of carrier confinement as in a DH laser and the outer two determine the optical cavity, as in a LOC laser (Fig. 2.32). This configuration, therefore, combines the advantages of DH and LOC lasers. A refinement in the structure can be made by using graded compositions in the outer pair of heterojunctions. Consequently, such a configuration is called a graded index, separate confinement heterojunction (GRIN-SCH) laser. By grading the composition of AlGaAs, it is also possible to obtain better waveguiding.

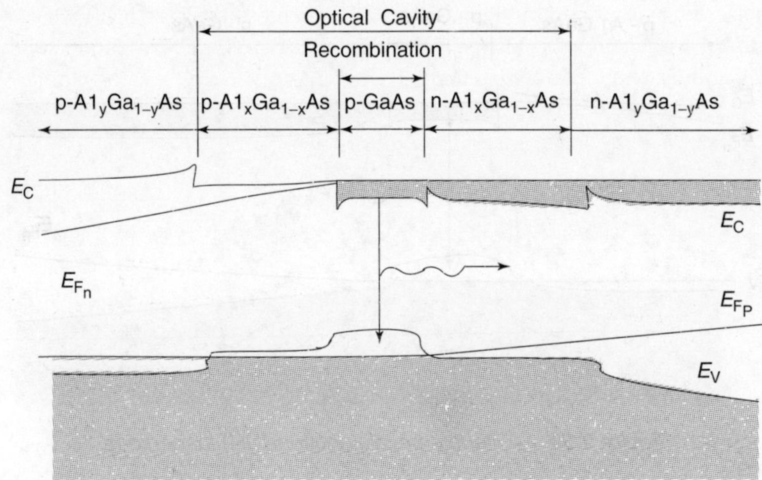

Figure 2.32 *The separate confinement heterojunction (SCH) laser diode*

(vi) Cleaved coupled cavity (C^3) laser This consists of two simple *pn* homojunction lasers placed with a gap of 5μ m between them. The two junctions are electrically controlled and independent of one another (Fig. 2.33). The first diode is operated above the threshold current density. The emitted radiation wavelength emitted by it has to fulfill the condition, $L = (n\lambda/2)$ where L measures the length of the optical cavity of the first laser. The emitted laser light would then consist of a number of longitudinal modes. To operate a laser diode in a single mode has been a long-standing problem. An attempt at a single mode operation is made in this type of configuration. By changing the input current density to the second diode, a change is brought about in its injected density of carriers which effectively controls the effective resonator length. It may then be possible to realize a situation where both the diodes emit the same wavelength. By changing the diode current, one diode may then be tuned to the other.

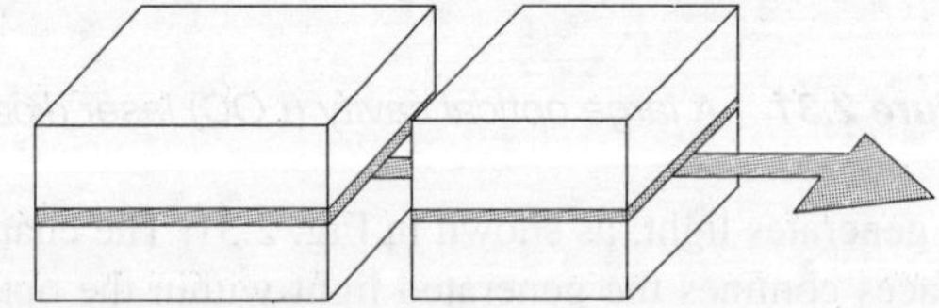

Figure 2.33 *A cleaved coupled cavity (C^3) laser diode*

(vii) Distributed feedback (DFB) laser Another approach to the single mode lasing is to use the distributed feedback (DFB) principle. Adjacent to the junction (active layer), a grating of the type shown in Fig. 2.34, is designed. The light reflected by successive grating elements would reinforce each other if the condition $2D = n\lambda$ is satisfied. The two reflected beams would then remain in phase provided their path difference $2D$ (approx) is an integral multiple of the wavelength of light. In this configuration, reflections from the grating are used instead of reflections from the end mirrors. The corrugations determine the coherent wavelength which are in turn determined by Bragg scattering and

they de-emphasize the role played by the Fabry–Perot mirrors. Thus, corrugations act like frequency selectors. The absence of end mirrors allows the integration of this type of laser on a semiconductor chip with optical waveguides and other components. It also allows for wavelength stability. By choosing a particular D, one can ensure that only one particular longitudinal mode exists.

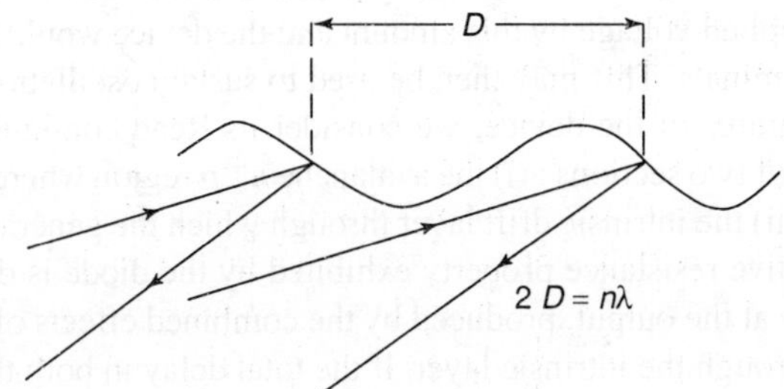

Figure 2.34 *A distributed feedback (DFB) laser diode*

(viii) Vertical cavity surface emitting laser (VCSEL) This is a laser with a cavity defined by multiple quantum wells which forms the active layer of the device. Light emitted due to electron-hole recombination has to undergo multiple reflections at the Bragg reflectors so that the laser output gets stabilized at a particular wavelength determined by the grating element (Fig. 2.35). The advantage of a laser of this kind is the realization of a $2D$ laser array, which is compatible with IC processing technology.

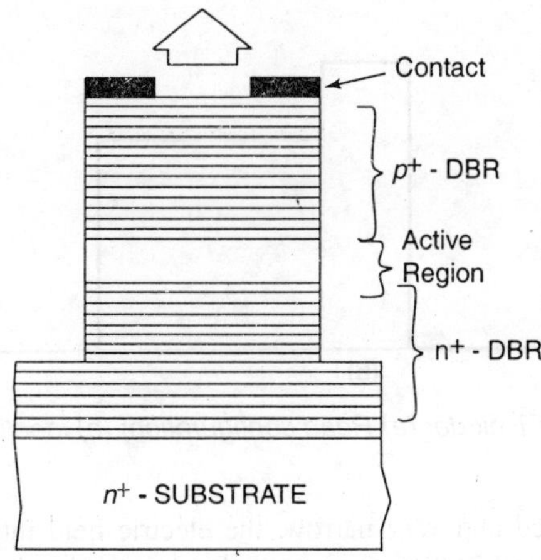

Figure 2.35 *A vertical cavity surface emitting laser (VCSEL)*

2.9 Impact avalanche and transit time (IMPATT) diodes

The name of the device is derived from the phrase, '*impact ionization by avalanche and transit time*', which incidentally defines its working principle. The device essentially is a modification of a *pn* junction reverse biased to the state of avalanche breakdown. Over the d.c. reverse bias, a small signal a.c. is also superimposed. Owing to the finite time required for the carrier generation in the impact ionization process, the current generated by it lags behind the applied a.c. signal. The generated carriers would also require a finite time to negotiate the bulk of the semiconductor to appear at the output. If the total delay in both the above processes is adjusted to be exactly π radians, the current at the output would also be found to lag behind the applied voltage by this amount and the device would start exhibiting a negative conductance across its terminals. This may then be used to sustain oscillations in a microwave cavity. To analyze the salient features of the device, we consider its Read configuration (Fig. 2.36). Such a diode essentially consists of two sections : (i) the avalanche $n^+ p$ region where the carrier multiplication actually takes place, and (ii) the intrinsic drift layer through which the generated carriers travel towards the p^+ contact. The negative resistance property exhibited by the diode is due to the phase lag of the current behind the voltage at the output, produced by the combined effects of avalanche multiplication and the drift of carriers through the intrinsic layer. If the total delay in both these processes is adjusted to be π radians, the device would start exhibiting a negative conductance behaviour.

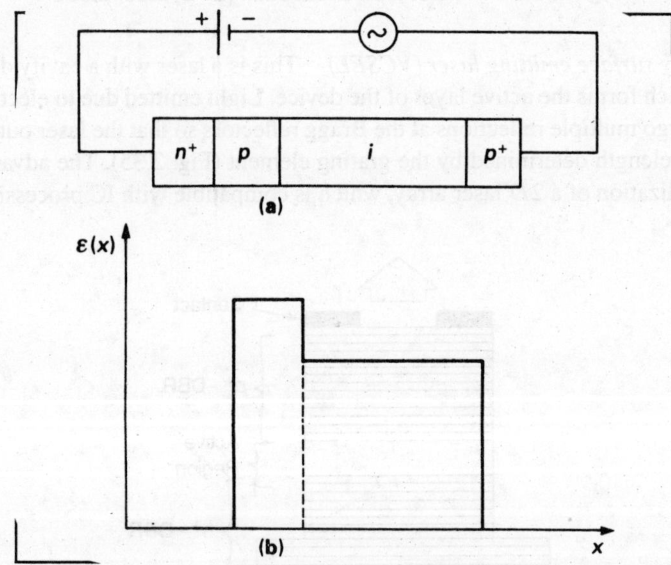

Figure 2.36 *IMPATT diode: (a) Read configuration; (b) idealized field distribution*

If the p-region is lightly doped and very narrow, the electric field intensity over it may be treated to remain almost uniform (Fig. 2.36(b)). On top of the d.c. field, which corresponds to the carrier multiplication region, a small signal microwave field derived from the associated resonant circuit is also superimposed. As the diode becomes more and more reverse biased due to the increasing a.c. biases, more and more carriers are generated by the impact ionization process. These generated carriers start drifting towards appropriate ends of the diode by the effect of the junction field. The height of the carrier pulse continues to grow as long as the net reverse bias across the diode exceeds the threshold value required for carrier multiplication. The notable feature about this growth is that the peak height of the carrier pulse is not attained in phase with the applied a.c. field but lags behind it due to inherent transmission delays. Let us, for example, presume that the hole pulse attains its peak height when the a.c. voltage has just completed one half of a cycle. Therefore, during the avalanche process itself, the generated current lags behind the applied voltage by a phase angle of $(\pi/2)$ radians. If an additional phase difference of $(\pi/2)$ radians is introduced during the transmission of holes through the i-layer, the device would start exhibiting the desired negative conductance property. This would be the case, if the length L of the i-layer is given by

$$\frac{L}{v_d} = \frac{1}{4f} \tag{2.182}$$

where v_d denotes the drift velocity of holes through the i-layer and f is the frequency of the imposed microwave signal. Therefore, in choosing an appropriate microwave cavity of a natural frequency f, the choice of L of the drift layer is extremely critical.

Analysis of the IMPATT diode

We now proceed to calculate the impedances offered by avalanche and drift layers and examine the situations where they tend to become negative.

(i) Avalanche region The current continuity equations for electrons and holes within the space-charge layers when carrier multiplication occurs is given by

$$\frac{\partial p}{\partial t} + \left(\frac{1}{q}\right)\left(\frac{\partial J_p}{\partial x}\right) = \alpha v_d(n+p) \tag{2.183}$$

and

$$\frac{\partial n}{\partial t} - \left(\frac{1}{q}\right)\left(\frac{\partial J_n}{\partial x}\right) = \alpha v_d(n+p) \tag{2.184}$$

where α measures the carrier multiplication rate (which measures the fractional increase in the carrier density per unit distance travelled). For the sake of simplicity of analysis, α is presumed to be equal both for electrons and holes. The thermal generation effects in the reverse biased pn junction is ignored in the above considerations. Adding (2.183) and (2.184) and integrating over the avalanche layer of width x_A, we get

$$\left(\frac{x_A}{v_d}\right)\left(\frac{\partial J}{\partial t}\right) + [J_p - J_n]_0^{x_A} = 2J_D\alpha_0 x_A \tag{2.185}$$

where α_0 denotes the average ionization rate over the space-charge layer and $J \cong J = qv_d(n+p)$ (where J_D measures the reverse saturation current density). Since, electrons and holes are produced in pairs by the impact ionization process, $[J_p - J_n]$ would remain the same on both ends of the depletion layer. Equation (2.185) then simplifies to

$$\tau_A\left(\frac{\partial J}{\partial t}\right) = 2J_D\alpha_0 x_A \tag{2.186}$$

where τ_A accounts for the time taken by the carriers to cover the avalanche region. When a small a.c. signal is superimposed on the applied d.c. bias, we get

$$\varepsilon = \varepsilon_D + \varepsilon_A \exp(j\omega t)$$
$$J = J_D + J_A \exp(j\omega t) \tag{2.187}$$

and

$$\alpha_0 = \alpha_D + \alpha_A \exp(j\omega t) \cong \alpha' \varepsilon_A \exp(j\omega t)$$

In the above equation, the d.c. ionization rate α_D is considered negligible compared to the a.c. ionization rate α_A. Combining (2.186) and (2.187), one finds

$$J_A = \frac{2\alpha' \varepsilon_A x_A J_D}{j\omega\tau_A} \tag{2.188}$$

The current generated by the avalanche process is thus seen to be reactive, varying inversely as ω through an inductor of self-inductance L_A which is given by

$$L_A = \frac{\tau_A}{2\alpha' A J_D} \tag{2.189}$$

where A denotes the junction area. On the other hand, the capacitance C_A offered by an avalanche region is given by

$$C_A = \frac{\kappa\varepsilon_0 A}{x_A} \tag{2.190}$$

The resonant circuit composed of L_A and C_A has a resonant frequency, given by

$$f_r = [2\pi(L_A C_A)^{1/2}]^{-1} = \frac{1}{2\pi}\left[\frac{2\alpha' v_d J_D}{\kappa\varepsilon_0}\right]^{1/2} \tag{2.191}$$

The resonant frequency is thus seen to be proportional to $(J_D)^{1/2}$. The impedance Z_A offered by the avalanche region may then be expressed as

$$\frac{1}{Z_A} = \frac{1}{j\omega L_A} + j\omega C_A = \frac{1 - \omega^2 L_A C_A}{j\omega L_A}$$

or

$$Z_A = j\omega L_A \left[1 - \frac{\omega^2}{\omega_r^2}\right]^{-1} \tag{2.192}$$

The ratio of the avalanche to the total current density (injection efficiency γ) may now be expressed as

$$\gamma = \frac{J_A}{J} = \frac{Z_A}{j\omega L_A} = \left[1 - \frac{\omega^2}{\omega_r^2}\right]^{-1} \tag{2.193}$$

Z_A may also be expressed in the following alternative form:

$$(Z_A)^{-1} = j\omega C_A[1 - (\omega^2 L_A C_A)^{-1}] = j\omega C_A \left[1 - \frac{\omega_r^2}{\omega^2}\right]^{-1} \tag{2.194}$$

(ii) Drift layer The a.c. hole current density generated by the avalanche process drifts through the i-layer. At any point of the drift layer, the alternating conduction current density may be expressed as

$$J_c(x) = J_A \exp\left[-j\omega\left(\frac{x}{v_d}\right)\right] \tag{2.195}$$

where J_A measures the avalanche current density at $x = 0$. The total current density crossing the i-layer is however independent of position. The difference between the above two currents (viz. the total and the conduction current densities) is due to the electric displacement. We may therefore write

$$J = J_c(x) + J_d(x) \tag{2.196}$$

But the displacement current density $J_d(x)$ may be expressed as

$$J_d(x) = \frac{\partial D}{\partial t} = \left(\frac{\partial}{\partial t}\right)[\kappa\varepsilon_0\varepsilon_D(x)\exp(j\omega t)]$$

or

$$J_d(x) = j\omega\kappa\varepsilon_0\varepsilon(x) \tag{2.197}$$

where $\varepsilon(x) = \varepsilon_D(x)\exp(j\omega t)$ denotes the electric field at any point of the drift layer. Now, combining (2.193), (2.195), (2.196) and (2.197), we get

$$\varepsilon(x) = \frac{J\left[1 - \gamma\exp\left(\frac{-j\omega x}{v_d}\right)\right]}{j\omega\kappa\varepsilon_0} \tag{2.198}$$

The net p.d. over the drift layer may now be expressed as

$$V_d = \int_0^L \varepsilon(x)dx = \frac{J}{j\omega\kappa\varepsilon_0}\left[L - \left\{1 - \left(\frac{\omega^2}{\omega_r^2}\right)\right\}^{-1}\left\{\frac{-\exp\left(\frac{-j\omega x}{v_d}\right)}{\left(\frac{j\omega}{v_d}\right)}\right\}_0^L\right]$$

or

$$V_d = \frac{JL}{j\omega\kappa\varepsilon_0}\left[1 - \left\{1 - \left(\frac{\omega^2}{\omega_r^2}\right)\right\}^{-1}\left\{\frac{1 - \exp(-j\theta)}{j\theta}\right\}\right] \tag{2.199}$$

where $\theta = (\omega L/v_d)$ measures the phase lag introduced between the current and the voltage by the i-layer. The capacitance offered by the i-layer may be expressed as

$$C_d = \frac{\kappa\varepsilon_0 A}{L} \tag{2.200}$$

The total impedance offered by the i-layer may be obtained by combining (2.199) and (2.200) as

$$Z_d = \left[\left(\frac{1}{\omega C_d}\right)\left\{\frac{(1-\cos\theta)}{\theta}\right\}\left\{1 - \left(\frac{\omega^2}{\omega_r^2}\right)\right\}^{-1}\right] + \left(\frac{j}{\omega C_d}\right)\left[-1 + \left(\frac{\sin\theta}{\theta}\right)\left\{1 - \left(\frac{\omega^2}{\omega_r^2}\right)\right\}^{-1}\right] \tag{2.201}$$

The above equation clearly states that the resistance offered by the drift layer is negative if $\omega > \omega_r$, except when $\theta = 2n\pi$. The impedance offered by the drift layer is however capacitive. The total impedance is then given by

$$Z = Z_A + Z_d + R_S$$

i.e.

$$Z = \frac{L^2}{2\kappa\varepsilon_0 A v_d} \left\{1 - \left(\frac{\omega^2}{\omega_r^2}\right)\right\}^{-1} \left\{\frac{(1-\cos\theta)}{\left(\frac{\theta^2}{2}\right)}\right\} + \left(\frac{j\omega}{C_d}\right)\left\{\left(\frac{\sin\theta}{\theta}\right) - 1\right\} \cdot$$

$$+ \left[\left\{\left(\frac{\omega_r^2}{\omega^2}\right) - 1\right\}^{-1} \left(\frac{\sin\theta}{\theta}\right) + \left(\frac{x_A}{L}\right)\right] + R_s \qquad (2.202)$$

where R_s denotes the series resistance of the device. As already mentioned, the first term in (2.102) measuring the active resistance becomes negative only for $\omega > \omega_r$. The reactive term then becomes capacitive. This is a desirable feature because IMPATT diodes are operated in conjunction with microwave cavities where the reactance is largely inductive.

We have explained the IMPATT operation in a simple Read diode configuration. But, a number of variations is possible in the device configuration. A *p-i-n* (Misawa) diode has also been used to generate microwave oscillations. In this case, the entire reverse voltage is available over the *i*-layer which serves both as the avalanche and the drift region for carriers. Sometimes this diode is said to operate in the TRAPATT *(trapped plasma avalanche and triggered transit)* mode. Instead of generating carriers by impact ionization, they may also be injected into the *i*-layer over a metal-semiconductor barrier. The device then is known as a BARITT *(barrier injection and transit time)* diode. If the avalanche region is extremely thin, carriers may also tunnel through it. The device then is known as a TUNNETT *(tunnelling and transit time)* diode. IMPATT diodes may also be available in various other configurations e.g. MITATT *(mixed tunnel avalanche transit time)* diode, DOVATT *(double velocity avalanche transit time)* diode and QWITT *(quantum well injection and transit time)* diode. In MITATT diodes, carriers are partly generated by impact ionization and partly by tunnelling through the avalanche region. In the case of a DOVATT diode, the drift region consists of two different materials in which carriers move with two different velocities. In a QWITT diode, the carriers are injected by resonant tunnelling through a quantum well.

2.10 Other configurations of *pn* diodes

(i) Planar doped barrier (PDB) diode and Camel diodes The planar doped barrier diode consists of a $n^+-i-p^+-i-n^+$ structure of GaAs. The middle p^+-layer is extremely thin (2∼10 nm) and, as such, it is fully depleted of free carriers. Such a thin, heavily doped layer can only be controlled by MBE or MOCVD growths. The device is endowed with a triangular barrier and therefore it is sometimes referred to as the triangular barrier diode. The camel diode differs from the PDB diode in its structure and consists of $n^{++} - p^+ - n$ configuration; once again, the p^+ layer is extremely thin. Unlike normal

pn junctions, current in them flows by the process of thermionic emission. These diodes are majority carrier devices and, therefore, do not have minority carrier storage effects. They are thus, capable of very high frequency operations. The barrier heights in these devices are easily controllable by adjusting the process variables during their fabrications.

(ii) p-i-n Diodes *p-i-n* Diodes are modifications of *pn* junctions for special applications. The presence of intrinsic layers substantially increases the breakdown voltage making them useful for high voltage applications. *p-i-n* diodes also find applications in RF switching. When the diode is forward biased, it is highly conducting and behaves as a short. At zero or reverse biases, it behaves as a capacitor or an open circuit. The value of the RF resistance offered by the device is solely determined by the superimposed d.c bias or current. The latter due to its storage effects controls the resistance offered by the device which cannot be altered by RF signals. Thus at RF frequencies, *p-i-n* diodes behave like pure resistors. This property is made use of to design phase shifters, limiters etc. A *p-i-n* diode has also been used as a nuclear radiation detector and as a common photodiode.
In a *p-i-n* photodiode there is no gain mechanism involved, since, on the average one electron-hole pair may be produced and collected by the junction for each photon absorbed. Thus, the gain is essentially unity. The response time in this case is dependent upon the width of the depletion layer.

(iii) Avalanche photodiodes When a *pn* diode is operated in the third quadrant of its I–V characteristic, the current is essentially independent of the voltage but is proportional to the optical generation rate. Such a device, called a photodiode, provides a useful means of measuring illumination levels or for converting the time-varying optical signals into electrical signals. Avalanche photodiodes have the advantage of providing gain through the avalanche multiplication effect. The disadvantage is the increased noise relative to *p-i-n* diodes due to the random fluctuations in the avalanche process. This noise can be reduced if the impact ionization in the high field region is due to only one type of a carrier, since more fluctuations in the ionization process occur when both electrons and holes participate. In Si, the ability of electrons to create EHPs in an impact ionization event is much higher than for holes. Therefore, Si avalanche photodiodes can be operated with a relatively high gain and a low noise. On the other hand, the ionization rates for the two carriers are fairly equal in most compound semiconductors. One creative way of overcoming the problem has already been depicted in the figure. By using a multilayered heterostructure with successive layers of AlGaAs graded from GaAs to wider band-gap AlGaAs compositions, it is possible to take advantage of the wider steps in the conduction band than in the valence band of the GaAs-AlGaAs heterojunction. When a large reverse voltage is applied to the diode, electrons enter each GaAs region high in the conduction band with enough energy to cause impact ionization (Fig. c). In contrast, holes enter the GaAs regions with lesser energies because the valence band discontinuity is much less. As a result, the avalanche multiplication in this diode is primarily due to electrons. In the figure, an electron entering the first GaAs layer causes multiplication, and in the process continues throughout the structure. The device is similar to a vacuum tube photomultiplier. Obviously, the gain of the device is high and the noise reduced compared to ordinary photodiodes but the bandwidth is also reduced.

2.11 Circuit applications of *pn* diodes

The ability of a *pn* diode to allow a current to flow through it only in a particular direction has made it possible to use it as a rectifier of alternating currents. A rectifier is a device that has a low impedance under a forward bias and a high impedance under a reverse bias.

(i) Half-wave rectifier When a sinusoidal voltage is applied to a *pn* diode, the latter conducts as long as the diode remains forward biased. As a result, a symmetric sinusoidal waveform becomes a half-wave (Fig. 2.37).

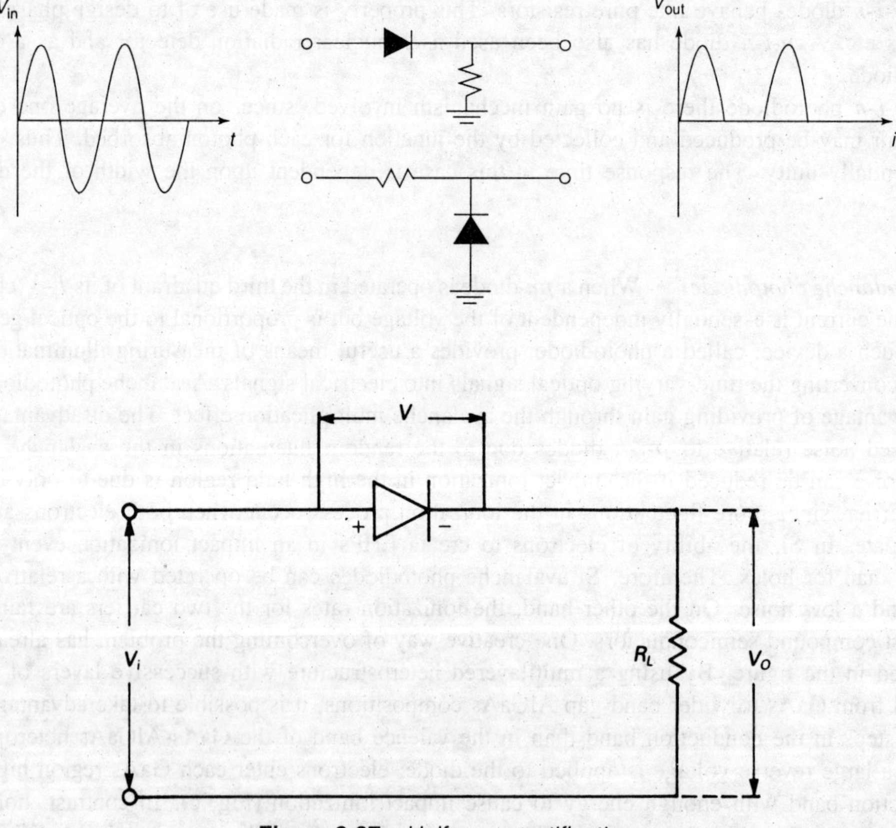

Figure 2.37 *Half-wave rectification*

(ii) Full-wave rectifier Here the circuit does not block the negative voltage, but changes its polarity. The circuit diagram of a full-wave rectifier is shown in Fig. 2.38. It is a more efficient a.c. to d.c. converter than a half-wave rectifier. Two popular versions are the bridge rectifier and the configuration using a center-tapped transformer.

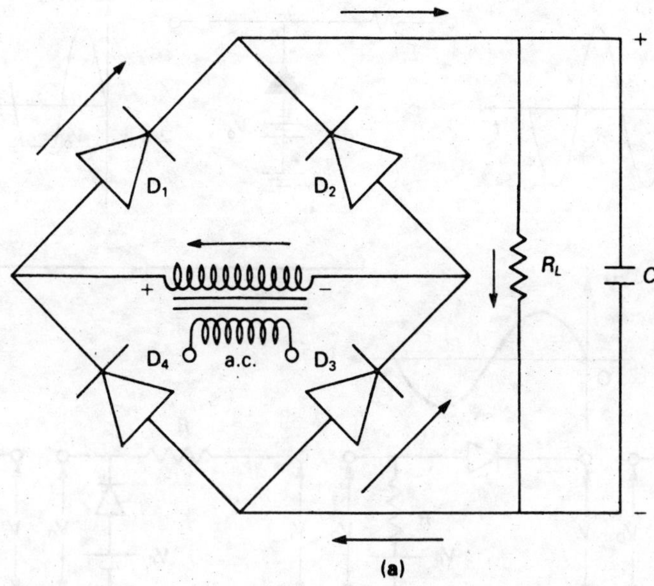

Figure 2.38 *The full-wave rectifier circuit with a capacitor circuit: (a) the circuit*

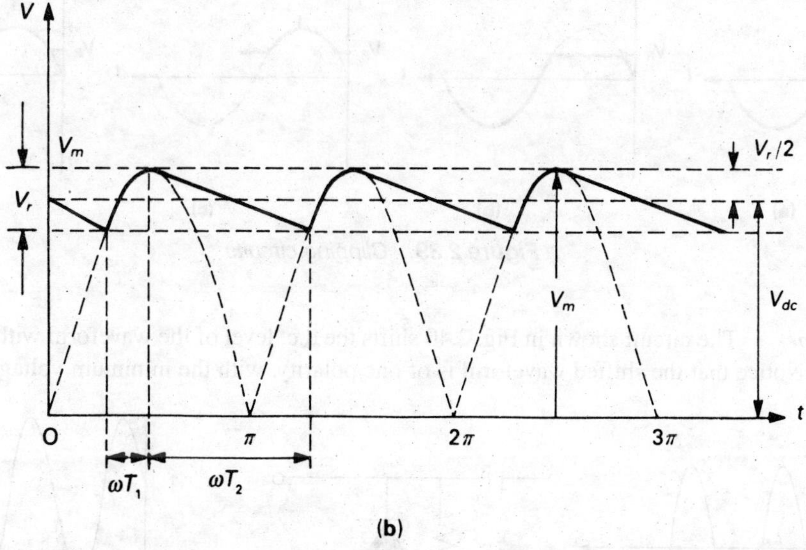

Figure 2.38 *continued (b) The rectifier output voltage waveform*

(iii) Clipper The circuit shown in Fig. 2.39 clips one polarity of the waveform to within a selected value, without distorting the rest of the waveform. When $V_0 = 0$, it becomes a half-wave rectifier.

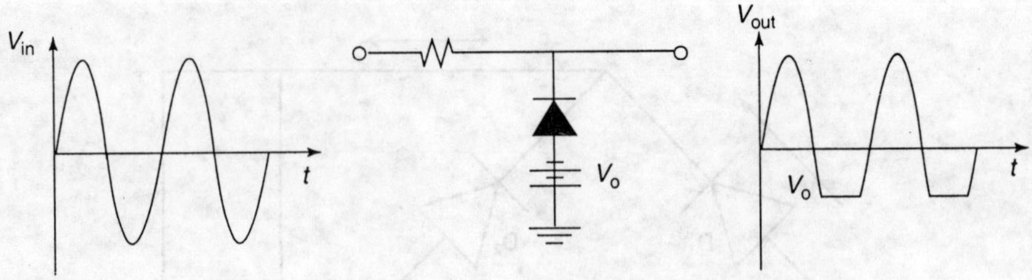

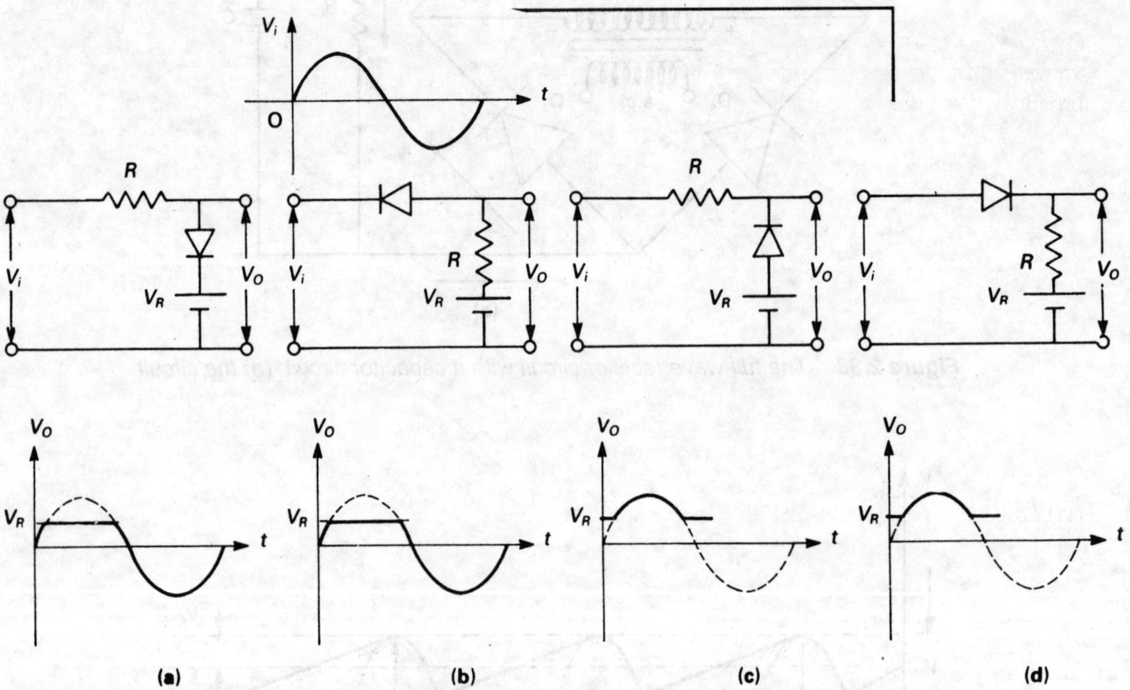

Figure 2.39 *Clipping circuits*

(iv) Clamper The circuit shown in Fig. 2.40 shifts the d.c. level of the waveform without distorting its shape. Notice that the shifted waveform is of one polarity, with the minimum voltage at zero. The

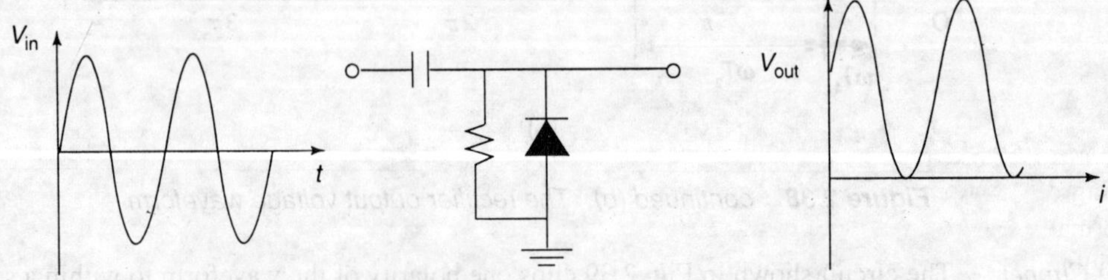

Figure 2.40 *A clamper circuit with input and output waveforms*

circuit can also be used in an a.c. to d.c. converter, as a "doubler", such that the d.c. value obtained is twice that of the original a.c. voltage. Assuming the diode to be ideal, the drop across the device is zero under the forward biased condition. Hence, the output cannot rise above V_R and is said to be clamped at this level. If the input voltage is sinusoidal with a peak value V_m and an average value of zero, then as indicated in Fig. 2.40, the output is sinusoidal with an average value of $(V_R - V_m)$. Such a waveform is realized subject to the following conditions: $R_f = 0$, $R_r = \infty$ and $V\gamma = 0$; the source impedance $R_s = 0$ and the RC time constant is much larger than the time period of the signal.

(v) Peak detector A circuit shown in Fig. 2.41 detects the local peak value of a fast signal. It can be viewed as a half-wave rectifier with a low pass filter. A practical example is the demodulation of AM broadcasting. The time constant of the output can be varied by changing R and C.

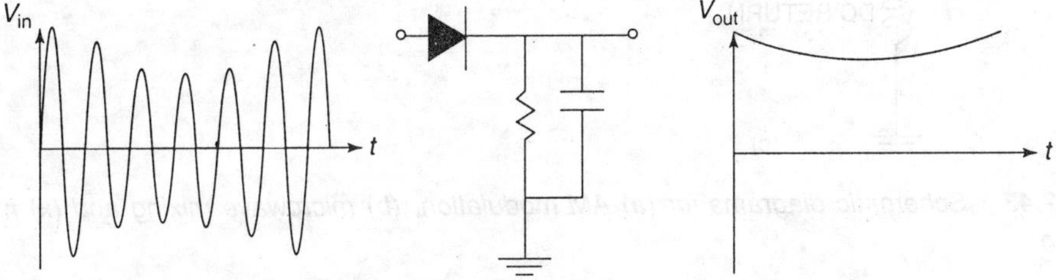

Figure 2.41 *peak detector circuit with input and output waveforms*

(vi) Logic Simple OR and AND logics can be implemented by using circuits shown in Fig. 2.42.

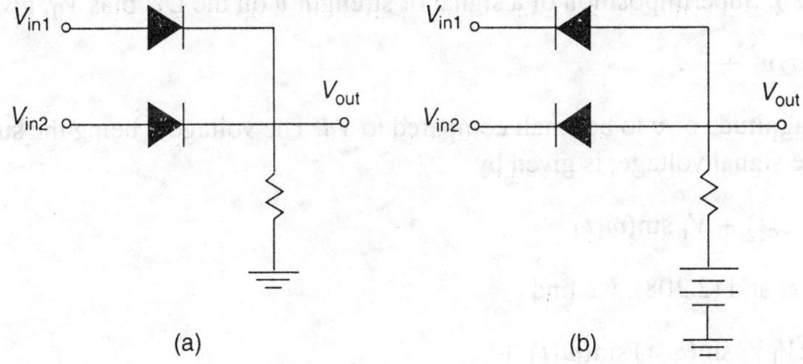

Figure 2.42 *Logic realizations for (a) OR gate and (b) AND gate*

(vii) Microwave modulation, mixing and detection Any non-linear device, not necessarily a rectifying device, can theoretically perform these functions. In broadcasting, the signal containing the information is modulated with a much higher frequency, called the carrier frequency. The advantages of modulation at these higher frequencies are: (i) more efficient transmission through the atmosphere, (ii) reduced antenna size and (iii) a larger number of channels being available. Popular modulation schemes

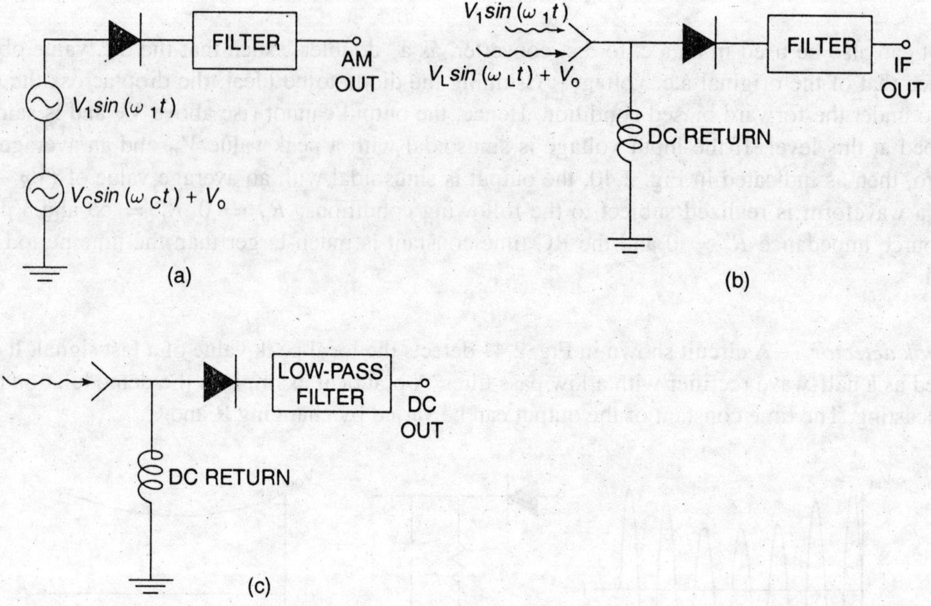

Figure 2.43 *Schematic diagrams for (a) AM modulation, (b) microwave mixing and (x) microwave detection*

are amplitude modulation (AM) and frequency modulation (FM). The circuit shown in Fig. 2.43(a) can produce amplitude modulation. Since the diode $I-V$ characteristic can be represented by an equation

$$I = I_0 \exp(\beta V_0) \tag{2.206}$$

where $\beta = (q/kT)$. Superimposition of a signal of strength v on the DC bias V_0, gives the current as

$$i = a_1 v + a_2 v^2 + \ldots \tag{2.207}$$

presuming the magnitude of v to be small compared to V_0. The voltage v being the superimposition of the carrier and the signal voltage, is given by

$$v = V_c \sin(\omega_c t) + V_1 \sin(\omega_1 t) \tag{2.208}$$

Combining (2.207) and (2.208), we find

$$i = \ldots + 2V_1 V_c \sin(\omega_c t) \sin(\omega_1 t) + \ldots \tag{2.209}$$

which contains the amplitude modulated output.
A heterodyne receiver has a mixer followed by a detector. The function of the mixer is to lower the microwave frequency to an intermediate value. This down conversion has a number of advantages: (a) ease of amplification, (b) ease in narrow band filtering and (c) ease in the variability of the local oscillator frequency, so that the system could be used for different carrier frequencies. In Fig. 2.43(b), the incoming signal is mixed with that from a local oscillator to generate a voltage v_1, given by

$$v_1 = V_1 \sin(\omega_1 t) + V_L \sin(\omega_L t) \tag{2.210}$$

Combining (2.207) and (2.210), one finds

$$i = \ldots + 2a_2 V_1 V_L \sin(\omega_1 t)\sin(\omega_L t) + \cdots$$
$$= \ldots + a_2 V_1 V_L \cos[(\omega_1 - \omega_L)t] + \ldots \quad (2.211)$$

The lowering of the frequency from ω_1 to $(\omega_1 - \omega_L)$ is obvious. Other unwanted frequencies are subsequently

filtered out. The current is proportional to the local oscillator voltage V_L which is much larger than V_1.

A microwave detector circuit is shown in Fig. 2.43(c). If the signal strength is small, we may presume

$$v_1 = V_1 \sin(\omega_1 t) \quad (2.212)$$

and therefore, the corresponding current would be given by

$$i_1 = a_1 v_1 + a_2 v_1^2$$
$$= a_1 V_1 \sin(\omega_1 t) + a_2 V_1^2 \sin^2(\omega_1 t) \quad (2.213)$$

The last term contains the demodulated component as it has a non-zero d.c. value. Because, the output is proportional to the square of the input signal, the device is often referred to as the square law detector (Fig. 2.44). For large signal detection, there is no d.c. bias and the device is sometimes called a zero bias detector. The output is filtered to obtain a d.c. output.

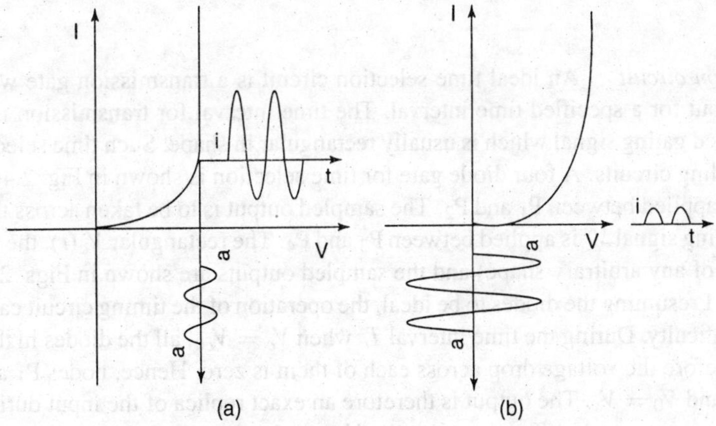

Figure 2.44 *(a) The small-signal response in modulation, mixing and detection. Note the non-linearity in the output current, (b) the large signal response in a zero-bias detector*

(viii) Comparator The diode circuit which is used for clipping can also be used to compare any two given voltages. A comparator circuit therefore helps one to mark the instant when a given waveform attains a particular reference level. To cite an example, in the diode circuit used for clipping (Fig. 2.40),

the input signal is taken as a ramp voltage. The input is seen to cross the voltage level $V_i = V_R + V_\gamma$ at an instant t_1 (Fig. 2.45). As a result of this, the diode output remains clamped at a voltage V_R until $t = t_1$. Therefore, a device to which a comparator voltage is applied will only respond if the output voltage exceeds V_0 after $t = t_1$.

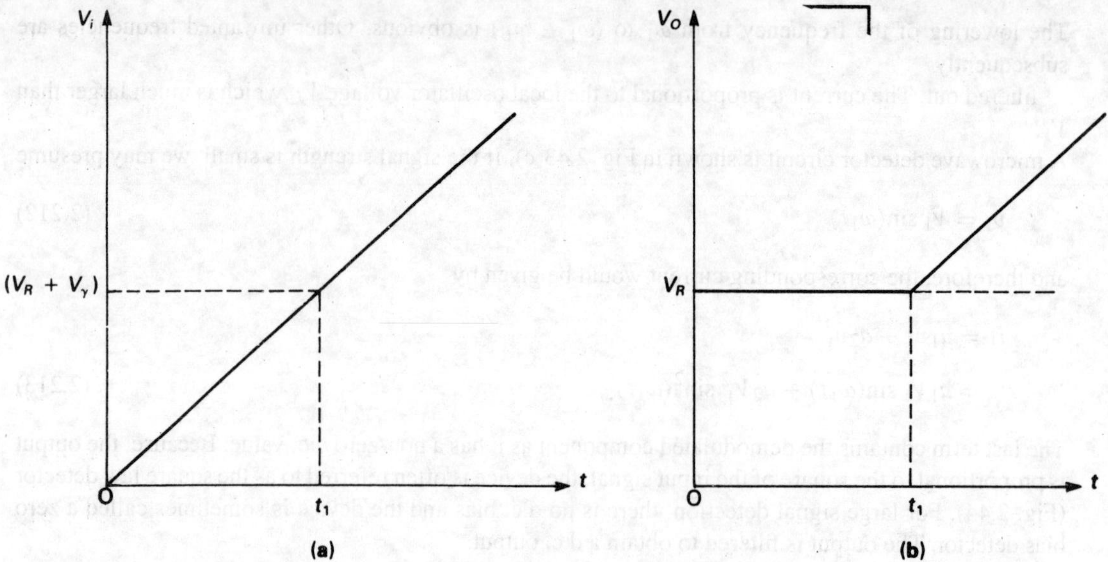

Figure 2.45 *(a) Input and (b) output voltages of a comparator circuit shown in Fig. 2.39(d)*

(ix) Time selection circuit An ideal time selection circuit is a transmission gate which is an exact replica of the input for a specified time interval. The time interval for transmission is selected by an externally imposed gating signal which is usually rectangular in shape. Such time selection circuits are also called sampling circuits. A four diode gate for time selection is shown in Fig. 2.46. The signal V_s to be sampled is applied between P_1 and P_2. The sampled output is to be taken across the load R_L. The control or the gating signal V_c is applied between P_3 and P_4. The rectangular $V_c(t)$, the sinusoidal $V_s(t)$ (which could be of any arbitrary shape) and the sampled outputs are shown in Figs. 2.46 (b), (c), and (d), respectively. Presuming the diodes to be ideal, the operation of the timing circuit can be understood without much difficulty. During the time interval T_c when $V_c = V_{c0}$, all the diodes in the bridge circuit conduct and therefore the voltage drop across each of them is zero. Hence, nodes P_1 and P_2 are at the same potentials and $V_0 = V_s$. The output is therefore an exact replica of the input during the selection time T_c. But during the interval T_n when $V_c = -V_n$, all the four diodes become reverse biased and as a result, effectively there is an infinite resistance between P_1 and P_2. Hence, for this period T_n, the output would be zero. In the above analysis, it is implicitly presumed that $|V_n| > V_{s0}$, otherwise, the diodes will not be reverse biased.

(x) Voltage regulator circuit A Zener diode, because of its very sharp breakdown characteristic, is used to regulate the voltage across a given load. A series regulator circuit is shown in Fig. 2.47. The source voltage V and the resistance R are so selected that the voltage across the Zener diode is the

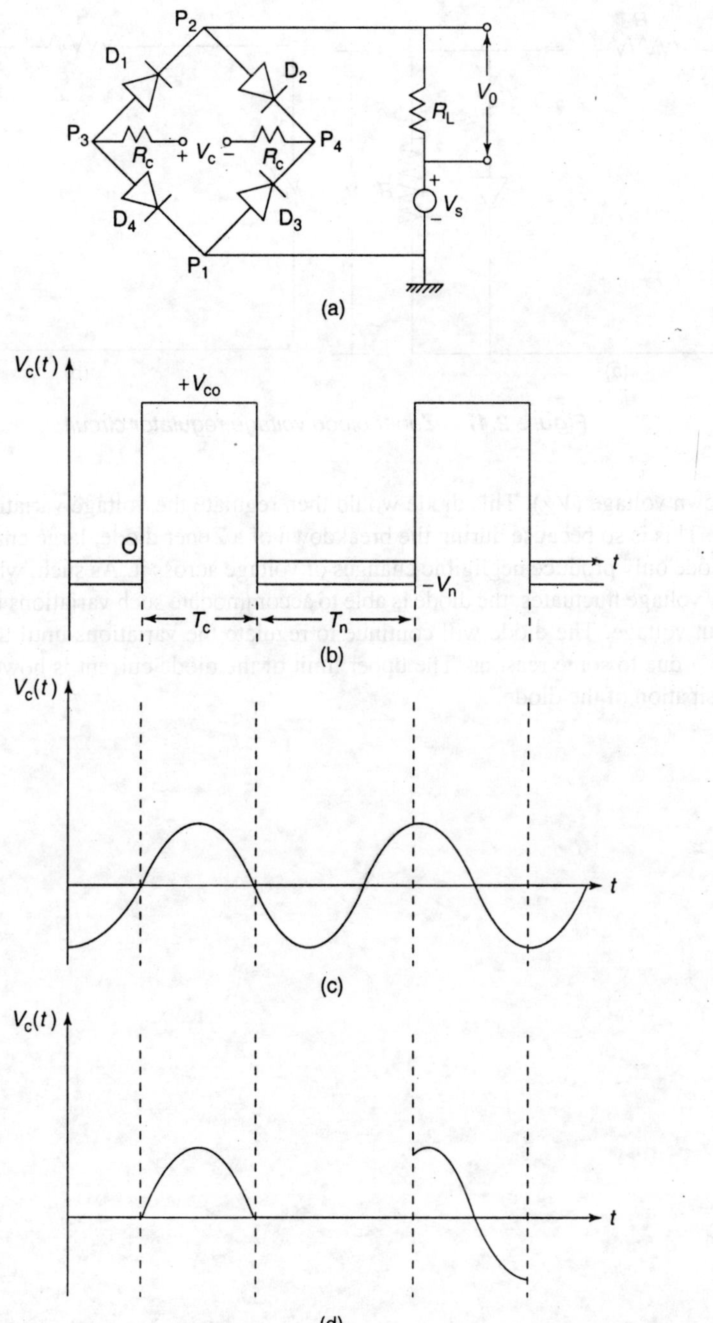

Figure 2.46 *The time selection circuit: (a) the network, (b), (c) & (d) different voltage waveforms*

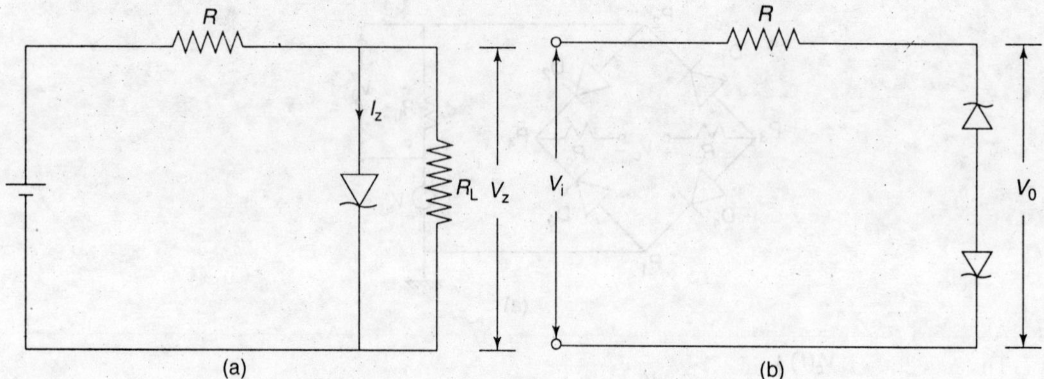

Figure 2.47 *Zener diode voltage regulator circuit*

Zener breakdown voltage (V_Z). This diode would then regulate the voltage variations across the load resistance R_L. This is so because during the breakdown of a Zener diode, large changes in the current through the diode only produce negligible changes of voltage across it. As such, when the load current and the supply voltage fluctuates, the diode is able to accommodate such variations to maintain a nearly constant output voltage. The diode will continue to regulate the variations until the voltage across it drops below V_Z due to some reasons. The upper limit of the diode current is however determined by the power dissipation of the diode.

Solved examples

2.1 Assume a p^+n junction with a graded n-region where the doping is described by $N_d(x) = Gx^m$. The depletion layer width W extends from the junction at $x = 0$ to the entire length of the n-region. Derive (i) an expression for the maximum electric field ε_m, (ii) the built-in junction potential Ψ_0 and (iii) the junction capacitance per unit area C_j.

Solution

The doping profile in the n-region of the one-sided abrupt p^+n junction is given by

$$N_d(x) = Gx^m \tag{1}$$

Owing to the one-sided nature of the p^+n junction, the width of the transition layer on the p-side may be neglected. The Poisson's equation on the n-side may then be expressed as

$$\frac{d^2\Psi(x)}{dx^2} = -\left(\frac{\rho}{\kappa\varepsilon_0}\right) = -\left(\frac{qGx^m}{\kappa\varepsilon_0}\right) \tag{2}$$

Integrating (2), we find

$$\frac{d\Psi(x)}{dx} = -\left(\frac{qG}{\kappa\varepsilon_0}\right)\left[\frac{x^{m+1}}{m+1}\right] + A_1 \tag{3}$$

where A_1 is a constant of integration. Since the electric field must disappear at the transition layer boundary on the n-side, we set $[d\Psi(x)/dx] = 0$ at $x = W$ to evaluate A_1. Thus,

$$A_1 = \left(\frac{qG}{\kappa\varepsilon_0}\right)\left[\frac{W^{m+1}}{m+1}\right] \tag{4}$$

Combining (3) and (4), we get

$$-\left[\frac{d\Psi(x)}{dx}\right] = \varepsilon(x) = \left[\frac{qG}{\kappa\varepsilon_0(m+1)}\right][x^{m+1} - W^{m+1}] \tag{5}$$

The maximum electric field at the junction may be obtained by setting $x = 0$ in (5). We then get

$$\varepsilon_m = -\left[\frac{qGW^{m+1}}{\kappa\varepsilon_0(m+1)}\right] \tag{6}$$

Integrating (5) once more, we find

$$\Psi(x) = \left[\frac{qG}{\kappa\varepsilon_0(m+1)}\right]\left[xW^{m+1} - \left(\frac{x^{m+2}}{m+2}\right) + A_2\right]$$

where the constant of integration A_2 can be set equal to zero by choosing $\Psi = 0$ at $x = 0$. We then get,

$$\Psi(x) = \left[\frac{qG}{\kappa\varepsilon_0(m+1)}\right]\left[xW^{m+1} - \left(\frac{x^{m+2}}{m+2}\right)\right] \tag{7}$$

The built-in junction potential Ψ_0 can be obtained from (7) by setting $x = W$. That is,

$$\Psi_0 = \frac{qGW^{m+2}}{\kappa\varepsilon_0(m+2)} \tag{8}$$

Finally, to derive an expression for the depletion layer capacitance, we observe that if we change the depletion layer width by dW, the change in the charge content per unit area of the depletion layer is given by

$$dQ = qN_d(W)dW = qGW^m dW \tag{9}$$

The corresponding change in the barrier potential can be obtained by differentiating (8) with respect to W. The result is given below:

$$d\Psi_0 = \left[\frac{qGW^{m+1}}{\kappa\varepsilon_0}\right]dW \tag{10}$$

Dividing (9) by (10), we find

$$C_j = \frac{dQ}{d\Psi_0} = \frac{\kappa\varepsilon_0}{W} \tag{11}$$

But from (8) we derive

$$W = \left[\frac{\kappa\varepsilon_0\Psi_0(m+2)}{qG}\right]^{1/(m+2)} \tag{12}$$

Combining (11) and (12) we find

$$C_j = \frac{k\varepsilon_0}{\left[\frac{k\varepsilon_0\Psi_0(m+2)}{qG}\right]^{1/(m+2)}}$$

or

$$\left(\frac{1}{C_j}\right)^{m+2} = \frac{(m+2)\Psi_0}{qG(\kappa\varepsilon_0)^{(m+1)}} \tag{13}$$

For a reverse biased pn junction, (13) may be rewritten as

$$\left(\frac{1}{C_j}\right)^{m+2} = \frac{(m+2)(\Psi_0 + V)}{qG(\kappa\varepsilon_0)^{(m+1)}} \tag{14}$$

Now if we choose $m = -(3/2)$, (14) reduces to

$$\left(\frac{1}{C_j}\right)^{1/2} = \left[\left(\frac{(\kappa\varepsilon_0)^{1/2}}{2qG}\right)(\Psi_0 + V)\right] = A(\Psi_0 + V) \tag{15}$$

for a reverse biased p^+n junction. Thus, if this C_j is used as a component of a LC tank circuit, its resonant frequency may be expressed as

$$f_r \propto \left(\frac{1}{C_j}\right)^{1/2} \propto V \tag{16}$$

if $V > \Psi_0$. Therefore the frequency of such a tank circuit can be changed by varying the reverse potential across the p^+n junction in a linear fashion.

2.2 Obtain expressions for the transition layer widths on the n the and p the sides and the differential junction capacitance of an abrupt p-i-n diode.

Solution

p-region The Poisson's equation in the p-region of a p-i-n diode may be expressed as

$$\frac{d^2\Psi_p(x)}{dx^2} = \frac{qN_a}{\kappa\varepsilon_0} \tag{1}$$

where κ denotes the dielectric constant of the semiconductor and $\varepsilon_0 = 8.854 \times 10^{-12}$ F/m is the permittivity of free space. Integrating (1) and defining $\varepsilon(x) = 0$ at $x = -x_p$, we get

$$\frac{d\Psi_p(x)}{dx} = \left(\frac{qN_a}{\kappa\varepsilon_0}\right)(x + xp) \tag{2}$$

Integrating (2) once more and taking $\Psi_p = 0$ at $x = 0$, we get

$$\Psi_p(x) = \left(\frac{qN_a}{\kappa\varepsilon_0}\right)\left(\frac{x^2}{2} + xx_p\right) \tag{3}$$

Putting $x = -x_p$, in (3), we get

$$\Psi_{p0} = -\left(\frac{qN_a x_p^2}{2\kappa\varepsilon_0}\right) \tag{4}$$

i-region In this case the Poisson's equation takes the following form:

$$\frac{d^2\Psi_i(x)}{dx^2} = 0 \tag{5}$$

Integrating (5), we get

$$\frac{d\Psi_i(x)}{dx} = A \tag{6}$$

Since the electric field at $x = 0$, must be continuous, we must get from (2)

$$\frac{d\Psi_i(x)}{dx} = \frac{qN_a x_p}{\kappa\varepsilon_0} \tag{7}$$

Integrating (7) once again, we find

$$\Psi i(x) = \left(\frac{qN_a x_p}{\kappa\varepsilon_0}\right) x \tag{8}$$

where the constant of integration is taken as zero, because $\Psi_i(x)$ is set to zero at $x = 0$.

n-region The Poisson's equation in this case may be written as

$$\frac{d^2\Psi_n(x)}{dx^2} = -\left(\frac{qN_d}{\kappa\varepsilon_0}\right) \tag{9}$$

Integrating (9) and identifying $[d\Psi_n(x)/dx] = 0$ at $x = x_n + W_i$ (where W_i is the width of the intrinsic layer), we get

$$\frac{d\Psi_n(x)}{dx} = -\left(\frac{qN_d}{\kappa\varepsilon_0}\right)[W_i + x_n - x] \tag{10}$$

Integrating once again, we find,

$$\Psi_n(x) = -\left(\frac{qN_d}{\kappa\varepsilon_0}\right)\left[W_i x + x x_n - \left(\frac{x^2}{2}\right) + B\right] \tag{11}$$

where B is a constant of integration. To evaluate it, we utilize the condition $\Psi_i(W_i) = \Psi_n(W_i)$. Comparing (8) and (11) we find

$$\left(\frac{qN_a x_p}{\kappa\varepsilon_0}\right) W_i = -\left(\frac{qN_d}{\kappa\varepsilon_0}\right)\left[W_i^2 + W_i x_n - \left(\frac{W_i^2}{2}\right) + B\right] \tag{12}$$

As the electric field within the intrinsic material has to be independent of x, the electric field at $x = 0$ and $x = W_i$ must be the same. We therefore derive from (2) and (10)

$$N_a x_p = N_d x_n \tag{13}$$

Such a result also follows on considering the space-charge layers on either side of the i-region and the overall charge neutrality of the semiconductor from the electrical point of view. Imposing (13) on (12), we get

$$B = -\left(\frac{W_i^2}{2}\right) \tag{14}$$

Substituting (14) in (11), we get

$$\Psi_n(x) = \left(\frac{qN_d}{\kappa\varepsilon_0}\right)\left[x(W_i + x_n) - \left(\frac{1}{2}\right)(x^2 + W_i^2)\right] \tag{15}$$

Setting $x = (W_i + x_n)$ in (15), we get

$$\Psi_{n0} = \left(\frac{qN_d x_n}{\kappa\varepsilon_0}\right)\left[\frac{W_i + x_n}{2}\right] \tag{16}$$

adding (4) and (16), we get for the total built-in potential of the p-i-n diode

$$\Psi_0 = |\Psi_{n0} + |\Psi_{po}| = \left(\frac{qN_a x_p^2}{2\kappa\varepsilon_0}\right) + \left(\frac{qN_d x_n W_i}{\kappa\varepsilon_0}\right) + \left(\frac{qN_d x_n^2}{2\kappa\varepsilon_0}\right)$$

or

$$\Psi_0 = \left(\frac{qN_d^2 x_n^2}{2\kappa\varepsilon_0 n^*}\right) + \left(\frac{qN_d x_n W_i}{\kappa\varepsilon_0}\right) \tag{17}$$

where n^* denotes the reduced doping density. The above equation may be expressed in the following quadratic form:

$$x_n^2 + \left(\frac{2n^* W_i x_n}{N_d}\right) + \left(\frac{2\kappa\varepsilon_0 n^* \Psi_0}{qN_d^2}\right) = 0 \tag{18}$$

The solution of (18) may now be expressed as

$$x_n = -\left(\frac{n^* W_i}{N_d}\right) + \left[\left(\frac{n^* W_i}{N_d}\right)^2 + \left(\frac{2\kappa\varepsilon_0 n^* \Psi_0}{qN_d^2}\right)\right]^{1/2} \tag{19}$$

The negative sign before the radical sign is inadmissible as x_n cannot be negative. Similarly, using $N_a x_p = N_d x_n$ in (17), one obtains

$$x_p = -\left(\frac{n^* W_i}{N_a}\right) + \left[\left(\frac{n^* W_i}{N_a}\right)^2 + \left(\frac{2\kappa\varepsilon_0 n^* \Psi_0}{qN_a^2}\right)\right]^{1/2} \tag{20}$$

Now if the transition layer width on the n-side changes by dx_n, the net change in the charge content per unit area of the depletion layer is given by

$$dQ_n = qN_d dx_n \tag{21}$$

Differentiating (19), we get

$$dx_n = \left(\frac{1}{2}\right)\left[\frac{d\Psi_0}{\left\{\left(\frac{n^* W_i}{N_d}\right)^2 + \left(\frac{2k\varepsilon e_0 n^* \Psi_0}{qN_d^2}\right)\right\}^{1/2}}\right]\left(\frac{2k\varepsilon_0 n^*}{qN_d^2}\right)$$

Combining the above equation with (19), we get

$$dx_n = \left[\frac{d\Psi_0}{\left(\frac{x_n + n^* W_i}{N_d}\right)}\right]\left(\frac{\kappa\varepsilon_0 n^*}{qN_d^2}\right)$$

Using this result in (21), we find

$$dQ_n = qN_d dx_n = \left(\frac{\kappa\varepsilon_0 n^*}{N_d}\right)\left[\frac{d\Psi_0}{\left(\frac{x_n + n^* W_i}{N_d}\right)}\right]$$

Therefore,

$$C_j = \frac{dQ_n}{d\Psi_0} = \frac{\kappa\varepsilon_0}{\left[W_i + \left(\frac{N_d x_n}{n^*}\right)\right]} = \frac{\kappa\varepsilon_0}{\left[W_i + \left(\frac{N_a x_p}{n^*}\right)\right]} \tag{22}$$

because $N_a x_p = N_d x_n$ for space-charge neutrality. Adding $N_a x_n$ to both sides of it, we get

$$N_a x_n + N_d x_n = N_a x_n + N_a x_p$$

i.e.

$$x_n(N_a + N_d) = N_a(x_n + x_p)$$

Dividing throughout by $N_a N_d$, we get

$$x_n\left[\frac{N_a + N_d}{N_a N_d}\right] = \left[\frac{x_n + x_p}{N_d}\right]$$

$$x_n + x_p = \frac{N_d x_n}{n^*}$$

Using this result in (22), we get

$$C_j = \frac{\kappa\varepsilon_0}{x_n + x_p + W_i} \tag{23}$$

This is the required expression for the capacitance of a *p-i-n* diode.

2.3 A Si *pn* junction has a linearly graded structure on the *p*-side with $(dN/dx) = 10^{19}\ \text{cm}^{-4}$ and a uniform doping of 3×10^{14}/c.c. on the *n*-side. If the depletion layer width is 0.8 μ m on the *p*-side at zero bias find the total width of the depletion layer, the built-in potential and the maximum field at zero bias.

Solution

p-side $x_p = 0.8\,\mu\text{m} = 8 \times 10^{-7}\,\text{m}, \kappa = 12, \varepsilon_0 = 8.854 \times 10^{-12}\,\text{F/m}, a = (dN/dx)$ $10^{19}\,\text{cm}^{-4} = 10^{27}\,\text{m}^{-4}$

$$\frac{d^2\Psi_p(x)}{dx^2} = -\left(\frac{\rho}{\kappa\varepsilon_0}\right) = -\left(\frac{qax}{\kappa\varepsilon_0}\right)$$

Integrating the above equation, we find

$$\frac{d\Psi_p(x)}{dx} = -\left(\frac{qax^2}{2\kappa\varepsilon_0}\right) + A_1$$

But since at $x = -x_p$, $[d\Psi_p(x)/dx] = 0$, we get $A_1 = (qax_p^2/2\kappa\varepsilon_0)$. Therefore, we get

$$\frac{d\Psi_p(x)}{dx} = -\left(\frac{qa}{2\kappa\varepsilon_0}\right)(x^2 - x_p^2) \tag{1}$$

Hence,

$$\varepsilon_{\max}(0) = -\left[\frac{d\Psi_p(x)}{dx}\right] = \frac{qax_p^2}{2\kappa\varepsilon_0} \tag{2}$$

Integrating (1) once more, we find

$$\Psi_p(x) = -\left(\frac{qa}{2\kappa\varepsilon_0}\right)\left[\left(\frac{x^3}{3}\right) - xx_p^2\right] \tag{3}$$

The constant of integration reduces to zero as the potential chosen to be zero at $x = 0$. Putting $x = -x_p$, we get

$$\Psi_{p0} = -\left(\frac{qax_p^3}{3\kappa\varepsilon_0}\right) \tag{4}$$

n-side The Poisson's equation in this case is

$$\frac{d^2\Psi_n(x)}{dx^2} = -\left(\frac{qN_d}{\kappa\varepsilon_0}\right) \tag{5}$$

Integrating (5), we get

$$\frac{d\Psi_n(x)}{dx} = -\left(\frac{qN_d x}{\kappa\varepsilon_0}\right) + A_2$$

Since, $[d\Psi_n(x)/dx] = 0$ at $x = x_n$, $A_2 = (qN_d x_n/\kappa\varepsilon_0)$. Therefore,

$$\frac{d\Psi_n(x)}{dx} = -\left(\frac{qN_d}{\kappa\varepsilon_0}\right)(x_n - x) \tag{6}$$

Hence,

$$\varepsilon_{\max}(0) = \frac{qN_d x_n}{\kappa\varepsilon_0} \tag{7}$$

Since the electric field has to be continuous across $x = 0$, comparing (2) and (7), we find that

$$\frac{qN_d x_n}{\kappa\varepsilon_0} = \frac{qax_p^2}{2\kappa\varepsilon_0}$$

or

$$N_d x_n = \frac{ax_p^2}{2} \tag{8}$$

Integrating (6) once more, we find

$$\Psi_n(x) = -\left(\frac{qN_d}{\kappa\varepsilon_0}\right)\left[\left(\frac{x_n^2}{2}\right) - xx_n\right] \tag{9}$$

because the potential is chosen to be zero at $x = 0$. Putting $x = x_n$ in (9), we find

$$\Psi_{n0} = -\left(\frac{qN_d}{\kappa\varepsilon_0}\right)\left(\frac{x_n^2}{2}\right) \tag{10}$$

Adding the magnitudes of (4) and (10), we find

$$\Psi_0 = |\Psi_{n0}| + |\Psi_{p0}| = \left(\frac{qN_d}{\kappa\varepsilon_0}\right)\left(\frac{x_n^2}{2}\right) + \left(\frac{qax_p^3}{3\kappa\varepsilon_0}\right) \tag{11}$$

But from (8), we find $x_n = (ax_p^2/2N_d)$. Using this result in (11), we get

$$\Psi_0 = \left(\frac{qax_p^3}{3\kappa\varepsilon_0}\right)\left[\left(\frac{3ax_p}{8N_d}\right) + 1\right] \tag{12}$$

Now making use of (12), we find

$$\Psi_0 = \left[\frac{1.6 \times 10^{-19} \times 10^2 \times 8 \times 10^{-7})^3}{3 \times 12 \times 8.854 \times 10^{-12}}\right]\left[\frac{3 \times 8 \times 10^{-7} \times 10^{27}}{(8 \times 3 \times 10^{20}) + 1}\right]$$

or $\quad \Psi_0 = 0.514$ V

We have noted that $x_n = (ax_p^2/2N_d) = 10^{27} \times (8 \times 10^{-7})^2/(2 \times 3 \times 10^{20}) = 1.067\ \mu$m and it is given that $x_p = 0.8\ \mu$m. Therefore, $W = |x_n| + |x_p| = (1.067 + 0.8)\ \mu\text{m} = 1.867\ \mu$m

Next,

$$\varepsilon_{\max}(0) = \frac{qN_d x_n}{\kappa\varepsilon_0} = \frac{1.6\times10^{-19}\times3\times10^{20}\times1.067\times10^{-6}}{12\times8.854\times10^{-12}}$$

$$= 4.82\times10^5 \text{ V/m}$$

Alternatively,

$$\varepsilon_{\max}(0) = \frac{qax_p^2}{2\kappa\varepsilon_0} = 1.6\times10^{-19}\times10^{27}\times\frac{(8\times10^{-7})^2}{2\times12\times8.854\times10^{-12}}$$

$$= 4.82\times10^5 \text{ V/m}$$

2.4 Consider a linearly graded *pn* junction where the impurity density in the transition region varies linearly with distance away from the junction. In other words, $N_1 = ax$ for $x < 0$ and $N_2 = bx$ for $x > 0$. Show that the depletion layer width W and the junction capacitance per unit area (C_T/A) are given by

$$W = \left[\frac{3\kappa\varepsilon_0 V(\sqrt{a}+\sqrt{b})^2}{qab}\right]^{1/3} \quad \text{and} \quad \frac{C_T}{A} = \frac{\kappa\varepsilon_0}{W}$$

respectively where $V = \Psi_0 \pm V_a$.

Solution

Since for $x < 0$, $N_1 = -ax$ (after assigning the negative sign to x), the Poisson's equation on the *n*-side may be written as

$$\frac{d^2\Psi_n(x)}{dx^2} = -\left(\frac{\rho}{\kappa\varepsilon_0}\right) = -\left(\frac{qN_1}{\kappa\varepsilon_0}\right) = \frac{qax}{\kappa\varepsilon_0} \tag{1}$$

Integrating (1), we find

$$\frac{d\Psi_n(x)}{dx} = \left(\frac{qax^2}{2\kappa\varepsilon_0}\right) + A_1 \tag{2}$$

Presuming $[d\Psi_n(x)/dx] = 0$ at $x = -x_n$, we find from (2), $A_1 = -(qax_n^2/2\kappa\varepsilon_0)$. Using this value in (2), we get

$$\frac{d\Psi_n(x)}{dx} = \left(\frac{qa}{2\kappa\varepsilon_0}\right)(x^2 - x_n^2) \tag{3}$$

Integrating once again, and selecting $\Psi_n(x) = 0$ at $x = 0$, we find

$$\Psi_n(x) = \left(\frac{qa}{2\kappa\varepsilon_0}\right)\left[\left(\frac{x^3}{3}\right) - xx_n^2\right] \tag{4}$$

Putting $x = -x_n$, in (3), we find

$$\Psi_{n0} = \frac{qax_n^3}{3\kappa\varepsilon_0} \tag{5}$$

For $x > 0$, $N_2 = bx$. The Poisson's equation in this case may be written down as

$$\frac{d^2\Psi_p(x)}{dx^2} = -\left(\frac{\rho}{\kappa\varepsilon_0}\right) = -\left(\frac{qN^2}{\kappa\varepsilon_0}\right) = -\left(\frac{qbx}{\kappa\varepsilon_0}\right) \tag{6}$$

Integrating (6), we find

$$\frac{d\Psi_p(x)}{dx} = -\left(\frac{qbx^2}{2\kappa\varepsilon_0}\right) + A^2$$

Since $[d\Psi_p(x)/dx] = 0$ at $x = x_p$, $A_2 = (qbx_p^2/2\kappa\varepsilon_0)$. Incorporating these results in the above relation, we find

$$\frac{d\Psi_p(x)}{dx} = \left(\frac{qb}{2\kappa\varepsilon_0}\right)(x_p^2 - x^2) \tag{7}$$

Integrating once more, we find

$$\Psi_p(x) = \left(\frac{qb}{2\kappa\varepsilon_0}\right)\left[xx_p^2 - \left(\frac{x^3}{3}\right)\right] \tag{8}$$

Since, $\Psi_p = 0$, at $x = 0$. Putting $x = x_p$ in (8), we get

$$\Psi_{p0} = \frac{qbx_p^3}{3\kappa\varepsilon_0} \tag{9}$$

The total built-in junction potential is then given by

$$\Psi_0 = |\Psi_{n0}| + |\Psi_{p0}| = \left(\frac{q}{3\kappa\varepsilon_0}\right)(ax_n^3 + bx_p^3) \tag{10}$$

For charge neutrality, the total ionized charge per unit area on the n-side (Q_n) must equal the total ionized charge on the p-side (Q_p). That is,

$$ax_n^2 = bx_p^2 \tag{11}$$

We may now rewrite (10) as follows:

$$\Psi_0 = \left(\frac{q}{3\kappa\varepsilon_0}\right)(ax_n^2x_n + bx_p^2x_p) = \left(\frac{q}{3\kappa\varepsilon_0}\right)(ax_n^2)(x_n + x_p)$$

or

$$\Psi_0 = \left(\frac{q}{3\kappa\varepsilon_0}\right)(ax_n^2)W \tag{12}$$

or

$$x_n = \left[\frac{3\kappa\varepsilon_0\Psi_0}{qaW}\right]^{1/2} \tag{13}$$

Similarly,

$$x_p = \left[\frac{3\kappa\varepsilon_0\Psi_0}{qbW}\right]^{1/2} \tag{14}$$

Adding (13) and (14), we get

$$x_n + x_p = W = \left[\frac{3\kappa\varepsilon_0\Psi_0}{qW}\right]^{1/2}\left[\frac{1}{\sqrt{a}} + \frac{1}{\sqrt{b}}\right]$$

Simplifying, we find

$$W = \left[\frac{3\kappa\varepsilon_0(\sqrt{a}+\sqrt{b})^2\Psi_0}{qab}\right]^{1/3} \tag{15}$$

When a voltage V_a is applied across the junction, the above expression may be rewritten as

$$W(V_a) = \left[\left\{\frac{3\kappa\varepsilon_0(\sqrt{a}+\sqrt{b})^2}{qab}\right\}(\Psi_0 \pm V_a)\right]^{1/3}$$

i.e.

$$W(V_a) = \left[\left\{\frac{3\kappa\varepsilon_0(\sqrt{a}+\sqrt{b})^2}{qab}\right\}V\right]^{1/3} \tag{16}$$

Next, the junction capacitance per unit area is given by

$$C_j = \frac{dQ_n}{d\Psi_0} = \frac{C_T}{A} \tag{17}$$

where

$$dQ_n = qN_1(x_n)dx_n \tag{18}$$

measures the change in the stored charge per unit area of the pn junction. From (13), we infer that

$$x_n = \left[\frac{3\kappa\varepsilon_0}{qa}\right]^{1/2}\left(\frac{\Psi_0}{W}\right)^{1/2}$$

From this and (15), we find

$$\frac{dx_n}{d\Psi_0} = \left[\frac{\kappa\varepsilon_0}{3\Psi_0 Wqa}\right]^{1/2} \tag{19}$$

Combining (17) and (19), we find

$$\frac{C_T}{A} = \frac{\kappa\varepsilon_0}{W} \tag{20}$$

Hence proved.

2.5 Calculate the impurity density and the lifetime of minority carriers on either side of a Ge *pn* junction whose depletion layer capacitance C per unit area varies as

$$\frac{1}{C^2} = 1.77 \times 10^{-8}\ [V(\text{volt}) + 0.314]\ (\text{cm})^4/(\mu\mu\text{F})^2$$

The diode reverse saturation current density at room temperature is $192\mu\ \text{A}/(\text{cm})^2$ and the diffusion capacitance per unit area at zero bias is $0.363\mu\text{F}/(\text{cm})^2$. ($n_i = 2.2 \times 10^{13}\ \text{cm}^{-3}$)

Solution

The depletion layer capacitance per unit area of an abrupt *pn* junction per unit area under reverse bias conditions is given by

$$\frac{1}{C^2} = \left[\frac{2}{\kappa\varepsilon_0 q n^*}\right](\Psi_0 + V) \tag{1}$$

Comparing (1) with the given expression, we find

$$\left[\frac{2}{\kappa\varepsilon_0 q n^*}\right] = 1.77 \times 10^{-8}(10^{-2}\ \text{m})^4/(10^{-12}\ \text{F})^2$$

or

$$\left[\frac{1}{\kappa\varepsilon_0 q n^*}\right] = 0.885 \times 10^{8}(\text{m})^4/(\text{F})^2 \tag{2}$$

and

$$\Psi_0 = 0.314\ \text{V} \tag{3}$$

From (2), it follows that

$$n^* = \frac{N_a N_d}{(N_a + N_d)} = (16 \times 8.854 \times 10^{-12} \times 1.6 \times 10^{-19} \times 0.885 \times 10^{8})^{-1}$$

$$= 4.987 \times 10^{20}/\text{m}^3 \tag{4}$$

But the built-in potential is given by

$$\Psi_0 = \left(\frac{kT}{q}\right)\ln\left(\frac{(N_a N_d)}{n_i^2)}\right)$$

From which we derive

$$N_a N_d = n_i^2 \exp\left(\frac{q\Psi_0}{kT}\right) \tag{5}$$

Substituting for appropriate parameters in (5), we get

$$N_a N_d = (2.2 \times 10^{19})^2 \exp\left(\frac{0.314}{0.026}\right) = 8.47 \times 10^{43}/\text{m}^6 \tag{6}$$

Combining (4) and (6), we get

$$N_a + N_d = \left[\frac{N_a N_d}{n^*}\right] = \frac{8.47 \times 10^{43}}{4.987 \times 10^{20}} = 1.7 \times 10^{23}/\text{m}^3 \qquad (7)$$

Also,

$$N_a - N_d = (N_a + N_d)^2 - 4(N_a N_d) = [(1.7 \times 10^{23})^2 - 4 \times 8.47 \times 10^{43}]^{1/2}$$
$$= 1.69 \times 10^{23}/\text{m}^3 \qquad (8)$$

Comparing (7) and (8) we notice that $N_a \gg N_d$. Therefore, we conclude that the p-side of the junction is more heavily doped than the n-side or it is a p^+n junction. We may therefore write

$$N_a = 1.7 \times 10^{23}/\text{m}^3$$

From (6), we next find

$$N_d = \frac{8.47 \times 10^{43}}{1.7 \times 10^{23}} = 4.98 \times 10^{20}\ \text{m}^3$$

Therefore, the reverse saturation current density of the p^+n junction may be written as

$$Js \cong J_{po} = 1.92\ \text{A/m}^2$$

But, the diffusion capacitance per unit area of the one-sided abrupt p^+n junction is given by

$$C_{d0} = \frac{qJ_{p0}\tau_p}{kT} = 0.363 \times 10^{-2}\ \text{F/m}^2$$

Therefore,

$$\tau_p = \frac{kTC_{d0}}{qJ_{p0}} = \frac{0.026 \times 0.363 \times 10^{-2}}{1.92} = 49.2\ \mu\text{s}$$

But,

$$\tau_p = \frac{p_n}{g_0} = \frac{n_i^2}{N_d g_0}$$

Therefore,

$$g_0 = \frac{n_i^2}{N_d \tau_p} \qquad (9)$$

Substituting the appropriate values of physical constants in (9), we find

$$g_0 = \frac{(2.2 \times 10^{19})^2}{4.98 \times 10^{20} \times 49.16 \times 10^{-5}} = 1.975 \times 10^{22}/\text{m}^3\ \text{s}$$

Thus,

$$\tau_n = \frac{n_p}{g_0} = \frac{n_i^2}{N_a g_0} = \frac{(2.2 \times 10^{19})^2}{1.7 \times 10^{23} \times 1.975 \times 10^{22}} = 0.144\ \mu\text{s}$$

2.6 Reverse biased diodes are frequently employed as electrically controllable variable capacitors. The depletion layer capacitance of an abrupt *pn* junction is 20 pF at 5 V. Compute the decrease in capacitance for 1 V increase in bias.

Solution

The depletion layer capacitance of a reverse biased *pn* junction may be expressed as

$$\frac{1}{C^2} = \left[\frac{2}{\kappa\varepsilon_0 q n^* A^2}\right](\Psi_0 + V) \tag{1}$$

where A denotes the junction area. Differentiating (1) with respect to V, we find

$$\frac{dC}{dV} = -\left[\frac{C^3}{\kappa\varepsilon_0 q n^* A^2}\right] \tag{2}$$

The negative sign in (2) indicates that C decreases with increase in V. Dividing (2) by (1), we get

$$\frac{dC}{dV} = -\left(\frac{C}{2V}\right) \tag{3}$$

for $V > \Psi_0$. Thus, if the applied voltage is 5 V and $C = 20$ pF, we get from (3),

$$\frac{dC}{dV} = \frac{-2\ pF}{V} \tag{4}$$

From (2) we get

$$\frac{1}{\kappa\varepsilon_0 q n^* A^2} = -\left[\frac{\left(\frac{dC}{dV}\right)}{C^3}\right] = \frac{2 \times 10^{-12}}{(20 \times 10^{-12})^3} = 2.5 \times 10^{20}\ \text{F}^{-2}\text{V}^{-1}. \tag{5}$$

Using (5), we get from (1) at a voltage of 6 V, $C = 18.257$ pF. Therefore, $\Delta C = (20 - 18.257) =$ 1.743 pF.

2.7 Derive an expression for the *pn* junction diode current as a function of the difference of the applied voltage and the built-in junction potential.

Solution

The Shockley equation giving the diode current is

$$I = Aq\left[\left(\frac{D_p p_n}{L_p}\right) + \left(\frac{D_n n_p}{L_n}\right)\right]\left[\exp\left(\frac{qV}{kT}\right) - 1\right] \tag{1}$$

The injected hole density on the n-side of the pn junction is given by

$$p(x_n) = p_n \exp\left(\frac{qV}{kT}\right) = n_i \exp\left[\left(\frac{q}{kT}\right)(\varphi_n - \Psi_n)\right] \exp\left(\frac{qV}{kT}\right) \tag{2}$$

Also, we know that

$$\Psi_0 = \left(\frac{kT}{q}\right) \ln\left[\frac{N_d N_a}{n_i^2}\right] = \left(\frac{kT}{q}\right) \ln\left[\frac{N_d N_a}{N_c N_v} \exp\left(\frac{E_G}{kT}\right)\right]$$

or

$$\Psi_0 = \left(\frac{kT}{q}\right) \ln\left[\frac{N_d N_a}{N_c N_v}\right] + \frac{E_G}{q}$$

or

$$E_G = q\Psi_0 - kT \ln\left[\frac{N_d N_a}{N_c N_v}\right]$$

or

$$\exp\left(\frac{-E_G}{kT}\right) = \exp\left(\frac{-q\Psi_0}{kT}\right) + \exp\ \ln\left[\frac{N_d N_a}{N_c N_v}\right] \tag{3}$$

Equation (1) may now be rewritten as

$$I = Aq\left[\left(\frac{D_p}{N_d L_p}\right) + \left(\frac{D_n}{N_a L_n}\right)\right] n_i^2 \left[\exp\left(\frac{qV}{kT}\right) - 1\right]$$

or

$$I = Aq\left[\left(\frac{D_p}{N_d L_p}\right) + \left(\frac{D_n}{N_a L_n}\right)\right] (N_c N_v) \exp\left(\frac{-E_G}{kT}\right)\left[\exp\left(\frac{qV}{kT}\right) - 1\right]$$

$$= Aq\left[\left(\frac{D_p}{N_d L_p}\right) + \left(\frac{D_n}{N_a L_n}\right)\right] (N_c N_v) \left[\exp\left(\frac{qV - E_G)}{kT}\right) - \exp\left(\frac{-E_G}{kT}\right)\right] \tag{4}$$

But from (3) we derive that

$$qV - E_G = q(V - \Psi_0) + kT \ln\left[\frac{N_d N_a}{N_c N_v}\right]$$

$$\exp\left[\frac{qV - E_G}{kT}\right] = \exp\left[\frac{q(V - \Psi_0)}{kT}\right] + \exp \ln\left[\frac{N_d N_a}{N_c N_v}\right] \tag{5}$$

Combining equations (3), (4) and (5),

$$I = Aq\left[\left(\frac{D_p}{N_d L_p}\right) + \left(\frac{D_n}{N_a L_n}\right)\right] (N_c N_v) \left[\exp\left\{\frac{-q(\Psi_0 - V)}{kT}\right\} - \exp\left\{-q\left(\frac{\Psi_0}{kT}\right)\right\}\right] \tag{6}$$

This is the required expression.

2.8 Find an expression for the electron current in the n-type material of a forward biased pn junction

Solution

The hole distribution on the n-side of a forward biased pn junction is given by

$$p_n(x) - p_n = p_n \left[\exp\left(\frac{qV}{kT}\right) - 1\right] \exp\left(\frac{-x}{L_p}\right) \tag{1}$$

where x has been measured from the space-charge layer boundary on the n-side. The diffusion current density at any point of the n-type material is given by

$$J_p(x) = -qD_p \left[\frac{\partial p_n(x)}{\partial x}\right] \tag{2}$$

Now from (1), we derive

$$\frac{\partial p_n(x)}{\partial x} = \left(\frac{-p_n}{L_p}\right)\left[\exp\left(\frac{qV}{kT}\right) - 1\right] \exp\left(\frac{-x}{L_p}\right) \tag{3}$$

Combining (2) and (3), we find

$$J_p(x) = -q\left(\frac{D_p p_n}{L_p}\right)\left[\exp\left(\frac{qV}{kT}\right) - 1\right] \exp\left(\frac{-x}{L_p}\right) \tag{4}$$

The electron current density over the n-layer is given by

$$J_n(x) = J - J_p(x) \tag{5}$$

Combining (4) and (5), we get

$$J_n(x) = q\left[\left(\frac{D_p p_n}{L_p}\right)(1 - e^{-x/Lp}) + \left(\frac{D_n n_p}{L_n}\right)\right]\left[\exp\left(\frac{qV}{kT}\right) - 1\right] \tag{6}$$

Multiplying (6) by the junction area, one gets the expression for the electron current.

2.9 Imagine a p^+n diode built with the n-layer of a very small length $L \ll L_p$. Solve the diffusion equation to obtain an expression for the minority carrier density stored over the n-layer. Also, derive an expression for the current crossing the junction.

Solution

The d.c. diffusion equation for holes in the n-region is expressed as

$$\frac{\partial^2 p(x)}{\partial x^2} = \frac{\{p(x) - p_n\}}{L_p^2} \tag{1}$$

where $L_p = (D_p\tau_p)^{1/2}$ measures the diffusion length in the n-region. The solution of the standard differential equation, given in (1) is

$$p(x) - p_n = A\exp\left(\frac{-x}{L_p}\right) + B\exp\left(\frac{x}{L_p}\right) \tag{2}$$

where A and B are constants whose values may be determined from boundary conditions. When $L \gg L_p$, it is customary to presume that $B = 0$, as the excess minority carriers cannot increase indefinitely with the increase in distance. But, for $L \ll L_p$, there is no justification for ignoring B. To determine these constants, we notice that at $x = 0$ (the transition region boundary on the n-side) $p(x_n) = p_n \exp(qV/kT)$. From (2), we therefore, obtain

$$A + B = p(x_n) - p_n \tag{3}$$

At the other extremity of the n-layer, (2), however predicts that

$$A\exp\left\{\frac{-(L-x_n)}{L_p}\right\} + B\exp\left\{\frac{(L-x_n)}{Lp}\right\} = 0 \tag{4}$$

where the length, L of the n-layer is measured from the centre of the junction. While writing (4), it is presumed that all the injected holes recombine on the surface of the n-layer. From (4), it therefore follows that

$$B = -A\left[\frac{\exp\left\{\frac{-(L-x_n)}{L_p}\right\}}{\exp\left\{\frac{(L-x_n)}{L_p}\right\}}\right] \tag{5}$$

Substituting this expression for B in (3), we get

$$A = [p(x_n) - p_n]\frac{\exp\left\{\frac{(L-x_n)}{L_p}\right\}}{\left[\exp\left\{\frac{(L-x_n)}{L_p}\right\} - B\exp\left\{\frac{-(L-x_n)}{L_p}\right\}\right]} \tag{6}$$

Next, combining (5) and (6) we get

$$B = -[p(x_n) - p_n]\frac{\exp\left\{\frac{-(L-x_n)}{L_p}\right\}}{\left[\exp\left\{\frac{(L-x_n)}{L_p}\right\} - B\exp\left\{\frac{-(L-x_n)}{L_p}\right\}\right]} \tag{7}$$

Substituting the expressions for A and B got from (6) and (7) in (2), we find

$$p(x) - p_n = \frac{p(x_n) - p_n}{\left[\exp\left\{\frac{(L-x_n)}{L_p}\right\} - B\exp\left\{\frac{-(L-x_n)}{L_p}\right\}\right]} x \left[\exp\left\{\frac{(L-x_n-x)}{L_p}\right\} - \exp\left\{\frac{-(L-x_n-x)}{L_p}\right\}\right] \tag{8}$$

This is the expression for the excess hole density stored in the short n-layer of a length L. It should however be remembered that we have presumed the excess injected holes to have decayed at the surface of the n-layer. Since the junction is of the p^+n type, the current may be regarded to consist mainly of holes which may be expressed as

$$J_p = -qD_p \left[\frac{\partial p(x)}{\partial x}\right]\Big|_{x=x_n} \tag{9}$$

But from (8), it follows that

$$\left[\frac{\partial p(x)}{\partial x}\right]\Big|_{x=x_n} = -\left[\frac{p(x_n) - p_n}{L_p}\right] \coth \left[\frac{L - x_n}{L_p}\right] \tag{10}$$

Combining (9) and (10) and remembering that $p(x_n) = p_n \exp(qV/kT)$, we get

$$J_p = q\left(\frac{D_p p_n}{L_p}\right)\left[\exp\left(\frac{qV}{kT}\right) - 1\right] \coth \left[\frac{L - x_n}{L_p}\right] \tag{11}$$

This is the required expression for the current density crossing the narrow base diode.

2.10 Show that the current flowing through a pn junction having very short n and p regions is independent of carrier lifetimes in those regions.

Solution

On the basis of the solution of the last problem, an the ideal diode equation representing the current flow through a very short base diode is given by

$$I = Aq\left[\left(\frac{D_p p_n}{L_p}\right) \coth\left(\frac{W_n}{L_p}\right) + \left(\frac{D_n n_p}{L_n}\right) \coth\left(\frac{W_p}{L_n}\right)\right]\left[\exp\left(\frac{qV}{kT}\right) - 1\right] \tag{1}$$

where $W_n = (W_1 - x_n)$ and $W_p = (W_2 - x_p)$; W_1 and W_2 are the widths of the neutral n and p regions respectively. When $W_n > 6L_p$ and $W_p > 6L_n$, (1) reduces to the ideal diode equation applicable to a large base diode. In a short base diode there is very little recombination in neutral n and p regions. Injected carriers mostly recombine at the ohmic contacts. When $W_n > 6L_p$ and $W_p > 6L_n$, coth terms in (1) may be expanded. Retaining only the first terms in the two expansions, (1) simplifies to

$$I = Aq\left[\left(\frac{D_p p_n}{W_n}\right) + \left(\frac{D_n n_p}{W_p}\right)\right]\left[\exp\left(\frac{qV}{kT}\right) - 1\right] \tag{2}$$

Thus, the current flowing through a short base diode is independent of the carrier lifetime in n and p regions.A short base diode may therefore be used for very high frequency rectification applications.

2.11 Show that the energy gap of a semiconductor can be estimated by measuring the temperature coefficient of the forward voltage of a *pn* diode at a constant current.

Solution

For relatively large forward biases, the *pn* junction current may be represented by the following equation:

$$I = I_s \exp\left(\frac{qV_F}{kT}\right) \tag{1}$$

Differentiating (1) with respect to T, one gets

$$\left(\frac{1}{I}\right)\left(\frac{dI}{dT}\right) = \left(\frac{1}{I_s}\right)\left(\frac{dI_s}{dT}\right) + \left(\frac{q}{kT}\right)\left[\left(\frac{dV_F}{dT}\right) - \left(\frac{V_F}{T}\right)\right] \tag{2}$$

But,

$$I_s = Aq\left[\left(\frac{D_p}{N_d L_p}\right) + \left(\frac{D_n}{N_a L_n}\right)\right](N_c N_v)\exp\left(\frac{-E_G}{kT}\right) \tag{3}$$

Since $(N_c N_v) \propto T^3$, (3) may be rewritten as

$$I_s = BT^3 \exp\left(\frac{-E_G}{kT}\right) \tag{4}$$

Differentiating (4) with respect to T, we get

$$\left(\frac{1}{I_s}\right)\left(\frac{dI_s}{dT}\right) = \left(\frac{1}{T}\right)\left[3 + \left(\frac{E_G}{kT}\right)\right] \tag{5}$$

Combining (2) and (5), we get

$$\left(\frac{1}{I}\right)\left(\frac{dI}{dT}\right) = \left(\frac{1}{T}\right)\left[3 + \left(\frac{E_G}{kT}\right)\right] + \left(\frac{q}{kT}\right)\left[\left(\frac{dV_F}{dT}\right) - \left(\frac{V_F}{T}\right)\right] \tag{6}$$

If the current is held constant i.e, $(dI/dT) = 0$. In this case, (6) reduces to

$$V_G = V_F - \left(\frac{3kT}{q}\right) - T\left(\frac{dV_F}{dT}\right) \tag{7}$$

Thus, by measuring the temperature dependence of the forward voltage at constant current, one may estimate the semiconductor energy gap $E_G = qV_G$.

2.12 For an abrupt *pn* junction, show that

$$\frac{dV_i}{dT} = \left[\frac{V_i - V_G}{T}\right] + \left(\frac{dV_G}{dT}\right) - \left(\frac{3k}{q}\right)$$

where V_i and V_G correspond to (E_i/q) and (E_G/q) respectively. For a Si *pn* junction with $N_d = 10^{15}\,\text{cm}^{-3}$, $N_a = 10^{18}\,\text{cm}^{-3}$, calculate (dV_i/dT) at 300 K and V_i at 305 K. Assume $(dV_G/dT) = -2.75 \times 10^{-4}\,\text{V(K)}^{-1}$; $n_i = 1.5 \times 10^{10}\,\text{cm}^{-3}$.

Solution

We know that $V_i = (kT/q)\ \ln\ (N_d N_a/n_i^2)$ where $n_i^2 = N_c N_v\ \exp\ (-E_G/kT)$.
Hence,

$$\frac{V_i - V_G}{T} = \left(\frac{k}{q}\right)\ \ln\ \left(\frac{N_d N_a}{N_c N_v}\right) \tag{1}$$

Differentiating (1) with respect to t, we get

$$\frac{dV_i}{dT} = \left(\frac{k}{q}\right)\ \ln\ \left(\frac{N_d N_a}{N_c N_v}\right) - \left(\frac{kT}{q}\right)\frac{d}{dT}[\ln\ (N_c N_v)] + \left(\frac{dV_G}{dT}\right) \tag{2}$$

Combining (1) and (2), we find

$$\frac{dV_i}{dT} = \left[\frac{V_i - V_G}{T}\right] + \left(\frac{dV_G}{dT}\right) - \left(\frac{kT}{q}\right)\frac{d}{dT}[\ln\ (N_c N_v)] \tag{3}$$

But, it may be shown that

$$\frac{d}{dT}[\ln\ (N_c N_v)] = \frac{3}{T} \tag{4}$$

Combining (3) and (4), one finds

$$\frac{dV_i}{dT} = \left[\frac{V_i - V_G}{T}\right] + \left(\frac{dV_G}{dT}\right) - \left(\frac{3k}{q}\right) \tag{5}$$

Now,

$$V_i(305\ \text{K}) = \left(\frac{kT}{q}\right)\ \ln\ \left(\frac{N_d N_a}{n_i^2}\right)$$

$$= \left[\frac{1.38 \times 10^{-23} \times 305}{1.6 \times 10^{-19}}\right] \ln \left[\frac{10^{15} \times 10^{18}}{2.25 \times 10^{20}}\right]$$

$$= 0.765\ \text{V}$$

Similarly,

$$V_i(300\ \text{K}) = 0.757\ \text{V}$$

Therefore from (3),

$$\frac{dV_i}{dT} = \left[\frac{0.757 - 1.12}{300}\right] + (-2.75 \times 10^{-4}) \left(\frac{3 \times 1.38 \times 10^{-23}}{1.6 \times 10^{-19}}\right)$$

$$= -17.3375 \times 10^{-4}\ \text{V/K}.$$

2.13 The donor and acceptor concentrations on n and p sides of a Si abrupt pn junction are equal to 10^{16} cm^{-3}.The whole of the semiconductor is uniformly illuminated such that the hole concentration in the neutral n-region rises to 10^{13} cm^{-3}. No current is allowed to flow out. What would be the reading of the voltmeter whose positive terminal is connected to the p-side and the negative terminal to the n-side at 300 K ($n_i(Si) = 1.5 \times 10^{10}$ cm^{-3}).

Solution

It is given that $n_n = 10^{16}/\text{cm}^3$, Therefore $p_n = (n_i^2/n_n) = (1.5 \times 10^{10})^2/10^{16} = 2.25 \times 10^4/\text{cm}^3$. Thus $p_n \ll n_n$. Now, from the law of the junction, we know that at the point x_n, one must have

$$n(x_n)p(x_n) = n_i^2 \exp\left(\frac{qV}{kT}\right) \tag{1}$$

where $n(x_n) = n_n + p(x_n)$. It is given that $p(x_n) = 10^{13}$ cm^{-3} whereas $n_n = 10^{16}$ cm^{-3}. Therefore $p(x_n) \ll n_n$. Hence $n(x_n) = n_n$. Using this in (1), we find

$$p(x_n) = \left(\frac{n_i^2}{n_n}\right) \exp\left(\frac{qV}{kT}\right) = p_n \exp\left(\frac{qV}{kT}\right)$$

or

$$V = \left(\frac{kT}{q}\right) \ln\left[\frac{p(x_n)}{p_n}\right] = 0.026 \ln\left[\frac{10^{13}}{2.25 \times 10^4}\right] \text{V}$$

or

$$V = 0.517\,\text{V}$$

2.14 A Ge sample with $n_0 = 10^{17}$ cm^{-3} is optically excited at 300 K such that $g_{op} = 10^{20}$ electron-hole pairs/cm^{3}s, $\tau_n = \tau_p = 10\mu$ s. What is the separation between the quasi Fermi levels?

Solution

We know that $\delta_n = \delta_p = g_{op}\tau_n = 10^{20} \times 10 \times 10^{-6} = 10^{15}$ cm^{-3}. Then, the hole density within the sample $p_0 = (n_i^2/n_0) = (2.10 \times 10^{20}/10^{17}) = 2.1 \times 10^3$ cm^{-3}.
Hence,

$$p = p_0 + \delta_p = 10^{15} = 2.1 \times 10^3 \exp\left[\frac{E'_F - E_F}{kT}\right]$$

or

$$\exp\left(\frac{\Delta E_F}{kT}\right) = \frac{10^{15}}{2.1 \times 10^3} = 4.76 \times 10^{11}$$

or

$$\frac{\Delta E_F}{kT} = 26.89$$

or

$$\Delta E_f = 0.699\,\text{eV} \tag{1}$$

2.15 Excess carriers are injected on one surface of a thin slice of a n-type Si with length L and extracted at the opposite face where $p_n(L) = p_{n0}$ (thermal equilibrium density of minority carriers). There is no electric field in the region $0 < x < L$. Derive expressions for the current densities at $x = 0$ and at $x = L$. Calculate the fraction of the injected current which reaches the opposite surface by diffusion. ($D_p = 50\,\text{cm}^2\text{s}^{-1}$; $\tau_p = 50 \times 10^{-6}$ s and $L = 0.1$ mm).

Solution

The injected holes diffuse according to the following law:

$$p_n(x) = p_n(0)\ \exp\left(\frac{-x}{L_p}\right) \tag{1}$$

Since at $x = L$, $p_n(x) = p_{n0}$, we have

$$p_{n0} = p_n(0)\ \exp\left(\frac{-L}{L_p}\right) \tag{2}$$

Therefore,

$$J_p(x) = -qD_p\left[\frac{dp(x)}{dx}\right] = q\left[\frac{p_n(0)}{L_p}\right]\ \exp\left(\frac{-x}{L_p}\right) \tag{3}$$

At $x = 0$,

$$J_p(0) = q\left[\frac{D_p p_n(0)}{L_p}\right] \tag{4}$$

At $x = L$,

$$J_p(L) = q\left[\frac{D_p p_n(L)}{L_p}\right] \tag{5}$$

Hence,

$$\left[\frac{J_p(L)}{J_p(0)}\right] = \left[\frac{p_n(L)}{p_n(0)}\right] = \exp\left(\frac{-L}{L_p}\right) \tag{6}$$

But,

$$L_p^2 = D_p\tau_p = 50 \times 50 \times 10^{-6}, \quad \text{or} \quad L_p = 50 \times 10^{-3}\ \text{cm} \tag{7}$$

Therefore, $[J_p(L)/J_p(0)] = \exp\,[-(0.1 \times 10^{-1})/(50 \times 10^{-3})] = \exp\,(-0.2) = 0.81873$. Thus, nearly 82% of the injected current reaches the other face by diffusion.

2.16 Assume a long p^+n diode which is illuminated uniformly, resulting in the generation of g_0 electron-hole pairs per m^3 per second at a bias of V volts. Derive an expression for the hole density distribution in the n-region.

Solution

If a steady state hole concentration generated due to irradiation is Δp, then according to the law of recombination, we have

$$-g_0 = \frac{dp}{dt} = -\left(\frac{\Delta_p}{\tau_p}\right) \quad \text{or} \quad \Delta_p = g_0\tau_p \tag{1}$$

As a result of irradiation, the thermal equilibrium density increases from p_n to $(p_n + g_0\tau_p)$. In the absence of any irradiation, the hole density distribution is given by

$$p(x) - p_n = p_n\left[\exp\left(\frac{qV}{kT}\right) - 1\right]\exp\left(\frac{-x}{L_p}\right) \tag{2}$$

where x is the distance measured from the transition region boundary on the n-side. To include the effect of irradiation, we have to rewrite it as

$$p(x) - p_n - g_0\tau_p = \left\{p_n\left[\exp\left(\frac{qV}{kT}\right) - 1\right] - g_0\tau_p\right\}\exp\left(\frac{-x}{L_p}\right)$$

$$p(x) - p_n = \left\{p_n\left[\exp\left(\frac{qV}{kT}\right) - 1\right] - g_0\tau_p\right\}\exp\left(\frac{-x}{L_p}\right) + g_0\tau_p \tag{3}$$

2.17 Calculate the avalanche breakdown voltage of a Ge pn step junction if $N_a = N_d = 10^{15}\,\text{cm}^{-3}$ when the critical field intensity for breakdown is 5×10^6 V/m. Repeat calculations if N_d is increased by a factor of 100. ($k = 16$, $n_i = 2.4 \times 10^{19}\,\text{m}^{-3}$)

Solution

For an abrupt pn junction, the maximum electric field intensity is given by

$$\varepsilon_m = \left[\frac{2qn^*\Psi_0}{\kappa\varepsilon_0}\right]^{1/2} \tag{1}$$

where

$$\Psi_0 = \left(\frac{kT}{q}\right)\ln\left[\frac{N_d N_a}{n_i^2}\right] \tag{2}$$

At a reverse bias of V volts, (1) modifies to

$$\varepsilon(V) = \left[\frac{2qn_*(\Psi_0 + V)}{\kappa\varepsilon_0}\right]^{1/2} \tag{3}$$

Dividing (3) by (1), we get

$$\varepsilon(V) = \varepsilon_m \left[1 + \left(\frac{V}{\Psi_0}\right)\right]^{1/2} \tag{4}$$

Thus, if V_b denotes the breakdown voltage, $\varepsilon(V_b)$ denotes the critical field intensity at breakdown. Now,

$$\Psi_0 = \left(\frac{kT}{q}\right) \ln \left[\frac{N_d N_a}{n_i^2}\right] = 0.026 \ln \left[\frac{10^{30}}{(2.4 \times 10^{13})^2}\right] = 0.19 \text{ V}$$

and

$$n^* = \left[\frac{N_d N_a}{N_d + N_a}\right] = \left(\frac{10^{15} \times 10^{15}}{2 \times 10^{15}}\right) = 5 \times 10^{20} \text{ m}^{-3}$$

Therefore,

$$\varepsilon_m = \left[\frac{2 \times 1.6 \times 10^{-19} \times 5 \times 10^{20} \times 0.19}{.16 \times 8.854 \times 10^{-12}}\right]^{1/2} = 4.63 \times 10^5 \text{ V/m}$$

To calculate the breakdown voltage, we next make use of (4) when it takes the following form:

$$\varepsilon(V_b) = \varepsilon_m \left[1 + \left(\frac{V_b}{\Psi_0}\right)\right]^{1/2}$$

or

$$5 \times 10^6 = 4.63 \times 10^5 \left[1 + \left(\frac{V_b}{0.19}\right)\right]^{1/2}$$

or

$$V_b = 21.96 \text{ V}$$

Next if $N_d = 10^{17}$ cm^{-3}, $N_a = 10^{15}$ cm^{-3}, $n^* = [N_d N_a/(N_d + N_a)] \cong N_a$, since $N_a \ll N_d$. Therefore $n^* = 10^{21}$ m^{-3} and $\Psi_0 = (kT/q) \ln [N_d N_a/n_i^2] = 0.026 \ln [10^{32}/(5.76 \times 10^{26})] =$ 0.31 V.

$$\varepsilon_m = \left[\frac{2qn^*\Psi_0}{\kappa\varepsilon_0}\right]^{1/2} = \left[\frac{2 \times 1.6 \times 10^{-19} \times 0.31 \times 10^{21}}{16 \times 8.854 \times 10^{-12}}\right]^{1/2} = 8.37 \times 10^5 \text{ V/m}$$

Hence,

$$\varepsilon(V_b) = \varepsilon_m \left[1 + \left(\frac{V_b}{\Psi_0}\right)\right]^{1/2}$$

yields

$$5 \times 10^6 = 8.37 \times 10^5 \left[1 + \left(\frac{V_b}{0.31}\right)\right]^{1/2}$$

or

$$V_b = 1.75 \text{ V}$$

2.18 For heterojunctions in the GaAs-AlGaAs system, the direct (Γ) band gap difference ΔE_G^{Γ} is accommodated approximately (2/3) in the conduction band and (1/3) in the valence band. For an Aluminium composition of 0.3, the AlGaAs is a direct semiconductor with $\Delta E_G^{\Gamma} = 1.85\,\text{eV}$ Sketch the band diagrams for two heterojunctions: (i) n^+-$Al_{0.3}Ga_{0.7}$ As on p^+-GaAs and (ii) n^+-$Al_{0.3}Ga_{0.7}$ As on n-GaAs.

Solution

Taking $\Delta E_G = 1.85(\text{AlGaAs}) - 1.43(\text{GaAs}) = 0.42\,\text{eV}$, the band offsets are $\Delta E_C = (2/3)\Delta E_G = (2/3) \times 0.14 = 0.28\,\text{eV}$; and $\Delta E_v = (1/3)\Delta E_G = (1/3)(0.42) = 0.14\,\text{eV}$.

2.19 The quarternary material $In_{1-x}Ga_xAs_yP_{1-y}$ is lattice matched to InP whenever $x = 0.45y$. The band gap is found to vary with y as $E_G(y) = 1.35 - 0.72y + 0.12y^2$. Find the composition of the active layer for semiconductor lasers designed to operate at 1.3 and 1.55μm wavelengths. What are the longest and shortest wavelengths at which these lasers can operate?

Solution

The band gaps corresponding to 1.3μm and 1.55μm respectively work out to be ($E_G = hc/\lambda$) 0.954 eV and 0.7998 eV respectively.
Now to solve for y we have to use

$$E_G(y) = 0.954 = 1.35 - 0.72y + 0.12y^2$$

Solving this quadratic equation for y one finds $y = 5.387$ and 0.6133. Since y need to be a fraction, the former value is inadmissible. Then $x = 0.45\ y = 0.45 \times 0.6133 = 0.276$. The formula of the alloy which would operate at 1.3μm would then be given by $In_{0.724}\,Ga_{0.276}\,As_{0.613}\,P_{0.387}$.
Similarly, for 1.55μ m, we may write

$$E_G(y) = 0.7998 = 1.35 - 0.72y + 0.12y^2$$

The solution of this quadratic equation yields, $y = 5.1$ or 0.9. As y has to be a fraction, the former value is inadmissible. Then $x = 0.45y = 0.45 \times 0.9 = 0.405$. The composition of the alloy capable of working at 155μm would then be given by $In_{0.595}Ga_{0.405}As_{0.9}P_{0.1}$.
We also see that y can vary between 0 and 1. Consequently, we find $E_G(0)$(maximum) $= 1.35\,\text{eV}$ and $E_G(1)$ (minimum) $= 0.75\,\text{eV}$. The shortest and the longest wavelengths are then given by $[h_c/E_G]$ and they respectively work out to be 0.918μ m (InP) and 1.653μ m ($In_{0.55}Ga_{0.45}As$).
Alternatively, we also have

$$0.12y^2 - 0.72y + (1.35 - E_G) = 0$$

The solution to this quadratic equation may be written as

$$y = \frac{0.72 \pm (0.48E_G - 0.128)^{1/2}}{0.24}$$

For y to be a fraction, we must have

$$0.72 - (0.48E_G - 0.128)^{1/2} < 0.24$$

which yields $E_G(\text{min}) = 0.746\,\text{eV}$, as obtained earlier.
We thus see that the lasing wavelength increases from 0.918μ m as the Arsenic concentration is increased from 0 and reaches a maximum value of 1.653μ m when a minimum Arsenic concentration is available in the alloy.
At the other extreme when $y = 0$, we find $E_G(\text{max}) = 1.35\,\text{eV}$.

2.20 A *pn* diode is made up of a material for which $E_G = 2\,\text{eV}$. Assuming a forward current of 1 mA flowing through the diode and assuming all the recombinations to be direct, calculate the light power emitted by the diode.

Solution

If J measures the current crossing the *pn* diode which is responsible for light emission, then

$$J = qv\Delta n = q\left(\frac{W}{\Delta t}\right)\Delta n \tag{1}$$

where the electrons of a density Δn negotiates the depletion layer of a width W in a time Δt .The recombination rate of electrons then follows from (1) to be

$$-\left(\frac{dn}{dt}\right) = \frac{J}{qW} = \frac{I}{AqW} \tag{2}$$

where A denotes the junction area. Presuming that every electron is responsible for the emission of a photon, (2) represents the number of radiative transitions per unit volume per unit time. Therefore, presuming that each transition releases $E_G = 2.0\,\text{eV}$ of energy, the net power emitted is given by

$$P' = \frac{IE_G}{AqW}\ \text{J/m}^3\text{s} \tag{3}$$

Hence, the light power emitted by the whole junction is given by

$$P = AWP' = \frac{IE_G}{q}\ \text{J/s} \tag{4}$$

Substituting the values of the appropriate parameters in (4), we get

$$P = \frac{10^{-3} \times 2 \times 1.6 \times 10^{-19}}{1.6 \times 10^{-19}}\ \text{J/s} = 2\,\text{mW}$$

2.21 Consider a Si *pn* junction solar cell of an area of $2\,\text{cm}^2$. If the dopings on both sides of the solar cell are $N_a = 1.7 \times 10^{16}\,\text{cm}^{-3}$, $N_d = 5 \times 10^{19}\,\text{cm}^{-3}$ and given that $\tau_n = 10\mu\,\text{s}$, $\tau_p = 0.5\mu\,\text{s}$, $\Delta_n = 9.3\,\text{cm}^2/\text{s}$, $\Delta_p = 2.5\,\text{cm}^2/\text{s}$ and $I_L = 95\,\text{mA}$, calculate the open circuit voltage and the maximum power output of the solar cell at room temperature.

Solution

The area of the solar cell $= A = 2\,\text{cm}^2 = 2 \times 10^{-4}\,\text{m}^2$. Therefore, the reverse saturation current is

$$I_s = Aq\left[\left(\frac{D_p}{\tau_p}\right)^{1/2}\left(\frac{1}{N_d}\right) + \left(\frac{D_n}{\tau_n}\right)^{1/2}\left(\frac{1}{N_a}\right)\right] n_i^2 \tag{1}$$

Substituting the values of the appropriate parameters in the above equation, we find $I_s = 3.816 \times 10^{-13}$ A.

The open circuit voltage is given by

$$V_{\text{OC}} = \left(\frac{kT}{q}\right) \ln\left[1 + \left(\frac{I_L}{I_S}\right)\right] \tag{2}$$

Substituting the values of the physical parameters in (2), we find, $V_{\text{OC}} = 0.622$ V. To calculate the maximum power output we use the following equation

$$P_{\text{mp}} = \frac{qI_S V_{\text{mp}}^2}{kT}\left[\frac{1 + \left(\dfrac{I_L}{I_S}\right)}{1 + \left(\dfrac{qV_{\text{mp}}}{kT}\right)}\right] \tag{3}$$

where V_{mp} is given by

$$\exp\left(\frac{qV_{\text{mp}}}{kT}\right) = \left[\frac{1 + \left(\dfrac{I_L}{I_S}\right)}{1 + \left(\dfrac{qV_{\text{mp}}}{kT}\right)}\right] = \frac{2.49 \times 10^{10}}{1 + \left(\dfrac{qV_{\text{mp}}}{kT}\right)} \tag{4}$$

To calculate V_{mp}, we first neglect it in the denominator of (4). Obtaining a value for it, we use it next in the denominator of (4) to obtain a better value V_{mp}. Repeating this procedure a number of times, we can derive a consistent value of the maximum power voltage. We thus find $V_{\text{mp}} = 0.54$ V in this case. We next use it in (3) to obtain the maximum power output of the solar cell, which works out to be 49.45 mW.

2.22 Holes are injected into the long n-region of a forward biased p^+n diode. The current is I at $t = 0$ and decays exponentially as $I(t) = I\,\exp(-t/\tau_p)$.

(a) Find the charge stored in the n-layer as a function of time;

(b) assuming $V(t) > (kT/q)$, also derive an expression for it.

Solution

The minority hole charge stored in the neutral n-region is given by

$$Q_p = Aqp_nL_p\left[\exp\left(\frac{qV}{kT}\right)-1\right] \tag{1}$$

whereas the diode current in the asymmetric p^+n diode is given by

$$I = Aq\left(\frac{D_p p_n}{L_p}\right)\left[\exp\left(\frac{qV}{kT}\right)-1\right] \tag{2}$$

Dividing (1) by (2), we get

$$I = \frac{Q_p}{\tau_p} = -\left(\frac{dQ_p}{dt}\right) \tag{3}$$

if Q_p decreases with t. Equation (3) in this case reduces to

$$\left(\frac{dQ_p}{dt}\right)+\left(\frac{Q_p}{\tau_p}\right)=0 \tag{4}$$

But is given that

$$I(t) = -\left(\frac{dQ_p}{dt}\right) = I\exp\left(\frac{-t}{\tau_p}\right)$$

Using this relation in (4), we find

$$Q_p(t) = I\tau_p\exp\left(\frac{-t}{\tau_p}\right) \tag{5}$$

Equation (5) gives the stored charge in the n-layer as a function of time. Next, to arrive at the expression for the time-dependent diode voltage, we combine (2) and (5), to obtain

$$Q_p(t) = I\tau_p\exp\left(\frac{-t}{\tau_p}\right) = Aqp_nL_p\left[\exp\left\{\frac{qV(t)}{kT}\right\}-1\right] \tag{6}$$

Presuming $V(t) \gg (kT/q)$, the above expression simplifies to

$$V(t) = -\left(\frac{kT}{q}\right)\left(\frac{t}{\tau_p}\right)+\left(\frac{kT}{q}\right)\ln\left[\frac{I\tau_p}{Aqp_nL_p}\right] \tag{7}$$

Thus, the diode voltage should decay linearly with t.

2.23 A pn diode at 300 K has a reverse saturation current of 5μA. Find the maximum and the minimum currents crossing the pn junction when a voltage wave 0.1 sin 314t is superimposed on a 2 V d.c. source applied to the diode. ($\tau_n = \tau_p = 100\mu$s)

Solution

The d.c. flowing through the diode at a forward bias of V_0 volts is given by

$$I_{dc} = I_s\left[\exp\left(\frac{qV_0}{kT}\right) - 1\right] \quad (1)$$

The alternating component of the current crossing the diode, on the other hand, is given by

$$I_{ac} = \left(\frac{qV_a}{kT}\right)\left[(I_{p0} + I_{n0}) + \left(\frac{j\omega}{2}\right)(\tau_p I_{p0} + \tau_n I_{n0})\right] \quad (2)$$

It is given that $I_s = (I_{p0} + I_{n0}) = 5 \times 10^{-6}$A. Substituting for I_s and V_0 in (1), we get

$$I_{dc} = 5 \times 10^{-6}\left[\exp\left(\frac{0.2}{0.026}\right) - 1\right] = 10.957\,\text{mA}$$

Similarly, $I_{ac} = (0.1/0.026)[(5 \times 10^{-6}) + j(314/2)(100 \times 10^{-6} \times 5 \times 10^{-6} \times 2)] = 0.019\,\text{mA}$

$$I_{max} = (I_{dc} + I_{ac}) = 10.957 + 0.019 = 10.976\,\text{mA}$$

and $$I_{min} = (I_{dc} - I_{ac}) = 10.957 - 0.019 = 10.938\,\text{mA}$$

2.24 Two Si *pn* diodes are connected in series opposition. A 0.05 V battery is impressed upon this arrangement. Find the voltage drop across each diode at room temperature.

Solution

To begin with we presume that the entire voltage drop is available across the reverse biased second diode. Hence,

$$I = I_s\left[\exp\left(\frac{qV_2}{kT}\right) - 1\right] = I_s\left[\exp\left(\frac{-0.05}{0.026}\right) - 1\right] = -0.853I_s$$

Next, let us presume that the voltage drop over the first diode is V_1. Then

$$0.853I_s = I_s\left[\exp\left(\frac{-V_1}{0.026}\right) - 1\right]$$

This yields, $V_1 = 0.016$ V. Hence $V_2 = 0.050 - 0.016 = 0.034$ V. Using this value as the drop across the second diode, the current flowing in the circuit is obtained as $I = 0.73I_s$. Using this current also to flow through the diode 1, one finds, $V_1 = 0.0143$ V. Hence, our new $V_2 = (0.05 - 0.0143)$ V $= 0.0357$ V.

Using this as the diode 2 voltage, the current flowing through it is $I = -0.747I_s$. In order that this current should also flow through the diode 1, the potential drop across it works out to be $V_1 = 0.014$ V. This gives the new $V_2 = (0.05 - 0.014)$ eV $= 0.036$ eV. Repeated calculations yield that these are the most consistent values of the diode voltages.

2.25 A voltage $200\sin(100\pi\, t)$ is applied to a half wave *pn* diode voltage rectifier. Assuming the load resistance to be $10\,\text{k}\,\Omega$ and the diode forward resistance to be negligible, calculate : (i) the maximum current flowing, (ii) the average value of the current ; (iii) its r.m.s. value; (iv) its rectifier efficiency; (v) form factor; (vi) ripple factor; and (vii) the voltage regulation, taking the diode resistance to be $2.5\,\Omega$

Solution

(i) The maximum diode current is

$$I_m = \frac{V_m}{(r_d + R)} = \frac{200}{10 \times 10^3} = 20\,\text{mA}$$

(ii) The average diode current is

$$I_{\text{av}} = \left(\frac{1}{2\pi}\right) \int_0^{\pi} I_m \sin\, \alpha\, d\alpha = \frac{I_m}{\pi} = \frac{20}{\pi} = 6.37\,\text{mA}$$

(iii)

$$I_{\text{rms}} = \left[\left(\frac{I_m^2}{2\pi}\right) \int_0^{\pi} \sin^2 \alpha\, d\alpha \right]^{1/2} = \frac{I_m}{2} = \frac{20}{2} = 10\,\text{mA}$$

(iv) The rectifier efficiency, $\eta = \left(\frac{P_{\text{dc}}}{P_{\text{ac}}}\right) \times 100\%$. Now $P_{\text{dc}} = I_{\text{av}}^2\, R$ and $P_{\text{ac}} = I_{\text{rms}}^2$ R. Therefore $\eta = 40.58\%$

(v) Form factor $= \dfrac{I_{rms}}{I_{av}} = \dfrac{10}{6.37} = 1.57$

(vi) Ripple factor $= \gamma = \dfrac{I'_{rms}}{I_{av}} = \dfrac{(I_{\text{rms}}^2 - I_{\text{av}}{}^2)^{1/2}}{I_{\text{av}}} = 1.21$

(vii) Voltage regulation $= [\{E_{\text{dc}}\,(\text{no load}) - E_{\text{dc}}\,(\text{full load})\}/E_{\text{dc}}\,(\text{full load})]$

Now, $E_{\text{dc}}(\text{no load}) = \left(\dfrac{E_m}{\pi}\right) = \left(\dfrac{200}{\pi}\right) = 63.66\,\text{V}$ and $E_{\text{dc}}(\text{full load}) = E_{\text{dc}}\,(\text{no load}) - I_{\text{av}} r_{\text{d}} = 63.64\,\text{V}$.
Hence the percentage voltage regulation = 0.0314%

Exercises

2.1 Consider a p-i-n diode which has a central region made up of an intrinsic material sandwiched between p and n regions and d as the width of the intrinsic layer. Show that the junction capacitance is equivalent to two capacitances in series or $(1/C_T) = (d/\varepsilon A) + (W/\varepsilon A)$ where W is the sum of the transition layer widths on n and p sides. Also, verify the relation:

$$V = V_d \pm V_a = \left(\frac{Qd}{\varepsilon}\right) + (N_1 + N_2)\frac{Q^2}{2e\varepsilon}N_1 N_2$$

where Q denotes the charge stored per unit area of the junction and N_1 and N_2 are the doping densities on either side of the junction, e = electronic charge and ε = dielectric constant of the material.

2.2 Show that the barrier height Ψ_0 of an abrupt pn junction is given by

$$q\Psi_0 = E_G - kT\ \ln\left[\frac{N_C N_V}{N_a N_d}\right]$$

where the symbols have their usual significance.

2.3 The central region of a Si p-π-n diode is 200 μm wide and has a resistivity of 1 kΩcm. The doping concentration in each side of the p^+ and n^+ regions are 10^{18} cm^{-3}. Calculate the zero bias capacitance and obtain an expression for the rate of change of the capacitance with voltage at zero bias.

[0.53 μ F/m^2; -0.0447 pF/V]

2.4 A Ge pn junction is made up of an alloyed p-region with a hole concentration of 2×10^{19} cm^{-3} and a base n-region of 1 Ωcm resistivity. Given $N_C = 1.05 \times 10^{19}$ cm^{-3} and the Fermi level on the p-side coincides with E_V. Calculate the built-in voltage V_d. Also, compute the width W of the space-charge region and the junction capacitance per unit area (C_T/A) at zero applied bias. What is the ratio of the extensions of space-charge regions into n and p layers?

[0.46 V; 71.35 μ m; 198.5μ F/ m^2; 1.25×10^4]

2.5 Calculate the junction capacitance per unit area (C_T/A) in a Ge pn diode with $N_a = 2\times 10^{19}\ \text{cm}^{-3}$ on the p-side and $N_d = 10^{15}\ \text{cm}^{-3}$ on the n-side for (a) forward bias of 0.2 V, (b) no applied voltage and (c) reverse voltage of 10 V. Also locate the positions of the maximum electric field in the junction and calculate its values for cases (a), (b) and (c).

[1.1886 Fd; 158.7 μ F; 32.93 μ F; 7.51 × 10^5 V/m; 10^6 V/m; 4.858 × 10^6 V/m]

2.6 Show that for an abrupt Si n^+p junction, the depletion layer capacitance is given by $C = 2.9\times 10^{-7}(N_a/\Psi_0)^{1/2}\ \text{pF/cm}^2$.

2.7 An abrupt Si pn junction at 300 K has an area of 1 mm^2. The measured junction capacitance C_j as a function of the bias is given by

$$\left(\frac{1}{C_j}\right)^2 = \left(\frac{5}{11}\right) \times 10^6\ (3 - 5V_a)$$

where C_j is expressed in μ F and V_a in volts. (a) Determine the built-in junction potential and the depletion layer width at zero bias. (b) Also calculate the doping concentration on two sides of the junction.

[0.6 V; 12.4 cm; $N_a = 4.56\times 10^{19}\ \text{m}^{-3}$; $N_d = 5.2\times 10^{10}\ \text{m}^{-3}$]

2.8 A Si abrupt pn junction has $N_a = 3\times 10^{18}\ \text{cm}^{-3}$ on the p-side and an area of $1.6\times 10^{-3}\ \text{cm}^2$. The junction capacitance is 18 pF at a reverse bias of 3.2 V and 12 pF at 8.2 V. Calculate the built-in voltage and the donor concentration on the n-side.

[0.8 V; $1.73\times 10^{15}\ \text{cm}^{-3}$]

2.9 Show that the hole component of the pn junction current can be calculated by integrating the charge stored in the steady state hole distribution and then dividing the charge by the hole lifetime τ_p.

2.10 For a narrow base diode, show that the current due to recombination at the ohmic contact is

$$I = \left[qA\left(\frac{D_p p_n}{L_p}\right)\ \text{cosech}\left[\frac{L - x_n}{L_p}\right]\right]\left[\exp\left(\frac{qV}{kT}\right) - 1\right]$$

2.11 For an ideal abrupt p^+n junction with $N_d = 10^{16}\ \text{cm}^{-3}$, find the stored minority carriers in the neutral n-region when a forward bias of 1V is applied. The length of the neutral n-region is 1 μ m and the diffusion length of holes is 5 μ m.

[$4.29\times 10^2\ \text{Coul/m}^2$]

2.12 Consider a *pn* diode which has identical dopings on both sides. Find the ratio of the hole to electron currents if both *p* and *n* regions happen to be extremely narrow. How is this ratio changed if both sides are wide?

$[(D_p/D_n); (D_p\tau_n/D_n\tau_p)^{1/2}]$

2.13 Show that the reverse saturation current in an ideal *pn* diode varies with temperature approximately as $I_S(T) = A(T)\ \exp(mT_C)$ where T_C measures the temperature in centigrades. Calculate $A(T)$ and m.

$[Aq\{(D_p/L_pN_d) + (D_n/L_nN_a)\}\exp(-E_G/273k); \{(E_G/(273)^2k)T_C\}]$

2.14 Assume that a *pn* junction has $N_a = 10^{17}\ \text{cm}^{-3}$ and $N_d = 10^{15}\ \text{cm}^{-3}$. Let it contain $10^{15}\ \text{cm}^{-3}$ of traps located at 0.02 eV above the intrinsic Fermi level of Si with $\sigma_n = \sigma_p = 10^{-15}\ \text{cm}^2$. If $V_{\text{th}} = 10^7$ cms/s, calculate the generation current at ±0.5 V. Also calculate the total forward and reverse currents for a junction area of $10^{-4}\ \text{cm}^2$.

$[2.2176 \times 10^{-2}\ \text{A/m}^2; 1.19 \times 10^{-2}\ \text{A/m}^2; 1.75\ \text{nA}; 0.28\ \text{nA}]$

2.15 A symmetrical abrupt Ge *pn* junction has an impurity concentration of 10^{15} atoms per cm^3 on both sides. Calculate the avalanche breakdown voltage, if the impurity concentration on the *n*-side remains the same but becomes $10^{19}\ \text{cm}^{-3}$ on the *p*-side.

[287.178 V]

2.16 Consider an abrupt Si p^+n junction diode at 300 K whose breakdown voltage is given by $V_B = (b/2\alpha_0)\ \exp(b/\varepsilon_{\text{mb}})$. Assuming $\alpha_0 = 1.2 \times 10^7\ \text{cm}^{-1}$ and $b = 1.5 \times 10^6\ \text{V cm}^{-1}$, calculate the doping concentration in the *n*-region that will make $V_B = 36$ V.

$[5.13 \times 10^{15}\ \text{cm}^{-3}]$

2.17 If the Zener breakdown voltage is V_z and it occurs at a peak field ε_z, show that $V_z = (k\varepsilon_0\varepsilon_z^2/2qN_a)$ where N_a denotes the acceptor density of an n^+p diode.

2.18 The ionization coefficient in GaAs can be approximated by $\alpha_n = \alpha_p = (\varepsilon_b/4)\ 6 \times 10^{-26}\ \text{cm}^{-1}$ where ε is expressed in V/cm. Calculate the breakdown voltage of a GaAs p^+n junction with a doping of $6 \times 10^{15}\ \text{cm}^{-3}$ on the lightly doped *n*-side.

[140 V]

2.19 A GaAs laser diode is required to lase at 8600 Å. The absorption coefficient of the semiconductor is $0.5\ \text{m}^{-1}$. Presuming the reflection coefficient and the probability of photon emission to be unity, calculate the threshold current density for lasing at $T = 0$ K. (Presume $W = 80$ Å and $\Delta\nu = 0.01\ \nu$)

$[0.1706\ \text{A/m}^2]$

2.20 The band gap of $Pb_{1-x}Sn_xTe$ at 77 K is found to vary with the mole fraction x as E_G (eV) = $0.22 - 0.55\,x$. At what wavelength would such a Pb salt laser operate when $x = 0.2$?

[11.27 μ m]

2.21 Calculate the optical frequencies for semiconductor lasers operating at 0.8, 1.55 and 10 μ ms. What should the bandgap of the active materials be in each case assuming that the photon energy nearly equals the bandgap energy?

[1.55 eV; 0.80 eV; 0.124 eV]

2.22 A Si solar cell has a short-circuit current of 100 mA and an open circuit voltage of 0.8 V under full illumination. The fill factor is 0.7. What is the maximum power delivered to a load by this cell?

[56 mW]

2.23 Consider a Si *pn* junction solar cell of an area 2 cm^2. If the dopings on both sides of the solar cell are $N_a = 1.7 \times 10^{16}\,\text{cm}^{-3}$, $N_d = 5 \times 10^{19}\,\text{cm}^{-3}$ and given that $\tau_n = 10\,\mu\text{s}$, $\tau_p = 0.5\,\mu\text{s}$, $D_n = 9.3\,\text{cm}^2/\text{s}$, $D_p = 2.5\,\text{cm}^2/\text{s}$ and $I_L = 95$ mA. Calculate the open-circuit voltage and the maximum power output of the solar cell, all at room temperature. ($n_i = 1.45 \times 10^{16}/\text{m}^3$)

[0.622 V; 44.38 mW]

2.24 The reverse saturation current density of a particular Si *pn* junction is 10 μ A. The open-circuit voltage developed when such a junction is used as a solar cell is 0.26 V. Calculate: (i) the short-circuit current of the junction, (ii) the current and the voltage under maximum power transfer conditions, (iii) the maximum power that may be developed within the solar cell, (iv) conversion efficiency when $P_{\text{in}} = 270$ mW and (v) the fillfactor of the cell.

[220 mA; 0.203 V and 192.08 mA; 38.99 mW; 14.44%, 0.68]

2.25 Consider a Si n^+p junction solar cell with 1 cm^2 area having $N_a = 2 \times 10^{18}\,\text{cm}^{-3}$, $\tau_n = 4 \times 10^{-7}$ s, $D_n = 50\,\text{cm}^2.\text{s}^{-1}$ and $G = 2.7 \times 10^{19}\,\text{cm}^{-3}\text{s}^{-1}$. Calculate the open-circuit voltage V_{OC}. Assume $T = 300$ K and $N_d = 2 \times 10^{19}\,\text{cm}^{-3}$.

[0.46 V]

2.26 A 1 cm^2 area of a Si *pn* junction solar cell has its dark current given by $10^{-8}[\exp(V_j/1.5V_T) - 1]$ A. The cell has a $I_L = 38$ mA under AMO condition at 300 K. Determine the maximum output power and the maximum value of the load resistance. Also determine the fill factor and the cell efficiency assuming 20% power loss due to the reflection at the surface.

[0.32 V; 8.94Ω; 0.77; 0.106%]

2.27 One *pn* junction solar cell has a $V_{OC} = 0.5$ V and an $I_L = 1$ A. Second cell has a $V_{OC} = 0.6$ V and an $I_L = 0.8$ A. Assume that both cells obey the ideal diode equation. Calculate the values of V_{OC} and I_{SC} when the two diodes are connected in (a) parallel and in (b) series.

[0.47 V, −1.8 A; 1057 V, 0.9 A]

2.28 Consider a n^+p junction solar cell made on a 150μ m thick *p*-Si substrate that has $L_n = 600\ \mu$ m. One cell exhibits an ohmic contact on the back while the other has a perfectly reflecting contact at the back. The first cell has a $V_{OC} = 0.55$ V and $I_L = 1.8$ A. If the second cell has $I_L = 2$ A, calculate the V_{OC} for this cell.

[0.567 V]

2.29 A Read diode is designed to generate oscillations at 10^{11} Hz. Presuming the carrier drift velocity to be 10^5 m/s, calculate the width of the intrinsic layer. A phase difference of $(\pi/4)$ may be presumed to be introduced during the avalanche process.

[0.75 μ m]

2.30 A forward current of 1 mA flowing through a p^+n junction is suddenly reversed. The reverse saturation current density is 1 μ A. Calculate the storage time. ($\tau_p = 5\ \mu$s).

[34.54 s.]

2.31 An abrupt p^+n junction long base diode is carrying a steady forward current I_F for $t < 0$. For $t > 0$, the diode currrent decays as $I_F \exp(-t/\tau_p)$. Determine the stored charge $Q_p(t)$. Also calculate the diode voltage as a function of time.

$[Q_p(t) = I_F\tau_p \exp(-t/\tau_p);\ V(t) = (kT/q) \ln[1 + \{I_F \exp(-t/\tau_p)/I_R\}]$

2.32 Consider an abrupt Si p^+n junction long base diode with a forward current of 2 mA at 300 K. The hole lifetime in the *n*-region is 10^{-7} s. Neglecting the depletion layer capacitance, calculate the diode impedances at frequencies of 140 kHz, 1.2 MHz and 350 MHz.

[12.96 Ω, 12.15 Ω, 0.118 Ω]

2.33 Ignoring the depletion layer capacitance, calculate the impedance of a Si abrupt p^+n junction diode at 500 MHz. The diode is carrying a forward current of 1 mA and has the following parameters: $W_n = 5\ \mu$ m, $\tau_p = 10^{-6}$ s, $D_p = 12\ \text{cm}^2/\text{s}$, $A = 3 \times 10^{-4}\ \text{cm}^2$ and $T = 300$ K. Taking $N_d = 2 \times 10^{15}\ \text{cm}^{-3}$ and the built-in voltage = 0.7 V, calculate the voltage at which the depletion layer capacitance becomes the diffusion capacitance. ($n_i = 1.45 \times 10^{16}\ \text{m}^{-3}$)

[0.98 V]

2.34 In a forward biased Si p^+n diode carrying a current of 1 mA, the diffusion capacitance is 1 μ F. Calculate the lifetime of holes in the n-region.

[26 μ s]

2.35 Show that the low frequency diffusion capacitance of an abrupt p^+n diode varies linearly with the forward current I_F. If the plot of C_D vs. I_F has a slope of 1.6 Fd/A, calculate the hole lifetime, the stored charge and the value of C_D at $I_F = 2$ mA.

[4.16×10^{-7} s.; 8.32×10^{-10} Coul; 32 nFd]

2.36 A pn diode at 300 K has a reverse saturation current of 10 μ A. An alternating voltage wave $0.1 \sin(314t)$ is superimposed upon a forward d.c.bias of 0.26 V. Calculate the ratio of a.c. to d.c flowing through the diode. What is the diode a.c. admittance? ($\tau_n = \tau_p = 50\,\mu$ s)

[1.75×10^{-4}; 384.6 μ mhos]

2.37 A Ge pn junction diode has a reverse saturation current of 10^{-6} A at 300 K. A parallel combination of two such diodes is connected to a 1 V battery in series with a 50 ohm resistor such that both the diodes are forward biased. Calculate the current through the circuit and the voltage drop across each diode.

[7.7 mA; 0.23 V; 0.77 V]

2.38 The reverse saturation current of a pn diode is 10 μ A. The diode is placed in series with an ohmic resistance of 5Ω and a 0.5 V d.c. source. Determine the diode current.

[0.055 A]

2.39 In a full-wave pn diode rectifier, the load resistance is 400Ω. The diode possesses a resistance of 3Ω each. The a.c. voltage applied to each diode is of the type $240 \sin(\pi t)$. Calculate (i) the rectifier efficiency, (ii) the form factor, (iii) percentage voltage regulation, (iv) the peak inverse voltage, and (v) the ripple factor.

[81.06%; 1.11; 0.755; 480 V; 0.4834]

2.40 A pn diode whose reverse saturation current is 10^{-5} A is connected in series with a resistor and a 1 V battery. The resulting current through the diode is found to be 100 mA. What is the value of the series resistance?

[8.8Ω]

References

[1] Bergh, A.A.,and Dean, P.J., 1976, *Light Emitting Diodes*, Clarendon, Oxford.

[2] Casey, H.C. Jr., and Panish, M.B., 1978, *Heterostructure Lasers*, Academic, New York.

[3] Chapin, D.M., Fuller,C.S., and Pearson, G.L., 1954, A New Si *pn* Junction Photocell for Converting Solar Radiation into Electrical Power, *J.Appl.Phys.*, **25**, 676.

[4] Gray, P.E., Dewitt, D., Boothroyd, A.R., and Gibbons, J.F., 1964, *Physical Electronics and Circuit Models of Transistors, Vol.2*, Semiconductor Electronics Education Committee, Wiley, New York.

[5] Hayashi, I., Panish, M.B., Foy, P.W. and Sumski, S.,1970, Junction Lasers which operate continuously at Room Temp., *Appl. Phys. Lett.*, **17**, 109.

[6] Johnston, R.L., DeLoach, B.C. Jr., and Cohen, B.G., 1965, A Silicon Diode Oscillator, *Bell System Tech. J.* **44**, 369.

[7] Millman, J. and Halkias, C.C., 1971, *Integrated Electronics: Analog and Digital Circuit Systems*, McGraw Hill, New York.

[8] Milnes, A.G. and Feucht, D.L.,1972, *Heterojunctions and Metal-Semiconductor Junctions*, Academic, New York.

[9] Moll, J.L., 1957, The Evolution of the Theory of Current-Voltage Characteristics of *pn* Junctions, *Proc.IRE (USA)*, **45**, 1228.

[10] Nanavati, R.P., 1963, *Introduction to Semiconductor Electronics*, McGraw Hill, New York.

[11] Nathan, M.I., Dumke, W.P., Burns, G., Dill, F. J. Jr., and Lasher, G.J., 1962, Stimulated Emission of Radiation from GaAs *pn* Junctions, *Appl. Phys. Lett*, **1**, 62.

[12] Phillips, A.B., 1962, *Transistor Engineering*, McGraw Hill, New York.

[13] Pulfrey, D.L., 1978, *Photovoltaic Power Generation*, D. Van Nostrand: New York.

[14] Read, W.T., 1958, A Proposed High Frequency Negative Resistance Diode, *Bell System Tech. J.*, **37**, 401.

[15] Sharma, B.L.,and Purohit, R.K.,1974, *Semiconductor Heterojunctions*, Pergamon, London.

[16] Shive, J.N., 1959, *Semiconductor Devices*, Van Nostrand, Princeton, N.J.

[17] Shockley, W., 1949, The Theory of *pn* Junctions in Semiconductors and *pn* Junction Transistors, *Bell System Tech.J. (USA)*, **28**, 435.

[18] Shockley, W., 1954, Negative Resistance Arising from Transit Time in Semiconductor Diodes, *Bell System. Tech. J.*, **33**, 799.

[19] Strutt, M.J.O, 1966, *Semiconductor Devices, Vol.1., Semiconductor and Semiconductor Diodes*, Academic Press, New York.

[20] Wang, S., 1966, *Solid State Electronics*, McGraw Hill, New York.

3 Transistor physics

The discovery of transistors (which is an acronym for the transfer of resistors) is one of the greatest achievements of mankind. The bipolar transistor's low input impedance coupled with a high output impedance and an unattenuated current transfer from the input to the output makes it an ideal device for amplification of alternating voltages. The output impedance of the device may also be controlled by appropriately biasing it. This property of transition from a high impedance state to a low impedance one and vice versa by applying an appropriate bias to the transistor enables one to design an electronic switch. In this chapter, we will be concerned with the study of the physical principles of operations of a transistor. To analyze the behaviour of a transistor in a circuit, we need to know its equivalent circuit forms. These have been derived here from three independent considerations, viz.,

(i) the device approach,
(ii) the black box approach and
(iii) the Ebers–Moll approach.

The equivalent circuit derived on the basis of the device approach is expressible in terms of the fundamental device parameters. As such, this would be useful from the point of view of design considerations of transistors. The second type of equivalent circuit is based on its terminal characteristics. Depending on the choices of independent variables in the form of transistor currents and voltages, a great variation is possible in this type of equivalent circuit. From the point of view of experimental measurements, however, the hybrid circuit parameters are the most convenient ones. The third type of equivalent circuit is useful in analyzing its switching characteristics. Having first described the low frequency transistor behaviour, the high frequency and the switching characteristics of transistors are analyzed. It will also be shown that if the transistor base has an impurity gradient instead of being homogeneously doped, there will be an improvement in its high frequency characteristics.

Field-effect transistors, unlike the junction types, are dependiant on the majority current carriers for their operation. They are somewhat similar in behaviour to vacuum tubes. They have a high input impedance, low noise figure, lower voltage gains, larger bandwidths, immunity to external radiations, etc. The physics of operations of the junction field-effect transistors (JFET) is presented in this chapter. The phototransistor, as an ultrasensitive optical device, has also been introduced in this chapter. The physics of uni-junction transistors and that of thyristors are somewhat related to those of junction transistors. Therefore, these devices have also been considered. They are well-known for their switching capabilities. Various other types of recently developed transistors are also briefly discussed.

A chapter on the physics of transistors will be incomplete without any mention of their applications. A few typical applications of transistors are therefore presented at the end.

3.1 Basic functions of a transistor

Fig. 3.1(a) shows the equivalent circuit of a hypothetical device having a low input impedance R_{in}, a high output impedance R_{out} and a near unity current gain for a load resistance $R_L (\ll 0.1 R_{out})$. Voltage gains can be realized if R_L is chosen such that $R_L I_{in}$ is considerably greater than the input voltage. In the ideal case, as shown in Fig. 3.1(b), the input approaches a short-circuit while the output, an open-circuit. Such a device is expected to function as an ideal voltage amplifier. If by appropriate biasing, the output impedance of the above mentioned device is changed from a very high to a very low value and vice versa, the device can function as a switch. These two operations viz., amplification and switching are at the root of many electronic functions of transistors.

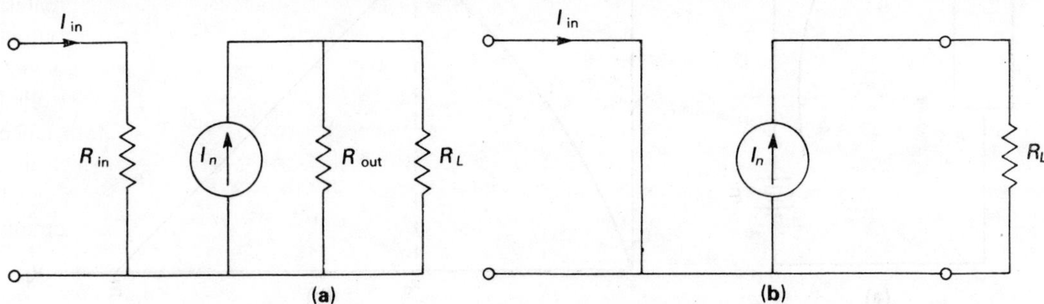

Figure 3.1 *Equivalent circuit: (a) hypothetical amplifier; (b) ideal amplifier*

To elaborate further on the above two potentialities of a transistor, let us consider a two-terminal device (Fig. 3.2(a)) that has a non-linear $I-V$ characteristic, as shown in Fig. 3.2(b). The non-linear I–V curve of the device may be traced out by experimentally measuring the device currents at various applied voltages. When such a device is connected in series with a resistance R and a bias E, the steady state values of the current (i_d) and the voltage (v_d) are obtained. To evaluate these steady state values, we consider the loop equation appropriate to the circuit of Fig. 3.2(a) which is

$$E = i_d R + v_d \tag{3.1}$$

This equation involves two unknowns viz., i_d and v_d. They may be evaluated by referring to the static I–V characteristic of the device, described by

$$i_d = f(v_d) \tag{3.2}$$

The steady state current I_d and the voltage V_d may now be obtained by solving the above two equations simultaneously by a graphical method, as shown in Fig. 3.2(b). Equation (3.1) is said to describe the load line of the circuit.

Let us next presume that a third terminal is being added to the device (Fig. 3.3(a)) to control its I–V characteristic. The control current i_T gives rise to a set of characteristics, as shown in Fig. 3.3(b). The load line of the circuit may still be represented by (3.1), which has been drawn on the set of curves of Fig. 3.3(b). The steady state current and the voltage are determined by i_T. Now if an a.c. source is superimposed on i_T at the input, large scale fluctuations in i_d at the output is possible by

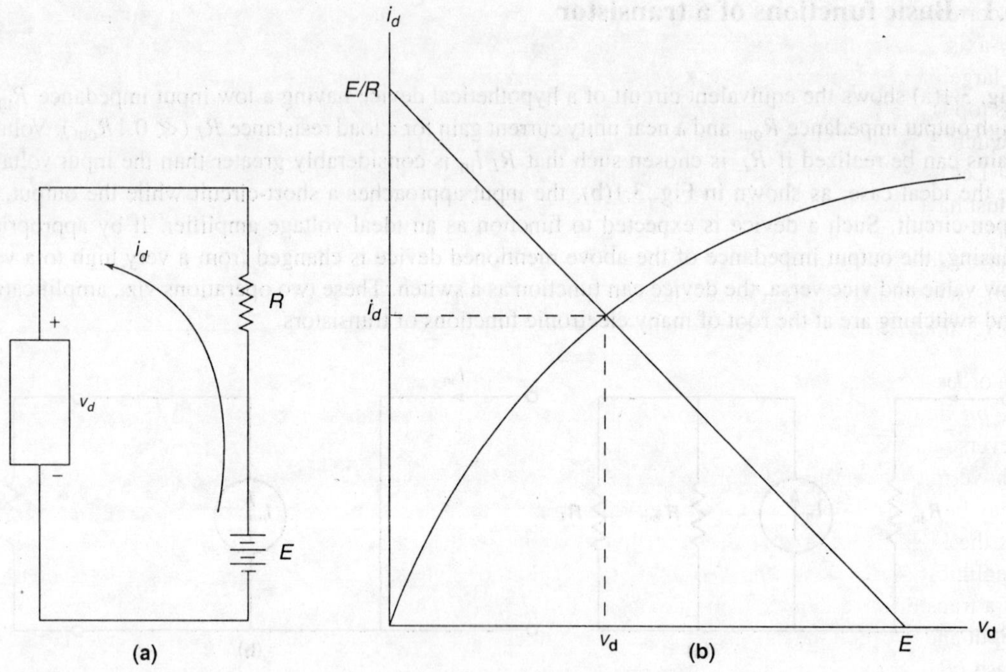

Figure 3.2 *A two-terminal non-linear device: (a) the biasing circuit, (b) the I–V characteristic and the loadline*

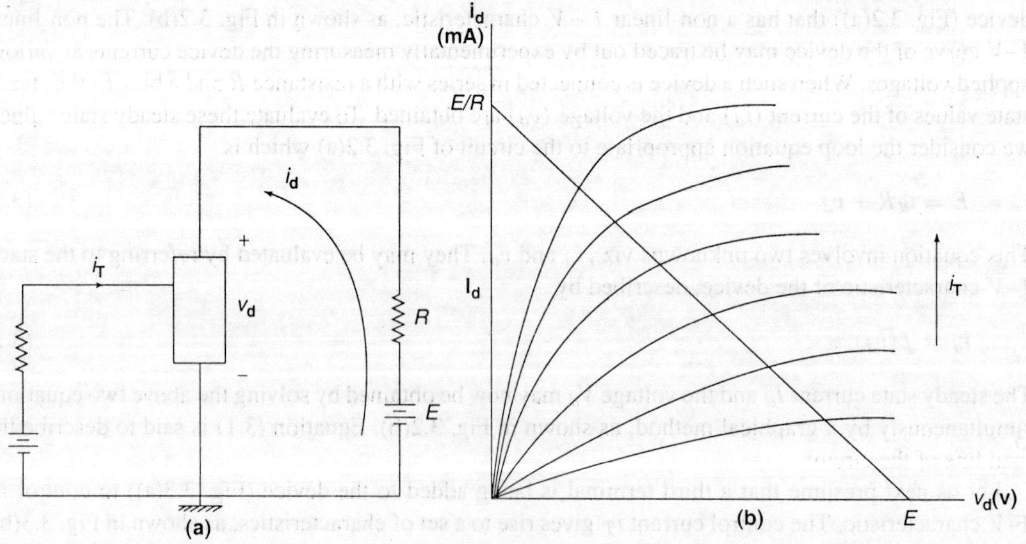

Figure 3.3 *A three terminal non-linear device whose I–V curve can be controlled by i_T: (a) biasing circuit, (b) its I–V characteristic and the load line*

a correspondingly small variation in i_T. If the curves for equal changes in i_T are equi-spaced on the i_d-axis, a faithful amplified version of the small control signal at the input can be obtained because of a large input impedance. Also, if we can turn the device from the bottom of the load line ($i_d = 0$) to its top ($i_d \cong E/R$), by changing the control signal appropriately, it can also function as an electronic switch. This type of switching is required in digital circuits.

Let us once again return to our discussion of an ideal voltage amplifier, as presented in Fig. 3.1. It must have the following three characteristics

a) a low input impedance,
b) a high output impedance, and
c) an unattenuated current transfer from the input to the output.

In order to realize this in practice, we have to carefully examine the I–V characteristics of pn diodes. A pn diode has a very low impedance in the forward biased condition while its impedance in the reverse biased state is very high. The first two requirements of an ideal voltage amplifier, as mentioned above, may therefore be realized very easily by suitably biased pn junctions. The third requirement may be fulfilled by inserting a very thin semiconducting layer between the two pn junctions serving as the input and output sections of the amplifier, so that the carriers lost in it by recombination are negligibly small. Such a pnp configuration is appropriately called a transistor because effectively there is a transfer of resistance from the output to the input. The forward biased pn junction serves as the input and is called the emitter (E) because it injects the carriers into the intervening n-layer called the base (B). The reverse biased np junction forms the output of the device. It collects the carriers that reach it via the base layer after surviving recombination and is called the collector (C) (Fig. 3.4(a)). Thus by using suitably biased pn junctions and an intervening semiconducting layer to connect them,

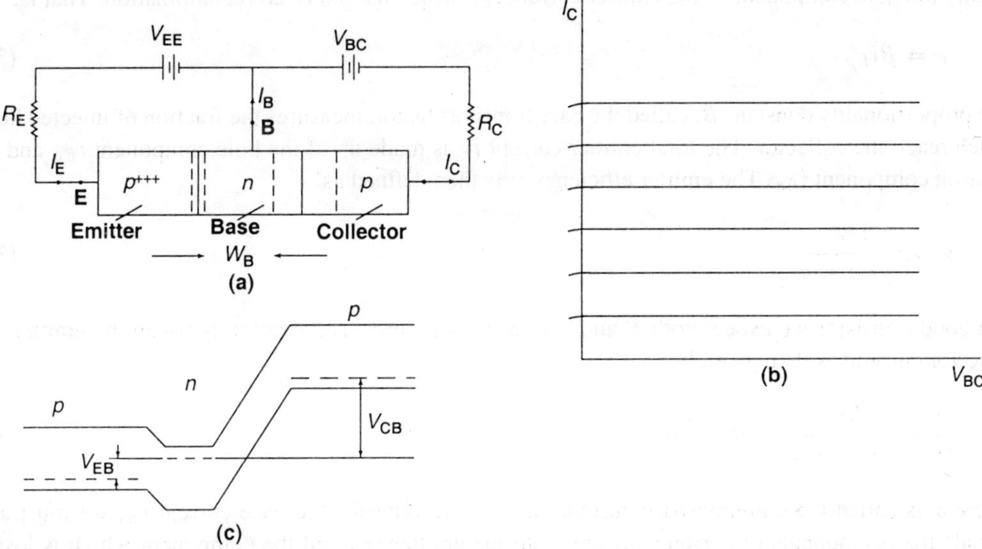

Figure 3.4 (a) A normally biased pnp transistor, (b) I–V characteristic of the reverse biased collector junction as a function of the emitter current, (c) the energy band diagram under normal operating conditions

we can design a transistor. An *npn* transistor may also be built similarly. The various current directions in it would however be opposite relative to that in a *pnp* transistor. Due to larger mobility of electrons, *npn* transistors are faster relative to the *pnp* ones.

A normally biased *pnp* transistor is shown in Fig. 3.4(a). Injection of holes by the emitter into the base layer supplies the minority carrier holes for the reverse current of the *np* collector junction. Of course, it is necessary that the injected holes in the base layer should not recombine in the n-region before they can diffuse to the depletion layer of the reverse biased *pn* junction. To ensure this, it is necessary to make the width of the base layer smaller than the hole diffusion length.

It is clear that I_E flows into the emitter and I_C flows out of the collector, so that $I_E \cong I_C$. In a good transistor, the base current I_B is required to be very small. This current plays the role of i_T in Fig. 3.3(a). The following three mechanisms are responsible in determining it

a) Some holes injected into the base layer may be lost to recombination with electrons even if $W_B \ll L_p$. The electrons lost to recombination with holes have to be replenished by their injection through the base contact (I_B).
b) Some electrons may be injected from the base into the emitter region even if the emitter is heavily doped compared to the base. These electrons also have to be supplied by I_B.
c) Some of the electrons which are thermally generated in the collector depletion layer are swept into the base layer by the junction field at the base collector junction. This latter effect, however, contributes to the lowering of I_B.

The resulting I–V characteristic and the energy band diagram have been shown in Figs. 3.4(b) and 3.4(c) respectively.

Now, we can relate small signal transistor currents i_E, i_B and i_C. We will, however, ignore the finite reverse saturation current crossing the base collector junction. The collector current would then consist of only the hole component of the emitter current i_{Ep} which has survived recombination. That is,

$$i_C = B i_{Ep} \tag{3.3}$$

The proportionality constant B, called the base transport factor, measures the fraction of injected holes which reach the collector. The total emitter current i_E is made up of the hole component i_{Ep} and the electron component i_{En}. The emitter efficiency γ is then defined as

$$\gamma = \frac{i_{Ep}}{i_{En} + i_{Ep}} \tag{3.4}$$

In a good transistor we expect both B and γ to approach unity. The relation between the emitter and collector currents is then given by

$$\frac{i_C}{i_E} = \frac{B i_{Ep}}{i_{En} + i_{Ep}} = B\gamma = \alpha \tag{3.5}$$

where α is called the common-base current gain. To account for the base current i_B, we must also include the components of currents injected into the emitter i_{En} and the component which is lost to recombination $(1 - B)i_{Ep}$. Therefore,

$$i_B = i_{En} + (1 - B) i_{Ep} \tag{3.6}$$

The relationship between the collector and the base current may be expressed as

$$\frac{i_C}{i_B} = \frac{B i_{Ep}}{i_{En} + (1 - B) i_{Ep}} = \frac{B\left[\frac{i_{Ep}}{i_{En}+i_{Ep}}\right]}{1 - \left[\frac{B i_{Ep}}{i_{En}+i_{Ep}}\right]} = \frac{B\gamma}{1 - B\gamma}$$

$$= \frac{\alpha}{1-\alpha} = \beta \tag{3.7}$$

where β is defined as the common-emitter current gain.

Now, we will explain how we can bring about large changes in i_C by small changes in i_B. From space-charge neutrality arguments of the base layer, it can be shown that i_B, in fact, controls i_C. Since the n-type base layer is electrostatically neutral between the two transition regions, the presence of excess holes during transit through the base layer calls for compensating electrons from the base contact. However, there is an important difference in the times that holes and electrons have to spend in the base layer. The excess holes spend a time τ_t, on the average, during their transit from the emitter to the collector. Since the base width is much smaller than the hole diffusion length, the transit time τ_t is much smaller than the average hole lifetime τ_p in the base layer. Thus, while an electron which is injected by the base contact, on the average, waits for τ_p for recombination with a hole, many holes may enter and leave the base layer in the mean time, each with an average transit time τ_t. In other words, for each electron injected by the base contact, (τ_p/τ_t) holes can pass from the emitter to the collector maintaining the space-charge neutrality of the base layer. Therefore,

$$\frac{i_C}{i_B} = \beta = \frac{\tau_p}{\tau_t} \tag{3.8}$$

Therefore, if the electron supply i_B is restricted, the traffic of holes from the emitter to the collector would be correspondingly reduced; otherwise, the space-charge neutrality of the n-base layer cannot be maintained.

Circuit representations of transistors We have just discussed the fundamental basis of operation of bipolar transistors and explained in a simplified way how it can be used to perform amplification of small a.c. signals and switching of currents from the off state to the on condition and vice-versa in an electronic circuit. Proper sign conventions used to represent transistors in circuits are given in Fig. 3.5. When a current I_E is fed through an emitter, the collector current is given by the algebraic sum of the reverse saturation current I which is already flowing across the base-collector junction, and a fraction of the emitter current I_E that survives recombination in the base layer. Using appropriate sign conventions (Fig. 3.5), we may write

$$I_C = I_{CO} + \alpha I_E \tag{3.9}$$

Since $I_{CO} \ll I_E$, (3.9) reduces to

$$|I_C| \cong \alpha I_E \tag{3.10}$$

as it also follows from (3.5). From Kirchoff's current law, we may now write

$$I_B = -(I_C + I_E) \tag{3.11}$$

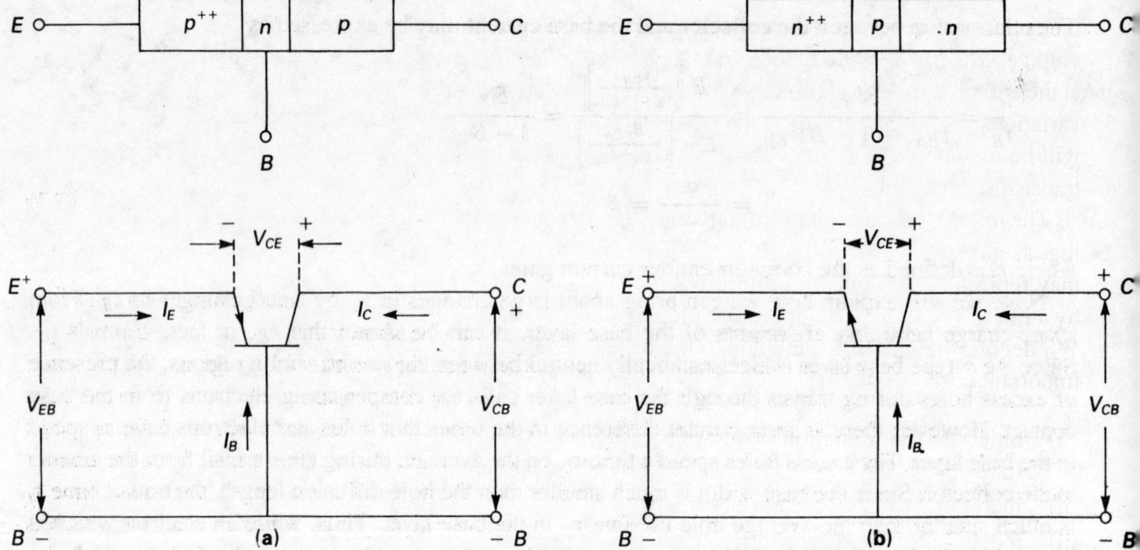

Figure 3.5 *Circuit representations of transistor and symbols : (a)* $p^{++}np$ *transistor; (b)* $n^{++}pn$ *transistor*

Multiplying both sides of (3.11) by α and then combining with (3.9), we get

$$I_C = \left[\frac{I_{CO}}{1-\alpha}\right] + \left[\frac{\alpha I_B}{1-\alpha}\right]$$

$$I_C = \beta I_B + (\beta + 1) I_{CO} \tag{3.12}$$

If $I_{CO} \ll I_B$, (3.12) simplifies to $I_C \cong \beta I_B$, as we have already found in (3.7). Now, if we take $\alpha = 0.98$, β works out to be 49. If α happens to change by 1%, the corresponding change in β works out to be 50%. Such a sensitive variation in β is caused due to the fact that I_B is the difference of two nearly equal currents which are large in magnitudes.

The current gains α and β are found to vary with injection level I_E. We have seen that the effective diffusion constant of the injected minority carriers increase with the injection level (2.96). As a result, the transit time of injected minority carriers is appropriately cut at higher injection levels giving them lesser time for recombination. Therefore, both α and β are expected to increase initially with the increase in the injection level. But with a substantial increase in I_E, the injected carriers may diffuse to meet the surface state levels. In this case, owing to the increase in the surface recombination rate, α and β after attaining a maximum value, start decreasing with increase in I_E.

3.2 Early effect and transistor characteristics

While discussing the a.c. behaviour of *pn* diodes in Section 2.4, we presumed that owing to the a.c. voltage magnitudes being small, the transition region boundaries of *pn* junctions can be regarded to be independent of the a.c. voltage variations. Such an assumption cannot however be extended to the collector junction of the transistor where the available voltage is the amplified version of the input voltage, which obviously is not too small. We may, therefore, presume that the transition layer boundary at the emitter end to be stationary while that at the collector end to be oscillating with the output voltage variations. As a result of this, the base width of the transistor will cease to remain stationary and it will be modulated as a function of the collector voltage. Such an effect has a profound influence on transistor behaviour.

The minority carrier distribution within the base layer of a transistor would be exponentially decaying, as already explained by (2.71). Since, the base of the transistor has to be extremely narrow, we may replace the exponential minority hole density variation in the n base region of a pnp transistor by a linear variation as an approximation, as shown in Fig. 3.6. W_B denotes the true base width while W'_B denotes its reduced value due to the increased collector voltage. Such an effect has the following important consequences:

i) reduced recombination of injected carriers from the emitter to the base, leading to an increase in α,
ii) increased density gradient of minority carriers within the base causing an increase in I_E and
iii) reduction of the base width to zero at a particular collector voltage making the transistor action impossible.

Such a phenomenon is known as "*punch-through*". However, if the reverse collector voltage is not large enough to give rise to "*punch-through*", the effect of the base width modulation due to the increased bias magnitude is to give rise to an increased α and I_E. This phenomenon is known as the "*Early effect*" and is basic to the understanding of the transistor I–V characteristics.

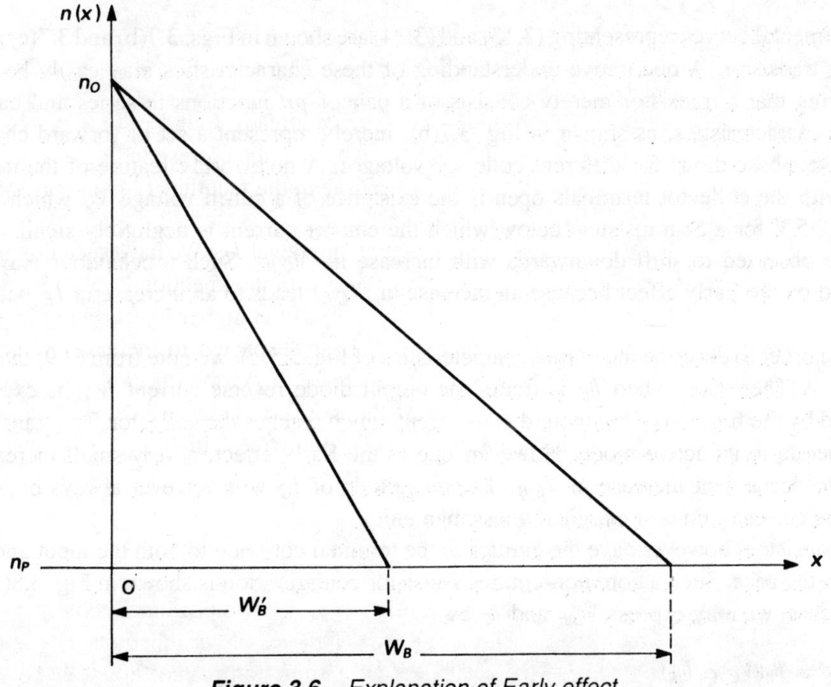

Figure 3.6 *Explanation of Early effect*

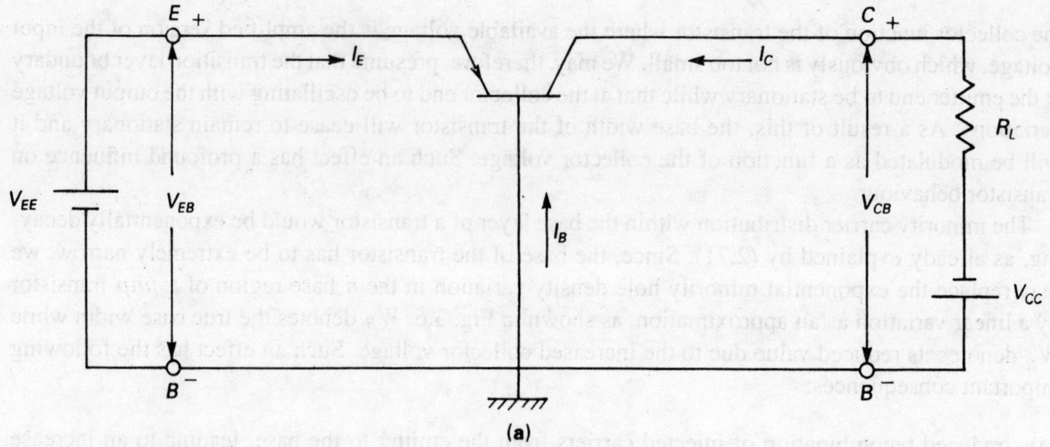

***Figure 3.7** pnp transistor in the common-base mode: (a) circuit configuration*

The grounded base transistor configuration along with its I–V characteristics are shown in Fig. 3.7. The emitter current I_E and the collector voltage V_{CB} may be taken as independent variables to express V_{EB} and I_C as

$$V_{EB} = f_1(V_{CB}, I_E) \tag{3.13}$$

$$I_C = f_2(V_{CB}, I_E). \tag{3.14}$$

The experimental curves representing (3.13) and (3.14) are shown in Figs. 3.7(b) and 3.7(c) respectively for a *pnp* transistor. A qualitative understanding of these characteristics may easily be reached by remembering that a transistor merely consists of a pair of *pn* junctions in series and back-to-back. The input characteristics, as shown in Fig. 3.7(b), merely represent a set of forward characteristics of the emitter-base diode for different collector voltages. A noteworthy feature of the input characteristics with the collector terminals open is the existence of a cut-in voltage V_γ which is 0.1 V for a Ge and 0.5 V for a Si transistor) below which the emitter current is negligibly small. The emitter curves are observed to shift downwards with increase in $|V_{CB}|$. Such a behaviour may readily be understood by the Early effect because an increase in $|V_{CB}|$ leads to an increase in I_E with V_{EB} held constant.

Next, in order to describe the output characteristics of Fig. 3.5(c), we note from (3.9) that $I_C = I_{CO}$ for $I_E = 0$. Therefore, when I_E is finite, the output diode reverse current I_{CO} is expected to be augmented by the fraction of the input diode current which reaches the collector. The transistor is then said to operate in its active mode. However, due to the Early effect, a very small increase in I_C is expected to occur with increase in V_{CB}. The magnitude of I_C will however always be less than I_E because the current gain α is marginally less than unity.

Most transistors however have the emitter as the terminal common to both the input and the output rather than the base. Such a common-emitter transistor configuration is shown in Fig. 3.8(a).

In this case, we may express V_{BE} and I_C as

$$V_{BE} = f_1(V_{CE}, I_B) \tag{3.15}$$

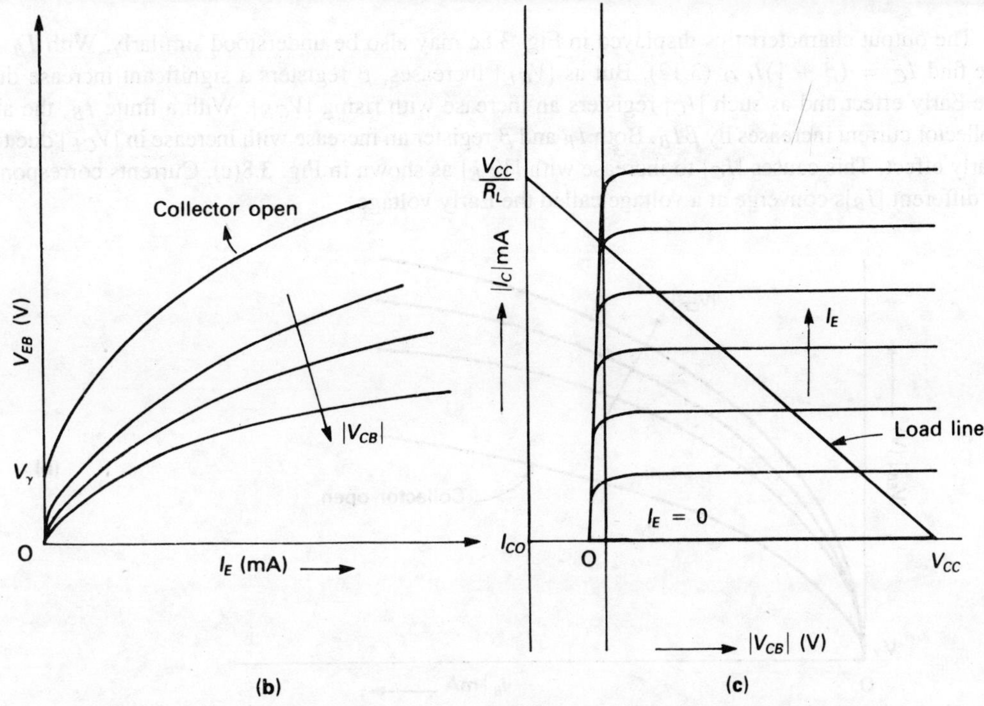

Figure 3.7 *continued (b) input characteristics and (c) output characteristics*

and

$$I_C = f_2(V_{CE}, I_B). \tag{3.16}$$

Equations (3.15) and (3.16) describe the input and the output characteristics for a *pnp* transistor in the common-emitter mode (Fig. 3.8(a)). We observe from Fig. 3.8(b), that with the collector open and the emitter diode forward biased, the transistor input characteristic is essentially the same as that of a forward biased diode. An increase in $|V_{CE}|$ with V_{BE} held constant, causes a decrease in the base width which results in the reduced recombination current I_B.

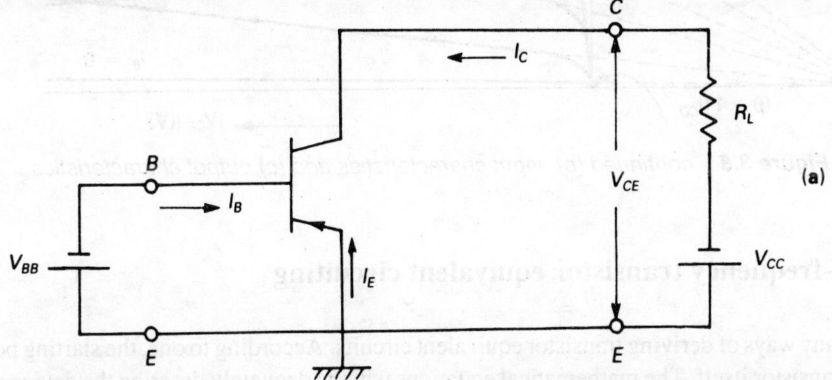

Figure 3.8 *pnp transistor in the common-emitter mode: (a) circuit configuration*

The output characteristics displayed in Fig. 3.8c may also be understood similarly. With $I_B = 0$, we find $I_C = (\beta + 1)I_{CO}$ (3.12). But as $|V_{CE}|$ increases, β registers a significant increase due to the Early effect and as such $|I_C|$ registers an increase with rising $|V_{CE}|$. With a finite I_B, the above collector current increases by βI_B. Both I_B and β register an increase with increase in $|V_{CE}|$ due to the Early effect. This causes $|I_C|$ to increase with $|V_{CE}|$ as shown in Fig. 3.8(c). Currents corresponding to different $|I_B|$s converge at a voltage called the Early voltage.

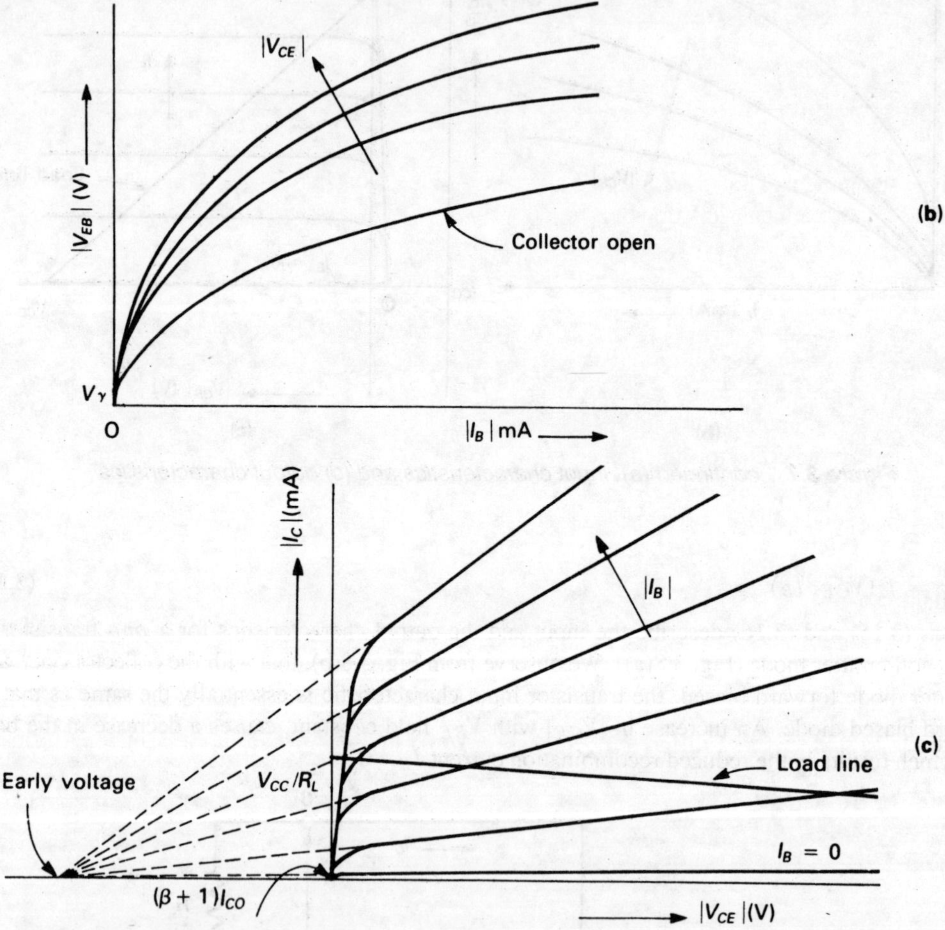

Figure 3.8 *continued (b) input characteristics and (c) output characteristics*

3.3 Low-frequency transistor equivalent circuiting

There are many ways of deriving transistor equivalent circuits. According to one, the starting point is the physics of transistor itself. The mathematical equations which adequately describe the device operation in terms of emitter and collector currents are first derived. One then looks for a suitable equivalent circuit that satisfies these equations. This is known as the device approach. Its advantage is that each component of the equivalent circuit becomes expressible in terms of the fundamental device parameters. The other way is to start from a prior knowledge of the terminal characteristics of the transistor and derive mathematical equations among various currents and voltages. We then look for a suitable circuit that satisfies these terminal relationships. Since one needs to know only the device's terminal behaviour to arrive at this form of the equivalent circuit, this is called the Black-box approach. Lastly, we will describe the Ebers–Moll model which is often used to predict the switching characteristics of transistors. In this model, the transistor is treated as two *pn* diodes connected back-to-back with two current sources shunting them.

3.3.1 The device approach

Basically, we assume that holes are injected into the base layer by the forward biased emitter and these holes diffuse to the collector junction of a *pnp* transistor. First, we find out the excess hole distribution in the base region by solving Poisson's equation. Next, the emitter and the collector currents are obtained from the gradients of the hole distributions on each side of the base. To simplify calculations the following assumptions are made

(i) holes diffuse from the emitter to the collector. The drift of carriers in the base layer is negligible;
(ii) the emitter current is mostly made up of holes;
(iii) the collector saturation current is negligibly small;
(iv) both emitter and collector junction areas are of uniform cross- section A and the flow of current is one dimensional; and
(v) all currents and voltages are steady.

The hole diffusion equation in the d.c. case for the base region of a *pnp* transistor may be expressed as (similar to (2.69)),

$$\frac{\partial^2 p(x)}{\partial x^2} - \frac{[p(x) - p_n]}{L_p^2} = 0 \tag{3.17}$$

The solution to this standard differential equation may now be expressed in the following different ways:

$$\begin{aligned} p(x) - p_n &= A \exp\left(\frac{x}{L_p}\right) + B \exp\left(\frac{-x}{L_p}\right) \\ &= C \cosh\left(\frac{x}{L_p}\right) + D \sinh\left(\frac{x}{L_p}\right) \\ &= E \sinh\left[\frac{\{(\frac{W}{2}) - x\}}{L_p}\right] + F \sinh\left[\frac{\{\frac{W}{2} + x\}}{L_p}\right] \end{aligned} \tag{3.18}$$

where W measures the effective transistor base width. We will prefer to use the last solution in (3.18) as it helps one to evaluate the constants E and F. Using equations similar to (2.65), we may write

$$p\left(\frac{-W}{2}\right) = p_E = p_n \exp\left(\frac{qV_E}{kT}\right) \tag{3.19}$$

and

$$p\left(\frac{+W}{2}\right) = p_C = p_n \exp\left(\frac{qV_C}{kT}\right) \tag{3.20}$$

where $(-W/2)$ and $(+W/2)$ respectively denote the emitter and the collector ends of the base layer. V_E and V_C respectively denote the forward biases applied to the emitter and the collector junctions. Using the above equations in (3.18), E and F can be found. With these values, the excess density at any point of the base layer is given by

$$p(x) - p_n = \left[(p_E - p_n) \sinh \left[\frac{\{(\frac{W}{2}) - x\}}{L_p} \right] + (p_C - p_n) \sinh \left[\frac{\{(\frac{W}{2}) + x\}}{L_p} \right] \frac{\sinh\left(\frac{\frac{W}{2}+x}{Lp}\right)}{\sinh\left(\frac{W}{Lp}\right)} \sinh\left(\frac{W}{L_p}\right) \right] \tag{3.21}$$

The emitter and the collector hole current densities may now be obtained from (3.21) by setting $x = (-W/2)$ and $x = (+W/2)$ respectively. Hence, we get

$$J_{pE} = \left(\frac{qD_p}{L_p}\right)\left[(p_E - p_n)\coth\left(\frac{W}{L_p}\right) - (p_C - p_n)\,\mathrm{cosech}\left(\frac{W}{L_p}\right)\right] \tag{3.22}$$

$$J_{pC} = \left(\frac{qD_p}{L_p}\right)\left[(p_E - p_n)\,\mathrm{cosech}\left(\frac{W}{L_p}\right) - (p_C - p_n)\coth\left(\frac{W}{L_p}\right)\right] \tag{3.23}$$

Since electron currents cross only one junction, they may be obtained from (3.22) and (3.23) by letting W approach infinity. We then obtain

$$J_{nE} = \left(\frac{qD_n}{L_{ne}}\right)(n_E - n_{pe}) \tag{3.24}$$

and

$$J_{nC} = -\left(\frac{qD_n}{L_{nc}}\right)(n_C - n_{pe}) \tag{3.25}$$

Appropriately combining (3.22) to (3.25), we get

$$I_E = a_{11}\left[\exp\left(\frac{qV_E}{kT}\right) - 1\right] + a_{12}\left[\exp\left(\frac{qV_C}{kT}\right) - 1\right] \tag{3.26}$$

and

$$I_C = a_{21}\left[\exp\left(\frac{qV_E}{kT}\right) - 1\right] + a_{22}\left[\exp\left(\frac{qV_C}{kT}\right) - 1\right] \tag{3.27}$$

where

$$a_{11} = qA\left[\left(\frac{D_p p_n}{L_p}\right)\coth\left(\frac{W}{L_p}\right) + \left(\frac{D_n n_{pe}}{L_{ne}}\right)\right]$$

$$a_{12} = -qA\left[\left(\frac{D_p p_n}{L_p}\right)\ \text{cosech}\left(\frac{W}{L_p}\right)\right]$$

$$a_{21} = qA\left[\left(\frac{D_p p_n}{L_p}\right)\ \text{cosech}\left(\frac{W}{L_p}\right)\right] \tag{3.28}$$

and

$$a_{22} = -qA\left[\left(\frac{D_p p_n}{L_p}\right)\coth\left(\frac{W}{L_p}\right) + \left(\frac{D_n n_{pc}}{L_{nc}}\right)\right]$$

where A denotes the cross-sectional area of the junction. It may now be noted that $a_{11} = -a_{22}$ and $a_{12} = -a_{21}$. We may now express (3.26) as

$$\left[\exp\left(\frac{qV_E}{kT}\right) - 1\right] = \left(\frac{I_E}{a_{11}}\right) - \left(\frac{a_{12}}{a_{11}}\right)\left[\exp\left(\frac{qV_C}{kT}\right) - 1\right]$$

Expressing it in a differential form, we find

$$\Delta V_E = \left(\frac{kT}{qa_{11}}\right)\exp\left(\frac{-qV_E}{kT}\right)\Delta I_E - \left(\frac{a_{12}}{a_{11}}\right)\left[\frac{\exp q(V_C - V_E)}{kT}\right]\Delta V_C \tag{3.29}$$

Similarly from (3.27), we get

$$I_C = \left(\frac{a_{21}}{a_{11}}\right)I_E + \left[a_{22} - \left(\frac{a_{12}a_{21}}{a_{11}}\right)\right]\left[\exp\left(\frac{qV_C}{kT}\right) - 1\right]$$

again expressing it in a differential form, we get

$$\Delta I_C = \left(\frac{a_{21}}{a_{11}}\right)\Delta I_E + \left(\frac{q}{kT}\right)\left[a_{22} - \left(\frac{a_{12}a_{21}}{a_{11}}\right)\right]\exp\left(\frac{qV_C}{kT}\right)\Delta V_C \tag{3.30}$$

For a transistor biased in the active region V_E is positive while V_C is negative. Equations (3.29) and (3.30) may now be expressed in the following simplified forms:

$$\begin{aligned}\Delta V_E &= h_{11}\Delta I_E + h_{12}\Delta V_C \\ \Delta I_C &= h_{21}\Delta I_E + h_{22}\Delta V_C\end{aligned} \tag{3.31}$$

where the various h (hybrid) parameters may be identified as

$$h_{11} = \left(\frac{kT}{qa_{11}}\right)\exp\left(\frac{-qV_E}{kT}\right)$$

$$h_{12} = -\left(\frac{a_{12}}{a_{11}}\right)\left[\frac{\exp q(V_C - V_E)}{kT}\right]$$

$$h_{21} = \left(\frac{a_{21}}{a_{11}}\right) \tag{3.32}$$

and

$$h_{22} = \left(\frac{q}{kT}\right)\left[a_{22} - \left(\frac{a_{12}a_{21}}{a_{11}}\right)\right]\exp\left(\frac{qV_C}{kT}\right)$$

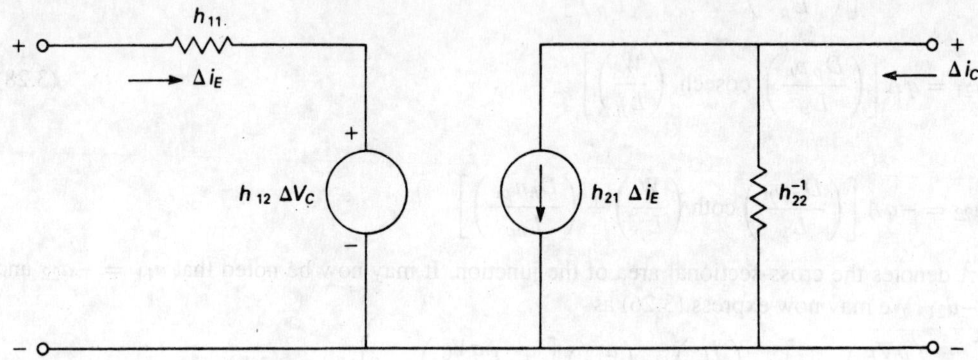

Figure 3.9 *Small-signal h-equivalent circuit of a transistor*

In (3.32), appropriate signs of the emitter and collector voltages must be used. The electrical network shown in Fig. 3.9 satisfies the pair of equations (3.31). These h parameters are seen to be related to the basic device parameters and, therefore, they may be used to design a particular transistor. Neglecting the electron components of the currents crossing the emitter junction, the emitter current may now be written as (3.22),

$$I_E = qA\left(\frac{D_p}{L_p}\right)\left[\Delta p_E \coth\left(\frac{W}{L_p}\right) - \Delta p_C \operatorname{cosech}\left(\frac{W}{L_p}\right)\right] \tag{3.33}$$

where $\Delta p_E = (p_E - p_n) = p_n[\exp(qV_E/kT) - 1]$ and $\Delta p_C = (p_C - p_n) = p_n[\exp(qV_C/kT) - 1]$ Similarly the collector current (3.23) may be expressed as

$$I_C = qA\left(\frac{D_p}{L_p}\right)\left[\Delta p_E \operatorname{cosech}\left(\frac{W}{L_p}\right) - \Delta p_C \coth\left(\frac{W}{L_p}\right)\right] \tag{3.34}$$

The base current equation may now be obtained as

$$I_B = I_E - I_C = qA\left(\frac{D_p}{L_p}\right)\left[(\Delta p_E + \Delta p_C)\left\{\coth\left(\frac{W}{L_p}\right) - \operatorname{cosech}\left(\frac{W}{L_p}\right)\right\}\right]$$

or

$$I_B = qA\left(\frac{D_p}{L_p}\right)(\Delta p_E + \Delta p_C)\tanh\left(\frac{W}{2L_p}\right) \tag{3.35}$$

If the collector is reverse biased, $\Delta p_C = -p_n$, which is usually small. In such cases, equations for I_E, I_C and I_B simplify to to the following simpler expressions:

$$I_E = qA\left(\frac{D_p}{L_p}\right)\Delta p_E \coth\left(\frac{W}{L_p}\right)$$

$$I_C = qA\left(\frac{D_p}{L_p}\right)\Delta p_E \operatorname{cosech}\left(\frac{W}{L_p}\right) \tag{3.36}$$

and

$$I_B = qA\left(\frac{D_p}{L_p}\right)\Delta p_E \tanh\left(\frac{W}{2L_p}\right)$$

For small values of (W/L_p), the basic base current expression simplifies to

$$I_B = \frac{qAW\Delta p_E}{2\tau_p} \tag{3.37}$$

This base current only takes into account the recombination in the base layer.

3.3.2 Black-box approach

Of the four parameters $(I_E,\ V_E)$ and $(I_C,\ V_C)$ needed for complete specifications of the terminal behaviour of a transistor, any two of them may be chosen as independent variables and the remaining two as the dependent ones. If we presume $V_E = f_1(I_E,\ I_C)$ and $V_C = f_2(I_E,\ I_C)$ to be dependent variables, we may write as a result of partial differentiation

$$\Delta V_E = r_{11}\Delta I_E + r_{12}\Delta I_C \tag{3.38}$$

and

$$\Delta V_C = r_{21}\Delta I_E + r_{22}\Delta I_C \tag{3.39}$$

where the r (or resistance) parameters are defined as

$$r_{11} = \left.\frac{\partial V_E}{\partial I_E}\right|_{\Delta I_C=0};\quad r_{12} = \left.\frac{\partial V_E}{\partial I_C}\right|_{\Delta I_E=0}$$

$$r_{21} = \left.\frac{\partial V_C}{\partial I_E}\right|_{\Delta I_C=0};\quad r_{22} = \left.\frac{\partial V_E}{\partial I_C}\right|_{\Delta I_E=0} \tag{3.40}$$

On the basis of (3.38) and (3.39), we can now derive an equivalent circuit. But, this is not a convenient one because it consists of two independent voltage sources of magnitudes $r_{12}\Delta I_C$ and $r_{21}\Delta I_E$. To derive a circuit with only one independent voltage source, we rewrite (3.38) by adding and subtracting $r_{12}\Delta I_E$. Next, (3.39) is also written by adding and subtracting $(\Delta I_E + \Delta I_C)r_{12}$. The equations then reduce to the following forms:

$$\Delta V_{EB} = (r_{11} - r_{12})\Delta I_E + r_{12}(\Delta I_E + \Delta I_C) \tag{3.41}$$

and

$$\Delta V_{CB} = r_{12}(\Delta I_E + \Delta I_C) + (r_{21} - r_{12})\Delta I_E + (r_{22} - r_{12})\Delta I_C \tag{3.42}$$

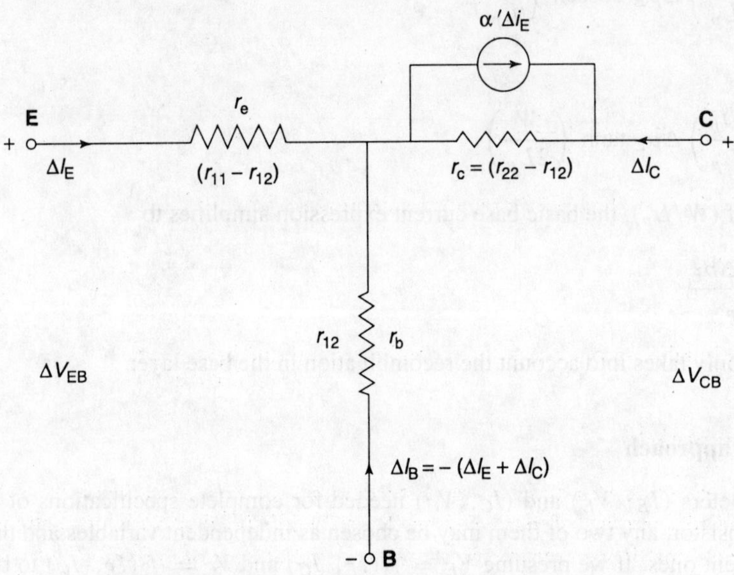

Figure 3.10 *The common base transistor*

Equations (3.41) and (3.42) are satisfied by the T-equivalent circuit given in Fig. 3.10. The circuit very much resembles a transistor operating in the common base mode with α', given by

$$\alpha' = \frac{r_{21} - r_{12}}{r_{22} - r_{12}} \tag{3.43}$$

which represents the common base current gain. But for $\Delta V_C = 0$, it follows from (3.39) that the common base current gain α should be given by

$$\alpha = \frac{r_{21}}{r_{22}} \tag{3.44}$$

Comparing (3.43) and (3.44) we notice that in the active region of the transistor, r_{12} is smaller than r_{21} and r_{22}. The equivalent circuit given in (3.10) may now be transformed to suit the common-emitter configurations by interchanging resistances r_e with r_b and replacing ΔI_E by $-(\Delta I_B + \Delta I_C)$. In this case, the constant current generator $\alpha' \Delta I_E$ is replaced by $\beta \Delta I_B$ with opposite polarity and r_c by $r_d = r_c(1 - \alpha)$. The resultant equivalent circuit is shown in Fig. 3.11. Its derivation is discussed below. Starting from (3.41), we write

$$\Delta V_{EB} = (r_{11} - r_{12})\Delta I_E + r_{12}(\Delta I_E + \Delta I_C)$$
$$= r_e \Delta I_E + r_b(\Delta I_E + \Delta I_C)$$

But as $\Delta I_E = -(\Delta I_B + \Delta I_C)$, the above relation reduces to

$$\Delta V_{EB} = -r_e(\Delta I_B + \Delta I_C) - r_b(\Delta I_B + \Delta I_C) + r_b \Delta I_C$$
$$= -r_e \Delta I_B - r_e \Delta I_C - r_b \Delta I_B$$
$$= -r_b \Delta I_B - r_e(\Delta I_B + \Delta I_C)$$

or

$$-\Delta V_{EB} = r_b \Delta I_B + r_e(\Delta I_B + \Delta I_C) \tag{3.45}$$

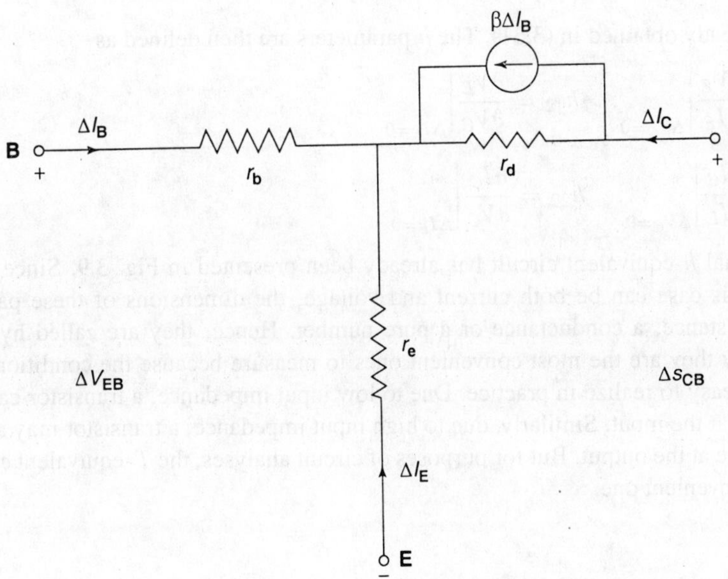

Figure 3.11 *The common-emitter transistor T-equivalent circuit*

Equation (3.45) explains the input section of Fig. 3.11. To explain the output section, we start from (3.42)

$$\Delta V_{CB} = r_{12}(\Delta I_E + \Delta I_C) + (r_{21} - r_{12})\Delta I_E + (r_{22} - r_{12})\Delta I_C$$
$$= -r_b \Delta I_B + \alpha r_c \Delta I_E + r_c \Delta I_C$$

Since the input voltage ΔV_{EB} is usually small, it follows from the input section of the common base equivalent circuit that $r_e \Delta I_E = r_b \Delta I_B$. Using it, the above relation simplifies to

$$\Delta V_{CB} = -r_e\Delta I_E + \alpha r_c \Delta I_E + r_c \Delta I_C$$
$$= -r_e\Delta I_E + \alpha r_c(-\Delta I_B - \Delta I_C) + r_c\Delta I_C$$
$$= -r_e\Delta I_E - \alpha r_c\Delta I_B - \alpha r_c \Delta I_C + r_c\Delta I_C$$
$$= r_e(\Delta I_B + \Delta I_C) - \left[\frac{\alpha}{1-\alpha}\right] r_c(1-\alpha)\Delta I_B + r_c(1-\alpha)\Delta I_C$$
$$= r_e(\Delta I_B + \Delta I_C) - \beta r_d \Delta I_B + r_d\Delta I_C \quad (3.46)$$

This equation explains the output section of Fig. 3.11. If we choose I_E and V_C as independent variables, we can write $V_E = f_1(I_E, V_C)$ and $I_C = f_2(I_E, V_C)$. Expressing these relations in a differential form, we get

$$\Delta V_E = h_{11}\Delta I_E + h_{12}\Delta V_C$$
$$\Delta I_C = h_{21}\Delta I_E + h_{22}\Delta V_C$$

as we have already obtained in (3.31). The h parameters are then defined as

$$h_{11} = \left.\frac{\partial V_E}{\partial I_E}\right|_{\Delta V_C=0}; \quad h_{12} = \left.\frac{\partial V_E}{\partial V_C}\right|_{\Delta I_E=0}$$
$$h_{21} = \left.\frac{\partial I_C}{\partial I_E}\right|_{\Delta V_C=0}; \quad h_{22} = \left.\frac{\partial I_C}{\partial V_C}\right|_{\Delta I_E=0} \quad (3.47)$$

The small signal h-equivalent circuit has already been presented in Fig. 3.9. Since the independent variables in this case can be both current and voltage, the dimensions of these parameters can be those of a resistance, a conductance or a pure number. Hence, they are called hybrid parameters. Experimentally they are the most convenient ones to measure because the conditions $\Delta I_E = 0$ and $\Delta V_C = 0$ are easy to realize in practice. Due to low input impedance, a transistor can be biased by a current source at the input. Similarly, due to high input impedance, a transistor may also be biased by a voltage source at the output. But for purposes of circuit analyses, the T-equivalent circuit is found to be the most convenient one.

3.4 High-frequency transistor behaviour

So far our discussions were restricted only to the d.c. cases. In this section, we shall analyze the flow of a small signal, low frequency a.c. through the transistor base. We would thereafter extend our analysis to the high frequency case.

In Section 2.4 we presented an analysis of small signal a.c. behaviour of pn diodes. We already noticed there that the a.c. component p_a of the hole density in the n base layer must satisfy the following a.c.diffusion equation:

$$\frac{\partial^2 p_a}{\partial x^2} - C_p^2 p_a = 0 \quad (3.48)$$

where

$$C_p^2 = \left[\frac{1 + j\omega\tau_p}{L_p^2}\right] \tag{3.49}$$

Following our arguments of writing the solution (3.18), the solution of (3.48) may be written as

$$p_a(x) = A \sinh\, C_p\left[\left(\frac{W}{2}\right) - x\right] + B \sinh C_p\left[\left(\frac{W}{2}\right) + x\right] \tag{3.50}$$

where A and B are two constants to be determined by employing the following boundary conditions:

$$p_a\left(\frac{+W}{2}\right) = p_c$$

and

$$p_a\left(\frac{-W}{2}\right) = p_e \tag{3.51}$$

where $p_c = (qp_C V_C/kT)$ and $p_e = (qp_E V_E/kT)$ respectively denote the amplitudes of a.c. densities of holes at the collector and the emitter ends of the base layer respectively. Imposing (3.51) in (3.50), the constants A and B may be calculated easily. With the values of A and B, substituted in (3.50), we get

$$p_a(x) = \frac{p_e \sinh C_p\left\{\left(\frac{W}{2}\right) - x\right\} + p_c \sinh C_p\left\{\left(\frac{W}{2}\right) + x\right\}}{\sinh(C_p W)}. \tag{3.52}$$

The a.c. diffusion current density due to holes may next be derived from (3.52) by using Fick's law of diffusion, as presented below:

$$J_{pa} = \frac{-qDp\partial p_a(x)}{\partial x} = \frac{qC_pD_p\left[p_e\, \sinh\, C_p\left\{\left(\frac{W}{2}\right) - x\right\} + p_c \sinh C_p\left\{\left(\frac{W}{2}\right) + x\right\}\right]}{\sinh(C_p W)} \tag{3.53}$$

The corresponding emitter and collector current densities may now be obtained from (3.53) by setting $x = -(W/2)$ and $+(W/2)$ respectively. Thus,

$$J_{pa}\left(\frac{-W}{2}\right) = qCpDp[p_e \text{ coth } (C_p W) - p_c \text{ cosech } (C_p W)] \tag{3.54}$$

and

$$J_{pa}\left(\frac{+W}{2}\right) = qCpDp[p_e \text{ cosech } (C_p W) - p_c \text{ coth } (C_p W)] \tag{3.55}$$

In the active region of the transistor, p_c approaches zero as V_C is large and negative. In that case (3.54) and (3.55) simplify to

$$J_{pe} = \left[\frac{q^2 C_p D_p p_E V_E}{kT}\right] \text{coth}(CpW) \tag{3.56}$$

and

$$J_{pc} = \left[\frac{q^2 C_p D_p p_E V_E}{kT}\right] \text{ cosech } (CpW) \tag{3.57}$$

where $p_E = p_n \exp(qV_E/kT)$. We can also compute the a.c. electron currents crossing the emitter and the collector junctions by letting W approach infinity and interchanging p s and n s, as electrons have to cross only one junction. Thus,

$$J_{ne} = \frac{q^2 C_{en} D_n n_E V_E}{kT} \tag{3.58}$$

where

$$C_{en}^2 = \frac{1 + j\omega\tau_{ne}}{L_{ne}^2} \tag{3.59}$$

τ_{ne} and L_{ne} denote the carrier lifetime and the diffusion length of electrons in the p-type emitter respectively. Similarly we find

$$J_{nc} = -\left[\frac{q^2 C_{cn} D_n n_C V_C}{kT}\right] \tag{3.60}$$

where

$$C_{cn}^2 = \frac{1 + j\omega\tau_{nc}}{L_{nc}^2} \tag{3.61}$$

τ_{nc} and L_{nc} refer to the electron lifetime and the diffusion length of electrons respectively in the p-type collector. We now define the emitter efficiency of the transistor as

$$\gamma = \frac{J_{pe}}{J_{pe} + J_{ne}} \tag{3.62}$$

and the base transport factor as

$$B = \frac{J_c}{J_{pe}} \tag{3.63}$$

so that the common-emitter current gain is given by

$$\frac{J_c}{J_e} = \frac{BJ_{pe}}{J_{pe} + J_{ne}} = B\gamma = \alpha \tag{3.64}$$

On the basis of earlier equations, we now obtain,

$$\gamma = \left[1 + \left(\frac{\sigma B}{\sigma E}\right)\left(\frac{C_{en}}{C_p}\right) \tanh\left\{(1 + j\omega\tau_p)^{1/2} \frac{W}{L_p}\right\}\right]^{-1} \tag{3.65}$$

where $\sigma_B = q\mu_n n, \sigma_E = q\mu_p p$. Thus to increase γ to unity, $\sigma_B \ll \sigma_E$. The transistor emitter is therefore required to be doped heavily compared to the base. Neglecting J_{nc}, the base transport factor works out to be

$$B = \text{sech}\,(C_p W) \tag{3.66}$$

By letting $W \to 0$, the results for the d.c. cases are

$$\gamma = \left[1 + \left(\frac{\sigma_B}{\sigma_E}\right)\left(\frac{L_p}{L_{ne}}\right)\tanh\left(\frac{W}{L_p}\right)\right]^{-1} \tag{3.67}$$

and

$$B = \text{sech}\left(\frac{W}{L_p}\right) \tag{3.68}$$

The transport factor is by far the most important parameter in determining the transistor current gain as γ is usually very close to unity.

Next, to derive the high frequency properties of the transistors, we know that

$$\cosh x = \prod_{n=1}^{\infty}\left[\frac{1+4x^2}{(2n-1)^2\pi^2}\right]$$

As the higher product terms are closer to unity than the first one, we need consider only the first term in the above expansion and write

$$\cosh x = \frac{1+4x^2}{\pi^2}$$

Utilizing the above result in (3.66), we get

$$\alpha = B = \text{sech}\,(C_p W) = [\cosh(C_p W)]^{-1} = \left[1 + \left(\frac{4}{\pi^2}\right)(C_p W)^2\right]$$

i.e.

$$\alpha = \frac{\alpha_0}{1 + j\left(\frac{\omega}{\omega_\alpha}\right)} \tag{3.69}$$

where

$$\alpha_0 = 1 - \left(\frac{4}{\pi^2}\right)\left(\frac{W}{L_p}\right)^2 \tag{3.70}$$

and

$$\omega_\alpha = \left[\left(\frac{1}{\tau_p}\right) + \left(\frac{\pi^2 D_p}{4W^2}\right)\right] \cong \left[\left(\frac{1}{\tau_p}\right) + \left(\frac{1}{\tau_t}\right)\right] \tag{3.71}$$

Equation (3.69) may also be put in the following simplified form:

$$\alpha = \left[\frac{\alpha_0}{\left\{1 + \left(\frac{\omega}{\omega_\alpha}\right)^2\right\}^{1/2}} \right]^{1/2} \exp(-j\theta)$$

where

$$\theta = tan^{-1}\left(\frac{\omega}{\omega_\alpha}\right) \tag{3.72}$$

Thus according to (3.72), the current gain of a transistor decreases with increase in frequency. At $\omega = \omega_\alpha$, the collector current falls to $(1/\sqrt{2})$ of its d.c.value. The frequency corresponding to this value of ω is called the half-power frequency or the alpha cutoff frequency. The results pertaining to the common-emitter mode may be derived similarly. We know that

$$\beta = \frac{\alpha}{1-\alpha} = \left[\left(\frac{1}{\alpha}\right) - 1\right]^{-1} = [\cosh\,(C_p W) - 1]^{-1} = \left[\left(\frac{4}{\pi^2}\right)(C_p W)^2\right]^{-1}$$

or

$$\beta = \frac{\beta_0}{1 + j\left(\frac{\omega}{\omega_\beta}\right)} \tag{3.73}$$

where

$$\beta_0 = \left(\frac{\pi^2}{4}\right)\left(\frac{L_p}{W}\right)^2 \tag{3.74}$$

and

$$\omega_\beta = \frac{1}{\tau_p} \tag{3.75}$$

Thus β_0 and ω_β denote the d.c. current gain and beta cutoff frequency respectively. We may now combine (3.71) and (3.75) as follows:

$$\omega_\alpha = \left[\left(\frac{1}{\tau_p}\right) + \frac{\pi^2 D_p}{4W^2}\right] = \left(\frac{1}{\tau_p}\right)\left[1 + \frac{\pi^2 L_p^2}{4W^2}\right] = \omega_\beta(\beta_0 + 1) \tag{3.76}$$

Since $\beta_0 \gg 1, \omega_\alpha \gg \omega_\beta$. Thus, by using common-emitter mode, one can realize higher gains at the expense of being used at lower frequencies. We have already noticed earlier that in order to increase γ, σ_E has to be considerably larger than σ_B. To derive information about the relative values of σ_B and σ_C for satisfactory transistor operation, we have to consider the expression for the reverse saturation current density crossing the collector junction when the emitter is left open (i.e. $I_E = 0$). Accordingly for a transistor biased in the active region, we get from (3.26),

$$\exp\left(\frac{qV_E}{kT}\right)-1=\frac{-q\left[\left(\frac{D_p p_n}{L_p}\right)\text{ cosech}\left(\frac{W}{L_p}\right)\right]}{q\left[\left(\frac{D_p p_n}{L_p}\right)\text{ coth}\left(\frac{W}{L_p}\right)+\left(\frac{D_n n_{pe}}{L_{ne}}\right)\right]} \tag{3.77}$$

Substituting this in (3.25), we get

$$I_{CO}=\frac{-qA\left[\left(\frac{D_p p_n}{L_p}\right)^2\text{ cosech}^2\left(\frac{W}{L_p}\right)\right]}{\left[\left(\frac{D_p p_n}{L_p}\right)\text{ coth}\left(\frac{W}{L_p}\right)+\left(\frac{D_n n_{pe}}{L_{ne}}\right)\right]+\left(\frac{qAD_n n_{pc}}{L_{nc}}\right)+\left(\frac{qAD_p p_n}{L_p}\right)\text{ coth}\left(\frac{W}{L_p}\right)} \tag{3.78}$$

But $(n_{pe}/p_n)=(n_n/p_{pe})\doteq(\sigma_B/\sigma_E)(\mu_p/\mu_n)\ll 1$. As a result of this, (3.78) simplifies to

$$I_{CO}=\left[\frac{q^2 D_p n_i^2 \mu_n}{L_p\sigma_B}\right]\tanh\left(\frac{W}{L_p}\right)+\left[\frac{q^2 D_p n_i^2 \mu_p}{L_{nc}\sigma_C}\right] \tag{3.79}$$

where we have used $p_n=[qn_i^2\mu_n/\sigma_B]$ and $n_{pc}=[qn_i^2\mu_n/\sigma_C]$. According to (3.79), I_{CO} can be significantly reduced by increasing σ_C as σ_B cannot be increased beyond a particular limit because it has to remain lower than σ_E.

Sometimes a quantity called the maximum frequency of oscillations (f_m) is used as a figure of merit for high frequency transistor work. An expression for it can be derived next from the fundamental device parameters. This is the maximum frequency upto which a transistor can be made to oscillate. At extremely high frequencies, the transistor h-equivalent circuit parameters assume the following values: $h_{11e}=r_b'$, $h_{12e}=0$, $h_{21e}=(\omega_\alpha/j\omega)$ and $h_{22e}=\omega_\alpha C_{tc}$. The h equivalent circuit is shown in Fig. 3.12. If the output of the transistor amplifier is fed back to the input, self-sustaining oscillations can start under certain conditions. For this to happen, the input and the output currents must have the

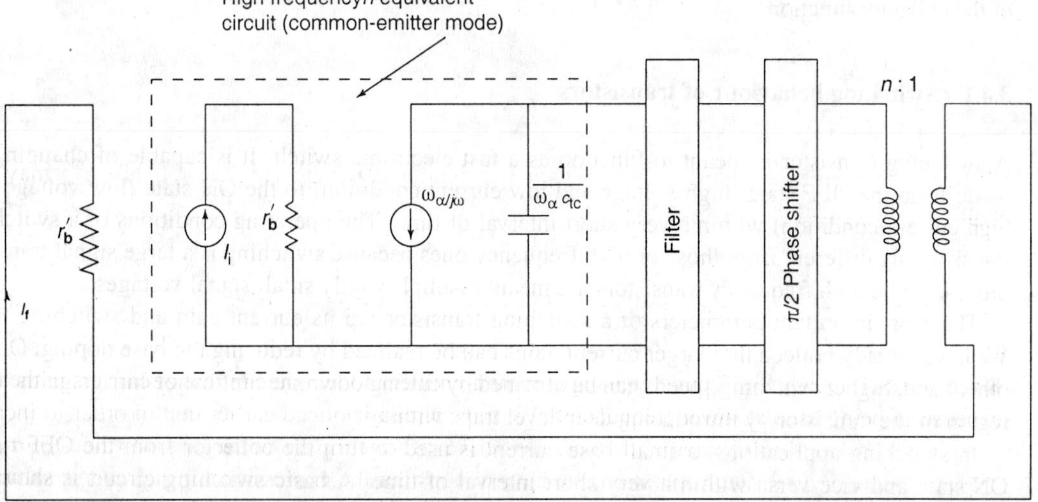

Figure 3.12 *Calculation of the maximum frequency (f_m) of oscillations*

same magnitudes and phase. As shown in Fig. 3.12, the output of the transistor is fed to an ideal filter which tunes out the effect of finite C_{tc} and then through a $(\pi/2)$ phase shifter which changes the phase just enough to cancel the imaginary part of the independent current source, so that the output and the input currents appear in the same phase. The output of the phase shifter is next fed through an ideal transformer whose output directly feeds the input of the transistor. From Fig. 3.12, we may directly write

$$\frac{I_f}{n} = \frac{\left(\frac{\omega_\alpha}{\omega}\right) I_i \left(\frac{1}{\omega_\alpha C_{tc}}\right)}{r'_b n^2 + \left(\frac{1}{\omega_\alpha C_{tc}}\right)} \tag{3.80}$$

For self-sustained oscillations, $I_i = I_f$. It then follows from (3.80) that

$$\omega = \frac{n\omega_\alpha}{1 + n^2 \omega_\alpha r'_\beta C_{tc}} \tag{3.81}$$

Now, we have to choose the turn ratio n to maximize ω. Differentiating ω with respect to n, we get

$$\frac{d\omega}{dn} = 0 = \omega_\alpha[1 + n^2 \omega_\alpha r'_b C_{tc}] - 2\omega_\alpha n^2 r'_b C_{tc}$$

Solving for n, we find

$$n = (\omega_\alpha r'_b C_{tc})^{-1/2} \tag{3.82}$$

Combining (3.81) and (3.82), we find

$$f_m = (f_\alpha / 8\pi r'_b C_{tc})^{1/2} \tag{3.83}$$

It thus turns out that the base resistance r'_b is an important high frequency transistor parameter. The asymptotic value of h_{11e} at very high frequencies gives r'_b. C_{tc} measures the transition layer capacitance of the collector junction.

3.4.1 Switching behaviour of transistors

A switching transistor is meant to function as a fast electronic switch. It is capable of changing its mode from the OFF state (high voltage and low current condition) to the ON state (low voltage and high current condition) within a very short interval of time. The operating conditions of a switching transistor are different from those of high frequency ones because switching is a large signal transient process while high frequency transistors are meant to amplify only small signal voltages.

The most important parameters of a switching transistor are its current gain and switching time. We have already noticed that larger current gains can be realized by reducing the base doping. On the other hand, higher switching speeds can be obtained by cutting down the lifetime of carriers in the base region of the transistor by introducing deep level traps within it.

In switching applications, a small base current is used to turn the collector from the OFF to the ON state and vice versa within a very short interval of time. A basic switching circuit is shown in Fig. 3.13 where the emitter-base voltage V_{EB} is suddenly changed from negative to positive values. In the OFF state, the collector current is very low because both emitter-base and collector-base junctions are reverse biased. When both junctions become forward biased, the collector current will increase by following the load line until the ON state is reached. Thus, the transistor is virtually open-circuited in the OFF state (cutoff mode) and short-circuited in the ON state (saturated mode) as it is expected of an ideal switch. To understand the switching behaviour of transistors, we first discuss below the Ebers–Moll model.

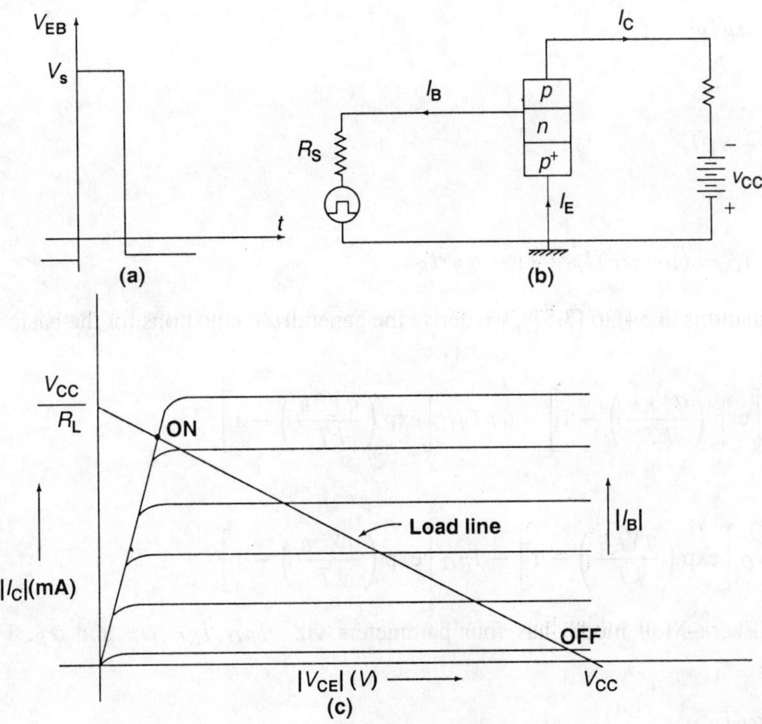

Figure 3.13 *(a) A switching pulse, (b) the basic switching circuit, (c) the collector characteristics*

Ebers–Moll model

The one dimensional *pnp* transistor can be represented as two *pn* junctions connected back-to-back with a common *n*-region. The current that flows through the emitter-base junction is shown as I_F. This depends on the emitter-base voltage V_{EB}. In the active mode of the transistor operation, a fraction of I_F, represented by $\alpha_F I_F$ flows into the collector. This is represented by the current generator $\alpha_F I_F$ in the base-collector circuit where α_F represents the forward common-emitter current gain. In the same way, the collector current I_R depends on the collector-base voltage V_{CB}. A fraction viz., $\alpha_R I_R$ flows into the emitter-base circuit. This has been represented by a constant current generator $\alpha_R I_R$ inserted into the input circuit where I_R is called the reverse common-base current gain. We may now write

$$I_F = I_{FO}\left[\exp\left(\frac{qV_{EB}}{kT}\right) - 1\right] \tag{3.84}$$

and

$$I_R = I_{RO}\left[\exp\left(\frac{qV_{CB}}{kT}\right) - 1\right] \quad (3.85)$$

The terminal currents are

$$I_E = I_F - \alpha_R I_R \quad (3.86)$$

and

$$-I_C = I_R - \alpha_F I_F \quad (3.87)$$

Therefore,

$$I_B = I_E - I_C = (1-\alpha_F)I_F + (1-\alpha_R)I_R \quad (3.88)$$

By combining equations (3.84) to (3.87), we derive the generalized equations for the basic Ebers–Moll model as

$$I_E = I_{FO}\left[\exp\left(\frac{qV_{EB}}{kT}\right) - 1\right] - \alpha_R I_{RO}\left[\exp\left(\frac{qV_{CB}}{kT}\right) - 1\right] \quad (3.89)$$

and

$$I_C = \alpha_F I_{FO}\left[\exp\left(\frac{qV_{EB}}{kT}\right) - 1\right] - I_{RO}\left[\exp\left(\frac{qV_{CB}}{kT}\right) - 1\right] \quad (3.90)$$

Thus, the basic Ebers–Moll model has four parameters viz., I_{FO}, I_{RO}, α_F and α_R. For an ideal transistor,

$$\alpha_F I_{FO} = \alpha_R I_{RO} \quad (3.91)$$

Next we shall consider the switching action of bipolar transistors based on this Ebers–Moll model (Fig. 3.14). Using (3.89) and (3.90), the coefficients α_F and α_R can be measured from the active and the inverted mode of transistor operations. The coefficients I_{FO} and I_{RO} can be obtained from two additional measurements of I_{EO} and I_{CO} where I_{EO} is the reverse saturation current crossing the emitter-base junction with collector open-circuited (i.e. $\exp(qV_{EB}/kT) \ll 1$ and $I_C = 0$). Similarly,

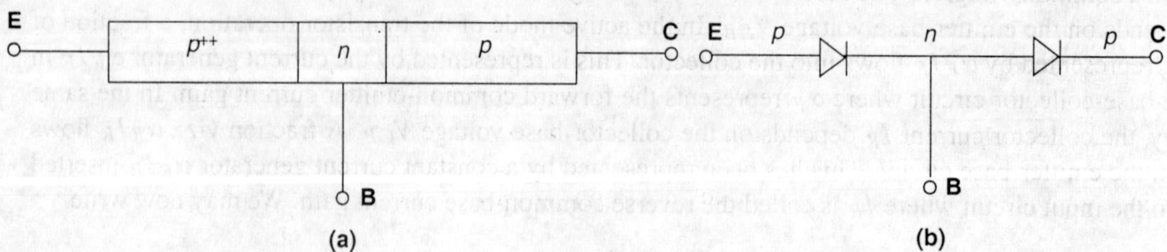

Figure 3.14 *(a) Cross-section of a p-n-p transistor, (b) a p-n-p transistor represented as two pn junctions conn ected back-to-back*

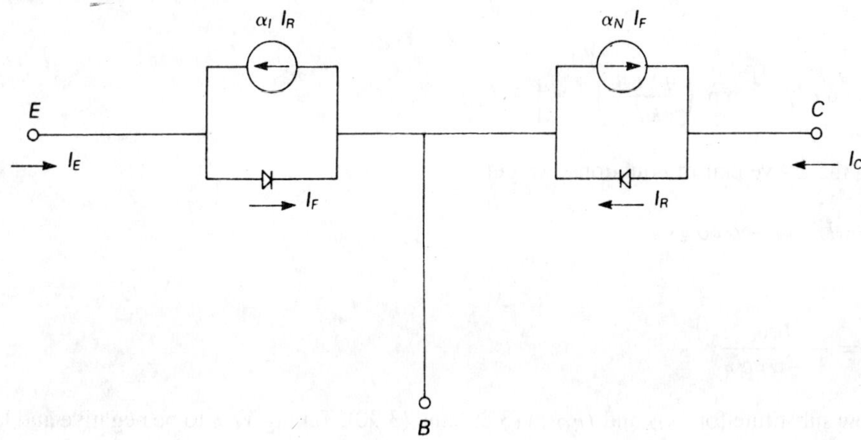

Figure 3.14 *continued (c) Circuit diagram for an Ebers–Moll model for a pnp transistor*

I_{CO} is the measured reverse saturation current crossing the base-collector junction with the emitter open-circuited (i.e., $\exp(qV_{CB}/kT) \ll 1$ and $I_E = 0$). Imposing the first condition in (3.89) and (3.90) we get

$$I_{E0} = -I_{FO} - \alpha_R I_{RO}\left[\exp\left(\frac{qV_{CB}}{kT}\right) - 1\right]$$

and

$$0 = -\alpha_F I_{F0} - I_{RO}\left[\exp\left(\frac{qV_{CB}}{kT}\right) - 1\right]$$

or

$$\alpha_F I_{F0} = -I_{RO}\left[\exp\left(\frac{qV_{CB}}{kT}\right) - 1\right]$$

Combining the above relations, we find

$$I_{E0} = -I_{FO} - \alpha_R(-\alpha_F I_{F0}) = -I_{FO} + \alpha_R\alpha_F I_{F0} = -I_{FO}(1 - \alpha_R\alpha_F)$$

or

$$I_{FO} = \frac{-I_{E0}}{1 - \alpha_R\alpha_F} \tag{3.92}$$

Next, imposing the second condition in (3.89) and (3.90), we get

$$0 = I_{FO}\left[\exp\left(\frac{qV_{EB}}{kT}\right) - 1\right] + \alpha_R I_{RO}$$

and

$$I_{C0} = \alpha_F I_{FO}\left[\exp\left(\frac{qV_{EB}}{kT}\right) - 1\right] + I_{RO}$$

Combining the above pair of equations, we get

$$I_{C0} = I_{RO}(1 - \alpha_F\alpha_R)$$

or

$$I_{RO} = \frac{I_{C0}}{1 - \alpha_F\alpha_R} \tag{3.93}$$

We may now substitute for I_{FO} and I_{RO} in (3.89) and (3.90). Taking V_{CB} to be negative and large, the above mentioned equations reduce to

$$I_E = -\left[\frac{I_{EO}}{1 - \alpha_F\alpha_R}\right]\exp\left(\frac{qV_{EB}}{kT}\right) + \frac{(1-\alpha_F)I_{EO}}{1 - \alpha_F\alpha_R} \tag{3.94}$$

and

$$I_C = -\left[\frac{\alpha_F I_{EO}}{1 - \alpha_F\alpha_R}\right]\exp\left(\frac{qV_{EB}}{kT}\right) + \frac{(1-\alpha_R)I_{CO}}{1 - \alpha_F\alpha_R} \tag{3.95}$$

Again, it follows from (3.89) that

$$I_{FO}\left[\exp\left(\frac{qV_{EB}}{kT}\right) - 1\right] = I_E + \alpha_R I_{RO}\left[\exp\left(\frac{qV_{CB}}{kT}\right) - 1\right]$$

Again from (3.90), we get

$$\alpha_F\, I_{FO}\left[\exp\left(\frac{qV_{EB}}{kT}\right) - 1\right] = I_C + I_{RO}\left[\exp\left(\frac{qV_{CB}}{kT}\right) - 1\right]$$

Combining the above pair of equations, we get

$$V_{CB} = \left(\frac{kT}{q}\right)\ln\left[1 + \frac{\alpha_F I_E - I_C}{I_{C0}}\right] \tag{3.96}$$

and

$$V_{EB} = \left(\frac{kT}{q}\right)\ln\left[1 + \frac{\alpha_R I_C - I_E}{I_{E0}}\right] \tag{3.97}$$

Three basic quantities viz., the OFF impedance, the ON impedance and the switching time are required to characterize the switching operation of a transistor. The impedance in the OFF condition may be obtained from (3.95) by setting $\exp(qV_{EB}/kT) \ll 1$. One then derives

$$R(\text{OFF}) = \frac{V_C}{I_C(\text{OFF})} = \frac{V_C(1 - \alpha_F\alpha_R)}{I_{C0}(1 - \alpha_R)} \tag{3.98}$$

Next, the impedance in the ON condition may be written as

$$R(\text{ON}) = \frac{V_{CE}(\text{ON})}{I_C(\text{ON})} = \frac{(V_{EB} - V_{CB})}{I_C} \tag{3.99}$$

But from (3.96) and (3.97), we get

$$V_{EC} = V_{EB} - V_{CB} = \left(\frac{kT}{q}\right) \ln \frac{I_{C0}\left[1 + (1 - \alpha_R)\left(\frac{I_C}{I_B}\right)\right]}{I_{E0}\left[(1 - \alpha_F)\left(\frac{I_C}{I_B}\right) - \alpha_F\right]}$$

where we have neglected (I_{E0}/I_B) and (I_{C0}/I_B) terms. Using the above result in (3.99), we find

$$R(\text{ON}) = \left(\frac{kT}{qI_C}\right) \ln \frac{I_{C0}\left[1 + (1 - \alpha_R)\left(\frac{I_C}{I_B}\right)\right]}{I_{E0}\left[(1 - \alpha_F)\left(\frac{I_C}{I_B}\right) - \alpha_F\right]} \tag{3.100}$$

Equation (3.98) suggests that the OFF impedance will be very high for a very low value of I_{C0}. According to (3.100), the ON impedance would be very low for larger values of I_C.

Finally, we proceed to calculate the switching time which is the time required by a transistor to switch from the OFF to the ON condition and vice versa. When a current pulse is applied to the base-emitter terminal at $t = 0$ (Fig. 3.15), the transistor is in the process of being turned ON from the OFF state. We shall show that the transient time is determined by the variation of the stored charge in the base layer. The total minority hole charge stored in the base layer is given by

$$Q_B = qA \int_0^W [p_n(x) - p_{n0}]\, dx$$

From (2.130), we may immediately write the charge control equation for the transistor as

$$i_B = \frac{dQ_B(t)}{dt} + \left[\frac{Q_B(t)}{\tau_p}\right] \tag{3.101}$$

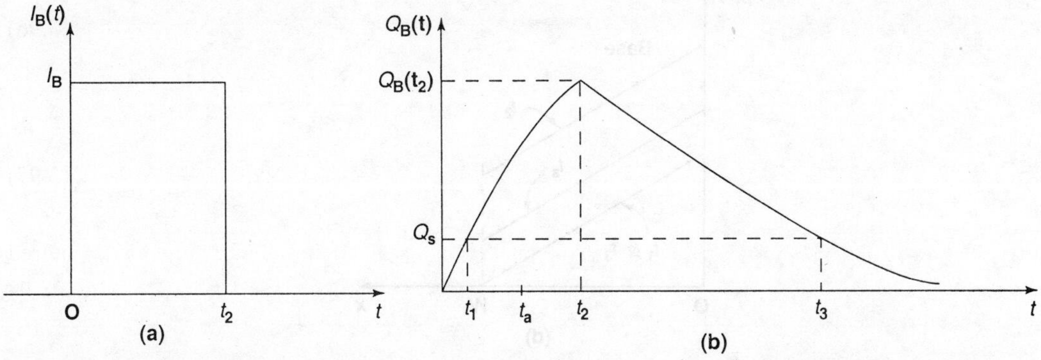

Figure 3.15 *The switching transients for a transistor: (a) the input current pulse, (b) the variation of the stored charge with time*

During the turn on transient, the base current is constant. Equation (3.101) may then be rewritten as

$$\frac{dQ_B(t)}{dt} = I_B - \left[\frac{Q_B(t)}{I_B}\right] \tag{3.102}$$

If $Q_B = 0$ at $t = 0$, the solution of (3.102) may be written as

$$Q_B(t) = I_B\tau_p\left[1 - \exp\left(\frac{-t}{\tau_p}\right)\right] \tag{3.103}$$

Thus for $t > \tau_p$, $Q_B(t) \to I_B\tau_p$, a plot of $Q_B(t)$ is shown in Fig. 3.15(b). For $Q_B(t) \ll Q_S$ where Q_S denotes the base charge when $V_{CB} = 0$ i.e. at the edge of saturation (as shown in Fig. 3.15(d)). If τ_t denotes the transit time for holes through the base layer, the collector current is obtained as

$$I_C(t) = \frac{Q_B(t)}{\tau_t} = \left[\frac{I_B\tau_p}{\tau_t}\right]\left[1 - \exp\left(\frac{-t}{\tau_p}\right)\right] \tag{3.104}$$

The variation of $I_C(t)$ as a function of time is plotted in Fig. 3.15(c). At $t = t_1$, the stored base charge reaches Q_S (which denotes the charge at which the transistor becomes saturated). Beyond this stage, the collector current remains essentially constant. For $Q_B > Q_S$, the device, therefore operates in the

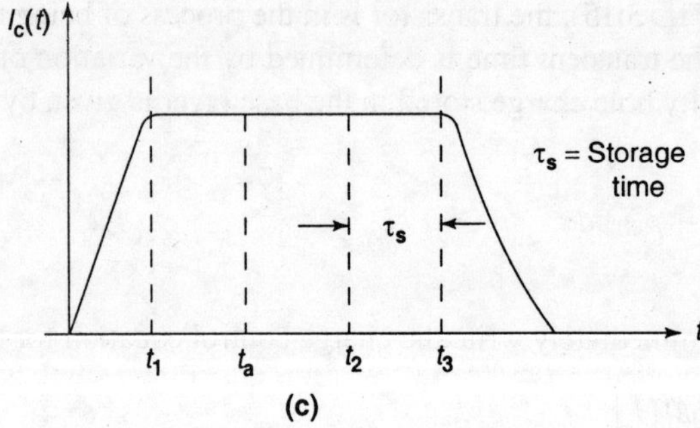

(c)

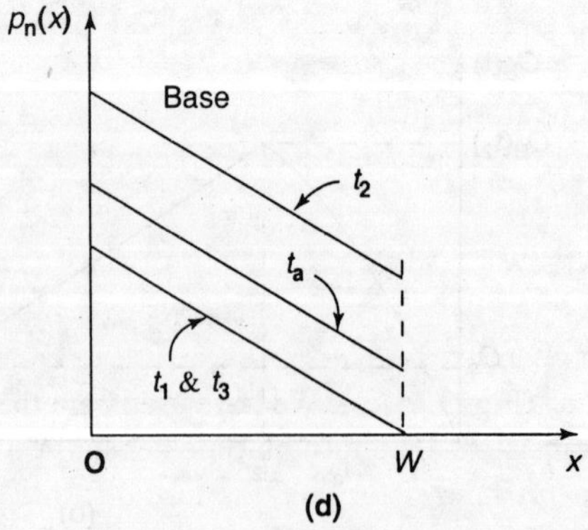

(d)

Figure 3.15 *continued (c) the variation of the output collector current with time, (d) the dependence of the minority carrier hole density as a function of distance for different times*

saturated mode. Fig. 3.15(d) shows that for any time greater than t_1 (say t_a), the hole distribution curve $p_n(x)$ vs. x will be parallel to that at $t = t_1$. Therefore, the gradients at any x and the emitter and the collector currents remain essentially the same. Putting $t = t_1$ in (3.103), we get

$$Q_S = I_B\tau_p\left[1 - \exp\left(\frac{-t_1}{\tau_p}\right)\right] \tag{3.105}$$

Solving for t_1, we obtain

$$t_1 = \tau_p \ln\left[1 - \left(\frac{Q_S}{I_B\tau_p}\right)\right]^{-1} = \tau_p \ln\left[1 - \left(\frac{I_C}{\beta I_B}\right)\right]^{-1} \tag{3.106}$$

where $I_B = (V_S/R_S)$ and $Q_S = (V_{CC}/R_L)t_t$ (see Fig. 3.13). According to (3.106), to reduce the turn on transient time t_1, the minority carrier lifetime τ_p and the stored charge Q_S must be reduced while the base current I_B has to be increased. During the turn off, the base current is suddenly switched off at $t = t_2$. The transient equation corresponding to this case may be obtained from (3.101) by putting $i_B = 0$. The solution to the resulting equation may then be written as

$$Q_B(t) = Q_B(t_2)\exp\left[\frac{-(t - t_2)}{\tau_p}\right] \tag{3.107}$$

where $Q_B(t_2)$ may be obtained from (3.103) by putting $t = t_2$. Beyond $t = t_2$, $Q_B(t)$ is plotted in Fig. 3.15(b). Since the transistor was initially in the saturated state, the collector current remains relatively unchanged till Q_B is reduced to Q_S at $t = t_3$. The duration between t_2 and t_3 is defined as the storage time t_s. When $Q_B < Q_S$, the device once again enters the active mode from the saturated state. The collector current in the interval between t_2 and t_3 is given by

$$I_C = \frac{Q_S}{t_t} = \beta I_B\left[1 - \exp\left(\frac{-t_1}{t_p}\right)\right] \tag{3.108}$$

which is constant. This is plotted in Fig. 3.15(c). The storage time t_s may be computed from (3.107) by putting $Q_B(t_3) = Q_S$. That is,

$$t_s = \tau_p \ln\left[\frac{Q_B(t_2)}{Q_S}\right] = \tau_p \ln\left[\frac{I_B\tau_p}{Q_S}\right] = \tau_p \ln\left[\frac{\beta I_B}{I_C}\right] \tag{3.109}$$

since the maximum charge that can be stored in the base layer is $I_B\tau_p$ (see (3.103)). Thus a small τ_p in the base layer is required to reduce t_s. Beyond $t = t_3$, when the transistor enters the active mode, the collector current decays exponentially as

$$I_C(t) = \left(\frac{Q_S}{\tau_t}\right)\exp\left(\frac{-t}{\tau_p}\right) = I_C \exp\left(\frac{-t}{\tau_p}\right) \tag{3.110}$$

with a characteristic time constant τ_p (Fig. 3.15(c)). We have used here the charge control equation to study the switching transients of transistors. The turn on time depends on how fast we can add holes (minority carriers) to the base of a *pnp* transistor, and the turn off time depends upon how fast we can remove holes by recombination. It is observed that the most important parameter for the study of switching transients is the minority carrier lifetime τ_p. One effective way of reducing it is by introducing efficient recombination traps near the energy gap centre.

We have just noticed that in order to explain the switching behaviour of transistors, their operations in the following three different modes have to be recognized

(i) the cutoff mode when both the emitter and the collector junctions are reverse biased;
(ii) the active mode when the emitter junction is forward biased and the collector junction is reverse biased; and finally
(iii) the saturated mode when both the emitter and the collector junctions can be regarded as forward biased.

The minority carrier density variation as a function of distance in the base region in the above three cases is shown in Fig. 3.16. It is explained in Fig. 3.16(b) how the minority carrier distribution in the saturated state can be regarded to be formed by the superpositions of minority carrier distributions due to the forward biased emitter and collector junctions.

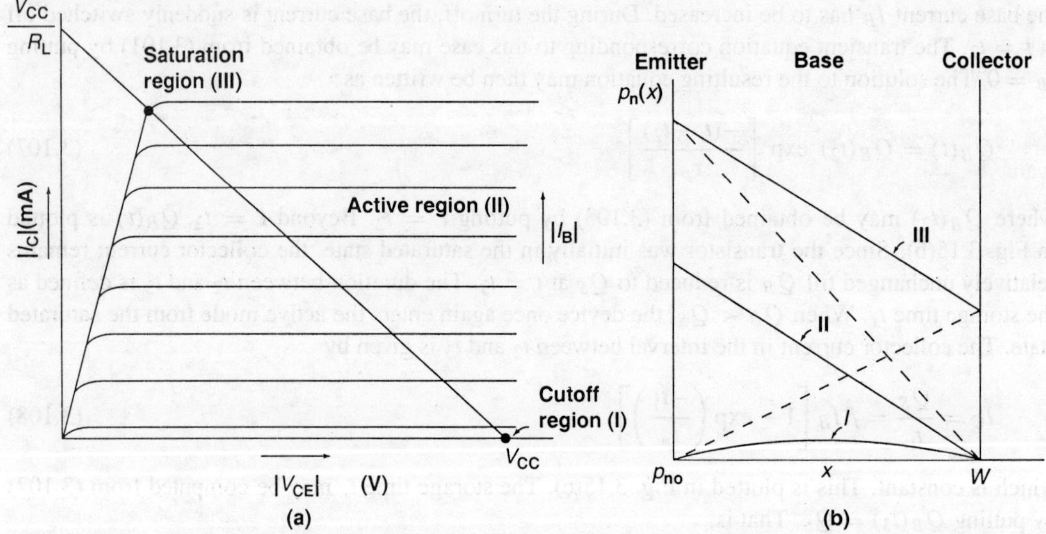

Figure 3.16 *(a) The operating modes of a transistor (b) the minority carrier distribution in the base region of a transistor for active, cut-off and saturated modes*

As the last example of the Ebers–Moll model, we would now employ it to explain the common-emitter transistor characteristics. While deriving (3.100), we used

$$V_{CE} = \left(\frac{kT}{q}\right) \ln \left[\frac{(1-\alpha)\left(\frac{I_C}{I_B}\right) - \alpha}{1 + (1-\alpha)\left(\frac{I_C}{I_B}\right)}\right] \tag{3.111}$$

where we presumed $I_{E0} \cong I_{C0}$ and $\alpha_F \cong \alpha_R = \alpha \sim 1$ (say). Since $\beta = \alpha/(1-\alpha) \cong (1-\alpha)^{-1}$, (3.111) can be simplified to

$$V_{CE} = \frac{kT}{q} \ln \left[\frac{\left(\frac{1}{\beta}\right)\left(\frac{I_C}{I_B}\right) - 1}{1 + \left(\frac{1}{\beta}\right)\left(\frac{I_C}{I_B}\right)}\right] \tag{3.112}$$

Solving for (I_C/I_B), we get

$$\left(\frac{I_C}{I_B}\right) = \left[\frac{\left\{1 + \exp\left(\frac{qV_{CE}}{kT}\right)\right\}}{\left(\frac{1}{\beta}\right)\left\{1 - \exp\left(\frac{qV_{CE}}{kT}\right)\right\}}\right] \tag{3.113}$$

Increasing V_{CE} increases the numerator but decreases the denominator. Consequently, for a given I_B, I_C increases monotonically with increase in V_{CE} until it stabilizes at βI_B for a moderately large value of V_{CE}. We have already described such an output characteristic in Fig. 3.16(a). But in order to increase the gentle rise of I_C with V_{CE} we may have to apply the Early effect.

Specifications for switching transistors While describing various types of switching times, we have neglected the charging time of the emitter junction capacitance in going from cutoff to saturation. Since the emitter junction is reverse biased during cutoff, it is necessary for the emitter space charge layer capacitance to be charged to the forward biased condition before the collector current starts flowing. Therefore, we must include a delay time t_d in Fig. 3.17 to account for this effect. The rise time t_r of a transistor is defined as the time required for the collector current to rise from 10% to 90% of its final value. A third specification is the fall time t_f, defined as the time required for the current to fall from $0.9I_C$ to $0.1I_C$.

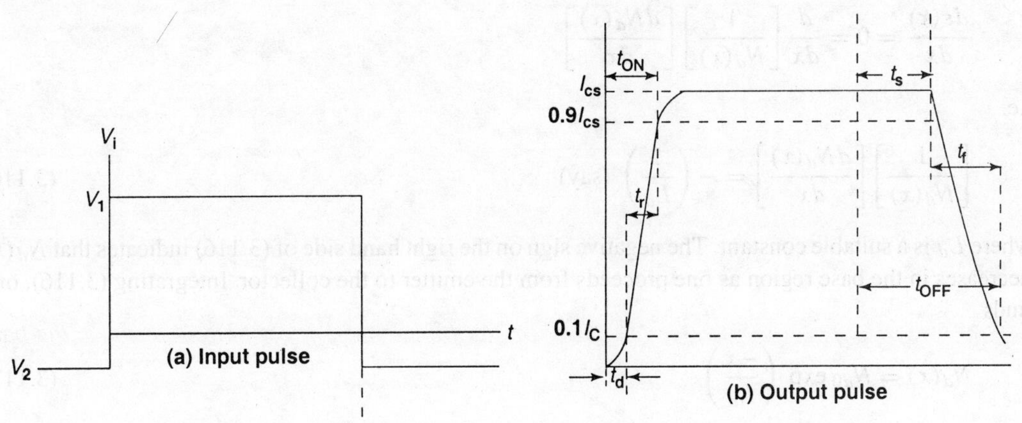

Figure 3.17 The collector current during a switching transient

3.5 Graded base transistors

Let us now consider a *pnp* transistor with a diffused base region instead of a homogeneously doped base one so that the impurity density over the base layer varies with distance instead of remaining constant. The density of donors and that of donated electrons are expected initially to be the same at every point in space. But, under room temperature conditions, the donor density gradient gets permanently locked up in space while the electrons remain mobile. As a result of this, electrons will have a tendency to diffuse over to the lower concentration side. Once a few electrons are able to do so, they expose the localized donor ions, thereby producing an electric field in the body of the base layer. Such an electric field would eventually tend to pull back the diffusing electrons producing a condition of dynamic equilibrium. At this stage, the drift and the diffusion components of electron currents become equal and opposite. But the creation of a local electric field to stop further diffusion of electrons enhances the hole flow in the body of the base layer. This consequently reduces their transit time, thereby increasing the gain and the cutoff frequency of the transistor.

The magnitude of the electric field intensity set up over the base layer may be obtained by presuming the net electron current density flowing over the base layer to zero. That is,

$$j_n(x) = 0 = q\mu_n n(x)\varepsilon(x) + qD_n \frac{dn(x)}{dx} \tag{3.114}$$

Solving for $\varepsilon(x)$, we find

$$\varepsilon(x) = -\left(\frac{kT}{q}\right)\left[\frac{1}{n(x)}\right]\left[\frac{dn(x)}{dx}\right] \tag{3.115}$$

By presuming complete ionization of donors, we may write $n(x) \cong N_d(x)$. Since the electron density variation with distance will be slightly displaced relative to that of the donor density variation, we may also presume $dn(x)/dx \cong dN_d(x)/dx$. To maximize the electric field $\varepsilon(x)$ in the base region, we must set

$$\frac{d\varepsilon(x)}{dx} = 0 = \frac{d}{dx}\left[\frac{1}{N_d(x)}\right]\left[\frac{dN_d(x)}{dx}\right]$$

i.e.

$$\left[\frac{1}{N_d(x)}\right]\left[\frac{dN_d(x)}{dx}\right] = -\left(\frac{1}{L_d}\right) \text{ (say)} \tag{3.116}$$

where L_d is a suitable constant. The negative sign on the right hand side of (3.116) indicates that $N_d(x)$ decreases in the base region as one proceeds from the emitter to the collector. Integrating (3.116), one finds

$$N_d(x) = N_{d0} \exp\left(\frac{-x}{L_d}\right) \tag{3.117}$$

where N_{d0} denotes the donor density in the emitter side of the base layer. Hence, the optimum impurity distribution to produce the maximum electric field in the base layer is given by (3.117) (Fig. 3.18).

The potential difference developed between the two ends of the base layer may then be obtained as

$$V_b = \int_0^W \varepsilon(x)dx = -\left(\frac{kT}{q}\right)\int_{N_d(0)}^{N_d(W)} \frac{dn(x)}{n(x)}$$

i.e.,

$$V_b = \left(\frac{kT}{q}\right) \ln\left[\frac{N_d(0)}{N_d(W)}\right] \tag{3.118}$$

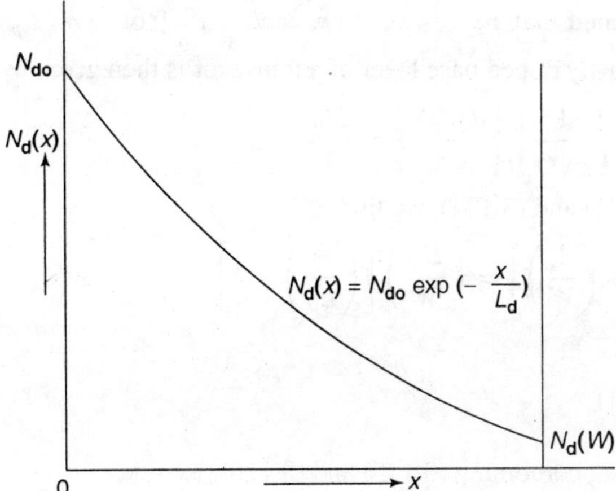

Figure 3.18 *Exponentially decaying donor concentration in the base region of a drift transistor*

The drift velocity of holes injected into the base layer will therefore be governed by V_b in accordance with the relation $1/2m_p^* v_d^2 = qV_b$. To minimize the hole transit time through the base layer, V_b has to be maximized while $N_d(W)$ is required to be a minimum. In Si transistors, it may be possible to increase $N_d(0)$ upto about $10^{18}/\text{cm}^3$ while the minimum value of $N_d(W)$ could only be n_i. Hence, the Fermi energy level resides near the conduction band edge at the emitter end, while at the collector end of the base layer it resides near the energy gap centre. Hence, the net built-in potential developed over the base layer due to non-uniform doping would be $(E_G/2q)$ at the most. The hole current density with the built-in field present is given by

$$j_p(x) = q\mu_p p(x)\varepsilon(x) - qD_p \frac{dp(x)}{dx} \tag{3.119}$$

Substituting for $\varepsilon(x)$ from (3.115), we find

$$j_p(x) = -qD_p p(x) \left[\left\{ \frac{1}{n(x)} \right\} \left\{ \frac{dn(x)}{dx} \right\} + \left\{ \frac{1}{p(x)} \right\} \left\{ \frac{dp(x)}{dx} \right\} \right] \tag{3.120}$$

For space-charge neutrality, the electron density at any point of the base layer would be $n(x) = N_d(x) + p(x)$. Hence, the hole velocity $u(x)$ through the base layer is given by

$$u(x) = \frac{j_p(x)}{qp(x)} = -D_p \left[\frac{1}{N_d(x)} \frac{d}{dx} (N_d(x) + p(x)) + \left(\frac{1}{p(x)} \right) \left(\frac{dp(x)}{dx} \right) \right] \tag{3.121}$$

In the low level injection condition $[p(x) \ll N_d(x)]$, the above expression reduces to

$$u(x) = -D_p \left[\frac{1}{N_d(x)} \frac{d}{dx} (N_d(x)) + \left(\frac{1}{p(x)} \right) \left(\frac{dp(x)}{dx} \right) \right] \tag{3.122}$$

For a normally biased *pnp* transistor, we derive from (3.22) that

$$J_{pE} = \left(\frac{qD_p}{L_p} \right) p_E \left(\frac{L_p}{W} \right) \tag{3.123}$$

where it has been presumed that $p_E \gg p_n > p_C$ and $\lim_{W\to 0}$ [coth (W/L_p)] $= (L_p/W)$. The drift velocity in a homogeneously doped base layer of a transistor is then given by

$$u = \frac{J_{pE}}{qp_E} = -D_p\left\{\frac{1}{p(x)}\right\}\left\{\frac{dp(x)}{dx}\right\} = \frac{D_p}{W} \tag{3.124}$$

If we now combine (3.122) and (3.124), we find

$$u = D_p\left[\left(\frac{1}{L_d}\right)+\left(\frac{1}{W}\right)\right] = \left(\frac{D_p}{W}\right)\left[\left(\frac{W}{L_d}\right)+1\right]$$

or

$$u = \left(\frac{D_p}{W}\right)[f+1] \tag{3.125}$$

where $f = (W/L_d)$. Also, combining (3.115) and (3.116), we find

$$\varepsilon = \frac{kT}{qL_d} \tag{3.126}$$

Equation (3.126) states that the maximum electric field is constant throughout the base layer. Therefore, we may also write

$$V_b = \varepsilon W = \frac{kTW}{qL_d} \tag{3.127}$$

Hence, according to (3.125), the velocity of the injected holes in the case of a graded base transistor increases $f+1$ fold, compared to the case of a homogeneously doped base transistor in the low level injection case. It is interesting to point out that for Si transistors f works out to be about 43. This shortening of the transit time can be a very important factor for high frequency applications (see (3.71)).

Current gains can also be increased if a heterojunction is used as the emitter of a transistor. The emitter efficiency is then automatically increased without the strict requirements on dopings of the emitter and the base regions. In a heterojunction emitter it is possible to get the barrier for electrons to be smaller compared to that for holes. Since the carrier injection varies exponentially with the barrier height, even a small difference between the heights of these two barriers can make a large change in the transport of electrons and holes across the emitter junction. In this case, one remains free to choose the doping of the base layer to reduce the base resistance and that of the emitter, to reduce the emitter capacitance. The high frequency characteristics of transistors can then be improved considerably. Heterojunction bipolar transistors can be fabricated from GaAs/AlGaAs systems.

3.6 Field-effect transistors

Bipolar junction transistors have revolutionized the electronic industry. But, its low input impedance and the difficulty in assembling them in integrated circuits are among the few problems which they pose to device engineers. Field effect transistors do not suffer from these disadvantages. They are available in various configurations. Here, we shall describe three types of geometries viz.,

(i) the junction field-effect transistor (JFET),
(ii) the modulation doped field-effect transistor (MODFET), and
(iii) the static induction transistor (SIT).

3.6.1 Junction field-effect transistor (JFET)

In order to describe the basic physical characteristics of the device we will consider here its rudimentary configuration consisting of a single crystal n-type semiconductor bar with ohmic contacts at both ends and two p^+ contacts applied at its opposite ends. The device in this form is shown in Fig. 3.19.

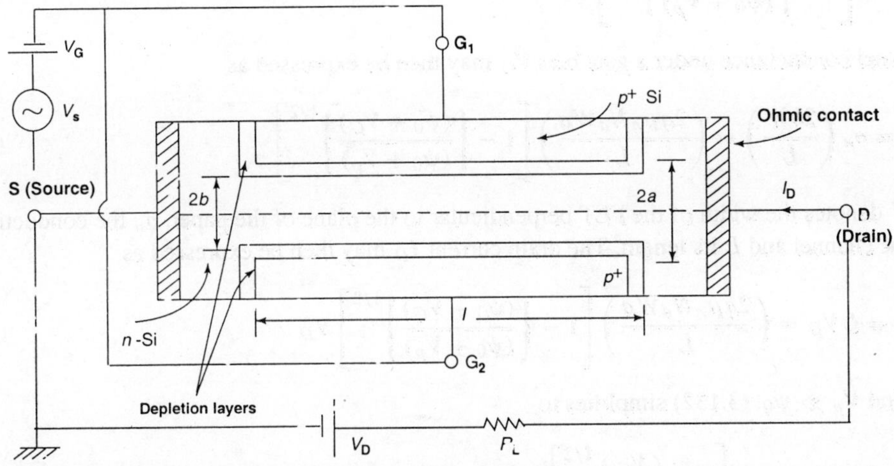

Figure 3.19 Configuration of a junction field effect transistor (JFET) with terminal connections to act as an amplifier

The two p^+ contacts, G_1 and G_2 are called gates and are connected to each other, as shown. A small positive voltage V_D is applied to the drain D relative to the source S. As a result of this, a current I_d flows through the channel. Due to a potential drop between the drain and the source along the channel, a potential gradient exists along the length of the channel. As such, the potential differences between the gate and the various points of the channel along its length are not the same. The magnitude of the gate channel reverse potential decreases as one moves from the drain D to the source S contact. Consequently, the conducting channel is expected to be wider at the source end relative to that at the drain end.

Let us consider the special case when the drain voltage is extremely small. In this case, we may ignore any potential variation along the channel length, so that the reverse potential between the gate and the various points of the channel is constant at all points. The channel cross-section can then be regarded to remain almost constant throughout. Since the channel is extremely lightly doped relative to the gate, most of the depletion layer widening due to the reverse bias at the gate would take place over the channel. The depletion layer width d_n under such an approximation is given by

$$d_n = (a - b) = \left[\frac{2\kappa\epsilon_0(\psi_0 + V_G)}{qN_d}\right]^{1/2} \tag{3.128}$$

where we have made use of (2.16). A pinch-off is said to occur when the gate voltage is of sufficient magnitude to reduce the channel thickness b to zero. In that case, we derive from (3.128) after writing $V_G = V_p$ and $b = 0$,

$$V_p = \left(\frac{qN_d a^2}{2\kappa\varepsilon_0}\right) - \psi_0 \tag{3.129}$$

Substituting for $(qN_d/2\kappa\varepsilon_0)$ from (3.129) into (3.128), we get

$$b = a\left[1 - \left\{\frac{(\psi_0 + V_G)}{(\psi_0 + V_p)}\right\}^{1/2}\right] \tag{3.130}$$

The channel conductance under a gate bias V_G may then be expressed as

$$G = \sigma_n\left(\frac{2bW}{L}\right) = \left(\frac{2q\mu_n N_d W a}{L}\right)\left[1 - \left\{\frac{(\psi_0 + V_G)}{(\psi_0 + V_p)}\right\}^{1/2}\right] \tag{3.131}$$

where W denotes the width of the FET perpendicular to the plane of the paper, σ_n the conductivity of the n-type channel and L its length. The drain current I_D may then be expressed as

$$I_D = GV_D = \left(\frac{2q\mu_n N_d W a}{L}\right)\left[1 - \left\{\frac{(\psi_0 + V_G)}{(\psi_0 + V_p)}\right\}^{1/2}\right] V_D \tag{3.132}$$

For V_G and $V_p \gg \psi_0$, (3.132) simplifies to

$$I_D = G\,V_D = G_0\left[1 - \left(\frac{V_G}{V_p}\right)^{1/2}\right] V_D \tag{3.133}$$

where

$$G_0 = \frac{2q\mu_n N_d W a}{L} \tag{3.134}$$

It should be remarked that (3.131) is only valid before pinch-off. Hence, according to (3.133) for smaller V_D and a constant V_G, I_D must vary linearly with V_D, as shown in Fig. 3.20(a). In this mode, the device may be made use of as a voltage controlled resistor or a varistor. The resistance is determined by the slope of the I_D–V_D curve which is a function of the gate voltage V_G. The I_D–V_G curve or the transfer characteristic is shown in Fig. 3.20(b). The curves are parabolic in nature.

Next, when the applied drain voltage V_D becomes larger, the potential gradient along the length of the channel can no longer be regarded as small. In this case, the reverse bias across the gate terminal and a point in the channel decreases in magnitude, as one moves from the drain to the source end. Consequently, the depletion layer assumes the shape of a characteristic wedge which tends to converge towards the drain end of the FET. To discuss the most general operating principles of the device, we will concentrate upon an infinitesimal length Δx of the channel where the potential is presumed to be $V(x)$. As a result, the reverse potential across the gate and the channel at that particular point becomes $[V_G + V(x)]$. We may however treat the channel length Δx to be of a uniform cross-section. Considering the potential drop to be ΔV over this length Δx of the channel, we may employ (3.132) to this case to find

$$I_D = \left(\frac{2q\mu_n N_d W a}{\Delta x}\right)\left[1 - \left\{\frac{V(x) + V_G}{V_p}\right\}^{1/2}\right]\Delta V(x) \tag{3.135}$$

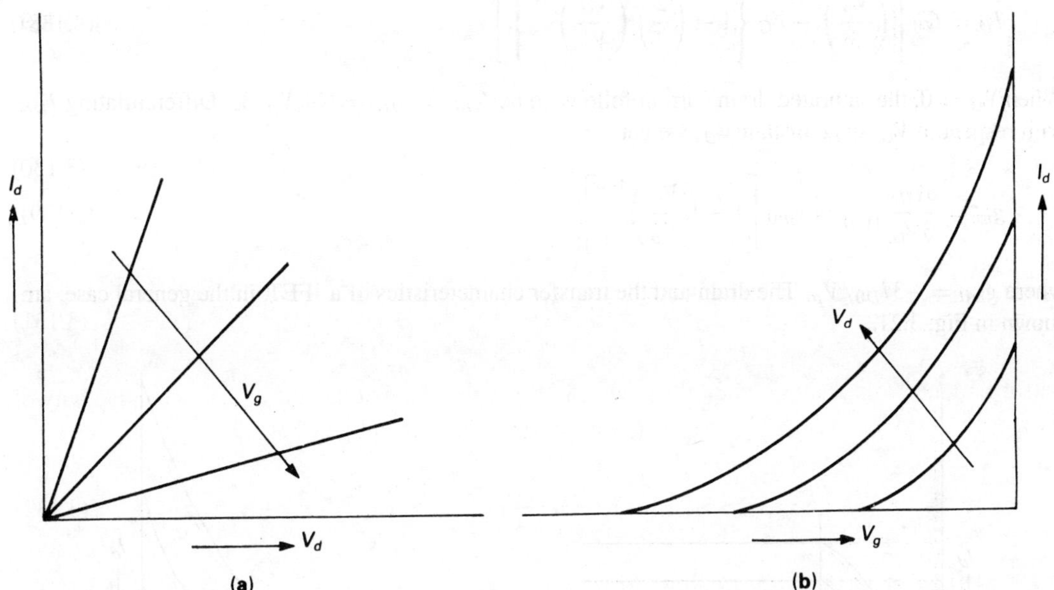

Figure 3.20 *Static characteristics of a JFET for smaller drain voltages: (a) drain characteristics; (b) transfer characteristics*

Rewriting (3.135), as given below and integrating between 0 to L (length of the channel), we get

$$\frac{I_D}{(2q\mu_n N_d W a)}\int_0^L dx = \int_0^{V_D}\left[1-\left\{\frac{V(x)+V_G)}{(V_p)}\right\}^{1/2}\right] dV(x)$$

Integrating, we find

$$I_D = G_0\left[V_D - \left(\frac{2}{3}\right)V_p\left\{\frac{V_D+V_G}{V_p}\right\}^{3/2} + \left(\frac{2}{3}\right)V_p\left(\frac{V_G}{V_p}\right)^{3/2}\right] \tag{3.136}$$

It should be remembered that (3.136) is also valid before pinch-off. The pinch-off voltage may be obtained from (3.136) by imposing the condition $(dI_D/dV_D) = 0$. It then follows that

$$V_p = V_D + V_G \tag{3.137}$$

as the pinch-off voltage. Detailed device analysis after pinch-off is extremely complicated. When $(V_D + V_G) > V_p$, the pinched-off point shifts towards the source end due to the overlapping of the depletion layers of the two gate junctions. However, at this stage, there is not much of a change in the channel current due to changes in the drain voltages because only a large change in the latter is capable of producing a very small shift in the pinched-off position. Combining (3.136) and (3.137), we obtain the saturated device current as

$$I_D = G_0 \left[\left(\frac{V_p}{3} \right) - V_G \left\{ 1 - \left(\frac{2}{3} \right) \left(\frac{V_G}{V_p} \right)^{1/2} \right\} \right] \tag{3.138}$$

When $V_G = 0$, the saturated drain current follows to be $I_{DS} = I_{DO} = G_0(V_p/3)$. Differentiating I_{DS} with respect to V_G at a constant V_D, we get

$$g_m = \frac{\partial I_{DS}}{\partial V_G}\Big|_{VD} = g_{m0} \left[1 - \left(\frac{V_G}{V_p} \right)^{1/2} \right] \tag{3.139}$$

where $g_{m0} = -3I_{D0}/V_p$. The drain and the transfer characteristics of a JFET, in the general case, are shown in Fig. 3.21.

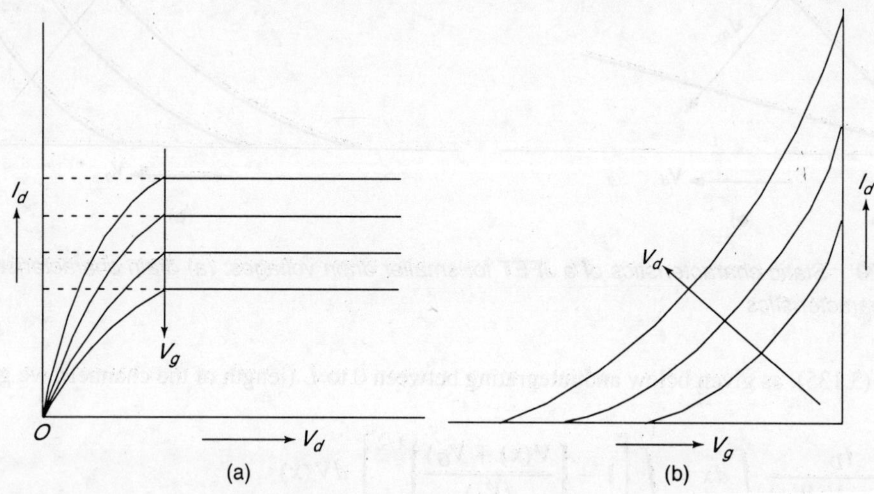

Figure 3.21 *General static characteristics of a JFET (a) drain characteristics; (b) transfer characteristics*

FETs are particularly well-suited for controlled switching between a conducting state and a non-conducting state, and are therefore useful in digital circuits. They are well-suited for integration with other semiconductor devices on a single chip. The operation of an FET differs from that of a conventional transistor in the following respects

(i) Its operation depends upon the flow of majority carriers only. It is therefore a unipolar device.
(ii) It is simpler to fabricate and occupies lesser space in integrated circuits than the conventional bipolar transistors.
(iii) Its input resistance is very high. Typically, it is about several megaohms.
(iv) It is less noisy than a bipolar transistor. The main disadvantage of an FET is its relatively small gain bandwidth product compared to that of a conventional transistor.

Short channel effects As the channel lengths of FETs are reduced, departures from the long channel behaviour are found to occur. They occur due to two dimensional potential distributions and high field effects in the channel region. For a given channel doping concentration, as the channel length is reduced, the depletion layer widths near the source and drain ends become comparable to the channel length. The potential distribution in the channel region now depends on both the transverse field $\varepsilon(x)$ (controlled by the gate voltage) and the longitudinal field $\varepsilon(y)$ (controlled by the drain bias). In other words, the potential distribution becomes two dimensional, and the gradual channel approximation is no longer applicable. Such a two dimensional potential distribution leads to the degradation of the sub-threshold behaviour, dependence of the threshold voltage on the channel length and the biasing voltages and failure of the current to saturate due to punch-through. As the electric field is increased, the channel mobility becomes field-dependent and eventually velocity saturation occurs. Increasing the field further, carrier multiplication near the drain end occurs, leading to the parasitic bipolar transistor action. High fields may also give rise to hot carrier injection into the oxide, leading to oxide charging and subsequent threshold voltage shift and transconductance degradation. Because the short channel effects complicate the device behaviour, these effects should be eliminated or minimized, if possible, so that a physical short channel device can preserve the electrical behaviour of a long channel one.

A variety of modifications to the simple theory of JFET operation must be made when the channel length is typically small ($< 1\,\mu$m). Until recently, these short channel effects were very commonly encountered in FETs. High field-effects occur in devices when 1 V appears across a channel of length 1 μm, giving rise to an electric field of 10^6 V/m. A simple piece-wise linear approximation to the velocity field curve assumes a constant mobility (linear) dependence upto some electric field ε_c and a constant velocity v_s at higher fields. A better approximation for Si is

$$v_d = \frac{\mu\varepsilon}{1 + \left(\frac{\mu\varepsilon}{v_s}\right)}$$

where μ denotes the low field mobility. These two approximations have been shown in the figure. If we presume that electrons negotiate the channel drift with a saturated velocity v_s, the drain current may be written as

$$I_D = qnv_dA = \frac{qnA\mu\varepsilon}{1 + \left(\frac{\mu\varepsilon}{v_s}\right)}$$

In this saturated velocity case, therefore, the drain current is reduced by a factor of $[1 + (\mu V_D/v_s L)]$, due to the field-dependent mobility effect where V_D represents the drain bias.

3.6.2 Modulation doped field-effect transistor (MODFET)

Other names for this device are high electron mobility transistor (HEMT), two dimensional electron gas field-effect transistor (TEGFET), and selectively doped heterojunction transistor (SDHT). Frequently, they are referred to as heterojunction field effect transistors (HFET). The unique feature of MODFET is the heterostructure in which the wider energy gap material is doped and the carriers diffuse to the undoped narrow energy gap material where the channel is formed. The net result of this modulation doping is that the carriers in the undoped heterointerface are spatially separated from the doped region and have extremely high mobilities as there is no impurity scattering. Lattice scattering is also minimized appropriately by reducing the temperature.

MODFET is fabricated by first growing an intrinsic layer of GaAs of about 1 μ m thick on a semi-insulating GaAs substrate, followed by a buffer layer of 30–60 Å of intrinsic AlGaAs. This layer ensures the separation of the heterointerface from the doped AlGaAs region and is critical for high carrier mobility. The doped AlGaAs layer is about 500 Å thick and has a concentration of about $2 \times 10^{18}/\text{cm}^3$ of donors. Since a precise control of film thickness is critical, the molecular beam epitaxy (MBE) is the preferred approach to fabricate such a device.

MODFET was originally developed for high speed applications. Commercially available MODFETs now operate at frequencies higher than 60 Hz, having channel lengths ranging from 0.25 μ m to 0.5 μm.

3.6.3 Static induction transistor (SIT)

This is basically a junction field-effect transistor with a very short channel length (Fig. 3.22). Multiple channels like this may be connected in parallel (Fig. 3.22(a)) to improve the power output. One major

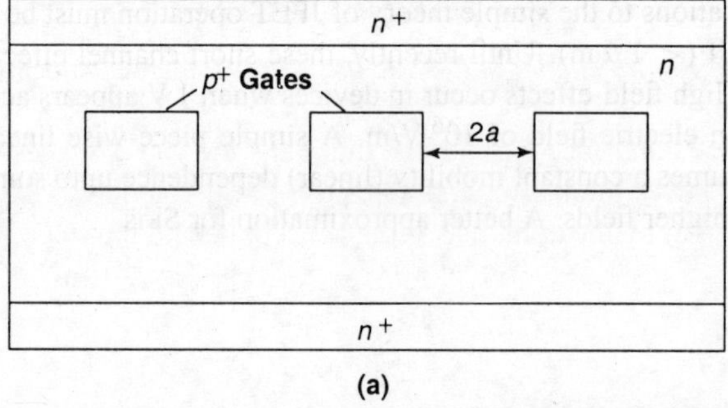

(a)

Figure 3.22 A static induction transistor (SIT): (a) the buried gate structure

difference in its structure from that of the conventional JFET is that the gates in this case do not extend closer to the source or the drain. This type of a transistor exhibits non-saturating I–V characteristics with increasing drain voltages (Fig. 3.23). The static induction transistors (SIT) are available in various configurations. The planar gate structure, shown in Fig. 3.22(b), is the most common type known today. The most critical parameters in a SIT are the spacing between the gates and the channel doping level. Since most SITs are designed normally ON, the doping of the channel is so chosen that the depletion regions from the gates do not merge with one another and there exists a narrow neutral channel opening even at zero gate bias. Typical gaps between gates are a few microns with a channel doping level in the $10^{15}/\text{cm}^3$ range. The figure shows that the gates are formed by pn junctions, but SIT operations may be generated to include metal gates and MIS gates as well. Most SITs are made on Si substrates, with GaAs being the next choice for high speed devices. Since the channel lengths are shorter, punch-through may occur with a high drain bias, even without any gate bias. The output characteristics of a SIT are shown in Fig. 3.23. At zero gate bias, the depletion region around the gates do not pinch-off the gap completely. A neutral n-region between the gates with zero gate bias provides a current path for a depletion mode device (normally ON). The current conduction is by drift and is similar to that as of an FET. With a negative bias on the gate, the depletion regions widen and pinch-off the channel and the electrons from the source face a potential barrier (Fig. 3.24). Once a barrier is formed, the current is controlled by diffusion and the barrier height ϕ_b is the controlling factor in supplying the carriers.

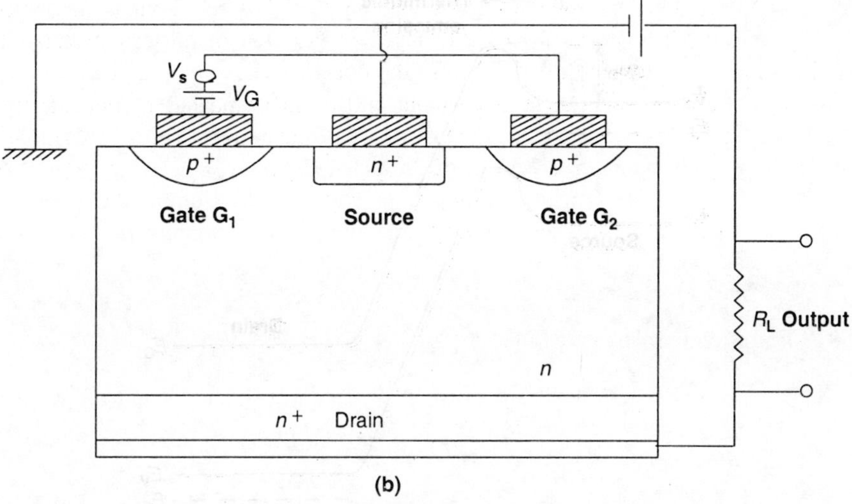

Figure 3.22 *continued (b) the planar gate structure with electrical connections to act as an amplifier*

The barrier height can be controlled by both the drain and the gate voltages. As shown in Fig. 3.25, a negative gate voltage raises the barrier and a positive drain voltage lowers the barrier height. The change of the barrier height by the drain bias is the concept behind the static induction principle. The

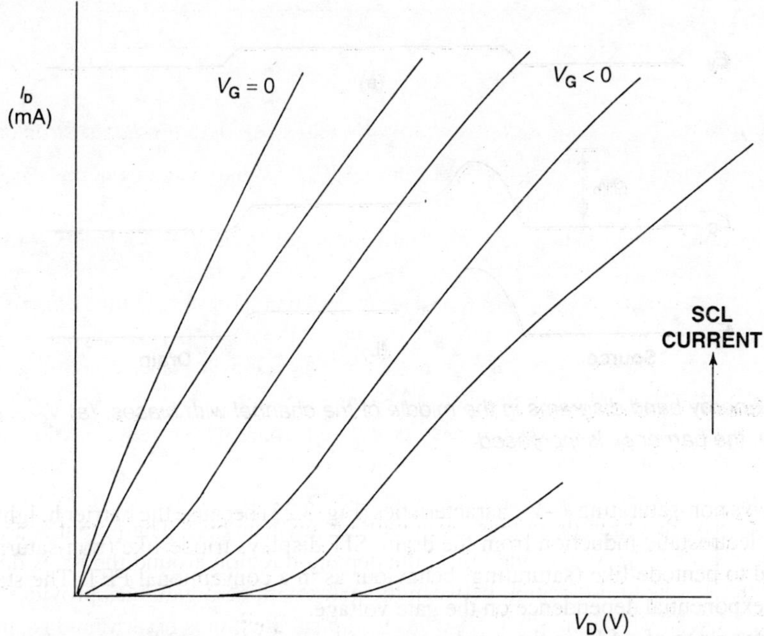

Figure 3.23 *Output characteristics of a Static Induction Transistor (SIT). At higher current levels, the space charge current is found to dominate*

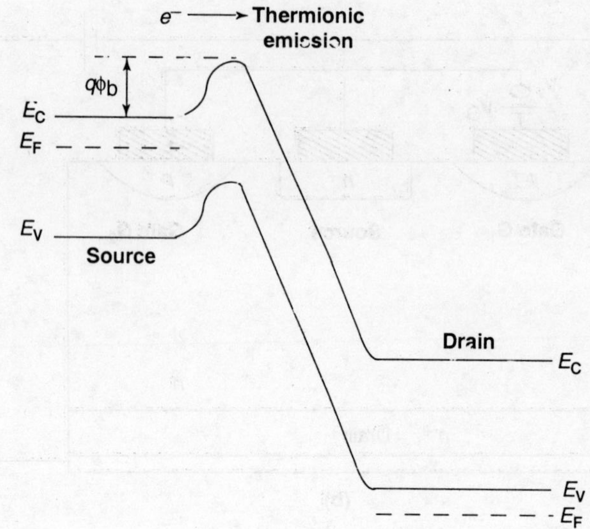

Figure 3.24 Energy band diagram from the source to the drain in the middle of the channel, between gates

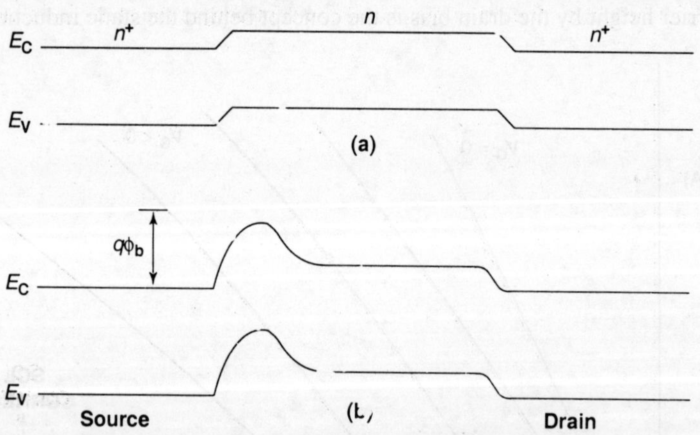

Figure 3.25 Energy band diagrams in the middle of the channel with biases, (a) $V_G = 0$, $V_D = 0$, (b) $V_G < 0$, $V_D = 0$, the barrier ϕ_b is increased

transistor displays non-saturating I–V characteristics (Fig. 3.23) because the barrier height for electrons is lowered by electrostatic induction from the drain. SIT displays triode-like (non-saturating) I_D–V_D plot as opposed to pentode-like (saturating) behaviour as in a conventional FET. The static induction current has an exponential dependence on the gate voltage.

The main advantage of a SIT is the combination of high voltage and high speed capabilities. The lower dopings cause breakdowns at voltages of about a few hundreds volts. The frequency of operations of these devices can be as high as 2 GHz. Most applications of SITs are in the power area. As an audio

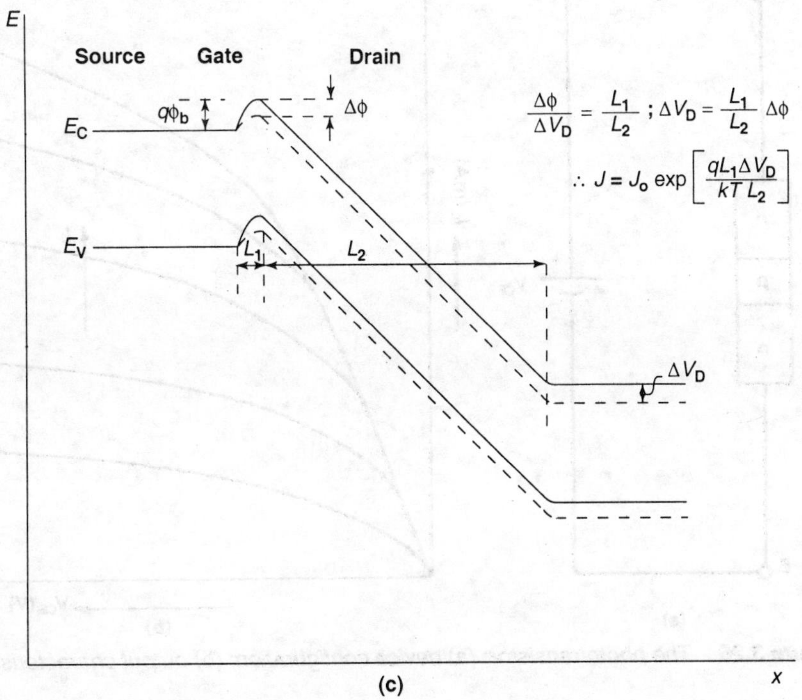

Figure 3.25 *continued (c) $V_G < 0$, $V_D > 0$, the barrier ϕ_b is decreased*

amplifier, SIT has a lower noise, a lower distortion and a lower output impedance. It can be used in high power oscillators required for broadcasting transmitters and microwave ovens. Other possible applications include logics, dynamic memory, image sensors and phototransistors.

3.7 Phototransistors

Both bipolar and unipolar transistors could be used suitably as phototransistors. They are found to be more sensitive than *pn* junction photodiodes. We illustrate in Fig. 3.26 how to convert a bipolar transistor into a phototransistor. We connect a junction in its common-emitter configuration and leave its base terminal open. The external radiation is directed towards the collector junction. The operation of the device can be understood by remembering that the emitter junction is slightly forward biased while the collector junction is reverse biased. To start with, let us presume that there is no radiant excitation. Since $I_B = 0$, it follows from (3.12) that

$$I_C = (\beta + 1) I_{CO} \tag{3.140}$$

If the light is now turned on to increase I_{CO} by I_L, the net collector current, follows to be

$$I_C = (\beta + 1)(I_{CO} + I_L) \tag{3.141}$$

Thus, because of the transistor action, the photoinduced current I_L is multiplied by a large factor $(\beta + 1)$. The family of curves shown in Fig. 3.26(b) corresponds to different values of the light intensity levels.

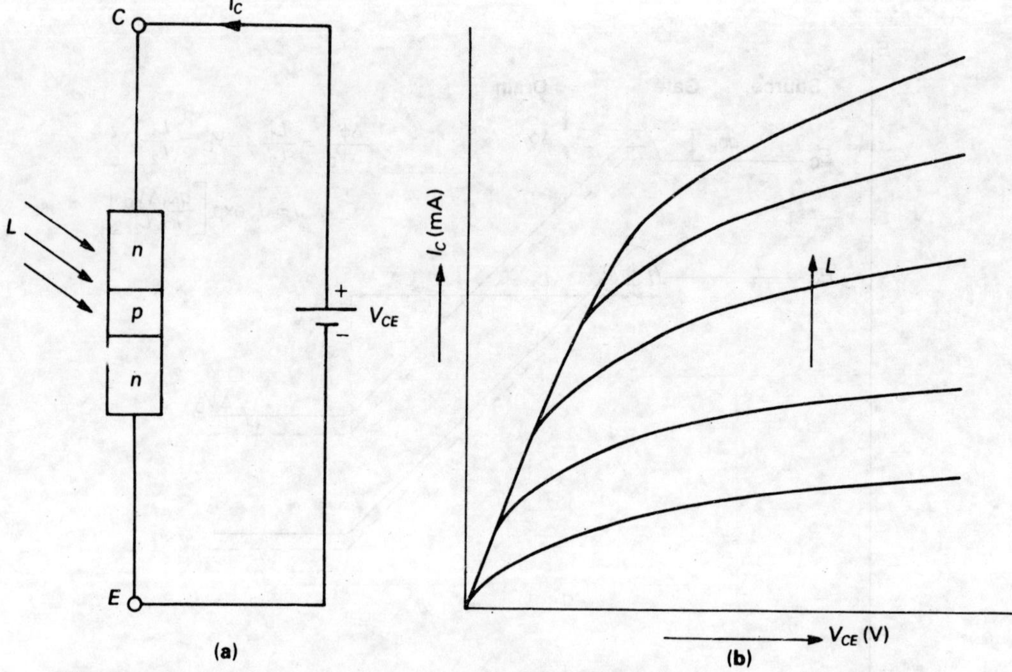

Figure 3.26 The phototransistor: (a) device configuration; (b) output characteristics

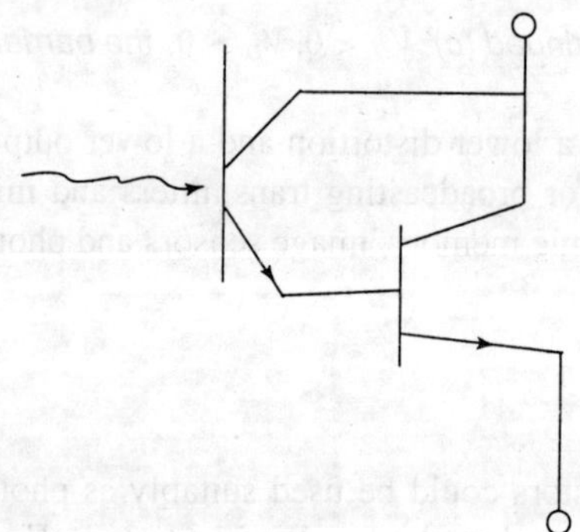

Figure 3.26 continued (c) Schematic diagram of a Darlington pair of phototransistors

It is also possible to bring out the base lead and to inject a base current I_B.The current expressed by (3.141) would then be increased by an additional term βI_B. A JFET may also be used suitably to respond to light intensities. Excitation of the channel doped with deep lying impurities by external radiation may also lead to a rise in the channel current as a function of the light intensity.

3.8 Unijunction transistor

The unijunction transistor (UJT) is a single junction, three terminal device (Fig. 3.27). In its I–V characteristic (Fig. 3.28), it has an S-shaped negative resistance region. Owing to this property, its applications in oscillators, multivibrators and timing circuits are extremely promising.

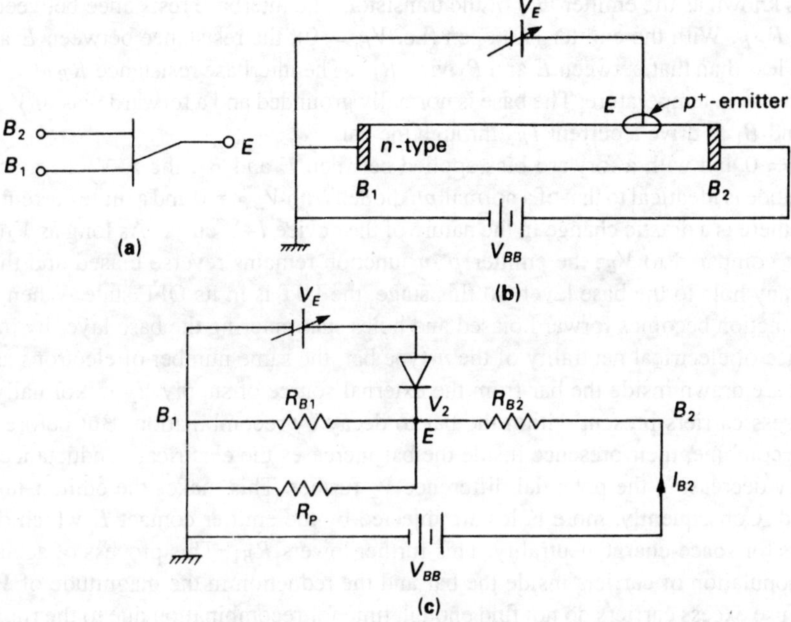

Figure 3.27 *The unijunction transistor (UJT): (a) device symbol; (b) biasing and (c) equivalent circuit*

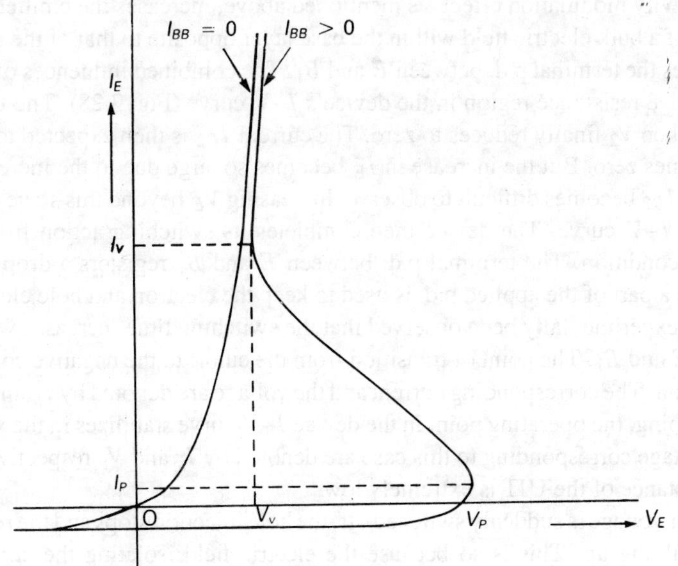

Figure 3.28 *The I–V characteristic of a UJT*

The UJT essentially consists of a high resistivity semiconductor bar (usually of Si) with ohmic contacts B_1 and B_2 at both of its ends. The device is well known as the filamentary transistor or a double base diode due to its particular shape. A single p^+n junction which is placed on the surface of the bar and closer to B_2 is known as the emitter (E) of the transistor. The interbase resistance between B_1 and B_2 is denoted by R_{BB}. With the emitter (E) open (i.e. $V_E = 0$), the resistance between E and B_2, viz., R_{B2} is always less than that between E and B_1 viz., R_{B1}. The interbase resistance $R_{BB}(= R_{B1} + R_{B2})$ decreases with rise in temperature. The base is normally grounded and a forward bias of V_{BB} is applied between B_2 and B_1 to drive a current I_{B2} through the bar.

With $V_{BB} = 0$ and with a forward bias applied between E and B_1, the I–V characteristic of the emitter-base diode is identical to that of a normal pn diode. With $V_{BB} \neq 0$ and a finite current I_{B2} flowing down the bar, there is a drastic change in the nature of the device I–V curve. As long as $V_2(= R_{B1} I_{B2})$ remains larger compared to V_E, the emitter p^+n junction remains reverse biased and the emitter E fails to inject any hole to the base layer. At this stage, the UJT is in its OFF state. When V_E exceeds V_2, the p^+n junction becomes forward biased and holes start entering the base layer by injection. For the maintenance of electrical neutrality of the n-type bar, the same number of electrons as that of the injected holes are drawn inside the bar from the external source of supply V_{BB}. Normally, we would expect the excess carriers present within the bar to decay by recombination. But before the carriers can actually recombine, their presence inside the bar increases the electrical conductance between E and B_1 thereby decreasing the potential difference V_2 further. This makes the emitter junction more forward biased. Consequently, more holes are injected by the emitter contact E which draws inside more electrons for space-charge neutrality. This further lowers R_{B1}. This process of accumulation of such a large population of carriers inside the bar and the reduction in the magnitude of V_2 continues unabated because excess carriers do not find enough time for recombination due to the runaway nature of the process. The electron and the hole gases collected inside the bar would respectively be attracted by E and B_1 contacts, producing a bulk electric field which is opposite to the applied external electric field. This conductivity modulation effect, as mentioned above, increases the emitter current I_E while the establishment of a bulk electric field within the base layer opposite to that of the externally applied electric field reduces the terminal p.d. between E and B_1. The combined influences of these two effects give rise to a negative resistance region in the device's I–V curve (Fig. 3.28). The UJT completes its switching action when V_2 finally reduces to zero. The current I_{B2} is then expected to increase slightly because R_{B1} becomes zero. But the increase in I_E becomes so large due to the increased hole density that the increase in I_{B2} becomes difficult to observe. Increasing V_E beyond this stage makes the emitter recover its normal I–V curve. The device then completes its switching action from the OFF to its ON (or saturated) condition. The terminal p.d. between E and B_1 registers a drop from the applied magnitude because a part of the applied p.d. is used to keep the electron and hole clouds isolated from one another. It has experimentally been observed that the switching time increases with the increasing distance between E and B_1. The point of transition from the cutoff to the negative conductance state is termed the peak point. The corresponding current and the voltage are denoted by I_p and V_p respectively. At the end of switching, the operating point in the device I–V curve stabilizes in the valley region. The current and the voltage corresponding to this case are denoted by I_v and V_v respectively. At the end of switching, the resistance of the UJT is extremely low.

When the emitter voltage is suddenly switched off, the hole injection stops and the resistance between E and B starts building up. This is so because the electric field isolating the carrier space-charge disappears, allowing excess electrons and holes to recombine freely with one another. Such a process would eventually cause the emitter junction to be reverse biased, as we had observed prior to the onset of switching. We then recover the peak point from the valley region and the device returns to its OFF state. The resistance in the OFF state may vary from several hundred kilo ohms to several mega ohms. But in the ON state, the device impedance is only about a few kilo ohms.

Analysis of the device From the design point of view it is desirable that an UJT must possess smaller (I_p, V_v) and larger (I_v, V_p) values. Mathematical expressions for the device parameters may be derived by referring to Fig. 3.27(c). The base current-voltage relation of the device is

$$I_{B2} = (V_{BB} - V_2)\, G_{B2} \tag{3.142}$$

and

$$I_E + I_{B2} = V_2(G_{B1} + G_p) \tag{3.143}$$

where the conductances used above are the reciprocals of the respective resistances. The emitter efiiciency γ may be expressed as

$$\gamma = \frac{I_{pE}}{I_E} = \frac{V_2 G_p}{I_E} \tag{3.144}$$

so that G_p is zero as long as the emitter remains reverse biased. Combining (3.142) and (3.143), we find

$$V_2 = \frac{I_E + I_{B2}}{G_{B1} + Gp} = \frac{I_E + (V_{BB} - V_2)G_{B2}}{G_{B1} + G_p}$$

Using (3.144) in the above equation, we find

$$V_2 = \left[\frac{G_{B2}V_{BB}}{G_{B1} + G_{B2}}\right] + \left[\frac{(1-\gamma)I_E}{G_{B1} + G_{B2}}\right] \tag{3.145}$$

We now define

$$\eta = \frac{G_{B2}}{G_{B1} + G_{B2}} = \frac{R_{B1}}{R_{B1} + R_{B2}} = \frac{R_{B1}}{R_{BB}} \tag{3.146}$$

as the intrinsic stand off ratio for the UJT. This is a measure of the interbase voltage that appears across R_{B1}. The emitter diode voltage V_D is however given by

$$V_D = \left(\frac{kT}{q}\right) \ln\left[\left(\frac{I_E}{I_{E0}}\right) + 1\right] \tag{3.147}$$

where I_{E0} measures the reverse saturation current crossing the emitter junction. The net emitter voltage may now be expressed as

$$V_E = V_2 + V_D \tag{3.148}$$

Combining (3.145), (3.147) and (3.148), we get

$$V_E = \eta V_{BB} - (1-\gamma)\,|I_E| \left(\frac{R_{B1}R_{B2}}{R_{BB}}\right) + \left(\frac{kT}{q}\right) \ln\left[\left(\frac{I_E}{I_{E0}}\right) + 1\right] \tag{3.149}$$

In the above equation, considering the relative signs of I_E and V_2, we find the second term to be negative. At the peak point of the I–V characteristic we can now set $[dV_E/dI_E] = 0$. We then find

$$I_p = \left[\frac{kT}{q(1-\gamma)}\right]\left[\left(\frac{1}{R_{B1}}\right) + \left(\frac{1}{R_{B2}}\right)\right] - I_{E0} \tag{3.150}$$

The current I_p at which the device turns ON may be minimized by making both R_{B1} and R_{B2} large. The expression for V_p follows from (3.149) by setting $I_E = I_p$.We then get,

$$V_p = \eta V_{BB} + V_D \tag{3.151}$$

assuming $I_p > I_{E0}$ and $(kT/q) < \eta V_{BB}$. Thus to make V_p larger, η should be as close to unity as possible. In other words, E must be situated as close to B_2 as possible. Next, the expression for the valley current I_v must be derived by setting $V_2 = 0$ in (3.145). We then get

$$I_v = \frac{V_{BB}}{(1-\gamma)R_{B2}} \tag{3.152}$$

Thus in order to increase I_v, R_{B2} must be reduced. This condition is in conformity with the requirement for larger V_p. Lastly, the valley voltage V_v follows from (3.149) on writing $I_E = I_v$. We then get

$$V_v = \left(\frac{kT}{q}\right) \ln\left[\left(\frac{I_E}{I_{E0}}\right) + 1\right] \tag{3.153}$$

To get a more accurate expression for V_v, the potential drop $I_v R_s$ over the device saturation resistance R_s, must be added to the right hand side of (3.153). The parameters I_p, V_p, I_v and V_v are known as the figures of merit of the device.

3.9 The four layer *pnpn* device

The four layer *pnpn* device's function is analogous to a *pn* diode rectifier, with the difference that its rectifying characteristics can be controlled externally. Devices working from a few milliamperes to several hundred amperes are now available. Therefore, this device is extremely useful for power switching applications.

Depending on the type of applications, its two, three or four terminal forms have been proposed. If it has two terminals the device is known as a Shockley diode. With three and four terminals it is respectively called semiconductor controlled rectifier (SCR) and semiconductor controlled switch (SCS). The different configurations of the device along with their I–V characteristics are shown in Fig. 3.29. The region OP of the curve represents the high impedance forward blocking state. The switching action begins at P where $dV/dI = 0$ at a voltage V_s (switching voltage) when the corresponding current is I_s. PQ represents the unstable negative conductance state. The operating point stabilizes at Q after switching. This point is known as the holding point. The corresponding voltage (V_h) and the current (I_h) are called the holding voltage and holding current respectively. Beyond Q, the device current rises as in an ordinary rectifier. The region QR is called the forward conducting state of the device. The device impedance at this stage is extremely low. Coming over to the reverse direction, we note that OS represents the reverse blocking state while ST corresponds to the state of junction breakdown.

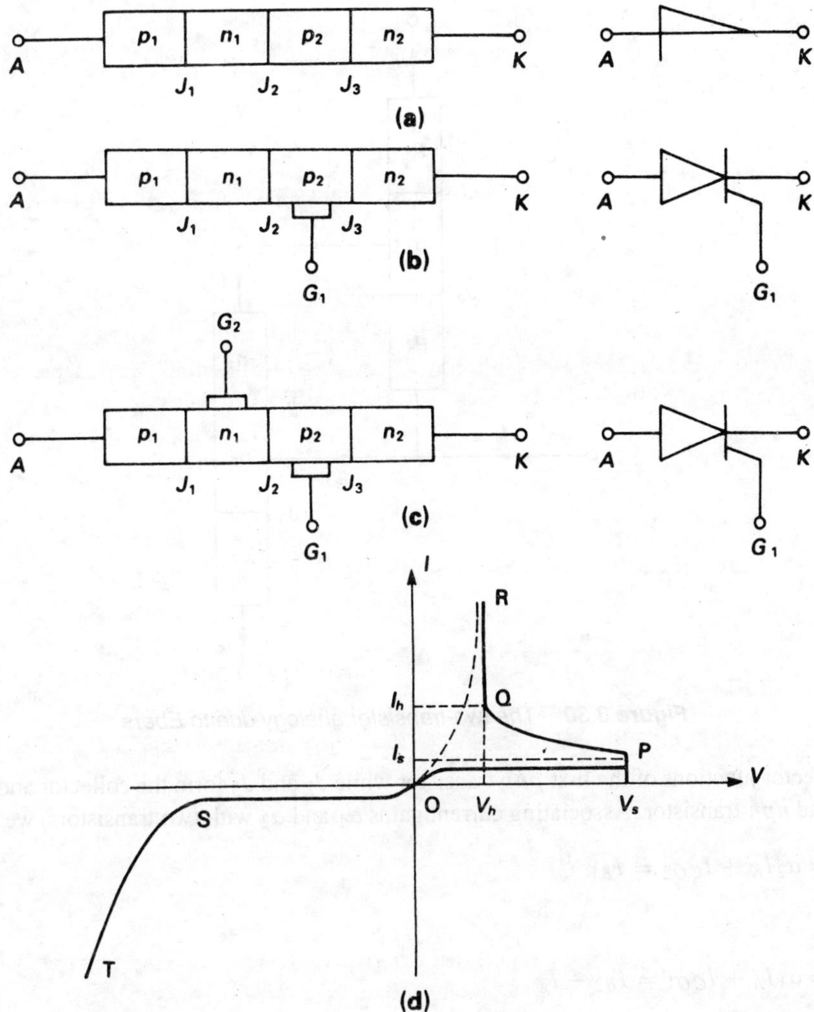

Figure 3.29 *(a) Shockley diode; (b) semiconductor-controlled rectifier (SCR); (c) semiconductor-controlled switch (SCS); (d) I–V characteristic of the device*

To explain the device I–V curve, as given in Fig. 3.29(d), we start by presuming that a reverse voltage is available between A and K. This places J_1 and J_3 under reverse bias a J_2 under forward bias. The device current is then restricted to reverse saturation currents crossing J_1 and J_3. This situation corresponds to the reverse blocking state OS of the device. At larger voltages, when the junctions breakdown, the device I–V characteristic is represented by ST. Next, with a forward bias between A and K, J_1 and J_3 become forward biased while J_2 becomes reverse biased. The device current is then restricted to the reverse saturation current crossing J_2 and is once again small. This corresponds to the forward blocking state OP of the device.

The switching action from the forward blocking to the forward conducting states was explained by Ebers using the two-transistor analogy as presented in Fig. 3.30. Here J_1 and J_2 represent the emitter

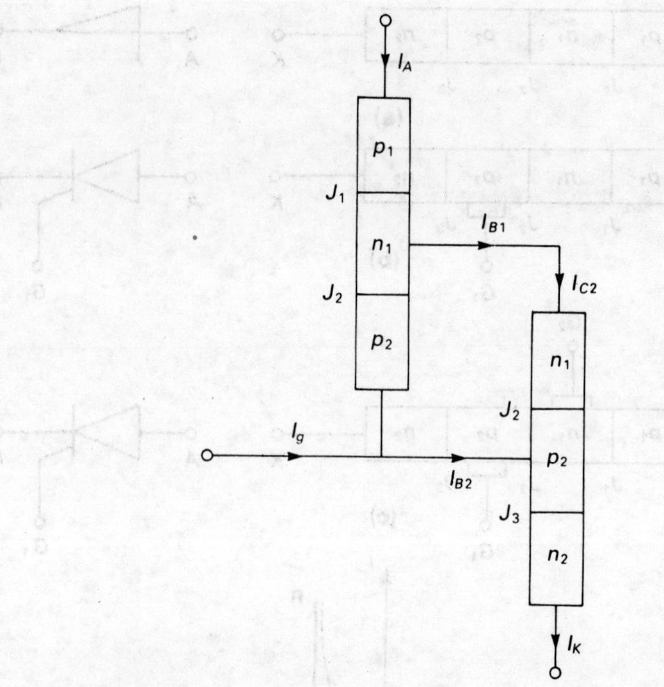

Figure 3.30 *The two-transistor analogy due to Ebers*

and the collector junctions of the first *pnp* transistor while J_2 and J_3 form the collector and the emitter of the second *npn* transistor. Associating current gains α_1 and α_2 with two transistors, we may write

$$I_{C2} = \alpha_2 I_K + I_{CO2} = I_{B1} \tag{3.154}$$

and

$$I_{C1} = \alpha_1 I_A + I_{CO1} = I_{B2} - I_g \tag{3.155}$$

Also

$$I_K = I_A + I_g \tag{3.156}$$

But

$$I_{B1} = I_A - I_{C1} = I_A - (\alpha_1 I_A + I_{CO1}) = (1 - \alpha_1) I_A - I_{CO1} \tag{3.157}$$

Comparing (3.154) with (3.157), we find

$$\alpha_2 I_K + I_{CO2} = (1 - \alpha_1) I_A - I_{CO1}$$

or

$$I_A = \frac{\alpha_2 I_g + I_{CO1} + I_{CO2}}{1 - (\alpha_1 + \alpha_2)} \tag{3.158}$$

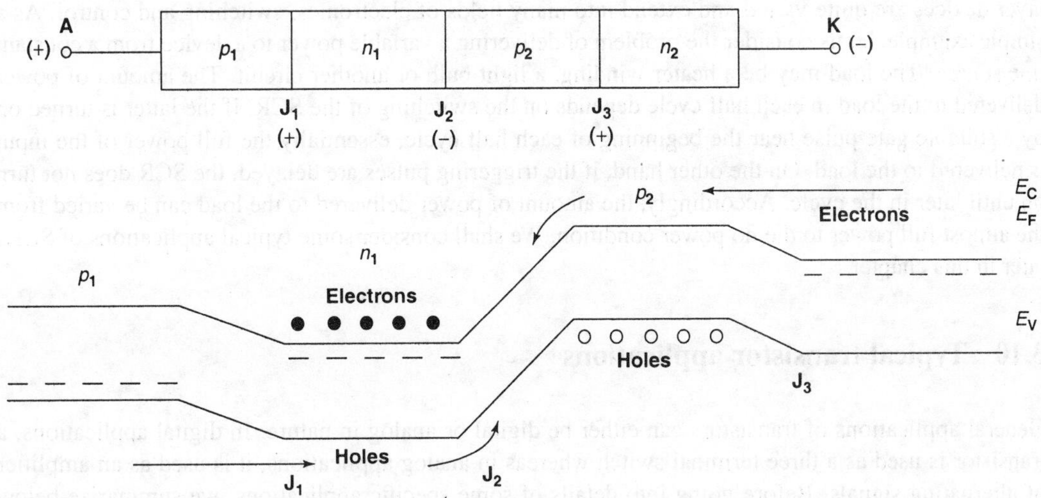

Figure 3.31 *The energy band diagram of a Shockley diode with J_1 and J_3 forward biased and J_2 reverse biased*

For a Shockley diode $I_g = 0$ since it contains only two electrodes. But the gate current is finite for an SCR and an SCS. The current gains α_1 and α_2 are in fact very small because the widths of different n and p regions are not very narrow as desired for a good transistor action. Hence, for a Shockley diode, (3.158) predicts the device current to consist of only $(I_{CO1} + I_{CO2})$. Increasing I_A, I_{CO1} and I_{CO2} first register a gentle rise due to carrier multiplication effect. Such an increase in I_A therefore causes transistor alphas to increase due to the effect of increasing diffusion constant as a function of the increasing injection level. On account of this, (3.158) predicts further increase in I_A which will lead to further rise in $(\alpha_1 + \alpha_2)$ once again. This cumulative effect of increasing alphas and I_A is responsible for the device switching. While I_A becomes very large, holes and electrons in appreciable proportions accumulate in p_2 and n_1 regions respectively (Fig. 3.31). The local electric field set up by these accumulated carriers opposes the external reverse bias across the n_1p_2 junction, thereby appreciably reducing the terminal voltage across the device. The combined effects of increasing I_A and the decreasing terminal voltage are responsible for the appearance of the negative conductance region PQ in the device I–V curve (Fig. 3.29(d)). At still higher injection levels when the internally developed field across the n_1p_2 junction is able to annul the reverse field developed across J_2 due to the external bias, it will start behaving like a forward biased p_2n_1 junction. The device then completes its switching action from the forward blocking to the forward conducting state. At this stage, it is necessary to restrict the device current to only low values by adding suitable external resistances so that the diode may not burn out. Beyond this stage, the diode starts behaving like a forward biased p_2n_1 junction.

To switch ON a Shockley diode at a specified voltage, we should be able to increase I_A by some external means. In an SCR and an SCS, the switching at a desired voltage can be initiated by applying appropriate pulses at the corresponding gate electrodes (Fig. 3.29(b) and 3.29(c)). At the same time, the device may be turned off by applying a suitable reverse pulse so that the device current drops below I_h. To secure a quicker turn off, minority carrier lifetimes in appropriate regions should be curtailed by doping them with any of the heavy elements e.g. Au, Ag or Ni. Applications of SCRs and other four layer devices are quite varied and extend into many fields of electronics, switching and control. As a simple example, let us consider the problem of delivering a variable power to a device from a constant line source. The load may be a heater winding, a light bulb or another circuit. The amount of power delivered to the load in each half cycle depends on the switching of the SCR. If the latter is turned on by a suitable gate pulse near the beginning of each half cycle, essentially the full power of the input is delivered to the load. On the other hand, if the triggering pulses are delayed, the SCR does not turn on until later in the cycle. Accordingly, the amount of power delivered to the load can be varied from the almost full power to the no power condition. We shall consider some typical applications of SCRs later in this chapter.

3.10 Typical transistor applications

General applications of transistors can either be digital or analog in nature. In digital applications, a transistor is used as a three terminal switch whereas in analog applications, it is used as an amplifier of alternating signals. Before going into details of some specific applications, we summarize below important functions of transistors.

3.10.1 A summary of various functions of transistors

1. *Logic* A digital computer needs logic building blocks e.g. OR, AND, NAND, NOT etc. circuits. These may be built by using a transistor as a primary component for them. Based on these building blocks, other digital circuits e.g. flip-flops, shift resistors and memory devices can be made.
2. *Control* As a switch, a transistor controls the passage of a signal through a given circuit. As a power device, a transistor controls the power to be delivered to the source.
3. *Amplifier* A transistor provides gain for a given input a.c. signal.
4. *Oscillators* An amplifier with a proper feedback can result in sustained oscillations so that a d.c. input can generate an a.c. output.
5. *Variable resistors* A transistor provides a resistance which can either be controlled by the base current (in a bipolar device) or the gate voltage (in a unipolar device). Simple examples are variable attenuators and variable phase shifters.
6. *Microwave applications* Being a nonlinear device, a transistor can be used for microwave mixing, detection and modulation.
7. *Impedance transformations* The source follower and the emitter follower circuits are special types of amplifiers where the voltage gain is approximately unity. The transistor merely transforms the output impedance to a much reduced value for the incoming signal.

Some important observations on transistors Transistors operating over 1 GHz (10^{12}C/s) are called microwave transistors. Since electron mobility is higher than that for holes in almost all semiconductors, all microwave transistors must be of the *npn* type. In order to reduce the series collector resistance, an epitaxial n-layer is grown on an n^+ substrate. In order to increase the emitter efficiency Arsenic must be used to dope the emitter of a Si transistor. A microwave transistor differs from its low frequency counterpart in the dimensions of its active areas and in the control of wafer and packaging parasites. To achieve microwave capability, the dimensions of active areas and the parasites have to be reduced considerably. Nowadays, the emitter strip width is found to be in the submicron range and the base thickness is as small as a few hundred angstroms. As the base width is reduced, it is necessary to get rid of the emitter-collector shorts caused by diffusion.

In contrast to the requirements for the microwave transistors, power transistors are designed to handle high voltages and large currents. In the latter, the main concern is with the absolute values of power and the limitation of operations imposed by the junction breakdown. With the increase in the power gain, the transistor temperature rises. The maximum operating temperature of a transistor is restricted by the temperature at which the base of a transistor becomes intrinsic in nature. Therefore, to improve the operation of power transistors, their encapsulations must provide an adequate heat sink for efficient thermal dissipation.

3.10.2 Common-emitter transistor amplifiers

A common-emitter *pnp* transistor voltage amplifier circuit is shown in Fig. 3.32(a). Let us presume that the applied voltage signal has a positive swing to start with. Consequently, the base-emitter current decreases causing a reduction in the output voltage. Thus, the input and the output voltages of a common-emitter amplifier will differ in phase by π radians. We next proceed to analyze the amplifier using its common-emitter T-equivalent circuit. Applying Kirchoff's voltage law (KVL) to this network, we find

$$V_{be} = (r_b + r_e)i_b + r_e i_c \tag{3.159}$$

$$V_{ce} = [r_e + r_c(1-\alpha)]i_c + (r_e - \alpha\, r_c)i_b \tag{3.160}$$

Writing $V_{ce} = -i_c R_L$, in (3.160), we get the current gain A_i of the transistor amplifier as

$$A_i = -\left(\frac{i_c}{i_b}\right) = \frac{r_e - \alpha\, r_c}{r_e + r_c(1-\alpha) + R_L} \tag{3.161}$$

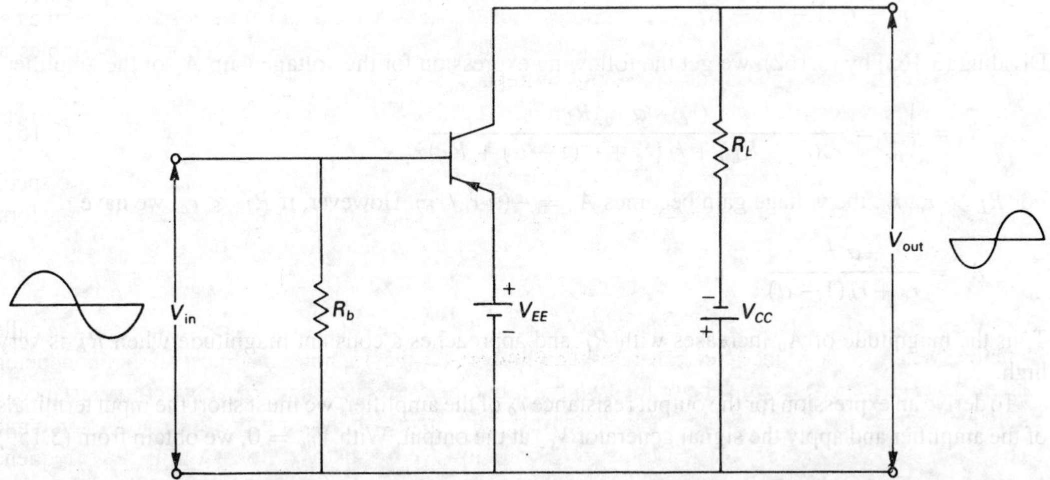

Figure 3.32 (a) Common-emitter *pnp* transistor amplifier

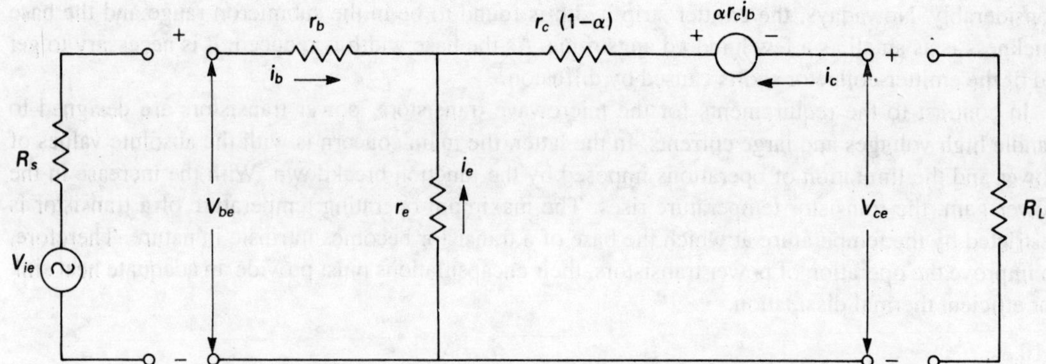

Figure 3.32 *continued (b) T-equivalent circuit of a common-emitter amplifier*

If $r_c \gg R_L$ and $r_e \ll \alpha\, r_c$, (3.161) simplifies to $A_i = -\alpha/(1-\alpha) = -\beta$, as expected. Substituting for i_c from (3.161) in (3.159), we get

$$V_{be} = (r_b + r_e)i_b - \left[\frac{r_e - \alpha\, r_c}{r_e + r_c(1-\alpha) + R_L}\right] i_b$$

Hence, the input impedance r_i of the amplifier is given by

$$r_i = \frac{V_{be}}{i_b} = r_b + \left[\frac{r_e - \alpha\, r_c}{r_e + r_c(1-\alpha) + R_L}\right] \tag{3.162}$$

If $R_L \gg r_c$, $r_i = (r_b + r_e)$. On the other hand if $R_L \ll r_c$, $r_i = r_b + [r_e/(1-\alpha)]$. Thus, as the load resistance R_L is decreased, the input resistance increases. Combining (3.160) and (3.161), we find

$$\frac{V_{ce}}{i_b} = \frac{(r_e - \alpha\, r_c)R_L}{r_e + r_c(1-\alpha) + R_L} \tag{3.163}$$

Dividing (3.163) by (3.162), we get the following expression for the voltage gain A_v of the amplifier

$$A_v = \frac{V_{ce}}{V_{be}} = \frac{(r_e - \alpha\, r_c)R_L}{r_e(r_c + R_L) + r_b\{r_e + r_c(1-\alpha) + R_L\}} \tag{3.164}$$

For $R_L \gg r_e, r_c$, the voltage gain becomes $A_v = -(\alpha\, r_c/r_b)$. However, if $R_L \ll r_c$, we have

$$A_v = \frac{-\alpha\, R_L}{r_e + r_b(1-\alpha)}$$

Thus the magnitude of A_v increases with R_L and approaches a constant magnitude when R_L is very high.

To derive an expression for the output resistance r_o of the amplifier, we must short the input terminals of the amplifier and apply the signal generator V_{ce} at the output. With $V_{be} = 0$, we obtain from (3.159)

$$i_b = -\left[\frac{r_e i_c}{r_e + r_b + R_s}\right]$$

where R_s denotes the series resistance of the input source. Substituting for i_b in (3.160), we get

$$r_o = \frac{V_{ce}}{i_c} = \frac{r_e r_c + \{r_e + r_c(1-\alpha)\}(r_b + R_s)}{r_e + r_b + R_s} \tag{3.165}$$

If $r_b \gg r_e$, and $r_c(1-\alpha) > r_e$, we get

$$r_o = r_c(1-\alpha) + \left[\frac{r_e r_c}{r_e + r_b + R_s}\right]$$

3.10.3 Common-collector amplifier

A grounded collector transistor amplifier, shown in Fig. 3.33, is analogous to a vacuum tube cathode follower circuit. The emitter is forward biased and the collector is reverse biased as usual. When the input signal strength is growing in the positive sense to increase the base-collector current, i_e must also increase for the space-charge neutrality in the base region. This would, therefore, require the emitter

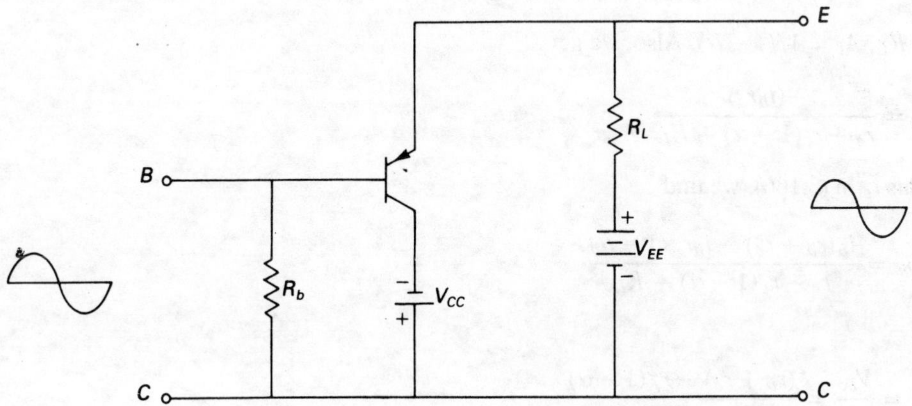

Figure 3.33 *(a) Common-collector amplifier circuit*

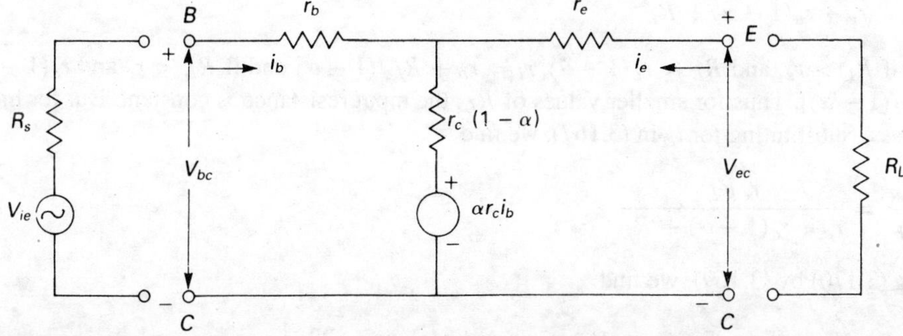

Figure 3.33 *continued (b) T-equivalent circuit of the common-collector amplifier*

emitter to be driven positive. Therefore, in this case, no phase reversal between input and output voltages is expected. Applying KVL to the equivalent circuit network, we find

$$V_{bc} = i_b(r_b + r_c) + i_e r_c(1 - \alpha) \tag{3.166}$$

and

$$V_{ec} = i_b r_c + i_e[r_e + r_c(1 - \alpha)] \tag{3.167}$$

where we have presumed $\alpha \sim 1$. Putting $V_{ec} = -R_L i_e$, in (3.167), we get

$$-R_L i_e = i_b r_c + i_e[r_e + r_c(1 - \alpha)]$$

or

$$A_i = -\left(\frac{i_e}{i_b}\right) = \frac{r_c}{r_e + r_c(1 - \alpha)} \tag{3.168}$$

If $r_c \gg R_L$, $A_i = 1/(1 - \alpha)$. Also, we get

$$i_e = \frac{-(i_b r_c)}{r_e + r_c(1 - \alpha) + R_L}$$

Using this i_e in (3.166), we find

$$V_{bc} = \frac{i_b(r_b + r_c) - i_b r_c^2(1 - \alpha)}{r_e + r_c(1 - \alpha) + R_L}$$

or

$$r_i = \frac{V_{bc}}{i_b} = \frac{(r_b + r_c) - r_c^2(1 - \alpha)}{r_e + r_c(1 - \alpha) + R_L}$$

or

$$r_i = \frac{r_b + r_c(r_e + R_L)}{r_e + r_c(1 - \alpha) + R_L} \tag{3.169}$$

Now if $R_L > r_e$, and $R_L < r_c(1 - \alpha)$, $r_i = r_b + R_L/(1 - \alpha)$ and if $R_L < r_e$ and $r_c(1 - \alpha)$, $r_i = r_b + [r_e/(1 - \alpha)]$. Thus for smaller values of R_L, the input resistance is constant. But for higher R_L, it increases. Substituting for i_e in (3.167), we find

$$\frac{V_{ec}}{i_b} = \frac{r_c R_L}{r_e + r_c(1 - \alpha) + R_L} \tag{3.170}$$

Dividing (3.170) by (3.169), we find

$$A_v = \frac{V_{ec}}{V_{bc}} = \left[1 + \left[\frac{r_b(r_e + R_L) + r_c\{r_e + (1 - \alpha)r_b\}}{r_c R_L}\right]\right]^{-1} \tag{3.171}$$

When $r_c \gg r_b$,

$$A_v = \left[\frac{1 + \{(1-\alpha)r_b\}}{R_L}\right]^{-1}$$

Thus the voltage gain of the common-collector amplifier works out to be less than unity. Finally to derive an expression for the output resistance r_o, we have to short circuit the input ($V_{bc} = 0$) terminals and then calculate (V_{ec}/i_c).

Putting $V_{bc} = 0$ in (3.166), we find

$$i_b = -\left[\frac{i_e r_c(1-\alpha)}{r_c + r_b + R_s}\right]$$

Using this i_b in (3.167), we get

$$V_{ec} = -\left[\frac{i_e r_c(1-\alpha)}{r_c + r_b + R_s}\right] r_c + i_e[r_e + r_c(1-\alpha)]$$

or

$$r_o = \frac{V_{ec}}{i_e} = r_e + \left[\frac{r_c(1-\alpha)(r_c + r_b + R_s - 1)}{r_c + r_b + R_s}\right] \tag{3.172}$$

If $r_c > r_b$, $r_o = r_e + r_c(1-\alpha)$. The output resistance of a common-collector amplifier is low while its input impedance is higher. As such, this amplifier is expected to be useful for impedance matching applications as its voltage gain is very close to unity.

3.10.4 Differential amplifier

This is used to amplify the difference between any two given voltages whose frequencies may extend from zero to several megahertz. This also serves as the basic stage of an integrated circuit operational amplifier (OPAMP). Fig. 3.34(a) represents a linear active network with two input signals V_1 and V_2 and one output signal V_0, each measured with respect to the ground potential. In an ideal differential amplifier, the output voltage V_0 is normally given by

$$V_0 = A_d(V_1 - V_2) \tag{3.173}$$

Figure 3.34 *(a) Block diagram of a differential amplifier*

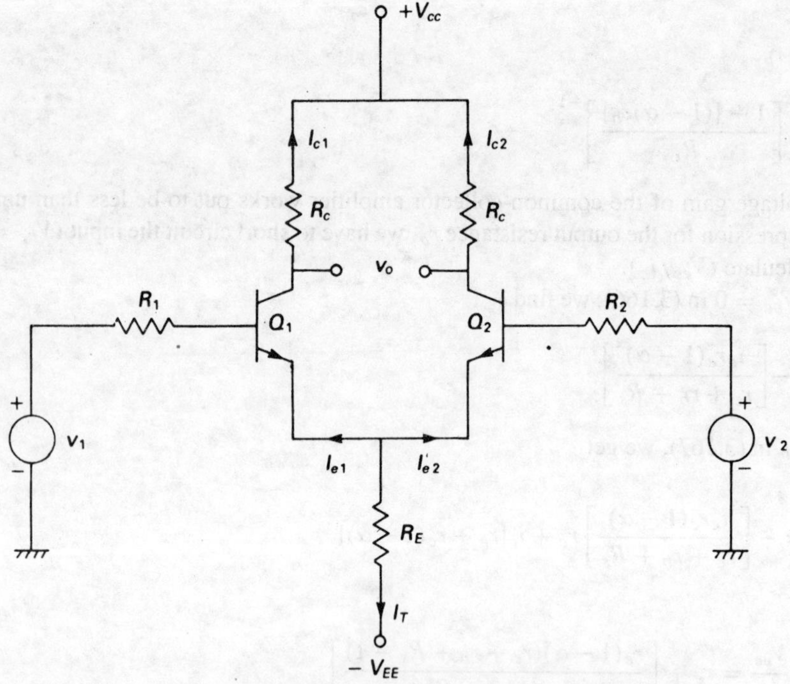

Figure 3.34 continued (b) Common-emitter differential amplifier

where A_d measures the gain of the differential amplifier. But a practical differential amplifier cannot be described by (3.173) because the output is not only expected to be given by the difference between the two input signals but should as a matter of fact be a linear combination of them. To consider this aspect, we next analyze an emitter-coupled differential amplifier (Fig. 3.34(b)). Since the amplifier circuit consists of two transistors, its voltage gain may be expressed as

$$V_0 = A_1 V_1 + A_2 V_2 \tag{3.174}$$

where A_1 and A_2 represent the voltage gains produced by two amplifiers using transistors Q_1 and Q_2 respectively when operating independently of one another. The base of two transistors have been shown grounded. We next define the common mode signal V_c as

$$V_c = \frac{1}{2}(V_1 + V_2) \tag{3.175}$$

We may now rewrite (3.174) as

$$V_0 = \frac{1}{2}[(A_1 - A_2)(V_1 - V_2) + (A_1 + A_2)(V_1 + V_2)]$$

i.e.,

$$V_0 = A_d V_d + A_c V_c \tag{3.176}$$

where $V_d = (V_1 - V_2)$; A_d and A_c respectively denote the gains of the difference and the common mode signals respectively, defined as

$$A_c = \frac{1}{2}(A_1 + A_2)$$

and

$$A_d = \frac{1}{2}(A_1 - A_2) \tag{3.177}$$

We may measure A_d directly by setting $V_1 = -V_2 = 0.5\,\text{V}$ (say), when $V_d = (V_1 - V_2) = 1.0\,\text{V}$ and $V_c = 1/2(V_1 + V_2) = 0$. Substituting these values in (3.176),we get $V_0 = A_d$. Thus, in this case, the output voltage gives a measure of the difference gain. Similarly, to measure A_c, we set $V_1 = V_2 = 1.0\,\text{V}$, so that $V_d = 0$ and $V_c = 1.0\,\text{V}$. We then get $V_0 = A_c$ from (3.176). For an ideal differential amplifier we desire A_d to be extremely large while A_c equal to zero, so that we retrieve (3.173). To characterize the ideality of the differential amplifier, we define a quantity ρ, called the common mode rejection ratio (CMRR) as

$$\rho = \left|\frac{A_d}{A_c}\right| \tag{3.178}$$

so that $\rho = \infty$, when $A_c = 0$. This serves as the figure of merit of the differential amplifier. To include ρ, in the expression for V_0, we rewrite (3.176) as

$$V_0 = A_d V_d \left[1 + \left(\frac{A_c V_c}{A_d V_d}\right)\right] = A_d V_d \left[1 + \left(\frac{1}{\rho}\right)\left(\frac{V_c}{V_d}\right)\right] \tag{3.179}$$

Thus, in order to realize a very large difference gain we must make $\rho \gg (V_c/V_d)$. The circuit shown in Fig. 3.34(b) serves as an excellent differential amplifier when R_E is made very large. To show that this statement is true, let us take $V_1 = V_2 = V$ (say) when $V_d = 0$ and $V_c = V$. Equation (3.176) then gives $V_0 = A_c V$. When $R_E \to \infty$, from the symmetry of the circuit, it follows that $I_{e1} = I_{e2}$. As such $I_{c1} = I_{c2}$ and $V_0 = 0 = A_c V$. Therefore, the CMRR, as defined by (3.178) becomes infinite as desired of an ideal differential amplifier.

3.10.5 FET amplifiers

A common source FET amplifier has been illustrated in Fig. 3.35(a). To analyze it, we must examine its small signal representation. We, therefore, express the drain current i_D as

$$i_D = f(V_{GS}, V_{DS}) \tag{3.180}$$

Expressing (3.180) in its differential form, we get

$$\Delta i_D = \left[\frac{\partial i_D}{\partial V_{GS}}\right]\bigg|_{V_{DS}} \Delta V_{GS} + \left[\frac{\partial i_D}{\partial V_{DS}}\right]\bigg|_{V_{GS}} \Delta V_{DS} \tag{3.181}$$

In the small-signal notation, (3.181) may be expressed as

$$i_d = g_m v_{gs} + \left(\frac{1}{r_d}\right) v_{ds} \tag{3.182}$$

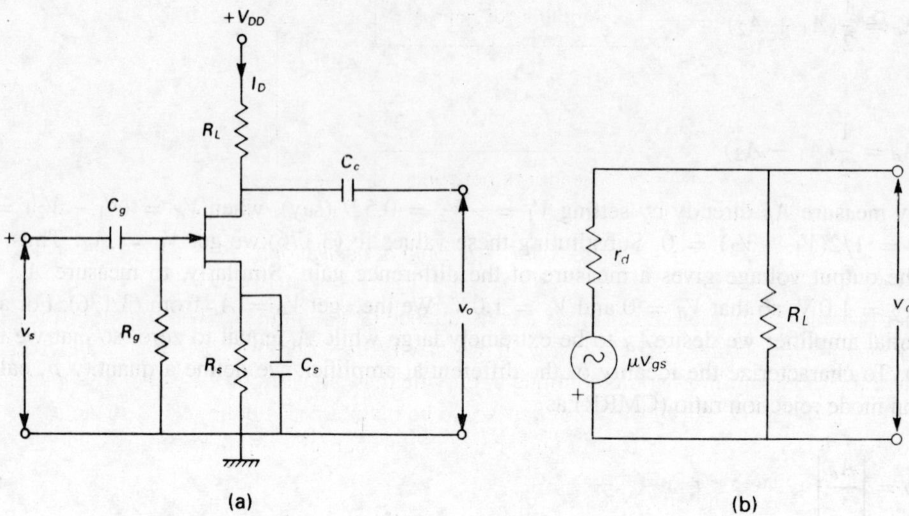

Figure 3.35 *(a) Common-source FET amplifier; (b) equivalent circuit*

where

$$g_m = \left[\frac{\partial\, i_D}{\partial\, V_{GS}}\right]\Bigg|_{V_{DS}} \quad \text{and} \quad r_d = \left[\frac{\partial\, V_{DS}}{\partial\, i_D}\right]\Bigg|_{V_{GS}} \tag{3.183}$$

g_m and r_d are called the transconductance and the drain resistance respectively. The amplification factor μ of the FET follows to be

$$\mu = -\left[\frac{\partial\, V_{DS}}{\partial\, V_{GS}}\right]\Bigg|_{i_D} = g_m r_d \tag{3.184}$$

From the equivalent circuit, the gain of the amplifier immediately follows to be

$$A_v = \frac{v_{ds}}{v_{gs}} = \frac{-\mu R_L}{r_d + R_L} = \frac{-g_m R_L}{1 + \left(\frac{R_L}{r_d}\right)} \tag{3.185}$$

The output resistance r_o of the amplifier may be obtained as usual by shorting the input and applying a signal generator across the output terminals. We then get

$$r_o = \frac{r_d R_L}{r_d + R_L} \tag{3.186}$$

The input resistance of the amplifier is however R_g.

3.10.6 Transistor oscillators

These are circuits meant to deliver an essentially sinusoidal output waveform without any signal excitation at the input. Fig. 3.36 shows the block diagram of an amplifier with a feedback network. The

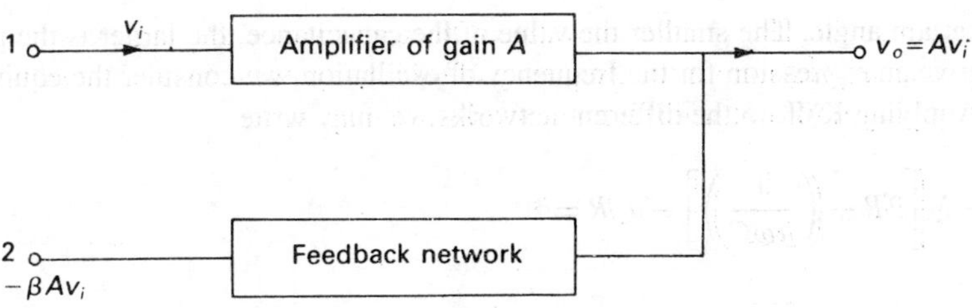

Figure 3.36 Principle of oscillations

amplifier provides an output signal V_0 as a consequence of the input V_i. The output of the feedback network provides a voltage $-\beta A V_i$. Now, if we satisfy the condition $\beta A = -1$ and connect the terminal 2 to 1, the amplifier would continue to provide the same output V_o, as before. In such a case, the oscillations at the output of the amplifier would be maintained indefinitely. The condition for the unity loop gain (i.e. $\beta A = -1$) is well known as the Barkhausen criterion and it gives the necessary condition for the onset of oscillations.

We select a phase shift oscillator as our illustrative example to explain the principle of oscillations. Figure 3.37 shows a conventional FET amplifier followed by three cascaded arrangements of capacitances and resistances. The output from the last RC network is returned to the gate. To obtain a positive feedback which is essential for oscillations, the feedback network must introduce a net phase shift of π radians. Such a phase shift is introduced by the three cascaded sections of RC networks. Each section consists of a series coupling capacitors C and a shunt resistance R, each shifting the phase by some angle. Such a phase shift is produced because each RC combination provides a current that leads the

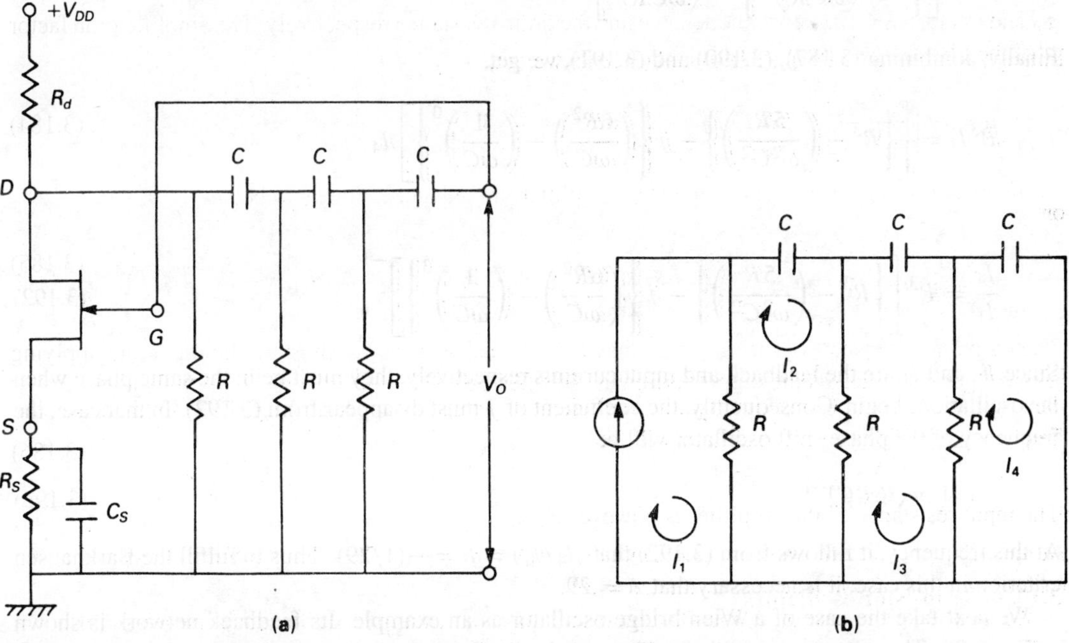

Figure 3.37 (a) RC phase shift oscillator; (b) equivalent circuit

voltage by a certain angle. The smaller the value of the capacitance, the larger is the phase lag of the current. To derive an expression for the frequency of oscillation, we consider the equivalent circuit of Fig. 3.33(b). Applying KVL to the different networks, we may write

$$-I_1 R + I_2\left[2R + \left(\frac{1}{j\omega C}\right)\right] - I_2 R = 0 \tag{3.187}$$

$$-I_2 R + I_3\left[2R + \left(\frac{1}{j\omega C}\right)\right] - I_4 R = 0 \tag{3.188}$$

and

$$-I_3 R + I_4\left[R + \left(\frac{1}{j\omega C}\right)\right] - I_2 R = 0 \tag{3.189}$$

From (3.189), we get

$$-I_3 = \left[1 - \left(\frac{i}{\omega C R}\right)\right] I_4 \tag{3.190}$$

Combining (3.188) and (3.190), we get,

$$I_2 = \left[\left\{1 - \left(\frac{1}{\omega C R}\right)^2\right\} - \left(\frac{3j}{\omega C R}\right)\right] I_4 \tag{3.191}$$

Finally, combining (3.187), (3.190) and (3.191), we get,

$$R^3 I_1 = \left[\left\{R^3 - \left(\frac{5R}{\omega^2 C^2}\right)\right\} - j\left\{\left(\frac{6R^2}{\omega C}\right) - \left(\frac{1}{\omega C}\right)^3\right\}\right] I_4$$

or

$$\frac{I_4}{I_1} = R^3\left[\left\{R^3 - \left(\frac{5R}{\omega^2 C^2}\right)\right\} - j\left\{\left(\frac{6R^2}{\omega C}\right) - \left(\frac{1}{\omega C}\right)^3\right\}\right]^{-1} \tag{3.192}$$

Since, I_4 and I_1 are the feedback and input currents respectively, they must be in the same phase when the oscillations begin. Consequently, the coefficient of j must disappear from (3.192). In that case, the frequency of the phase shift oscillator will be

$$f = [2\pi\sqrt{6}RC]^{-1} \tag{3.193}$$

At this frequency, it follows from (3.192) that $(I_4/I_1) = \beta = -(1/29)$. Thus to fulfill the Barkhausen criterion in this case, it is necessary that $A = 29$.

We next take the case of a Wien bridge oscillator as an example. Its feedback network is shown in Fig. 3.38. The advantage of this oscillator is that its frequency can be varied over a range of 1 to 10. The desired oscillations may be obtained by arranging the network and the associated amplifier

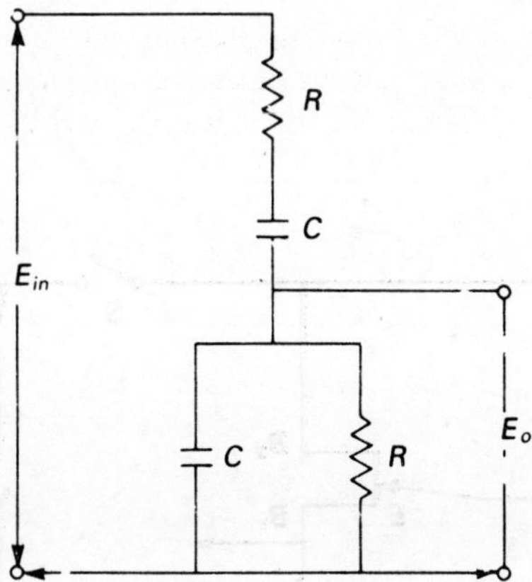

Figure 3.38 Network of a Wien bridge oscillator

circuit in such a way as to introduce a zero phase shift. E_{in} denotes the output of a common source FET amplifier while $\beta - E_{in}$ denotes the voltage fedback to the gate-source circuit of the amplifier. It is easy to find out from Fig. 3.38 that

$$\beta = \frac{Z_2}{Z_1 + Z_2} = \frac{\left[\left(\frac{1}{R}\right) + j\omega C\right]^{-1}}{\left[\left\{R + \left(\frac{1}{j\omega C}\right)\right\} + \left\{\left(\frac{1}{R}\right) + j\omega C\right\}^{-1}\right]}$$

or

$$\beta = [3 + j\{(\omega CR) - (\omega CR)^{-1}\}]^{-1} \tag{3.194}$$

In order that β becomes independent of j (or the input and the fedback portion of output comes in the same phase) we must have

$$\omega CR = (\omega CR)^{-1}$$

or

$$f = [2\pi RC]^{-1} \tag{3.195}$$

At this frequency $\beta = (1/3)$ as we find from (3.194). From the Barkhausen criterion, the gain of the amplifier must, therefore, be at least 3 for the maintenance of oscillations.

3.10.7 Applications of unijunction transistors

A few of the applications of an UJT are presented below. We have illustrated a simple UJT oscillator circuit in Fig. 3.39. The value of V_{BB} and R_1 in it must be so chosen that

$$V_{BB} - \frac{V_p}{R_1} > I_p \tag{3.196}$$

and

$$V_{BB} - \frac{V_v}{R_1} < I_v \tag{3.197}$$

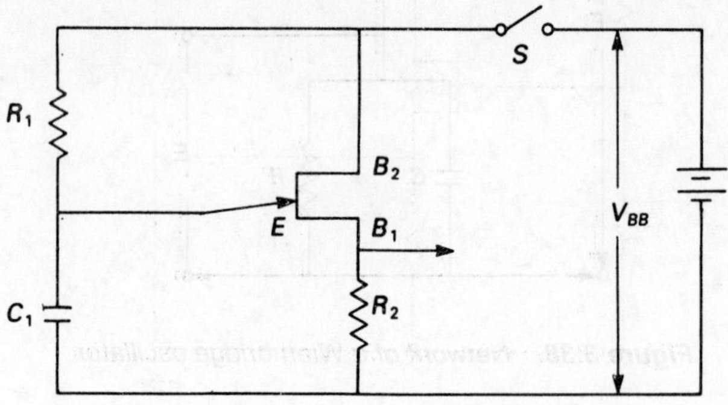

Figure 3.39 *A typical UJT relaxation oscillator*

If the first condition cannot be met, the UJT cannot fire and if the second one is not realized, the UJT cannot be turned off once it is switched on. When the switch S is closed C_1 begins charging itself to the level of the interbase voltage V_{BB}.The voltage across C_1 provides the emitter voltage V_E for the UJT. When $V_E = V_p$, the emitter becomes forward biased and the resistance between E and B_1 rapidly drops. This, therefore, provides a low resistance for the capacitor to discharge through R_{B1} and R_2 to the ground, When the residual voltage across C_1 falls below V_v, the UJT is turned off, stopping any further discharge of the capacitor C_1. The voltage across C_1 starts building up as before to repeat the earlier operation. Sharp pulses of voltages would thus be available across R_2. From the theory of charging of a condenser through a resistor, the time interval between successive voltage pulses follows to be

$$T = R_1 C_1 \ln \left[\frac{V_{BB} - V_v}{V_{BB} - V_p} \right] \tag{3.198}$$

Thus, by varying R_1, the time interval between successive pulses can be conveniently altered. The duration of the pulses may be calculated similarly. But, it should be remembered that during the discharge of the condenser C_1, the resistance between E and B_1 contact varies from R_{B1} to 0. Typically, the duration of these pulses is about a few microseconds. Such UJT relaxation oscillator circuits, capable of delivering sharp pulses of voltages, are often used to turn SCRs ON and OFF at desired voltage levels. The positive pulses across B_1, may be used to turn on SCRs while negative pulses across B_2 are useful in turning SCRs OFF. The pulse heights and their durations can be adjusted by appropriately choosing R, R_1, R_2, C and V_{BB}.

3.10.8 Application of semiconductor controlled rectifiers

As already discussed in section 3.9, the SCR is an active switching device capable of controlling a large amount of power flow though an electronic circuit. A simple SCR firing circuit is shown in Fig. 3.40.

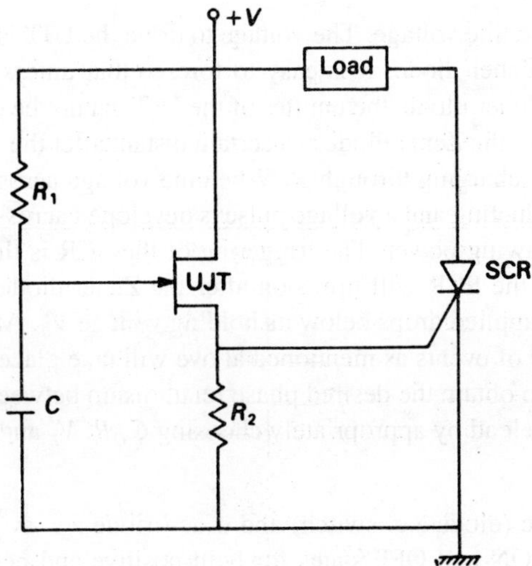

Figure 3.40 *A typical SCR trigger circuit*

When a full wave rectified voltage is available at $+V$, no current can flow through the load as both the SCR and the UJT are in their OFF states. The capacitor C however, continues charging through R_1 as the voltage wave grows in magnitude. Once the voltage across C becomes V_p, the UJT switches to its conducting state and a voltage is delivered across R_2. This voltage is applied to the gate of the SCR. Consequently, the SCR is turned ON at a desired voltage level allowing the current to flow through the load. The SCR will turn OFF once the voltage wave at A drops below V_h of the SCR. The load will then stop drawing any more power. The above sequence of events would once again be repeated with the growth of a new voltage wave at A.

The circuits which have been designed to provide triggers to SCRs are numerous. But, the circuits employing UJT are the simplest to provide reliable triggering. In some SCR applications, synchronization and phase control of the input signal relative to the output may become necessary. Such a circuit is shown in Fig. 3.41. A full wave rectified voltage is applied at the input. The load is connected in series

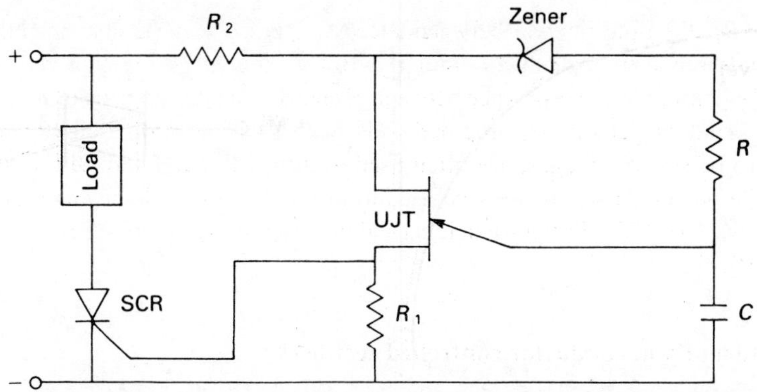

Figure 3.41 *A synchronized trigger circuit with phase control*

with the SCR and across the line voltage. The voltage to drive the UJT is obtained through a regulator combination of R_2 and a Zener diode. It is easy to foresee that unless the line voltage exceeds the breakdown voltage of the Zener diode, the emitter of the UJT cannot be driven. The Zener breakdown voltage V_z is available across the Zener diode at a certain instant after the voltage is applied at the input. The capacitor C then starts charging through R. When the voltage across C reaches the peak voltage V_p of the UJT, it starts conducting and a voltage pulse is developed across R_1. This pulse turns the SCR ON, and the load starts drawing power. The triggering of the SCR is therefore, determined by R, C and V_z. If RC is reduced, the SCR will fire soon after the Zener diode starts conducting. The SCR turns off when the voltage applied drops below its holding voltage V_h. At the next cycle of the applied voltage, the same sequence of events as mentioned above will take place. Thus, with the circuit given in Fig. 3.41, it is possible to obtain the desired phase relationship between the applied voltage and the current flowing through the load by appropriately choosing C, R, V_z and the SCR turn on voltage V_s.

Diac and Triac The diac (diode a.c. switch) and triac (triode a.c. switch) are bi-directional SCRs (or thyristors). They have ON and OFF states for both positive and negative voltages on the anode (Fig. 3.42). Therefore, they prove to be useful for a.c. applications. When the gate electrode is missing,

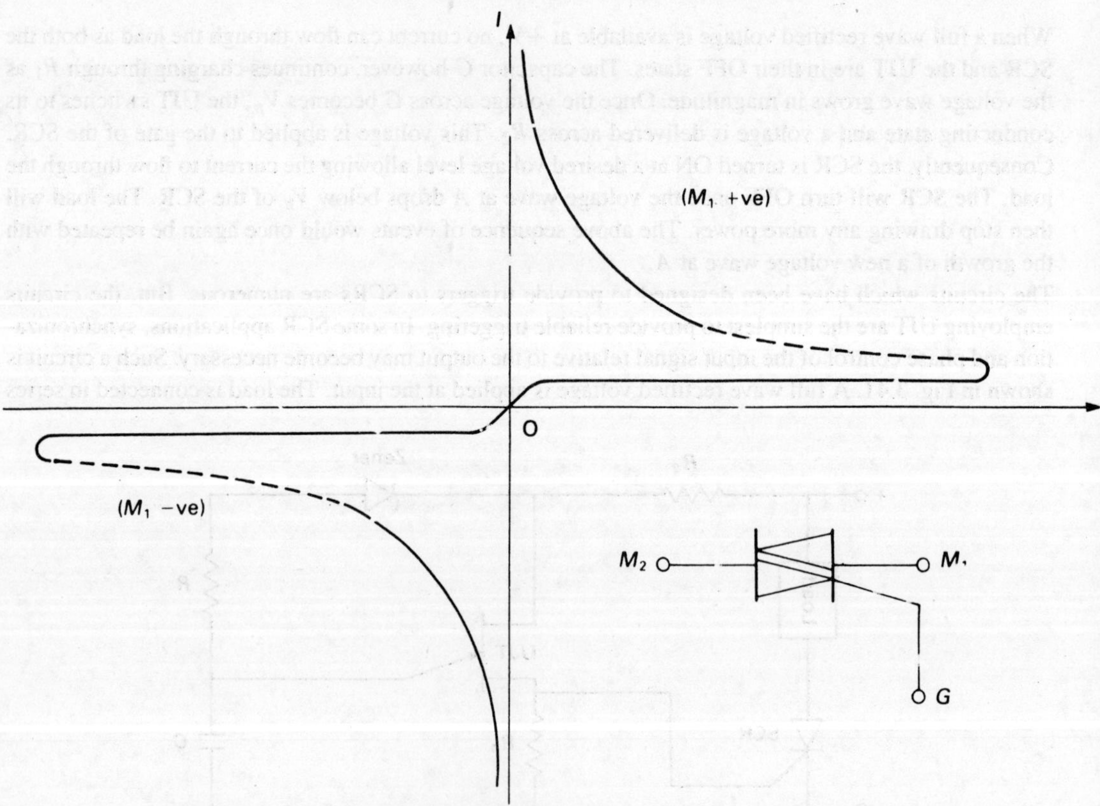

Figure 3.42 (a) *I–V characteristics and the circuit symbol of a triac*

the device is termed a diac (Fig. 3.42(b)). The cross-section of a triac is shown in Fig. 3.42(c). The diac is shown to possess a five layered structure. This can be considered as two Shockley diodes connected in parallel. For the positive polarity on M_2 and the negative on M_1, the above four layers behave as an SCR. Interchanging the polarities of M_1 and M_2, the lowermost layers function as an SCR.

The triac is a diac with a gate electrode to control the switching voltage. As shown in Fig. 3.42(c), the gate contact is made on the p-type base. It has a special property that both the positive and the negative gate voltages can lower the device switching voltage.

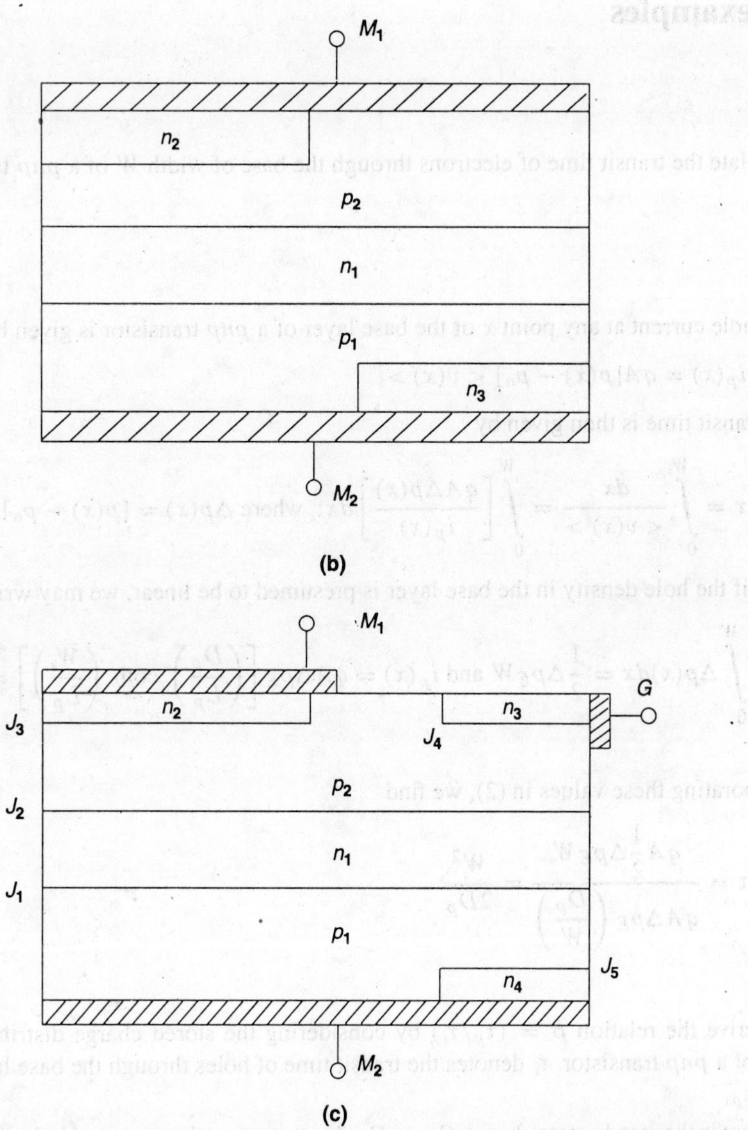

Figure 3.42 *continued (b) Structure of a DIAC, (c) Structure of a TRIAC*

Solved examples

3.1 Calculate the transit time of electrons through the base of width W of a *pnp* transistor.

Solution

The hole current at any point x of the base layer of a *pnp* transistor is given by

$$i_p(x) = qA[p(x) - p_n] < v(x) > \tag{1}$$

The transit time is then given by

$$\tau = \int_0^W \frac{dx}{< v(x) >} = \int_0^W \left[\frac{qA\Delta p(x)}{i_p(x)}\right] dx; \text{ where } \Delta p(x) = [p(x) - p_n] \tag{2}$$

Now, if the hole density in the base layer is presumed to be linear, we may write

$$\int_0^W \Delta p(x)dx = \frac{1}{2}\Delta p_E W \text{ and } i_p(x) = qA\Delta p_E \left[\left(\frac{D_p}{L_p}\right) \coth \left(\frac{W}{L_p}\right)\right] = qA\Delta p_E \left(\frac{D_p}{W}\right) \tag{3}$$

Incorporating these values in (2), we find

$$\tau = \frac{qA\frac{1}{2}\Delta p_E W}{qA\Delta p_E \left(\frac{D_p}{W}\right)} = \frac{W^2}{2D_p} \tag{4}$$

3.2 (a) Derive the relation $\beta = (\tau_p/\tau_i)$ by considering the stored charge distribution in the base layer of a *pnp* transistor. τ_i denotes the transit time of holes through the base layer. Assume that $\tau_n = \tau_p$.

(b) What is the steady state charge $Q_n = Q_p$ due to excess electrons and holes in the neutral base region for the transistor?

Solution

(a) In the steady state condition, there are excess holes and electrons stored in the base layer. The charge Q_n due to electron distribution is replaced every τ_p second in the base layer. Therefore, the base current is $i_B = (Q_n/\tau_p)$. On the other hand, the charge Q_p due to hole distribution is collected every τ_i second. Thus, $i_C = (Q_p/\tau_i)$. But for the space-charge neutrality of the base layer we must have $Q_n = Q_p$ at every instant of time. Therefore, the common-emitter current gain β is given by

$$\beta = \frac{i_C}{i_B} = \frac{\dfrac{Q_p}{\tau_i}}{\dfrac{Q_n}{\tau_p}} = \frac{\tau_p}{\tau_i}$$

Hence proved.

(b) The steady state charge distribution is given by

$$Q_n = Q_p = i_C\tau_i = i_B\tau_p$$

3.3 Obtain an expression for the transit time of minority carriers having an exponential distribution in the base layer of a transistor.

Solution

For an exponential impurity distribution in the base layer, the carrier drift velocity through it is given by

$$u = \left(\frac{D_p}{W}\right)(f+1) \quad (1)$$

where W denotes the base width and $f = (W/L_d)$ where L_d is defined by the following relation:

$$N_d(x) = N_{d0}\exp\left(\frac{-x}{L_d}\right) \quad (2)$$

Hence, the transit time of carriers through the base layer is given by

$$\tau = \frac{W}{u} = \frac{W^2}{D_p(f+1)} \quad (3)$$

The above analysis is intended for a *pnp* transistor.

3.4 A Si p^+np transistor has impurity concentrations of 5×10^{18}, 10^{15} and 10^{16} cm^{-3} in the emitter, base and collector regions respectively. The base width W_B is 10.0 μm and the device cross-sectional area is 3 mm^2. When the emitter-base junction is forward biased to 0.5 V, and the base-collector junction is reverse biased to 5 V, calculate

i) the neutral base width,
ii) the minority carrier density in the emitter and
iii) the minority carrier charge in the base. ($L_p = 2\,\mu$ m)

Solution

(a) For a forward biased emitter-base junction, the transition layer width on the emitter side of the base is negligibly small and can be ignored. This is however not the case on the collector side of the base due to the reverse biasing of the collector-base junction. For the collector-base junction, we have

$$n^* = \frac{N_a N_d}{N_a + N_d} = \frac{10^{15} 10^{16}}{10^{15} + 10^{16}} \cong 10^{15}\ \text{cm}^{-3} = 10^{21}\ \text{m}^{-3}$$

while $n_i(Si) = 1.45 \times 10^{16}\ \text{m}^{-3}$. Hence

$$\Psi_0 = \left(\frac{kT}{q}\right) \ln \left[\frac{N_a N_d}{n_i^2}\right] = 0.026 \ln \left[\frac{10^{21} 10^{22}}{(1.45 \times 10^{16})^2}\right] = 0.64\ \text{V} \quad \text{and}$$

$$x_n = \left[\left(\frac{2\kappa\varepsilon_0}{q}\right)\left(\frac{N_a}{N_d}\right)\left\{\frac{\Psi_0 + V}{N_a + N_d}\right\}\right]^{1/2}$$

$$= \left[\left\{\frac{2 \times 12 \times 8.854 \times 10^{-12}}{1.6 \times 10^{-19}}\right\}\left(\frac{10^{22}}{10^{21}}\right)\left(\frac{5.64}{10^{22}}\right)\right]^{1/2} = 2.737\ \mu\text{m}$$

Therefore, the neutral base width $= (10 - 2.737)\ \mu\text{m} = 7.263\ \mu$ m

(b) The minority carrier density in the transition region boundary of the emitter $= n_p$ exp $(qV_{EB}/kT) = (n_i^2/N_a)$ exp $(qV_{EB}/kT) = (1.45 \times 10^{16})^2\ /(5 \times 10^{24})$ exp $(0.5/0.026) = 9.45 \times 10^{15}\ \text{m}^{-3}$

(c) The minority carrier charge stored in the base layer is given by

$$Q_B = qp_n L_p \left[\exp\left(\frac{qV_{EB}}{kT}\right) - 1\right]$$

But

$$p_n = \frac{n_i^2}{N_d} = \frac{1.45 \times 10^{16}}{10^{21}} = 2.1 \times 10^{11}\ \text{m}^{-3}$$

Then

$$Q_B = 1.6 \times 10^{-19} \times 2 \times 10^{11} \times 2 \times 10^{-6} \left[\exp\left(\frac{0.5}{0.026}\right) - 1\right] = 1.44 \times 10^{-5}\ \text{C/m}^2$$

3.5 A potential difference of V_E volts is applied between the base-emitter leads of a p^+np transistor in the common-base mode. Presuming the emitter efficiency to be unity, calculate the current through the emitter lead. The base-collector junction is joined by a resistor R and no bias is applied across this junction. How does the current divide between the base and the collector leads?

Solution

Presuming the emitter efficiency $\gamma = [i_{pE}/(i_{pE} + i_{nE})] = 1$, i_{nE} reduces to zero. We may then write

$$I_E = I_{pE} = qA\left(\frac{D_p}{L_p}\right)(p_E - p_n) \coth\left(\frac{W}{L_p}\right) \text{ as } V_{BC} = 0$$

i.e.

$$I = I_E = qA\left(\frac{D_p}{L_p}\right)\Delta p_E \coth\left(\frac{W}{L_p}\right) \tag{1}$$

where

$$\Delta p_E = p_n\left[\exp\left(\frac{qV_E}{kT}\right) - 1\right]$$

Similarly,

$$I_C = qA\left(\frac{D_p}{L_p}\right)\Delta p_E \operatorname{cosech}\left(\frac{W}{L_p}\right) \tag{2}$$

Therefore,

$$I_B = I_E - I_C = qA\left(\frac{D_p}{L_p}\right)\Delta p_E\left[\coth\left(\frac{W}{L_p}\right) - \operatorname{cosech}\left(\frac{W}{L_p}\right)\right]$$

or

$$I_B = qA\left(\frac{D_p}{L_p}\right)\Delta p_E \tanh\left(\frac{W}{2L_p}\right) \tag{3}$$

For smaller base widths, one may assume $\tanh(W/2L_p) = (W/2L_p)$. In this case, (3) simplifies to

$$I_B = \frac{qA\Delta p_E W}{2\tau_p} \tag{4}$$

Again for $(W/L_p) \ll 1$, $\operatorname{cosech}(W/L_p) = (L_p/W)$. Equation (2) then simplifies to

$$I_C = \frac{qAD_p\Delta p_E}{W} \tag{5}$$

so that

$$\beta = \frac{I_C}{I_B} = \frac{2D_p\tau_p}{W^2} = \frac{\tau_p}{\dfrac{W^2}{D_p}} = 2\left(\frac{L_p}{W}\right)^2 \tag{6}$$

3.6 Assume that a *pnp* transistor is doped such that the emitter doping is ten times that in the base, the hole mobility in the emitter is half that of the electron mobility in the base and the base width is one-tenth the minority carriers diffusion length. The carrier lifetimes are equal. Calculate α and β for the transistor.

Solution

It is given that for the *pnp* transistor, $(p_{pE}/n_n) = 10$, $(\mu_{pe}/\mu_n) = (1/2)$ and $W = (L_p/10)$. The expressions for the emitter efficiency (γ), the transport factor (β^*) and the common-base current gain (α) are

$$\gamma = \left[1 + \left(\frac{\sigma_B}{\sigma_E}\right)\left(\frac{L_p}{L_{ne}}\right) \tanh \left(\frac{W}{L_p}\right)\right]^{-1},$$

$$\beta^* = \left[1 - \frac{1}{2}\left(\frac{W}{L_p}\right)^2\right], \quad \text{and } \alpha = \beta^*\gamma \text{ respectively.}$$

Now the expression for the emitter efficiency simplifies to

$$\gamma = \left[1 + \left(\frac{\mu_n}{\mu_{pe}}\right)\left(\frac{n_n}{p_{pE}}\right)\left(\frac{W}{L_p}\right)\right]^{-1} = \left[1 + 2\left(\frac{1}{10}\right)\left(\frac{1}{10}\right)\right]^{-1} = \frac{50}{51}$$

Next the transport factor is

$$\beta^* = \left[1 - \frac{1}{2}\left(\frac{W}{L_p}\right)^2\right] = \left[1 - \left(\frac{1}{2}\right)\left(\frac{1}{10}\right)^2\right] = 1 - \left(\frac{0.5}{100}\right) = \frac{199}{200}$$

Therefore the common-emitter current gain becomes

$$\alpha = \beta^*\gamma = \left(\frac{199}{200}\right)\left(\frac{50}{51}\right) = 0.975$$

The common-emitter current gain is then given by

$$\beta = \frac{\alpha}{1-\alpha} = \frac{0.975}{1 - 0.975} = \frac{0.975}{0.025} = 39$$

3.7 For a particular Si *npn* transistor, the punch-through voltage is found to be 30 V. Assuming the collector doping to be relatively higher than that of the base, which contains 10^{21} acceptors/m^3, estimate the base width at zero applied voltage.

Solution

The depletion layer width of a reverse biased *pn* junction is given by

$$W = \left[\frac{2\kappa\varepsilon_0(\Psi_0 + V)}{qn^*}\right]^{1/2} \tag{1}$$

for a reverse voltage of V volts. Since the base doping is usually smaller compared to that of the collector

$$n^* = \frac{N_a N_d}{N_a + N_d} \cong \frac{N_a N_d}{N_d} \cong N_a \quad (\text{since } N_a \ll N_d)$$

Also usually $V \gg \Psi_0$, With these approximations (1) reduces to

$$W = \left[\frac{2\kappa\varepsilon_0 V}{qN_a}\right]^{1/2} \tag{2}$$

Substituting the values of the appropriate parameters in (2), we get

$$W = \left[\frac{2 \times 12 \times 8.854 \times 10^{-12} \times 30}{1.6 \times 10^{-19} \times 10^{21}}\right]^{1/2} = 6.31\ \mu\text{m}$$

At zero applied voltage, the effective base width is therefore 6.31 μm.

3.8 The emitter and the collector regions of an alloyed Si *pnp* transistor are heavily doped and the impurity concentration in the base layer is 10^{15} cm^{-3}. Calculate the base width that will make the avalanche breakdown voltage equal to the punch-through voltage. Assume that the avalanche breakdown occurs when the maximum field strength in the depletion layer becomes 5×10^4 V/cm. What minority carrier diffusion length and lifetime in the base layer are required to obtain $\alpha = 0.95$? Assume $\gamma = 0.99$ and a reverse bias of 1.5 V at the collector-base junction.

Solution

The breakdown voltage of a *pn* junction may be expressed as

$$V_B = \frac{\kappa\varepsilon_0\varepsilon_c^2}{2qN_d} \tag{1}$$

Substituting the values of the appropriate parameters in (1), we find

$$V_B = \frac{12 \times 8.854 \times 10^{-12} \times (5 \times 10^6)^2}{2 \times 1.6 \times 10^{-19} \times 10^{21}} = 8.3\,\text{V} \tag{2}$$

If this happens to be the punch-through voltage, the base width must be given by

$$W_B = \left[\frac{2\kappa\varepsilon_0 V_B}{qN_d}\right]^{1/2} \tag{3}$$

Substituting the values of the appropriate parameters in (3), we get

$$W_B = \left[\frac{2 \times 12 \times 8.854 \times 10^{-12} \times 8.30}{1.6 \times 10^{-19} \times 10^{21}}\right]^{1/2} = 3.32\,\mu\text{m}.$$

For a 1.5 V reverse bias at the collector base junction, the transition layer width over the base layer is given by

$$W'_B = \left[\frac{2\kappa\varepsilon_0 V}{qN_d}\right]^{\frac{1}{2}} = \left[\frac{2 \times 12 \times 8.854 \times 10^{-12} \times 1.5}{1.6 \times 10^{-19} \times 10^{21}}\right]^{1/2} = 1.411\,\mu\text{m}$$

Therefore, the effective base width at 1.5 V reverse bias $W = (3.32 - 1.411)\,\mu\text{m} = 1.909\,\mu\text{m}$
Now,

$$\beta^* = \frac{\alpha}{\gamma} = \text{sech}\left(\frac{W}{L_p}\right) \text{ or } \cosh\left(\frac{W}{L_p}\right) = \frac{\gamma}{\alpha}$$

or

$$L_p = \frac{W}{\cosh^{-1}\left(\frac{\gamma}{\alpha}\right)} = \frac{1.909}{\cosh^{-1}\left(\frac{0.99}{0.95}\right)} = 6.606\,\mu\text{m}$$

Next

$$\tau_p = \frac{L_p^2}{D_p} = \frac{(6.606 \times 10^{-6})^2}{47 \times 10^{-4}} = 9.28 \times 10^{-9}\,\text{s}$$

3.9 An *npn* transistor has a base width of 3 μm and $D_B = 10\,\text{cm}^2\,\text{s}^{-1}$ at 300 K. The minority carrier lifetime in the base layer is 0.1 μ s, and γ is nearly unity. Determine f_α and the magnitude and the phase of α at a frequency of 15 MHz.

Solution

The alpha cutoff frequency f_α is given by

$$2\pi f_\alpha = \omega_\alpha = \left(\frac{1}{\tau_n}\right) + \left\{\frac{\pi^2}{4}\right\}\left(\frac{D_B}{W^2}\right)$$

or

$$f_\alpha = \frac{1}{2\pi}\left[\left(\frac{1}{\tau_n}\right) + \left\{\frac{\pi^2}{4}\right\}\left(\frac{D_B}{W^2}\right)\right] \tag{1}$$

or

$$f_\alpha = \frac{1}{2 \times 3.14}\left[\frac{1}{10^{-7}} + \frac{9.89 \times 10 \times 10^{-4}}{4 \times (3 \times 10^{-6})^2}\right]$$

or

$$f_\alpha = 45\,\text{MHz}$$

The current gain is given by

$$\alpha = \frac{\alpha_0}{1 + j\left(\dfrac{\omega}{\omega_\alpha}\right)} = \frac{\alpha_0}{1 + \left(\dfrac{\omega}{\omega_\alpha}\right)^{1/2}} \exp(-j\phi) \tag{2}$$

where

$$\phi = \tan^{-1}\left(\frac{\omega}{\omega_\alpha}\right) \tag{3}$$

But the d.c current gain α_0 is given by

$$\alpha_0 = \beta^* \gamma \tag{4}$$

where

$$\beta^* = \text{sech}\left(\frac{W}{L_p}\right) = 1 - \frac{1}{2}\left(\frac{W}{L_p}\right)^2 \quad \text{and } \gamma = 1$$

But

$$L_p = (D_B \tau_n)^{1/2} = (10 \times 10^{-4} \times 10^{-7})^{1/2} = 10^{-5}\,\text{m} = 10\,\mu\text{m}$$

Therefore

$$\beta^* = \text{sech}\left(\frac{3}{10}\right) = 1 - \frac{1}{2}\left(\frac{3}{10}\right)^2 = 0.955$$

Thus

$$\alpha_0 = \beta^* \gamma = 0.955$$

Hence

$$|\alpha| = \frac{|\alpha_0|}{\left\{1 + \left(\dfrac{f}{f_\alpha}\right)^2\right\}^{1/2}} = \frac{0.955}{\left\{1 + \left(\dfrac{15}{45}\right)^2\right\}^{1/2}} = 0.90725$$

and

$$\phi = \tan^{-1}\left(\frac{15}{45}\right) = 18.43^\circ$$

3.10 A switching transistor has a base width of 0.5 μm and a diffusion constant of 10 cm^2/s. The minority carrier lifetime in the base layer is 10^{-7} s. The transistor is biased with $V_{CC} = 5$ V and a load resistor of 10 kΩ. If a base current pulse of 2 μA has a duration of 2 μs, find the stored base charge and the storage time delay.

Solution

The stored base charge $Q_B(t)$ decays according to the following relation

$$Q_B(t) = I_B\tau_p\left[1 - \exp\left(\frac{-t}{\tau_p}\right)\right] \tag{1}$$

Since $t = 2\,\mu\text{s} > \tau_p$ $(= 10^{-7}\text{s})$, $\exp(-t/\tau_p) \cong 0$. Therefore

$$Q_B(t) = I_B\tau_p = 2 \times 10^{-13}\,\text{C}$$

The storage time delay t_s in such a case is given by

$$t_s = \ln\left[\frac{I_B\tau_p}{Q_s}\right] \quad \text{where} \quad Q_s \cong \left(\frac{V_{CC}}{R_L}\right)\tau_t = \left(\frac{V_{CC}}{R_L}\right)\left(\frac{W^2}{2D_p}\right)$$

Therefore

$$Q_s = \left(\frac{5}{10^4}\right)\frac{(0.5 \times 10^{-6})^2}{2 \times 10 \times 10^{-4}} = 6.25 \times 10^{-14}\,\text{C}$$

Hence

$$t_s = \ln\left[\frac{I_B\tau_p}{Q_s}\right] = 10^{-7}\ln\left[\frac{2 \times 10^{-13}}{6.25 \times 10^{-14}}\right] = 1.16 \times 10^{-7}\,\text{s}$$

3.11 (i) A transistor is operating in its cutoff state with both emitter and collector junctions reverse biased by a few tenths of a volt. Find expressions for emitter and collector currents.

(ii) Obtain an expression for the emitter junction voltage required to produce cutoff.

Solution

The Ebers–Moll equation may be written down as

$$I_E = \alpha_I\, I_C + I_{E0}\left[\exp\left(\frac{qV_{EB}}{kT}\right) - 1\right] \tag{1}$$

and

$$I_C = \alpha_N\, I_E - I_{C0}\left[\exp\left(\frac{qV_{CB}}{kT}\right) - 1\right] \tag{2}$$

where

$$\alpha_N I_{ES} = \alpha_I I_{CS}, \quad I_{E0} = (1 - \alpha_I \alpha_N) I_{ES}, \quad \text{and} \quad I_{C0} = (1 - \alpha_I \alpha_N) I_{CS}$$

Equations (1) and (2) may also be written as

$$I_E = I_{ES}\left[\exp\left(\frac{qV_{EB}}{kT}\right) - 1\right] - \alpha_I I_{CS}\left[\exp\left(\frac{qV_{CB}}{kT}\right) - 1\right] \tag{3}$$

and

$$I_C = \alpha_N I_{ES}\left[\exp\left(\frac{qV_{EB}}{kT}\right) - 1\right] - I_{CS}\left[\exp\left(\frac{qV_{CB}}{kT}\right) - 1\right] \tag{4}$$

If both V_{EB} and V_{CB} are negative by a few tenths of a volt, equations (3) and (4) reduce to,

$$I_E = -I_{ES} + \alpha_I I_{CS} \tag{5}$$

and

$$I_C = -\alpha_N I_{ES} + I_{CS} \tag{6}$$

Using the property $\alpha_N I_{ES} = \alpha_I I_{CS}$, (5) and (6) simplify to

$$I_E = -I_{ES}(1 - \alpha_N) \tag{7}$$

and

$$I_C = I_{CS}(1 - \alpha_I) \tag{8}$$

Substituting for I_{ES} and I_{CS} in terms of I_{E0} and I_{C0}, we obtain

$$I_E = -\frac{I_{E0}(1 - \alpha_N)}{1 - \alpha_I \alpha_N} \tag{9}$$

and

$$I_C = -\frac{I_{C0}(1 - \alpha_I)}{(1 - \alpha_I \alpha_N)} \tag{10}$$

These are the required expressions for the currents.

(ii) With the collector junction reverse biased, the emitter and the collector currents are given by

$$I_E = -\left[\frac{I_{E0}}{1 - \alpha_I \alpha_N}\right] \exp\left(\frac{qV_{EB}}{kT}\right) + \left[\frac{I_{E0}(1 - \alpha_N)}{1 - \alpha_I \alpha_N}\right] \tag{11}$$

and

$$I_C = \left[\frac{\alpha_N I_{E0}}{(1 - \alpha_I \alpha_N)}\right] \exp\left(\frac{qV_{EB}}{kT}\right) + \left[\frac{I_{C0}(1 - \alpha_I)}{(1 - \alpha_I \alpha_N)}\right] \tag{12}$$

Combining (9) and (11) at cutoff we get

$$V_{EB} = \left(\frac{kT}{q}\right) \ln\left[2(1 - \alpha_N)\right] \tag{13}$$

This is the required emitter-base voltage required to produce cutoff.

3.12 The reverse saturation current of the collector junction of a transistor is I_{CO}. We know that when the base is floating, the current through the transistor is large. Show that the potential of the floating base is $V_{BE} = (kT/q)\ \ln\ (\beta_0 I_{CO}/I_{E0})$.

Solution

The expression for the collector current is

$$I_C = \beta_0 I_B + (\beta_0 + 1) I_{CO} \tag{1}$$

As the base is floating, $I_B = 0$. Since $\beta_0 \gg 1$,

$$I_C \cong \beta_0 I_{CO} \tag{2}$$

As the base is floating, the collector current will be the emitter current. That is

$$I_C \cong \beta_0 I_{CO} = I_{E0}\ \exp\left(\frac{qV_{BE}}{kT}\right)$$

or

$$V_{BE} = \left(\frac{kT}{q}\right)\ \ln\ \left[\frac{\beta_0 I_{CO}}{I_{E0}}\right] \tag{3}$$

3.13 The reverse saturation current of a Ge *npn* transistor is 2 μA at 25℃ and it doubles for each temperature increase of 10℃. The bias $V_{BB} = 5$ V. Find the minimum allowable value of R_B if the transistor is to remain at the cutoff state at 75℃. If $V_{BB} = 1$ V and $R_B = 50\,\text{k}\Omega$, how high may the temperature rise before the transistor comes out of the cutoff state?

Solution

Since the reverse saturation current doubles for every rise of 10℃ from its value at 25℃, we may express it in the following generalized form:

$$I_{CO}(t) = 2^{(t-25)/10} I_{CO}(25℃) \tag{1}$$

Therefore,

$$I_{CO}(75℃) = 2^{(75-25)/10} I_{CO}(25℃) = 64\ \mu\text{A} \tag{2}$$

Next, applying Kirchoff's voltage law (KVL) to the emitter circuit, we find

$$-5 + I_{CBO} R_B + V_{BE,\text{cutoff}} = 0 \tag{3}$$

Remembering that $V_{BE,\text{cutoff}} = -0.1$ V, we find

$$-5 + 64 \times 10^{-6} R_B - 0.1 = 0$$

or

$$R_B = 79.7\,\text{k}\Omega \tag{4}$$

This is the required value of the resistance that keeps the transistor at the cutoff state at 75℃. On the contrary, if $V_{BB} = 1$ V and $R_B = 50\,\text{k}\Omega$, we get on applying the Kirchoff's voltage law (KVL) to the emitter circuit of the transistor in the cutoff state

$$-1 + 50 \times 10^3 I_{Co} - 0.1 = 0$$

or

$$I_{CO} = 0.022 \times 10^{-3}\ \text{A} \tag{5}$$

Substituting this value in (1), we find

$$0.022 \times 10^{-3} = 2^{(t-25)/10} \times 2 \times 10^{-6} \tag{6}$$

or

$$2^{t-25/10} = 11$$

or

$$\left[\frac{t-25}{10}\right] \log_{10} 2 = \log_{10} 11$$

or

$$t = 59.6℃ \tag{7}$$

If the junction temperature rises above 59.6℃, I_{CO} would increase further. As a result, I_E will be non-zero and the transistor will come out of the cutoff state.

3.14 An *npn* transistor is operated in the common-emitter (CE) mode. The d.c collector bias V_{CC} applied across $R_C = 2\,\text{k}\Omega$ is 12 V while the d.c. emitter bias V_{BB} applied across a resistance $R_b = 100\,\text{k}\Omega$ is 6 V. Presuming $I_{CO} = 20$ nA and $\beta = 50$, calculate the various transistor currents ($V_{BE} = 0.7$ V).

Solution

Applying Kirchoff's voltage law (KVL) to the emitter-base circuit (Fig. 3.43), we find

$$100 \times 10^3 I_B + V_{BE} = 6 \tag{1}$$

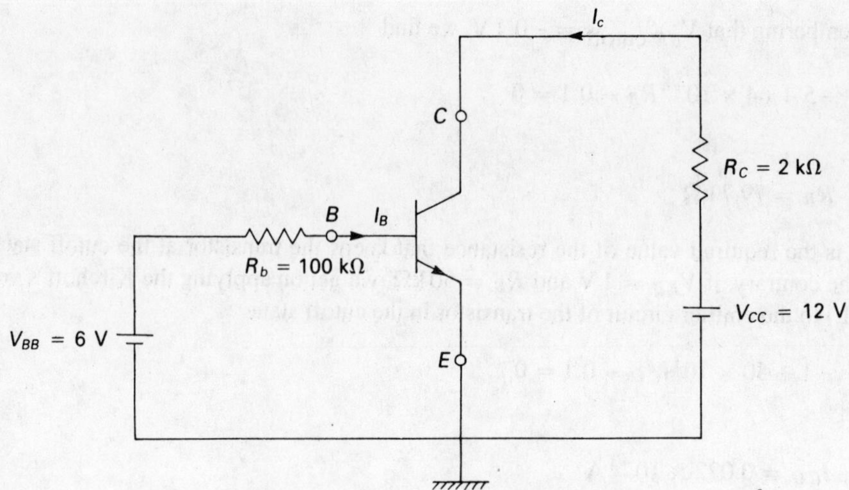

Figure 3.43 *Transistor bias circuit*

Taking $V_{BE} = 0.7$ V for a Si transistor, it follows from (1) that $I_B = 0.053$ mA
But,

$$I_C = \beta_0 I_B + (\beta_0 + 1) I_{CO} \tag{2}$$

Substituting the appropriate values of the parameters in (1), we find, $I_C = 2.65$ mA. But the equation used is valid only for the active region of the transistor. We must therefore calculate V_{CB} and show that it is positive. It will then really be proved that the transistor is biased in the active region. Applying KVL to the collector loop, we find

$$2 \times 10^3 I_C + V_{CB} + V_{BE} = 12 \tag{3}$$

or

$$V_{CB} = +6.0 \text{ V}$$

For an *npn* transistor, a positive V_{CB} suggests a reverse biased collector junction. Hence, the given transistor is operating in its active region, as already presumed.

3.15 A Si *npn* transistor with $\beta = 100$ is used in the given transistor circuit. Find the minimum value of R_c for which the transistor remains in the saturated state. ($V_{BE,\text{sat}} = 0.8$ V, $V_{CE,\text{sat}} = 0.2$ V)

Solution

We proceed by presuming that the transistor is in the saturated state (Fig. 3.44). Applying KVL to the base and the emitter circuits, we get

$$200 \times 10^3 I_B + V_{BE,\text{sat}} = 5 \tag{1}$$

and

$$I_C R_C + V_{CE,\text{sat}} = 10 \tag{2}$$

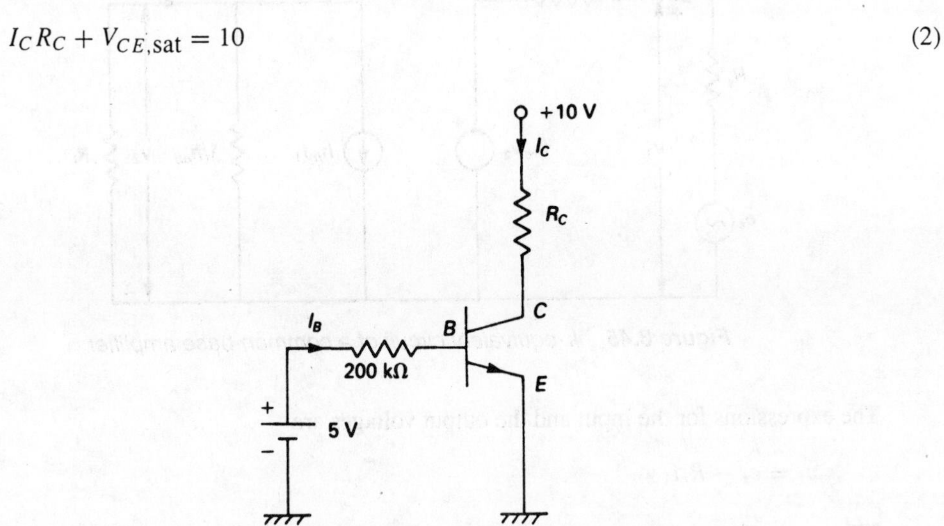

Figure 3.44 Saturated transistor

From the first equation, we derive, $I_B = 0.021$ mA. Therefore, $I_C = \beta I_B = 2.1$ mA. Using the value of I_C in the second equation, we find, $R_C = 4.67\,\text{k}\Omega$. If R_C exceeds $4.67\,\text{k}\Omega$, both I_C and I_B would increase and the transistor will no longer remain biased in the saturated state.

3.16 Draw the h-equivalent circuit of a small signal, low frequency transistor amplifier circuit in the grounded base configuration. Derive expressions for its

i) current gain,
ii) input impedance,
iii) voltage gain and
iv) output impedance.

Solution

The equations satisfying the h-equivalent circuit (Fig. 3.45) are

$$v_1 = h_{ib}\, i_1 + h_{rb}\, v_2 \tag{1}$$

and

$$i_2 = h_{fb}\, i_1 + h_{ob}\, v_2 \tag{2}$$

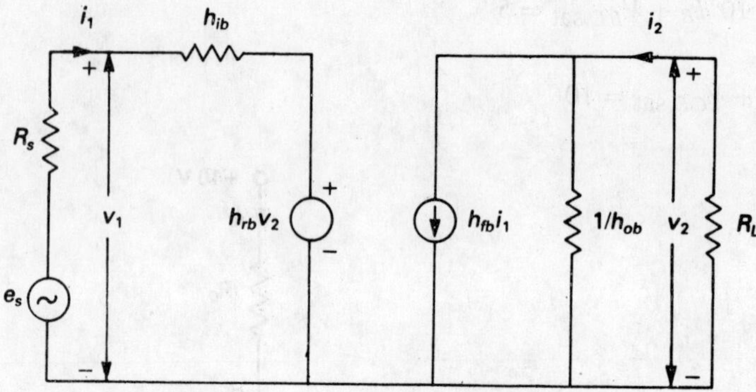

Figure 3.45 *h-equivalent circuit of a common-base amplifier*

The expressions for the input and the output voltages are

$$v_1 = e_s - R_s i_1 \tag{3}$$

and

$$v_2 = -R_L i_2 \tag{4}$$

(i) *Current gain* Combining (2) and (4), we get

$$i_2 = h_{fb}\, i_1 - h_{ob} R_L i_2$$

or

$$A_{ib} = -\left(\frac{i_2}{i_1}\right) = -\frac{h_{fb}}{1 + h_{ob} R_L} \tag{5}$$

(ii) *Input impedance* From (1), we find

$$R_{ib} = \frac{v_1}{i_1} = h_{ib} + h_{rb}\left(\frac{v_2}{i_1}\right) \tag{6}$$

From (2), we derive

$$v_2 = \frac{i_2 - h_{fb}\, i_1}{h_{ob}} \tag{7}$$

Substituting for i_2 from (4) in (7), we get

$$v_2 = \frac{(-v_2/R_L) - h_{fb}\, i_1}{h_{ob}}$$

or

$$\frac{v_2}{i_1} = -\frac{R_L\, h_{fb}}{1 + R_L\, h_{ob}} \tag{8}$$

Combining (6) and (8), we get

$$R_{ib} = h_{ib} + h_{rb}\left[-\frac{R_L h_{fb}}{1 + R_L h_{ob}}\right]$$

or

$$R_{ib} = \frac{h_{ib} + R_L \Delta}{1 + R_L h_{ob}} \tag{9}$$

where

$$\Delta = h_{ib}\, h_{ob} - h_{rb}\, h_{fb} \tag{10}$$

Equation (9) may also be put in the following form

$$R_{ib} = h_{ib} + R_L\, A_{ib}\, h_{rb} \tag{11}$$

(iii) *Voltage gain* The voltage gain may be expressed as

$$A_{vb} = \frac{v_2}{v_1} = \left(\frac{v_2}{i_1}\right)\left(\frac{v_1}{i_1}\right) = -\left[\frac{R_L h_{fb}}{h_{ib} + R_L \Delta}\right] \tag{12}$$

Multiplying (11) and (12), we find

$$R_{ib}\, A_{vb} = R_L\, A_{ib}$$

or

$$A_{vb} = R_L \left(\frac{A_{ib}}{R_{ib}}\right) \tag{13}$$

(iv) *Output impedance* To calculate the output impedance, we have to transfer the signal generator from the input to the output terminals and place a series resistance R_s across the input terminals. Equations (1) and (2) then simplify to the following forms:

$$0 = (R_s + h_{ib})i_1 + h_{rb}\, v_2 \tag{14}$$

and

$$i_2 = h_{fb}\, i_1 + h_{ob}\, v_2 \tag{15}$$

From (14), we find

$$i_1 = -\frac{h_{rb} v_2}{R_s + h_{ib}} \tag{16}$$

Substituting for i_1 in (15), we find

$$i_2 = -\left[\frac{h_{fb}\, h_{rb}\, v_2}{R_s + h_{ib}}\right] + h_{ob}\, v_2$$

or

$$\frac{1}{R_{ob}} = \frac{i_2}{v_2} = -\left[\frac{h_{fb}\, h_{rb}}{R_s + h_{ib}}\right] + h_{ob}\, v_2 = \frac{\Delta + R_s\, h_{ob}}{R_s + h_{ib}} \tag{17}$$

3.17 Relate the common-emitter h-equivalent circuit parameters with those of the common-base ones.

Solution

The equations defining two types of h-parameters are

$$v_{eb} = h_{ib}\, i_e + h_{rb}\, v_{cb} \tag{1}$$
$$i_c = h_{fb}\, i_e + h_{ob}\, v_{cb} \tag{2}$$

and

$$v_{be} = h_{ie}\, i_b + h_{re}\, v_{ce} \tag{3}$$
$$i_c = h_{fe}\, i_b + h_{oe}\, v_{ce} \tag{4}$$

Equations (1) and (2) define common-base h-parameters while equations (3) and (4) identify common-emitter h-parameters. We are required to relate them. From (3), we notice that

$$h_{re} = \left(\frac{v_{be}}{v_{ce}}\right)\bigg|_{i_b=0} = \left|\frac{v_{ce} - v_{cb}}{v_{ce}}\right|_{i_b=0} = \left|1 + \left(\frac{v_{bc}}{v_{ce}}\right)\right|_{i_b=0} \tag{5}$$

If $i_b = 0$, $i_c = -i_e$. Using this result in (2), we get

$$-i_e = h_{fb}\, i_e + h_{ob}\, v_{cb}$$

or

$$-(1 + h_{fb})\, i_e = h_{ob}\, v_{cb} \tag{6}$$

But

$$v_{ce} = v_{cb} + v_{be}$$

or

$$v_{be} = -v_{eb} = v_{ce} - v_{cb}$$

Using this result in (1), we get

$$v_{cb} - v_{ce} = h_{ib}\, i_e + h_{rb}\, v_{cb} \tag{7}$$

Substituting for i_e from (6) in (7), we get

$$v_{cb} - v_{ce} = v_{cb}\left[\frac{h_{rb} - (h_{ib}\, h_{ob})}{1 + h_{fb}}\right]$$

or

$$-\left(\frac{v_{bc}}{v_{ce}}\right) = \frac{1 + h_{fb}}{(1 - h_{rb})(1 + h_{fb}) + (h_{ib}\, h_{ob})}$$

Substituting this result in (5), we get

$$h_{re} = \frac{(h_{ib}\, h_{ob}) - h_{rb}(1 + h_{fb})}{(h_{ib}\, h_{ob}) + (1 - h_{rb})(1 + h_{fb})} \tag{8}$$

An approximate form of (8) may be obtained by noting that $h_{rb} \ll 1$ and $(h_{ib}h_{ob}) \ll (1 + h_{fb})$. In this case, we find

$$h_{re} = \left[\frac{h_{ib}\, h_{ob}}{1 + h_{fb}}\right] - h_{rb} \tag{9}$$

Next, we notice from (4) that

$$h_{oe} = \left|\frac{i_c}{v_{ce}}\right|_{i_b=0} = \left|\frac{i_c}{v_{cb} + v_{be}}\right|_{i_b=0} = \frac{1}{\left\{\left(\frac{v_{cb}}{i_c}\right) + \left(\frac{v_{be}}{i_c}\right)\right\}_{i_b=0}} \tag{10}$$

Since, $i_b = 0$, $i_e = -i_c$. Therefore, we get from (6),

$$\frac{v_{cb}}{i_e} = -\left(\frac{v_{cb}}{i_c}\right) = -\left[\frac{1 + h_{fb}}{h_{oe}}\right] \tag{11}$$

From (1), we find

$$v_{eb} = h_{ib}\, i_e + h_{rb}\, v_{cb} = -h_{ib}\, i_c + h_{rb}\, v_{cb}$$

Substituting for v_{cb} from (6) in the above equation, we find

$$v_{eb} = -h_{ib}\, i_c + h_{rb}\left\{\frac{1 + h_{fb}}{h_{ob}}\right\} i_c \tag{12}$$

Therefore

$$\left(\frac{v_{eb}}{i_c}\right)_{i_b=0} = -\left(\frac{v_{be}}{i_c}\right)_{i_b=0} = -h_{ib} + h_{rb}\left\{\frac{1 + h_{fb}}{h_{ob}}\right\} \tag{13}$$

Combining (10), (11) and (13), we find

$$h_{oe} = \frac{h_{ob}}{(1 + h_{fb}) + (h_{ib}\, h_{ob}) - h_{rb}(1 + h_{fb})} \tag{14}$$

Since, $h_{rb} \ll 1$ and $(h_{ib}\, h_{ob}) \ll (1 + h_{fb})$, equation (14) simplifies to

$$h_{oe} = \frac{h_{ob}}{1 + h_{fb}} \tag{15}$$

Next, we observe from (3) that,

$$h_{ie} = \left(\frac{v_{be}}{i_b}\right)_{V_{ce}=0} \tag{16}$$

When $v_{ce} = 0$, $v_{cb} = -v_{be}$. Therefore, we get from (1)

$$-v_{be} = h_{ib}\, i_e + h_{rb}(-v_{be})$$

or

$$i_e = -(i_b + i_c) = -\left[\frac{1 - h_{rb}}{h_{ib}}\right] v_{be} \tag{17}$$

Substituting for i_c from (17) in (2), we get

$$-i_b + \left[\frac{1 - h_{rb}}{h_{ib}}\right] v_{be} = h_{fb}\, i_e + h_{ob}\, v_{cb} \tag{18}$$

Next, substituting for i_c from (17) in (18), we find

$$i_b = \left[\left\{\frac{1 - h_{rb}}{h_{ib}}\right\} + \left\{\frac{h_{fb}(1 - h_{rb})}{h_{ib}}\right\} + h_{ob}\right] v_{be} \tag{19}$$

Therefore

$$h_{ie} = \left.\frac{\partial v_{be}}{\partial i_b}\right|_{V_{ce}=0} = \left[\left\{\frac{1 - h_{rb}}{h_{ib}}\right\} + \left\{\frac{h_{fb}(1 - h_{rb})}{h_{ib}}\right\} + h_{ob}\right]^{-1} \tag{20}$$

Again, since $h_{rb} \ll 1$, $(h_{ib}\, h_{ob}) \ll (1 + h_{fb})$, (20) reduces to

$$h_{ie} = \frac{h_{ib}}{1 + h_{fb}} \tag{21}$$

Finally, we note from (17) and (3)

$$i_b + i_c = \left\{\frac{1 - h_{rb}}{h_{ib}}\right\} v_{be} = \left\{\frac{1 - h_{rb}}{h_{ib}}\right\} h_{ie}\, i_b$$

when $v_{ce} = 0$. Therefore

$$i_c = i_b\left[\frac{(1 - h_{rb})h_{ie}}{h_{ib}} - 1\right] \tag{22}$$

or

$$h_{fe} = \left.\frac{i_c}{i_b}\right|_{V_{ce}=0} = -\frac{h_{fb} - h_{rb}}{1 + h_{fb}} \tag{23}$$

If $h_{rb} \ll h_{fb}$ (23) reduces to

$$h_{fe} = -\frac{h_{fb}}{1 + h_{fb}} \tag{24}$$

We now summarize below the relations

$$h_{ie} = \frac{h_{ib}}{1 + h_{fb}}$$

$$h_{re} = \left[\frac{h_{ib} h_{ob}}{1 + h_{fb}}\right] - h_{rb}$$

$$h_{fe} = -\frac{h_{fb}}{1 + h_{fb}}$$

and

$$h_{oe} = \frac{h_{ob}}{1 + h_{fb}}$$

3.18 A common-base transistor amplifier has a load resistance R_L and is fed by a signal source having an internal resistance R_S. Obtain expressions for the voltage gain and the input impedance of the amplifier using its T-equivalent circuit.

Solution

The transistor T-equivalent has been shown in Fig. 3.10. Applying Kirchoff's voltage law (KVL) to the emitter-base loop, we find

$$\Delta i_E\,(r_e + r_b + R_S) + \Delta i_C\, r_b = V_S \tag{1}$$

Next, applying KVL to the collector-base loop, we find

$$\Delta i_E\,(r_b + \alpha r_c) + \Delta i_C\,(r_c + R_L + r_b) = 0 \tag{2}$$

From (2) we derive

$$\Delta i_E = -\Delta i_C \left[\frac{r_c + r_b + R_L}{r_b + \alpha r_c}\right] \tag{3}$$

Combining (1) and (3), we get

$$\Delta i_C = V_S \left[\frac{r_b - \{(r_e + r_b + R_S)(r_c + r_b + R_L)\}}{(r_b + \alpha r_c)}\right]^{-1} \tag{4}$$

The voltage gain A_V of the amplifier is given by

$$A_V = \frac{R_L \Delta i_C}{V_S} = \frac{(r_b + \alpha r_c)R_L}{(r_e + r_b + R_S)(r_c + r_b + R_L) - r_b(r_b + \alpha r_c)} \tag{5}$$

Substituting for Δi_C from (3) in (1), we get

$$\Delta i_E \left[(r_e + r_b + R_S) - \left\{ \frac{r_b(r_b + \alpha r_c)}{(r_c + r_b + R_L)} \right\} \right] = V_S \tag{6}$$

The input resistance of the amplifier is then given by

$$r_i = \frac{V_S}{\Delta i_E} = \left[(r_e + r_b + R_S) - \left\{ \frac{r_b(r_b + \alpha r_c)}{r_c + r_b + R_L} \right\} \right] \tag{7}$$

This is the expression for the input impedance of the amplifier.

3.19 For a p-channel Si FET with $a = 5 \times 10^{-4}$ cm and the channel resistivity of 10 Ω cm find the pinch-off voltage. Repeat your calculations for a p-channel Ge FET with $\rho = 2\,\Omega$ cm, $\mu_n(\text{Si}) = 0.15\,\text{m}^2/\text{Vs}$, $\mu_n(\text{Ge}) = 0.39\,\text{m}^2/\text{V s}$.

Solution

The pinch-off voltage for an FET is given by

$$V_P = \left[\frac{qN_d a^2}{2\kappa\varepsilon_0} - \Psi_0 \right] \cong \frac{qN_d a^2}{2\kappa\varepsilon_0}$$

on neglecting Ψ_0. But, $(1/\rho) = (q\mu_n N_d)$. Therefore

$$V_P = \frac{a^2}{2\kappa\varepsilon_0\rho\mu_n} = \frac{(5 \times 10^{-6})^2}{2 \times 12 \times 8.854 \times 10^{-12} \times 10 \times 10^{-2} \times 0.15} = 7.84\text{ V}$$

Similarly, for Ge, $\kappa = 16$. Therefore,

$$V_P = \frac{a^2}{2\kappa\varepsilon_0\rho\mu_n} = \frac{(5 \times 10^{-6})^2}{2 \times 16 \times 8.854 \times 10^{-12} \times 10 \times 10^{-2} \times 0.39} = 2.26\text{ V}$$

3.20 If two FETs are connected in parallel, find out the effective transconductance g_m, the effective resistance r_d and the amplification factor μ of the combination.

Solution

Let us presume two FETs with mutual conductances g_{m1} and g_{m2} and resistances r_{d1} and r_{d2} are connected in parallel, as shown in Fig. 3.46(a). Since the two drain resistances are in parallel, the total current flowing through the circuit is given by

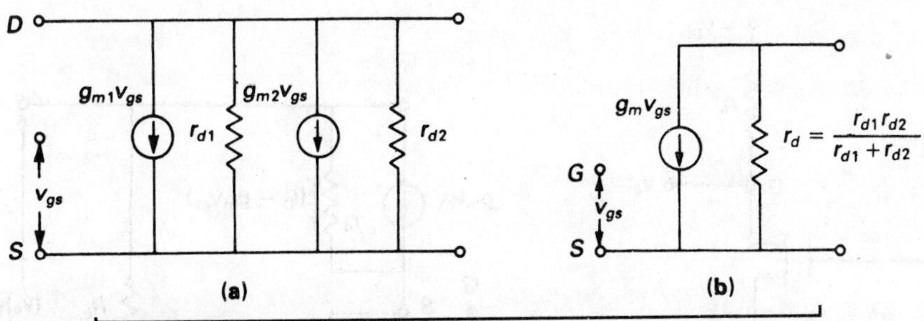

Figure 3.46 *(a) Two FETS in parallel; (b) equivalent circuit*

$$(g_{m1} + g_{m2})\, V_{gs} = g_m V_{gs}$$

and the effective drain resistance is

$$r_d = \frac{r_{d1}\, r_{d2}}{r_{d1} + r_{d2}}$$

The equivalent circuit is shown in Fig. 3.46(b).
In this case, the amplification factor μ of the combination is given by

$$\mu = g_m\, r_d = (g_{m1} + g_{m2}) \left[\frac{r_{d1}\, r_{d2}}{r_{d1} + r_{d2}}\right]$$

$$= \frac{(g_{m1}\, r_{d1}) r_{d2} + (g_{m1}\, r_{d2}) r_{d1}}{r_{d1} + r_{d2}}$$

or

$$\mu = \frac{\mu_1\, r_{d2} + \mu_2\, r_{d1}}{r_{d1} + r_{d2}}$$

3.21 A common-drain amplifier uses an FET having $r_d = 200\,\mathrm{k\Omega}$ and $\mu = 20$. The load resistance R_L is placed in the drain circuit. Compute the output impedance and the voltage gain of the amplifier for $R_L = 100\,\mathrm{k\Omega}$ and $R_S = 150\,\mathrm{k\Omega}$.

Solution

To analyze a common-source and a common-drain amplifier jointly, we have given the generalized circuit and its equivalent form in the figures 3.47(a) and 3.47(b) respectively. It is presumed that the circuits are properly biased in the linear region. For the common-source amplifier $R_S = 0$ and the output voltage is collected across the drain terminal D. In the case of the common-drain amplifier, the output $(V_O)_2$ is picked up across the source terminals. Applying Kirchoff's law to the output of Fig. 3.47(b), we get

$$I_D R_L + (I_D - g_m V_{gs}) r_d + I_D R_S = 0 \tag{1}$$

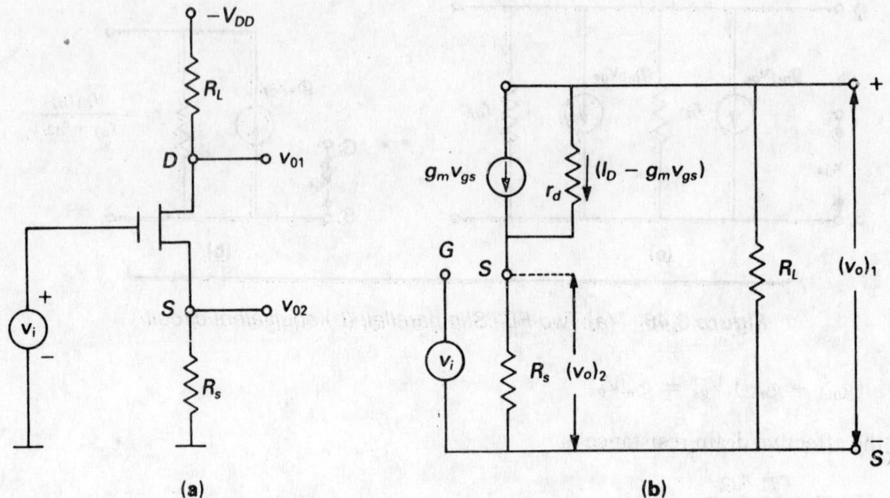

Figure 3.47 *A generalized FET amplifier: (a) circuit diagram; (b) equivalent circuit*

But

$$V_{gs} = V_i - I_D R_S \tag{2}$$

Combining (1) and (2), we get

$$I_D = \frac{\mu V_i}{R_L + r_d + (\mu + 1)R_S} \tag{3}$$

For the case of the common-drain amplifier, the output is taken across R_S and is given by

$$(V_0)_2 = I_D R_S = \frac{\mu V_i R_S}{R_L + r_d + (\mu + 1)R_S} \tag{4}$$

Therefore, the voltage gain A_V is given by

$$A_V = \frac{(V_0)_2}{V_i} = \frac{\mu R_S}{R_L + r_d + (\mu + 1)R_S} \tag{5}$$

Equation (4) may also be rewritten as

$$(V_0)_2 = \left[\frac{\mu}{\mu + 1}\right] \frac{V_i R_S}{\dfrac{R_L + r_d}{\mu + 1 + R_S}} \tag{6}$$

Equation (6) suggests that we cannot simplify the equivalent circuit further by imagining an equivalent source of e.m.f. $[\mu/(\mu + 1)]V_i$ to be applied across R_S and $[(R_L + r_d)/(\mu + 1)]$ connected in series. The latter therefore measures the cutput resistance of the common-drain amplifier. Using (5), we get

$$A_V = \frac{20 \times 150 \times 10^3}{(100 + 200 + 21 \times 150)10^3} = 0.87$$

Next, the output resistance is given by

$$R_0 = \frac{R_L + r_d}{\mu + 1} = \frac{(100 + 200) \times 10^3}{21} = 14.286\,\text{k}\Omega$$

3.22 An UJT has $R_{BB} = 10\,\text{M}\Omega$, $R_{B1} = 8\,\text{M}\Omega$, and $V_{BB} = 5\,\text{V}$. Calculate its figure of merit for $\gamma = 0.9999$ at the valley point. ($I_{EO} = 2.5\,\text{nA}$ at 300 K)

Solution

The switching voltage (V_P) of the UJT is given by

$$V_P = V_{BB} + V_D \cong \left(\frac{R_{B1}}{R_{BB}}\right) V_{BB} \tag{1}$$

Using the appropriate values of the parameters in (1), we find

$$V_P = \left(\frac{8}{10}\right) \times 5 = 4.0\,\text{V}$$

The expression for the corresponding current (I_P) is

$$I_P \cong \left[\frac{kT}{q(1-\gamma)}\right]\left[\left(\frac{1}{R_{B1}}\right) + \left(\frac{1}{R_{B2}}\right)\right] \tag{2}$$

before switching, $\gamma = 0$. Therefore,

$$I_P = 0.026\left[\left(\frac{1}{8}\right) + \left(\frac{1}{2}\right)\right] \times 10^{-6}\,\text{A} = 0.01625\,\mu\text{A}$$

Next, the valley current (I_V) is given by

$$I_V = \frac{V_{BB}}{(1-\gamma)R_{B2}} = \frac{5}{(1 - 0.9999) \times 2 \times 10^6} = 25\,\text{mA} \tag{3}$$

Finally, the valley voltage is given by

$$V_V = \left(\frac{kT}{q}\right) \ln\left[\left(\frac{I_V}{I_{E0}}\right) + 1\right] \tag{4}$$

Substituting appropriate values, we get

$$V_V = 0.026 \ln\left[\frac{25 \times 10^{-3}}{(2.5 \times 10^{-9}) + 1}\right] = 0.42\,\text{V} \tag{5}$$

Thus, all the figures of merit are evaluated.

3.23 For a four layer $p_1n_1p_2n_2$ transistor, $\alpha_2 = 0.4$ and $\alpha_1 = 0.5(L_p/W)^{1/2} \ln(J/J_0)$, where $L_P = 25\ \mu$m and $J_0 = 5 \times 10^{-6}$ A/cm^2. Find the cross-sectional area of the thyristor that will switch at a current of $I = 1$ mA. $W = 80\ \mu$m.

Solution

I = Switching current = JA (junction area) = 10^{-3} A or $J = 10^{-3}/A$ A/m^2.
But, $\alpha_1 = 0.5(L_p/W)^{1/2} \ln(J/J_0) = 0.5(25/80)^{1/2} \ln[(10^{-3}/A)/5 \times 10^{-2}] = 0.2795 \ln(1/50A)$

The necessary condition for the device to switch is $(\alpha_1 + \alpha_2) = 1$. That is

$$0.2795 \ln\left(\frac{1}{50A}\right) + 0.4 = 1.0$$

or

$$\ln\left(\frac{1}{50A}\right) = 2.147$$

or

$$A = 23.36\,\text{cm}^2$$

3.24 An SCR is to fire at a 30° conduction angle. During the conduction, the SCR voltage drop is negligible. The applied voltage is 200 V r.m.s and the load is a 50 Ω resistor. Calculate (i) the readings of an a.c. ammeter connected in series with the load, (ii) the readings of the d.c. ammeter connected in series with the load, (iii) the reading of the a.c. voltmeter connected across the load, (iv) the reading of a d.c. voltmeter connected across the load, and (vi) the total power dissipated in the load resistor.

Solution

A typical SCR trigger circuit is shown in Fig. 3.48. The peak voltage applied $V_m = 200\sqrt{2} = 282.84$ V

(i) The a.c. ammeter connected in series with the load would measure the r.m.s value of the current given by

$$i_{\text{rms}} = \left(\frac{1}{50}\right)\left[\frac{(282.84)^2}{2\pi}\int_{\pi/6}^{\pi} \sin^2\alpha\, d\alpha\right]^{1/2} = 2.32\text{ A}$$

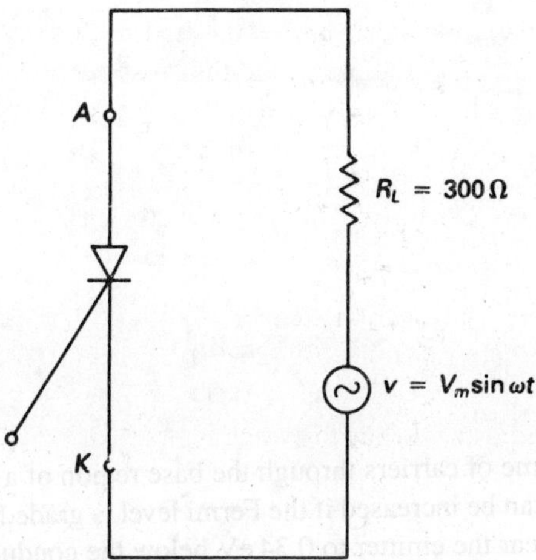

Figure 3.48 *A typical SCR trigger circuit*

(ii) The d.c ammeter connected in series with the load would give the average value of the current, given by

$$i_{av} = \left(\frac{1}{50}\right)\left[\frac{(282.84)}{2\pi}\int_{\pi/6}^{\pi} \sin \alpha \, d\alpha\right] = 1.68 \text{ A}$$

(iii) During the conduction through the SCR, no voltage is measured across it. During the remaining part of the applied a.c. cycle, the line voltage is available across it. The a.c. voltmeter connected across the load would measure the r.m.s value of the line voltage, given by

$$V_{rms} = \left[\frac{(282.84)^2}{2\pi}\int_{\pi/6}^{\pi} \sin^2 \alpha \, d\alpha\right]^{1/2} = 139.37 \text{ V}$$

(iv) The average voltage across the load would be

$$V_{av} = \frac{282.84}{2\pi}\int_{\pi/6}^{\pi} \sin \alpha \, d\alpha = 72.74 \text{ V}$$

(v)

$$P_{d.c} = V_{av} \times i_{av} = 72.74 \times 1.68 = 122.2 \text{ Watts}$$

(vi)

$$P_{a.c} = \frac{(282.84)^2}{50 \times 2\pi}\int_{\pi/6}^{\pi} \sin^2 \alpha \, d\alpha = 388.4$$

Exercises

3.1 Calculate the transit time of carriers through the base region of a transistor for a drift field ε and find out how much f can be increased if the Fermi level is graded uniformly from 0.24 eV below the conduction band near the emitter to 0.34 eV below the conduction band at the collector end. What impurity distribution would give rise to such a field?
[$N_d(x) = N_{d0} \exp(-x/L_d)$; $f = 3.846$]

3.2 Calculate the current amplification factor α of an *npn* Ge transistor with the following parameters: $N_a = 2 \times 10^{15}$ cm^{-3}, $N_d = 10^{17}$ cm^{-3}, $\tau_{ne} = 5\,\mu$ s, $\tau_p = 1\,\mu$ s and $W = 5\,\mu$m. How much deviation of α is due to recombination losses? How much of it is due to incomplete injection?
[$\gamma = 0.9998$; $\beta = 0\,9973$; $\alpha = 0.9971$]

3.3 A symmetrical Ge *pnp* transistor with emitter-base and collector-base junctions, each 1 mm in diameter has an impurity concentration of 5×10^{15} cm^{-3} in the base and 10^{18} cm^{-3} in the emitter and the collector respectively. The base width is 10 μm, $\tau_B = 4\,\mu$ s, $\tau_E = 10^{-8}$ s. and the emitter region is much wider than the diffusion length L_E. Calculate the current gains α and h_{FE} of the transistor. Take $D_B = 47$ cm^2/s and $D_E = 52$ cm^2/s.
[$\alpha = 0.9972$; $h_{FE} = 356.14$]

3.4 A Si n^+pn transistor has a base width of 150 μm, and a base doping of 10^{14} cm^{-3}. A reverse bias of 500 V is applied to the base-collector junction. Calculate the minority carrier lifetime in the base that will give a common-emitter current gain of 40.
[19.9 μ s]

3.5 An *npn* Ge transistor has base and collector conductivities given by $\sigma_E = 100\,(\Omega\,\text{cm})^{-1}$ and $\sigma_B = 5\,(\Omega\,\text{cm})^{-1}$. Calculate the emitter efficiency of the transistor.
[$\gamma = 0.952$]

3.6 For an *npn* transistor of the alloy type in which the resistivity ρ_B of the base is much larger than that of the collector, derive an expression for the punch-through voltage as a function of the transistor base width W_B. Calculate the punch-through voltage if $W_B = 5\,\mu$m and $\rho_B = 1\,\Omega$cm.
[$V = (1/2\kappa\varepsilon_0\mu_p)(W^2/\rho_B)$; 235 V.]

3.7 Obtain an expression for the punch-through voltage of a transistor when the doping in the base is linearly graded as $N(x) = Bx$. $[V_{pt} = 2qBW^3/3\kappa\varepsilon_0]$

3.8 The punch-through voltage of a Ge alloyed *pnp* transistor is 25 V, the base doping is 10^{15} cm^{-3} and the emitter and the collector doping concentrations are 10^{19} cm^{-3} each. Calculate the zero bias base width and the α of the transistor at a 10 V reverse bias across the collector-base junction. Assume $\tau_B = 10^{-6}$ s. and $T = 300$ K. [6.654 μm; 0.99939]

3.9 An *npn* transistor of Si with uniformly doped emitter, base and collector regions has a collector-base junction punch-through voltage of 60 V and $h_{FE} = 40$ at a reverse bias of 5 V. Determine the reverse bias voltage at which h_{FE} becomes 80. [14.82 V]

3.10 Calculate the alpha cutoff frequency of a graded base transistor having an exponential impurity (N_d) distribution within the base layer. The difference between the Fermi levels at the emitter and collector ends of the base is 0.1 V. (Given : $W = 5\,\mu$m, $(kT/q) = 0.26$ V; $\mu p = 0.18$ m^2/ Vs; $\tau_p = 10^{-6}$ s) [3.564×10^8 Hz]

3.11 For an ion-implanted *npn* transistor, the net impurity doping in the neutral base region is given by $N_a = N_{a0}$ exp $(-x/L)$ where $N_{a0} = 2 \times 10^{18}$ cm^{-3} and $L = 0.3\,\mu$m. (a) Find the total amount of impurities in the neutral base layer per unit area for a neutral base width of 0.8 μm. (b) Find the average impurity density in the neutral base region. (c) If $L_E = 1\,\mu$m, $N_E = 10^{19}$ cm^{-3}, $D_E = 1$ cm^2/ s, the average lifetime in the base is 10^{-6} s, find the common-emitter current gain.

[49]

3.12 Show that: (i) $\alpha_N = (I_{CEO} - I_{CO})/I_{CEO}$; and (ii) $\alpha_I = [1 - (I_{CO}/I_{CES})]/\{1 - (I_{CO}/I_{CEO})]$ where I_{CEO} = collector-emitter current with the base open and I_{CES} = collector-emitter current with a short-circuited base.

3.13 Calculate the base spreading resistance r'_b for the transistor shown in Fig. 3.49, in which the base is connected on one side and all the base current flows along the base region to this contact. Assume low injection, so that emitter crowding is negligible.

$[r'_b = (\rho_b L/6ZW_b)]$

3.14 We wish to find the overall values of α and β for the composite *pnp* transistor (see Fig. 3.50). Assume that the terminal currents of the lateral *pnp* transistor are related by α_1 and β_1 (neglect saturation currents); similarly, let α_2 and β_2 describe the *npn* type. Find: (a) α and β for the composite *pnp* transistor, (b) Show that when $\alpha_2 = 1$, the overall $\alpha = 1$ and $\beta = \beta_1\beta_2$.

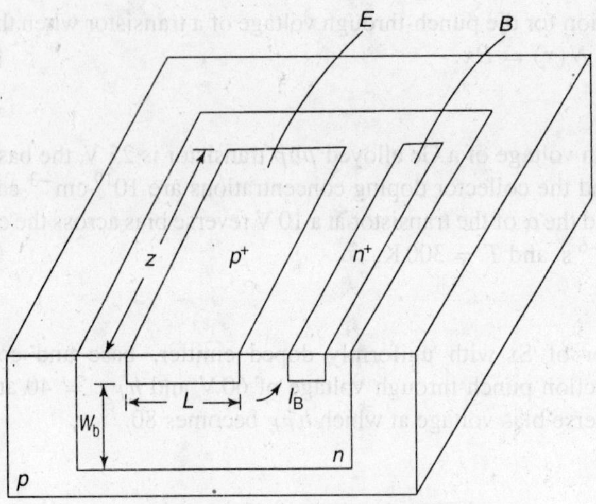

Figure 3.49 *Exercise 3.13*

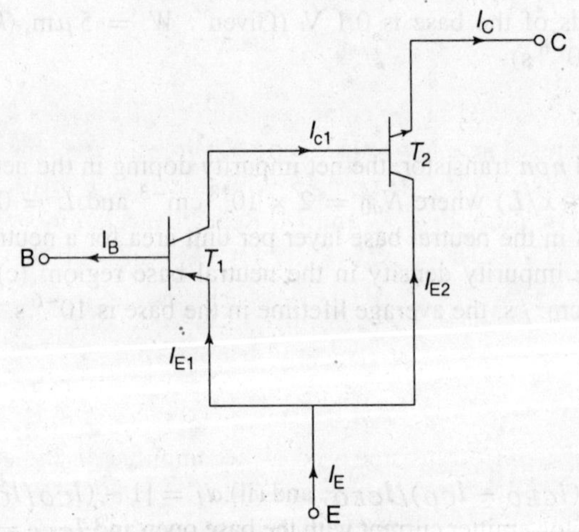

Figure 3.50 *Exercise 3.14*

3.15 A Si *pnp* transistor is operated in the common-emitter mode. The d.c. collector bias V_{CC} applied across $R_C = 1\ \text{k}\Omega$ is 8 V while the d.c. emitter bias V_{BB} applied across $R_b = 60\ \text{k}\Omega$ is 4 V. Calculate the various transistor currents. Repeat calculations with a resistance $R_e = 3\ \text{k}\Omega$ connected to the emitter leg. ($\beta = 100$, $I_{CO} = 2$ nA, $V_{BE} = 0.7$ V).

[0.055 mA, 5.5 mA; 0.009 mA, 0.9 mA]

3.16 For the transistor circuit shown in Fig. 3.51, assuming $\beta = 100$, (i) find out whether Si transistor is in the cutoff, saturated or in the active region, (ii) find V_0 and (iii) calculate the minimum value of R_e for which the transistor operates in the active region ($V_{BE} = 0.7$ V).

[active region; 2 V; $R_e = 0$]

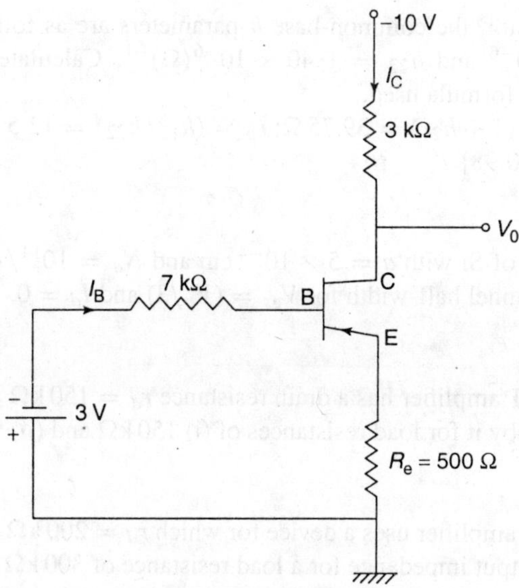

Figure 3.51 *Exercise 3.16*

3.17 An *npn* transistor is operated in the common-emitter (CE) mode. The d.c. collector bias V_{CC} applied across a load resistance $R_C = 4\,\text{k}\Omega$ is 13 V, while the d.c. emitter bias V_{BB} applied across a resistance $R_b = 40\,\text{k}\Omega$ is 4 V. Presuming $\beta = 98$ and $I_{CO} = 10\,\text{nA}$, determine whether or not the transistor is in saturation. Find I_B and I_C. Repeat calculations with 1 kΩ emitter resistance added. ($V_{BE,\text{sat}} = 0.8\,\text{V}$ and $V_{CE,\text{sat}} = 0.2\,\text{V}$ for a Si transistor)

[0.08 mA, 3.2 mA; saturated state; 0.0237 mA, 2.3266 mA]

3.18 The *h*-parameters of a *pnp* transistor used as an amplifier in the common-emitter mode are $h_{ie} = 800\,\Omega$, $h_{re} = 5.4 \times 10^{-4}$, $h_{fe} = 46$ and $h_{oe} = 80 \times 10^{-6}\Omega^{-1}$. If $R_L = 1\,\text{k}\Omega$ and $R_s = 500\,\Omega$, calculate the: (i) current gain, (ii) input resistance, (iii) voltage gain and (iv) output resistance of the amplifier. [−42.59, 777 Ω, −54.8, 16.42 kΩ]

3.19 Relate the common-base *h* parameters with the common-emitter ones.

[$h_{rb} = h_{ie}h_{oe}/(1 + h_{fe}) - h_{re}$; $h_{ob} = h_{oe}/(1 + h_{fe})$; $h_{ib} = h_{ie}/(1 + h_{fe})$; $h_{fb} = -h_{fe}/(1 + h_{fe})$]

3.20 Relate the common-emitter *h*-parameters with the common-collector ones.

[$h_{rc} = (1 + h_{re}) \cong 1$; $h_{oc} = h_{oe}$; $h_{ic} = h_{ie}$; $h_{fc} = -1/(1 + h_{fe})$]

3.21 For a particular transistor, the common-base h-parameters are as follows: $h_{11} = 40\,\Omega, h_{21} = -0.98, h_{12} = 5 \times 10^{-6}$ and $h_{22} = 0.40 \times 10^{-6}(\Omega)^{-1}$. Calculate its T- equivalent circuit parameters. Derive the formula used.
[$r_e = h_{11} - (h_{12}/h_{22})(1 + h_{21}) = 39.75\,\Omega$; $r_b = (h_{12}/h_{22}) = 12.5\,\Omega$; $r_c = (1 - h_{12})/h_{22} = 2.5\,\text{M}\Omega$; $\alpha = -h_{21} = 0.98$]

3.22 For an n-channel FET of Si with $a = 5 \times 10^{-4}$ cm and $N_d = 10^{14}/\text{cm}^3$, find (i) the pinch-off voltage and (ii) the channel half-width for $V_{gs} = (V_p/3)$ and $I_d = 0$. [1.88 V; 2.11×10^{-6} m]

3.23 A common-source FET amplifier has a drain resistance $r_d = 150\,\text{k}\Omega$ and $\mu = 15$. Calculate the voltage gain produced by it for load resistances of (i) $150\,\text{k}\Omega$ and (ii) $900\,\text{k}\Omega$. [7.5; 12.857]

3.24 A common-drain FET amplifier uses a device for which $r_d = 200\,\text{k}\Omega$ and $\mu = 20$. Calculate the voltage gain and its output impedance for a load resistance of $300\,\text{k}\Omega$. ($R_s = 750\,\text{k}\Omega$).
[0.923; $23.81\,\text{k}\Omega$]

3.25 A given UJT has an interbase resistance of $8\,\text{k}\Omega$, $R_{B1} = 6\,\text{k}\Omega$ when $I_E = 0$. Determine (a) the UJT current if $V_{BB} = 16$ V and $V_E < V_p$, (b) the intrinsic stand off ratio and (c) the peak voltage.
[$\eta = 0.75$; $V_p = 12$ V; $I = I_{EO}$.]

3.26 A UJT has $R_{B1} = 900\,\text{k}\Omega$, and $R_{B2} = 100\,\text{k}\Omega$. This is to be used to design a relaxation oscillator. Calculate R_1 if the applied interbase voltage is 10 V. You may presume $(1 - \gamma) = 10^{-4}$ in the conducting state of the UJT. ($I_{E0} = 1$nA at 300 K)
[$V_p = 9$ V; $I_p = 0.23\,\mu$A; $I_v = 1$ A, $V_v = 0.54$ V; $4.34 \times 10^6\,\Omega > R_1 > 9.46\,\Omega$]

3.27 An SCR is required to supply power to a $300\,\Omega$ load resistor from a 200 V power supply. If the trigger voltage is so adjusted that the conduction begins at 45° after the start of each cycle, calculate the following: (i) the ammeter reading connected in series with the load, (ii) the voltmeter reading connected in parallel to SCR, (iii) the reading of the wattmeter inserted in the circuit so as to read the total power delivered by the a.c. supply. [0.49 A; 119.58 V; 73.33 W]

References

[1] Adler, R.B., Smith, A.C., and Longini, R.A., 1966, Introduction to Semiconductor Physics, *(SEEC***1**), Wiley, New York.

[2] Bardeen, J., Brattain, W.H., 1948, *Phys. Rev*. (USA), **74**, 230

[3] Blicher, A., 1976, *Thyristor Physics*, Springer, New York.

[4] Cooke, H.F., 1971 Microwave Transistors: Theory and Design, *Proc. IRE*, **59**, 1163

[5] Early, J.M., 1952, Effects of Space-charge Layer Widening in Junction Transistor Characteristics, *Proc. IRE*, **42**, 1761

[6] Ebers, J.J., 1950, Four Terminal *pnpn* Transistors, *Proc. IRE*, **40**, 1361.

[7] Gandhi, S.K., 1977, *Semiconductor Power Devices*, Wiley, New York.

[8] Gartner, W.W., 1960, *Transistors:Principles, Design and Applications*, D. Van Nostrand, Princeton, N.J.

[9] Gentry, F.E., Gutzweiler, F.W., Holonyak, N.H. and Von Zastrow, E.E., 1964. *Semiconductor Controlled Rectifiers*, Prentice Hall, Englewood Cliff. N.J.

[10] Gray, P.E., DeWitt, D., Boothroyd, A.R., and Gibbons, J.F., 1966, Physical Electronics and Circuit Models of Transistors (*SEEC* **2**), Wiley, New York

[11] Lesk, I.A., and Mathis, V.P., 1953, The Double Base Diode-A New Semiconductor Device, *IRE Conv. Rec*. **6**, 2

[12] Moll, J.L., Tannenbaum, M., Goldley, J.M., and Holonyak, N.,1956, *pnpn* Transistor Switches, *Proc. IRE*, **40**, 1361

[13] Morant M.J., 1964, *Introduction to Semiconductor Devices*, Addison Wesley, Reading, Mass.

[14] Pritchard, R.L., 1967, *Electrical Characteristics of Transistors*, McGraw Hill, New York

[15] Searle, C.A., Boothroyd, A.R., Angelo, E.J., Gray, P.E., and Pederson, D.E., 1966, Elementary Circuit properties of Transistors (*SEEC* **3**), Wiley, New York

[16] Sevin, L.J., 1965, *Field Effect Transistors*, McGraw Hill, New York

[17] Shockley W., Pearson, G.L., and Haynes J. R., Hole Injection in Ge-Qualitative Studies and Filamentary Transistors, *Bell System Tech*. J (USA), **28**, 344

[18] Thronton, R.D., DeWitt, D., Chenette, E.R., and Gray, P.E., 1966, *Characteristics and Limitations of Transistors*, Wiley, New York.

[19] Wallmark, J.T., and Johnson, H., 1966, *Field Effect Transistor*, Prentice Hall, Englewood Cliff, N.J.,

[20] Webster, W.M., 1954, On the variation of Junction Transistor Current Amplification Factor with the Emitter current, *Proc. IRE*, **42**, 914.

4 Metal-semiconductor devices

In the earlier chapters, we were only concerned with the flow of charge carriers over potential barriers formed by *pn* junctions. A potential barrier is also formed when a metal and a semiconductor are brought into intimate contact. Like *pn* junctions, the current flow over such barriers is unidirectional in nature and is a function of the applied voltage. The metal-insulator-semiconductor (MIS) structure was first proposed as a voltage variable capacitor. Later, they were also found to be useful for the study of semiconductor surfaces. Since the metal-semiconductor (MESFET) and the metal-insulator-semiconductor (MOSFET) transistors are important elements of microprocessors, semiconductor memories and power devices, their physics are discussed in detail in this chapter. Ohmic contacts in semiconductor devices are also formed of metal-semiconductor junctions. Charge-coupled devices (CCDs) which form the two-dimensional imaging systems of video cameras are basically made up of MOS units. Their physics has also been dealt with briefly.

4.1 Metal-vacuum boundary : Schottky effect

For a metal-vacuum system at $T = 0\,\mathrm{K}$, metal work function ($q\,\varphi_m$) is defined as the minimum energy required by an electron to escape from an initial state at the Fermi energy into vacuum. Its value is however found to be extremely sensitive to surface contamination.

When an electron is situated in vacuum at a distance x from a plane metallic surface, it induces a positive charge on the surface. The effect of the induced positive charge on the metal can be accounted for by presuming that there is a point positive charge of the same magnitude as the electronic charge at a distance $(-x)$ behind the plane metallic surface. For all practical purposes, this may be regarded as the electrical image of the electron. The electrostatic force of attraction between the electron and its image charge can be expressed as

$$F(x) = -\left[\frac{q^2}{4\pi\varepsilon_0}(2x)^2\right] = -\left[\frac{q^2}{16\pi\varepsilon_0 x^2}\right] \tag{4.1}$$

where ε_0 denotes the permittivity of free space ($= 8.854 \times 10^{-12}$ F/m). Now, the work done in bringing an electron from infinity to a point distant x from the metal would be

$$V_i(x) = \int_{\infty}^{x} F(x)\,dx = -\left[\frac{q^2}{16\pi\varepsilon_0 x}\right] \tag{4.2}$$

However, in the presence of an external electric field ε tending to pull out electrons from the metal, the potential energy expression (4.2) modifies to

$$V_i(x) = -\left[\frac{q^2}{16\pi\varepsilon_0 x}\right] - q\varepsilon x \tag{4.3}$$

According to (4.3), the variation of $V_i(x)$ with x is parabolic in nature. This is illustrated in Fig. 4.1. The position where the potential energy would be a maximum can be obtained by stipulating that $[dV_i(x)/dx] = 0$. We then get

$$x_m = \left[\frac{q}{16\pi\varepsilon_0\varepsilon}\right]^{1/2} \tag{4.4}$$

The maximum potential energy corresponding to $x = x_m$ can now be obtained from (4.3) as

$$V_m = -q\left[\frac{q\,\varepsilon}{4\pi\varepsilon_0}\right]^{1/2} = -q\,\Delta\phi \tag{4.5}$$

where

$$\Delta\phi = 2\,\varepsilon\,x_m \tag{4.6}$$

Thus, under the presence of an external electric field, the maximum potential energy is lowered by $\Delta\phi$. This lowering of the work function of a metal by an external electric field is called the Schottky effect (Fig. 4.1). At metal-vacuum boundaries, such a lowering could be significant at times. But, when a solid dielectric replaces vacuum, the Schottky lowering is considerably reduced because of the higher dielectric constants of those materials.

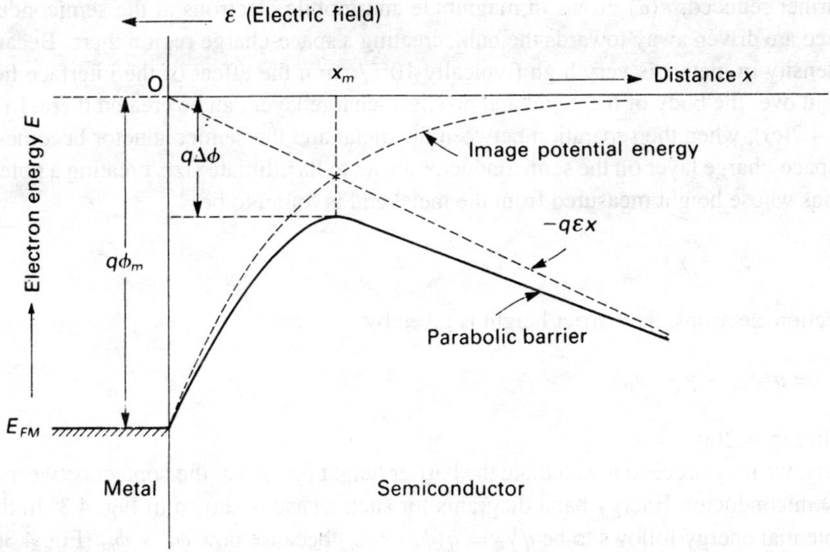

Figure 4.1 The energy distance diagram of a metal-vacuum contact

4.2 Metal-semiconductor boundary : Ohmic contact

To be able to analyze the characteristics of metal-semiconductor devices, we must first discuss the physics of their interfaces. They are often associated with surface states. Their presence in some cases could be minimized by proper surface treatments but they cannot be eliminated altogether. We will examine here the metal-semiconductor interfaces in the following two extreme cases:

a) the surfaces are ideal or the surface state density at the interface is zero, and
b) the surfaces are most imperfect and maximum surface state density exists at the interface.

The conditions relevant for the intermediate case may then be derived without much difficulty.

Case (a)

Figure 4.2(a) depicts the energy band diagrams of a metal and an n-type semiconductor before any physical contact between them has actually been made. As the metal and the semiconductor are progressively brought closer, electron tunnelling may set in between them once their separation δ becomes comparable to the electron wavelength when tunnelling is most likely to occur. This current flow is required to equalize the Fermi levels on both sides of the interface. Consequently, the Fermi energy level on the semiconductor side is lowered by an amount $q(\phi_m - \phi_s)$ relative to that at the metal end Fig. 4.2(b). Such a potential difference is defined as the contact potential. Due to this potential difference an electric field ε is set up between the interfaces, given by

$$\varepsilon(\delta) = \frac{\phi_m - \phi_s}{\delta} \tag{4.7}$$

As δ is further reduced, $\varepsilon(\delta)$ grows in magnitude and mobile electrons at the semiconductor end of the interface are driven away towards the bulk, creating a space-charge region there. Because, the free electron density in metals is very high (typically $10^{23}/\text{cm}^3$), the effect of the interface field is easily screened out over the body of the metal and no space-charge layer can be created there. In the limiting case (Fig. 4.2(c)), when the separation between the metal and the semiconductor becomes practically zero, the space-charge layer on the semiconductor grows to its ultimate size, creating a potential barrier for electrons whose height measured from the metal end is found to be

$$q\phi_{Bn} = q(\phi_m - \chi) \tag{4.8}$$

For conduction electrons, the barrier height is given by

$$q\phi_{bi} = q(\phi_m - \chi - V_n) \tag{4.9}$$

as shown in Fig. 4.2(c).

Similarly, we may proceed to calculate the barrier height formed at the contact between a metal and a p-type semiconductor. Energy band diagrams for such a case is shown in Fig. 4.3. In this case, the contact potential energy follows to be $qV_c = q(\phi_s - \phi_m)$ because now $\phi_s > \phi_m$ (Fig. 4.3(b)). As δ is reduced, the electric field (V_c/δ) at the interface grows in magnitude and ultimately it sweeps out holes from the semiconductor interface towards the bulk of p-Si, producing a space-charge layer there.

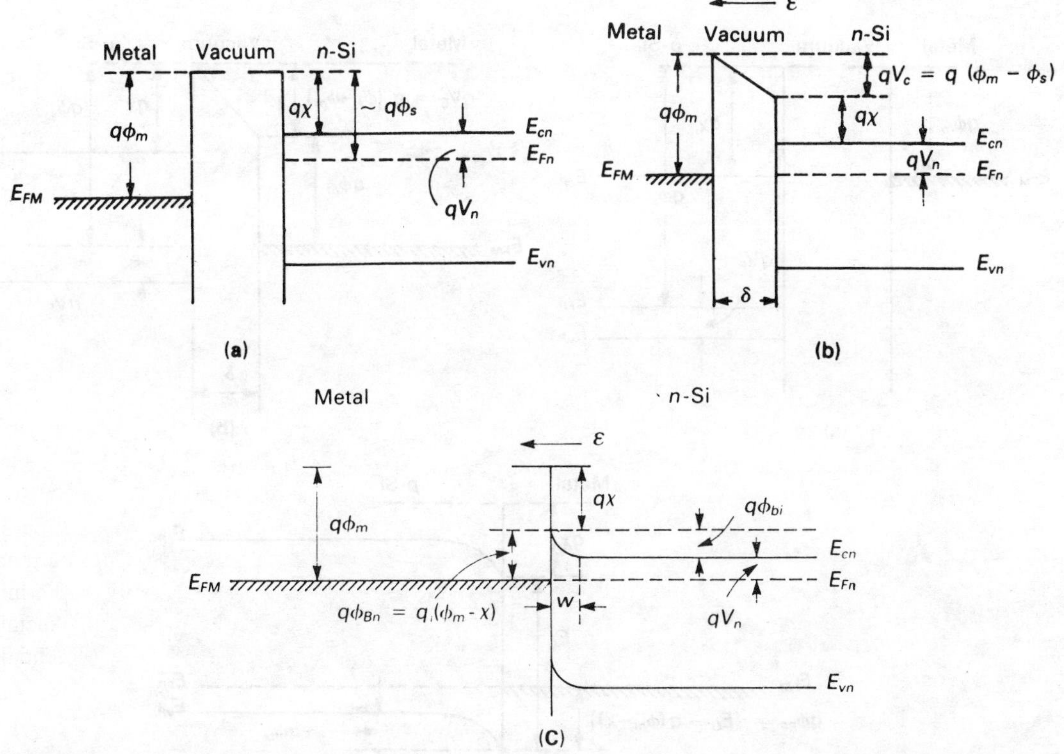

Figure 4.2 *Metal and an n-type semiconductor in contact: (a) metal and semiconductor are widely separated; (b) metal and semiconductor placed very close to each other so that there is carrier tunnelling between them; (c) metal and semi-conductor placed in intimate contact.*

As argued already, an electric field cannot be developed over the metallic body. When the space-charge layer is fully developed (Fig. 4.3(c)), the barrier height for holes from the metal end is given by

$$q\phi_{Bp} = [E_G - q(\phi_m - \chi)] \tag{4.10}$$

Adding (4.8) and (4.10), we find

$$q(\phi_{Bn} + \phi_{Bp}) = E_G \tag{4.11}$$

Thus, according to (4.11), the sum of the barrier heights for electrons and holes as formed at the metal-semiconductor interfaces with a particular semiconductor is equal to the semiconductor energy gap and is independent of the semiconductor dopings and the metal work functions.

The shape of the potential barrier, the maximum electric field at the junction, the depletion layer widths, etc. may now be obtained by solving the one-dimensional Poisson's equation within the space-charge layer of n-Si (Fig. 4.2(c)) which is given by

$$\frac{d^2\psi(x)}{dx^2} = -\frac{\rho}{\kappa\varepsilon_0} = \frac{-qN_d}{\kappa\varepsilon_0} \tag{4.12}$$

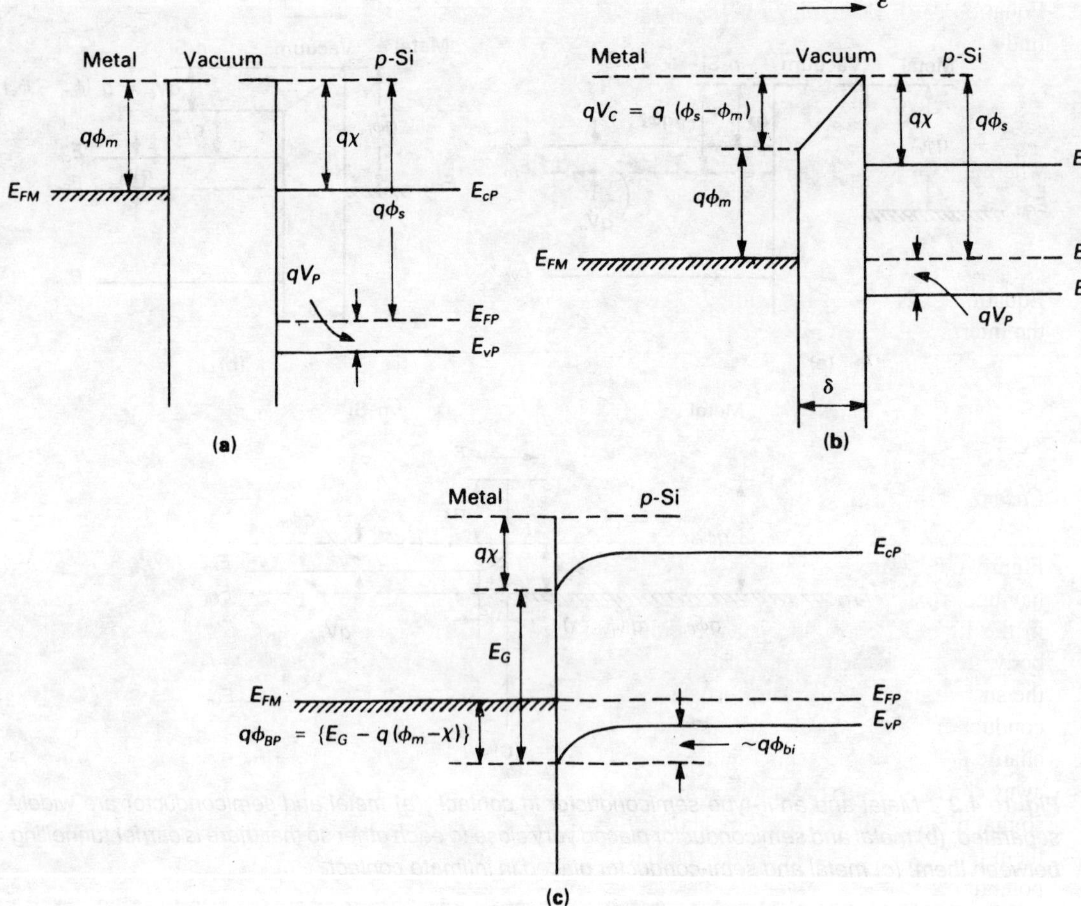

Figure 4.3 *Metal and a p-type semiconductor in contact: (a) metal and semiconductor are widely separated; (b) metal and semiconductor placed very close to each other so that there is carrier tunnelling between them; (c) metal and semi-conductor placed in intimate contact.*

where $\psi(x)$ represents the electrostatic potential, N_d the donor density in n-type Si and κ measures the dielectric constant of Si. Integrating (4.12), we find

$$\varepsilon(x) = -\left[\frac{d\psi(x)}{dx}\right] = \left(\frac{qN_d}{\kappa\varepsilon_0}\right)x + \text{const.}$$

The value of the constant of integration may be evaluated by presuming $\varepsilon(x) = 0$ at $x = W$ (depletion layer width). We then get

$$\varepsilon(x) = -\left(\frac{qN_d}{\kappa\varepsilon_0}\right)(W - x) \tag{4.13}$$

Equation (4.13) also suggests that $\varepsilon(x)$ decays with increase in x. Integrating (4.13) once again, we find

$$\psi(x) = \left(\frac{qN_d}{2\kappa\varepsilon_0}\right)(W - x)^2 \tag{4.14}$$

where it is presumed that $\psi(x) = 0$ at $x = W$. We know that at $x = 0$, $\psi(x) = \phi_{bi}$. Therefore,

$$W = \frac{2\kappa\varepsilon_0\,\phi_{bi}}{qN_d} \tag{4.15}$$

Equation (4.15) gives the width of the depletion layer. Setting $x = 0$ in (4.13), the maximum field at the interface is given by

$$\varepsilon_m = -\left[\frac{qN_dW}{\kappa\varepsilon_0}\right] = -\left[\frac{2qN_d\,\phi_{bi}}{\kappa\varepsilon_0}\right]^{1/2} \tag{4.16}$$

Case (b)

Figure 4.4(a) shows the energy band diagrams of a metal and an n-type semiconductor with a surface having an exceedingly large density of surface states. They are shown to be isolated from one another in the figure. Even under such a situation, a space-charge layer develops over the semiconductor body. This is caused by the carrier exchanges taking place between the main conduction band and the surface state levels. The surface states being of the acceptor type absorb electrons from the main conduction band thereby exposing their parent donor atoms. This results in the creation of the space-charge layer over the semiconductor body. The direction of the developed electric field tends to drive away electrons from the semiconductor surface. Bringing the metal and the semiconductor very close, so that they are spaced apart by about an electron wavelength, electron tunnelling will ensue between them tending to align the metal and the semiconductor Fermi levels. Once that is realized, a contact potential $V_c = (\phi_m - \phi_s)$ develops across the interface (Fig. 4.4(b)). This, in its turn, generates an electric field $[(\phi_m - \phi_s)/\delta]$ across the interface which grows stronger and stronger as δ is reduced. But this field will never be comparable to that which is already existing over the bad semiconductor surface. Hence, no significant modification in the already developed space-charge layer will take place when the metal and the semiconductor are brought into intimate contact (Fig. 4.4(c)). The Fermi level is then said to be pinned at the semiconductor-insulator interface. Therefore, in this case, the barrier height at the interface is determined mainly by the nature of the semiconductor surface and is independent of the metal work function. Referring to Fig. 4.4(c), we note that

$$q\phi_{Bn} = E_G - q\,\phi_0 \tag{4.17}$$

where ϕ_0 denotes the neutral potential. This is the potential difference between (E_{Fn}/q) and (E_{vn}/q) at the semiconductor surface. The barrier heights calculated so far have to be reduced by $q\Delta\phi$ in order to consider the Schottky effect (see (4.5)). In real life situations neither is a semiconductor surface ideal (the surface state density zero) nor is it perfectly non-ideal (the surface state density infinite). For surfaces having intermediate defect densities, the barrier height across the interface may be written down by combining (4.8) and (4.17) as follows:

$$\phi_{Bn} = C(\phi_m - \chi - \Delta\phi) + (1 - C)(E_G - q\,\phi_0 - \Delta\phi) \tag{4.18}$$

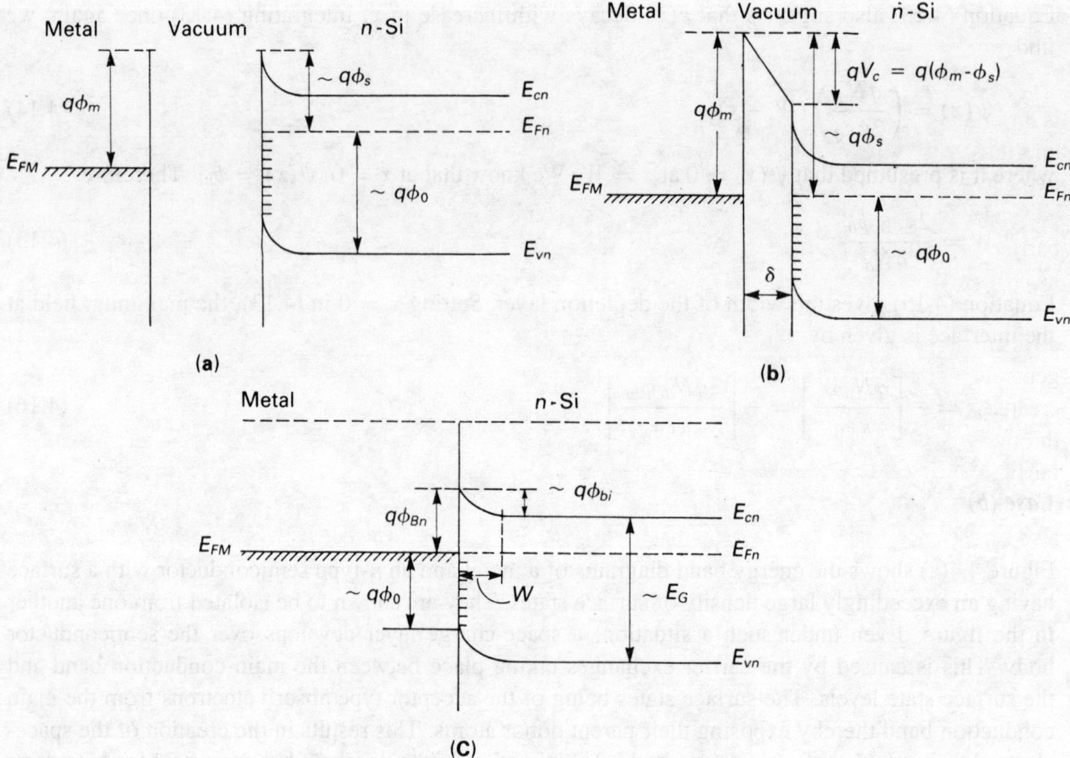

Figure 4.4 *Metal and n-type semiconductor in contact (the semiconductor is endowed with a very bad surface): (a) when they are widely separated; (b) brought very close for the carrier tunnelling; (c) metal and semiconductor in intimate contact with one another.*

where C is a constant determining the ideality of a semiconductor surface. Evidently, $C = 1$, for an ideal surface and $C = 0$ for an exceedingly bad surface. C must therefore acquire a value between 0 and 1 in real problems. The equation (4.18) may further be simplified and expressed as

$$\phi_{Bn} = C\phi_m - \left\{\left(\frac{E_G}{q}\right) - \phi_0 - \Delta\phi\right\} - C\left\{\left(\frac{E_G}{q}\right) + \chi - \phi_0\right\}$$

i.e.

$$\phi_{Bn} = C\phi_m + C' \tag{4.19}$$

where C' is an appropriate constant whose value depends upon the semiconductor energy gap, neutral level (surface state density), electron affinity etc.

Ohmic contact When bringing semiconductor devices in contact with metals, it is desired that the contact must have a linear I–V characteristic in both biasing directions and a negligible series resistance. A good ohmic contact should not affect the device performance. The specific contact resistance $\bar{R}_c$, defined as

$$R_c = \left[\frac{dJ}{dV}\right]^{-1}_{V=0} \tag{4.20}$$

is an important figure of merit of the ohmic contact. Studies shows that to obtain a low value of R_c one must use a higher doping concentration in the semiconductor or a lower barrier height. These two cases of ohmic contacts are illustrated in Fig. 4.5. It is difficult to make ohmic contacts on wide gap semiconductors. A metal does not generally exist with a low enough work function to yield a low barrier. In such cases, the general technique for making an ohmic contact involves the establishment of a heavily doped surface layer on the semiconductor upon which an ohmic contact is desired. Structures, such as, metal-n^+-n or metal-p^+-p are prepared for that purpose by various methods viz. shallow diffusion, alloy regrowth, ion implantation etc. Depositing a layer of a heavily doped semiconductor generates a potential well for carriers. In Fig. 4.5(a), for example, a potential well for electrons has been created. If the triangular barrier thickness of height ϕ_{Bn} is quite narrow, electron tunnelling may occur through it. The contact resistance of such a junction is usually very small and its I–V characteristic is fairly linear both for forward and reverse biases. If a metal of a very low work function is available, the barrier height at the contact would be fairly low (Fig. 4.5(b)). Such a contact, in some cases may also serve as an ohmic contact.

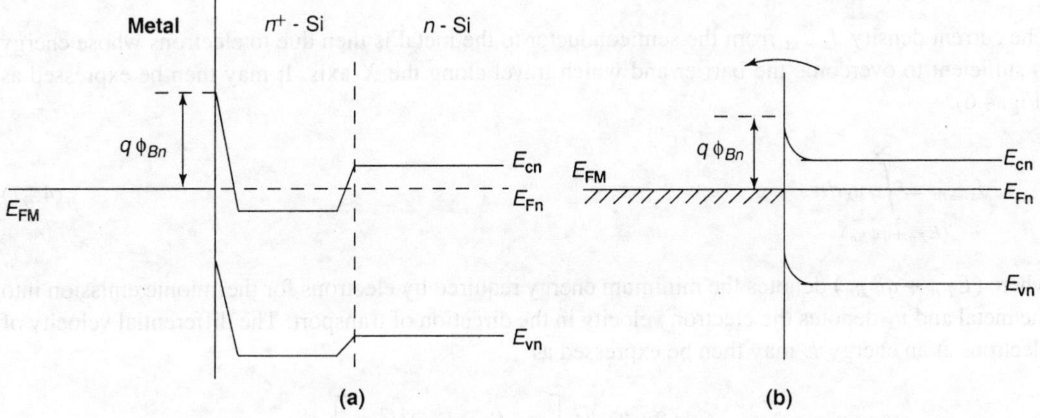

Figure 4.5 Ohmic contacts: (a) higher doping; (b) lower barrier height

4.3 Current transport across a metal-semiconductor boundary

When the mobility of carriers is reasonably high, the current transport over metal-semiconductor barriers observed to be due to thermionic emission. The theory of the current flow is derived here on the basis of the following assumptions

(i) The barrier height is sufficiently greater than the average thermal energy of carriers;

(ii) The current flow over the barrier does not disturb the thermal equilibrium of carriers existing on both sides of the interface;

(iii) The current is independent of the barrier shape and depends only on the barrier height.

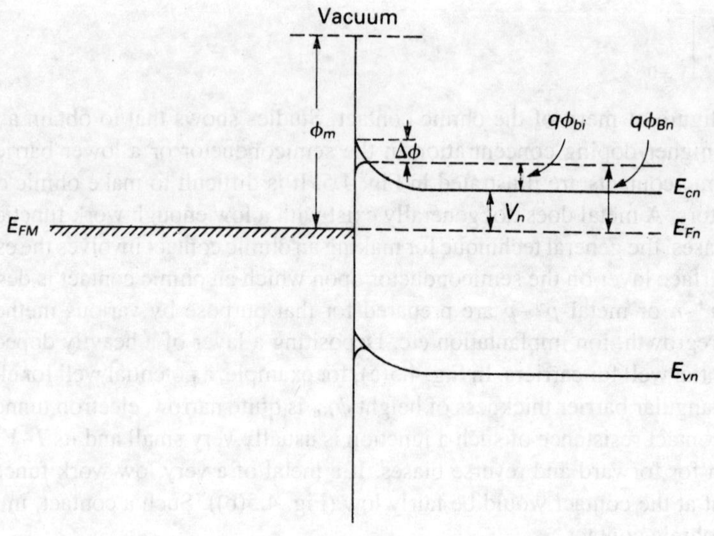

Figure 4.6 *Thermionic emission over a potential barrier*

The current density $J_{s\rightarrow m}$ from the semiconductor to the metal is then due to electrons whose energy is sufficient to overcome the barrier and which travel along the X-axis. It may then be expressed as (Fig. 4.6),

$$J_{s\rightarrow m} = \int_{(E_{Fn}+q\phi_{Bn})}^{\infty} q v_x dn \tag{4.21}$$

where $(E_{Fn} + q\phi_{Bn})$ denotes the minimum energy required by electrons for thermionic emission into the metal and v_x denotes the electron velocity in the direction of transport. The differential velocity of electrons at an energy E may then be expressed as

$$dn = \rho_c(E) f_n(E)\, dE = 4\pi \left(\frac{2m_n^*}{h^2}\right)^{3/2} \left[\frac{(E - E_{cn})^{1/2}}{1 + \exp\left(\frac{E - E_{Fn}}{kT}\right)}\right] dE$$

Presuming that the carriers obey Maxwell–Boltzman statistics instead of Fermi–Dirac statistics, the above expression simplifies to

$$dn = 4\pi \left(\frac{2m_n^*}{h^2}\right)^{3/2} \exp\left(\frac{-qV_n}{kT}\right) \left[(E - E_{cn})^{1/2} \left[\exp\left\{-\frac{(E - E_{cn})}{kT}\right\}\right]\right] dE \tag{4.22}$$

where $qV_n = (E_{cn} - E_{Fn})$ (Fig. 4.6). Presuming that the electron energy in the conduction band is only kinetic, we may write,

$$E - E_{cn} = \frac{1}{2} m_n^* v^2$$

such that $dE = m_n^* v dv$. Substituting these results in (4.22), we find

$$dn = 2\left(\frac{m_n^*}{h}\right)^3 \exp\left(\frac{-qV_n}{kT}\right) \exp\left[-\left(\frac{m_n^* v^2}{2kT}\right)\right] 4\pi\, v^2\, dv \tag{4.23}$$

Evidently, (4.23) gives the differential density of electrons whose speeds lie between v and $v + dv$ which are distributed in all possible directions, such that

$$v^2 = v_x^2 + v_y^2 + v_z^2$$

where v_x varies between $v_{0x} = [2(E_{Fn} + q\,\phi_{Bn})/m_n^*]^{1/2}$ and ∞ while both v_y and v_z lie between $-\infty$ to $+\infty$. Using the above relation in (4.23) we get

$$dn = 2\left(\frac{m_n^*}{h}\right)^3 \exp\left(\frac{-qV_n}{kT}\right) \exp\left[\frac{-m_n^*(v_x^2 + v_y^2 + v_z^2)}{2kT}\right] dv_x dv_y dv_z \tag{4.24}$$

since $4\pi\, v^2\, dv = dv_x dv_y dv_z$.

Combining (4.21) and (4.24), we find

$$J_{s\to m} = 2q\left(\frac{m_n^*}{h}\right)^3 \exp\left(\frac{-qV_n}{kT}\right) \int_{V_{0x}}^{+\infty} v_x \exp\left[\frac{-(m_n^* v_x^2)}{2kT}\right] dv_x$$

$$\int_{-\infty}^{+\infty} \exp\left[\frac{-(m_n^* v_y^2)}{2kT}\right] dv_y \int_{-\infty}^{+\infty} \exp\left[\frac{-(m_n^* v_z^2)}{2kT}\right] dv_z \tag{4.25}$$

Integrating (4.25) appropriately, we get

$$J_{s\to m} = \left[\frac{4\pi m_n^* k^2}{h^3}\right] T^2 \exp\left(\frac{-qV_n}{kT}\right) \exp\left[-\frac{(m_n^* v_{0x}^2)}{2kT}\right] \tag{4.26}$$

where v_{0x} must also satisfy the following relation

$$\frac{1}{2} m_n^* v_{0x}^2 = q(\phi_{bi} - V) \tag{4.27}$$

V being the applied forward bias on the semiconductor relative to that on the metal. Combining (4.26) and (4.27), one gets

$$J_{s\to m} = A^* T^2 \exp\left(\frac{-q\phi_{Bn}}{kT}\right) \exp\left(\frac{qV}{kT}\right) \tag{4.28}$$

where ϕ_{Bn} is the barrier height measured from the metal end and A^* is the effective Richardson's constant given by

$$A^* = \frac{4\pi m_n^* k^2}{h^3} \tag{4.29}$$

For electrons in a metal, this constant is designated by A, whose value works out to be $1.26 \times 10^6 \text{Am}^{-2}\text{T}^{-2}$. Introducing the image force lowering effect, the barrier height is lowered by $\Delta\phi$. Since the barrier height for electrons moving from the metal end is independent of the applied bias, the current flowing into the semiconductor would be the same as at $V = 0$. Hence, putting $V = 0$, in (4.28), we get

$$J_{m \to s} = A^* T^2 \exp\left(\frac{-q\phi_{Bn}}{kT}\right) \tag{4.30}$$

Hence, the net current density flowing from the semiconductor to the metal when a forward voltage V is applied to the semiconductor, can be obtained by taking the algebraic sum of (4.28) and (4.30) and expressed as

$$J = A^* T^2 \exp\left(\frac{-q\phi_{Bn}}{kT}\right)\left[\exp\left(\frac{qV}{kT}\right) - 1\right] \tag{4.31}$$

Equation (4.31) is similar to the current transport equation in a *pn* junction but the expressions for the saturation current densities in the two cases are quite different.

4.4 Metal-insulator-semiconductor (MIS) system

An ideal MIS system is shown in Fig. 4.7(a). Across an ideal MIS diode it is presumed that

(i) the difference between the metal and the semiconductor workfunctions viz., $\phi_{ms} = (\phi_m - \phi_s)$ is zero when no bias is applied,

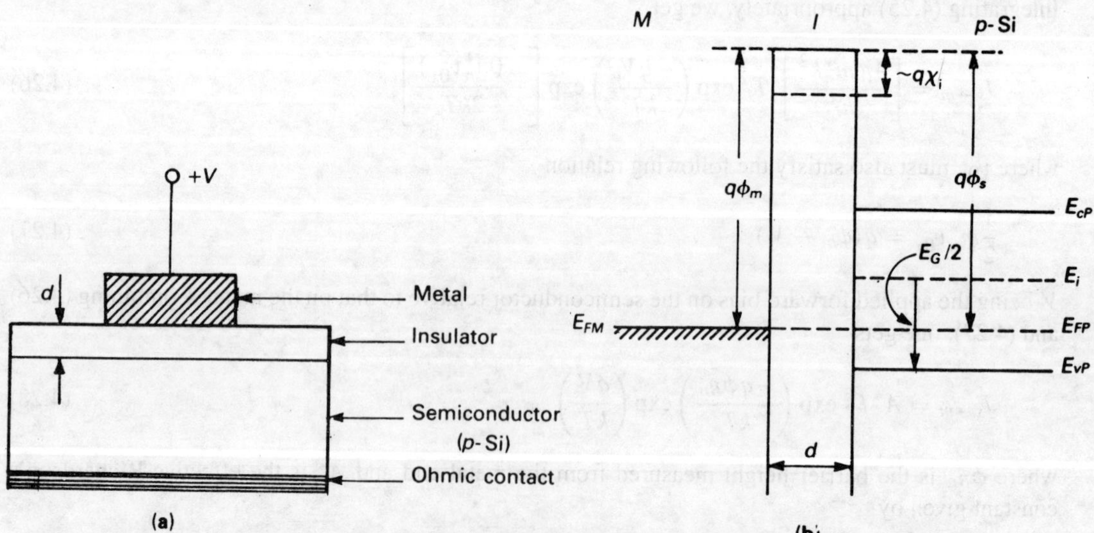

Figure 4.7 An ideal MIS contact: (a) device configuration; (b) energy band diagram

(ii) the only charges which exist at the interfaces are those on the semiconductor and the metal ends of the interfaces adjacent to the insulator under any biasing condition, and

(iii) no charge transport is possible through the insulator under the d.c. condition (Fig. 4.7(b)).

When an ideal MIS system is biased, three different kinds of space-charge distributions may arise at the semiconductor-insulator interface. Fig. 4.8 shows three cases using a p-type semiconductor as the substrate. When a small negative voltage ($V < 0$) is applied on the metal relative to that on the p-type semiconductor, holes get collected adjacent to the insulator. The energy band diagram corresponding to this case is shown in Fig. 4.8(a). The layer adjacent to the semiconductor is called the accumulation layer for holes.

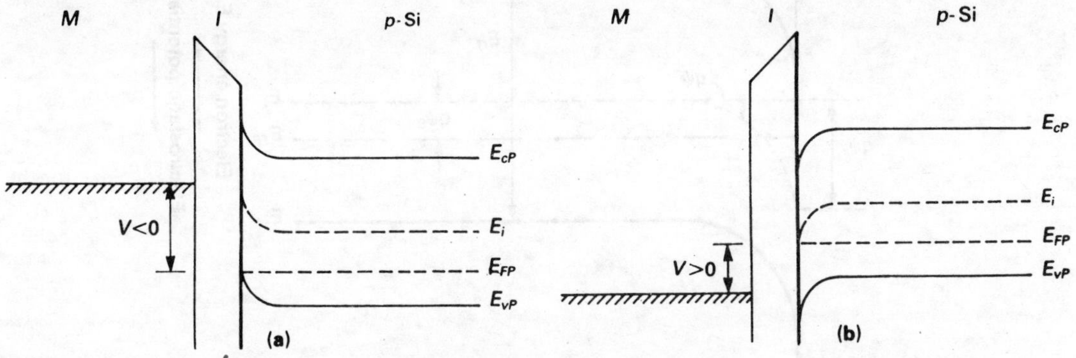

Figure 4.8 *Band diagrams of an ideal MIS contact: (a) accumulation of holes: (b) depletion of holes*

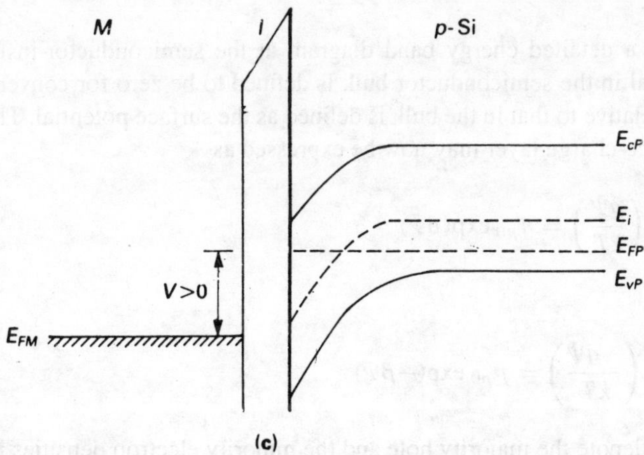

Figure 4.8 *continued (c) formation of an inversion layer*

When a small positive voltage ($V > 0$) is applied on the metal plate relative to the p-type semiconductor, holes are repelled away from the semiconductor-insulator interface, producing a depletion layer for holes, as shown in Fig. 4.8(b). Now, when the magnitude of the forward bias is sufficiently increased so that the Fermi level cuts across the intrinsic level (Fig. 4.8(c)) at the semiconductor-insulator interface, bringing the conduction band close to the Fermi energy, a part of the semiconductor close to the interface, starts behaving as an inversion layer (n-type). Similar energy diagrams with n-type semiconductor substrate may also be drawn.

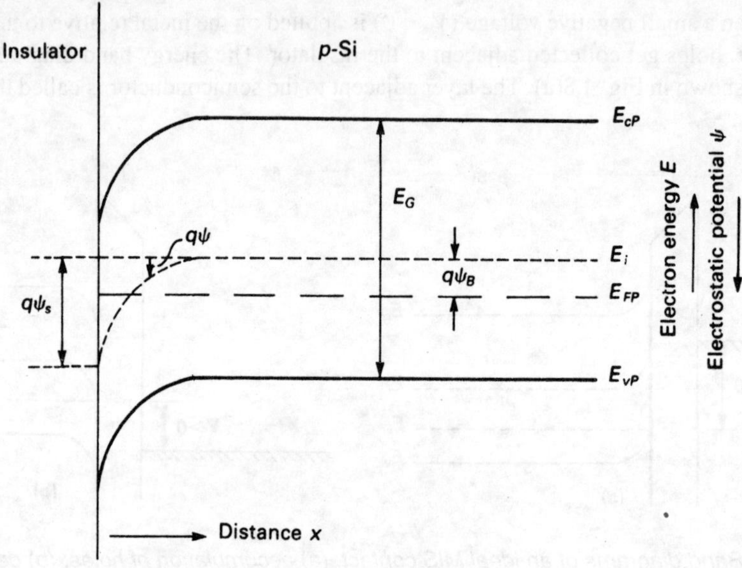

Figure 4.9 *Detailed band diagram at the semiconductor-insulator interface*

Figure 4.9 gives a detailed energy band diagram at the semiconductor-insulator interface. The electrostatic potential in the semiconductor bulk is defined to be zero for convenience. The potential Ψ_s at the interface relative to that in the bulk is defined as the surface potential. The carrier densities at any point of the space-charge layer may now be expressed as

$$n_p = n_{p0} \exp\left(\frac{q\Psi}{kT}\right) = n_{p0} \exp(\beta\Psi) \tag{4.32}$$

and

$$p_p = p_{p0} \exp\left(\frac{-q\Psi}{kT}\right) = p_{p0} \exp(-\beta\Psi)$$

where n_{p0} and p_{p0} denote the majority hole and the minority electron densities in the semiconductor bulk respectively and $\beta = (q/kT)$. The carrier densities on the semiconductor surface may be obtained by setting $\Psi = \Psi_s$ in (4.32). Now, on the basis of our earlier discussions, we may identify the following five electrostatically distinct regions at the semiconductor-insulator interface:

(i) $\Psi_s < 0$: accumulation of holes,
(ii) $\Psi_s = 0$: flat band condition,

(iii) $\Psi_B > \Psi_s > 0$: depletion of holes,
(iv) $\Psi_s = \Psi_B$: formation of an inversion layer.

The one-dimensional Poisson's equation in the space-charge layer may now be written as

$$\frac{d^2\psi(x)}{dx^2} = -\left[\frac{\rho(x)}{\kappa\varepsilon_0}\right] \tag{4.33}$$

where

$$\rho(x) = q[N_d^+ - N_a^- + p_p - n_p] \tag{4.34}$$

and N_d^+ and N_a^- denote the densities of ionized donors and acceptors respectively within the space-charge layer. But the charge neutrality condition must be satisfied in the semiconductor bulk. Hence (4.34) reduces to

$$N_d^+ - N_a^- = n_{p0} - p_{p0} \tag{4.35}$$

Next, combining (4.32), (4.34) and (4.35), we get

$$\rho(x) = q[p_{p0}\{\exp(-\beta\Psi) - 1\} - n_{p0}\{\exp(\beta\Psi) - 1\}] \tag{4.36}$$

Substituting for $\rho(x)$ from (4.36) in (4.33), multiplying throughout by $2[d\psi(x)/dx]$ and finally integrating, one obtains

$$\left[\frac{d\psi(x)}{dx}\right]^2 = -\left(\frac{2q}{\kappa\varepsilon_0}\right)\int_0^{\Psi}[p_{p0}\{\exp(-\beta\Psi) - 1\} - n_{p0}\,\{\exp(\beta\Psi) - 1\}]\,d\Psi$$

i.e.,

$$\varepsilon^2 = \left(\frac{2kT}{q}\right)^2\left(\frac{q\,n_{p0}\beta}{2\kappa\varepsilon_0}\right)\left[\{\exp(-\beta\Psi) + (\beta\Psi) - 1\} + \left(\frac{n_{p0}}{p_{p0}}\right)\{\exp(\beta\Psi) - (\beta\Psi) - 1\}\right.$$

i.e.,

$$\varepsilon(x) = \pm\left(\frac{2kT}{qL_d}\right)F\left[\beta\Psi, \left(\frac{n_{p0}}{p_{p0}}\right)\right] \tag{4.37}$$

where the characteristic Debye length L_d is given by

$$L_d = \frac{2\kappa\varepsilon_0}{q\,p_{p0}\beta} \tag{4.38}$$

and

$$F\left[\beta\Psi, \left(\frac{n_{p0}}{p_{p0}}\right)\right] = \left[\{\exp(-\beta\Psi) + (\beta\Psi) - 1\} + \left(\frac{n_{p0}}{p_{p0}}\right)\{\exp(\beta\Psi) - (\beta\Psi) - 1\}\right]^{1/2} \tag{4.39}$$

In (4.37), we have to use the positive sign for $\varepsilon(x)$ when Ψ is positive and vice versa. Now, the space-charge density Q_s at the semiconductor surface required to produce the maximum field ε_s at the interface may be obtained from Guass's law of electrostatics as

$$Q_s = \kappa\varepsilon_0\,\varepsilon_s = \pm\left(\frac{2\kappa\varepsilon_0 kT}{qL_d}\right)F\left[\beta\Psi,\left(\frac{n_{p0}}{p_{p0}}\right)\right] \tag{4.40}$$

A few general cases of interest may now be derived from (4.40).

Case I During accumulation of holes ($\Psi_s < 0$), it follows from (4.40) that

$$Q_{sc} \sim \kappa\varepsilon_0\,\varepsilon_s \sim \exp\left(\frac{q|\Psi_s|}{kT}\right) \tag{4.41}$$

because in this case, only the first term in (4.39) dominates.

Case II During hole depletion ($\Psi_s > 0$), only the second term in (4.39) dominates so that we get

$$Q_{sc} \sim |\Psi_s|^{1/2} \tag{4.42}$$

Case III During inversion ($\Psi_s > \Psi_B$), the fourth term in (4.39) dominates. In that case, we get

$$Q_{sc} \sim \left[-\exp\left(\frac{q|\Psi_s|}{kT}\right)\right] \tag{4.43}$$

The variation of the surface charge density $|Q_{sc}|$ as a function of the surface potential Ψ_s is shown in Fig. 4.10.

Now, the total capacitance of a MIS diode is the series combination of the insulator capacitance $C_i(=\varepsilon_0\varepsilon_i/d)$ and the space-charge layer capacitance C_D. The capacitance of the combination is given by

$$C = \frac{C_i C_D}{C_i + C_D} \tag{4.44}$$

But for a given insulator thickness C_i remains a constant. The space-charge layer capacitance C_D may however be defined as

$$C_D = \frac{dQ_s}{\Psi_s} \tag{4.45}$$

But, from (4.40), we find

$$Q_s = \pm\left(\frac{2\kappa\varepsilon_0 kT}{qL_d}\right)\{\exp(-\beta\Psi_s)+(\beta\Psi_s)-1\}+\left(\frac{n_{p0}}{p_{p0}}\right)[\{\exp(\beta\Psi_s)-(\beta\Psi_s)-1\}]^{1/2} \tag{4.46}$$

Differentiating (4.46) with Ψ_s, we get

$$C_D = \frac{dQ_s}{d\Psi_s} = \left(\frac{\kappa\varepsilon_0}{L_d}\right)\left[\frac{\{1-\exp(-\beta\Psi_s)+\left(\frac{n_{p0}}{p_{p0}}\right)\{\exp(\beta\Psi_s)-1\}}{F\left\{\beta\Psi_s,\left(\frac{n_{p0}}{p_{p0}}\right)\right\}}\right] \tag{4.47}$$

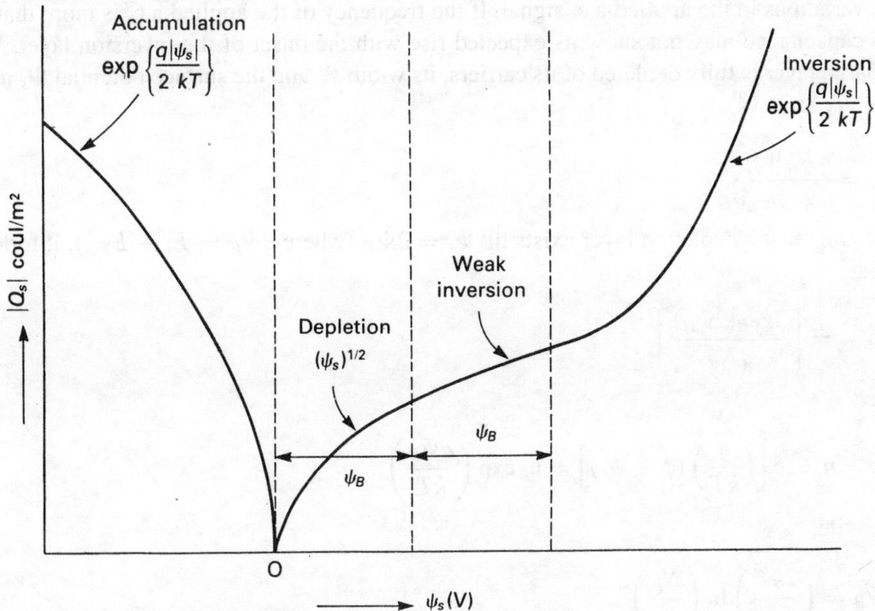

Figure 4.10 *Dependence of* $|Q_s|$ *on* ψ_s

To obtain the capacitance corresponding to the flat band case ($\Psi_s = 0$), the exponentials in (4.47) are expanded and the smaller power terms retained. We then get

$$C_D = C_{FB} = \frac{\sqrt{2}\kappa\varepsilon_0}{L_d} \tag{4.48}$$

The total MIS capacitance in the flat band case may then be obtained from (4.44) as

$$C_0 = \frac{\varepsilon_0\varepsilon_i}{d + \frac{\varepsilon_i L_d}{\sqrt{2}\kappa}} \tag{4.49}$$

Next, to describe the variation of the MIS capacitance as a function of the applied bias, we start with a negative voltage on the metallic electrode so that an accumulation layer for holes is developed at the interface of the insulator and the p-type semiconductor. $C = C_i$, because the contribution of the space-charge layer capacitance is practically nil. This then corresponds to the maximum capacitance of the MIS system. As the negative bias on the metallic electrode is gradually reduced so that the energy bands tend to become flat, the MIS capacitance drops in magnitude. In the flat band case, the MIS capacitance is given by (4.49). When the polarity of the voltage on the metallic electrode is such that Ψ_s becomes positive, a depletion layer for holes is formed at the semiconductor-insulator interface. MIS capacitance is further reduced as C_D is finite. The MIS capacitance continues to decrease with increase in Ψ_s until it acquires a minimum value. It starts increasing thereafter as an inversion layer nucleates at the semiconductor-insulator interface. It should be understood that the increase of capacitance of the MIS system depends upon the ability of the electron concentration in the inversion layer to follow the variations of a.c. applied to the system. The generation-recombination rate of carriers must keep up with the variations in the applied a.c. signal. If the frequency of the applied a.c. is more than 100 Hz, the MIS capacitance may not show its expected rise with the onset of the inversion layer. When the space-charge layer is fully depleted of its carriers, its width W and the surface potential Ψ_s are related to each other as (4.14),

$$\Psi_s = \frac{qN_aW^2}{2\kappa\varepsilon_0} \tag{4.50}$$

If we presume that a depletion layer exists till $\Psi_s = 2\Psi_B$ (where $q\Psi_B = E_i - E_{Fp}$), it follows from (4.50) that

$$W_{\max} = \left[\frac{2\kappa\varepsilon_0(2\Psi_B)}{qN_a}\right]^{1/2} \tag{4.51}$$

But, since

$$p_s = n_i \exp\left[\left(\frac{q}{kT}\right)(\phi - \psi_s)\right] = n_i \exp\left(\frac{q\Psi_B}{kT}\right)$$

we may write,

$$2\Psi_B = \left(\frac{2kT}{q}\right)\ln\left(\frac{N_a}{n_i}\right) \tag{4.52}$$

Combining (4.51) and (4.52), we get

$$W_{\max} = \left[\frac{4\kappa\varepsilon_0 kT\ln\left(\frac{N_a}{n_i}\right)}{q^2N_a}\right]^{1/2} \tag{4.53}$$

In practice, $W_{\max}$ is found to lie between 5 μ m to 0.01 μ m in the doping ranges of 10^{14} to $10^{18}/\text{cm}^3$. The corresponding minimum capacitance of the MIS system is then given by (4.44),

$$C_{\min} = \frac{\varepsilon_0\varepsilon_i}{d + \dfrac{\varepsilon_i W_{\max}}{\kappa}} \tag{4.54}$$

The variation of (C/C_i) for the MIS capacitance as a function of Ψ_s has been shown in the Fig. 4.11.

The relationship between the surface potential and the applied voltage V on the MIS system may now be computed as follows:

Presuming that a part of the applied voltage V_i is available over the insulator, the charge Q_M developed per unit area of the electrode, is given by Gauss's law of electrostatics as

$$Q_M = \varepsilon_0\varepsilon_i\left(\frac{V_i}{d}\right) \tag{4.55}$$

Similarly, the charge developed at the semiconductor end of the insulator interface is given by

$$Q_S = \kappa\varepsilon_0\left(\frac{qNaW}{\kappa\varepsilon_0}\right) = qNaW \tag{4.56}$$

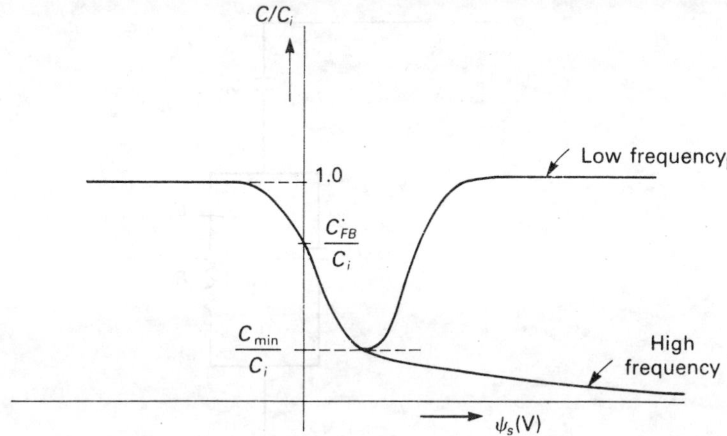

Figure 4.11 *Variation of MIS capacitance with ψ_s*

where we have used (4.16). Now, for electrical neutrality over the insulating layer, we must have $|Q_M| = |Q_S|$. Comparing (4.55) and (4.56), we get

$$V_i = \left(\frac{d}{\varepsilon_0 \varepsilon_i}\right)(2\kappa\varepsilon_0\, qNa\Psi_S)^{1/2} \tag{4.57}$$

But the applied voltage V is shared between the insulator (V_i) and the semiconductor (V_S). Therefore, we may write

$$V = V_i + V_S \tag{4.58}$$

where the potential drop V_S over the semiconductor body is given by

$$V_S = \int \frac{dQ_S}{C_S} = \int \frac{qN_a dW}{\frac{\kappa\varepsilon_0}{W}} = \frac{qN_a W^2}{2\kappa\varepsilon_0} = \Psi_S \tag{4.59}$$

according to (4.50). Next, combining (4.57), (4.58) and (4.59), we get

$$V = \Psi_S + \left(\frac{d}{\varepsilon_0 \varepsilon_i}\right)(2\kappa\varepsilon_0\, qNa\, \Psi_S)^{1/2} \tag{4.60}$$

Thus, if V is known, (4.60) may be used to evaluate Ψ_S by solving the quadratic equation.

However all these discussions are valid only for ideal semiconductor surfaces. In practical MIS diodes there may be

a) surface states which will exchange charges with the semiconductor bulk, or
b) mobile sodium ions inside the insulating layer.

To derive the information on surface states, we may either use capacitance-voltage or conductance-voltage measurements. However, when the surface state density is low ($\sim 10^{14}$ states/m^2 eV), we find the following conductance measurement technique to give more accurate results:

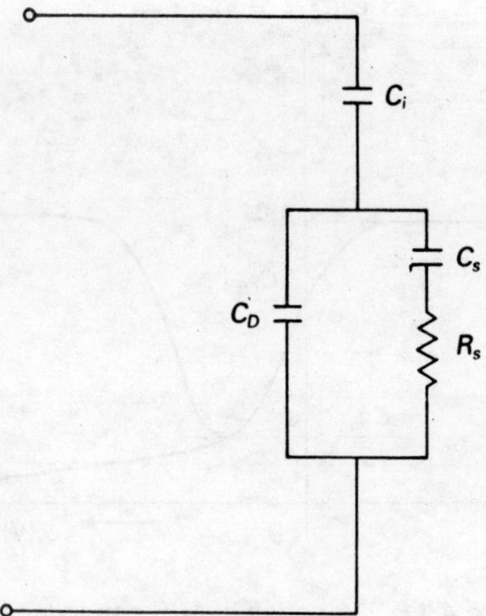

Figure 4.12 *The equivalent circuit of a non-ideal MIS contact*

Figure 4.12 shows the equivalent circuit of a MIS diode including the effects of surface states. The capacitance C_S and the resistance R_S take into account the effects. The impedance Z of the parallel branch of the equivalent circuit may now be expressed as

$$(Z)^{-1} = j\omega C_D + [R_S + (j\omega C_S)^{-1}]^{-1} = j\omega C_D + \frac{j\omega C_S}{1 + j\omega C_S\, R_S}$$

or

$$(Z)^{-1} = j\omega C_D + \frac{(j\omega C_S)(1 - j\omega C_S R_S)}{1 + \omega^2 C_S^2 R_S^2}$$

or

$$(Z)^{-1} = \left[\frac{\omega^2 C_S^2 R_S}{1 + \omega^2 C_S^2 R_S^2}\right] + j\omega\left[C_D + \left\{\frac{C_S}{1 + \omega^2 C_S^2 R_S^2}\right\}\right]$$

or

$$Y = G_p + j\omega C_p \tag{4.61}$$

where G_p and C_p may easily be identified. Thus, in order to evaluate the surface states density associated with semiconductor surfaces, the admittance of an MIS diode is first to be evaluated. The insulator capacitance C_i is easily measured by driving the diode to the case of accumulation. The total admittance of the MIS system may then be expressed as

$$Y_T = j\omega C_i + Y = G_p + j\omega(C_i + C_p) \tag{4.62}$$

It is easy to see that the conductance of the system may be expressed as

$$\frac{G_p}{\omega} = \frac{\omega C_S^2 R_S}{1 + \omega^2 C_S^2 R_S^2} \tag{4.63}$$

Thus, if (G_p/ω) is evaluated as a function of frequency, the former will acquire a maximum value of $[(\omega C_S^2 R_S)/2]$ when $(\omega C_S R_S) = 1$. In this case, $(G_p/\omega) = (C_S/2)$. Having thus expressed C_S, R_S can be found out from the relation $R_S = (\omega C_S)^{-1} = (2G_p)_{\max}$. Such a measurement therefore directly yields the values of R_S and C_S. The surface state density N_{SS} per cm^2 per V may then be derived from the above measurements, as discussed below: Due to the presence of the surface states, the charge accumulated on per unit area of the semiconductor surface in the energy interval $d\Psi_S$ is expressed as

$$dQ_{SS} = q\, N_{SS}\, d\Psi_S \tag{4.64}$$

Therefore, the capacitance C_S per unit area associated with the surface states is given by

$$C_S = \left(\frac{dQ_{SS}}{d\Psi_S}\right) = q\, N_{SS} = 2\left(\frac{G_p}{\omega}\right)_{\max}$$

or

$$N_{SS} = \left(\frac{2}{q}\right)\left(\frac{G_p}{\omega}\right)_{\max} \tag{4.65}$$

For an ideal MIS diode the work function difference ϕ_{ms} between the metal and the semiconductor was taken to be zero. If this is not so, the space-charge layer would appear over the semiconductor even before the application of any bias across the junction. As a result, a space-charge density Q_S will develop on the semiconductor-insulator interface, which would be given by

$$Q_S = C_i \phi_{ms} \tag{4.66}$$

The voltage giving the flat band capacitance would shift appropriately by an amount ϕ_{ms}. The voltage corresponding to (C_0/C_i) (Fig. 4.11) therefore gives a direct measure of ϕ_{ms}.

A MOS capacitor can be used as a varactor. Compared to other forms of varactors, such as, the *pn* junction and Schottky barrier diodes, the MOS capacitor has a much improved leakage and a wider capacitance range. It is also the 'heart' of a MOSFET and is widely used as a powerful analytical tool to study semiconductor surfaces and dielectrics. An MOS capacitor can be used as a fixed-value capacitor by doping the substrate heavily. A very important application of an MOS device is as a storage capacitance in a DRAM cell. In this particular example, the surface area is to be maximized for a large capacitance.

4.5 Metal-semiconductor field-effect transistor (MESFET)

Figure 4.13 shows the configuration of a GaAs MESFET. The starting GaAs substrate is slightly doped with an *n*-type (chromium) so that the Fermi level is very near the energy gap centre, resulting in a very high resistivity material (10^8 ohm cm), generally called semi-insulating GaAs. On this poorly conducting substrate, a thin layer of a lightly doped *n*-type GaAs is grown epitaxially to form the channel region of the FET. Common metals for the Schottky gate in GaAs are Al or alloys of Ti, W(tungsten) and Au. The ohmic source and drain contacts may be alloys of Au and Ge. GaAs is preferred over Si in fabricating this type of an FET because of its higher electron mobility. Also, the operating temperatures of GaAs devices are higher relative to those of Si ones. Since no diffusion process of impurities are involved in the fabrication of the device, close geometrical tolerances in device structures may be realized without much difficulty. Gate lengths of $L \leq 1\,\mu$ m are common in these types of devices. This feature is very important for their very high frequency operation capabilities as both the drift time and the capacitances can be kept to their minimum values.

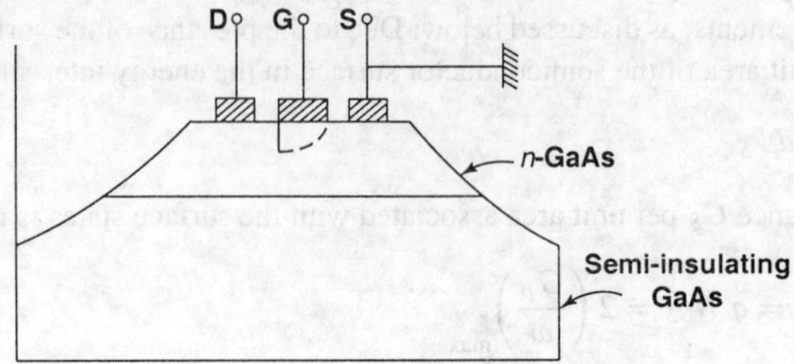

Figure 4.13 *The GaAs MESFET*

It is also possible to avoid epitaxial growth of the n-type layer by using ion implantation. Starting with a semi-insulating GaAs substrate, a thin n-layer can be formed by implanting a column VI donor impurity, such as Se. The ion implantation requires a post-annealing process to remove the radiation damages. The source and the drain contacts may further be improved by implanting n^+ impurities in appropriate regions. GaAs MESFETs are commonly used in integrated circuits.

A MESFET is similar to a JFET except that (i) it has a single gate electrode and (ii) the gate is formed by a metal-semiconductor junction. The transistor current between the source and the drain is mainly controlled by the gate. The gate bias modulates the depletion layer width underneath so that the channel opening is varied (Fig. 4.13). If the potential variation along the channel is much smaller than in the perpendicular direction, the gradual channel approximation may be used in the one-dimensional analysis. Using (4.15), the depletion layer width W_d at a distance x from the source is given by

$$W_d(x) = \left[2\kappa\varepsilon_0 \frac{\{\phi_{bi} - V_G + V(x)\}}{qN_d} \right]^{1/2} \tag{4.67}$$

where V_G denotes the negative gate bias and $V(x)$ represents the semiconductor channel potential with respect to the source, and ϕ_{bi} is given by

$$\phi_{bi} = \phi_{bn} - V_n = \phi_{bn} - \left(\frac{kT}{q}\right) \ln\left(\frac{N_c}{N_d}\right) \tag{4.68}$$

where ϕ_{bn} is the Schottky barrier height. The resistance along the channel is controlled by the channel cross-sectional area $A(x)$, given by (Fig. 4.14). The differential resistance dR over a length dx may be expressed as

$$dR = \left[\frac{\rho}{A(x)}\right] dx = \frac{dx}{q\,\mu_n N_d W\{a - W_d(x)\}} \tag{4.69}$$

where W measures the width of the FET normal to the plane of the diagram. The potential variation along the length is then given by

$$dV(x) = I_D\,dR = \frac{I_D\,dx}{q\mu_n N_d W\{a - W_d(x)\}} \tag{4.70}$$

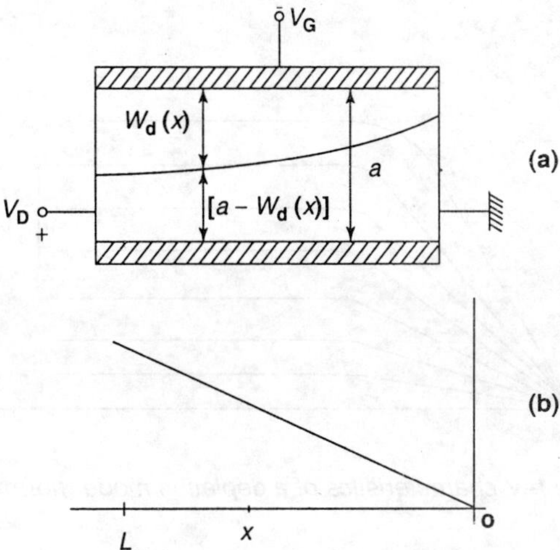

Figure 4.14 *The channel opening as a function of the drain bias, (b) the channel potential* $V(x)$ *with respect to the grounded source*

Integration of (4.70) from the source to the drain gives

$$I_D = G_0 \left[V_D - \left(\frac{2}{3} \sqrt{V_p} \right) \{(V_D + \phi_{bi} - V_G)^{3/2} - (\phi_{bi} - V_G)^{3/2}\} \right] \tag{4.71}$$

where

$$G_0 = \frac{(q\mu_n N_d Wa)}{L} \tag{4.72}$$

is the full channel conductance when $W_d = 0$. V_p is called the pinch-off voltage, which is given by

$$V_p = \frac{qN_d a^2}{2\kappa\varepsilon_0} \tag{4.73}$$

It is the net value of the potential difference $(V_D + \phi_{bi} - V_G)$ across the gate junction corresponding to the pinch-off condition $(dI_D/dV_D = 0 \text{ or } W_d = a)$.

The output characteristics of MESFET are analogous to those of JFET and are shown in Fig. 4.15. Equation (4.71) describes these characteristics from a very small drain bias till saturation. For small drain voltages, i.e. $V_D \ll (\phi_{bi} - V_G)$, equation (4.71) reduces to

$$I_D = G_0 \left[1 - \left\{ \frac{(\phi_{bi} - V_G)}{V_p} \right\}^{1/2} \right] V_D \tag{4.74}$$

In this region ohmic characteristics are observed. The transconductance in the linear region is given by

$$g_m = \frac{G_0 V_D}{2} \{(\phi_{bi} - V_G)V_p\}^{1/2} \tag{4.75}$$

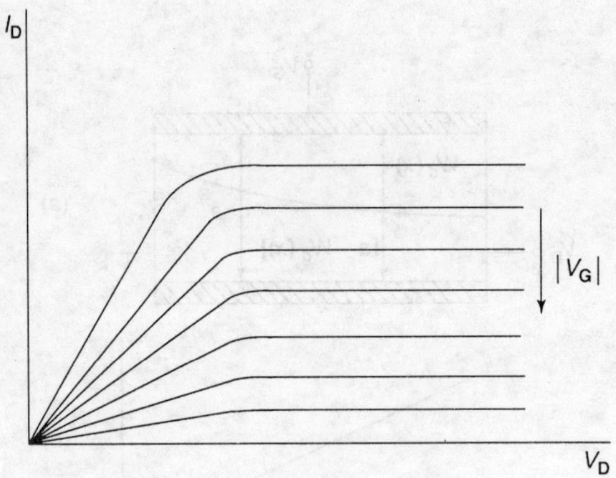

Figure 4.15 *The I–V characteristics of a depletion mode (normally ON) MOSFET*

The transistor is turned off at a gate voltage V_T when $(\phi_{bi} - V_T) = V_p$
or

$$V_T = \phi_{bi} - V_p \tag{4.76}$$

The transistor current is observed to saturate (i.e. $dI_D/dV_D = 0$) when $V_p = (V_D + \phi_{bi} - V_G)$
or

$$V_{D,\,\mathrm{sat}} = V_p + \phi_{bi} - V_G = V_G - V_T \tag{4.77}$$

The current in the saturation region may be obtained on substituting for V_D in (4.71). Thus,

$$I_{\mathrm{sat}} = G_0\left[\left(\frac{V_p}{3}\right) - (\phi_{bi} - V_G)\left[1 - \left(\frac{2}{3}\right)\left\{\frac{(\phi_{bi} - V_G)}{V_p}\right\}^{1/2}\right]\right] \tag{4.78}$$

and

$$g_{m,\,\mathrm{sat}} = \frac{dI_{\mathrm{sat}}}{dV_G} = G_0\left[1 - \left\{\frac{(\phi_{bi} - V_G)}{V_p}\right\}^{1/2}\right] \tag{4.79}$$

Qualitatively, for drain biases higher than $V_{D,\,\mathrm{sat}}$, the pinch-off point starts migrating towards the source end. However, the potential at the pinch-off point remains $V_{D,\,\mathrm{sat}}$, independent of V_D. This is due to the reduction in the effective channel length, which is measured between the source and the pinch-off point.

Specific applications of MESFETs include microwave power amplifiers, oscillators, switches and mixers. Commercial microwave amplifiers working upto 40 GHz are already available, with the possibility of going till 100 GHz for 0.25 μ m channel length devices.

4.6 Metal-oxide-semiconductor field-effect transistor (MOSFET)

The structure of a MOSFET is shown in Fig. 4.16. The metallic electrodes are completely insulated from the semiconducting ones by means of a thin insulating layer between them. Owing to this, the device is sometimes referred to as the insulated gate field-effect transistor (IGFET). A positive voltage applied to the gate may induce a conducting channel in the semiconductor substrate under suitable circumstances. In the planar configuration of the device, as shown in the figure, the two diffused n^+ regions of the device serve as the source (S) and the drain (D) electrodes. To analyze the device behaviour, we presume complete absence of surface states from the semiconductor-insulator interface. It is easy to notice that with a drain-source voltage of any polarity, no conduction through the channel is ever possible, because of the placements of two pn junctions back-to-back in series. Applying a positive voltage on the gate electrode, mobile holes underneath it in the p-channel tend to be driven away towards the bulk of the semiconductor, exposing the negatively charged acceptor ions sitting there. When the gate bias is increased sufficiently, all the mobile holes are driven away from the interface. Almost all of the negatively charged acceptor ions are then exposed. When these negative ionic charges are unable to compensate for the effects of increasing positive bias on the gate electrode, mobile electrons are drawn towards the interface from the bulk semiconductor. An interfacial layer of electrons is thus created connecting the source to the drain. Applying a suitable drain source voltage at this stage, electrical conduction through the channel becomes possible. Now, it is not difficult to realize that with the increase in the gate voltage ($+V_G$), the channel conductance would increase.

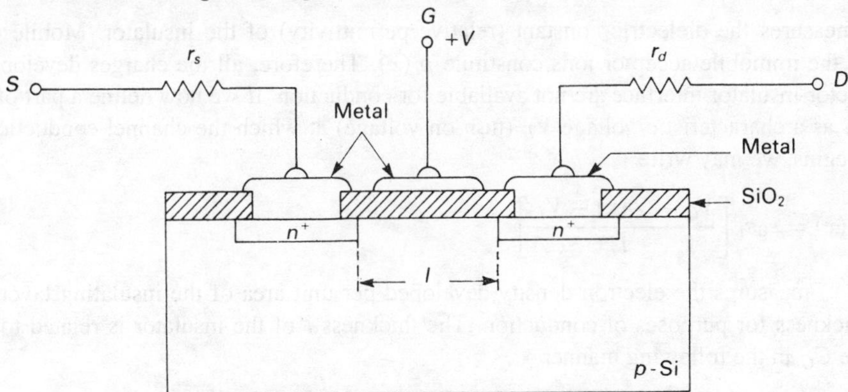

Figure 4.16 *Configuration of a MOSFET*

Next, to arrive at the I–V relation of the device, we presume that the voltage at any point x in the channel (measured from the source end) is $V(x)$, so that the transverse voltage across the insulator at that point would be $[V_G - V(x)]$. If the uniform thickness of the oxide layer is t at that point, the electric field intensity there becomes (Fig. 4.17)

$$\varepsilon(x) = \frac{V_G - V(x)}{t} \tag{4.80}$$

The surface charge density induced at the semiconductor-insulator interface by the electric field is obtained from Gauss's law of electrostatics as

$$\rho_i(x) = \varepsilon_0\, \varepsilon_i\, \varepsilon(x) \tag{4.81}$$

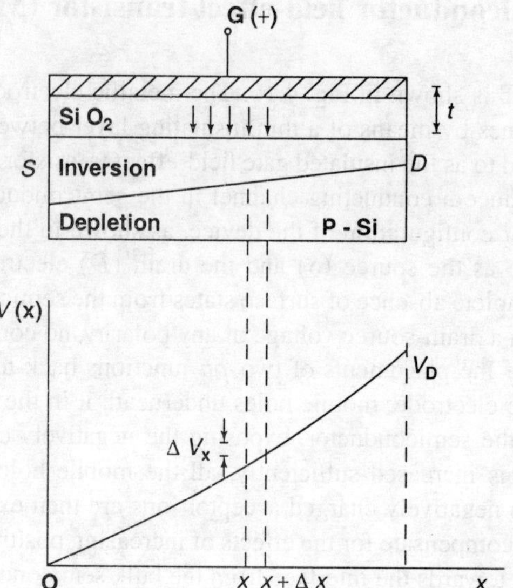

Figure 4.17 *Schematic view of an n-channel MOSFET*

where ε_i measures the dielectric constant (relative permittivity) of the insulator. Mobile electrons along with the immobile acceptor ions constitute $\rho_i(x)$. Therefore, all the charges developed at the semiconductor-insulator interface are not available for conduction. If we now define a part of the gate voltage V_G as a characteristic voltage V_T (turn-on voltage) at which the channel conduction due to electrons begins, we may write

$$q\Delta n(x) = \varepsilon_0\varepsilon_i \left[\frac{V_G - V(x) - V_T}{t}\right] \tag{4.82}$$

where $\Delta n(x)$ measures the electron density developed per unit area of the insulating layer per unit channel thickness for purposes of conduction. The thickness t of the insulator is related to the gate capacitance C_G in the following manner

$$C_G = \varepsilon_0\varepsilon_i \left[\frac{LW}{t}\right] \tag{4.83}$$

where W is the width of the gate electrode normal to Fig. 4.16. Substituting for 't' from (4.83) in (4.82), we find

$$q\Delta n(x) = \left(\frac{C_G}{LW}\right)[V_G - V(x) - V_T] \tag{4.84}$$

Next, let us concentrate on a length Δx of the channel of unit thickness inside p-Si. Its conductance may then be expressed as

$$G(x) = \sigma(x)\left[\frac{W.1}{\Delta x}\right] = q\mu_n \Delta n(x)\left[\frac{W}{\Delta x}\right] \tag{4.85}$$

Combining (4.84) and (4.85), we find

$$G(x) = \left(\frac{\mu_n C_G}{L}\right)\left[\frac{V_G - V(x) - V_T\}}{\Delta x}\right] \tag{4.86}$$

The channel current I_D under the influence of the drain voltage ΔV (available over Δx) is given by

$$I_D = G(x)\,\Delta V = \left(\frac{\mu_n C_G}{L}\right)[V_G - V(x) - V_T]\left(\frac{\Delta V}{\Delta x}\right) \tag{4.87}$$

Integrating (4.87) over the length L of the channel, we get

$$I_D = \left(\frac{\mu_n C_G}{L^2}\right)\left[V_G - V_T - \left(\frac{V_D}{2}\right)\right]V_D \tag{4.88}$$

where V_D measures the drain source voltage. The parasitic resistance associated with the source and the drain viz., r_s and r_d may be neglected if the doping levels of n^+ regions, forming the source and the drain are relatively high. Imposing the condition $dI_D/dV_D = 0$ in (4.88), we find that the drain current saturates when $V_D = (V_G - V_T)$. The saturated drain current from (4.88) is given by

$$I_{DS} = \left(\frac{\mu_n C_G}{L^2}\right)\left[\frac{(V_G - V_T)^2}{2}\right] \tag{4.89}$$

The transconductance g_m in the saturated state may be obtained from (4.89) as

$$g_m = \left(\frac{dI_{DS}}{dV_G}\right)_{VD} = \left(\frac{\mu_n C_G}{L^2}\right)(V_G - V_T) \tag{4.90}$$

The observed g_m is however found to be lower than predicted by (4.90). This is partly due to the finite parasitic resistances r_s and r_d associated with the source and the drain contacts and partly due to the lowering of the carrier mobility due to scattering at the oxide surfaces within the channel. The plots of $I_D - V_D$ curves are shown in Fig. 4.18. In this type of FET, we saw that the drain currents increased with the gate voltages. Hence, it is said to operate in the enhancement mode. We have already noticed the depletion mode of operations for JFET and MESFET.

The conductance in this type of an FET begins when the voltage applied to the gate is just sufficient to generate an inversion layer within the channel. We have already seen that an inversion layer is generated when $\Psi_S = \Psi_B = (kT/q)\ln(N_a/n_i)$. Using this condition in (4.60), we find that the gate turn-on voltage is given by

$$V_T = 2\Psi_B + \left(\frac{WL}{C_G}\right)[2\kappa\varepsilon_0 q N_a \Psi_B]^{1/2} \tag{4.91}$$

From (4.82) we notice that for $V(x) \ll V_G$, $\Delta n(x)$ is just finite when V_G just exceeds V_T. Hence V_T, given by (4.91) gives the turn-on voltage for the MOSFET.

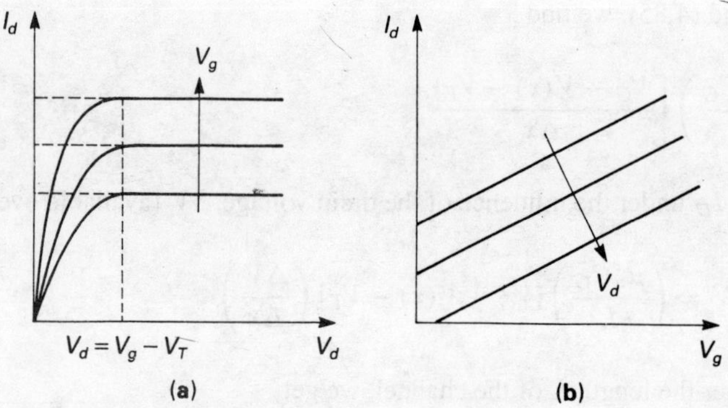

Figure 4.18 *MOSFET: (a) drain and (b) transfer characteristics*

As the channel lengths of MOSFETs are reduced, the depletion layer widths of the source and the drain junctions become comparable to them. The potential distribution within the channel is now controlled by both the longitudinal field ε_x along the channel length and the transverse field ε_y perpendicular to it. The potential distribution inside the channel then becomes two-dimensional. Because of the high electric field within the channel, the electron mobility very soon becomes field-dependent and eventually velocity saturation takes place. These phenomena complicate the device operation and degrade device performance. They should either be minimized or eliminated altogether so that physically short channel devices may preserve the characteristics of the long channel ones.

Types of MOSFETs

An equivalent circuit of a MOSFET is shown in Fig. 4.19. The differential transconductance g_m has already been introduced and discussed. The input conductance G_{IN} is caused by leakages through the gate insulator and is very negligible. G_{OUT} corresponds to the drain conductance.

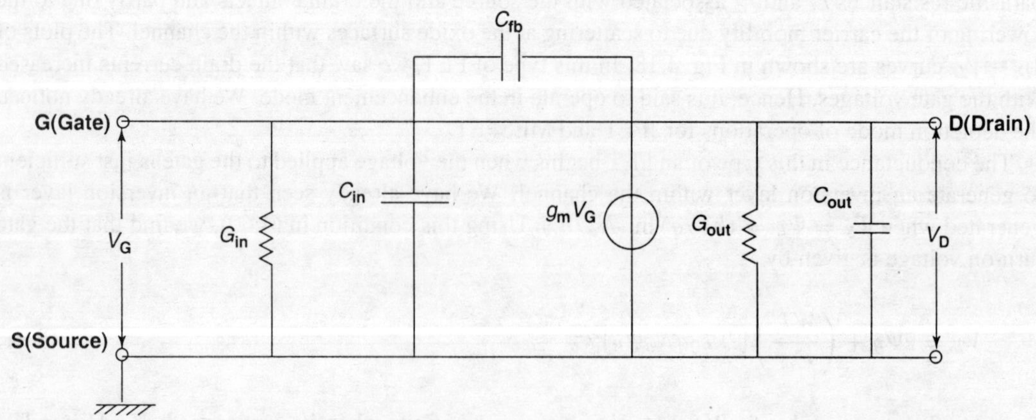

Figure 4.19 *The equivalent circuit of a MOSFET (the common-source configuration)*

There are basically four different types of MOSFETs, depending on the type of the inversion layer. If at zero gate bias, the channel conductance is very low, we must apply a positive gate voltage to form the n-channel. This type is called a normally-OFF (enhancement mode) n-channel MOSFET. If an n-channel exists at zero bias, we must apply a negative bias to the gate to deplete the carriers in order to reduce the channel conductance. This type of device is called the normally-ON (depletion mode), n-channel MOSFET. These two types of FETs are shown in Fig. 4.20(a). Similarly, we have the p-channel, normally-OFF (enhancement mode) and normally-ON (depletion mode) MOSFETs (Fig. 4.20(b)). The device symbols are also shown alongside.

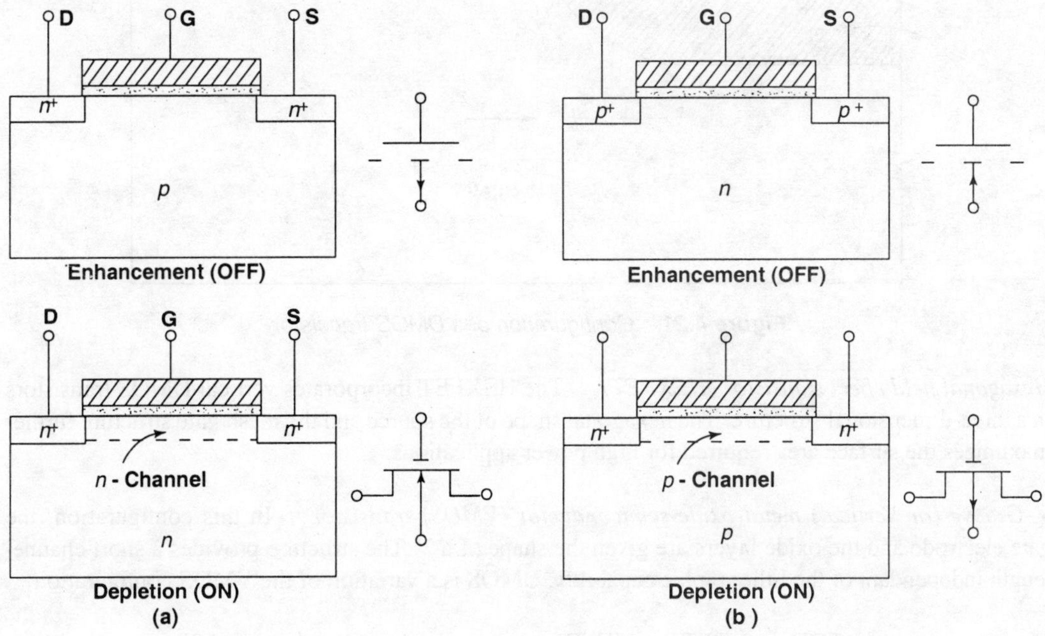

Figure 4.20 *The basic types of MOSFETs: (a) n-channel, (b) p-channel*

A MOSFET enjoys a wide range of applications in the electronics industry and is the most common transistor in the commercial integrated circuits. In terms of performance, it has high speed capability, extremely high input resistance, and a relatively constant output impedance. It is relatively inexpensive to produce these devices and one gets a high yield without much of an effort. It occupies very little space and consumes very low power. MOSFETs are exclusively used for SRAMs and DRAMs.

Related devices

Double diffused metal oxide semiconductor (DMOS) transistor The high frequency performance of MOSFETs improves with decreased channel lengths. A DMOS transistor achieves very short channel lengths by using diffusion properties. Figure 4.21 shows a DMOS structure where the channel length L is determined by the higher rate of diffusion of Boron compared to that of Phosphorus. The channel is followed by a lightly doped n-region, which serves as a part of the drain electrode. DMOS is useful for high power and high frequency applications.

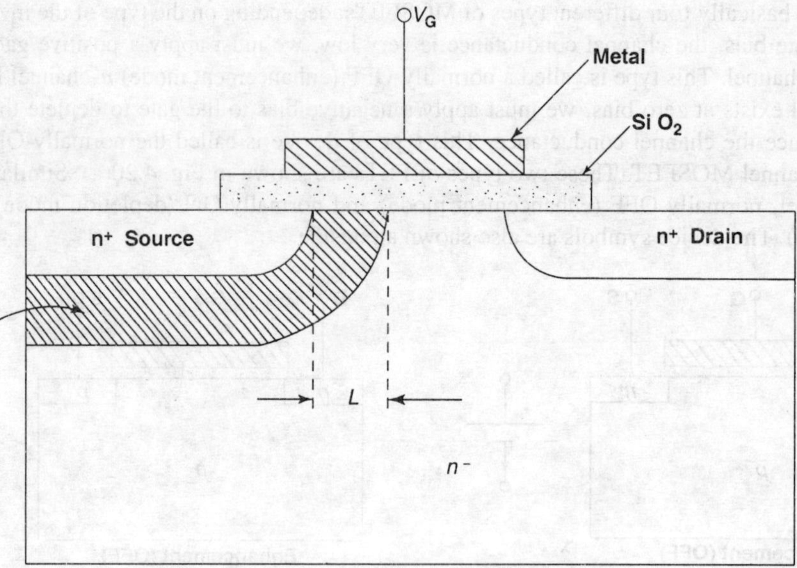

Figure 4.21 *Configuration of a DMOS transistor*

Hexagonal field effect transistor (HEXFET) The HEXFET incorporates vertical DMOS transistors in a three-dimensional structure. The hexagonal shape of the source and the mesh gate structure further maximizes the surface area required for high power applications.

V-Groove (or Vertical) metal-oxide-semiconductor (VMOS) transistor In this configuration, the gate electrode and the oxide layers are given the shape of a V. The structure provides a short channel length independant of the lithographic capability. UMOS is a variation of the VMOS configuration.

Thin film transistor (TFT) A TFT is an IGFET whose active layer is a deposited film on an insulator substrate or a layer. Since the film is non-crystalline, the device performance is inferior to that of the bulk devices. The current drive is much smaller and the speed is lower. The structure of a TFT is shown in Fig. 4.22. The gate insulator can either be a thermal oxide or a deposited dielectric.

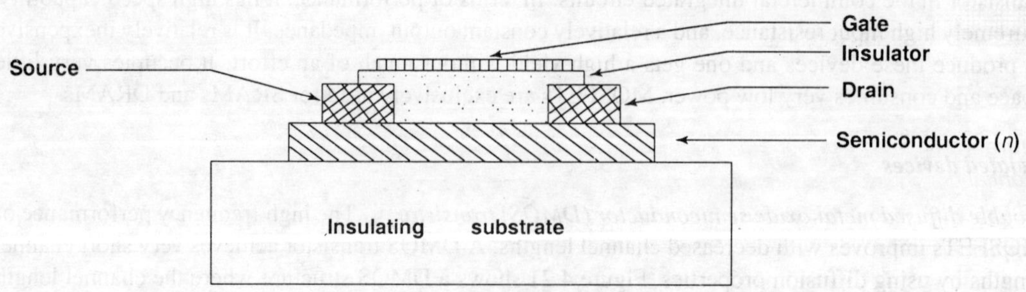

Figure 4.22 *An n-channel thin film transistor (TFT)*

Metal-nitride-oxide-semiconductor (MNOS) transistor This belongs to a group of metal-insulator-oxide-semiconductor (MIOS) structures having a special feature of dual gate dielectric-insulator on the oxide. With the nitride being the most popular, other insulators include alumina, tantalum oxide and titanium oxide. The MNOS transistor is used as a non-volatile memory. The oxide layer thickness is in the range of 20–50 Å and is thermally grown on the Si substrate. The purpose of this oxide film is to provide a good interface to the semiconductor and to prevent back tunnelling of the injected charge for better charge retention. Typically, the deposited nitride layer ranges from 200 Å to 600 Å.

Silicon-on-insulator MOSFET Many silicon-on-insulator (SOI) devices have been proposed, including silicon-on-sapphire, silicon-on-nitride and silicon-on-oxide structures. Its configuration is analogous to a TFT except that the semiconductor material, used in this case, is crystalline in nature. The devices are made using the standard MOS processes.

Ideal static induction transistor (ISIT) This is another form of an FET with channel dimensions much smaller than the mean free path of electron-phonon collision of the carriers so that the carrier conduction may be regarded as ballistic. The device configuration is shown in Fig. 4.23 and is analogous to its junction counterpart, discussed earlier. In an ISIT device, therefore, carriers travel without encountering lattice vibrations on their way. The device can be used for amplification till about 1000 Hz. The carriers in this device move with an ultrahigh speed in the thermion emission mode. Dimensions of an SIT is very small. Consequently, it has a very small operating voltage, a high transconductance and a high cutoff frequency.

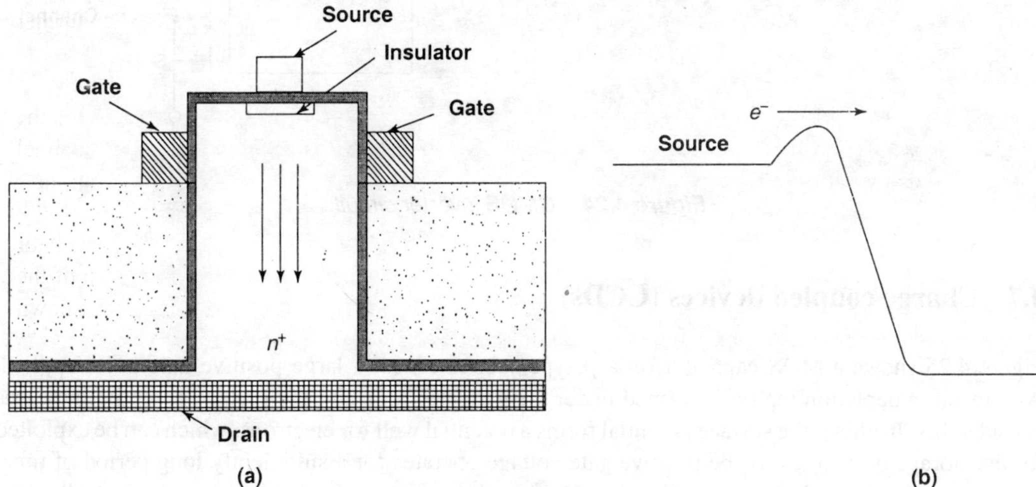

Figure 4.23 *(a) The schematic cross-section of an ideal static induction transistor (ISIT), (b) the potential distribution from the source to the drain along the centre of the channel*

Complementary MOS (CMOS) devices A particularly useful device for digital applications is a combination of n-channel and p-channel MOS transistor in adjacent regions on the same chip. The CMOS combination is illustrated in the basic inverter circuit of Fig. 4.24. In this circuit the drains of the two transistors are connected together to form the output, while the input terminal is common to the transistor gates. The p-channel device has a negative threshold voltage and the n-channel transistor has a positive threshold voltage. Therefore, a zero voltage input ($V_{IN} = 0$) gives zero gate voltage to the n-channel device, but the voltage between the gate and the source of the p-channel device is V. Thus, the p-channel device is ON and the n-channel device is OFF, and the full voltage is measured at V_{OUT} (i.e. V appears across the non-conducting n-channel transistor). Alternatively, a positive value of V_{IN} turns the n-channel transistor ON and the p-channel one, OFF. The output voltage measured across the ON n-channel device is essentially zero. Thus, the circuit operates as an inverter. With a binary 1 at the input, the output is in the 0-state and vice versa. It is to be noted that one of the devices is turned off in either condition. Since the devices are connected in series, no drain current flows in the steady state.

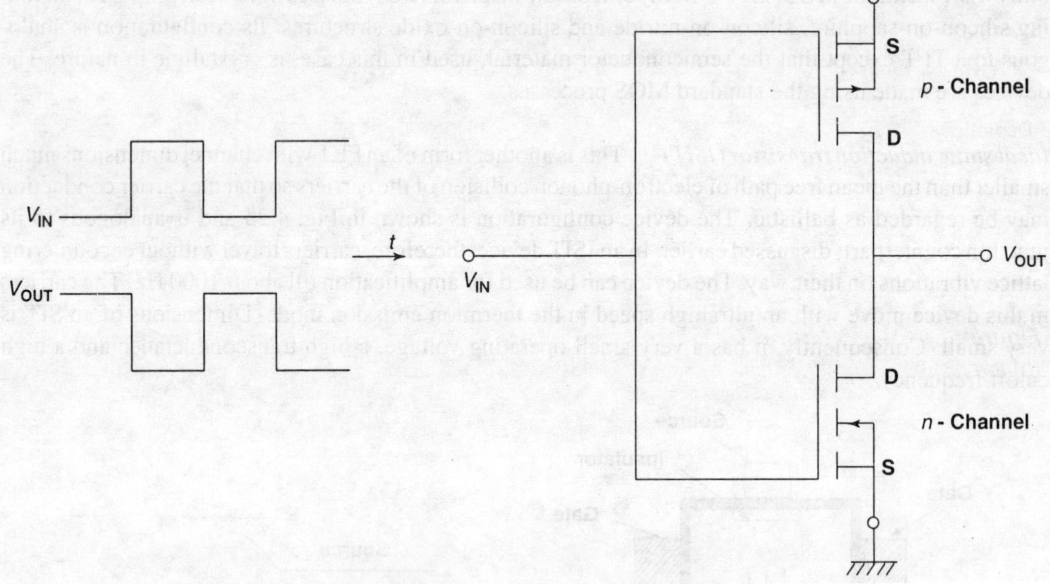

Figure 4.24 *CMOS inverter circuit*

4.7 Charge coupled devices (CCDs)

Figure 4.25 shows a MOS capacitor on a p-type substrate with a large positive gate pulse applied. As a result, a depletion region is formed under the gate electrode and the surface potential increases considerably. In effect, the surface potential forms a potential well for electrons, which can be exploited for the storage of charges. If the positive gate voltage operates for a sufficiently long period of time, carriers may be thermally generated near the semiconductor surface and electrons may start filling up the well. The time required to fill up the well in this manner is called the thermal relaxation time. If we can inject electrons into this potential well by any other means e.g., either electrically or optically, they will be stored there. The storage would have to be temporary because we must move the electrons out to another storage location as soon as possible, before thermal generation becomes appreciable there. Therefore, what is needed is a process required to transfer the charge from one potential well to an adjacent location as quickly as possible without losing much charge. The original CCD structure consists of a series of metal electrodes forming an array of MOS capacitors, as shown in Fig. 4.25. Voltage pulses are now supplied to three lines L_1, L_2, and L_3 each connected to G_1, G_2 and G_3

respectively. These voltages are clocked to provide potential wells, which vary with time, as shown in Fig. 4.26. At t_1, the potential well exists under the G_1 electrode, and we presume that this well contains packets of electrons produced by some means. At t_2, a potential V_2 is applied to the adjacent electrode G_2, so that the charge equalizes between G_1 and G_2 well. At t_3, when $V_1 < V_2$, the charge is gradually transferred from well 1 to 2. At t_4 when V_1 is zero and V_2 is positive, the charge is completely transferred to the well under G_2. This way, the charge could be transferred to the adjacent well on the right one after another, and detected at the other end.

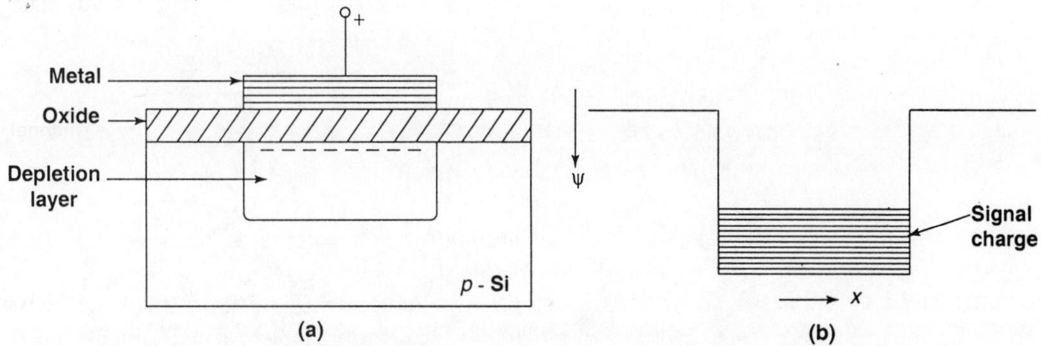

Figure 4.25 *An MOS capacitor with a positive gate bias (a) the depletion region and the surface charge, (b) the potential well at the interface, partially filled with electrons corresponding to the surface charge*

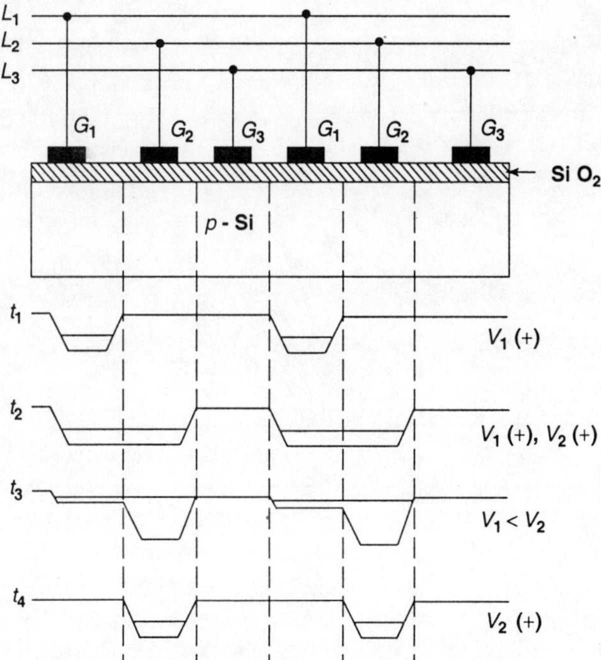

Figure 4.26 *Configuration of a basic Charge Coupled Device (CCD) composed of a linear array of MOS capacitors*

Applications The video camera, where the image is scanned and converted into an electrical signal, is probably the most important application of CCDs. The output wave form, after a chain of CCDs can be delayed compared to the input. A delay as long as 1 second may be realized. It is also used in signal processing, memories and logic.

Solved examples

4.1 Calculate the electric field intensity that must be applied perpendicular to a metal surface to reduce its work function to half its original value. ($\phi_m = 5.0\,\text{eV}$)

Solution

The externally applied electric field reduces the barrier height due to the Schottky effect. The expression for the Schottky lowering is given by

$$\Delta\varphi = \left(\frac{q\varepsilon}{4\pi\varepsilon_0}\right)^{1/2} \tag{1}$$

We want to calculate ε such that

$$\Delta\varphi = \frac{\phi_m}{2} \tag{2}$$

Combining (1) and (2), we find

$$\left(\frac{q\varepsilon}{4\pi\varepsilon_0}\right)^{1/2} = \frac{\phi_m}{2} \tag{3}$$

Squaring (3), we find

$$\varepsilon = \frac{\pi\varepsilon_0\phi_m^2}{q} \tag{4}$$

Substituting appropriate values in (4), we get

$$\varepsilon = \frac{3.14 \times 8.854 \times 10^{-12} \times 25}{1.6 \times 10^{-19}} = 4.34 \times 10^9\ \text{V/m} \tag{5}$$

4.2 A sample of n-type ($N_d = 10^{20}/\,\text{m}^3$) Si is brought into intimate contact with a metal ($\phi_m = 5\,\text{eV}$). Calculate

(i) the contact potential,
(ii) the barrier height from the semiconductor end,
(iii) the barrier height from the metal end,

(iv) the barrier height from the metal end when the contact is made with a p-type sample,
(v) the depletion layer width,
(vi) the maximum electric field at the junction,
(vii) the drift current over the barrier at 300 K,
(viii) the thermionic current density over the barrier at 300 K.

(Given : $\chi = 4.05\,\text{eV}$, $\phi_s = 4.06\,\text{eV}$, $\mu_n = 0.15\,\text{m}^2/\text{V.sec}$., $m^* = 1.1.2\,\text{m}$, $kT = 0.026\,\text{eV}$)

Solution

(i) The contact potential: $V_C = (\phi_m - \phi_s) = (5 - 4.06)\,\text{eV} = 0.94\,\text{eV}$;

(ii) $\phi_{bi} = (\phi_{bn} - V_n) = [(\phi_m - \chi) - (\phi_s - \chi)] = (\phi_m - \phi_s) = (5 - 4.06) = 0.94\,\text{eV}$

(iii) $\phi_{bn} = (\phi_m - \chi) = (5 - 4.05) = 0.95\,\text{eV}$

(iv) $\phi_{bp} = \left[\left(\dfrac{E_G}{q}\right) - \phi_{bn}\right] = (1.12 - 0.95) = 0.17\,\text{eV}$

(v) $W = \left(\dfrac{2\kappa\varepsilon_0\phi_{bi}}{qN_d}\right)^{1/2} = \left[\dfrac{2 \times 12 \times 8.854 \times 10^{-12} \times 0.94}{1.6 \times 10^{-19} \times 10^{20}}\right]^{1/2} = 3.53\,\mu\text{m}$

(vi) $\mathcal{E}_m(o) = \left[\dfrac{2qN_d(\phi_m - \chi)}{\kappa\varepsilon_0}\right]^{1/2} = \left[\dfrac{2 \times 1.6 \times 10^{-19} \times 10^{20} \times 0.95}{12 \times 8.854 \times 10^{-12}}\right]^{1/2}$
$= 5.349 \times 10^5\,\text{V/m}$

(vii) $J_{\text{drift}} = q\mu_n N_d \exp\left(\dfrac{-q\phi_{bi}}{kT}\right)\varepsilon(0) = 1.6 \times 10^{-19} \times 0.15 \times 10^{20} \exp\left(\dfrac{-0.94}{0.026}\right) \times 5.35 \times 10^5\,\text{A/m}^2 = 2.55 \times 10^{-10}\,\text{A/m}^2$

(viii) $J_{\text{th}} = \left[\dfrac{4\pi m^* q k^2 T^2}{h^3}\right] \exp\left(\dfrac{-q\phi_{bi}}{kT}\right)$ at $V = 0$. Therefore,

$$J_{\text{th}} = 4 \times 3.14 \times 9 \times 10^{-31} \times 1.6 \times 10^{-19} \times (1.38 \times 10^{-23})^2 \times \frac{(300)^2}{(6.62 \times 10^{-34})^3}$$

$$= 2.127 \times 10^{-5}\,\text{A/m}^2$$

It may thus be seen that $J_{\text{th}} \gg J_{\text{drift}}$. Therefore, at any applied bias, the thermionic current will dominate over the drift current.

4.3 A thin oxide layer is grown on the surface of a uniformly doped p-Si sample of $10\,\Omega$ cm resistivity. A positive charge in the oxide raises the surface electron concentration to $3 \times 10^{15}\,\text{cm}^{-3}$. Calculate the magnitude and the sign of the surface potential.

Solution

The bulk hole density p_B is given by

$$p_B = \frac{1}{\rho q \mu_p} = (10 \times 10^{-2} \times 1.6 \times 10^{-19} \times 0.13)^{-1} = 4.8 \times 10^{20}\,/\,\text{m}^3$$

But, the surface hole density, $p_s = 30 \times 10^{20}/\,\text{m}^3$ where,

$$p_s = p_B \exp\left(\frac{q\Psi_s}{kT}\right)$$

Therefore,

$$\Psi_s = \left(\frac{kT}{q}\right)\ln\left(\frac{p_s}{p_B}\right)$$

Substituting the values of the appropriate parameters in the above equation, we get

$$\Psi_s = 0.026\ln(6.25) = 0.047\,\text{eV}$$

The sign of Ψ_s must be negative.

4.4 An n-type Si sample has a uniform donor concentration of $N_d = 5 \times 10^{15}\,\text{cm}^{-3}$. Calculate the surface potential required

a) to make the surface behave intrinsically and
b) to bring strong inversion at the surface.

Also, calculate the corresponding applied voltages. ($d = 300$ Å)

Solution

We know that $n \cong N_d = N_C \exp[-(E_C - E_F)/kT]$ where $N_C = 2.8 \times 10^{19}\,\text{cm}^{-3}$ (Si); therefore, $[(E_C - E_F)/kT] = \ln(N_C/N_d) = \ln(2.8 \times 10^{19}/5 \times 10^{15}) = 5.6 \times 10^3$ or $(E_C - E_F) = 0.026 \times 8.63 = 0.224\,\text{eV}$. Hence, $q\Psi_B = [(E_G/2) - (E_C - E_F)] = [(1.12/2) - 0.224] = 0.336\,\text{eV}$. Therefore, the surface potential Ψ_S required to make the surface an intrinsic sample is $\Psi_B = \Psi_S = 0.336$ V
The strong inversion begins at the surface when $\Psi_S = 2\Psi_B = 2 \times 0.336 = 0.672\,\text{eV}$. Alternatively Ψ_S may also be obtained in the following way: We know that $n \cong N_d = n_i \exp[(q/kT)(\Psi - \phi_n)] = n_i \exp[(q\Psi_B/kT)]$ or $\Psi_B = (kT/q)\ln(N_d/n_i)$. Substituting for appropriate parameters in this equation, we get

$$\Psi_B = 0.026\ln\left[\frac{5 \times 10^{21}}{1.45 \times 10^{16}}\right] = 0.331\,\text{eV}$$

For the intrinsic case, $\Psi_B = \Psi_S = 0.331$ V. To bring about strong inversion, $\Psi_S = 2\Psi_B = 2 \times 0.331 = 0.663\,\text{eV}$. Now, the corresponding voltages may be computed by using the following relation:
For the intrinsic case,

$$V = \Psi_S + \left(\frac{d}{\varepsilon_i\varepsilon_0}\right)(2\kappa\varepsilon_0 q N_d \Psi_S)^{1/2} = 0.331 + \frac{300 \times 10^{-10}}{3.95 \times 8.854 \times 10^{-12}} \times (2 \times 12 \times 8.854 \times 10^{-12} \times 1.6 \times 10^{-19} \times 5 \times 10^{21} \times 0.331)^{1/2} = 0.541\,\text{V}$$

Next, for strong inversion,

$$V = \Psi_S + \left(\frac{d}{\varepsilon_i \varepsilon_0}\right)(2\kappa\varepsilon_0 q N_d \Psi_S)^{1/2} = 0.663 + \frac{300 \times 10^{-10}}{3.95 \times 8.854 \times 10^{-12}} \times$$

$$(2 \times 12 \times 8.854 \times 10^{-12} \times 1.6 \times 10^{-19} \times 5 \times 10^{21} \times 0.663)^{1/2} = 0.951 \text{ V}$$

4.5 An ideal Al-SiO_2-Si (p-type) junction is formed such that the thickness of the insulating layer is 1000 Å. The acceptor density of p-type Si is 10^{22} / m^3. Calculate the

(i) maximum capacitance,
(ii) flat band capacitance and
(iii) minimum capacitance of the MIS system. What would be the potential drop over the insulating layer if 1 V is applied across the MIS junction? ($n_i = 10^{16}$ / m^3, $\varepsilon_i = 3.95$ and $\varepsilon_s = 12$)

Solution

(i) The maximum capacitance of the ideal MIS junction is given by

$$C_{\max} = \frac{\varepsilon_i \varepsilon_0}{d} \text{ F/m}^2 \tag{1}$$

Substituting the values of the parameters in (1), we get

$$C_{\max} = \frac{3.95 \times 8.854 \times 10^{-12}}{1000 \times 10^{-10}} = 349.73 \ \mu \text{ F/m}^2$$

(ii) The flat band capacitance C_{FB} is given by

$$C_{FB} = \frac{\varepsilon_i \varepsilon_0}{d + \left(\frac{\varepsilon_i}{\varepsilon_s}\right)\left(\frac{L_d}{\sqrt{2}}\right)} \tag{2}$$

where

$$L_d = \left[\left(\frac{kT}{q}\right)\left\{\frac{(2\varepsilon_s \varepsilon_0)}{(q p_{p0})}\right\}\right]^{1/2} \tag{3}$$

Substituting appropriate values in (3), we get

$$L_d = \left[\frac{2 \times 12 \times 8.854 \times 10^{-12} \times 0.026}{1.6 \times 10^{-19} \times 10^{22}}\right]^{1/2} = 5.876 \times 10^{-8} \text{ m}$$

Using this L_d in (2), we find

$$C_{FB} = \left[\frac{3.95 \times 8.854 \times 10^{-12}}{10^{-7} + \left(\frac{3.95}{12}\right)\left(\frac{5.876 \times 10^{-8}}{\sqrt{2}}\right)}\right] = 307.70 \ \mu \text{ F/m}^2$$

(iii) The minimum capacitance is given by

$$C_{\min} = \frac{\varepsilon_i \varepsilon_0}{\left[W_{\max} + \left(\frac{\varepsilon_i}{\varepsilon_s}\right)\left(\frac{L_d}{\sqrt{2}}\right)\right]} \tag{4}$$

where

$$W_{\max} = \left[\frac{4\varepsilon_0 \varepsilon_s kT \ln\left(\frac{N_a}{n_i}\right)}{q^2 N_a}\right]^{1/2} \tag{5}$$

From (5), we find

$$W_{\max} = \left[\frac{4 \times 12 \times 8.854 \times 10^{-12} \times 0.026 \times 2.3}{1.6 \times 10^{-19} \times 10^{22}} \ln\left(\frac{10^{22}}{10^{16}}\right)\right]^{1/2}$$

$$= 3.08 \times 10^{-7} \text{ m}$$

Therefore,

$$C_{\min} = \frac{3.95 \times 8.85 \times 10^{-12}}{\left\{(3.08 \times 10^{-7} + \left(\frac{3.95}{12}\right)\left(\frac{5.876 \times 10^{-8}}{\sqrt{2}}\right)\right\}}$$

$$= 108.72\ \mu\text{F/m}^2$$

(iv) Now, if V is the external voltage applied across the MIS junction, we have,

$$V = V_i + V_S = V_i + \Psi_S \tag{6}$$

where V_i = voltage available across the insulator and V_S = voltage drop over the semiconductor. Therefore,

$$V = \Psi_S + \left(\frac{d}{\varepsilon_i \varepsilon_0}\right)(2\varepsilon_s \varepsilon_0 q N_a \Psi_S)^{1/2} \tag{7}$$

Thus, to evaluate V_i, we must first determine Ψ_S by solving (7). Substituting the values of the appropriate parameters in (7), we get

$$1.0 = \Psi_S + \left(\frac{10^{-7}}{3.95 \times 8.854 \times 10^{-12}}\right)(2 \times 12 \times 8.854 \times 10^{-12} \times 1.6 \times 10^{-19} \times 10^{22} \Psi_S)^{1/2}$$

or

$$4\Psi_S^2 - 4.779\Psi_S + 1 = 0 \tag{8}$$

Solving this quadratic equation, one finds, Ψ_S = 1.174 or 0.5205 V. Since, Ψ_S cannot exceed V, it must be 0.5205 V. Using this value in (6), we find

$$V_i = (1 - 0.5205) = 0.4795 \text{ V}$$

4.6 In an experiment with a non-ideal MIS diode, the measured capacitance associated with the surface states is found to be 100 pF/cm^2. Estimate the surface state density. The C–V plot of the same MIS diode shows a shift in the flat band capacitance by 0.8 V. Determine the work function difference between the metal and the semiconductor.

Solution

The capacitance associated with the surface states is given by

$$C_S = \frac{dQ_{SS}}{d\Psi_S} = \frac{qN_{SS}d\Psi_S}{d\Psi_S} = qN_{SS}$$

Therefore,

$$N_{SS} = \frac{C_S}{q} \tag{1}$$

Thus, $N_{SS} = (100 \times 10^{-12})/(1.6 \times 10^{-19}) = 62.5 \times 10^7$ (F/cm^2 C) $= 0.625 \times 10^9$ states/ cm^2 V. Since, the surface state density is small, the shift of C_{FB} along the voltage axis gives a measure of ϕ_{ms}. Hence, in our case $\phi_{ms} = 0.8$ V.

4.7 The p-channel of a Si MOSFET is doped with 10^{13} acceptors/c.c and the thickness of the oxide layer is 3 μ m. Considering the surface state density to be negligible, calculate the gate voltage at which the channel conduction begins. ($\varepsilon_s = 12$, $\varepsilon_i = 4$, $n_i = 10^{10}$ cm^{-3})

Solution

The gate turn-on voltage is given by

$$V_{GT} = \Psi_B + \left(\frac{t}{\varepsilon_i \varepsilon_0}\right)(2\varepsilon_s \varepsilon_0 q N_a \Psi_B)^{1/2} \tag{1}$$

where

$$\Psi_B = \left(\frac{kT}{q}\right) \ln\left(\frac{N_a}{n_i}\right) \tag{2}$$

From (2),

$$\Psi_B = 0.026 \ln\left(\frac{10^{19}}{10^{16}}\right) = 0.026 \ln (10^3)$$

i.e.,

$$\Psi_B = 0.1796 \text{ V} \tag{3}$$

Using this value in (1), we get

$$V_{GT} = 0.1796 + 0.0847 \times 106\ (61.063 \times 10^{-12})^{1/2} = 0.8415 \text{ V}$$

4.8 An n-channel GaAs MESFET has $\phi_{Bn} = 0.9\,\text{V}$, $N_d = 10^{17}\,\text{cm}^{-3}$, $a = 0.2\,\mu\text{m}$, $Z = 10\,\mu\text{m}$.

a) Is this an enhancement mode or adepletion mode device?
b) Find the threshold voltage of operation.
c) Find the maximum conductance at $V_G = 0$.
d) Calculate the cutoff frequency. ($L = 1\mu$ m)

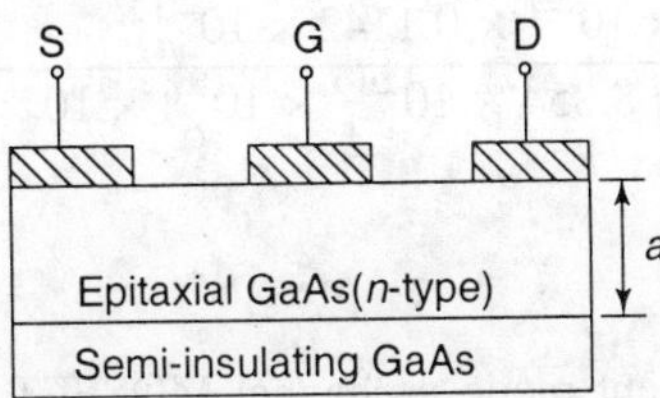

Solution

The figure shows a cross-section of a GaAs MESFET. The device is fabricated by growing an n-type epitaxial layer on a high resistivity GaAs substrate which may be either n- or p-type. The source and the drain contacts are made by depositing a suitable material by vacuum evaporation and by alloying it under a subsequent heat treatment. The metal gate offers a number of advantages. First, the formation of a Schottky barrier contact can be realized at much lower temperatures than those required for pn junction fabrication. Second, the length of the gate electrode can be controlled as desired. It can even be reduced to submicron dimensions. Depending on the thickness of the epitaxial layer, a MESFET may be designed to operate either in the depletion mode (normally on) device or enhancement mode (normally off) device. In a depletion mode device, the thickness of the epilayer is more than the zero bias depletion layer width of the Schottky barrier gate and the transistor has a conducting channel even at $V_G = 0$. Conduction of the channel is initiated by small positive values of V_G. Enhancement devices are useful for low power, high frequency applications. But, in most cases MESFETs are of the depletion types. The depletion layer width of the space-charge region under the gate is given by

$$W = \left[\frac{2\kappa\varepsilon_0\phi_{Bn}}{qN_d}\right]^{1/2} = \left[\frac{2 \times 13.1 \times 8.854 \times 10^{-12} \times 0.9}{1.6 \times 10^{-19} \times 10^{23}}\right]^{1/2} = 0.1142\,\mu\,\text{m}$$

Since, W,A, the device must be of depletion mode type. It will always be in the ON state. Therefore, the threshold voltage of operation $V_{GT} = 0$. The maximum device conductance is given by

$$G_m = \sigma_n\left(\frac{Za}{L}\right) = (q\mu_n N_d)\left(\frac{Za}{L}\right) = (1.6 \times 10^{-19} \times 0.85 \times 10^{23})$$
$$\frac{(10 \times 10^{-6} \times 0.2 \times 10^{-6})}{10^{-6}} = 2.72\,\text{mho}$$

If C_{in} measures the input capacitance of the MESFET, then the cutoff frequency f_T, is defined by the relation

$$2\pi f_T C_{\text{in}} = G_m$$

or

$$f_T = \left(\frac{1}{2\pi}\right)\left(\frac{G_m}{C_{\text{in}}}\right) = \left(\frac{1}{2\pi}\right)\left(\frac{G_m W}{\varepsilon_s L Z}\right)$$

or

$$f_T = \frac{2.72 \times 10^{-2} \times 0.1142 \times 10^{-12}}{2 \times 3.14 \times 13.1 \times 8.854 \times 10^{-12} \times 10^{-6} \times 10 \times 10^{-6}}$$

$$= 0.42\,\text{MHz}.$$

4.9 An aluminium gate enhancement mode n-channel MOSFET has a substrate concentration of $N_a = 6 \times 10^{15}\,\text{cm}^{-3}$ and an oxide thickness of 0.01μ m. The SiO_2 has 10^{10} charges/cm^2. Determine the threshold voltage of the transistor. When the transistor is operated in the linear region with $V_D = 0.5\,\text{V}$, calculate the gate voltage to obtain a drain current of 2 mA. Assuming $L = 10\mu$ m, $\mu_n = 500\,\text{cm}^2/\text{Vs}$ and $Z = 100L$, calculate the g_m of the device and the maximum frequency of oscillation.

Solution

Z = width of the channel = 100 $L = W$; $t = 0.1\mu$ m. The important expressions for the MOSFET are

$$(V_{GT} - V_{g0}) = \Psi_B + \left(\frac{WL}{C_g}\right)(2k\varepsilon_0 q N_a \Psi_B)^{1/2} \quad (1)$$

$$\Psi_B = \left(\frac{kT}{q}\right) \ln\left(\frac{N_a}{n_i}\right) \quad (2)$$

$$Cg = \frac{\varepsilon_0 \varepsilon_i (LW)}{t} \quad (3)$$

$$I_d = \mu_n C g \frac{(V_g - V_{GT})}{L^2} \quad (4)$$

$$f_T = \frac{g_m}{2\pi C_{\text{in}}} = \left(\frac{\mu_n}{2\pi L^2}\right)(V_g - V_{GT}) \quad (5)$$

$$g_m = \left(\frac{\mu_n C g}{L^2}\right)(V_g - V_{GT}) \quad (6)$$

and

$$\rho_s = \varepsilon_i \varepsilon_0 \left(\frac{V_{g0}}{t}\right) = \left(\frac{Cg}{LW}\right) V_{g0} \quad (7)$$

Next, using (3), we find $C_g = 3.95 \times 8.854 \times 10^{-12} \times 10 \times 10^{-6} \times 100 \times 10 \times \dfrac{10^{-6}}{0.1} \times 10^{-6} =$ 3.49 pF

Similarly, using (7), we get $V_{g0} = \left(\dfrac{LW}{Cg}\right)\rho_s = 100 \times 10^{-6} \times 100 \times 10 \times 10^{-6} \times 10^{14} \times 1.6 \times \dfrac{10^{-19}}{3.49} \times 10^{-12} = 0.0458$ V

Using (2), we get $\Psi_B = \left(\dfrac{kT}{q}\right) \ln\left(\dfrac{Na}{n_i}\right) = 0.026 \ln\left(\dfrac{6 \times 10^{15}}{1.5 \times 10^{10}}\right) = 0.335$ V

Now from (1), we find

$$
\begin{aligned}
V_{GT} - V_{g0} &= 0.335 + \left[\frac{100 \times (10 \times 10^{-6})^2}{3.49 \times 10^{-12}}\right] \\
&\quad (2 \times 12 \times 8.854 \times 10^{-12} \times 1.6 \times 10^{-19} \times 6 \times 10^{21} \times 0.335)^{1/2} \\
&= 0.335 + 0.749 \\
&= 1.084 \text{ V}
\end{aligned}
$$

Hence, the threshold voltage is $V_{GT} = (1.084 + 0.0458) = 1.1298$ V

Now, the drain current may be computed from the following expression:

$$
I_d = \left(\frac{\mu_n Cg}{L^2}\right)(V_g - V_{GT} - V_D)V_D \tag{8}
$$

or

$$
2 \times 10^{-3} = \left[\frac{0.05 \times 3.49 \times 10^{-12}}{(10 \times 10^{-6})^2}\right][V_g - 1.46 - 0.5]
$$

Solving, we get for the gate voltage, $V_g = 4.25$ V

From (6), we find for the transconductance

$$
g_m = \left(\frac{\mu_n Cg}{L^2}\right)(V_g - V_{GT})
$$

or

$$
g_m = \left[\frac{0.05 \times 3.49 \times 10^{-12}}{(10 \times 10^{-6})^2}\right](4.25 - 1.46) = 4.87 \times 10^{-3} \text{ mho}
$$

Finally, for the cutoff frequency, we get from (5)

$$
f_T = \left(\frac{\mu_n}{2\pi L^2}\right)(V_g - V_{GT})
$$

Therefore,

$$
f_T = \left[\frac{0.05}{2 \times 3.14 \times (10 \times 10^{-6})^2}\right](4.25 - 1.46) = 2.22 \times 10^8 \text{ Hz}
$$

4.10 Calculate the voltage to be applied to a CCD to attain the deepest potential well under the insulator if the semiconductor doping is $10^{20}\,\text{m}^{-3}$. What is the depth of the potential well? ($d = 1\mu$ m, $\varepsilon_s = 12$, $\varepsilon_i = 3.95$, $n_i = 10^{16}\,\text{m}^{-3}$).

Solution

Applying a gate voltage to a CCD, the surface potential changes. When $\Psi_S = 2\Psi_B = 2(E_i - E_{F_p})/q$, the deepest potential well develops under the insulator. The gate voltage V corresponding to this interface potential is given by

$$V = 2\Psi_B + \left(\frac{d}{\varepsilon_i\varepsilon_0}\right)[2\varepsilon_S\varepsilon_0 q N_a(2\Psi_B)]^{1/2} \tag{1}$$

where

$$2\Psi_B = \left(\frac{2kT}{q}\right)\ln\left(\frac{N_a}{n_i}\right) \tag{2}$$

The maximum width of the well is however given by

$$W_{\max} = \left[\frac{4\varepsilon_0\varepsilon_s\Psi_B}{qN_a}\right]^{1/2} \tag{3}$$

From (2), we find, $2\Psi_B = (2kT/q)\ln(N_a/n_i) = 2 \times 0.026 \ln(10^{20}/10^{16}) = 0.48$ V. Using this value in (1), we get

$$V = 0.48 + \left(\frac{10^{-6}}{3.95 \times 8.854 \times 10^{-12}}\right)(2 \times 12 \times 8.854 \times 10^{-12} \times 10^{20}$$

$$\times 1.6 \times 10^{-19} \times 0.48)^{1/2} = 1.63\text{ V}$$

Finally from (3), we get

$$W_{\max} = \left[\frac{4\varepsilon_0\varepsilon_s\Psi_B}{qN_a}\right]^{1/2} = \left[\frac{4 \times 12 \times 8.854 \times 10^{-12} \times 0.24}{1.6 \times 10^{-19} \times 10^{20}}\right]^{1/2} = 2.524\,\mu\text{ m}$$

4.11 Analyze a common-source amplifier circuit with MOSFET at high frequencies and calculate : (i) voltage gain, (ii) input admittance, (iii) input capacitance and (iv) output admittance.

Solution

(i) *Voltage gain* The output voltage is given by

$$V_0 = IZ_L \tag{1}$$

where I is the current short-circuiting D and S terminals (Fig. 4.27). Its constant current generator equivalent circuit is shown in Fig. 4.28. Z denotes the impedance between the two terminals when all the voltage sources in the circuit are shorted and the current sources are made open-circuited. We may then write

$$I = (j\omega C_{gd})V_i - g_m V_i \tag{2}$$

and

$$\frac{1}{Z} = \left(\frac{1}{Z_L}\right) + \left(\frac{1}{r_d}\right) + (j\omega C_{ds}) + (j\omega C_{gs}) \tag{3}$$

The voltage gain is then given by

$$A_V = \frac{V_0}{V_i} = \frac{IZ}{V_i} = \frac{-g_m + Y_{gd}}{Y_L + Y_{ds} + Y_{gd} + g_d} \tag{4}$$

where Y_S stands for corresponding admittances.

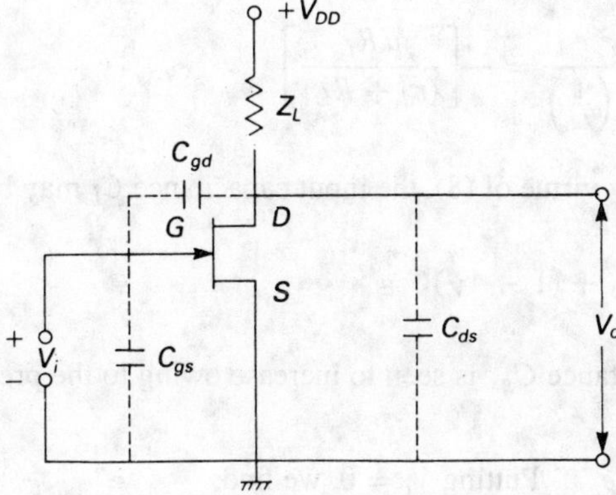

Figure 4.27 *Common-source MOSFET amplifier with different interelectrode capacitances*

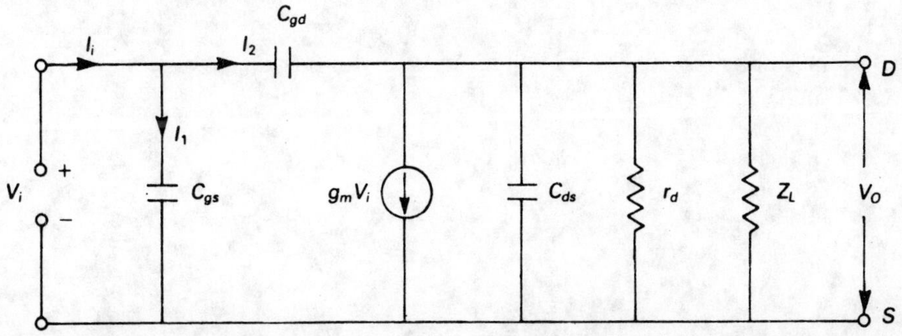

Figure 4.28 *Constant current generator equivalent circuit*

(ii) *Input admittance*

$$I_1 = V_i(j\omega C_{gs}) = V_i\, Y_{gs} \tag{5}$$

and

$$I_2 = (V_i - V_0)(j\omega C_{gd}) = (1 - A_V)V_i\, Y_{gd} \tag{6}$$

Therefore,

$$I_i = I_1 + I_2 = [Y_{gs} + (1 - A_V)Y_{gd}]V_i \tag{7}$$

The input admittance is then given by

$$Y_i = \frac{I_i}{V_i} = Y_{gs} + (1 - A_V)Y_{gd} \tag{8}$$

Thus, if Y_i is required to be small, both Y_{gs} and Y_{gd} also have to be small enough to be negligible.

(iii) *Input capacitance* If $z = R_L$, equation (4) reduces to

$$A_V = \frac{-g_m}{\left(\frac{1}{R_L}\right) + \left(\frac{1}{r_d}\right)} = -\left[\frac{\mu R_L}{(r_d + R_L)}\right] \tag{9}$$

at low frequencies. By virtue of (8), the input capacitance C_i may be expressed as

$$C_i = \frac{Y_i}{j\omega} = C_{gs} + (1 - A_V)C_{gd} \tag{10}$$

Thus the input capacitance C_{gs} is seen to increase owing to the presence of C_{gd}. This is known as the Miller effect.

(iv) *Output admittance* Putting $V_i = 0$, we find,

$$Y_0 = Y_{ds} + Y_{ds} + g_d \tag{11}$$

Exercises

1. An electric field of intensity 10^8 V/ m is applied perpendicular to a plane metallic surface so as to extract electrons out of it into vacuum. Calculate the Schottky lowering and its position relative to the metallic surface. Repeat your calculations when the vacuum is replaced by Si.
[18.96 Å, 0.38 V; 5.47 Å, 0.11 V]

2. A metal of $\phi_m = 4.5$ eV is brought into intimate contact with n-GaP ($\chi = 4$ eV). Calculate

   i) the contact potential,
   ii) the barrier height from the semiconductor end,
   iii) the barrier height from the metal end,
   iv) the barrier height from the metal end when the contact is made with p-type material of arbitrary doping,
   v) the width of the depletion layer,
   vi) the maximum electric field across the junction,
   vii) the drift current over the barrier at 300 K and
   viii) the thermionic current density over the barrier at 300 K.

   ($\phi_s = 4.1$ eV, $\mu_n = 110\,\text{cm}^2/\,\text{Vs}$, $N_d = 10^{20}/\,\text{m}^3$, $m^* = 0.082$ m, $E_G = 2.24$ eV, $\epsilon_s = 11.1$)
   [0.4 eV, 0.4 eV, 0.5 eV, 1.74 eV, 2.216 μ m, 4.03 × 10^5 V/m, 1.47 × 10^{-2}A/m^2, 1.825 × 10^3A/m^2]

3. A metal ($\phi_m = 5.0$ eV) forms a Schottky barrier with a semiconductor ($\chi = 4.05$ eV) doped with donors but having an imperfect surface. By a photoelectric measurement the Schottky barrier height from the metal end is observed to be 0.68 eV. Determine the ideality factor of the semiconductor surface ($E_G = 1.12$ eV and $\phi_0 = 0.7$ eV) [0.49]

4. A sample of n-type Si forms a Schottky barrier with a metal of $\phi_m = 5$ eV. By a photoelectric measurement the Schottky barrier height as determined from the metal end is found to be 0.7 eV. Calculate the ideality factor of the semiconductor surface.($E_G = 1.12$ eV, $\phi_0 = 0.75$ eV, $\chi = 4$ eV)
[0.524]

5. A Schottky barrier diode is fabricated on an n-type Si with $N_d = 1.5 \times 10^{16}\,\text{cm}^{-3}$ by evaporating a metal with $\phi_m = 4.9$ eV. Neglecting the effects due to interface states, calculate the built-in voltage, the barrier height, and the depletion layer width at zero bias. (Assume $T = 300$ K, $\chi = 2.9$ eV, $V_n = 0.01$ eV) [2 eV, 1.99 eV, 4.19 × 10^{-7} m]

6. A 0.5 μ m thick oxide layer is grown on a uniformly doped n-type Si with $N_d = 1.5 \times 10^{15}\,\text{cm}^{-3}$ Assuming the oxide to be charge free, calculate the surface potential and the gate voltage for

a) making the surface intrinsic and
b) creating a strong inversion layer at the surface. Also calculate the maximum width W_m of the surface depletion region. [0.3043 eV, 0.6086 eV; 7279.7Å]

7. Consider an MOS capacitor of area 1 cm^2 made over Si (n-type) with $N_d = 1.5 \times 10^{14}$ cm^{-3} and Al gate. The SiO_2 layer is 0.2 μ m thick. The Si is 20 μ m thick and is grown epitaxially on an n^+Si substrate having $N_d = 10^{-19}$ cm^{-3}. Neglecting interface charges between Si and SiO_2, determine the flat band capacitance, C_{min} and C_{max} for the structure.
[174 pF, 169 pF, 531.24 pF]
8. An ideal MIS junction is formed with p-Si ($N_a = 10^{15}$ cm^{-3}). Calculate

(i) the characteristic Debye length within the semiconductor,
(ii) the flat band capacitance of the junction when the insulator thickness is 2000 Å,
(iii) the potential drop across the semiconductor if a bias of 2.0 V is applied across the MIS junction,
(iv) the charge induced on the metal end of the insulator and
(v) the depletion layer width of the semiconductor.

($\varepsilon_s = 12, \varepsilon_i = 4$)
[1858 Å, 145.3 μ F/ m^2, 0.37 V, 288.64 μ C/ m^2, 7009.9 Å]
9. The surface state density associated with a semiconductor is 10^{10}/ cm^2 V. Such a sample is used to form a non-ideal MIS contact. Calculate the capacitance associated with the surface states. If the work function difference between the metal and the semiconductor is 0.8 eV, calculate by how much the point corresponding to C_{FB} will shift. [1.6 nF/ cm^2, 0.8 eV]
10. A MOSFET which turns on at a gate bias of 1.0 V is conducting a particular current under a drain voltage of 0.1 V. What will be the gate voltage at which the drain current saturates? Also, find out the gate voltage at which the drain current reaches half its saturated value. [1.1 V, 1075 V]
11. A MOSFET has its channel doped with acceptors to a concentration of 10^{20} m^{-3}. The thickness of the oxide layer is 10,000 Å. Presuming the semiconductor surface state density to be negligible, calculate the gate voltage at which the channel conduction begins. ($\varepsilon_i = 3.95$, $\varepsilon_s = 12$ and $n_i = 10^{16}$ m^{-3})
[1.057 V]
12. A MOSFET which turns on at a gate voltage of 1.5 V is operating under a gate voltage of 1.6 V. Calculate the drain voltage at which the current saturation occurs. Find out the ratio of the drain current to its saturated value when $V_d = 0.05$ V. [0.1 V, 0.75]
13. It is desired to produce a potential well in the p-channel of a Si CCD of 1μ m depth. What should be

a) the doping of the channel, and
b) the gate bias needed for this purpose?

($d = 1\mu$ m, $\varepsilon_i = 4$, $\varepsilon_s = 12$ and $n_i = 10^{16}$ m^{-3}) [2.2×10^{13} cm^{-3}, 0.54 V]
14. A Si Schottky barrier photodiode with a junction area of 0.5 0cm^2 has a 100 Å thick Au film to form a barrier. The Si sample is 100 μ m thick, n-type and has a resistivity of 200 Ω cm. The back side of the diode employs a transparent ohmic contact. The front surface of the diode is uniformly illuminated with 0.95μ m light and the incident power is 80 m W. Neglecting the losses in the Au film and assuming unit quantum efficiency and $\alpha = 150$ cm^{-1}, calculate the photocurrent at a reverse voltage of 200 V. [9.48×10^4A/ m^2]

15. Show that the power conversion efficiency of a Schottky barrier solar cell increases with the increasing barrier height and reaches its maximum value when the barrier height becomes equal to the band gap of the semiconductor.
16. A common-source MOSFET amplifier has the following parameters: $g_m = 1.8\,\text{mA/V}$, $r_d = 50\,\text{k}\Omega$, $C_{gs} = 5\,\text{pF}$, $C_{gd} = 3\,\text{pF}$, $R_L = 150\,\text{k}\Omega$ and the amplifier operates at 50 Hz. Calculate the voltage gain and the input capacitance. [2.52, 0.44 pF]
17. Analyze a common-drain MOSFET amplifier at high frequencies and obtain expressions for: (i) voltage gain, (ii) input admittance (iii) input capacitance and (iv) output admittance of the amplifier. [$A_V = (g_m + j\omega C_{gs})R_S/[1+(g_m+g_d+j\omega C_T)R_S]$ where $C_T = (C_{Sn}+C_{ds}+C_{gs})$ $Y_i = [j\omega C_{gd} + (1 - A_V)j\omega C_{gs}]$; $C_i = [C_{gd} + (1 - A_V)C_{gs}]$; $Y_O = (g_m + g_d + j\omega C_T)$]
18. A common-drain MOSFET amplifier has the following parameters : $g_m = 1.5\,\text{mA/V}$, $r_d = 50\,\text{k}\Omega$, $C_{gs} = 3\,\text{pF}$, $C_{ds} = 1\,\text{pF}$, $C_{gd} = 1\,\text{pF}$, $C_{Sn} = 1\,\text{pF}$. $R_S = 100\,\text{k}\Omega$. The amplifier operates at 50 Hz. Calculate: (i) the voltage gain (ii) the input admittance, (iii) the input capacitance, and (iv) the output admittance. [0.99, j $(103\pi \times 10^{-12})$ mho, 1.03 pF, 1.5×10^{-3} mho]

References

[1] Barbe, D.F., 1975, Imaging Devices Using the Charge-Coupled Concept, *Proc. IRE*, **63**, 38.

[2] Beynon, J.D.E., 1975, The Basic Principles of Charge-Coupled Devices, *Micro-electronics*, **7**, 7.

[3] Boyle, W.S., and Smith, G.E., 1970, Charge-Coupled Devices, *Bell System Tech. J.* **49**, 587.

[4] Brews, J.R., 1981, Physics of the MOS Transistors in D.Kahng ed., *Applied Solid-State Science*, Sup.2A, Academic, New York.

[5] Forhman-Bentchkowsky, D., 1970, The Metal-Nitride-Oxide-Silicon (MNOS) Transistor Characteristics & Applications, *Proc. IEEE*, **58**, 207.

[6] Garett, C.G.B. and Brattain, W.H., 1955, Physical Theory of Semiconductor Surfaces, *Phys. Rev.* **99**, 376.

[7] Goetzberger, 1966, Ideal MOS Curves for Si, *Bell Syst. Tech. J.* **45**, 1097.

[8] Grove, A.S., Deal, B.E., Snow, E.H., and Sah, C.T., 1965, Investigation of Thermally Oxidized Silicon Surfaces using MOS Structures, *Solid State Electronics*, **8**, 145.

[9] Hofstein, S.R., and Heiman, F.P., 1963, The Si Insulated-Gate Field-Effect Transistor, *Proc. IEEE*, **51**, 1190.

[10] Ihantola, H.K.J. and Moll, J.L., 1964, Design Theory of a Surface Field-Effect Transistor, *Solid State Electronics*, **7**, 423.

[11] Kim, C.K., 1979, *The Physics of Charge Coupled Devices* in M.J.Howes and D.V. Morgan eds., p.1. Wiley, New York.

[12] Kingston, R.H., and Neustadter, S. F., 1955, Calculation of Space-Charge Electric Field and the Free Carrier Concentration at the Surface of a Semiconductor, *J. Appl., Phys.* **26**, 718.

[13] Mead, C.A., 1966, Schottky Barrier Gate Field-Effect Transistor, *Proc. IEEE*, **54**, 307.

[14] Moll, J.L., 1959, Variable Capacitance with a Large Capacity Change, *Wes. Conv. Rec. Pt*, **3**, 32.

[15] Moore, G., 1979, VLSI Some Fundamental Changes, *IEEE Spectrum*, **16** (4), 30.

[16] Nicolian, E.H., and Brews, J.R., 1982, *MOS Physics & Technology*, Wiley, New York.

[17] Pfann, W.G., and Garrett, C.G.B., 1959, Semiconductor Varactor Using Space-Charge Layers, *Proc. IRE*, **47**, 2011.

[18] Richman, P., 1973, *MOSFETs and Integrated Circuits*, Wiley, New York.

[19] Sequin, C.H., and Tompsett, M.F., 1975, *Charge-Transfer Devices*, Academic, New York.

[20] Terman, L.M., 1962, An Investigation of Surface States at a Si/SiO_2 Interface Employing MOS Diodes, *Solid State Electronics*, **5**, 285.

5 Semiconductor tunnel devices

Electric currents in semiconductor devices flow by various mechanisms. These are tabulated below

Table 5. 1 *Electric current conduction mechanisms in semiconductor devices*

Mechanism	Examples
Drift	Resistors
Diffusion	*pn* Junctions
Thermionic emission	Schottky barrier diodes
Tunnelling	Tunnel diodes
Recombination	LEDs and semiconductor lasers
Generation	Solar cells
Avalanche	IMPATT diodes

Since this chapter will be fully devoted to the description of semiconductor tunnel devices, we will first critically examine the mechanism of the quantum mechanical tunnelling effect. A one-dimensional potential barrier diagram is shown in Fig. 5.1 for this purpose. A microscopic particle, say an electron, is incident upon it with a kinetic energy E such that $E < V_0$ (the barrier height). If the incident particle is a massive one (like a piece of a stone), it is common experience that the particle would be unable to negotiate the barrier region as the latter would reflect it backwards almost immediately after its incidence on it. But, when microscopic particles of a reasonable dimension are incident upon a barrier, it is observed experimentally that a certain fraction of it is always transmitted to the other side of it. Since this phenomenon is believed to be associated with the wave nature of microscopic particles, it is called quantum mechanical tunnelling or tunnelling, in short.

Conventional physics of analyzing this effect rests on the idea that the particle energy is measurable throughout the process of tunnelling and remains constant during its motion as required by the principle of conservation of energy. Since energy is presumed to be measurable at every stage of tunnelling, it is equivalent to assuming that the microscopic particle retains its wave-particle duality while negotiating the potential barrier. Therefore, the Schrodinger's time-independent wave equation, which incorporates the idea of wave-particle duality is employed to analyze the process physically. Wave functions, obtained as solutions of these equations in appropriate regions of space in and around the potential barrier, are matched at appropriate points where the particles appear to enter or leave it. The transmission coefficient or the tunnelling probability of particles is then defined as

$$Z = \frac{|\Psi_{\text{trans}}|^2}{|\Psi_{\text{inc}}|^2} \tag{5.1}$$

where Ψ_{inc} and Ψ_{trans} denote the wave functions at the incident and the transmitted ends of the barrier respectively. Similarly, the reflection coefficient R from the barrier surface is defined by

$$R = \frac{|\Psi_{\text{refl}}|^2}{|\Psi_{\text{inc}}|^2} \tag{5.2}$$

As the total density of particles must be conserved throughout the process, one must have

$$R + Z = 1 \tag{5.3}$$

In this analysis of transmission through a potential barrier, the particle density as well as its energy (or velocity) is considered to be measurable at every point inside it. As such, the tunnelling current density through the barrier should be expressible as,

$$J = J_i Z \tag{5.4}$$

where J_i denotes the incident current density $(= qv_i)$. This theory of tunnelling has, however, failed to account adequately for the current flow through *pn* tunnel junctions and in several other cases.

The problem with the theory can, at once, be traced if one carefully examines the nature of the barrier wave function obtained by the time-independent formalism of the theory. For a rectangular potential barrier, the wave function inside it is expressible as

$$\Psi(x) = C \exp(-\chi x) + D \exp(+\chi x) \tag{5.5}$$

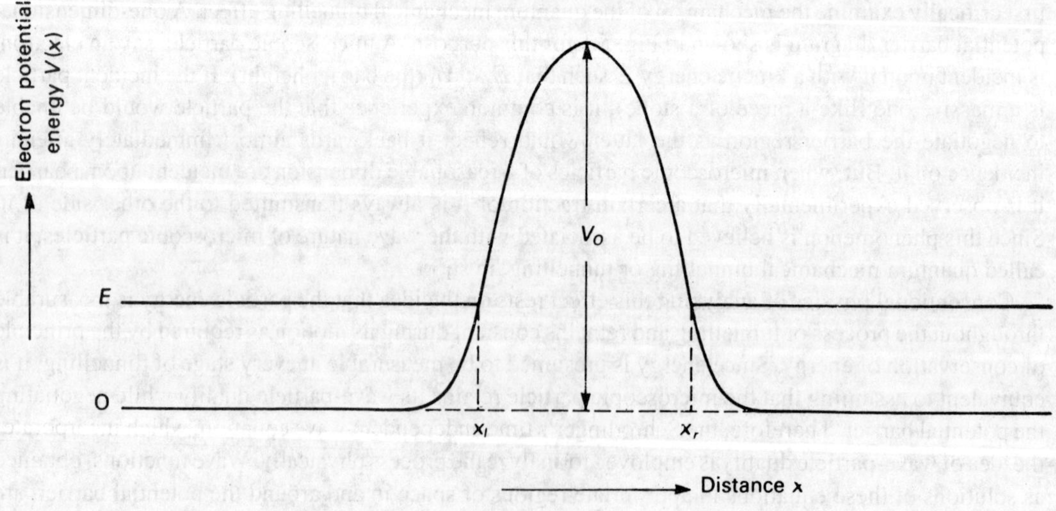

Figure 5.1 A potential barrier of an arbitrary shape

where the symbols have their usual meanings. The physical form of this wave function does not suggest a motion of any known kind through the barrier region. From this equation, when we try to identify the particle wave vector inside the barrier, it turns out to be an imaginary quantity $(i\chi)$. If, at all, there is a real flow of microscopic particles through the barrier, corresponding to the incident wave vector $k = (2mE/h^2)^{1/2}$, (as suggested by (5.4)) it should have been possible to express the barrier wave function as

$$\Psi(x) = [C\ \exp(-\chi x) + D\ \exp(+\chi x)]\ \exp(ikx) \tag{5.6}$$

so that the particles may continue to tunnel through the barrier as a propagating matter wave (corresponding to the wave vector k) with its amplitude being constantly damped. It may however be interesting to note that $|\Psi(x)|^2$, obtained either from (5.5) or (5.6) yields the same result. But, Schrodinger's equation written inside a rectangular barrier will never yield (5.6) as its solution. Since the nature of propagation through the barrier during tunnelling seems very much uncertain, (5.4) cannot be taken as the definition of the tunnel current density. A new description of the tunnelling phenomenon thus seems very much necessary to circumvent the above mentioned problem. With this end in view, we will first examine electron tunnelling through a barrier from the point of view of the principle of quantum measurement and observations. Thereafter, we would analyze the physics of heavily doped semiconductors because not only are they the starting materials for laser diodes but for tunnel diodes, as well. The description of the tunnel effect through a tunnel diode would next be presented on the basis of both the new and the conventional ideas. The physics of other related semiconductor tunnel devices would thereafter be reviewed. This chapter will finally conclude with a description of typical tunnel diode applications.

5.1 Tunnelling from the point of view of quantum measurement

In the beginning, we will first review the conceptual aspects of particles and waves as used in classical and quantum physics. Besides having certain invariant attributes like rest mass, electric charge, etc., a particle in classical physics also occupies a finite extension in space, which cannot be occupied by any other particle simultaneously. It can transfer all or a part of its total momentum and kinetic energy to another particle during a collision. During motion, it describes a definite path or a trajectory characterized by certain constants of motion e.g. its energy and/or angular momentum. The path of the particle during the motion is determined by Hamilton's principle of least action. Particles are regarded as localized bundles of energy and momentum and at any instant of time they are described by the state parameters x (position) and (dx/dt) (velocity). As the motion continues, they evolve continuously following some standard equations based on Newton's laws. Therefore, if the initial values of x and (dx/dt) are known, the particle trajectory may at once be derived.

A wave, in contrast, is a disturbance spread over space and time. It is described by a wave function $\Psi(r, t)$ which characterizes the wave at a position distant r from a reference point and at any time t. Its frequency ν and the wavelength λ are related to one another by the relation

$$u = \nu\ \lambda \tag{5.7}$$

where u denotes the phase velocity of the wave. For a propagating wave, the wave function $\Psi(r, t)$ may be expressed as

$$\Psi(r, t) = A\ \cos\ (k, r - \omega t) \tag{5.8}$$

where A denotes the real amplitude of the wave, $k(= 2\pi/\lambda)$ represents its wave vector and $\omega(= 2\pi/T = 2\pi\nu)$ stands for its angular frequency. Equation (5.8) satisfies the classical wave equation viz.,

$$\nabla^2\Psi(r,t) = \left(\frac{1}{u^2}\right)\left[\frac{\partial^2\Psi(r,t)}{\partial t^2}\right] \tag{5.9}$$

Now, if $\Psi_1,\ \Psi_2,\ \Psi_3...$ represent the probable solutions of (5.9), then a linear superposition of these functions also represents an allowed solution of it. A linear superposition of these wave functions may be represented as

$$\phi(r,t) = \Sigma_i\, C_i\, \Psi_i\,(r,t) \tag{5.10}$$

where C_i s are real constants. The function $\phi(r,t)$ is also a solution of (5.9). Equation (5.10) embodies the principle of superposition. It is interesting to notice that while no two particles can coexist at a certain position in space at a given time, any number of waves, according to (5.10), can coexist at a particular point.

In quantum mechanics, on the other hand, a piece of matter is considered to exhibit wave-particle dualism depending on circumstances. As regards its dual nature, there are two schools of interpretations available. One is led by Albert Einstein and is well known as the statistical interpretation of quantum mechanics. It maintains that a given material entity can either behave as a classical wave or a classical particle at a given instant of time and the quantum theory deals with the statistical properties of the ensemble of identical particles but not with the individual motions of the constituent particles.

The other school, which is led by Neils Bohr (also known as the Copenhagen interpretation), advocates that the laws of quantum mechanics are applicable to individual particles or waves in an ensemble. When a quantum measurement is carried out on a physical parameter (e.g. the energy or the momentum), a wave-packet is generated in the process. The physical dimensions of such a wave-packet is determined by the procedure undertaken to carry out a particular quantum measurement and they are related to one another through the Heisenberg's uncertainty relations, expressed by the following two inequalities:

$$\Delta x\,\Delta p_x \geq h \tag{5.11}$$

and

$$\Delta t\,\Delta E \geq h \tag{5.12}$$

Equations (5.11) and (5.12) are dependent on each other. Because of these relations, it is not difficult to conceive that a plane matter wave in the position (or time) space possesses a delta-function amplitude spectrum in the momentum (or energy) space and vice versa. It must, however, be mentioned at this stage that when a quantum measurement of the aforesaid physical variables are carried out, it is impossible to describe how p_x (or E) and x (or t), as contained in (5.11) and (5.12), vary as continuous functions of their conjugate variables. This is so because h is the least measurable quantum of action. Therefore, while studying a quantum fluctuation phenomenon, one must be able to know beforehand the total fluctuation in one of its variables say, ΔE (or Δp_x) which is likely to occur, so as to be able to follow the changes in its corresponding conjugate variables t (or x). The observation by quantum measurement is regarded to be complete once the uncertainty products contained in (5.11) and (5.12) are realized. A wave-packet, possessing particle characteristics, is produced as a result of such a quantum measurement. Therefore, one may notice that the property of wave-particle duality exhibited by matter is contained in these uncertainty relations. Such a relationship between the wave and the particle characteristics cannot be reconciled on the basis of our classical ideas of particles and waves mentioned earlier. The behaviour of matter at a particular instant of time can either be particle-like or wave-like depending upon the circumstances. If the dimensions of the interacting object, employed for quantum measurement, are larger compared to the matter wavelength, the behaviour of the entity will be particle-like. On the other hand, if the said dimensions are comparable to the particle wavelength, the entity will display its wave characteristics. The present day quantum mechanics rests on Heisenberg's uncertainty relations, expressed by (5.11) and (5.12).

Uncertainties, referred to in the above equations, correspond to individual quantum measurements of the physical variables. If the said physical variables are measured a large number of times, the averages of uncertainties of the different physical variables will not differ much from zero, in the end. Therefore, if quantum averages of physical variables are taken into account, one may still use the classical descriptions of microscopic objects as contained in Newton's equations of motions without any ambiguity (Ehrenfest's theorem).

Now, extending our discussions on quantum measurement, let us next describe the case of the electron diffraction at a one-dimensional slit of width 'a' (say) (Fig. 5.2). An electron beam of a well-defined energy E and momentum p_x is presumed to be incident upon the slit from the left. Since the electron beam has a well-defined momentum p_x to start with, its position uncertainties viz., Δx, Δy and Δz upon measurement in the beginning, turn out to be extremely large. Therefore, the incident electron beam may be regarded to behave almost as an ideal wave, having infinite extensions in all possible directions, but propagating only along the X-axis. If the slit's opening has been set along the Y-axis, the passage of the electron beam through it would require its spatial extension (or the uncertainty) along the Y-direction to be restricted to the slit's width 'a'. Stated mathematically, this implies

$$\Delta y \cong a \tag{5.13}$$

Consequently, the Y-component of electron's momentum, which was initially known precisely, now becomes uncertain by an amount

$$\Delta p_y \cong \frac{h}{a} \tag{5.14}$$

Figure 5.2 illustrates the electron diffraction at a linear slit. An observation screen S is placed parallel to the linear slit at a distance much larger than the slit width. Diffracted electron beams from various portions of the slit would reach the screen at a point P. For the sake of analysis, let us divide the slit into two equal halves. PC makes an angle θ with the horizontal. The path difference between the rays AP and PC is $\Delta = (a/2)\sin\theta$. Now, if

$$\left(\frac{2\pi}{\lambda}\right)\Delta = \left(\frac{2\pi}{\lambda}\right)\left[\left(\frac{a}{2}\right)\sin\,\theta\right] = \pi \tag{5.15}$$

i.e.

$$\theta \cong \frac{\lambda}{a} \tag{5.16}$$

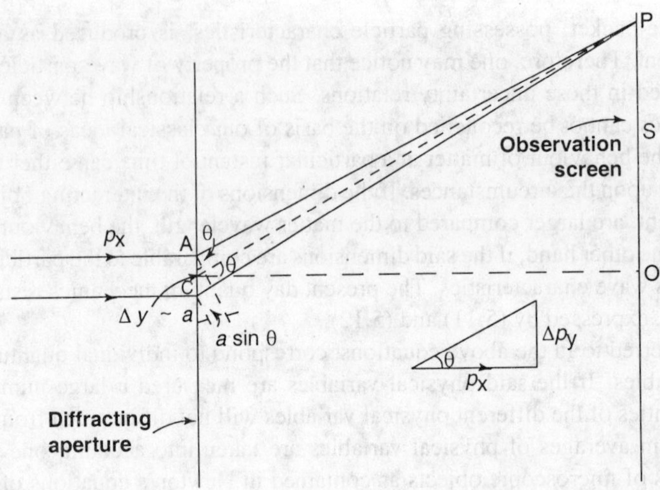

Figure 5.2 *The electron diffraction at a linear slit*

the electron beams at P would interfere destructively, producing a minimum intensity there. The same argument is applicable to all rays which originate from the slit as we move progressively from A to C and from C to B. Hence, when the condition (5.16) is realized, the resultant electron intensity at P, due to diffraction by the slit will be zero. From the triangle of vectors (shown in the inset of Fig. 5.2), we get

$$\theta \cong \frac{\lambda}{a} = \frac{\Delta p_y}{p_x}$$

or

$$\Delta p_y \cong \frac{h}{a} \tag{5.17}$$

which is the same result as given in (5.14). Thus, the conclusion we arrive at from the diffraction approach corroborates that obtained from the uncertainty relation. Therefore, the problem of diffraction at a linear slit can be treated as one of quantum measurement of physical variables of the electron like energy, momentum, position and the corresponding time.

On the basis of the foregoing analysis, we notice that immediately after the diffraction, the Y co-ordinates of the electron's position and momentum which were known precisely beforehand, become uncertain by Δy and Δp_y respectively, as given by (5.13) and (5.14). The diffracting slit in this case, thus behaves as an apparatus intended to determine (or to measure) the position and the momentum co-ordinates of the electron as the latter undergoes a quantum measurement by it. But, the fluctuations produced in the position and the momentum co-ordinates of the electron during the process must be within the limits set by the Heisenberg's uncertainty relations. Owing to such a spread produced in the momentum values, the electron energy, which was precisely known to be E beforehand, must now lie within a range ΔE of it, after diffraction (or quantum measurement), which is given by

$$\Delta E = \frac{(\Delta p_y)^2}{2m} = \frac{h^2}{2ma^2} \tag{5.18}$$

For measurements of Δy, Δp_y, and ΔE, the electron wave must interact with the diffracting aperture for a specific interval of time Δt, which is given by

$$\Delta t \cong \frac{h}{\Delta E} \cong \frac{2ma^2}{h} \cong \frac{a}{\frac{\Delta p_y}{2m}} \tag{5.19}$$

Thus, according to (5.19), the y-component of the electron's velocity which was known to be exactly zero beforehand now becomes uncertain by an amount $[(\Delta p_y)/2m]$, immediately after diffraction.

We may thus note that electrons whose energies were accurately known to be E before incidence upon the slit, find their energies distributed in a range between $(E + \Delta E)$ and $(E - \Delta E)$ immediately after diffraction. The energy range of fluctuation ΔE, according to (5.18), however depends upon the slit width 'a'. We have also noted with interest that due to a finite time Δt, required for such measurements, no information on E, Δp_y or y of electrons can ever be obtained unless the said time Δt elapses.

A question may arise at this stage! Experimentally, the diffraction effect of a mono-energetic electron beam across a narrow slit has been observed but no change in its energy (or frequency) (since $\Delta E = h\,\Delta\nu$) has ever been noticed. The answer to this question may be found by taking the following numerical example: Let us take a slit of width $a = 0.1\,\text{mm} = 10^{-4}\,\text{mm} = \Delta y$. The corresponding uncertainty in its momentum then works out to be $\Delta p_y = (h/a) = 6.62 \times 10^{-30}$ kg m/s. This predicts an energy spread of $\Delta E = [(\Delta p_y)^2/2\,\text{m}] = 1.5 \times 10^{-10}$ eV to be observable after a time interval $\Delta t \cong (h/\Delta E) = 2.76 \times 10^{-5}$ s. If we consider the electrons to be propagating with a velocity of 10^6 m/s, it will have a kinetic energy $E = (1/2\,\text{mv}^2) = 2.8\,\text{eV}$. Thus, we notice that the predicted $\Delta E(1.5 \times 10^{-10}\,\text{eV})$ is too small compared to its kinetic energy E (2.8 eV), to be recorded experimentally. This ΔE is also inversely proportional to the square of the slit width. Let us next consider the case when the width of the slit $a = \Delta y = \lambda$ (the electron wavelength). In this case the intensity of the diffracted spectrum would be too weak to be observable. But, it is interesting to evaluate ΔE. The electron wavelength corresponding to $v = 10^6$ m/s then works out to be $\lambda = 0.73 \times 10^{-9}$ m. The corresponding uncertainty in momentum then follows to be $\Delta p_y \cong (h/a) \cong (h/\lambda) \cong 9.07 \times 10^{-25}$ kg m/s. The energy uncertainty corresponding to this Δp_y then is $\Delta E = [(\Delta p_y)^2/2m] = 2.8\,\text{eV}$, which turns out to be the same as its kinetic energy E. This would be observable after a time interval of $\Delta t \cong (h/\Delta E) \cong 1.465 \times 10^{-14}$ s. We may then conclude that if $\Delta y \cong a \cong \lambda$, $\Delta p_y \cong (h/a) \cong (h/\lambda) \cong p_x$, then $\Delta E = [(\Delta p_y)^2/2m] \cong [(p_x)^2/2m] = E$.

We may express the same fact in the following words: If the slit width is of the order of the electron wavelength, the energy uncertainty of electrons, as a result of diffraction (or quantum measurement), follows to be of the order of the incident electron energy itself. But such an energy uncertainty is observable only after a lapse of time $\Delta t \cong (h/\Delta E)$. This diffraction effect, where a plane matter wave interacts with a one-dimensional slit (which acts as the measuring apparatus) for a definite interval of time and then collapses into a wave packet formed due to the superposition of a large number of scattered plane matter wavelets, is indeed an example of quantum measurement of physical parameters of electrons. The plane waves constituting the wave packet have a continuously varying but limited phase difference among themselves. As concluded earlier, the dimensions of the wave packet (viz., Δy, Δp_y, ΔE and Δt) are however set by the width a of the diffraction aperture. The reason why the aperture is technically called an apparatus and the process, a quantum measurement must now be obvious.

We may now examine the tunnel effect on the basis of quantum measurement as laid down above. The example of diffraction at a single slit clearly illustrated how an electron wave can be scattered directly into the position space. Since, the variables E, t, p_y and y for an electron are mutually interdependent through Heisenberg's uncertainty relations, similar diffraction effects could equally well be observed in the energy, momentum or the time spaces under appropriate conditions. But, in order to generate quantum fluctuations in the energy space, we require an apparatus in that space (like the linear slit in the diffraction experiment). A potential barrier as shown in Fig. 5.1 provides such an apparatus. A stream of electrons of kinetic energy $E(< V_0)$ is shown to be incident upon it at $x = x_l$. Beyond this position, electrons as classical particles face a forbidden region of energy height $(V_0 - E)$. At $x = x_l$, electrons are expected to be reflected totally if they behave as classical particles because they would be incapable of propagating with a negative kinetic energy through the barrier region. But, for microscopic particles, like electrons, fluctuations in their physical variables are allowed during a quantum measurement within the framework of the Heisenberg's uncertainty relations, as discussed above. As electrons of a specific kinetic energy $E(< V_0)$ approaches a potential barrier, it slows down gradually until its kinetic energy (or velocity) vanishes at $x = x_l$. Beyond this position, the barrier demands that the electron must acquire a negative kinetic energy if it happens to penetrate it and propagate thereafter. As this is impossible for a material particle, the electron energy E is set into an oscillation about its original value with an amplitude

$$\Delta E \cong (V_0 - E). \tag{5.20}$$

As already discussed earlier, this quantum fluctuation in energy cannot be observed as long as the electron wave interacts with the barrier. On the basis of Heisenberg's uncertainty relation, the time for the electron-barrier interaction must be given by

$$\tau = \Delta t \geq \frac{h}{V_0 - E} \tag{5.21}$$

As the electron energy during its interaction with the potential barrier is in a state of measurement, we may regard the barrier electron states to be under evolution. As the time-dependent energy scattering (or the quantum measurement of energy) continues for the duration of τ seconds and takes place over a distance $W[= (x_r - x_l)$, the barrier width], the speed of measurement (which can be recorded only after τ seconds) may be expressed as (W/τ). Also, if Δp represents the corresponding momentum fluctuation introduced by the quantum measurement process, the group velocity of the generated wave packet with which it will move after τ seconds, works out to be $(\Delta E/\Delta p)$. Hence, the velocity of electron tunnelling, which becomes observable after the process may be expressed as

$$v = \frac{\Delta E}{\Delta p} = \frac{W}{\tau} \tag{5.22}$$

Since, $\Delta E \tau \geq h$, it follows from (5.22) that

$$\Delta p \, W \geq h \tag{5.23}$$

But, we know that

$$\Delta p = (2m\Delta E)^{1/2} = [2m\,(V_0 - E)]^{1/2} = \hbar\chi \text{ (say)} \tag{5.24}$$

where χ is defined as the barrier penetration constant and measures the maximum uncertainty introduced in the electron wave vector during the quantum measurement process. Combining (5.23) and (5.24), one finds

$$\chi W \geq 2\pi \tag{5.25}$$

Equation (5.25) connects the barrier height to its width and sets a lower limit to χW for the observation of the tunnel effect. Combining (5.22) and (5.24), we get

$$v = \frac{\Delta E}{(2m\Delta E)^{1/2}} = \left[\frac{\Delta E}{2m}\right]^{1/2} = \frac{h\chi}{2m} \tag{5.26}$$

5.2 Analysis of the tunnel effect

Conventionally, while describing tunnelling of microscopic particles through a potential barrier, their potential energies inside the barrier are identified exactly as given by the barrier shape. The particles, while tunnelling are believed to follow a linear trajectory passing through the classical turning points x_ℓ and x_r of the potential barrier (Fig. 5.1). Based on this contention, two seemingly distinct but physically identical formalisms viz., time-independent and time-dependent perturbation formalism came into use. In the time-independent approach, we employ Schrodinger's time-independent wave equation in the barrier region to describe the tunnel effect as it takes care of the wave-particle dualism, which is presumed to be displayed by electrons during tunnelling. In the time-dependent perturbation formalism, on the other hand, two barrier states X_l and X_r (obtained by solving time-independent Schrodinger's equation in the barrier region) are identified. The tunnelling transition, from one to the other, is presumed to be initiated by a perturbing term $H_1(t)$ in the Hamiltonian (not identified). Due to this time-dependent perturbation, the barrier states are presumed to belong to two different energies, which differ by an infinitesimal amount (as induced by the perturbing term of the Hamiltonian). The barrier wave function is thereafter formulated on the basis of the laws of the time-dependent perturbation theory. In the limit when $H_1(t)$ tends to zero, both the above mentioned approaches of studying tunnelling become exactly identical to one another.

The problem with the conventional tunnelling description should now be obvious because it regards the particle trajectory to exist inside the barrier. Such a particle motion through a barrier can never be traced or observed by any experiment. On account of this, the conventional ways of defining the tunnelling time and the tunnelling current density seems inappropriate.

The conventional theories of tunnelling have failed to account for the limit of resolution of the field emission microscope. Esaki's formula, representing the tunnelling current density through a *pn* tunnel diode, also cannot be explained by the prevailing notions of the tunnelling theory. The latter also failed to account adequately for the flow of a super-current through a Josephson junction. It now remains to see whether our theory of tunnelling, based on quantum measurement, introduced in this chapter, is able to account for these unexplained effects satisfactorily.

In the last section, we analyzed the problem of tunnelling qualitatively, in the light of quantum measurement principles, where we regarded the barrier electronic states to undergo evolution over the tunnelling period of τ seconds. As a result of the quantum measurement, the incident electron energy E of electrons undergoes a time-dependent scattering by the potential barrier such that the energy of the transmitted electrons lies anywhere between $(E + \Delta E)$ and $(E - \Delta E)$ after τ seconds where $\Delta E = (V_0 - E)$. In other words, in such a case, the transmitted electron energy is required to be different from the incident one. At first sight, such a notion seems to violate the principle of conservation of energy, which is followed very rigorously in the tunnelling studies. But, considering the tunnelling of a very large number of particles, their average energy uncertainty after the process is not expected to be much different from zero. Thus the classical laws become operative when the quantum averages of physical variables are taken into account. Due to the energy fluctuation effect, the time-dependent part of the barrier wave function during tunnelling may be represented as

$$T(t) = T_0 \exp\left[-\left(\frac{i}{\hbar}\right)(E_l \pm \Delta E)t\right] \tag{5.27}$$

which becomes an observable only after τ seconds. In (5.27), E_l denotes the incident electron energy from the left. Writing (5.27) in a differential form, we get

$$\left[\frac{i\hbar}{T(t)}\right]\left[\frac{dT(t)}{dt}\right] \pm \Delta E = E_l \tag{5.28}$$

The electron kinetic energy (T_k) and the potential energy (V_P) also undergo fluctuations during tunnelling, so that the total electronic energy remains constant throughout the process. That is,

$$\Delta T_k + \Delta V_P = E_l \tag{5.29}$$

where ΔT_k and ΔV_P represent fluctuations in kinetic and potential energies of an electron respectively, produced during tunnelling. The fluctuations in the potential energy may range from 0 to V_0 (the maximum height of the barrier). Expressing (5.29) in the operator formalism, we find

$$-\left(\frac{\hbar^2}{2m}\right)\left(\frac{d^2}{dx^2}\right) + V_0 = E_l \tag{5.30}$$

Unlike in conventional physics of tunnelling, one now allows a range of values to the kinetic and potential energies of the tunnelling electron. As already mentioned, the effects of such energy fluctuations are observable only after a time of τ seconds (the time required for the electron-barrier interaction to be over). Now, if we presume the space part of the barrier wave function to be $X(x)$, we may use (5.30) to write

$$-\left(\frac{\hbar^2}{2m}\right)\left[\frac{d^2X(x)}{dx^2}\right] + V_0\,X(x) = E_l\,X(x)$$

Rearranging, we may write

$$-\left(\frac{\hbar^2}{2m}\right)\left[\frac{1}{X(x)}\right]\left(\frac{d^2}{dx^2}\right) + V_0 = E_l \tag{5.31}$$

Combining (5.28) and (5.31), we may now write

$$-\left(\frac{\hbar^2}{2m}\right)\left[\frac{1}{X(x)}\right]\left(\frac{d^2}{dx^2}\right) + V_0 = \left[\frac{i\hbar}{T(t)}\right]\left[\frac{dT(t)}{dt}\right] \pm \Delta E = E_l \tag{5.32}$$

If $\Psi(x,t) = X(x)T(t)$ denotes the total barrier wave function, we get after multiplying (5.32) by $\Psi(x,t)$

$$\left[-\left(\frac{\hbar^2}{2m}\right)\left(\frac{\partial^2}{\partial x^2}\right) + V_0 \pm \Delta E\right]\Psi(x,t) = i\hbar\left[\frac{\partial\Psi(x,t)}{\partial t}\right]$$

i.e.,

$$H\,\Psi(x,t) = [H(x) + H(t)]\,\Psi(x,t) = i\hbar\left[\frac{\partial\Psi(x,t)}{\partial t}\right] \tag{5.33}$$

We may now identify the tunnelling barrier Hamiltonian as

$$H = \left[-\left(\frac{\hbar^2}{2m}\right)\left(\frac{\partial^2}{\partial x^2}\right) + V_0 \pm \Delta E\right] \tag{5.34}$$

where the space and the time parts of the Hamiltonian may be identified as

$$H(x) = -\left(\frac{\hbar^2}{2m}\right)\left(\frac{\partial^2}{\partial x^2}\right) + V_0 \tag{5.35}$$

and

$$H(t) = \pm\,\Delta E \tag{5.36}$$

respectively. The space part of the wave equation (5.31) may now be put in the following standard form:

$$\frac{d^2X(x)}{dx^2} - \chi^2\,X(x) = 0 \tag{5.37}$$

where

$$\chi^2 = \left(\frac{2m}{\hbar^2}\right)[V_0 - E] \tag{5.38}$$

The allowed solutions of (5.37) are given by

$$X_l(x) = \alpha\,\exp\,(-\chi x) \tag{5.39}$$

and

$$X_r(x) = \beta\,\exp\,(+\chi x) \tag{5.40}$$

where α and β are two suitable constants. Combining (5.39) and (5.40) appropriately with (5.27), we may write the time-dependent barrier wave function as

$$\Psi(x,t) = a_l(t)X_l(x)\,\exp\left(\frac{-iE_lt}{\hbar}\right) + a_r(t)X_r(x)\,\exp\left(\frac{-iE_rt}{\hbar}\right) \tag{5.41}$$

where $a_l(t)$ and $a_r(t)$ are the time-dependent coefficients which determine the rate of time- dependent scattering from the incident to the transmitted end. While writing (5.41), we presumed

$$E_r = E_l \pm \Delta E = E_l \pm \left(\frac{\hbar}{\tau}\right) \tag{5.42}$$

Equation (5.41) clearly expresses the fact that the second part of the wave function is built up at the expense of the first one as the quantum measurement (or the time-dependent scattering) by the potential barrier progresses. $a_r(t)$ grows to its fullest size at $t = \tau$ seconds when a quantum just manages to tunnel through. This phenomenon is repeated periodically after every τ seconds as the tunnelling of subsequent quanta follow. The wave function (5.37) becomes an observable after every τ seconds.

5.2.1 Tunnelling probability

In usual tunnelling problems, $a_r(t)$ (scattered wave amplitude) is very small compared to $a_l(t)$. We may then regard $a_l(t)\sim 1$, and $d/dt[a_l(t)] = 0$. Combining (5.33) and (5.41) and imposing the above approximations, we obtain

$$i\hbar \frac{d}{dt}[a_r(t)]\, X_r(x) = (\pm\Delta E)\, X_\ell(x)\, \exp(-i\omega_{lr}t) \tag{5.43}$$

where $\omega_{lr} = (\omega_l - \omega_r) = (E_l - E_r)/\hbar$. Multiplying (5.43) by $X_r^*(x)\,dx$ and integrating over the barrier extremities, one obtains

$$i\hbar \frac{d}{dt}[ar(t)] \int_{X_\ell}^{X_r} |X_r(x)|^2\, dx = T_{\ell r}\, \exp(-i\omega_{\ell r}t) \tag{5.44}$$

where

$$T_{lr} = \int_{X_l}^{X_r} X_r^*(\pm\Delta E)\, X_\ell dx = \pm\,\alpha\beta^*(V_0 - E)W = \pm\,\alpha\beta^*\left(\frac{\hbar^2\chi^2}{2m}\right)W \tag{5.45}$$

Next, integrating a_r(t) in (5.44), we find

$$a_r(t) = \left[\frac{T_{lr}\delta}{(\hbar\,\omega_{lr})S}\right][\exp(-i\omega_{lr}t) - 1] \tag{5.46}$$

where

$$S = \int_{X_l}^{X_r} |X_r(x)|^2 dx \tag{5.47}$$

and δ introduces an unaccounted phase difference between $a_\ell(t)$ and $a_r(t)$. Equation (5.46) may further be simplified as

$$a_r(t) = \left[\frac{(-2i\delta)T_{lr}\ \exp\left(\dfrac{-i\omega_{lr}t}{2}\right)}{\hbar S}\right]\left[\sin\frac{\left(\dfrac{\omega_{lr}t}{2}\right)}{\omega_{lr}}\right] \tag{5.48}$$

Substituting for T_{lr} and S from (5.45) and (5.47), one obtains

$$\beta\, a_r(t) = \left[\frac{(-i\delta)\,\alpha\,\hbar\,\chi^2\,\tau\ \exp\left(\dfrac{-i\omega_{lr}\tau}{2}\right)}{m\ \exp\,(2\chi W)}\right]\left[\frac{\sin\left(\dfrac{\omega_{lr}\tau}{2}\right)}{\dfrac{\omega_{lr}\tau}{2}}\right] \tag{5.49}$$

While deriving (5.49), it was presumed that $\chi W \sim 1$. Such a relation follows immediately from Heisenberg's uncertainty relation $\Delta k.\Delta x \sim 1$. The uncertainty in electron's position during tunnelling is $\Delta x = W$ (barrier width) while the uncertainty in the electron's wave vector Δk is χ. The unknown coefficient α may now be evaluated by matching the incident wave with the barrier wave function. The former may be represented as

$$\Psi_{\text{inc}}(x,t) = [\exp\,(ikx) + R\ \exp\,(-ikx)]\ \exp\,(-i\omega_l t) \tag{5.50}$$

Presuming $a_r(t) \ll a_\ell(t)$, we find as a result of matching (5.41) with (5.50) at $x = x_\ell$

$$\alpha = \left[\frac{2k}{k+i\chi}\right]\ \exp\,(ikx_l) \tag{5.51}$$

Next, substituting $\delta = -\ \exp\,(i\theta_0)$ (say) and $\tau = (\hbar/2\Delta E) = (m/\hbar\chi^2)$ in (5.49) and substituting for α from (5.51) in (5.49), we get

$$\beta\, a_r(t) = i\alpha\ \exp\,(-2\chi W)\ \exp\left[-i\left\{\left(\frac{\omega_{lr}\tau}{2}\right) - \theta_0\right\}\right]\left[\frac{\sin\left(\dfrac{\omega_{lr}\tau}{2}\right)}{\left(\dfrac{\omega_{lr}\tau}{2}\right)}\right] \tag{5.52}$$

Taking $a_l(t) \sim 1$, the barrier wave function (5.41) may be expressed as

$$\Psi(x,t) = X_l(x)\ \exp\,(-i\omega_l t) + a_r(t)X_r(x)\ \exp\,(-i\omega_r t) \tag{5.53}$$

Using (5.53) we may immediately write the expression for the tunnelling probability at the far end of the barrier as

$$\begin{aligned} Z(W,\tau) = |\Psi(w,\tau)|^2 &= |X_l|^2 + |a_r(\tau)|^2|X_r|^2 \\ &+ [X_l^* X_r a_r(\tau)\ \exp\,(i\omega_{lr}\tau) + X_l X_r^* a_r^*(\tau)\ \exp\,(-i\omega_{lr}\tau)] \end{aligned} \tag{5.54}$$

Substituting for X_l and X_r from (5.39) and (5.40) in (5.54), we find

$$Z(W,\tau) = |\alpha|^2 \exp(-2\chi W) + |\beta|^2 |a_r(\tau)|^2 \exp(2\chi W) + \alpha\beta^* a_r^*(\tau) \exp(-i\omega_{lr}\tau) + a^*\beta a_r(\tau) \exp(i\omega_{lr}\tau) \tag{5.55}$$

Substituting for α and $\beta a_r(\tau)$ from (5.51) and (5.52) in (5.55), we obtain

$$Z(W,\tau) = \left[\frac{4k^2}{k^2+\chi^2}\right] \exp(-2\chi W) \left[1 + \left\{\frac{\sin^2\left(\frac{\omega_{lr}\tau}{2}\right)}{\left(\frac{\omega_{lr}\tau}{2}\right)^2}\right\} - 2\sin\left\{\left(\frac{\omega_{lr}\tau}{2}\right) + \theta_0\right\} \frac{\sin\frac{\omega_{lr}\tau}{2}}{\left(\frac{\omega_{lr}\tau}{2}\right)}\right] \tag{5.56}$$

At the energy of incidence i.e., $\omega_{lr} = 0$, the above equation reduces to

$$Z(W) = \left[\frac{8k^2}{(k^2+\chi^2)}\right] \exp(-2\chi W)(1 - \sin\theta_0) \tag{5.57}$$

Since (5.57) is also applicable to a rectangular potential barrier, this must lead to the following tunnelling probability expression

$$Z(W) = \left[\frac{16k^2\chi^2}{(k^2+\chi^2)^2}\right] \exp(-2\chi W) \tag{5.58}$$

Since, both the expressions are the same, it follows that

$$\sin\theta_0 = \frac{(k^2-\chi^2)^2}{(k^2+\chi^2)^2} \tag{5.59}$$

Solving for θ_0, one obtains,

$$\theta_0 = \left(\frac{\pi}{2}\right) - 2\tan^{-1}\left(\frac{\chi}{k}\right) \tag{5.60}$$

An independent evaluation of θ_0 also confirms this value.

According to the quantum measurement analysis, the tunnelling probability, given by (5.56), is independent of the barrier shape and it depends only on the barrier height and the width. This equation presents the whole probability spectrum of electron emission at the far end of the potential barrier as a result of tunnelling. This equation clearly predicts that an electron incident at the energy E_l has a finite probability of tunnel emission at any energy E_r around it.

5.2.2 Tunnelling current density

Firstly this type of current density has to be distinguished from the conventional one. Conventional current densities are caused due to the flow of real particles through any given region of space. By now, it should be easy to recognize that tunnelling is not caused by any real flow of material particles. The particle probability density, in fact, grows during tunnelling and it becomes observable only after the particle-barrier interaction is over. Hence, the rate of growth of the probability density in the barrier region at the end of tunnelling, integrated over its width, multiplied by the electronic charge must give the required tunnelling current density. This may readily be obtained from the equation of continuity expressed as

$$\left(\frac{dJ}{dx}\right) - q\frac{\partial}{\partial t}(\Psi\Psi^*) = 0 \tag{5.61}$$

As the probability density becomes an observable quantity after every τ second, the tunnelling current density should be expressed as

$$J = q\int_{X_l}^{X_r} \frac{\partial}{\partial t}(\Psi\Psi^*)|_{t=\tau} dx \tag{5.62}$$

In the above expression (q) denotes the charge carried by each electron. Using (5.54), we may now write at any point of the barrier

$$\begin{aligned}(\Psi\Psi^*) &= |\alpha|^2 \exp[-2\chi(x-x_l)] + |\beta|^2\,|a_r(t)|^2 \exp[2\chi(x-x_l)]\\ &\quad + [\alpha\beta^* a_r^*(t)\exp(-i\omega_{lr}t) + \alpha^*\beta a_r(t)\exp(i\omega_{lr}t)]\end{aligned} \tag{5.63}$$

To obtain the tunnelling current density, we differentiate (5.63) with respect to t, to obtain,

$$\begin{aligned}\frac{\partial}{\partial t}(\Psi\Psi^*) &= |\beta|^2\frac{d}{dt}\,|a_r(t)|^2 \exp[2\chi(x-x_l)]\\ &\quad + \left[\alpha\beta^*\left(\frac{d}{dt}\right)a_r^*(t)\exp(-i\omega_{lr}t) + \alpha^*\beta\left(\frac{d}{dt}\right)a_r(t)\exp(i\omega_{lr}t)\right]\\ &\quad + [-i\omega_{lr}\alpha\beta^* a_r^*(t)\exp(-i\omega_{lr}t) + i\omega_{lr}\alpha^*\beta a_r(t)\exp(i\omega_{lr}t)]\\ &= E_1 + F_1 + G_1 \text{ (say)}\end{aligned} \tag{5.64}$$

From (5.48), one may obtain

$$\begin{aligned}|a_r(t)|^2 &= \left[\frac{4\,|T_{lr}|^2}{\hbar^2 S^2}\right]\left[\frac{\sin^2\left(\frac{\omega_{lr}t}{2}\right)}{(\omega_{lr})^2}\right]\\ &= \frac{[4\hbar^2|\alpha|^2\chi^4]}{[m^2|\beta|^2\exp(4\chi W)]}\left[\frac{\sin^2\left(\frac{\omega_{lr}t}{2}\right)}{(\omega_{lr})^2}\right]\end{aligned}$$

where we have substituted for $|T_{lr}|^2$ from (5.45) and S from (5.47). We next differentiate $|a_r(t)|^2$ with respect to t, to obtain,

$$\frac{d}{dt}\,|a_r(t)|^2 = \left[\frac{h^2|\alpha\,|^2 2\,\chi^4}{m^2\,|\beta|^2\exp(4\chi W)}\right]\left\{\frac{\sin(\omega_{lr}t)}{\omega_{lr}}\right\}$$

We may then write

$$E_1 = \left[\frac{2h^2|\alpha|^2\chi^4 \exp\{2\chi(x - x_l)\}}{m^2 \exp(4\chi W)}\right]\left\{\frac{\sin(\omega_{lr}t)}{\omega_{lr}}\right\} \tag{5.65}$$

Next, to derive an expression for F_1, we differentiate $|a_r(t)|$ in (5.48) with respect to time to get

$$\frac{d}{dt}[a_r(t)] = -\left[\frac{i\hbar\,\delta\,\alpha\,\chi^2 \exp(-i\omega_{lr}t)}{m\beta \exp(2\chi W)}\right] \tag{5.66}$$

We then get

$$F_1 = -\left[\frac{2\,|\alpha|^2\,\hbar\chi^2 \exp(-2\chi W)}{m}\right]\sin\theta_0 \tag{5.67}$$

Finally, to determine G_1, we notice from (5.46) that

$$a_r(t) = \left[\frac{(-\delta)\,T_{lr}\,\{1 - \exp(-i\omega_{lr}t)\}}{(\hbar\,\omega_{lr})\,S}\right]$$

$$= \alpha\,\hbar\,\chi^2\left[\frac{\exp(i\theta_0) - \exp\{-i\,(\omega_{lr}t - \theta_0)\}}{m\beta\omega_{lr}\exp(2\chi W)}\right]$$

Hence,

$$G_1 = \left[\frac{2\,|\alpha|^2\,\hbar\chi^2 \exp(-2\chi W)}{m}\right][\sin\theta_0 + \sin(\omega_{lr}t + \pi + \theta_0)] \tag{5.68}$$

Combining E_1, F_1, G_1 in (5.64), we get

$$\frac{\partial}{\partial t}(\Psi\Psi^*)\Big|_{t=\tau} = \left[\frac{2\hbar^2\,|\alpha|^2\,\chi^4\tau \exp\{2\chi(x - x_l)\}}{m^2 \exp(4\chi W)}\right]\left\{\frac{\sin(\omega_{lr}\tau)}{(\omega_{lr}\tau)}\right\}$$

$$+\left[\frac{2\,|\alpha|^2\,\hbar\chi^2 \exp(-2\chi W)}{m}\right][\sin\,\theta_0 + \sin(\omega_{lr}\tau + \pi + \theta_0)] \tag{5.69}$$

Substituting (5.69) in (5.62), we obtain after necessary simplifications,

$$J = J_{01}\left[\frac{\sin(\omega_{lr}\tau)}{\omega_{lr}\tau}\right] + J_{02}\,\sin(\omega_{lr}\tau + \phi_0)] \tag{5.70}$$

where

$$\phi_0 = (\pi + \theta_0) = \pi + \left(\frac{\pi}{2}\right) - 2\tan^{-1}\left(\frac{\chi}{k}\right)$$

$$= \left(\frac{3\pi}{2}\right) - 2\tan^{-1}\left(\frac{\chi}{k}\right) \tag{5.71}$$

$$J_{01} = \frac{q\hbar^2\chi^3\tau\ |\alpha|^2\ \exp(-2\chi W)}{m^2} = \frac{4q\hbar k^2\chi \exp(-2\chi W)}{m\ (k^2+\chi^2)} \tag{5.72}$$

$$= q\left(\frac{\hbar k}{m}\right)\left[\frac{16qk^2\chi^2 \exp(-2\chi W)}{(k^2+\chi^2)^2}\right]\left[\frac{k^2+\chi^2}{4k\chi}\right] \tag{5.73}$$

$$= J_{\text{conv}}\left[\frac{k^2+\chi^2}{4k\chi}\right] \tag{5.74}$$

and

$$J_{02} = \frac{2q\hbar\chi^2 W\ |\alpha|^2\ \exp(-2\chi W)}{m} = \frac{8q\hbar k^2\chi^2 W \exp(-2\chi W)}{m\ (k^2+\chi^2)} \tag{5.75}$$

$$= q\left(\frac{\hbar k}{m}\right)\left[\frac{16qk^2\chi^2 \exp(-2\chi W)}{(k^2+\chi^2)^2}\right]\left[\frac{(k^2+\chi^2)W}{2k}\right] \tag{5.76}$$

$$= J_{\text{conv}}\left[\frac{(k^2+\chi^2)W}{2k}\right] \tag{5.77}$$

where the conventional tunnelling current density is given by $J_{\text{conv}} = q(\hbar k/m)Z$. Comparing (5.74) and (5.77), we find

$$J_{02} = (2\chi W)\ J_{01} \tag{5.78}$$

Equation (5.70) represents the tunnelling current density generated by a single incident electron, incident at an energy E_l and tunnelling at the energy E_r on the other side such that the difference between them is infinitesimally small, because of a large time of 1 second required for the tunnelling current density to develop.

5.2.3 Resonant tunnelling

During the normal electron tunnelling across a potential barrier, we have noticed that when an electron of a kinetic energy E falls upon the potential barrier of any shape but of a height V_0, (such that $E < V_0$), the electron energy undergoes a time-dependent scattering for a specified period of time to appear at any energy between $(E + \Delta E)$ and $(E - \Delta E)$ where $\Delta E = (V_0 - E)$ denotes the barrier height for the electron. Such a scattering in energy is due to the incapability of the electron to acquire a negative kinetic energy during tunnelling as dictated by the potential barrier and be still moving inside it. The consequent growth of the electron probability density in the scattered states gives rise to a spectrum in the transmission coefficient of the field-emitted electrons. We have also seen that the time rate of the growth of the probability density in the scattered states, on the other hand, also determines the tunnelling current density The minimum time for scattering before the effects due to quantum measurement becomes observable determines the tunnelling time.

During single electron tunnelling across a potential barrier, the electron intensity decreases significantly. Therefore, when the question of electron tunnelling across a pair of symmetrical barriers is

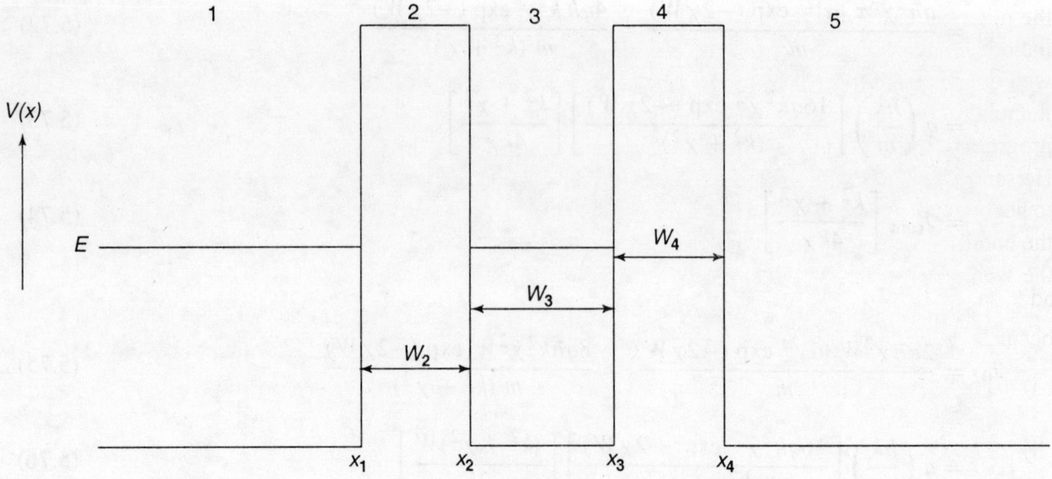

Figure 5.3 *A double barrier model*

considered (Fig. 5.3), not enough tunnelling is expected to occur through them. But, the results are quite different when the following conditions are satisfied viz.,

$$\chi_2 W_2 = \chi_4 W_4 \tag{5.79}$$

where

$$\chi_2^2 = \chi_4^2 = \left(\frac{2m}{\hbar^2}\right)(V_0 - E) \tag{5.80}$$

This condition is easily realized if the barriers of the double barrier system are of equal heights and widths respectively. Secondly,

$$k_1 = \chi_2 = k_3 = \chi_4 = k_5 \tag{5.81}$$

implies that the electron energy is equal to the effective barrier height faced by the electron. Thirdly, the condition

$$k_3 W_3 = \left(n + \frac{1}{2}\right)\pi \tag{5.82}$$

must be realized. We, however, know that at a quantum well state, one must always realize the condition $k_3 W_3 = n\pi$. Now, when an electron enters the quantum well at the quantum well energy at $x = x_2$ and meets a wave reflected at x_3, the net phase difference between them becomes $[(2\pi/\lambda)(2W_3) + \pi] = [2k_3 W_3 + \pi] = (2n + 1)\pi$. Hence, the two waves destroy each other by the destructive interference process. In this case, the condition $k_3 W_3 = n\pi$, reduces to (5.82) as the effects of reflections at x_3 (the interface between the rarer and a denser medium) is considered. When the above-mentioned three conditions are simultaneously satisfied, an unattenuated electron transfer through the double barrier system is predicted. Such a phenomenon is known as the resonant transmission. Although the potential barrier 2 tends to induce a quantum fluctuation to energy E by $\Delta E = (V_0 - E)$ of the incident electron incident from the region 1, the availability of a very narrow energy level within the well does not allow the electron to appear, unless the width of the wave packet generated by quantum fluctuation within the barrier 2, matches with the width of the quantum well energy level. As time progresses, the energy width of the wave packet decreases according to a linear relation (given by the Heisenberg's uncertainty principle). Consequently, the incident electron from region 1 would be able to negotiate the barrier 2 and appear in region 3 after a reasonably long period of time, as determined by the energy level width of the quantum well. Also, on account of multiple reflections occurring within the well, the electron wave amplitude inside it constantly builds up. Under such circumstances, and when the above mentioned three conditions are simultaneously fulfilled, the following set of events occur

i) The currents due to the forward and reflected waves within the well (region 3) almost cancel one another, leaving only the incident current upon the barrier to be propagating in the right direction;
ii) The current reflected at the interface of region 3 and 4 tunnel back through the barrier 2 to completely annul the reflected current at the interface of region 1 and allowing only the incident current to flow there (region 1).

The ongoing current within the well whose amplitude is already augmented due to the multiple reflection effect tunnels out of the barrier 4, producing a current in region 5 which is of the same magnitude as the incident current. As a result of all these effects, a current equal in magnitude as the incident current, flows through every region of space of the double barrier system, giving rise to the phenomenon of resonant tunnelling.

5.3 Heavy-doping effects

Semiconductor tunnel and laser diodes use substrates which are doped with impurities in excess of a concentration of $10^{18}/\text{cm}^3$. The properties of these semiconductors are somewhat different from the lightly doped ones. The important consequences of heavier dopings are: (i) the location of the Fermi energy level within the main semiconductor bands, and (ii) the narrowing of the semiconductor energy gap. At lower impurity densities ($\sim 10^{15}/\text{cm}^3$), the impurity states existing within the semiconductor energy gap are shallow and discrete. In such a case, the electrostatic interaction among different impurity ions distributed throughout the semiconductor bulk is negligibly small as they are situated reasonably far away from each other. Carriers contributed by these impurity atoms are also smaller in number. In other words, as the carriers are distinguishable from each other, the Maxwell-Boltzman statistics is able to describe their behaviour. With the increase in the doping level, the average distance between different impurity atoms starts decreasing. It is then reasonable to presume that the electronic wave functions bound to neighboring impurity atoms begin to overlap on each other, giving rise to an impurity band. The Fermi energy level, which maintains its steady drift towards the band edges with increasing doping concentrations, ultimately penetrates the main semiconductor bands (conduction or valence bands). The density of carriers available for conduction is then expected to rise with increasing doping density. Beyond a certain doping concentration, it may not be possible to distinguish carriers from one another. The Fermi–Dirac statistics then become applicable to the carrier gas. Owing to this change in properties, the gas of carriers is believed to change their class or to enter a degenerate state from a non-degenerate one (so to say).

The impurity concentrations averaged over a big enough part of the crystal may be taken as a constant. But there may be appreciable fluctuations over smaller volumes. Such fluctuations in the impurity density is believed to introduce potential wells of variable depths inside the semiconductor where carriers may be suitably trapped. But, because of the presence of a very large density of free carriers available within a heavily doped semiconductor, the effects of the above-mentioned potential fluctuations may not be felt at all by the mobile carriers. However, in a non-crystalline semiconductor sample, where the free electron density is not very high, random variations in the defect density within the sample is known to introduce an exponential or a Gaussian energy band tail to the electron energy spectrum.

5.3.1 Optical properties of heavily doped semiconductors

(a) Absorption An incident photon is expected to be absorbed by a semiconductor when it is about to lift an electron from its valence to the conduction band. But, if the semiconductor is a degenerate one, having metallic properties, the photons may be absorbed by free carriers as well, if the former is unable to lift an electron from the valence to the conduction band. In an n-type degenerate semiconductor, however, a photon may lift an electron from the top of the valence band to states within an energy range of kT of the Fermi level in the conduction band where the vacant states for an electron can exist. Therefore, as the doping level is gradually increased, the Fermi level penetrates deeper into the conduction band, and the energy of the absorbed photon gradually increases. Such a shift in the absorbed photon energy is known as the *Burstein shift*.

(b) Reflection The effective mass of carriers in a heavily doped semiconductor sample may be evaluated by measuring the reflection coefficient R of the incident infrared radiation incident upon it. Ignoring any absorption, one obtains

$$\frac{1+\sqrt{R}}{1-\sqrt{R}} = \kappa\varepsilon_0 - \frac{nq^2\lambda^2}{m^*\pi^2c^2\varepsilon_0} \tag{5.83}$$

where λ is the wavelength of the infrared radiation and c is the velocity of light. Other symbols in (5.83) have their usual significance.

(c) Faraday rotation The rotation of the plane of polarization of a beam of polarized light passing parallel to the length of a heavily doped semiconductor sample which is oriented along the length of an external magnetic field is known as the Faraday rotation. A simple analysis expresses the angle of rotation as

$$\theta = \frac{Bn\,l\,q^3\lambda^2}{8\pi c^3\,\kappa\varepsilon_0(\mu_r\mu_0)^2m^{*2}} \tag{5.84}$$

where l = length of the semiconductor sample, B = flux density parallel to l. The other symbols have their usual significance. Thus, by measuring θ, one may estimate either n or m^*.

5.3.2 Mott transition

When the carrier densities are extremely high, a lattice of hydrogen-like atoms may behave like metals under suitable circumstances. But if the carrier density is extremely low when carriers are mostly localized to ions, the same type of the lattice may behave as an insulator, as well. If the bound carriers are somehow ionized by lattice vibrations, the liberated carriers in the solid may be able to partly screen the attraction between the carriers and the parent ions. Such a process will lead to a further lowering of the binding energy of the bound carriers and an increase in their density within the solid. The runaway nature of this process may ultimately convert the insulator into a metal when the carrier binding energy drops to zero, in the limit. Such a phenomenon whereby an insulator may make a sudden transition to a metallic state is known as the Mott transition. A similar effect may also be observed in semiconductors as their doping levels are gradually raised.

In donor-doped semiconductors, the carrier density is built up by carrier ionization from the donor states. When the density of such carriers becomes extremely high, the dielectric screening of the long-range Coulomb potential of the type discussed above occurs. Therefore, beyond a particular carrier density the carrier ionization energy may be presumed to drop to zero. All the donors may then be regarded to have contributed their carriers to the conduction band. The characteristic impurity density at which impurities are ionized is called the delocalization concentration. This may be estimated by ESR measurements, as discussed below. Beyond a particular impurity density in semiconductors, a single ESR line is observed whose width starts decreasing with increasing impurity concentrations. The concentration at which the minimum line width is recorded, corresponds to the delocalization impurity density. Beyond this impurity concentration, shallow impurity states, originally existing within the semiconductor energy gap, may be assumed to disappear altogether. Such a vanishing of the ionization energy has been reported experimentally by Pearson and Bardeen on the basis of their electrical resistivity and Hall effect measurements on Si samples doped with B and P between 87 K to 900 K. X-ray studies clearly reveal that during doping, the Phosphorus atoms replace Silicon ones substitutionally. They noticed that the energy required to ionize acceptor atoms suddenly drops to zero around a concentration of $5 \times 10^{18}/\text{cm}^3$. Similar studies have also been reported by Debye and Conwell in n-type Germanium. They measured the electrical resistivity and Hall coefficient between 11 K to 300 K, and found the ionization of carriers to drop suddenly to zero around $1.5 \times 10^{18}/\text{cm}^3$. To explain the variation of the ionization energy with doping, they suggested the following mechanisms to be responsible

i) As the doping density is increased, the residual potential energy of attraction between the electrons and the donors gradually decreases until it completely disappears at a particular doping concentration;
ii) The neutral centres, if polarized by free carriers, may also be screened out in a similar fashion.

Due to these effects, an electron cannot remain bound to a charged atomic centre. The variation in the impurity ionization energy with doping can be expressed by the following empirical formula

$$E_d(N_d) = E_{d0} - \beta N_d^{1/3} \tag{5.85}$$

where E_{d0} denotes the ionization energy at a very low doping density and $\beta = 4.30 \times 10^{-6}$ eV m. Debye and Conwell have however found that $\beta = 2.35 \times 10^{-6}$ eV m. Equation (5.85) readily follows on the model of the electrostatic screening of mobile carriers mentioned earlier. The ionization energy of carriers bound to ions is inversely proportional to the distance between the ion and the carrier. If N_d denotes the ionic density, the volume of the semiconductor available to each ion becomes $(1/N_d)$. Therefore, the distance between the carrier and the ion becomes inversely proportional to one-third power of the density of ionized donors. Hence, the decrease in ionization energy at a particular doping density may be expressed by (5.85). The effectiveness of the electrostatic screening was observed to be greater at lower temperatures. It has been noticed experimentally that the carrier ionization occurs when half the distance between two neighboring impurity ions is of the order of the first Bohr radius for electrons in semiconductors.

5.3.3 Impurity ionization energy

We will now derive an expression for the variation of the impurity ionization energy as a function of doping in a semiconductor sample. On the basis of Bohr's hydrogen atom model, the motion of an electron about a positively charged ion can be expressed as

$$\frac{m^* v^2}{r} = \frac{\partial V(r)}{\partial r} = \frac{\partial}{\partial r}\left[-\left(\frac{q^2}{4\pi\varepsilon_0}\right)\left[\frac{\exp(-\lambda r)}{r}\right]\right] \tag{5.86}$$

where it is presumed that the electrostatic interaction between the ion and the electron is screened by the mobile carriers. The screening constant λ is given by

$$\lambda = \left[\frac{q^2 n}{\varepsilon_0 kT}\right]^{1/2} = \left(\frac{1}{L_d}\right) \tag{5.87}$$

for a non-degenerate semiconductor. When the doping becomes degenerate, the expression for the screening constant changes to

$$\lambda = \left[\frac{m^* q^2}{\pi\varepsilon_0 \hbar^2}\right]^{1/2}\left(\frac{3n}{\pi}\right)^{1/6} = 2\left(\frac{3n}{\pi a_B^3}\right)^{1/6} \tag{5.88}$$

where the symbols have their usual significance. Next, Bohr's quantization condition applied to the first Bohr radius reads

$$m^* v r = \hbar \tag{5.89}$$

Combining (5.86) and (5.89), we get

$$\left(\frac{m^* q^2 r}{4\pi\varepsilon_0 \hbar^2}\right)(1 + \lambda r) = \exp(\lambda r) \tag{5.90}$$

The solution of this transcendental equation yields impurity Bohr radius (Fig. 5.4) r_H. According to (5.87) and (5.88), the screening constant λ increases with doping. For a larger λ, $\exp(\lambda r)$ increases very rapidly with r. In such a case, the left-hand side of (5.90) is unable to keep pace with it and no finite solution of (5.90) can be expected. The doping density at which (5.90) fails to yield a finite and definite solution gives the required delocalization density. The electron energy in the first Bohr orbit may now be expressed as

$$E = \frac{1}{2} m^* v^2 - \left(\frac{q^2}{4\pi\varepsilon_0 r_H}\right)\exp(-\lambda r_H) \tag{5.91}$$

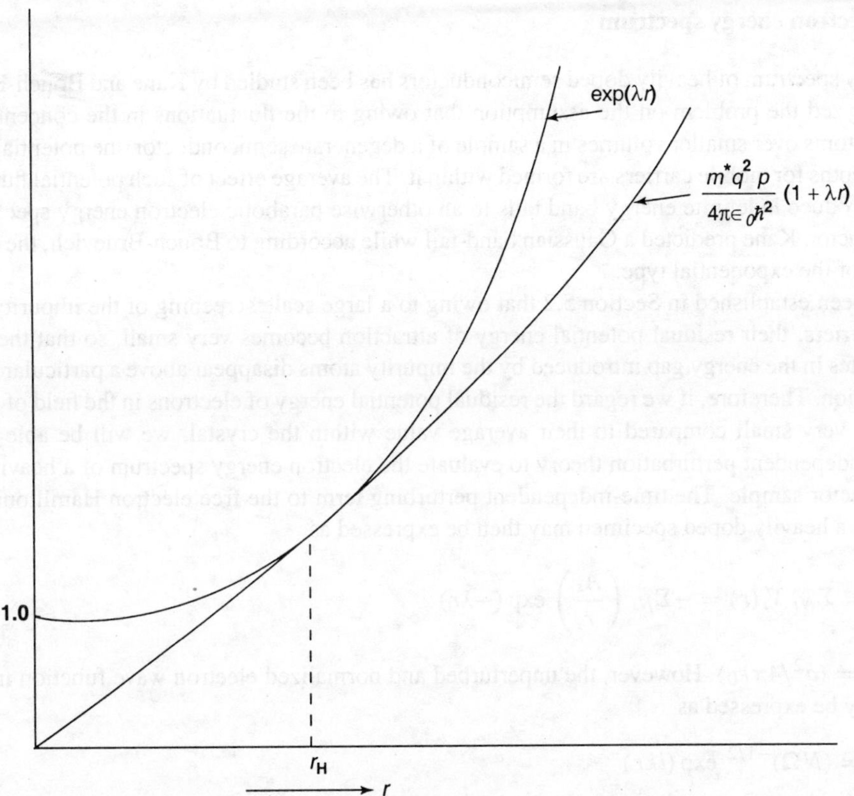

Figure 5.4 *The calculation of the impurity Bohr radius*

Combining (5.89), (5.90) and (5.91), we find

$$E = -\left(\frac{\hbar^2}{2m^* r_H^2}\right)\frac{(1-\lambda r_H)}{(1+\lambda r_H^2)} \tag{5.92}$$

From (5.92), it follows that the impurity ionization energy drops to zero when

$$\lambda r_H = 1 \tag{5.93}$$

Equation (5.93) clearly states that the impurity ionization energy drops to zero when the screening parameter is equal to the reciprocal of the impurity Bohr radius. This condition also confirms our earlier observation that the impurity ionization energy drops to zero when the distance between the two neighboring impurity ions is twice the impurity Bohr radius r_H. The former is found to be $(2/\lambda)$. Consequently, an ion would fail to bind an electron if $r_H > (1/\lambda)$. On the contrary, if $r_H < (1/\lambda)$, the electron will remain bound to the ion. The doping density corresponding to carrier delocalization may be estimated by combining (5.93) with (5.88).

5.3.4 Electron energy spectrum

The energy spectrum of heavily doped semiconductors has been studied by Kane and Bonch-Bruevich. They analyzed the problem on the assumption that owing to the fluctuations in the concentration of impurity atoms over smaller volumes in a sample of a degenerate semiconductor, the potential wells of random depths for mobile carriers are formed within it. The average effect of such potential fluctuations was to introduce indefinite energy band tails to an otherwise parabolic electron energy spectrum of a semiconductor. Kane predicted a Gaussian band-tail while according to Bonch-Bruevich, the band-tail would be of the exponential type.

It has been established in Section 5.2 that owing to a large scale screening of the impurity ions by mobile carriers, their residual potential energy of attraction becomes very small, so that the discrete energy states in the energy gap introduced by the impurity atoms disappear above a particular impurity concentration. Therefore, if we regard the residual potential energy of electrons in the field of screened ions to be very small compared to their average value within the crystal, we will be able to apply the time-independent perturbation theory to evaluate the electron energy spectrum of a heavily doped semiconductor sample. The time-independent perturbing term to the free electron Hamiltonian of an electron in a heavily doped specimen may then be expressed as

$$H_1 = \Sigma_{Ni}\ V_i(r) = -\Sigma_{Ni} \left(\frac{A_s}{r}\right) \exp(-\lambda r) \tag{5.94}$$

where $A_s = (q^2/4\pi\varepsilon_0)$. However, the unperturbed and normalized electron wave function inside the crystal may be expressed as

$$\Psi_{oi} = (N\Omega)^{-1/2} \exp(ikr) \tag{5.95}$$

where Ω measures the unit cell volume and N represents the atomic density within the crystal. Now, on the basis of the time-independent perturbation theory, the first order energy correction is given by

$$E_{1i} = \int \Psi_{oi}\ H_1\ \Psi^*_{oi}\ dv = -\left[\frac{4\pi N_i A_s}{\Omega N \lambda^2}\right] \tag{5.96}$$

This energy correction is clearly seen to be independent of the electron wave-vector. As a result of this, the entire unperturbed electron energy spectrum moves down into the energy gap by an amount given by (5.96). The corrected first order density of states function is then given by

$$\rho(E) = \left[\frac{\sqrt{2}(m^*)^{3/2}}{\pi^2 \hbar^3}\right]\left[E + \left(\frac{4\pi N_i A_s}{\Omega N \lambda^2}\right)\right]^{1/2} \tag{5.97}$$

where E continues to be measured from the original unperturbed band edge. Next, the second order energy correction is given by

$$E_{2i} = \Sigma_j\ |H'_{ij}|^2\ (E_{0i} - E_{0j})^{-1} \tag{5.98}$$

where

$$|H'_{ij}| = \int \Psi^*_{oi}\ H_1\ \Psi_{oj}\ dv \tag{5.99}$$

Simplifying (5.98), one obtains

$$E_{2i} = -\left[\frac{4\pi N_i A_s^2}{\Omega N \lambda}\right]\left[\frac{m^*}{\hbar^2(\lambda^2 + 4k_i^2)}\right] \tag{5.100}$$

Unlike the first order energy correction, the second order correction is dependent upon the electron wave vector. Next, regarding the first order corrected band edge as our new origin, the density of states function for the heavily doped sample works out to be

$$\rho(E) = \left(\frac{m^*}{2\pi^2\hbar^2}\right) \times \left[\frac{1 + \left\{\left(\frac{m^*E}{\hbar^2}\right) + \left(\frac{\lambda^2}{8}\right)\right\}}{\left[\left\{\left(\frac{m^*E}{\hbar^2}\right) + \left(\frac{\lambda^2}{8}\right)\right\}^2 + \left(\frac{2\pi m^{*2} N_i A_s^2}{\hbar^4 \Omega N \lambda}\right)\right]^{1/2}}\right]$$
$$\times \left[\left\{\left(\frac{m^*E}{\hbar^2}\right) - \left(\frac{\lambda^2}{8}\right)\right\} + \left[\left\{\left(\frac{m^*E}{\hbar^2}\right) + \left(\frac{\lambda^2}{8}\right)\right\}^2 + \left(\frac{2\pi m^{*2} N_i A_s^2}{\hbar^4 \Omega N \lambda}\right)\right]^{1/2}\right]^{1/2} \tag{5.101}$$

where $N\Omega = 1$. For N_i and λ tending to zero, (5.101) reduces to the standard expression for the density of states function in a normal semiconductor. Plotting $\rho(E)$ as a function of E, it is observed that it deviates from its characteristic parabolic dependence to a linear dependence on E.

5.3.5 Fermi level in heavily doped semiconductors

The Fermi level is an important parameter in characterizing a sample of a heavily doped semiconductor. We may calculate it with respect to the band edge by presuming that the maximum allowed energy of electrons at $T = 0\,\text{K}$ in semiconductors is the Fermi energy. If the impurity density within the semiconductor sample is N_i, presuming their complete ionization, the volume accessible to each electron becomes $(2/N_i)$, where the factor of 2 accounts for two possible spin orientations of electrons. But the limiting phase space volume of electrons is

$$\Delta p_x \, \Delta p_y \, \Delta p_z \cong \left(\frac{4}{3}\right)\pi\,(\Delta p)^3 \cong \left(\frac{\hbar^3}{\Delta V}\right) \tag{5.102}$$

where ΔV denotes the maximum volume available to each electron. If we now set $\Delta V = (2/N_i)$, as already argued, the maximum volume of the momentum space which would be available to electrons is given by

$$\left(\frac{4}{3}\right)\pi(\Delta p)^3_{\text{max}} = \frac{\hbar^3}{\frac{2}{N_i}}$$

i.e.,

$$(\Delta p)_{\text{max}} = \hbar\, k_F = \hbar\left(\frac{3N_i}{8\pi}\right)^{1/3} \tag{5.103}$$

The E–k relation calculated on the basis of the second order perturbation theory relative to the first order band edge is then given by

$$E = \left(\frac{\hbar^2 k^2}{2m^*}\right) - \left[\frac{4\pi N_i A_s^2}{\Omega N \lambda}\right]\left[\frac{m^*}{\hbar^2(\lambda^2 + 4k^2)}\right] \tag{5.104}$$

Setting $k = k_F$ in the above relation, we find, E'_{F0} where k_F is given by (5.103). To get the second order band edge, relative to that of the first order, we set $k = 0$ in (5.100) to get

$$\Delta E_2 = -\left[\frac{4\pi m^* N_i A_s^2}{\Omega N \hbar^2 \lambda^3}\right] \tag{5.105}$$

The Fermi level E_{F0} must be situated above the second order band edge by an amount

$$E_{F0} = E'_{F0} + |\Delta E_2| = \left(\frac{\hbar^2}{2m^*}\right)\left(\frac{3N_i}{8\pi}\right)^{2/3} + \left[\frac{4\pi m^* N_i A_s^2}{\Omega N \hbar^2 \lambda^3}\right] - \left[\frac{4\pi m^* N_i A_s^2}{\Omega N \lambda \hbar^2}\right]\left[\frac{1}{\left\{\lambda^2 + 4\left(\frac{3N_i}{8\pi}\right)^{2/3}\right\}}\right] \tag{5.106}$$

It is clearly seen that if $\lambda > 2k_F$, the heavily doped semiconductor has a metallic character and the Fermi energy in that case is given by the first term in (5.106) only. The above equation however gives the Fermi energy in a heavily doped semiconductor sample at $T = 0\,\text{K}$. The Fermi level at any finite temperature may be evaluated by using the following relation:

$$E_F = E_{F0} - \left[\frac{(\pi kT)^2}{6}\right]\left[\frac{\partial}{\partial E}\rho(E)\right]_{E_F = E_{F0}} \tag{5.107}$$

5.4 Tunnel diodes

While studying the reverse breakdown characteristics of heavily doped Ge *pn* junctions, Esaki observed a negative resistance region in their forward I–V characteristics. As he identified that part of the characteristic was due to quantum mechanical tunnelling, he named the device as a tunnel diode. From the point of view of circuit applications, the following features of a tunnel diode appear interesting

i) a negative resistance region at low dissipation levels,
ii) the capability of operating at microwave frequencies or even higher,
iii) a low noise figure and
iv) a relative invariance of their I–V characteristics with changing temperatures.

Tunnel diodes have been used for low power microwave amplification, oscillation, high speed switching and for binary memory applications. The tunnelling current through the diode was found to change reversibly with changes in pressure. This property has been utilized in the design of pressure-to-current transducer. Tunnel diodes have also been used as an aid in semiconductor research. Many physical processes, such as, phonon interaction in crystals may be studied and several other band structure parameters can be evaluated directly from the experimental tunnel diode I–V characteristics. Their detailed analyses have yielded a great deal of information on the properties of heavily doped semiconductors. It is also interesting to note that an effort to understand the mechanism of the current flow through the device has thrown a new light on the mechanism of charge carrier tunnelling through a potential barrier.

Tunnel diodes have been fabricated successfully with Si, InSb, GaAs, InAs, PbTe, GaSb and SiC. Their I–V characteristics have been analyzed in terms of interband tunnel current, excess current and the flow of thermal current over the potential barrier.

The main effectiveness of a tunnel diode apart from its negative differential resistance is that it is a majority carrier device and it does not suffer from minority carrier storage effects. Quantum mechanical tunnelling is a very fast process and is not limited by the drift time. The drawbacks of tunnel diodes are

i) a low oscillator power because of a lower tunnelling current,
ii) being a two terminal device, the input and the output are not isolated from one another,
iii) the device cannot be fabricated in large numbers.

Even though the device appeared quite promising in the 1960's, it has been replaced by transferred electron devices (TEDs) and IMPATT diodes as oscillators, and FETs, as switching elements.

A tunnel diode is a *pn* junction such that both of its *p* and *n* regions are degenerately doped. Typical concentrations are higher than $5 \times 10^{19}/\text{cm}^3$. Depletion layer widths of *pn* junctions at such concentrations is in the range of 50 to 100 Å. Due to a smaller depletion layer width, the capacitance of a tunnel diode is usually very high. Therefore, for high frequency applications, a smaller diode area is required.

5.4.1 Qualitative explanation of the tunnel diode $I - V$ characteristic

The energy band diagram of a *pn* tunnel diode is shown in Fig. 5.5. Since the materials on both sides of the junction are degenerate, the Fermi levels must lie within the main bands. Typical Fermi level penetrations in them are about a few kT with respect to the band edges. The I–V characteristic of the device is shown in Fig. 5.6. The current through it first increases with increase in voltage till V_p (peak voltage). Thereafter, the current decreases to a minimum value I_v (valley current) at a voltage V_v (valley voltage). Thus, the diode has a voltage-controlled N-shaped differential negative conductance. When the applied voltage is increased beyond V_v, the current is found to rise once again but now exponentially. The characteristic is nearly symmetrical near the origin for both forward and reverse directions. Figure 5.7 shows that the device's I–V curve can be analyzed in terms of three basic components:

i) band-to-band (or interband) tunnel current,
ii) excess current and
iii) thermal current.

The component giving rise to the negative differential conductance is the tunnelling of electrons between the conduction and valence bands. The electrons in the conduction bands face a triangular

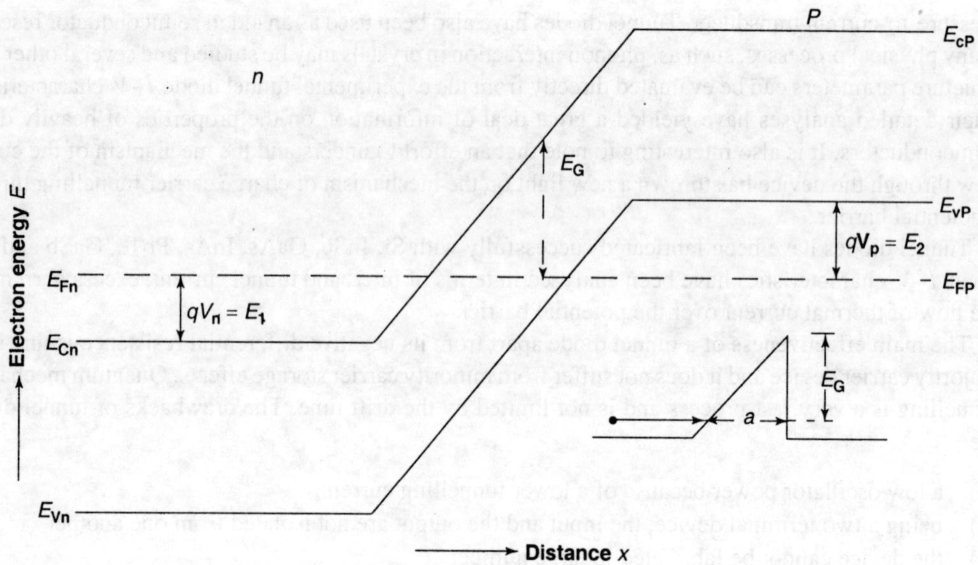

Figure 5.5 *The energy distance diagram of a pn tunnel diode*

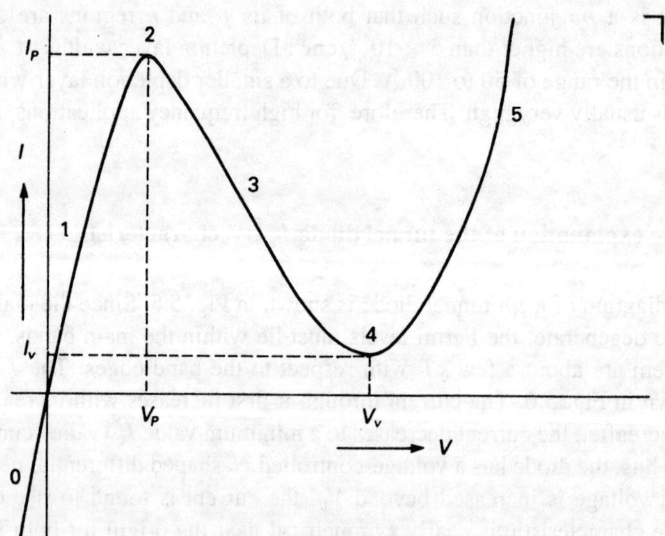

Figure 5.6 *The static I–V curve of a tunnel diode*

potential barrier of a height E_G (semiconductor energy gap) and a width 'a' (depletion layer width) (Fig. 5.5). To observe a larger tunnelling current, it is desirable to have a smaller E_G and 'a'. A stringent requirement for the tunnelling current to flow is the availability of vacant states on the other side of the potential barrier almost at the same energy for electrons to tunnel to. For individual electrons, there is a quantum fluctuation of energy produced during tunnelling. But, a tunnelling current density is caused by

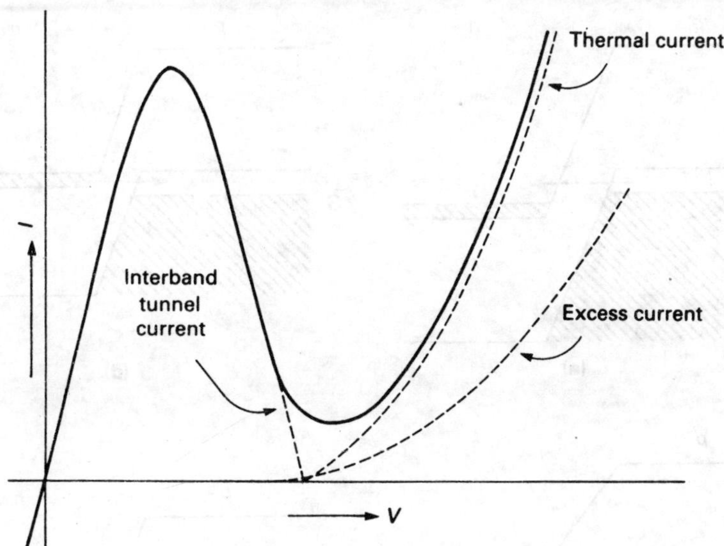

Figure 5.7 *Decomposition of the main tunnel diode current into three basic components*

a cumulative superposition of a large number of electron waves tunnelling out over a period of $\Delta t = 1$ second. Consequently, the energy fluctuation of the wave group formed by their superpositions will be $\Delta E \sim (\hbar/\Delta t)$, which will not be much different from zero. As such, the tunnel current density appears only in the vicinity of the incident energy, as it is also confirmed experimentally. These requirements are easily met when both sides of a pn junction are doped degenerately.

The general I–V characteristics of a tunnel diode, shown in Fig. 5.6, can be explained qualitatively by the energy band diagrams of Fig. 5.8. The numerals of Fig. 5.6 correspond to various band energy diagrams of Fig. 5.8. For the sake of analysis, a low temperature for the diode ($T \sim 0$ K) is being presumed so that the Fermi distribution may be regarded to remain abrupt and the states above the Fermi level may be regarded to remain empty while those below, are full. At a reverse bias (Fig. 5.8(a)), electrons tunnel from the valence band of the p-type material to the conduction band in the n-type material and the current increases monotonically with the increase in the reverse bias. With forward biases till V_p, electrons from the conduction band find increasing available empty states in the valence band and the current increases to the peak value I_p when E_{Fn} lines up with E_{vp} (Figs. 5.8(b) & and (c)). Beyond that point, the available empty states (at the same energy level as the incident electrons) start decreasing (Fig. 5.8(d)). When E_{cn} lines up with the E_{vp} (Fig. 5.8(e)), there is no empty state available on the other side and the tunnelling current is expected to drop down to zero. But, due to the presence of the defect states within the semiconductor energy gap, some current is noticed to flow even at the valley point and beyond. Such a current is therefore called an 'excess current'. At a forward voltage when bands uncross (Fig. 5.8(f)), the normal diffusion current is found to flow over the potential barrier as in a normal pn diode.

By virtue of the Fig. 5.7, the tunnelling current at a certain specified forward bias may be expressed as

$$J = J\,(\text{tunnel}) + J\,(\text{excess}) + J\,(\text{thermal}) \tag{5.108}$$

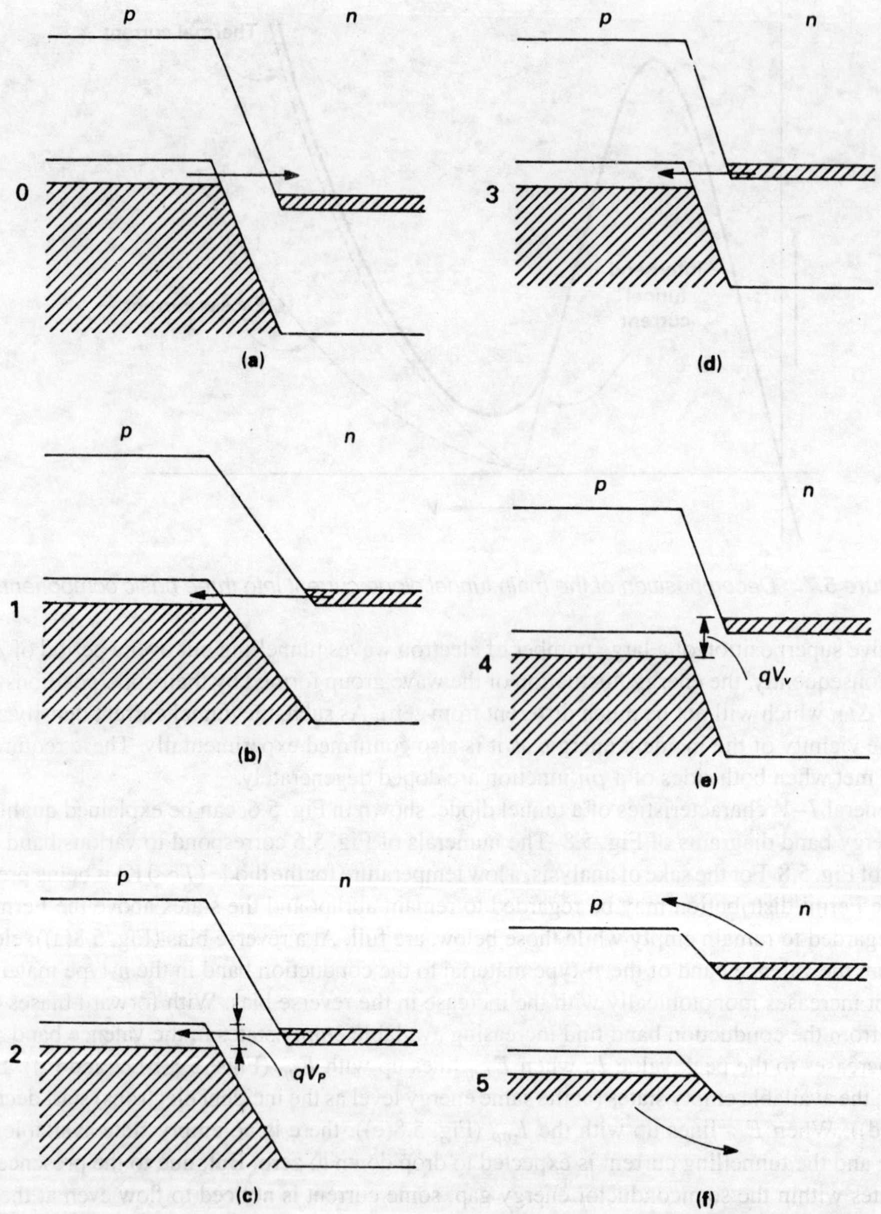

Figure 5.8 *Band profiles of a tunnel diode at different biases: (a) reserve current; (b) forward current; (c) peak current; (d) negative differential conductivity (n.d.c.) region; (e) valley region; (f) forward current*

where J may be expressed empirically as

$$J\text{ (tunnel)} = J_p \left(\frac{V}{V_p}\right) \exp\left[1 - \left(\frac{V}{V_p}\right)\right] \tag{5.109}$$

where J_p and V_p denote peak voltage and the peak current respectively. The peak voltage is found to be (Fig. 5.6)

$$V_p = \frac{E_1 + E_2}{3q} \tag{5.110}$$

According to Fig. 5.8(f), the valley voltage is given by

$$V_v = \frac{E_1 + E_2}{q} \tag{5.111}$$

As mentioned earlier, in practical devices the valley current I_v is never zero due to the 'excess current' resulting from tunnelling to bulk semiconductor states within the energy gap. This component may also be expressed as

$$J\,(\text{excess}) = J_v \exp\left[\alpha\,(V - V_v)\right] \tag{5.112}$$

where α is an appropriate constant. J_v bears a direct relationship to the density of trap levels within the energy gap. The empirical expression representing the thermal current density is

$$J\,(\text{thermal}) = J_s \exp\left(\frac{qV}{\eta kT}\right) \tag{5.113}$$

where $1 < \eta < 2$. A useful figure of merit for a tunnel diode is the peak-to-valley (I_p/I_v) current ratio.

5.4.2 Quantitative explanation of the tunnelling I–V characteristic

The tunnelling current density produced by a single electron of energy E_l (and of wave vector k) when incident upon a potential barrier of any arbitrary shape but of a height V_0 and a width W was expressed in (5.70) as

$$J = J_{01}\left[\frac{\sin\gamma}{\gamma}\right] + J_{02}\,\sin(\gamma + \phi_0) \tag{5.114}$$

where $\gamma = (\omega_{lr}t) = (\varepsilon_r t/\hbar)$ measures the phase difference between electrons incident at E_l and appearing at an energy E_r after the tunnelling time interval of t second. It has already been argued earlier, that a tunnelling current density appears only in the vicinity of the incident energy, (i.e., $\omega_{lr} \to 0$). In that case, the corresponding tunnelling time will lie anywhere between $-\infty$ and $+\infty$. If a group of incoherent beam of electrons falls upon a potential barrier, the phase differences of its various subgroups which tunnel out successively may be represented by $\gamma_1, \gamma_2 \ldots$ etc. These phase differences would then be found to vary between $-\infty$ to $+\infty$. So, if the electrons' emission is restricted only to the vicinity of E_l, the phase term should be rewritten as $\gamma = (\varepsilon_r t/\hbar)$ where t (time) is now the new variable to account for the random appearances of the electrons (which are incoherent) beyond the far side of the barrier as a result of tunnelling. The net tunnelling current density produced by all the subgroups taken together can now be found by summing (5.114) for γ varying between $-\infty$ to $+\infty$, after multiplying it w[illegible]he subgroup density $\rho_l(E_l)\ f_l\ (E_l)\ dE_l$. That is,

$$dJ(E_l) = \rho_l(E_l)\, f_l(E_l)\, dE_l \sum_{-\infty}^{+\infty} \left[J_{01} \left(\frac{\sin\gamma}{\gamma} \right) + J_{02}\, \sin(\gamma + \phi_0) \right] \tag{5.115}$$

To convert the summation in (5.115) into an appropriate integral we multiply it by

$$\frac{\hbar d\gamma}{\varepsilon_r \tau} = 1 \tag{5.116}$$

as $dt \sim \tau$. ε_r measures the minimum energy difference between electron energy levels at the transmitted end. Combining (5.114) and (5.115), we get

$$dJ(E_l) = \left(\frac{\hbar}{\varepsilon_r \tau} \right) \rho_l(E_l)\, f_l(E_l)\, dE_l \int_{-\infty}^{+\infty} \left[J_{01} \left(\frac{\sin\gamma}{\gamma} \right) + J_{02}\, \sin(\gamma + \phi_0) \right] d\gamma \tag{5.117}$$

Integrating, (5.117), we find

$$dJ(E_l) = \left(\frac{\pi\hbar}{\varepsilon_r \tau} \right) J_{01}\, \rho_l(E_l)\, f_l(E_l)\, dE_l \tag{5.118}$$

To derive an expression for ε_r, we next consider a group of vacant energy levels around E_l in the energy interval dE_l and within a volume element Ω_r at the transmitted end. Their number follows to be $\rho_r(E_l)[1 - f_r(E_l)]dE_l\Omega_r$. We may then write,

$$\varepsilon_r = \frac{dE_l}{\rho_r(E_l)\{1 - f_r(E_l)\}\, dE_l \Omega_r} = [\rho_r(E_l)[1 - f_r(E_l)]\, \Omega_r]^{-1} \tag{5.119}$$

Combining (5.118) and (5.119), we obtain

$$dJ(l \to r) = \left(\frac{\pi\hbar\Omega_r}{\tau} \right) J_{01}\, \rho_l(E)\, f_l(E)\, \rho_r(E)[1 - f_r(E)]\, dE \tag{5.120}$$

Similarly, an expression for the reverse tunnel current density may also be written down. Presuming the current from the left to right to be predominant, we find for the net tunnelling current density, if $\Omega_l = \Omega_r = \Omega$(say),

$$dJ = \left(\frac{\pi\hbar\Omega}{\tau} \right) J_{01}[f_l(E) - f_r(E)]\, \rho_l(E)\, \rho_r(E) dE \tag{5.121}$$

Substituting for J_{01} from (5.72) and using (5.58), we get

$$\left(\frac{\pi\hbar\Omega}{\tau} \right) J_{01} = \frac{\pi q \hbar^3 \Omega Z \chi^3}{m^{*2}} \tag{5.122}$$

The net tunnelling current density may now be obtained by integrating (5.122) over appropriate ranges of E at the incident end. Hence, the final expression for the tunnel current density across a *pn* tunnel diode reduces to (Fig. 5.9)

$$J = \left[\frac{\pi q \hbar^3 \Omega Z \chi^3}{m^{*2}}\right] \int_{E_{vp}}^{E_{cn}} [f_\ell(E) - f_r(E)]\, \rho_\ell(E)\, \rho_r(E) dE \tag{5.123}$$

Equation (5.123) may thus be used to evaluate the tunnelling part of the I–V characteristic of a tunnel diode.

We will next attempt to arrive at (5.143) from the point of view of semiconductor physics. Equation (5.114) gives the tunnelling current density produced by an electron incident at E_l and appearing at E_r at the transmitted end. The energy band diagram of ae forward biased tunnel diode is shown in Fig. 5.9. We consider electrons incident at E_l and appearing at E_r such that $(E_l - E_r) = \varepsilon_r$, an infinitesimally small energy. For a possible tunnelling current, an electron must be available at E_l and a vacant energy state must exist at E_r. Presuming the available electron density around E_l to be $\rho_l(E_l) f_l(E_l) dE_l = 1$, and the available vacant state at the transmitted end to be also $\rho_r(E_r)[1 - f_r(E_r)] dE_r \Omega_r = 1$(where Ω_r = volume of the electrode at the transmitted end), the net tunnelling current density originating at E_l and terminating at E_r, for a given phase γ for the incident electron is given by

$$dJ(E_l, E_r) = [\rho_l(E_l) f_l(E_l)\, dE_l]\; J(E_l, E_r)\; [\rho_r(E_r)\{1 - f_r(E_r)\} dE_r]\, \Omega_r \tag{5.124}$$

Equation (5.124) justifies the fact that the differential tunnelling current density flowing in a tunnel diode is proportional to the differential densities of electrons and holes on both sides of the *pn* tunnel junction. Such an assumption seems obvious from the point of view of semiconductor physics. Combining (5.123) and (5.124), we obtain

$$dJ(E_l, E_r) = [\rho_l(E_l) f_l(E_l)\, dE_l] \left[J_{01} \left(\frac{\sin \gamma}{\gamma}\right) + J_{02} \sin(\gamma + \phi_0) \right] [\rho_r(E_r)\{1 - f_r(E_r)\}\, dE_r]\, \Omega_r \tag{5.125}$$

At the incident end, electrons of different phases measured relative to that present at the transmitted end would be available. To take into consideration their composite effect, (5.125) has to be summed over

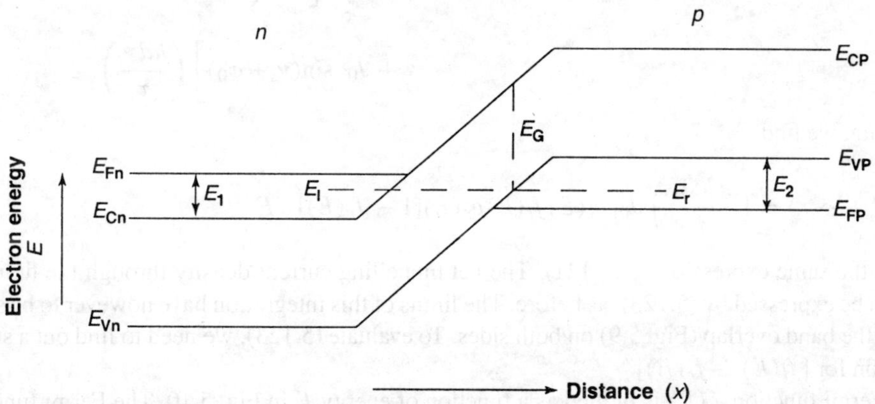

Figure 5.9 The energy band diagram of a tunnel diode.

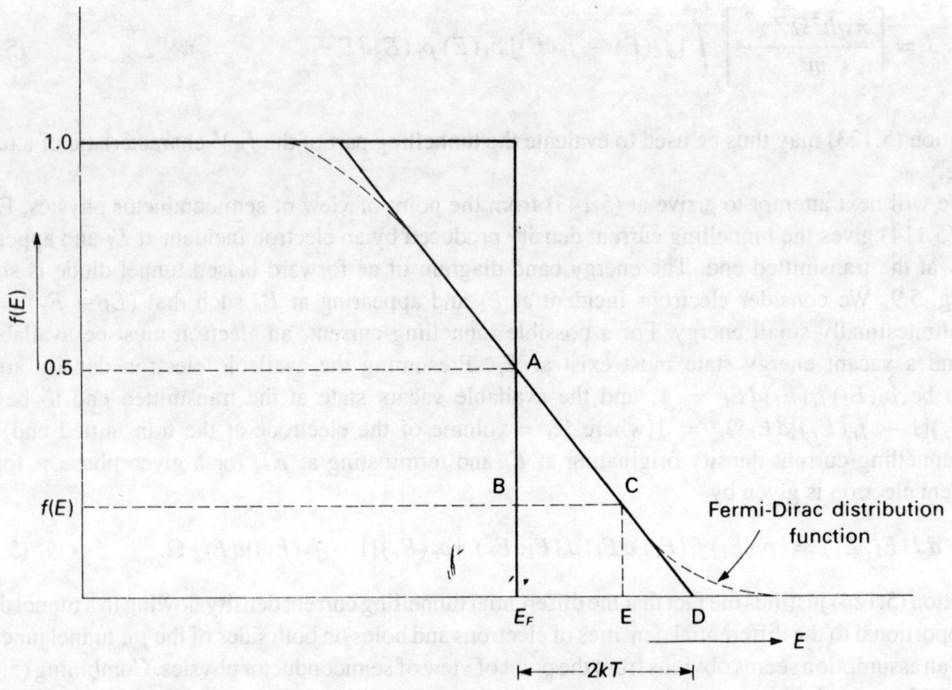

Figure 5.10 *Linearization of Fermi function*

all possible values of γ. Since, E_ℓ and E_r, differ only by an infinitesimal amount, we can replace E_r by E_l without much difficulty. Also, we note from our earlier considerations that $dE_r = \varepsilon_r = (\hbar d\gamma/\tau)$. Substituting for dE_r, (5.125) may therefore be written as

$$dJ(E_l) = \rho_l(E_l) f_l(E_l)\, dE_l \rho_r(E_l)[1 - f_r(E_l)]\, \Omega_r \int_{-\infty}^{+\infty} \left[J_{01}\left(\frac{\sin\gamma}{\gamma}\right) + J_{02}\sin(\gamma+\phi_0)\right]\left(\frac{\hbar d\gamma}{\tau}\right)$$

Integrating, we find

$$dJ(l \to r) = \left(\frac{\pi\hbar\Omega_r}{\tau}\right) J_{01}\rho_l(E) f_l(E)\rho_r(E)[1 - f_r(E)]\, dE$$

which is the same expression as (5.121). The net tunnelling current density through the tunnel diode may then be expressed by (5.123), as before. The limits of this integration have however to be set by the range of the band overlap (Fig. 5.9) on both sides. To evaluate (5.123), we need to find out a simplified expression for $[f_l(E) - f_r(E)]$.

The Fermi function $f(E)$ is plotted as a function of energy E in Fig. 5.10. The Fermi function can be linearized in the following way: Let us consider the triangles ABC and AE_FD of Fig. 5.10. Since the triangles are similar, we may write

$$\frac{\text{AB}}{\text{AE}_\text{F}} = \frac{\text{BC}}{\text{E}_\text{F}\text{D}}; \quad \text{or} \quad \frac{0.5 - f(E)}{0.5} = \frac{(E - E_F)}{2kT}$$

i.e.,

$$f(E) = \left(\frac{1}{2}\right) - \left[\frac{E - E_F}{4kT}\right] \tag{5.126}$$

Using this relation, we may write

$$f_l(E) - f_r(E) = \frac{E_{Fn} - E_{Fp}}{4kT} = \frac{qV}{4kT} \tag{5.127}$$

To compute (5.123) we must also use $\rho_l(E) = 4\pi(2m_n^*/h^2)^{3/2}E^{1/2} = C_1E^{1/2}, \rho_r(E) = 4\pi(2m_p^*/h^2)^{3/2}(\Delta E - E)^{1/2} = C_2(\Delta E - E)^{1/2}$, where $\Delta E = (E_1 + E_2 - qV) = (E_{vp} - E_{cn})$, gives the range of the band overlap in the forward biased condition. Incorporating all these results in (5.123), we get

$$J = \left[\frac{\pi q\hbar^3 \Omega Z\chi^3}{m^{*2}}\right] C_1C_2\left(\frac{qV}{4kT}\right)\int_0^{\Delta E} E^{1/2}(\Delta E - E)^{1/2}\, dE \tag{5.128}$$

The integral in (5.128) may be evaluated by putting $E = \Delta E \sin^2\theta$. Simplifying (5.128) and presuming that the electron and the hole effective masses are equal to m*, we find

$$J = \left[\frac{\pi q^2(\Omega\chi^3)m^*}{2\hbar^3 kT}\right] ZV(E_1 + E_2 - qV)^2 \tag{5.129}$$

If $(\Omega\chi^3)\sim 1$, the conventional tunnelling current density expression in a tunnel diode and (5.129) yield identical results. This is expected because in the conventional theory it is assumed that the electron from the incident end makes the tunnelling transition to a single quantum state at the transmitted end. An electron at the transmitted end must then require at least a volume $(\Delta x)^3$ (the uncertainty volume) which it will occupy after tunnelling. In that case $(\Delta x)^3 = \Omega$. The uncertainty in the electron wave vector Δk as a result of tunnelling, we know, is χ. Hence, $(\Omega\chi^3)\sim 1$, is nothing but a restatement of the principle of uncertainty which the electron after tunnelling must obey.

5.4.3 Tunnelling in a resonant tunnelling diode

During resonant tunnelling, an electron incident from one side of a double barrier heterostructure, traverses it at an energy corresponding to one of the quantized metastable states within the well (created by the spatial confinement of an electron by a pair of barriers, as shown in Fig. 5.11), without any attenuation in its intensity. In order that these quantized energy levels remain distinct to be identified, the energy separations between any two quantized energy levels within the well must exceed their thermal spread, produced by collisional effects inside the crystal. The energy separation between two consecutive quantized energy levels within the well is however given by

$$\Delta E \cong \frac{\hbar^2}{2m^* W_3^2} \tag{5.130}$$

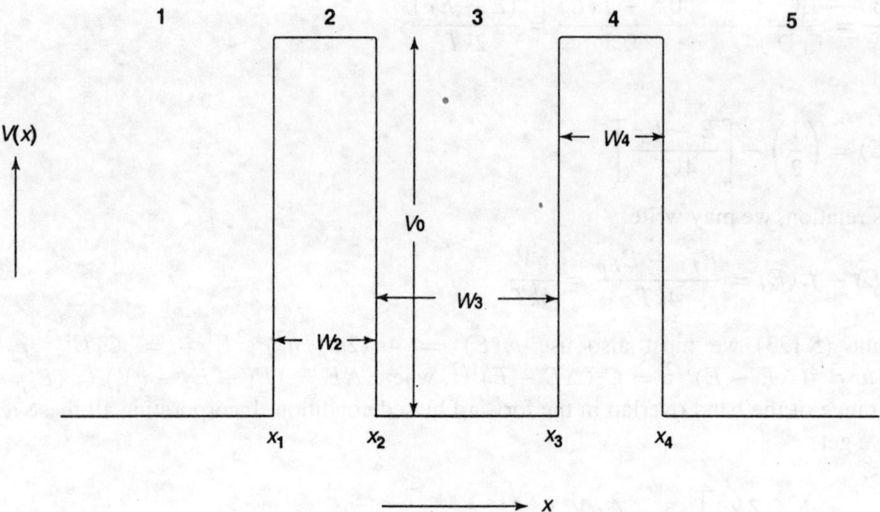

Figure 5.11 *The double barrier model*

The level spread due to the collisional effects ΔE_c, on the other hand, works out to be

$$\Delta E_c \cong \frac{\hbar}{\tau_s} \tag{5.131}$$

where τ_s ($\sim 10^{-13}$ second) measures the mean time between electron-phonon collision. For the quantized energy levels to remain distinct, one must therefore require $\Delta E > \Delta E_c$. The well width W_3 must then satisfy the following condition:

$$W_3 < \left[\frac{\hbar \tau_s}{2m^*}\right]^{1/2} \tag{5.132}$$

Taking $m^* \sim 0.1\ m_0$ (where m_0 denotes the free electron mass) for GaAs, one obtains $W_3 < 7.6$ nm. Also, if the electron velocity within the well is presumed to be 10^5m/s, the electron wavelength works out to be 73 nm, which is seen to be much larger than the well width. The ground state energy within the well is, however, given by

$$E = \frac{\pi^2 \hbar^2}{2m^* W_3^2} \tag{5.133}$$

With the appropriate values of the parameters, E works out to be 64.5 meV, which is relatively larger compared to the average carrier thermal energy ($\sim$26 meV at 300 K). This is also as per our requirements for the size quantization effects so that the carriers may not be excited thermally from one state to another. Due to the coupling of wave functions of electrons in the quantized states within the well with those existing on both sides of the potential barriers in the double barrier model, the metastable states are also found to exhibit a broadening $\delta E \sim (\hbar/\tau_b)$ (characterized by a time constant τ_b). The resonant tunnelling is said to be coherent if $\delta E > \Delta E_c$ or ($\tau_b < \tau_s$) i.e., when the carriers are not significantly scattered by phonons. On the other hand, if $(\tau_b > \tau_s)$, the resonant tunnelling is said to be incoherent or sequential. Obviously, the coherent resonant tunnelling will be faster than the sequential one. Therefore, to secure coherent resonant tunnelling, the coupling of wave functions of electrons within the well with those on both sides of it beyond the barriers must be strong enough to secure a larger δE (or a smaller τ_b). For this to be realized, the barrier width must also be of nanometre dimensions. Since both the barrier and the well widths have to be of the same nanometre dimensions for coherent resonant tunnelling to take place, the device is sometimes called a nanostructure. The quality of a double barrier resonant tunnelling diode (DBRTD) is usually characterized by its peak current density and the peak-to-valley current ratio (J_p/J_v). For a high speed operation J_p must be as high as 10^8 A/cm^2 and (J_p/J_v) ratio, as high as possible. Essential conditions for resonant tunnelling to occur have already been considered in section 5.2.3. The tunnelling current through barriers 2 and 4 flow by the mechanism of quantum scattering while through well 3 (Fig. 5.11) by the conventional drift mechanism. The principle of current continuity demands that the one particle current density through the various regions of the double barrier system must be identical. The differential resonant tunnelling current density at energy E can also be represented by (5.118) which is appended below for convenience

$$dJ_R(E) = \left(\frac{\pi\hbar}{\varepsilon_r \tau}\right) J_{01}\rho(E) f_l(E) dE \tag{5.134}$$

where

$$J_{01} = q\left(\frac{\hbar k}{m^*}\right) \tag{5.135}$$

and τ denotes the resonant tunnelling time. The other symbols in (5.134) have their usual meanings. The resonant tunnelling time is the sum of the tunnelling times through barriers 2 and 4. The former is given by $\tau_2 \sim (\hbar/\delta E)$ (where δE measures the tunnelling induced broadening),while the latter by $\tau_4 \sim [\hbar/(V_0 - E)] \sim (\hbar/\Delta E)$. Since, $\delta E \ll (V_0 - E)$, $\tau \cong \tau_2 \cong (\hbar/\delta E)$. Making use of this relation in (5.134), we get

$$dJ_R(E) = \left(\frac{\delta E}{\varepsilon_r}\right) J_{01}\rho_l(E) f_l(E) dE \tag{5.136}$$

For coherent resonant tunnelling, δE has to be broader than the collisional (thermal) energy level broadening. In the case $\delta E \sim \varepsilon_r$, the conventional drift and the resonant tunnelling current densities become almost the same. In a typical example, the peak resonant tunnelling current density works out to be around 10^8 A/cm^2.

5.4.4 Indirect tunnelling

So far, we considered the interaction of an electron with a potential barrier giving rise to a tunnelling current. This is found to be given by the rate of the growth of the probability density integrated over the barrier region at the end of quantum measurement. Such a process is termed direct tunnelling. But, there are instances when some other agencies present inside the barrier may also interact with the tunnelling electron, thereby opening up separate channels for tunnelling. Such cases are referred to as due to indirect tunnelling. The agencies which interact with a tunnelling electron may be any of the following

i) quantized lattice vibrations,
ii) photons and
iii) molecular excitations.

As a result of their interactions with the tunnelling electron, we observe breaks in the experimental tunnel diode's I–V characteristics observed at liquid He (4.2 K) temperatures. A break in the I–V curve is noticed at a bias of V volts when

$$qV = h\nu \tag{5.137}$$

where ν denotes the frequency of the interacting agency present inside the barrier. To fully understand the implications of (5.137), let us imagine a forward biased *pn* tunnel diode immersed in a liquid He bath at 4.2 K. Because such low temperatures are being used for observations, the Fermi functions on both sides of the junction are step-like and the difference between the Fermi levels on both sides of the junction gives the applied bias. So, as the forward bias is raised gradually, filled and vacant states become available at the same time at the same energy on both sides of the junction, thereby fulfilling the necessary condition for the direct current to flow across the junction. However, the moment the energy difference between the Fermi levels on both sides of the junction viz., $(E_{FL} - E_{FR}) = qV$, becomes equal to the energy quantum $h\nu$ of the interacting agency present inside the barrier, the incident electron undergoes a scattering by it, opening up an additional indirect channel for the tunnelling current to flow. This is explained in Fig. 5.12. Thus, the tunnel diode I–V curves at very low temperatures yield the spectra of molecular vibrations of a crystal. We may, therefore, expect such data to be related to the infrared and/or Raman spectra of materials forming the potential barrier. Such experimental findings have led to the development of a new branch of investigations, now known as the inelastic electron tunnelling spectroscopy (IETS). To reveal minute discontinuities in the I–V curves, one has to measure $[(dI/dV) - V]$ and $[(d^2I/dV^2) - V]$ characteristics of tunnel junctions at liquid helium temperatures. The typical nature of these curves are illustrated in Fig. 5.12. The advantages and the usefulness of this technique in evaluating molecular spectra lie in its greater sensitivity.

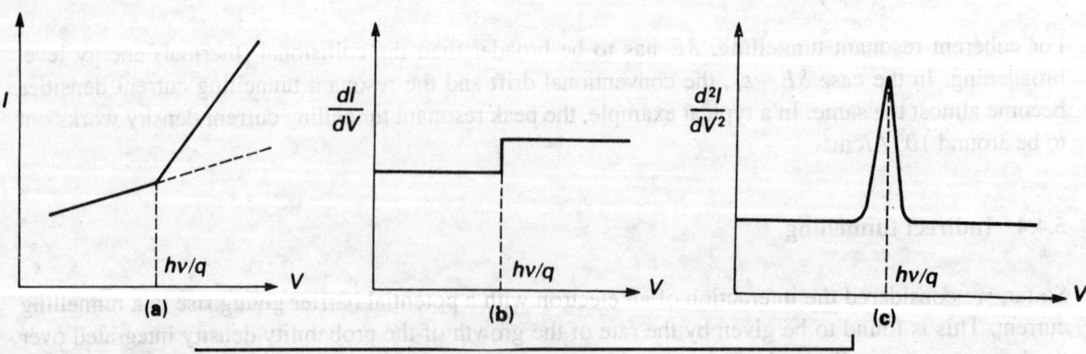

Figure 5.12 *Expected patterns of (a) of I–V; (b) $(dI/dV) - V$; (c) $(d^2I/dV^2) - V$ characteristics of a junction with indirect tunnelling*

5.4.5 Excess current

If there is no energy gap state within the semiconductor, the current in a tunnel diode must drop to zero at a forward bias of V_v (valley voltage) $= (E_1 + E_2)/q$. But, in real tunnel diodes, a finite current is found to flow even at this voltage. The observed current being in excess of the expected current, is called the 'excess current'. The origin of such a current flow is traced to the following two causes

i) tunnelling between band-tail states and
ii) carrier tunnelling by the way of energy gap states.

It has already been noticed earlier that the effect of heavy doping of a semiconductor crystal is to reduce the energy gap of the material which, in fact, acts as the potential barrier in a tunnel diode. Owing to this, an enhanced tunnelling current in the form of an excess current is found to flow across the tunnel diode at a voltage in the vicinity of V_v. But the most important contribution to the excess current is made available by way of the energy states existing in the energy gap region. The electrons from the conduction band on the n-side may tunnel to some of these, before finally dropping to some of the vacant states in the valence band on the p-side of the junction. As a variation of this process, an electron may also jump from the conduction band to one of the vacant band-gap states, before tunnelling to an available state on the p-side of the junction (Fig. 5.13). The band-gap states mostly originate from

i) donor and acceptor impurities which end up interstitially between atoms,
ii) unwanted chemical impurities which are unavoidably present,
iii) crystal defects generated by slipped atomic planes, missing atoms, etc. and
iv) surface states that are unavoidably present on the surface finite lattices.

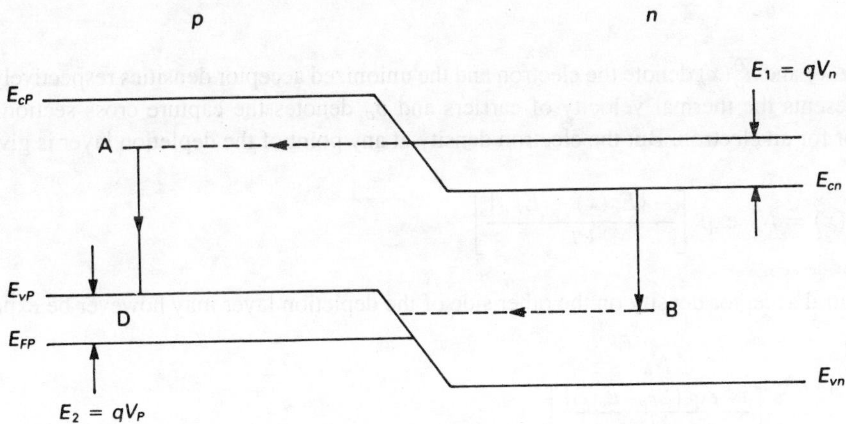

Figure 5.13 *Possible routes for carrier tunnelling explaining excess current flow*

The exponential increase of the excess current with the voltage was established experimentally by Chynoweth et. al. A theoretical calculation of the excess current in a tunnel diode is not an easy task because the physical model to represent the band-gap states in the energy gap region cannot be set up easily. But, in any case, the excess current density can be represented mathematically by (5.112), where α is a suitable constant given by $\alpha = (2/\hbar)(m^* \kappa \varepsilon_0 / n^*)^{1/2}$.

When the band-gap states exist in the energy gap region, a second negative resistance region in the excess current part of the tunnel diode's I–V curve may also be observed. A careful study of the tunnel diode I-V characteristic may, therefore, enable one to determine the distribution of states in the energy gap region of a semiconductor crystal. Also, this excess current is found to depend on the stress applied to the tunnel junction because the energy gap of a semiconductor is stress-dependent.

5.4.6 Thermal current in a tunnel diode

Beyond the valley point, the current in a tunnel diode mainly consists of excess current and diffusion current. With the rise in the forward bias magnitude, the diffusion current becomes more and more important. Interestingly enough, the thermal portion of the tunnel diode I-V curve retains its normal shape even down to 4.2 K. Based on the conventional diode theory of Shockley, the thermal current density at such low temperatures is expected to be quite low.

The low temperature thermal part of the tunnel diode I–V curve can however be explained by the theory of direct recombination of carriers within the depletion layer as proposed by Meyehoffer et al., According to his theory, holes recombine with electrons in the unionized donor states on the n-side and electrons are presumed to recombine with holes attached to the unionized acceptor states on the p-side of the junction. According to them, the thermal electron recombination current density across the junction is given by

$$J_e = \frac{1}{2}\int_0^\infty q v_x n(x)\sigma_a n_a^0(x)dx \tag{5.138}$$

where $n(x)$ and $n_a^0(x)$ denote the electron and the unionized acceptor densities respectively (Fig. 5.14), v_x represents the thermal velocity of carriers and σ_a denotes the capture cross-section of a neutral acceptor for an electron. But the electron density at any point of the depletion layer is given by

$$n(x) = N_c \exp\left[\frac{-\{E_c(x) - E_{Fn}\}}{kT}\right] \tag{5.139}$$

The neutral acceptor density on the other side of the depletion layer may however be expressed as

$$n_a^0(x) = \frac{N_a}{\left[\dfrac{1+\exp\{E_{Fp}-E_v(x)\}}{kT}\right]} \tag{5.140}$$

where N_a denotes the acceptor density. But, since $(E_{Fn} - E_{Fp}) = qV$, we may write

$$n(x)n_a^0(x) = N_a N_c \exp\frac{\left[\dfrac{-\{E_c(x)-E_{Fn}\}}{kT}\right]}{\left[\dfrac{1+\exp\{E_{Fn}-E_v(x)-qV\}}{kT}\right]} \tag{5.141}$$

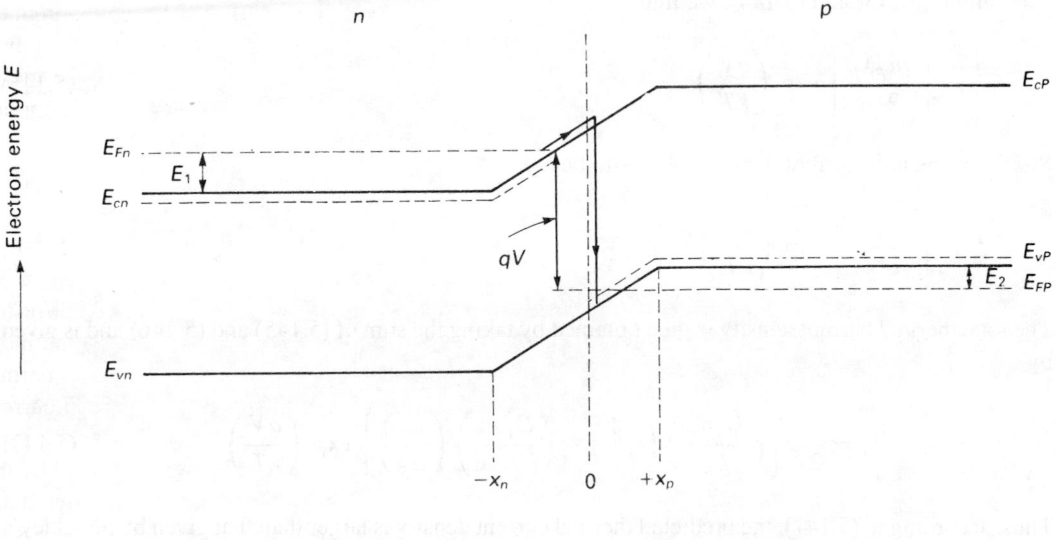

Figure 5.14 *Thermal current flow in a tunnel diode*

If, however, $(E_{Fn} - qV) = E_{Fp} > E_v(x)$, (5.162) simplifies to

$$n(x)n_a^0(x) = N_a N_c \exp\left[\frac{-(E_G)}{kT}\right] \exp\frac{(qV)}{kT}\Bigg] \tag{5.142}$$

The product $n(x)n_a^0(x)$ is seen to remain independent of x as long as $E_{Fp} > E_v(x)$. For $E_{Fp} \ll E_v(x)$, the exponent in the denominator of (5.140) becomes negligible and can be ignored. In that case, due to the increase in $\{E_c(x) - E_{Fn}\}$ with x, the product $n(x)n_a^0(x)$ suddenly drops to zero. The quantity $\{E_c(x) - E_{Fn}\}$ cannot however increase with x indefinitely because electrons possessing lower thermal energies are unable to reach the barrier top. Since the point of transition of the product $n(x)n_a^0(x)$ from the finite value, as given by (5.142) to zero is close to x_p, we need to integrate (5.138) from 0 to x_p only. The result of integration is

$$J_e = \frac{1}{2}\, q v_x N_a n_p \sigma_a x_p \exp\left(\frac{qV}{kT}\right) \tag{5.143}$$

where we have used

$$n_p = N_c \exp\left[\frac{-(E_{Cp} - E_{Fp})}{kT}\right] \cong Nc \exp\left(\frac{-E_G}{kT}\right)$$

But since $(N_a v_x \sigma_a)$ carriers recombine per second, their lifetime should be expressed as

$$\tau_n = (N_a v_x \sigma_a)^{-1} \tag{5.144}$$

Combining (5.143) and (5.144), we find

$$J_e = \left[\frac{q n_p x_p}{2\tau_n}\right] \exp\left(\frac{qV}{kT}\right) \tag{5.145}$$

Similarly, the hole current density follows to be

$$J_h = \left[\frac{q p_n x_n}{2\tau_p}\right] \exp\left(\frac{qV}{kT}\right) \tag{5.146}$$

The total thermal current density is then obtained by taking the sum of (5.145) and (5.146) and is given by

$$J = J_e + J_h = \frac{1}{2} q \left[\left(\frac{D_n n_p}{L_n}\right)\left(\frac{x_p}{L_n}\right) + \left(\frac{D_p p_n}{L_p}\right)\left(\frac{x_n}{L_p}\right)\right] \exp\left(\frac{qV}{kT}\right) \tag{5.147}$$

Thus, according to (5.147), the predicted thermal current density is larger than that given by Shockley's diode theory because $x_p > L_n$ and $x_n > L_p$. But, the exponential nature of the voltage dependence of the current remains unaffected. The effects of temperature in decreasing n_p and p_n are more than compensated by larger than unity ratio of (x_p/L_n) and (x_n/L_p).

5.4.7 Dependence of tunnel diode characteristics on various parameters

(i) Doping The doping profile of a tunnel diode is that of an abrupt *pn* junction. As such, the average barrier field is proportional to $(n^*)^{1/2}$. Consequently, the peak tunnelling current density is expected to increase as $\exp\,[-K(n^*)^{-1/2}]$. The switching speed of the tunnel diode is found to be inversely proportional to the diode RC time constant. As the negative resistance magnitude R is inversely proportional to the peak current, a larger switching speed implies a smaller diode RC time constant or a larger (I_p/C) value which is defined as the speed index.

Another figure of merit of the diode is the (I_p/I_v) ratio, which determines the current gain of the tunnel diode amplifier. This ratio is small for both low as well as higher dopings, while it attains a maximum value for some intermediate doping density. As I_p is smaller for lower doping levels and I_v is larger for larger doping levels, the (I_p/I_v) ratio would be smaller at these two extreme cases, acquiring a maximum at some intermediate doping level. The peak diode voltage $Vp = [(E_1 + E_2)/3q]$ increases with doping since the Fermi level penetrations E_1 and E_2, both rise with the doping level.

(ii) Temperature The peak tunnel current density of a tunnel diode was found to increase as well as decrease with rising temperatures. At higher doping levels, the semiconductor band-gap decreases with rising temperatures causing I_P to increase. In lightly doped junctions, on the other hand, E_1 and E_2 decrease with the rise in the temperature causing I_P also to drop off along with it. But, with rising temperatures, as the carrier injection over the barrier increases monotonically, I_v has a positive temperature coefficient. In lightly doped tunnel junctions, the diode peak voltage is also found to register a decrease with increasing temperatures because of decreasing Fermi level penetrations.

(iii) Electron bombardment, pressure and other effects Electron bombardment to the tunnel junctions introduces deep lying energy states within the energy gap of a semiconductor. The presence of these states increases the diode excess current. Therefore, the diode valley current I_v serves as a sensitive indicator of the distribution of the defect states in the energy gap of the material of the diode. Application of a mechanical stress across a tunnel junction also causes both the peak and the valley current densities to increase reversibly. The valley current increases because increasing stresses introduce more lattice defects. The peak current density, on the other hand, rises due to the decrease in the energy gap of the material. Annealing a tunnel diode around 300°C, the peak current decreases while the excess current increases. The peak current drops because the barrier width or the depletion layer width increases due to the diffusion of impurities. In the course of diffusion, the impurity atoms introduce lattice defects, which are responsible for increasing I_v. Owing to these reasons, a tunnel diode must be operated below 150°C. Permanent degradation of tunnel diodes has also been recorded under room temperature conditions. Such an effect is associated with a decreasing (I_p/I_v) ratio, as already discussed. This is due to the displacement of impurity atoms by the energy released during electron-hole recombination. It was experimentally observed that the exposure of GaAs tunnel diodes at 455°C in air for two minutes produces drastic degradation effects. This has been attributed to the diffusion of oxygen atoms in the *pn* junction. The original tunnel diode I–V characteristic may however be recovered by deep etching or cleaving of the exposed surface of the diode.

5.5 Backward and Zener diodes

When doping levels of *n* and *p* regions of a *pn* diode fall short of degeneracy, the forward diode current becomes smaller than the reverse tunnel current at the same bias level. In other words, such diodes are found to conduct more in the reverse direction than in the forward direction. As such, they have been called backward diodes. The typical I–V characteristic of the device is shown in Fig. 5.15(a). The forward current through such a diode consists of

i) the tunnelling current to band-gap levels and
ii) the normal diode diffusion current.

Under reverse bias conditions, the energy bands of *n* and *p* regions of the backward diode overlap, just as in the case of tunnel diodes, generating an interband tunnelling current. However, when the doping levels of a *pn* tunnel diode are around $10^{16}/\text{cm}^3$, the forward characteristic of the diode remains unaltered. But, in the reverse direction, we first observe a very small current upto a certain bias level before obtaining a very sharp increase in the current with rising voltages leading to a junction breakdown (Fig. 5.15(b)). Such a diode is called a Zener diode. It, therefore, possesses a very high resistance in the reverse direction upto a certain bias level, beyond which it behaves almost as a short-circuit. Unlike typical rectifier applications where the forward diode characteristic is important, the breakdown characteristic of Zener diodes is the focus of interest. The junction breakdown in this case is caused by interband tunnelling of carriers due to a very high junction field ($\sim 10^6$ V/cm). In such diodes, heavier dopings considerably reduce the junction width. As such, the collision of carriers with the ionized impurity atoms within the depletion layer are fewer. The energy acquired by them is also not sufficient to produce carrier multiplication by impact ionization in such a case. Diodes breaking down below 5V do so predominantly by the tunnel mechanism. But, the breakdown at higher voltages is caused by a mixture of avalanche and tunnelling mechanisms of carriers. A typical I–V characteristic of a Zener diode is shown in Fig. 5.11(b). In the forward biased condition, the energy bands on the n and p sides of a Zener diode do not overlap. Therefore, in such a case, the normal diode current mainly consists of the diffusion current. In the reverse biased condition to begin with, bands on both sides of the pn junction also do not overlap. Therefore, in such a case, the normal reverse current flows by the same diffusion mechanism. But, when the reverse voltage is increased sufficiently to produce a band overlap, a current due to the quantum mechanical tunnelling effect flows through the junction, as through a normal tunnel diode. Such a current is known to increase exponentially with voltage.

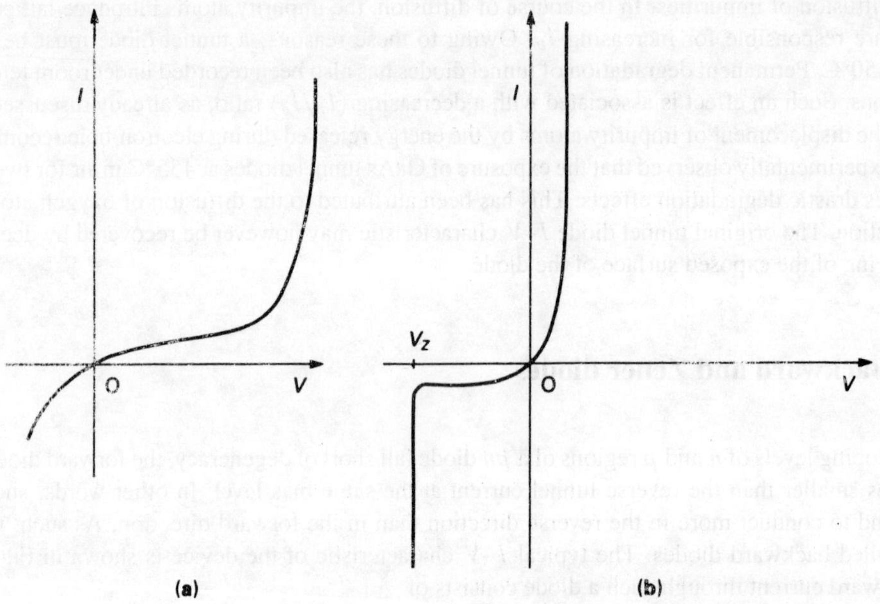

Figure 5.15 I–V characteristics of (a) backward diode; (b) Zener diode

5.6 Metal insulator semiconductor (MIS) tunnel diodes

MIS junctions can be fabricated over non-degenerate and degenerate semiconductor substrates through which the current may flow by the quantum mechanical tunnelling effect. We will be discussing both these types of junctions here.

5.6.1 Tunnelling to a non-degenerate semiconductor substrate

Such an MIS device is very useful in converting solar energy into useful electricity. Under an unbiased condition, the current flowing through the MIS junction with a very thin insulating layer will be detail-balanced. Applying an external voltage across an MIS sandwich, a net current due to tunnelling starts flowing through the device which may disturb the thermal equilibrium of carriers at the semiconductor-insulator interface. A potential drop over the semiconductor substrate will then develop. Since the potential drop over the metal and the insulating layer are negligibly small, we may presume the applied p.d. to be available only over the semiconductor space-charge layer as well as on the semiconductor substrate for the purpose of calculating the device current. Since a finite current flows through the semiconductor substrate, the Fermi level in it has to be position-dependent (Fig. 5.16). The energy difference between the extreme ends of the Fermi level over the body of the semiconductor gives the potential drop across it.

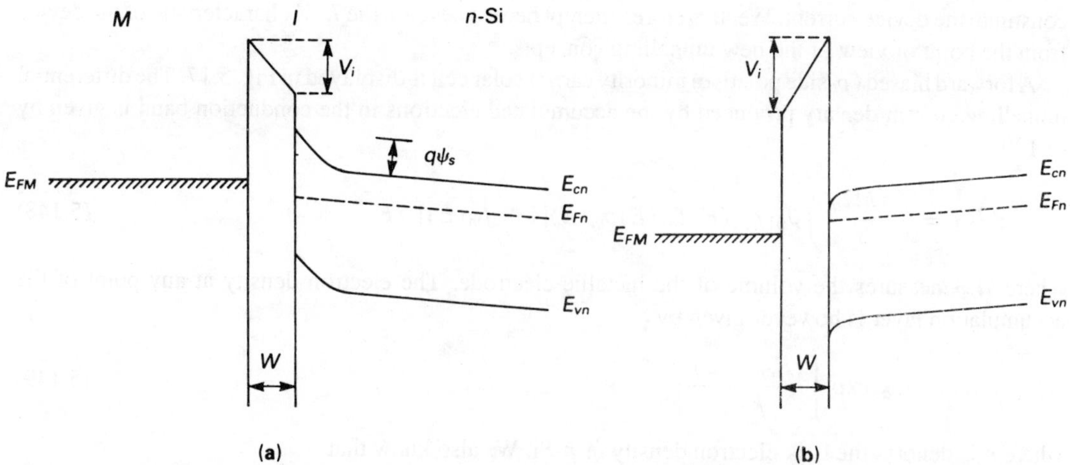

Figure 5.16 *Energy band diagrams of MIS junctions: (a) metal end negative; (b) metal end positive*

When the metal is made negative with respect to the semiconductor, E_{FM} moves up with respect to E_{Fn} (Fig. 5.16(a)) causing a depletion layer to grow at the semiconductor-insulator interface. This enhances electron tunnelling current flowing from the metal to the semiconductor, while the reverse current almost saturates. Such a current flow disturbs the thermal equilibrium of carriers existing at the semiconductor-insulator interface. The local electron density may then be represented by a quasi-Fermi level as in a *pn* tunnel diode.

On the other hand, when the metal is made positive with respect to the semiconductor, the metal Fermi level E_{FM} moves down relative to E_{Fn}, producing an accumulation layer for electrons at the interface (Fig. 5.16(b)).

In the absence of any applied bias, when such an MIS junction is irradiated by an external light source (e.g. Sun), electron-hole pairs are generated in the semiconductor causing the thermal equilibrium of carriers to be disturbed there. This produces a relative shift between E_{FM} and E_{Fn}, thereby producing an open-circuit voltage. A current through the MIS junction can then be realized even when its external terminals are shorted. The physical parameters of the MIS diode determining the development of an open-circuit voltage are

i) the metal work function ϕ_m,
ii) the insulator layer thickness,
iii) the density of surface states etc.

Smaller metal work function, lower surface state density and a larger resistivity of the semiconductor substrate are required to generate a larger open-circuit voltage. Schewchun et. al. have however discovered that minority carrier MIS tunnel diodes are the most convenient ones for the photovoltaic energy conversion applications.

The energy conversion potentialities of the minority carrier MIS and SIS junctions are due to their *pn* diode-like behaviour. Shewchun et. al. have however derived their *I–V* characteristic by considering carrier diffusion and their subsequent recombination in the semiconductor bulk, where the thermal equilibrium of carriers is disturbed owing to a large scale carrier tunnelling through the insulating layer. Due to the principle of continuity, the tunnelling current through the insulating layer must also constitute the device current. We, therefore, attempt here to develop the *I–V* characteristic of the device from the point of view of the new tunnelling concepts.

A forward biased (*p*-side positive) minority carrier solar cell is displayed in Fig. 5.17. The differential tunnelling current density produced by the accumulated electrons in the conduction band is given by (5.120),

$$dJ_{CT} = \left(\frac{\pi\hbar\Omega_m}{\tau}\right) J_{01}\rho_{cs}(E) f_{cs}(E)\rho_m(E)[1 - f_m(E)]\, dE \tag{5.148}$$

where Ω_m measures the volume of the metallic electrode. The electron density at any point of the accumulation layer is however given by

$$n(E) = n_{po}\, \exp\left[\frac{(E_{cp} - E)}{kT}\right] \tag{5.149}$$

where n_{po} denotes the bulk electron density in *p*-Si. We also know that

$$dn(E) = \rho_{cs}(E) f_{cs}(E) dE \tag{5.150}$$

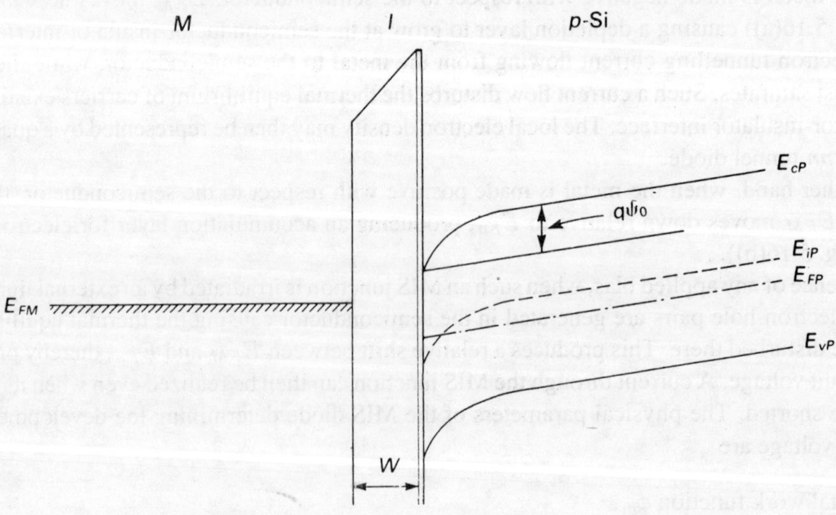

Figure 5.17 *A forward-biased minority carrier solar cell*

Combining (5.148) and (5.150), we may write

$$dJ_{CT} = \left(\frac{\pi\hbar}{\varepsilon_m \tau}\right) J_{01} dn(E) \tag{5.151}$$

where

$$\varepsilon_m = \rho_m(E)[1 - f_m(E)]\Omega_m \tag{5.152}$$

Next, differentiati: (5.149) with respect to E, and substituting in (5.151), we get

$$dJ_{CT} = -\left(\frac{\pi\hbar}{\varepsilon_m \tau}\right) J_{01} \left(\frac{n_{po}}{kT}\right) \exp\left[\frac{E_{cp} - E}{kT}\right] dE \tag{5.153}$$

Remembering that $k^2 = (2m_n^* E/\hbar^2)$ and $\chi^2 = (2m_i^*/\hbar^2)(V_0 - E)$, we get, from (5.73)

$$J_{01} = \left[\frac{16\sqrt{2\pi^2} \tau q m_n^* V_0^{1/2} \exp(-2\chi W)}{mi^{*3/2}\hbar}\right] E = CE \text{ (say)} \tag{5.154}$$

Combining (5.153) and (5.154) and integrating over appropriate limits, we find

$$dJ_{CT} = -\left[\frac{16\sqrt{2\pi^3} q n_{po} m_n^* V_0^{1/2} E_{cp}}{kT \varepsilon_m m_i^{*3/2}}\right] \exp(-2\chi W) \int_0^{q\Psi_s} \exp\left[\frac{E_{cp} - E}{kT}\right] dE \tag{5.155}$$

where E is measured from E_{cp}. In the pre-exponential factor, we have also presumed $E \sim E_{cp}$, because $q\Psi_s$ is small. Integrating (5.155), we find

$$J_{CT} = J_{CO}\left[\exp\left(\frac{q\Psi_s}{kT}\right) - 1\right] \tag{5.156}$$

where

$$J_{CO} = \left[\frac{16\sqrt{2\pi^3} q n_{po} m_n^* V_0^{1/2} E_{cp}}{\varepsilon_m m_i^{*1/2}}\right] \exp(-2\chi W) \tag{5.157}$$

The dependence of the insulator potential V_i on the interface potential has already been expressed in (4.57). Since the bulk of the applied potential develops over the semiconductor body of length L, we may also write

$$J_{CT} \cong \sigma_p \left[\frac{V - \Psi_s}{L}\right] \tag{5.158}$$

because the potential drop over the space-charge layer is Ψ_s. Combining (5.156) and (5.158), we find

$$\exp\left(\frac{q\Psi_s}{kT}\right) = \left[\frac{1 + \sigma_p(V - \Psi_s)}{J_{CO}L}\right] \tag{5.159}$$

The interface potential Ψ_s, developed with an external bias of V volts in an MIS tunnel diode is given by (5.159). This equation, however, is a transcendental one and can be solved either graphically or by the method of successive approximations.

The above discussions are however applicable to ideal semiconductor surfaces and when $\phi_{ms} = (\phi_m - \phi_s) = 0$. In practical problems we must account for the non-ideality of the insulator-semiconductor interfaces. If Ψ_s denotes the interface potential developed due to the finite work function difference ϕ_{ms}, the charge developed per unit area of the interface would be given by

$$Q_s = qN_aW = [2\kappa\varepsilon_0 qN_a\Psi_s]^{1/2} \tag{5.160}$$

In writing (5.160), we made use of (4.50) and (4.56). Also, if the work function difference is ϕ_{ms}, associated with the finite surface charges Q_{ss} per unit area, then we must have

$$Q_s + Q_{ss} = C_i\phi_{ms} \tag{5.161}$$

where C_i denotes the insulator capacitance per unit area. Solving (5.160) and (5.161) simultaneously, we obtain

$$\Psi_s = [2\kappa\varepsilon_0 qN_a]^{-1}(C_i\,\phi_{ms} - Q_{ss})^2 \tag{5.162}$$

Therefore, if the charge density Q_{ss} due to surface states, the work function difference ϕ_{ms} and the insulator capacitance C_i are known, the interface potential Ψ_s may easily be computed by using (5.162). For non-ideal semiconductor surfaces, the nature of the I–V relation (5.156) remains the same. But J_{C0} has now to be multiplied by $\exp(-q\Psi_{ss}/kT)$ where Ψ_{ss} is the surface potential with surface states.

In Fig. 5.17, we see that an inversion layer can be formed by applying an appropriate positive bias on the metal electrode. If now the MIS junction is irradiated by light, electron-hole pairs would be generated at the interface. This makes the inversion layer less n-type and causes the Fermi level near the semiconductor electrode to shift down slightly. Presuming the semiconductor to be originally biased negatively, the effect of photogeneration is equivalent to reducing the applied bias or to produce a reverse current density J_L through the MIS junction. Hence, the I–V relation of the MIS junction when illuminated by light may be expressed as

$$J_{CT} = J_C\left[\exp\left(\frac{q\Psi_s}{kT}\right) - 1\right] - J_L \tag{5.163}$$

where $J_C = J_{C0}\exp(-q\Psi_{ss}/kT)$ and J_L measures the current density produced by steady irradiation of the MIS junction. Equation (5.163) thus displays the solar cell-like feature of the MIS tunnel diodes. To derive an expression for the surface potential corresponding to the open-circuit voltage, we set the left-hand side of (5.163) to zero to obtain

$$\Psi_s = \left(\frac{kT}{q}\right)\ln\left[1 + \left(\frac{J_L}{J_C}\right)\right] \tag{5.164}$$

Next, combining (5.159) and (5.164), we obtain

$$V_{OC} = \left(\frac{kT}{q}\right)\ln\left[1 + \left(\frac{J_L}{J_C}\right)\right] + \left(\frac{J_{C0}}{J_C}\right)\left(\frac{LJ_L}{\sigma_p}\right) \tag{5.165}$$

Similarly, in order to derive an expression for the short-circuit current J_{SC} flowing through a non-ideal MIS diode, we set $V = 0$ in (5.159) and evaluate Ψ_s. Using that particular Ψ_s in (5.163), we get

$$J_{SC} = -\left[J_L + \left(\frac{J_C}{J_{C0}}\right)\left(\frac{\sigma_p \Psi_s}{L}\right)\right] \tag{5.166}$$

where Ψ_s is to be obtained by solving the following transcendental equation

$$\exp\left(\frac{q\Psi_s}{kT}\right) = 1 - \left[\left(\frac{\sigma_p \Psi_s}{J_{C0} L}\right)\right] \tag{5.167}$$

Following the procedure adopted for the *pn* junction solar cell, we may also calculate its efficiency and the fill factor (FF).

The majority carrier MIS solar cells may also be fabricated by growing thin oxide layers (~50 Å) in dry oxygen at 700 – 900°C on chemically prepared *p*-Si wafers of orientations $< 111 >$ and $< 100 >$. Metal contacts are next evaporated through appropriate metal masks. After the growth of the oxide layer, an inversion layer is formed over the entire *p*-Si surface which is presumably caused by the positive charges present over the thermal oxide layer. The inversion layer from areas remote from the top metal contact can be eliminated by exposing the diode to the atmosphere for several hours. To have a fine metal grating structure over the oxide layer, the photolithographic technique is employed. The MIS grating solar cell using Mg as the contact electrode spaced 200 μm apart on a SiO_2 film with SiO as the antireflection coating is fabricated experimentally on *p*-type Si substrates. The fabricated SIS solar cells differ from MIS ones in the technique of depositing the Indium Tin Oxide (ITO) layers. These are grown by spraying $SnCl_4$ and $InCl_3$ mixtures on *p*-type Si substrates. The oxide is normally modelled as bulk stoichiometric SiO_2. But, since the oxide layer is extremely thin, it is believed to be grossly non-stoichiometric, with pin holes present in them.

5.6.2 Tunnelling to degenerate semiconductor substrates

Pure SnTe and GeTe essentially behave as *p*-type degenerate semiconductors with a hole density of $10^{20}/\text{cm}^3$. MIS junctions on these materials may be fabricated by evaporating a metal electrode after oxidizing them. Such MIS junctions are found to display negative resistance characteristics under suitable circumstances. To describe their I–V characteristics qualitatively, we refer to Fig. 5.18. Application of the positive voltage on the metal electrode results in the electron tunnelling from the semiconductor valence band into the metal (Fig. 5.18(b)). The tunnelling current is then expected to rise monotonically with increasing positive voltage on the metal electrode because of the increasing availability of the vacant states on the metal end.

Let us next examine the effect of applying a negative bias on the metal electrode (Fig. 5.18(c)). Metallic electrons tunnel into unoccupied states of the valence band. But, with increasing negative voltages, the effective barrier height for electron tunnelling is increased and as a result of this, the electron tunnelling current decreases. Due to this effect, a negative resistance region appears in the device I–V curve. Such an effect is further augmented due to the non-availability of the vacant electronic states within the energy gap of the material. When the applied negative bias on the metal is sufficiently increased so that the conduction electrons are able to participate in the tunnelling process, the tunnelling current starts rising once again (Fig. 5.18(d)). Consequently, an N-shaped negative resistance is expected in the device I–V curve.

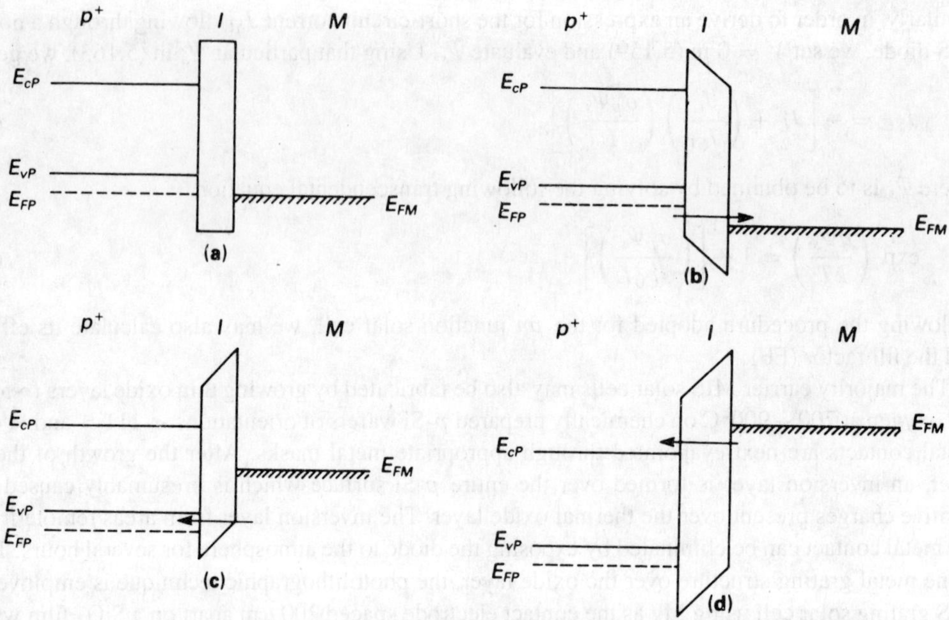

Figure 5.18 *Band diagrams of an MIS (p^{++}) diode*

5.7 Metal-insulator-semiconductor-switch (MISS) diode

In 1972, Yamamoto et al., reported a high speed Si device possessing an S-shaped negative resistance characteristic. It essentially consists of an MIS tunnel diode of the type already discussed and a pn junction in series. The final form of the device may then acquire a $n^+ - p - i - M$ or a $p^+ - n - i - M$ configuration. In its behaviour, it is somewhat similar to a silicon-controlled rectifier(SCR) having its switching and sustaining voltages in the range of 2 to 20 V respectively. Its I–V characteristic could be explained in a number of ways. A method developed here for analyzing the device I–V curve presumes ideal conditions to prevail at the semiconductor-insulator interface. Also, it is presumed that no pin holes exist within the insulator. The energy band diagram of the device is shown in Fig. 5.19, the cross-section of the MISS diode is presented in Fig. 5.20 and its I–V characteristic is given in Fig. 5.21.

(i) Reverse mode With a reverse voltage applied to the device (n^+ end positive), almost the entire applied voltage becomes available over the high resistance of the reverse biased n^+p junction. Consequently, the diode reverse saturation current constitutes the device current. On the basis of our deliberations in Chapter 2, this current density may be expressed as

$$J = q\left[\left\{\frac{D_p}{n_n L_p}\right\} + \left\{\frac{D_n}{p_p L_n}\right\}\right] n_i^2 + \left(\frac{q n_i}{\tau_i}\right)\left[\frac{2\kappa\varepsilon_0(\Psi_0 + V)}{qNa}\right]^{1/2} \tag{5.168}$$

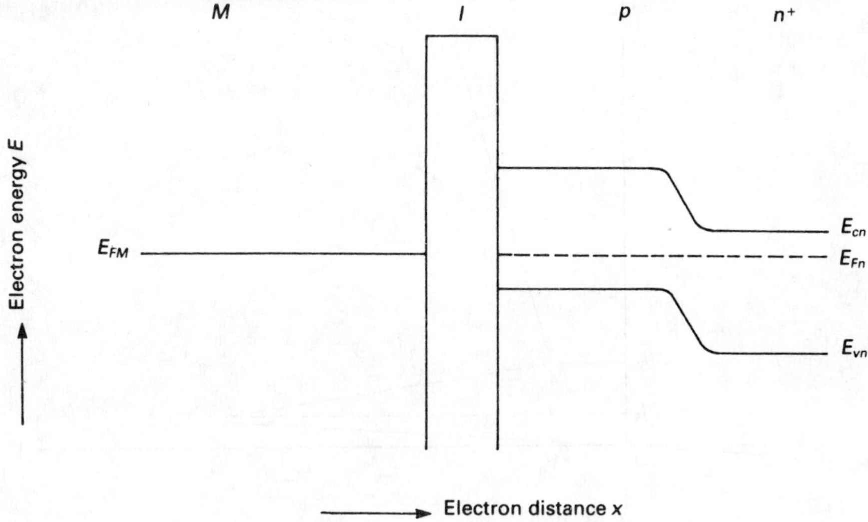

Figure 5.19 Energy band diagram of a MISS diode

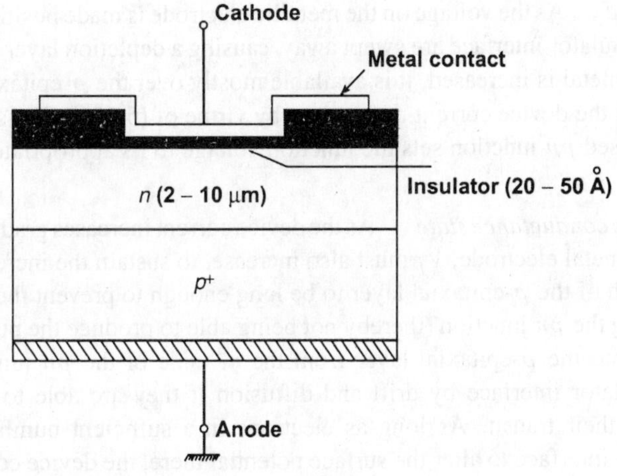

Figure 5.20 The cross-section of a MISS diode

The first term denotes the diode reverse saturation current while the second one accounts for the generation current within the depletion layer. This current also flows through the insulating layer and adjusts the surface potential Ψ_s at the semiconductor-insulator interface by virtue of (5.156).

(ii) Forward mode It consists of three parts:

a) high impedance state,
b) a switching or a negative conductance state and
c) a conducting or a low impedance state

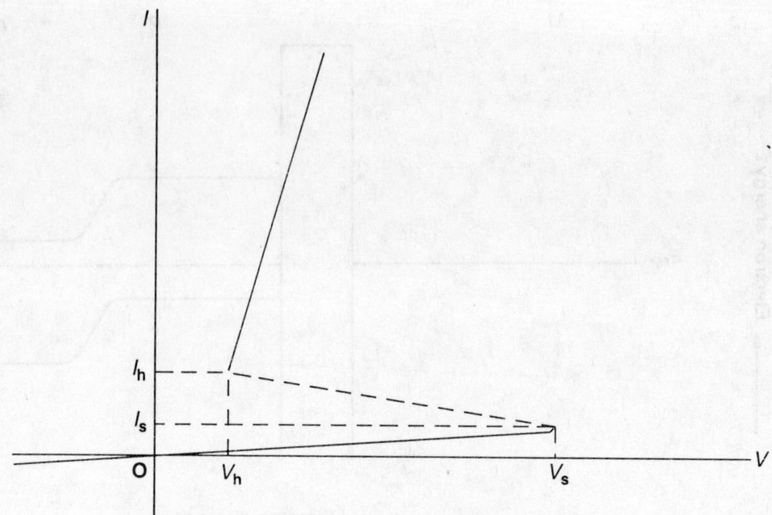

Figure 5.21 *The I–V characteristic of a MISS diode*

(a) High impedance state As the voltage on the metallic electrode is made positive, the holes existing at the semiconductor-insulator interface are swept away, causing a depletion layer to grow there. As the forward voltage on the metal is increased, it is available mostly over the *p*-epitaxial layer causing the surface potential Ψ_s and the device current J_{CT} to rise by virtue of (5.156). The same current flowing through the forward biased *pn* junction sets the junction voltage to its appropriate level V_j.

(b) Switching or negative conductance state As the device current increases gradually with increasing forward voltage on the metal electrode, V_j must also increase, to sustain the increased device current. If we presume the length of the *p*-epitaxial layer to be long enough to prevent the widening depletion layer on it from reaching the *pn* junction (thereby not being able to produce the punch-through effect), the electrons injected into the *p*-epitaxial layer from the n^+ side of the *pn* junction move towards the semiconductor-insulator interface by drift and diffusion if they are able to survive recombination with holes during their transit. As long as electrons in a sufficient number do not reach the semiconductor-insulator interface to alter the surface potential there, the device continues to remain in its forward blocking or OFF state. This is clearly explained by the following relation

$$n_p \exp\left(\frac{q\Psi'_s}{kT}\right) - n_p \exp\left(\frac{q\Psi_s}{kT}\right) = \exp\left[\left(\frac{qV_j}{kT}\right) - \left(\frac{L}{L_n}\right)\right] \tag{5.169}$$

where $L_n = (D_n \tau_n)^{1/2}$. Thus, according to (5.169), we see that as long as $(qV_j/kT) < (L/L_n)$, we have $\Psi'_s \sim \Psi_s$, and the device continues to be in its OFF state. However, when $(qV_j/kT) > (L/L_n)$, the increased surface potential Ψ'_s causes the tunnelling current through the insulator to increase in accordance with (5.156). When this current rises, V_j must also increase, so that it is able to maintain the same current flow through the *pn* junction. Increased electron injection by the *pn* junction further raises Ψ'_s, causing V_j to increase once again. Thus, once the condition $(qV_j/kT) \geq (L/L_n)$ is realized, the surface potential starts increasing of its own accord without any further increase in the source voltage.

The device then undergoes automatic switching from its OFF state to the ON condition. The switching voltage can be computed in the following manner: The *pn* junction current giving rise to switching is computed for a voltage $V_j = (kT/q)(L/L_n)$. The corresponding Ψ_s to maintain the same current is next computed from (5.156). The switching voltage may then be derived using (5.159).

The switching of the device entails large-scale electron and hole injections over the *p*-epitaxial layer, such that the electrons are collected at the semiconductor-insulator interface, while holes are collected at the opposite end. The switching occurs so rapidly that these carriers are unable to recombine with each other. Instead, they drift through the *p*-epilayer and get collected at opposite ends of it producing an internal field, opposing the externally applied field. This causes the terminal voltage of the device to be reduced appreciably. The increasing device current coupled with decreasing terminal voltage is responsible for the onset of the negative conductance state in the device I–V curve. The remainder of the applied voltage is used up in keeping electrons and holes isolated from one another over the *p*-epitaxial layer. At the end of the switching, the terminal or the holding voltage may be expressed as

$$V_h = V_i + V_s + V_j \tag{5.170}$$

where $V_s = \Psi'_s$. If both V_i and V_j are smaller than V_s, one gets $V_h \cong \Psi'_s$. The device current corresponding to this Ψ'_s gives the device holding current. However, the above approximations may not generally be true.

(c) Low impedance state The device switching concludes when the n^+p junction has stopped injecting an increasing number of electrons with higher biases. This will be the case when $V_j \cong \Psi_0$ (the built-in junction potential). The corresponding *pn* junction current gives the holding current I_h of the device. Using this I_h in (5.156), we may easily compute the final Ψ'_s which has developed at the end of the device switching. From (4.57), we may also compute V_i corresponding to this Ψ'_s. It is then easy to calculate V_h using (5.170). Beyond this stage, the MISS diode starts behaving like a normal MIS diode whose current increases with increasing applied bias.

Alternative explanation

In the above discussions, the switching action of the MISS diode was explained as being caused due to the electron injection from the forward biased n^+p junction over the *p*-epilayer to overcome their subsequent recombination losses on their way towards the insulating layer. Switching of the device has also been explained either due to the extension of the surface depletion region to the *pn* junction (punch-through effect) or due to avalanching on the semiconductor surface layer near the insulator. In order to understand these switching mechanisms, let us consider the energy band diagrams of Fig. 5.22. Fig. 5.22(a) shows the idealized band diagram at thermal equilibrium. Fig. 5.22(b) illustrates the diode with a positive gate voltage on the metal electrode. If the conductivity of the tunnel insulator is much greater than that of the reverse biased p^+n junction, most of the applied voltage will be available over the p^+n junction. The I–V characteristic of the device is then essentially the same as that of a reverse biased p^+n junction (as already mentioned earlier). The generation current within the depletion layer is given by

$$J = \frac{qn_iW_j}{\tau_i} = \left(\frac{qn_i}{\tau_i}\right)\left[\frac{2\kappa\varepsilon_0(\Psi_0 + V)}{qN_d}\right]^{1/2} \tag{5.171}$$

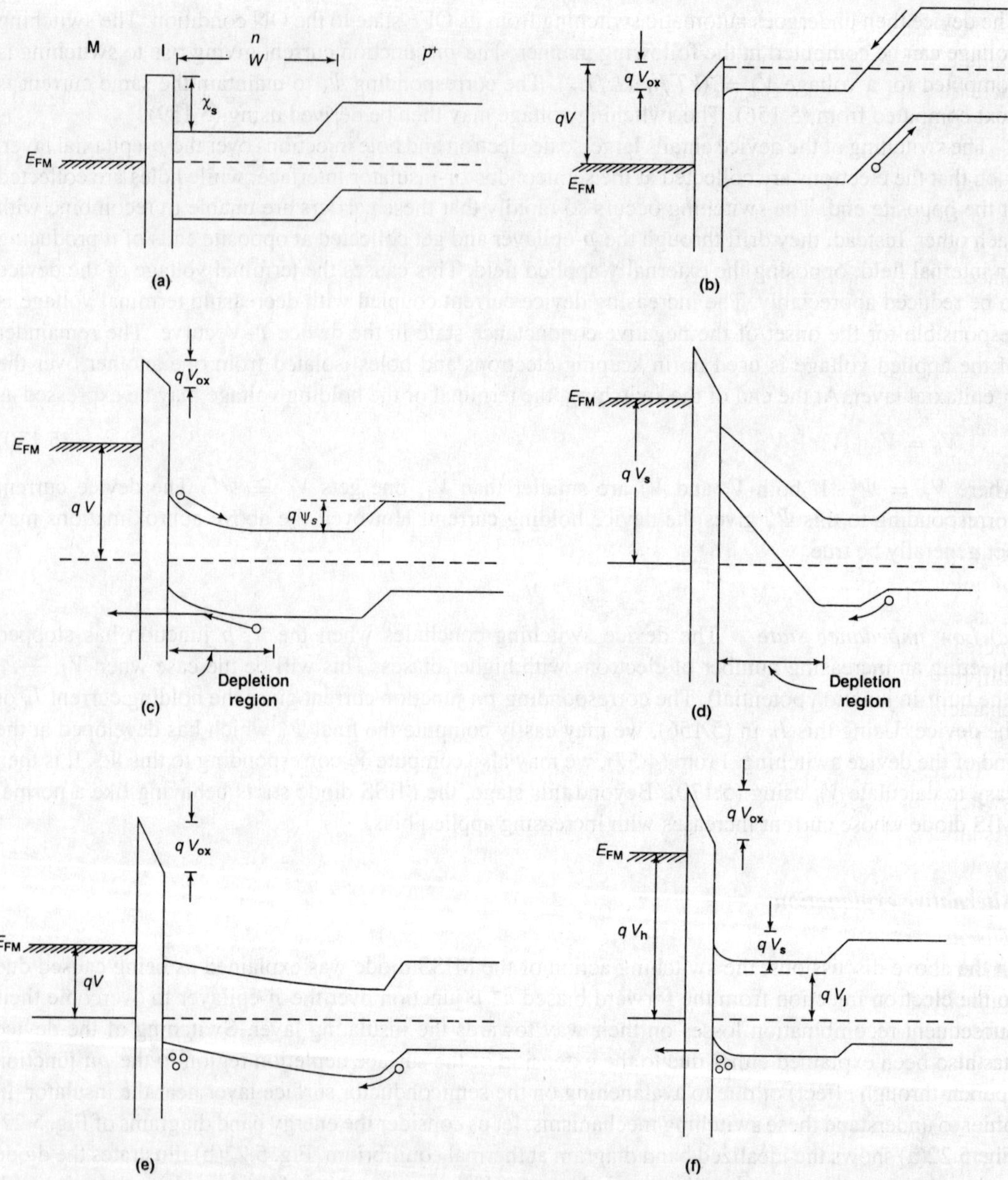

Figure 5.22 *Energy band diagrams of a MISS diode under different biasing conditions*

When the gate voltage increases negatively (Fig. 5.22(c)), the free electrons are swept out of the n-epitaxial layer through the p^+n junction and a depletion region grows under the gate electrode. Electron-hole pairs are then generated within this depletion layer. Electrons are swept towards the p^+n junction while the holes are swept towards the $SiO_2 - Si$ interface. For thicker oxide layers

(> 50Å), the generated holes accumulate at the interface and give rise to an inversion layer. If the oxide is thin enough, holes tunnel through it. Thus, as the negative gate voltage on the metal electrode increases, the surface n-layer becomes more and more depleted rather than becoming inverted. Under these conditions, the generated current is still given by (5.171) but now $(\Psi_0 + V)$ is replaced by Ψ_S (surface potential). The current is once again weakly dependent on the voltage corresponding to the forward blocking state.

When a sufficiently high voltage is applied, the depletion layer under the oxide extends upto the p^+n junction (Fig. 5.22(d)). The device then is at the condition of punch-through and switching takes place. The corresponding voltage is given by

$$V_S = \frac{qN_d(W - W_j)^2}{2\kappa\varepsilon_0} \tag{5.172}$$

where W measures the width of the n-epilayer and W_j represents the depletion layer width of the p^+n junction at zero applied bias. After the punch-through condition, the injected holes by the p^+n junction increases exponentially with the voltage across it. The field across the oxide, at this stage, is insufficient to allow the relatively larger injected holes to pass through the insulator. Consequently, a little increase in the voltage will cause the holes to accumulate at the $Si - SiO_2$ interface. Such a build up of holes moves the surface layer from the condition of deep depletion towards inversion (Fig. 5.22(e)). Consequently, Ψ_S and the voltage across the device, decreases. The voltage drop across the oxide increases, allowing a larger current to flow through the p^+n junction, thus turning the junction ON still further. This regenerative feedback mechanism causes the device to display its negative resistance characteristic. The holding condition is shown in Fig. 5.22(f), and the holding voltage is given by (5.170).

Under avalanching condition, similar regenerative mechanism is responsible for switching. The switching voltage in (5.172) will then be replaced by the avalanche breakdown voltage of the n-epilayer. As already mentioned previously, the thickness of the oxide layer is a key parameter determining the switching behaviour of the device.

Discussion In the given explanations, the increase of the surface potential (driving the semiconductor underneath the gate to a condition of deep depletion) is not regarded as the cause of the increased tunnelling through the insulator (according to 5.156). Also, the mechanism of the negative resistance effect is far from clear in these explanations. After switching, the terminal voltage is supposed to drop to the applied voltage. This is unlike the behaviour of other negative resistance devices.

The key issue giving rise to the switching action of the MISS device is noticed to be the change in the surface potential at the insulator-semiconductor interface due to the collection of excess charges there. These charges, as has already been discussed, originate from the following three causes

i) injection of carriers by the pn junction,
ii) punch-through effect produced over the epilayer which drives the pn junction more and more forward biased, and
iii) avalanche effect set up over the epilayer.

When these generated carriers, after surviving recombination, are able to reach the semiconductor-insulator interface to alter the surface potential there, switching begins. Increasing surface potential gives rise to increasing tunnelling current which drives the pn junction more and more forward biased causing the current to increase further and so on. Due to the runaway nature of this process, switching begins. The carriers of opposite polarity then collect on opposite ends of the epilayer. The energy required to keep them separated draws a part of the applied voltage, thereby reducing the terminal p.d. Thus the effects of increasing current combined with that of decreasing terminal potential ultimately gives rise to the negative conductivity region in the $I-V$ characteristics of the device. The device behaviour after switching remains the same as already discussed.

5.8 Tunnel devices of different types

(i) MIM tunnel diode The metal-insulator-metal tunnel diode is a thin-film device in which the electrons from the first metal can tunnel through the insulator and be collected by the second metal. Figure 5.23 shows the basic energy diagram of a MIM diode with identical metal electrodes. For very high voltages, the tunnelling resistance decreases abruptly. The MIM tunnel diodes are used to study the energy-momentum relation in the forbidden energy gap of a single crystal insulator.

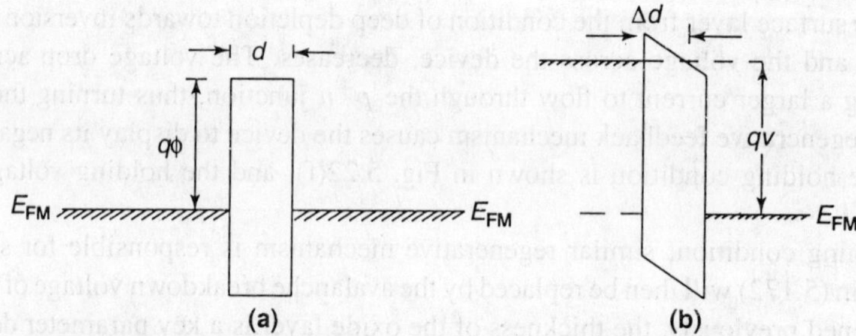

Figure 5.23 *The MIM tunnel diode (a) $V = 0$ (zero bias), (b) $V > \phi$*

(ii) Tunnel transistors The first tunnel transistor was proposed by Mead as early as 1960. Fig. 5.24 shows the device. The current flowing through the first MIM junction is due to tunnelling. After tunnelling from the emitter to the base, electrons have energies more than a few kT above the Fermi level in the base region; these are therefore, hot electrons as they are not in thermal equilibrium with the lattice. This transistor is therefore, referred to as the hot electron transistor. It was suggested that the current gain of such a transistor could be improved greatly by replacing the collector electrode with a Schottky barrier semiconducting layer.

(iii) Double barrier resonant tunnelling diode (DBRTD) The negative differential resistance of a resonant tunnelling diode was predicted by Tsu and Esaki in 1973. A resonant tunnelling diode requires band edge discontinuity at the conduction or valence band to form a quantum well and thus requires heteroepitaxy. The most popular material combination used is GaAs-AlGaAs followed by GaInAs-AlInAs. The central quantum well thickness is typically about 50 Å and the barrier layers range from 15 to 25 Å (Fig. 5.25). The well layer and the barrier layers are all undoped. The device is either fabricated by MBE or MOCVD.

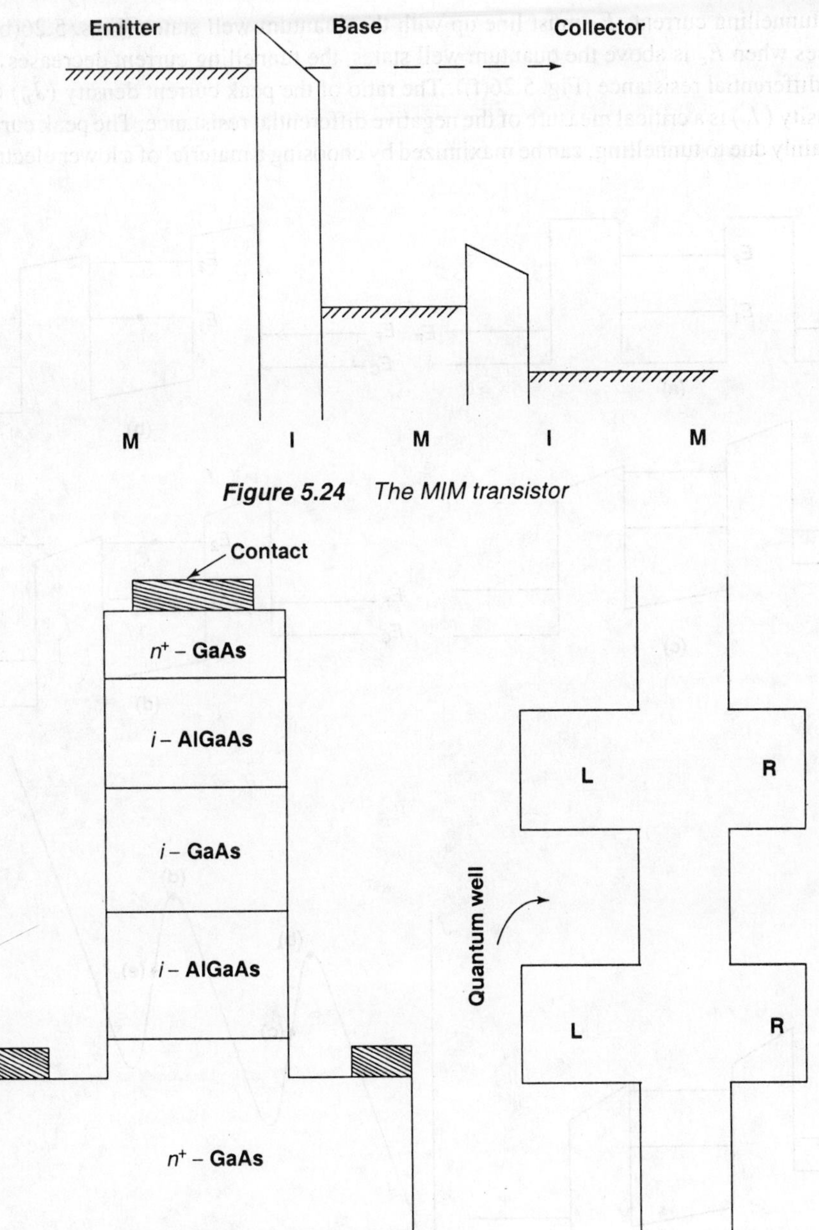

Figure 5.24 *The MIM transistor*

Figure 5.25 *Structure of a resonant tunnelling diode.*

A resonant tunnelling diode utilizes the quantization of energy states in a quantum well. In practice, ΔE_c lies in the energy range of $0.2 - 0.5\,\text{eV}$. Under biased conditions, carriers can tunnel from one electrode to another via some energy states within the well. The energy band diagrams and the nature of the I–V characteristic of a resonant tunnelling diode is shown in Fig. 5.26. It is clear that for the maximum tunnelling current, E_c must line up with the quantum well states (Figs. 5.26(b) & (d)). At higher biases when E_c is above the quantum well states, the tunnelling current decreases, resulting in a negative differential resistance (Fig. 5.26(f)). The ratio of the peak current density (J_p) to the valley current density (J_v) is a critical measure of the negative differential resistance. The peak current density, which is mainly due to tunnelling, can be maximized by choosing a material of a lower electron effective

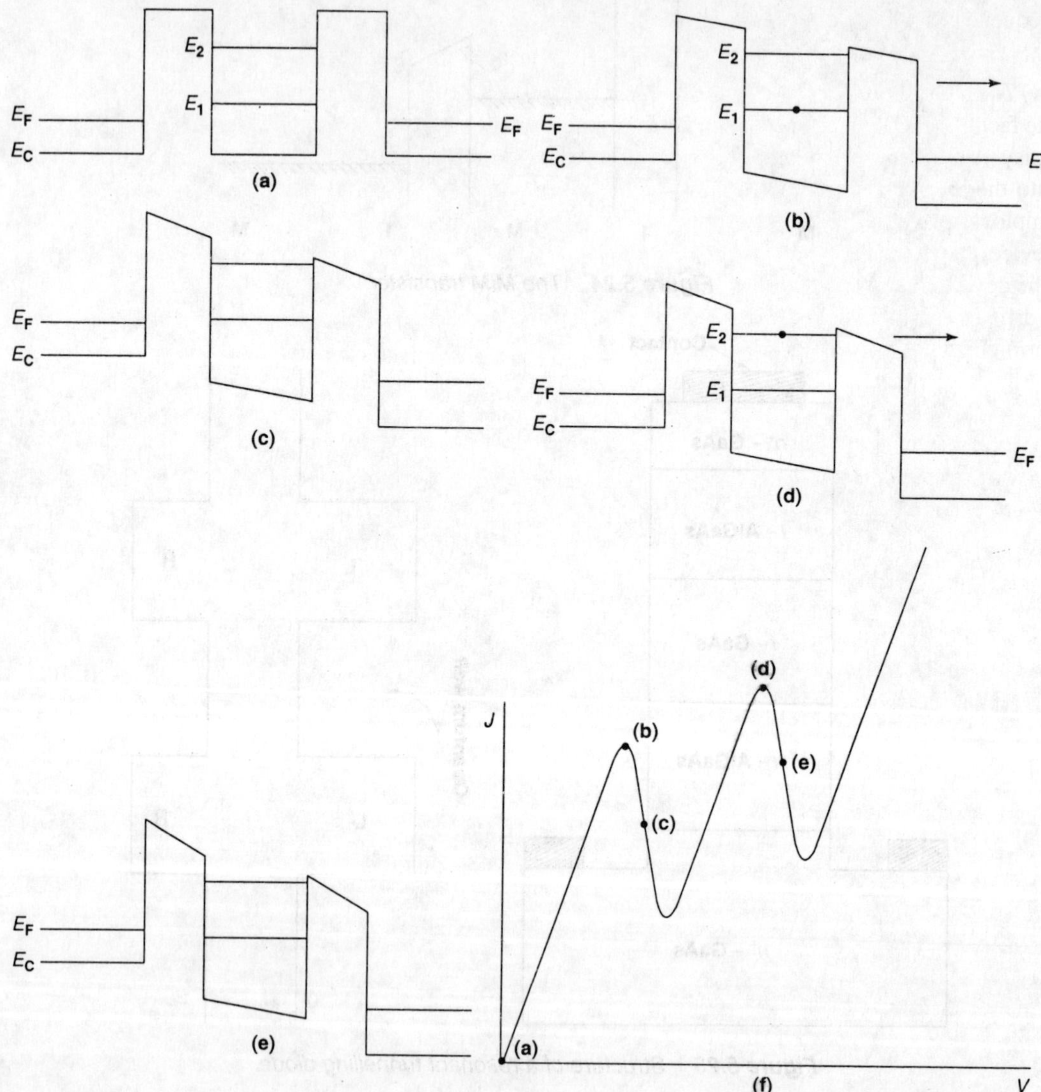

Figure 5.26 *The energy band diagrams of a resonant tunnelling diode and its I–V characteristics: (a) at equilibrium, (b) the resonant tunnelling through E_1, (c) the first negative resistance region, (d) the resonant tunnelling through E_2, (e) the second negative resistance region, (f) the I–V characteristic of a resonant tunnelling diode.*

mass. The non-zero valley current density is mainly due to the thermionic emission over the barriers and so it has a larger temperature dependence, unlike the peak tunnelling current density. Another small but conceivable contribution to the valley current density is due to the tunnelling of electrons to higher quantized levels. Even though the number of electrons available for tunnelling at energies higher than E_F is very small, there is a thermal distribution tail, especially when the quantized levels are close together. The maximum (J_p/J_v) ratio is about 50 under room temperature conditions. Maximum frequency of oscillations recorded with a DBRTD oscillator is expected to be around 10^{12} Hz.

(iv) The QWITT diode A major drawback of the IMPATT diode for very high frequency operations is the fact that the avalanche process, which depends upon random impact ionization events is inherently noisy. A variety of approaches have been investigated to find alternative methods for injecting carriers into the drift region without relying on the avalanche mechanism. A particularly interesting device employs resonant tunnelling through a quantum well to inject electrons into the drift region. This device, called quantum well injection transit time (QWITT) diode is shown schematically in Fig. 5.27. The device consists of a single GaAs quantum well between two Al_xGa_{1-x} As barriers, in series with a drift region of undoped GaAs. This structure is then placed between two n^+ – GaAs regions to form contacts. If an appropriate bias is applied so that the Fermi level in GaAs (n^+) is below E by

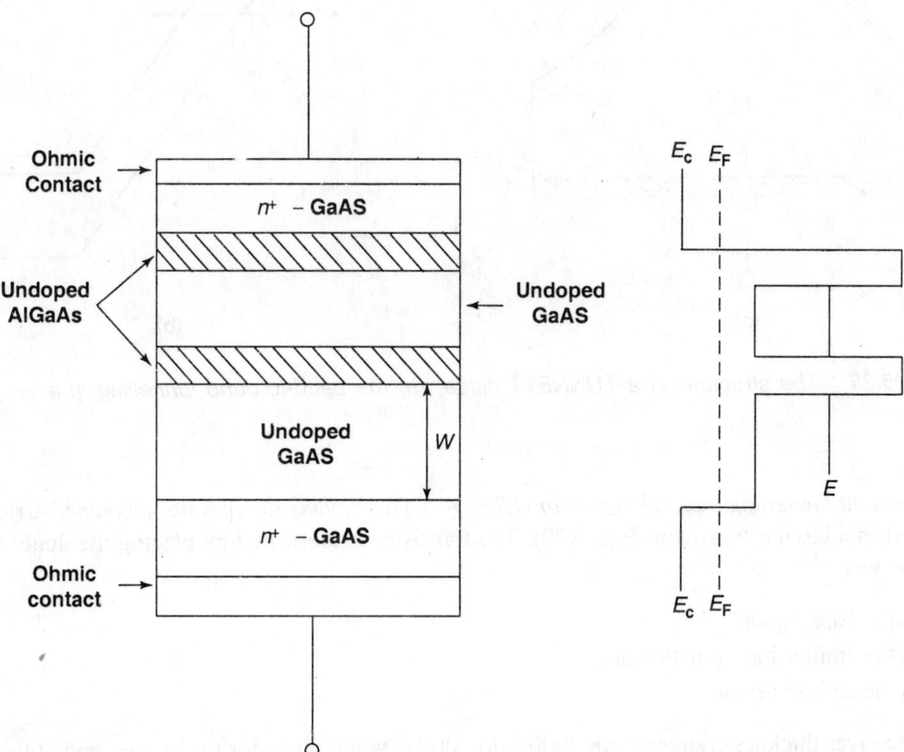

Figure 5.27 *Configuration of a QWITT diode, (b) the energy band diagram of the device with no applied bias*

an amount V_{RF} and an a.c. signal $V_{RF}\sin(\omega t)$ is superimposed upon the d.c. bias, then the resonant tunnelling current density through the well will peak at an injection angle $(\pi/2)$ in the a.c. cycle. The electrons would then drift through the i-layer (of appropriate length) resulting in the dynamic negative resistance.

(v) Tunnel injection transit time (TUNNETT) diode In a TUNNETT diode, the injection current is by tunnelling across a single barrier. The configuration of the device has been shown in Fig. 5.28(a). The advantage of a TUNNETT diode is its high frequency capability. Another advantage is its low voltage operation. This can operate at a voltage as low as 2 V. The limitation of the device is the low power handling capability due to a lower tunnelling current.

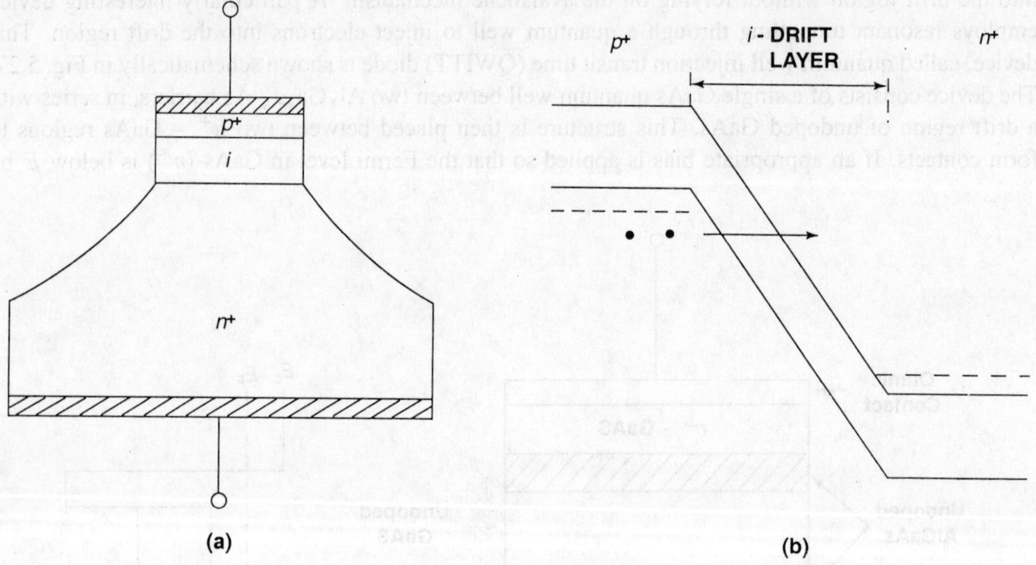

Figure 5.28 *The structure of a TUNNETT diode, (b) the band-to-band tunnelling in a pn junction injector*

(vi) Resonant tunnelling bipolar transistor (RTBT) This device incorporates a double barrier quantum well in a bipolar transistor (Fig. 5.29). The transistor is fabricated by placing the double barrier quantum well

a) in the base region,
b) at the emitter-base junction and
c) in the emitter region.

The base layer thickness ranges from 2000 Å to 3000 Å while those for the emitter and collector are slightly larger. The typical quantum well thickness is about 50 Å. It is surrounded by two barriers, whose widths lie in the range of 20–50 Å. All the three layers, which form the quantum well are undoped. Like all other quantum well devices, RTBTs are also fabricated using MBE.

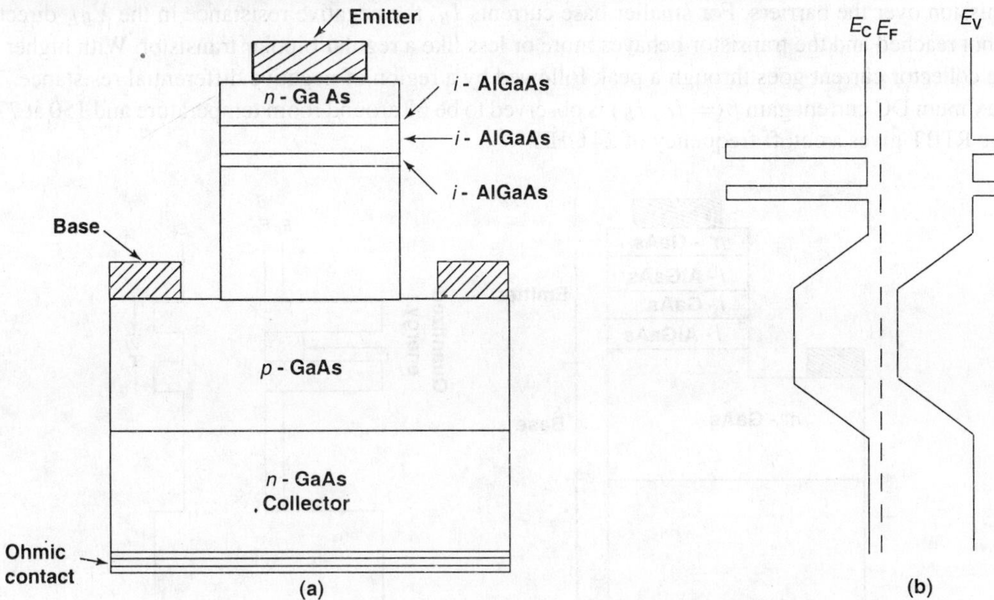

Figure 5.29 *(a) The RTBT configuration, (b) the energy band diagram*

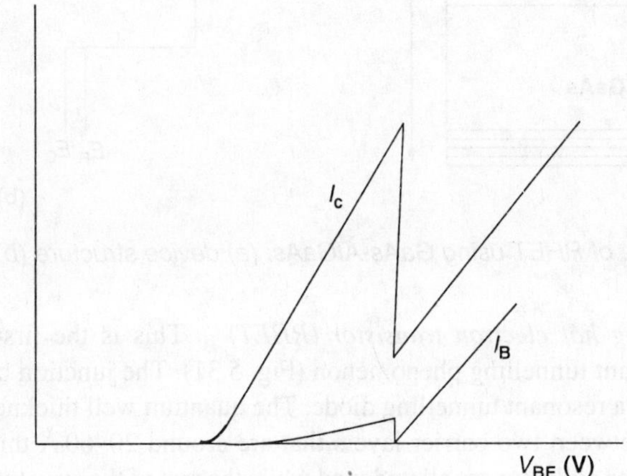

Figure 5.30 *The collector and the base currents as a function of V_{BE}*

In Fig. 5.30, the terminal characteristics all show a negative differential conductance as a function of the emitter-to-base voltage V_{BE}. This can be explained by using the energy band diagram shown in Fig. 5.29(b). Inside the quantum well, the energy sub-bands are quantized. Maximum tunnelling occurs when the conduction band edge E_c in the outer emitter layer aligns with the quantized level. Beyond that V_{BE}, the electron states within the quantum well are not available for resonant tunnelling, and hence the tunnelling current starts decreasing giving rise to a negative transconductance. With further increase in V_{BE}, the current goes through a valley point and rises once again. The second rise could be due to resonant tunnelling through the second quantized level, inelastic tunnelling or thermionic emission over the barriers. For smaller base currents I_B, the negative resistance in the V_{BE} direction is not reached and the transistor behaves more or less like a regular bipolar transistor. With higher I_B, the collector current goes through a peak followed by a region of negative differential resistance. The maximum DC current gain $\beta(= I_C/I_B)$ is observed to be 60 around room temperature and 150 at 77 K. The RTBT gives a cutoff frequency of 24 GHZ.

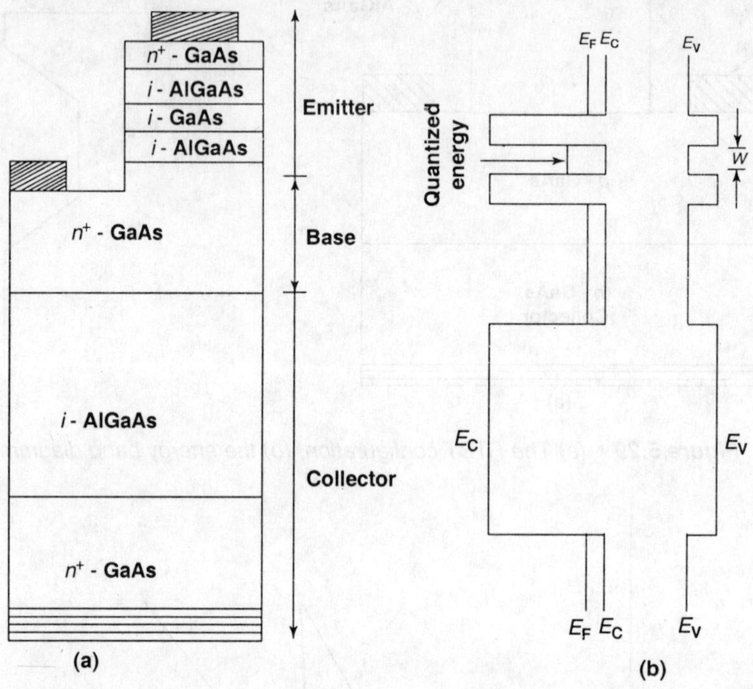

Figure 5.31 *Structure of RHET using GaAs-AlGaAs: (a) device structure (b) energy band diagram*

(vii) Resonant tunnelling hot electron transistor (RHET) This is the first three-terminal device making use of the resonant tunnelling phenomenon (Fig. 5.31). The junction between the emitter and the base is equivalent to a resonant tunnelling diode. The quantum well thickness is typically between 20–60 Å, sandwiched between two barrier layers that are around 20–60 Å thick. These three layers, plus the barrier layer in the collector are all undoped while the rest of the structure is heavily doped with n-type impurities. There is also an intrinsic GaAs spacer layer (~15 Å), inserted between the quantum well barrier layer (i-GaAs) and n^+-emitter or base, to prevent dopant diffusion to barrier layers. The degenerate base layer has a thickness in the range of 100–1000 Å. The collector usually has a transition layer (~50 Å) of graded composition to minimize quantum mechanical reflections arising from a sharp potential interface. The barrier layer within the collector is reasonably thick ranging from 2000 Å to 3000 Å, to ensure a high breakdown voltage between the collector and the base. Since ultrathin layers are required to fabricate this transistor, MBE must be used.

The injection current from the emitter is a resonant tunnelling current through quantized energy sub-bands in a quantum well. The barrier in the collector serves to prevent leakage between the base and the outer collector, both of which are heavily doped and are of the same type. With increasing V_{BE}, when the conduction band edge E_c at the emitter approaches the quantized energy level within the well, maximum electron injection occurs (Fig. 5.32). A further increase in V_{BE} reduces the resonant tunnelling current.

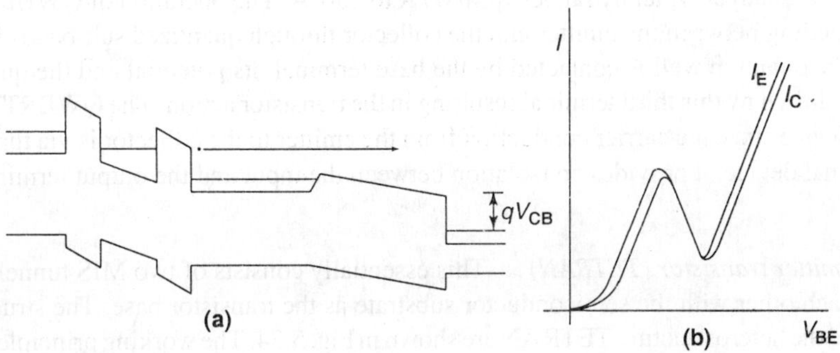

Figure 5.32 *(a) The energy band diagrams of a RHET for the maximum resonant tunnelling, (b) the terminal currents as a function of V_{BE} (for a fixed V_{CB})*

This is a basis for a negative differential transconductance. The collector-to-base voltage is applied to attract the emitted electrons efficiently. It is found that a barrier thickness of less than 30 Å is required to give a collector current density of 2×10^5 A/cm^2. The ratio (I_C/I_B) is found to be 10 at room temperature while it is 25 at 77 K.

(viii) Quantum well base resonant tunnelling transistor (QWBRTT) This device is basically a resonant tunnelling diode with a third terminal connected to the quantum well which is used as a base to control its potential. The quantum well base can either be doped with the same type of impurity as is used to dope the emitter and collector, or with the opposite type. The former is often referred to as a unilateral device and the latter as bipolar (Fig. 5.33). Unlike the DBRTD, the QWBRTT needs

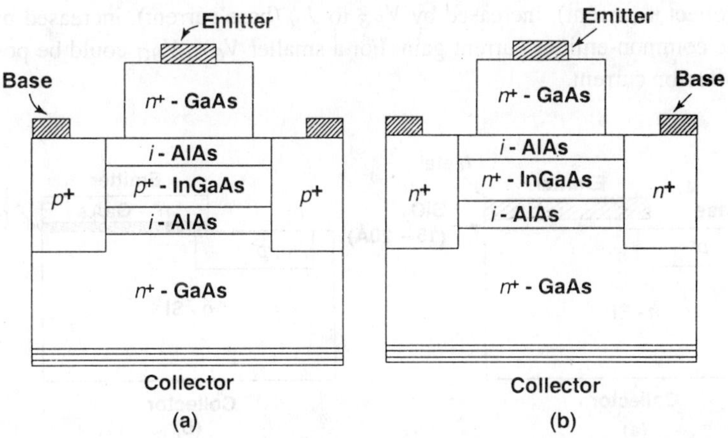

Figure 5.33 *The structures showing the two embodiments of QWBRTT: (a) the bipolar device with a p-type base, (b) the unipolar device with an n-type base.*

a heterosructure made from three layers with different energy gaps. The barrier layers must have the largest energy gap while the base layer must have a smaller energy gap than the emitter and the collector to reduce the leakage current from the base. An example is the GaAs-AlAs-InGaAs system, shown in Fig. 5.33. The base layer typically ranges from 60 Å to 150 Å. The operation of QWBRTT is based on resonant tunnelling between the emitter and the collector through quantized sub-bands in the quantum well. Since the quantum well is contacted by the base terminal, its potential and the quantized energy levels can be shifted by this third terminal resulting in the transistor action. The QWBRTT is potentially an ultrafast device since the carrier conduction from the emitter to the collector is via tunnelling. Being a three-terminal device, it provides an isolation between the input and the output terminals.

(ix) Tunnel emitter transistor (TETRAN) This essentially consists of two MIS tunnel diodes placed adjacent to each other with the semiconductor substrate as the transistor base. The structures for MIS TETRAN and the heterostructure TETRAN are shown in Fig. 5.34. The working principle of a TETRAN can best be demonstrated by the energy band diagrams of Fig. 5.35, using the MIS TETRAN as an example. It can be seen in Fig. 5.35(a), that under equilibrium, the semiconductor surface is depleted and there is no base region: With a high emitter-collector negative bias V_{CE} but no base emitter bias V_{BE}, the semiconductor is driven into a state of deep depletion with little change in the oxide field. The applied emitter-collector bias is shared between the oxide layer and the semiconductor surface as

$$V_{CE} = V_{OX} + \Psi_s \tag{5.173}$$

The hole tunnelling current density J_{tp} in this condition is practically zero as there is no net supply of holes. The electron current also does not increase significantly because Ψ_s absorbs most of the applied V_{CE}. The situation is depicted in Fig. 5.35(b). In Fig. 5.35(c), a base-emitter bias increases the supply of holes and reduces the semiconductor band bending Ψ_s, thereby increaing the oxide field and consequently the electron tunnelling current. In addition to the higher field, another factor that increases J_{tn} is the larger range of energy in which electrons can tunnel. The hole tunnelling current is also increased by the same V_{BE}, but the current level is much lower. The reasons for this are that the available holes for tunnelling are less abundant and the barrier height for holes is larger. The ratio of J_{tn} (or the collector current), increased by V_{BE} to J_{tp} (base current), increased by the same V_{BE}, is defined as the common-emitter current gain. For a smaller V_{CE}, V_{BC} could be positive and I_h is a forward-bias diffusion current.

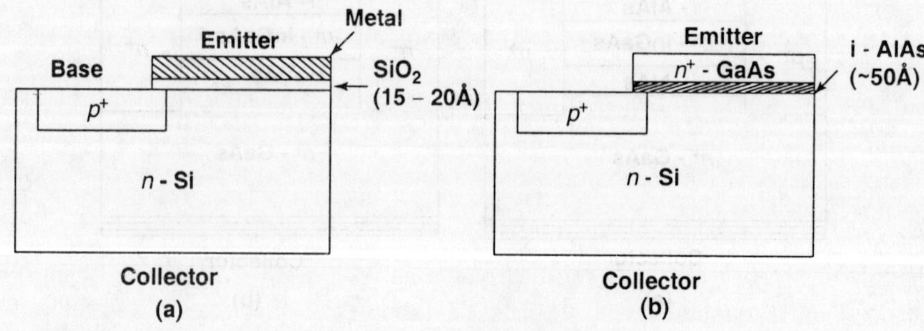

Figure 5.34 *The structures for (a) MISTETRAN and (b) heterostructure TETRAN*

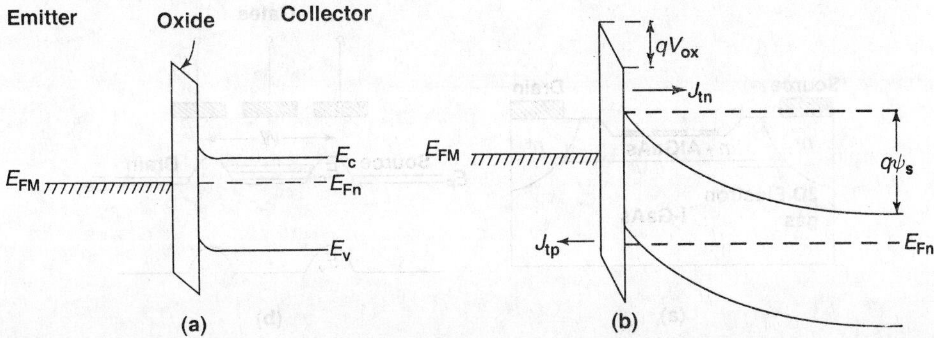

Figure 5.35 *The energy and band diagram of MIS TETRAN under different biasing conditions: (a) at equilibrium, (b) for a large* V_{CE}, V_{BE} *(or* $I_B = 0$*),*

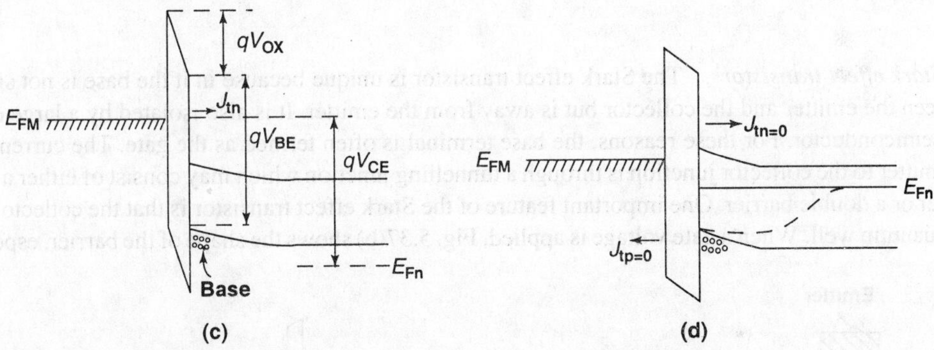

Figure 5.35 *continued (c) for, a larger* V_{CE} *with* $V_{BE} \neq 0$*; a base is formed as an inversion layer, (d) a smaller* V_{CE} *with* $V_{BE} \neq 0$

(x) Lateral resonant tunnelling field effect transistor (LRTFET) Structurally, LRTFET is an FET with discontinuous but closely spaced grating gates. Most stuctures reported are built on a GaAs-AlGaAs MODFET channel as shown in Fig. 5.36, but other FET channels such as that of a MOSFET can also be used. The LRTFET can be generalized to include a single quantum well or serial multiple quantum wells. The example shown in the figure has a single quantum well which is controlled by three gates. The two outer gates control the barriers while the middle gate controls the potential. In some cases, the middle gate may be omitted. The gate sizes and their spacing are critical for resonant tunnelling phenomenon. The smallest dimension achievable so far for either the gate or the space, is around 50 nm, and is obtained by X-ray lithography or electron beam lithography, together with dry etching. The n-doped AlGaAs layer is typically 40 nm with an additional intrinsic spacer layer of 7 nm, adjacent to the GaAs channel.

In the LRTFET, the current between the source and the drain is due to resonant tunnelling via quantized levels in the quantum well which is field induced by the gates. LRTFET provides a continuously tunnelable quantum well that is flexible and is useful for studying the resonant tunnelling phenomenon.

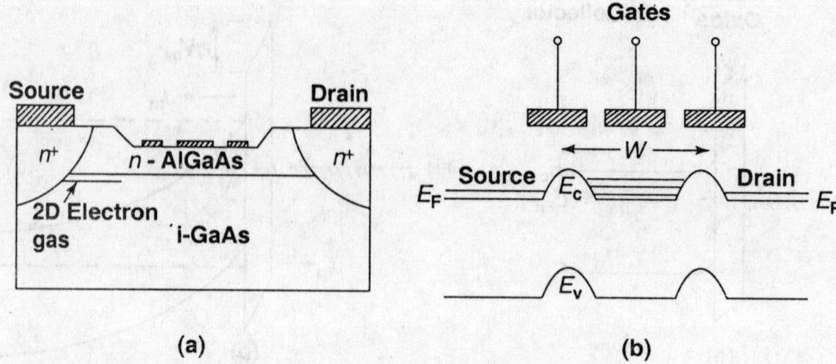

Figure 5.36 *(a) The structure of LRTFET using a GaAs-AlGaAs MODFET as an example, (b) the energy band diagram of LRTFET along the MODFET channel, showing the quantum well induced by the gate potential.*

(xi) Stark effect transistor The Stark effect transistor is unique because in it the base is not situated between the emitter and the collector but is away from the emitter. It is also isolated by a large energy gap semiconductor. For these reasons, the base terminal is often termed as the gate. The current from the emitter to the collector junction is through a tunnelling junction which may consist of either a single barrier or a double barrier. One important feature of the Stark effect transistor is that the collector layer is a quantum well. When a gate voltage is applied, Fig. 5.37(b) shows the shape of the barrier, especially

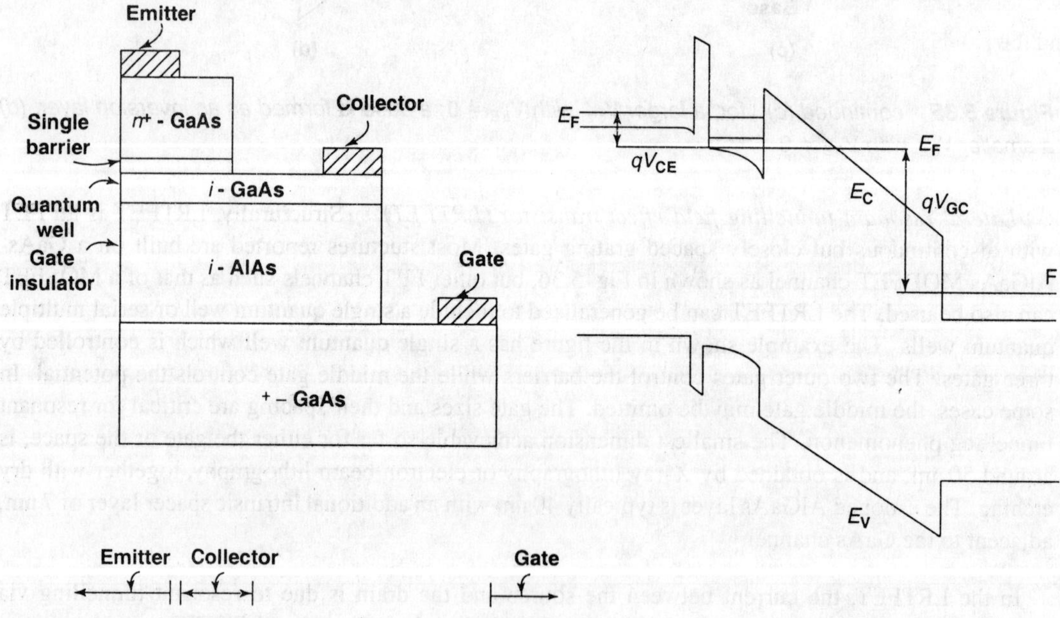

Figure 5.37 *(a) The structures of a Stark effect transistor, (b) the energy band diagram of the Stark effect transistor under a positive gate-to-collector bias V_{GC} and the collector-to-emitter bias V_{CE}.*

between the collector and the gate, and the shape of the well as drastically changed, inducing shifts of sub-bands within the collector quantum well. This phenomenon of the change of the energy band structure by an external field is called Stark effect and is responsible for the transistor action. When the collector sub-bands are scanned up and down, the resonant tunnelling current changes accordingly.

5.9 Tunnel diode applications

5.9.1 Tunnel diode amplifiers

To demonstrate the use of tunnel diode amplifiers, let us consider the circuit of Fig. 5.38. The circuit represents a generator of an internal conductance G_g connected in parallel to a negative conductance G of a tunnel diode and the load conductance G_L. The output power across the load may now be written as

$$P_{\text{out}} = \frac{I_L^2}{G_L} = \frac{I_g^2 G_L}{(G_g + G_L - G)^2} \tag{5.174}$$

To calculate the power delivered by the transistor, it is presumed that the condition of maximum power transfer viz., $G_g = (G_L - G)$ is satisfied. Hence, the input power is

$$P_{\text{in}} = \frac{I_g^2}{4G_g} \tag{5.175}$$

and the power gain is given by

$$PG = \frac{P_{\text{out}}}{P_{\text{in}}} = \frac{4G_g G_L}{(G_g + G_L - G)^2} \tag{5.176}$$

Thus, for a certain set of values of G_g, G_L and G, a power gain would follow. The operating point in the negative conductance region may however be stabilized by a proper choice of G_L.

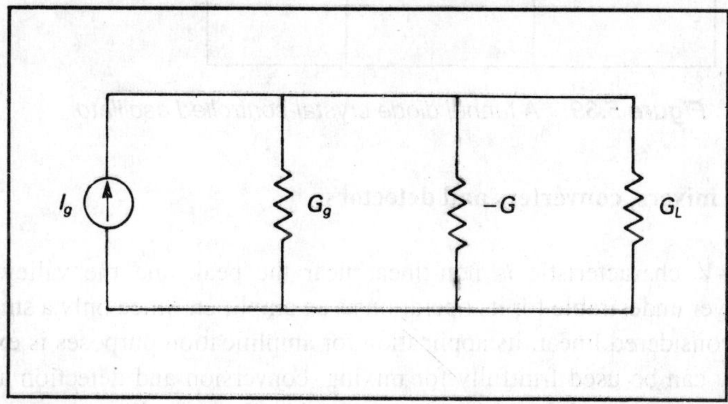

Figure 5.38

5.9.2 Tunnel diode oscillators

The stability of the operating point is an important consideration for using a tunnel diode as a voltage amplifier. But self-sustaining oscillations are necessary for a tunnel diode oscillator. To select the operating point for an oscillator see the worked example No.10. We find there that the necessary condition for the self-sustaining oscillations is

$$\left(\frac{|G|}{C}\right) - \left(\frac{R}{L}\right) > 0 \tag{5.177}$$

The corresponding frequency of oscillation is the given by

$$f = \frac{1}{2\pi}\left[\left\{\frac{(1 - R|G|)}{LC}\right\} - \frac{1}{4}\left\{\left(\frac{R}{L}\right) - \left(\frac{|G|}{C}\right)\right\}^2\right]^{1/2} \tag{5.178}$$

The oscillations build up in the negative conductance region as long as (5.177) is valid. When oscillations extend to regions where $[(|G|/C) - (R/L)]$ tends to be negative, oscillations get stabilized. A tunnel diode crystal-controlled oscillator is shown in Fig. 5.39. For stabilizing the frequency, a piezoelectric crystal is employed.

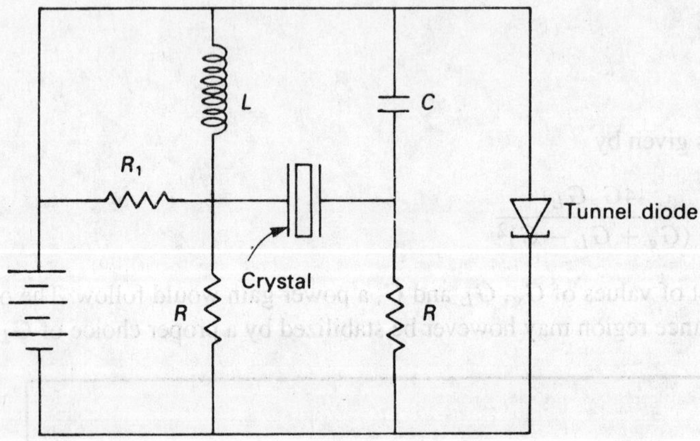

Figure 5.39 *A tunnel diode crystal-controlled oscillator*

5.9.3 Tunnel diode mixers, converters and detectors

The tunnel diode I–V characteristic is non-linear near the peak and the valley points. Such a non-linearity is however undesirable for its operation as an amplifier. Since only a small portion of the n.d.c. region can be considered linear, its application for amplification purposes is extremely limited. But, the non-linearity can be used fruitfully for mixing, conversion and detection applications. The non-linear I–V curve of the tunnel diode can be expressed mathematically as

$$I = a_0 + a_1 V + a_2 V^2 + a_3 V^3 + a_4 V^4 + \dots \tag{5.179}$$

The I–V curve of a tunnel diode shows that $(dI/dV) = 0$ for two values of V. Hence, the minimum number of terms in the polynomial describing the I–V curve must be three. It is therefore necessary to determine a_1, a_2, and a_3, since $a_0 = 0$ when $I = 0$ and $V = 0$. The remarkable features of a tunnel diode mixer are its low noise figure, high gain and low local oscillator power requirements. If a part of the n.d.c region is employed, a conversion gain may also be realized. But for that purpose, the operating point needs to be stabilized. A typical tunnel diode mixer circuit is shown in Fig. 5.40. The radio frequency and the local oscillator signals are mixed with each other in a tunnel diode, which is biased in its stable non-linear region near the peak point. The signals of different frequencies undergo mixing by virtue of (5.179). The resulting current may be obtained by writing $V = V_1 \sin(\omega_1 t) + V_0 \sin(\omega_0 t)$. Consequently, an intermediate signal output corresponding to the frequency $\omega_2 = (\omega_1 - \omega_0)$ is obtained across the output. The difference between a mixer and a converter is that a mixer requires an external local oscillator signal while a converter generates one. The following functions are simultaneously performed in a converter circuit

i) Oscillation at f_0,
ii) amplification of the r.f. signal f_1,
iii) mixing of two signals, and
iv) amplification of the intermediate frequency signal f_2 before it is transferred to the output.

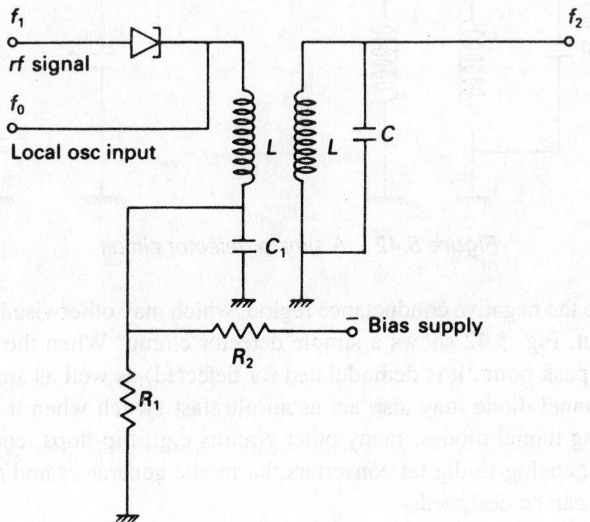

Figure 5.40 *A tunnel diode mixer circuit*

A simple converter circuit is shown in Fig. 5.41. It consists of a tank circuit (L_2, C_2) resonant at the intermediate frequency f_2 and another tank circuit (L_1, C_1) resonant at the intermediate frequency f_1. The tunnel diode is biased in its non-linear negative conductance region and is made to oscillate at the local oscillator frequency f_0. The non-linearity of the I–V characteristic near the peak point suggests the possibility of the device being used as a low-level detector. An examination of the tunnel diode I–V characteristic shows that unless a device is biased very close to the peak point, its detection efficiency is extremely poor. The peak amplitude of the modulated r.f. signal has to be restricted suitably

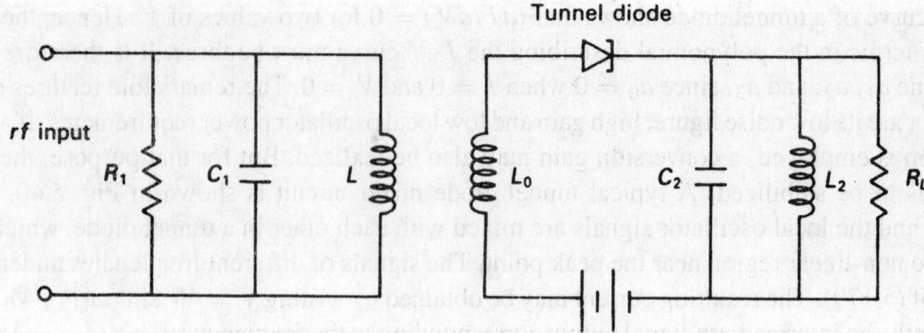

Figure 5.41 *A tunnel diode converter circuit*

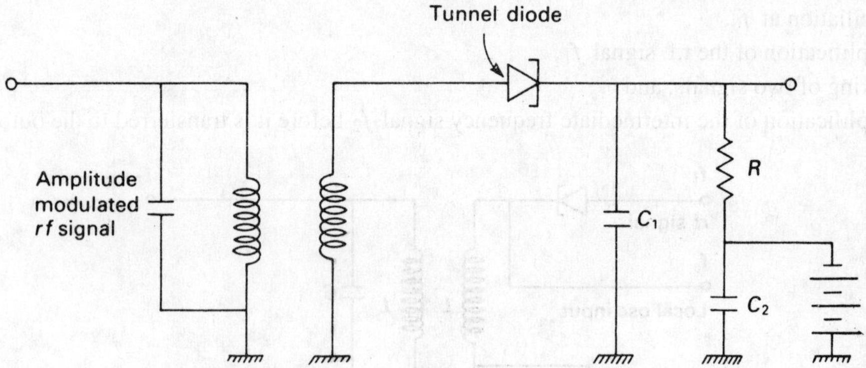

Figure 5.42 *A simple detector circuit*

to avoid excursions into the negative conductance region, which may otherwise introduce unwarranted distortions at the output. Fig. 5.42 shows a simple detector circuit. When the amplitude modulated signal swings over the peak point, it is demodulated (or detected) as well as amplified. In addition to these applications, a tunnel diode may also act as an ultrafast switch when it is made to operate in its bistable mode. Using tunnel diodes, many other circuits e.g., flip-flops, counters, shift resistors, zero-crossing detectors, analog-to-digital converters, harmonic generators and d.c. to a.c. converters, with many advantages, can be designed.

Solved examples

5.1 Discuss the condition for the exhibition of wave-particle dualism by microscopic entities.

Solution

According to the De Broglie relation, the wavelength associated with a microscopic particle of a momentum p is given by

$$\lambda = \frac{h}{p} \tag{1}$$

Now, if the probability of locating the particle within a distance λ is non-zero, then it is normally observed that the entity is capable of exhibiting wave-particle dualism. In other words, the uncertainty Δx in locating the particle must be λ. That is,

$$\Delta x \cong \lambda \tag{2}$$

Combining (1) and (2), we find

$$\Delta x = \frac{h}{p} \tag{3}$$

But, by virtue of Heisenberg's uncertainty relation, we know that

$$\Delta x \cong \frac{h}{\Delta p} \tag{4}$$

Comparing (3) and (4), one may easily conclude that the necessary condition for a material particle to exhibit wave-particle dualism is

$$p \cong \Delta p \tag{5}$$

If $p \gg \Delta p$, the wave nature of the particle becomes perceptible. On the other hand, if $p \ll \Delta p$, the particle nature is displayed by the microscopic entity. By similar arguments, one may establish that if $E \gg \Delta E$, then the entity will behave wave-like while if the opposite is true, its behaviour is corpuscular.

5.2 In barrier penetration problems, estimate the number of scattered wavelets which are generated as a result of the quantum measurement carried out by a potential barrier.

Solution

If incident matter waves interact with a potential barrier for a period of $\Delta t (= \tau)$seconds, we must have

$$\Delta t = \tau = nT = (n \pm \Delta n)(T \pm \Delta T) \tag{1}$$

where T is the period of a matter wave of frequency ν, and ΔT is the corresponding spread in the time period. It follows from equation (1) that

$$\frac{T}{\Delta T} = \left(\frac{n}{\Delta n}\right)\left[1 \pm \left(\frac{\Delta n}{n}\right)\right] = \left(\frac{n}{\Delta n}\right)(1 \pm f) = s\left(\frac{n}{\Delta n}\right) \text{ (say)} \tag{2}$$

where $f = (\Delta n/n)$ and $s = (1 \pm f) \sim 1$.
But,

$$\nu = \frac{1}{T} \tag{3}$$

Therefore,

$$\begin{aligned}\left|\frac{\Delta \nu}{\nu}\right| = \frac{\Delta T}{T} = \frac{\Delta n}{sn} = \frac{\Delta n\lambda}{s(n\lambda)} = \frac{\Delta n\lambda}{s\Delta x} = \frac{\Delta n\lambda}{s(\nu \Delta t)} \\ = \frac{(\Delta n\lambda)}{s\nu\lambda\Delta t} = \frac{\Delta n}{s\nu\Delta t}\end{aligned} \tag{4}$$

or

$$\Delta \nu \Delta t = \frac{\Delta n}{s} \sim \Delta n \tag{5}$$

where Δn denotes the number of scattered wavelets. Combining (2) and (4), one finds

$$\frac{\Delta n}{n} = \frac{\Delta \nu}{\nu} \tag{6}$$

From (6), we derive

$$\frac{\Delta n}{\left(\frac{\Delta x}{\lambda}\right)} = \frac{\left(\frac{\Delta E}{h}\right)}{\left(\frac{E}{h}\right)} = \frac{\Delta E}{E}$$

or

$$\Delta n = \left(\frac{\Delta x}{\lambda}\right)\left(\frac{\Delta E}{E}\right) \tag{7}$$

gives the number of scattered wavelets as a result of the quantum measurement by the potential barrier. The number n of waves of a wavelength λ is, however, given by

$$n = \frac{\Delta x}{\lambda} \sim \frac{W}{\lambda} \tag{8}$$

5.3 For an even function $F(t)$, the frequency spectrum can be found by the use of the Fourier integral theorem

$$g(\omega) = \left[\frac{1}{\sqrt{(2\pi)}}\right] \int_{-\infty}^{+\infty} F(t) \exp(-j\omega t) dt$$

Show that if $F(t) = A$, for $-a < t < a$ and zero elsewhere, one must have

$$g(\omega) = A \left(\frac{2}{\pi}\right)^{1/2} \left[\frac{\sin(\omega a)}{\omega}\right]$$

Plot $g(\omega)$ as a function of ω. We define the bandwidth $\Delta\omega$ such that at $\omega = \pm(\Delta\omega/2)$, $g(\omega)$ reduces to zero. Also, show that the product $\Delta\nu\Delta t = 1$, where $\Delta t \sim a$ and $\nu = (\omega/2\pi)$.

Solution

Fourier integral theorem : We start with the complex Fourier series expansion $F(t)$ expressed as

$$F(t) = \sum_{n=-\infty}^{n=+\infty} a_n \exp(nj\omega t) \tag{1}$$

where the coefficient a_n is given by

$$a_n = \left(\frac{1}{T}\right) \int_{-(T/2)}^{+(T/2)} F(u) \exp(-nj\omega u)\, du \tag{2}$$

Substituting (2) in (1), we find

$$F(t) = \sum_{n=-\infty}^{n=+\infty} \left(\frac{1}{T}\right) \int_{-(T/2)}^{+(T/2)} F(u) \exp\left\{\left(\frac{2\pi}{T}\right) nj(t-u)\right\} du \tag{3}$$

Let us next put

$$\frac{1}{T} = \Delta s \tag{4}$$

If $T \to \infty$, $\Delta s \to 0$ so that $n\,\Delta s = s$ (say). Making these substitutions in (4), we find

$$F(t) = \sum_{n=-\infty}^{n=+\infty} \Delta s \int_{-[1/(2\Delta s)]}^{[1/(2\Delta s)]} F(u) \exp\{j(2\pi\, n\, \Delta s)(t-u)\}\, du$$

$$= \int_{-\infty}^{+\infty} \exp j(2\pi st) ds \int_{-\infty}^{+\infty} F(u) \exp j(-2\pi su)\, du \tag{5}$$

Let us consider a pulse of height A which begins at $t = -a$ and ends at $t = +a$. Hence, we may write

$$F(t) = \begin{array}{lll} 0 & \text{for} & t < -a \\ a & \text{for} & -a \leq t \leq a \\ 0 & \text{for} & t > +a \end{array} \tag{6}$$

Substituting (6) in (5), we find

$$F(t) = \int_{-\infty}^{+\infty} \exp j(2\pi st)ds \int_{-a}^{+a} F(u) \exp j(-2\pi su)\, du \tag{7}$$

Now, put $2\pi s = v$. Equation (7) then reduces to

$$F(t) = \left[\frac{A}{2\pi j}\right] \int_{-\infty}^{+\infty} \exp\,[jv(t+a) - \exp \frac{[jv(t-a)]}{v}\, dv \tag{8}$$

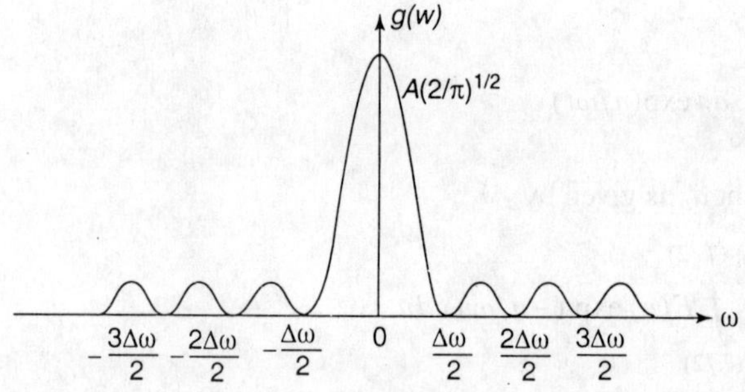

This is the Fourier integral representation of (6). If we now introduce a new variable $\omega = 2\pi s$, the equation (5) takes the following form:

$$F(t) = \left[\frac{1}{\sqrt{(2\pi)}}\right] \int_{-\infty}^{+\infty} g(\omega) \exp(-j\omega t)\, dt \tag{9}$$

where

$$g(\omega) = \left[\frac{1}{\sqrt{(2\pi)}}\right] \int_{-\infty}^{+\infty} F(u) \exp(-j\omega u) du \tag{10}$$

$g(\omega)$ (Fourier transform) gives the frequency spectrum of the function $F(t)$.
Now, the frequency spectrum of the pulse function, shown in the figure is given by

$$g(\omega) = \left[\frac{1}{\sqrt{(2\pi)}}\right] \int_{-a}^{+a} F(u) \exp(-j\omega u) du = A \left(\frac{2}{\pi}\right)^{1/2} \left[\sin \frac{(\omega a)}{\omega}\right] \tag{11}$$

The function $g(\omega)$ is plotted in the figure. According to (11), since $g(\omega) = 0$ for $\omega = \pm(\Delta\omega/2)$, we get

$$\left(\frac{\Delta\omega}{2}\right) a = \pi$$

i.e.,

$$\Delta\omega\Delta t = 2\pi \tag{12}$$

since, $a \sim \Delta t$. Also, since $\omega = 2\pi\nu$, it follows from (12) that

$$\Delta\nu\Delta t = 1 \tag{13}$$

5.4 Imagine a monochromatic beam of electrons of energy 500 meV to be incident upon a potential barrier of an arbitrary shape but of a height 1 eV. Calculate

(i) the tunnelling time of electrons through it,
(ii) the velocities of incident and transmitted electrons through it,
(iii) their transmission coefficients at the energy of incidence and
(iv) the order of magnitude of the barrier width.

Solution

The effective height of the barrier = $(V_0 - E) = (1 - 0.5) = 0.5$ eV. Therefore, the penetration constant χ is given by

$$\chi = \frac{[2m(V_0 - E)]^{1/2}}{\hbar} \tag{1}$$

Substituting the appropriate values of parameters in (1), we get

$$\chi = \frac{(2 \times 9.11 \times 10^{-31} \times 0.5 \times 1.6 \times 10^{-19})^{1/2}}{1.05 \times 10^{-34}} = 3.638 \times 10^9 \text{ m}^{-1}$$

(i) The tunnelling time τ of electrons through the barrier is given by

$$\tau \geq \frac{\hbar}{V_0 - E} \tag{2}$$

Substituting the values of the appropriate parameters in it, we get

$$\tau \geq \frac{6.62 \times 10^{-34}}{0.5 \times 1.6 \times 10^{-19}} \geq 8.28 \times 10^{-15} \text{ s}$$

(ii) The velocity of incident electrons is given by

$$v = \left(\frac{2E}{m}\right)^{1/2} \tag{3}$$

With appropriate value of parameters in (3), we get

$$v = \left[\frac{2 \times 500 \times 1.6 \times 10^{-22}}{9.11 \times 10^{-31}}\right]^{1/2} = 4.19 \times 10^5 \text{ m/s}$$

The velocity of the transmitted electrons is given by

$$v_t = \frac{\hbar \chi}{2m} = \frac{1.05 \times 10^{-34} \times 3.638 \times 10^9}{2 \times 9.11 \times 10^{-31}} = 2.096 \times 10^5 \text{ m/s}$$

(iii) The transmission coefficient at the energy of incidence is given by

$$Z = 16\, k^2 \chi^2 \exp \frac{(-2\chi W)}{k^2 + \chi^2} \tag{4}$$

Since, tunnelling takes place by quantum measurement

$$W \sim \frac{2\pi}{\chi} \tag{5}$$

Hence,

$$W \sim \frac{2 \times 3.14}{3.638 \times 10^9} = 17.27 \text{ Å}$$

and

$$k = \frac{mv}{\hbar} = \frac{4.19 \times 10^5 \times 9.11 \times 10^{-31}}{1.05 \times 10^{-34}} = 3.635 \times 10^9 \text{ m}^{-1}$$

Therefore,

$$Z = \frac{16 \times (3.635 \times 10^9)^2 \times (3.638 \times 10^9)^2 \exp(-2 \times 17.27 \times 10^{-10} \times 3.638 \times 10^9)}{(3.635 \times 10^9)^2 + (3.638 \times 10^9)^2}$$

$$= 1.4 \times 10^{-5}$$

5.5 Presuming the work function of tungsten to be 4.5 eV, estimate the magnitude of the external electric field to be applied to its tip placed in vacuum, in order to observe the field-emission from it.

Solution

Quantum mechanical tunnelling by quantum measurement is believed to occur across a metal-vacuum interface if the fluctuation Δp in the momentum of the electron is given by

$$\Delta p = (2m\phi_m)^{1/2} \tag{1}$$

Now, if ε and W denote the magnitude of the electric field intensity to be applied and the barrier width at the metal-vacuum interface respectively, we must have

$$q\,\varepsilon W = \phi_m \tag{2}$$

But, during tunnelling, the electron must satisfy the following inequality

$$\Delta p\ W{\sim}\hbar \tag{3}$$

Combining equations (1), (2) and (3), we find

$$\varepsilon{\sim}\frac{(2m)^{1/2}(\phi_m)^{3/2}}{q\hbar} \tag{4}$$

Substituting the values of the appropriate physical parameters in (4), we find

$$\varepsilon{\sim}\frac{(2\times 9.11\times 10^{-31})^{1/2}(4.5\times 1.6\times 10^{-19})^{3/2}}{(1.6\times 10^{-19})(6.26\times 10^{-34})} \leq 7.8\times 10^{9}\ \text{V/m}$$

5.6 A field-emission microscope (FEM) consists of a tungsten ($\phi = 4.5\,\text{eV}$) point emitter with a radius of curvature 1000 Å placed at the centre of an evacuated glass vacuum tube with a radius of curvature 10 cm. Calculate

i) the voltage to be applied between the fluorescent screen and the metallic tip to generate field-emission,
ii) the magnification and
iii) the limit of resolution of the microscope.

Solution

(i) The field generated and the voltage applied are known to be related by

$$\varepsilon = \frac{V}{KR} \tag{1}$$

where $K = 5$ (a constant) and R = radius of curvature of the tip. We have just seen that the field required to generate field-emission is 7.8×10^{9} V/m. Therefore,

$$V = \varepsilon KR = 7.8\times 10^{9}\times 5\times 1000\times 10^{-10} = 3,900\ \text{V}$$

(ii) The magnification of the microscope is given by

$$M = \frac{R'}{\beta R} \tag{2}$$

where R' measures the radius of the tube = 10 cm = 0.1 m, $\beta = 1.0$ and $R = 1000 \times 10^{-10} = 10^{-7}$ m. Substituting these values in (2), we get

$$M = \frac{0.1}{10^{-7}} = 10^6$$

5.7 Derive an expression for the Fermi energy in a metal presuming the maximum electron energy at $T = 0\,K$ is the metal Fermi energy.

Solution

According to Heisenberg's uncertainty relation, the uncertainty in an electron's position and its momentum must always be related to one another as follows:

$$\begin{aligned} \Delta x \Delta p_x &\geq h \\ \Delta y \Delta p_y &\geq h \\ \Delta z \Delta p_z &\geq h \end{aligned} \tag{1}$$

Multiplying the above three relations, we find

$$(\Delta x \Delta y \Delta z)(\Delta p_x \Delta p_y \Delta p_z) \geq (h)^3$$

or

$$\Delta p_x \Delta p_y \Delta p_z) \geq \frac{h^3}{\Delta V} \tag{2}$$

where $\Delta V = (\Delta x \Delta y \Delta z)$ measures the minimum uncertainty in the volume of the electron. In such a case, the uncertainty product in the momentum space would be a maximum. If n denotes the density of electrons in a metal, we must have

$$\Delta V_{\min} = \frac{2}{n} \tag{3}$$

where the factor 2 accounts for two possible spin orientations. Combining (2) and (3), we find

$$(\Delta p_x \Delta p_y \Delta p_z)_{\max} = \left(\frac{4\pi}{3}\right)(\Delta p)^3 \quad {}_{\max} \geq \frac{(h)^3}{\Delta V_{\min}} \geq \frac{n(h)^3}{2}$$

or

$$(\Delta p)_{\max} \geq h\left(\frac{3n}{8\pi}\right)^{1/3} = \hbar\ k_F \tag{4}$$

where k_F denotes the Fermi wave vector. The Fermi level E_F in a metal is then given by

$$E_F = \frac{\hbar^2 k_F^2}{2m} = \left(\frac{\hbar^2}{2m}\right)\left(\frac{3n}{8\pi}\right)^{2/3} \tag{5}$$

This is the required relation.

5.8 Calculate Debye lengths in

i) intrinsic Si ($n_i = 10^{16} m^{-3}$) and
ii) Copper ($n = 10^{29}\ m^{-3}$).

Solution

(i) The expression for the Debye length in intrinsic Si is given by

$$L_d = \left[\frac{\kappa \varepsilon_0 kT}{q^2 n_i}\right]^{1/2} \tag{1}$$

Substituting appropriate values in (1), we get

$$L_d = \left[\frac{12 \times 8.854 \times 10^{-12} \times 0.0260}{91.6 \times 10^{-19} \times 10^{16}}\right]^{1/2} = 41.55\ \mu\text{m}$$

(ii) The expression for the intrinsic Debye length in copper is given by

$$\frac{1}{L_d} = \left[\frac{mq^2}{\pi \varepsilon_0 \hbar^2}\right]^{1/2} \left(\frac{3n}{\pi}\right)^{1/6} \tag{2}$$

With proper values in (2), we find

$$\frac{1}{L_d} = \left(\frac{9.11 \times 10^{-31}}{3.14 \times 8.854 \times 10^{-12}}\right)^{1/2} \frac{1.6 \times 10^{-19}}{1.05 \times 10} \left(\frac{3 \times 10^{29}}{3.14}\right)^{1/6}$$

or

$$L_d = 0.526\ \text{Å}$$

5.9 Derive the condition of degeneracy of an electron gas.

Solution

In order that an electron gas may behave as degenerate, the volume available to each electron (i.e., n^{-1}) must be smaller than the uncertainty volume. Therefore, in the three-dimensional case, we have

$$\frac{1}{n} \leq \Delta x \Delta y \Delta z \tag{1}$$

But, by virtue of the Heisenberg's uncertainty relation we know that

$$\Delta x \Delta y \Delta z \geq \frac{h^3}{\Delta p_x \Delta p_y \Delta p_z} \tag{2}$$

But, for the exhibition of wave-particle dualism, we must have

$$\Delta p_x \cong p_x = (2mE_x)^{1/2} = (mkT)^{1/2} = \Delta p_y = \Delta p_z \tag{3}$$

Combining (2) and (3), we find

$$\Delta x \Delta y \Delta z \geq \frac{h^3}{\Delta p_x \Delta p_y \Delta p_z} = \frac{(h)^3}{(mkT)^{3/2}} \tag{4}$$

Imposing (4) in (1), we get

$$n \geq \frac{(mkT)^{3/2}}{h^3} \tag{5}$$

By similar arguments, for a 2D and 1D electron gases one may have

$$n \geq \frac{mkT}{h^2} \tag{6}$$

and

$$n \geq \frac{(mkT)^{1/2}}{h} \tag{7}$$

5.10 Discuss the application potentialities of a negative resistance device such as a tunnel diode.

Solution

A simple bias circuit of a tunnel diode along with its I–V characteristic is shown in Fig. 5.43. The input impedance of the negative resistance device may be expressed as

$$Z_{\text{in}} = \left[R \pm \frac{G}{G^2 + \omega^2 C^2}\right] + j\omega\left[L - \frac{C}{(G^2 + \omega^2 C^2)}\right] \tag{1}$$

In the n.d.c region the real part of the impedance in (1) must be negative. The real part of the impedance is seen to vanish at a frequency f_c given by

$$f_c = \frac{|G|}{2\pi C}\left[\frac{1}{R|G|} - 1\right]^{1/2} \tag{2}$$

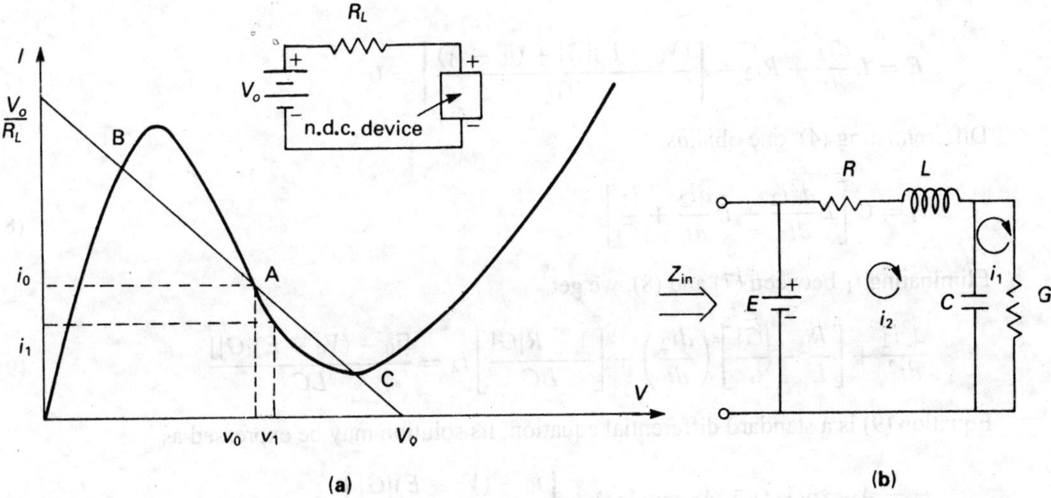

Figure 5.43 *(a) The biasing and (b) the the equivalent circuit of a negative resistance device*

where f_c is defined as the resistive cutoff frequency. On the other hand, the reactive part of the impedance is found to be zero at a frequency f_r, given by

$$f_r = \frac{1}{2\pi}\left[\frac{1}{LC} - \frac{|G|^2}{C^2}\right]^{1/2} \tag{3}$$

The operating point in the n.d.c region is normally unstable. But, it may be stabilized under suitable conditions.To find them, we apply Kirchoff's voltage law to the network to obtain

$$E = L\frac{di_2}{dt} + Ri_2 + \frac{1}{C}\left[\int (i_2 - i_1)dt\right] \tag{4}$$

Presuming the I–V characteristic to be linear near the operating point, we derive

$$|G| = \frac{i_0 - i_1}{V_1 - V_0} \tag{5}$$

Also,

$$CV_1 = \int (i_2 - i_1)dt \tag{6}$$

Combining (4) and (6), we find

$$E = L\frac{di_2}{dt} + Ri_2 + V_1$$

Using (5) and (6), the above relation simplifies to

$$E = L\frac{di_2}{dt} + Ri_2 + \left[\frac{i_0 - i_1}{|G| + V_0}\right]$$

or

$$E = L\frac{di_2}{dt} + Ri_2 + \left\{\frac{(V_0 - E)|G| + (i_0 - i_1)}{|G|}\right\} = 0 \tag{7}$$

Differentiating (4), one obtains

$$i_1 = C\left[L\frac{d^2 i_2}{dt^2} + R\frac{di_2}{dt} + \frac{i_2}{C}\right] \tag{8}$$

Eliminating i_1 between (7) and (8), we get

$$\frac{d^2 i_2}{dt^2} + \left[\frac{R}{L} - \frac{|G|}{C}\right]\left(\frac{di_2}{dt}\right) + \left[\frac{1 - R|G|}{LC}\right] i_2 = \frac{[i_0 - (V_0 - E)|G|]}{LC} \tag{9}$$

Equation (9) is a standard differential equation. Its solution may be expressed as

$$i_2 = A_1 \exp(\lambda_1 t) + A_2 \exp(\lambda_2 t) + \left\{\frac{i_0 - (V_0 - E)|G|}{LC}\right\} \tag{10}$$

where A_1 and A_2 are arbitrary constants whose values are settled from initial conditions, and we have

$$\lambda_1 \text{ or } \lambda_2 = \frac{1}{2}\left[\frac{|G|}{C} - \frac{R}{L}\right] \pm \left[\frac{1}{4}\left\{\frac{R}{L} - \frac{|G|}{C}\right\}^2 + \left\{\frac{1 - R|G|}{LC}\right\}\right]^{1/2} \tag{11}$$

Now, depending on the values of λ_1 and λ_2 , the following four cases may arise

(i) If λ_1 and λ_2 are real and positive quantities, according to (10),any initial transient would cause i_2 to grow exponentially. Therefore, the operating point at A would very soon be thrown out of the n.d.c region such that either it stabilizes at B or C. This is known as the bistable mode of operation and is useful for switching applications of the n.d.c device.

(ii) If λ_1 and λ_2 are real and negative quantities, any initial transient, according to (10), must die out in no time and the operating point gets stabilized at A. This mode of operation of the n.d.c device is useful for applications in amplifiers, mixers, converters and detectors.

(iii) If λ_1 and λ_2 are complex quantities with negative real parts, the device current i_2 is of a decaying sinusoidal type and the operating point gets quickly stabilized as in case (ii).

(iv) If λ_1 and λ_2 are complex quantities with positive real parts, the sinusoidal oscillations of the device current builds up so that in this mode, the device could be used as an oscillator.

Thus, to acquire a stable operating point in the n.d.c region, either the condition (ii) or (iii) need to be satisfied. From (11), we may infer that

$$\frac{|G|}{C} - \frac{R}{L} < 0 \tag{12}$$

and

$$1 - R|G| > 0 \tag{13}$$

Combinations of (12) and (13) yield

$$\frac{L}{C}|G| < R < \frac{1}{|G|} \tag{14}$$

Thus, if the resistance R is selected in accordance with (14), the operating point in the n.d.c region can be permanently stabilized.

Exercises

5.1 Assuming the electron gas in a Si sample to be a degenerate one, determine the Fermi level position in it at T = 0 K. ($n = 10^{26} m^{-3}$, $m^* = 0.01$ m) [19.75 meV]

5.2 Presuming the density of states function in a degenerate semiconductor to be varying linearly with energy, determine the Fermi level position in it at $T = 0\,K$. [$P(E) = CE$, $E_{FO} = (2n/C)^{1/2}$]

5.3 The reflection coefficient of infrared radiation ($\lambda = 8000$Å) from the surface of a Si sample was found to be 0.49. Calculate the electron effective mass. ($\kappa = 12$, $n = 10^{25}/\,\text{m}^3$). [$m^* = 0.011$ m]

5.4 Show that a sample of a degenerate semiconductor will have a metallic character if λ is greater than 2 k_F.

5.5 Imagine a unit positive charge $+q$ (of the same magnitude as the electronic charge) to be surrounded by an electron gas of a uniform density n. Obtain an expression for the net electrostatic potential energy of the electron gas in the field of a positive ion. [$-kT$]

5.6 Derive an expression for the energy gap narrowing of a heavily doped semiconductor sample.

$$\left[\Delta E_G = \frac{4\pi N_i A_s}{\Omega N \lambda^2} + \frac{4\pi\, m^* N_i\, A_s^2}{\Omega N \lambda^3\, \hbar^2}\right]$$

5.7 An n.d.c device is connected in series with a resistance R and a d.c.voltage source. The magnitude of the average negative resistance of the device was found to be 40 Ω. The series inductance and the capacitance of the n.d.c device are 100 mH and 100 μ F respectively. Estimate R for stabilizing the operating point in the n.d.c region. What are the resistive cutoff and the self-resonant frequency of the device? [25 Ω $< R <$ 40 Ω; 22.97 Hz; 30.79 Hz]

References

[1] Bonch Bruevich, V.L., 1964, *The Electronic Theory of Heavily Doped Semiconductors*, American Elsevier Co, New York.

[2] Burstein E., and Lundqvist, S., ed., 1969, *Tunnelling Phenomena in Solids*, Plenum Press, New York.

[3] Chow, W.F., 1964, *Principles of Tunnel Diode Circuits*, John Wiley, New York.

[4] Chynoweth, A.G., Feldman, W.L., and Logan, R.A., 1961, Excess tunnel current in Si Esaki Junctions, *Phys. Rev.*, **121**, 684.

[5] Demassa, T.A., and Knott, D.P., 1970, The Prediction of Tunnel Diode I–V Characteristics, *Solid State Electronics*, **14**, 520.

[6] Duke, C.B., 1969, *Tunnelling in Solids*, Solid State Physics Supplement No.10, Academic, New York.

[7] Esaki, L., 1958, New Phenomenon in Narrow Germanium *pn* Junctions, *Phys.Rev.*, **109**, 603, 1974; Long Journey into Tunnelling, *Proc. IEEE*,**62**, 825, 1976.

[8] Esaki, L., Miyahara, Y., 1960, A New Device using the Tunnelling Process in Narrow *pn* Junctions, *Solid State Electronics*, **1**, 13.

[9] Esaki, L., Stiles, P.J., 1966, New Type of Negative Resistance in Barrier Tunnelling, *Phys. Rev. Lett.*, **16**, 1108.

[10] Green, M.A., King, F.D., and Shewchun, J., 1974, Minority carrier MIS Tunnel Diodes and their Applications to Photovoltaic Energy Conversions Applications:I Theory, *Solid State Electronics*, **17**, 551:II Experiment, *Solid State Electronics*, **17**, 563.

[11] Kane, E.O., 1961, Theory of Tunnelling, *J.Appl. Phys.*, **38**, 2384.

[12] Meyerhofer, D., Brown, G.A., and Sommers Jr., H.S., 1962, Degenerate Ge I, Tunnel, Excess and Thermal Currents in Tunnel Diodes, Phys. Rev., 126, 1329.

[13] Morgan, J.V., and Kane, E.O., 1959, Observation of Direct Tunnelling in Ge, *Phys. Rev.Lett.*, **3**, 466.

[14] Roy, D.K., 1986, *Quantum Mechanical Tunnelling and its Applications*, World Scientific, Singapore.

[15] Roy, D.K., 1977, *Tunnelling and Negative Resistance Phenomena in Semiconductors*, Pergamon Press, Oxford, England.

[16] Roy, D.K., 1971, On the Prediction of Tunnel Diode I–V Characteristics, *Solid State Electronics*, **14**, 520.

[17] Simmons, J.G., et. al., 1977, Theory of Switching Phenomena in Metal Semiconductor n-p^+-Si Devices, *Solid State Electronics*, **120**, 955; 1977; Experimental Studies of Switching in Metal Semiconducting np^+ Si Devices, *Solid State Electronics*, **20**, 963; 1979, Theory of Switching Phenomena in *pn*-Insulator-(Tunnel)-Metal Devices, *Solid State Electronics*, **22**, 181.

[18] Solymar, L., 1972, *Superconductive Tunnelling and Applications*, Chapman and Hall, U.K.

[19] Thronber, K.K., Thomas C.McGill and Mead, C.A, 1967, The Tunnelling Time of an Electron, *J.Appl. Phys.*, **38**, 2384.

[20] Yamamoto, T. and Morimoto, M., 1972, Thin MIS Structure Si Negative Resistance Device, *Appl. Phys. Lett.*, **20**, 269.

Appendix I
Amorphous semiconductors

In crystalline solids, the atoms are stacked together in a regular manner, forming a three-dimensional pattern which is obtained by a repetition of a certain basic structural unit in space (Fig. A.1.1(a)). When the periodicity of the pattern extends throughout a given piece of material, one speaks of a single crystal. In polycrystalline materials, on the other hand, the periodicity of the structure is interrupted at the grain boundaries. The sizes of the grains in which the structure remains periodic may vary from microscopic dimensions to several angstroms. When the sizes of the grains or crystallites become comparable to the size of the basic structural unit, one can no longer talk of crystals any more because the essential feature of a crystal is the periodicity of the basic unit in its structure. The specimen then becomes an amorphous one. Long range order in the periodic arrangement of the atoms within the solid is missing. For most solids, the crystalline state is the most natural one since the energy of the atomic arrangement is lower than that of irregular packing of atoms. However, if the atoms are not given an opportunity to arrange themselves regularly by suddenly reducing their mobilities appreciably, the material is amorphous (Fig. A.1.1(b)). The terms amorphous solid, non-crystalline solid, disordered solid or liquid have no precise structural meaning beyond that the structure is non-crystalline on a significant scale. The principal structural order present is imposed by approximately constant nearest neighbour atoms or molecules. In amorphous Si, for example, groups of four atoms are tetrahedrally bonded at the proper interatomic separation (i.e., no internal dangling bond and no bond angle distortion greater than 20° is present). Such a state is nearer to the state of perfect short range order. The patterns of the neighbouring atoms are analogous to the crystal in the structural sense. The X-ray or the neutron diffraction pattern of an amorphous solid consists of one or more broad diffuse rings when viewed on a plane normal to the incident X-ray beam. The pattern is different from the diffraction pattern of a powdered crystalline material, which shows a large number of fairly sharp rings. Although the X-ray diffraction pattern of a typical amorphous material is distinctly different from that of a typical crystalline material, there is no sharp division between them.

Amorphous semiconductors can be prepared by thin film evaporation or sputtering. They can also be made by quenching (supercooling) a melt, condensation from the vapour phase onto a cooled substrate, chemical vapour deposition (CVD) or by means of a glow discharge from a silane gas (SiH_4). Since a regular crystalline order is missing in a sample of an amorphous material, the Bloch theorem is not applicable to it. Allowed energy bands and energy gaps are still formed because the nature of the density of states function vs. energy is determined most strongly by the local electronic bonding configurations. Both electrons and holes can carry current in an amorphous material. The carriers are more readily

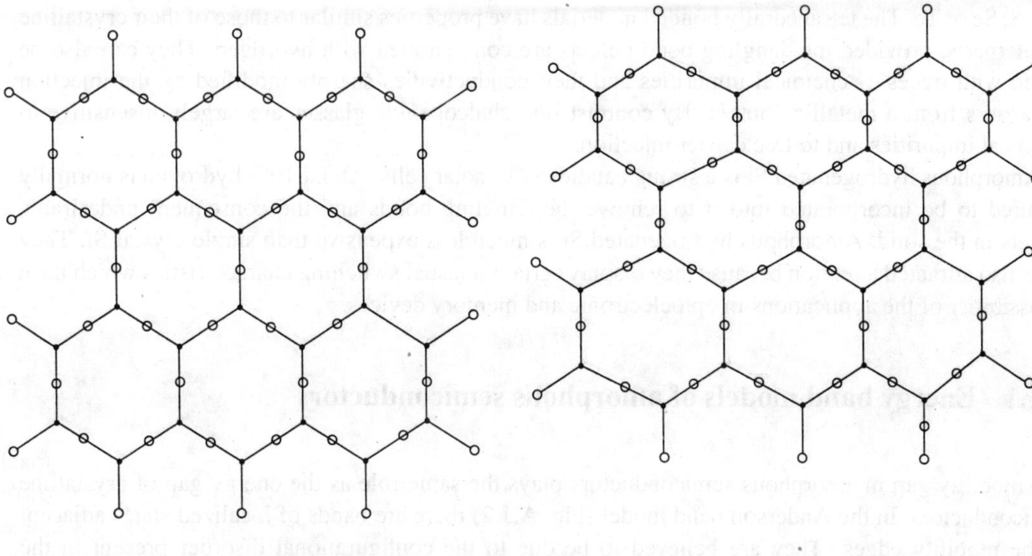

(a) (b)

Fig. A.1.1 *Schematic illustration of the differences between (a) crystal and (b) an amorphous material*

scattered by the disordered structure so that the mean free paths in such cases may sometimes be of the order of scale of the disorder. At the boundaries between individual crystallites of an amorphous material, the orientations of the lattice planes change giving rise to enhanced scattering of carriers. Consequently, the drift mobility of carriers is appreciably less in a sample of amorphous material than in a single crystal. Anderson proposed that the states near the band edges are localized and do not extend throughout the crystal. Conduction in these states occur by the thermally assisted hopping process.

Amorphous materials appear to behave like intrinsic semiconductors with the Fermi level existing near the energy gap centre. However, such a pinning of the Fermi level is known to arise from the presence of defects such as dangling bonds and other misfits present in the structure which produce localized states within the gap. A dangling bond is a broken or an unsatisfied bond in the covalent solid. A simple dangling bond normally contains one electron. Defects like this can introduce electron states deep inside the energy gap region. The nature of such defects and the techniques used for their passivations will be discussed later. The presence of the above mentioned defect states along with the tendency of the covalent alloys to satisfy the local valence requirements necessitates the use of special techniques for the preparation of the doped amorphous specimens.

Amorphous semiconductors can be classified into the following categories: (a) Elemental amorphous semiconductors e.g. Ge and Si; (b) Covalent amorphous semiconductors e.g., As_2Se_3 and GeTe (binary); (c) Covalent amorphous semiconductors (multicomponent) e.g., chalcogenides, borides and arsenide glasses and (d) ionic amorphous semiconductors e.g., Al_2O_3, V_2O_5 and other transition metal oxides. Since ionic bonds are relatively stronger, electrons in amorphous semiconductors are unable to participate in the conduction process. Therefore, only two distinct classes of amorphous semiconductors are widely studied. They are tetrahedrally bonded amorphous solids e.g., Ge & Si and the chalcogenide glasses. The latter are multi-component solids whose one major constituent is a chalcogen element viz., S, Se or Te. The tetrahedrally bonded materials have properties similar to those of their crystalline counterparts, provided the dangling bond defects are compensated with hydrogen. They can also be doped with traces of chemical impurities and their conductivities sharply modified by the injection of carriers from a metallic contact. By contrast, the chalcogenide glasses are largely insensitive to chemical impurities and to free carrier injection.

Amorphous hydrogenated Si is a strong candidate for solar cells. About 10% hydrogen is normally required to be incorporated into it to remove the dangling bonds and the consequent undesirable defects in the solid. Amorphous hydrogenated Si is much less expensive than single crystal Si. They have also attracted attention because they display certain unusual switching characteristics which have a possibility of the applications in optoelectronic and memory devices.

A.1.1 Energy band models of amorphous semiconductors

The mobility gap in amorphous semiconductors plays the same role as the energy gap of crystalline semiconductors. In the Anderson band model (Fig. A.1.2) there are bands of localized states adjacent to the mobility edges. They are believed to be due to the configurational disorder present in the semiconductor material and they form tails above the normal valence band and below the normal conduction band. At $T = 0\,K$ the mobility at the tails drops to zero. The sharp conduction and valence band edges with a well-defined energy gap which are the typical characteristics of crystalline semiconductors are conspicuous by their absence here. Such a feature is a consequence of short and long range orders of the crystal. In an amorphous material the long range order is destroyed.

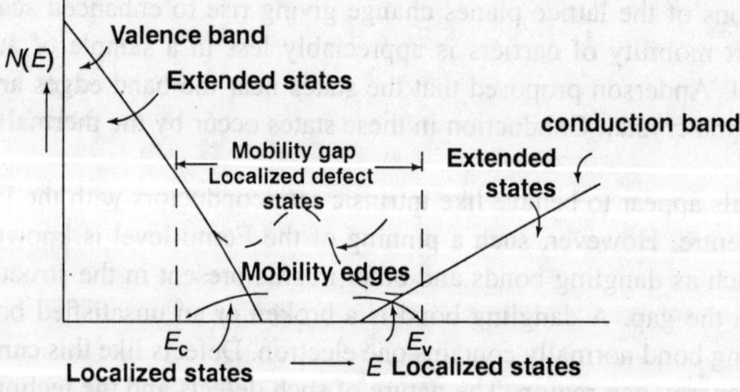

Fig. A.1.2. The density of states function $N(E)$ Vs the energy E of an amorphous material (Anderson's model)

According to the Davis and Mott model (Fig. A.1.3), the carrier conduction in a sample of an amorphous material can occur by three different methods. Their relative contributions to the total conductivity will predominate at different temperatures. At very low temperatures, the conduction can occur between states near the Fermi energy by the mechanism of thermally assisted tunnelling process. At higher temperatures charge carriers are excited to the localized states in the band tails. Carriers in these localized states can participate in the electrical transport only by the hopping mechanism. At still higher temperatures, carriers may be excited over the mobility edges to the extended states where normal carrier conduction may begin.

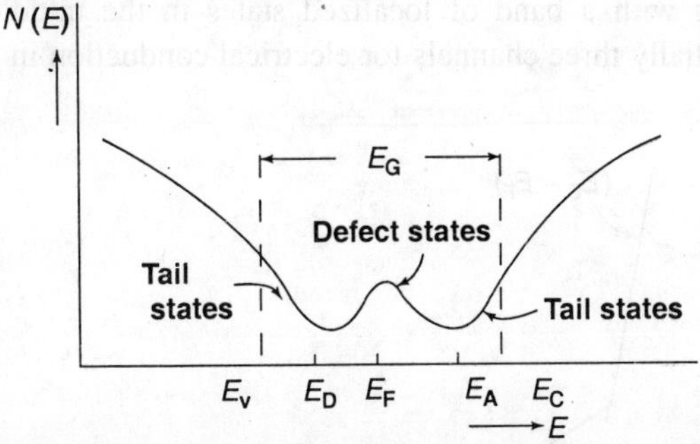

Fig. A.1.3 *The density of states function $N(E)$ Vs the energy E of an amorphous material (Davis and Mott model)*

The Cohen–Fritzsche–Ovinishky (CFO) model (Fig. A.1.4) is derived from the experimental observations that amorphous semiconductors are transparent in the infrared region of the electromagnetic spectrum and they exhibit thermally assisted hopping conductivity. Transitional and compositional disorders are presumed to cause fluctuations in the crystal potential energy leading to the tailings of the conduction and valence bands into the gap. The localized states are presumed to be created by the random potential variations within the crystal. This model predicts that at higher temperatures, the material would behave like an intrinsic semiconductor. The model is expected to be obeyed by alloy glasses which have both compositional and structural disorders.

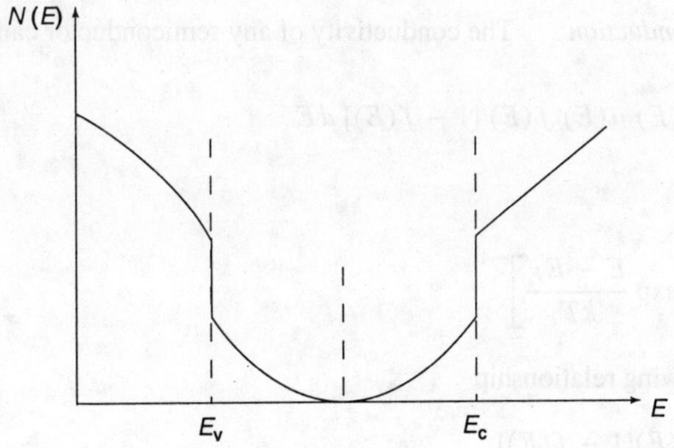

Fig. A.1.4 *The density of states function $N(E)$ Vs the energy E of an amorphous material (Cohen–Fritzsche–Ovinishky model)*

A.1.2 Temperature dependence of the dc conductivity of the amorphous material

The essential features of the Davis and Mott model for the band structure of amorphous semiconductors are that the narrow band-tails of localized states exist at the extremities of conduction and valence bands along with a band of localized states in the middle of the energy gap. This model gives rise to essentially three channels for electrical conduction in amorphous semiconductors (Fig. A.1.5).

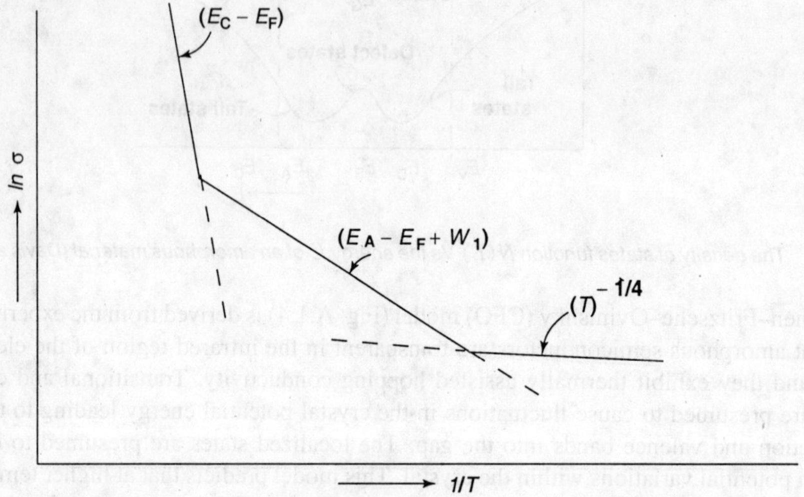

Fig. A.1.5 *A typical plot of* $\ln\sigma$ *Vs* $(1/T)$ *according to Davis–mott model*

(a) Extended state conduction The conductivity of any semiconductor can be expressed as

$$\sigma = -q \int N(E)\,\mu(E)\,f(E)\,[1 - f(E)]\,dE \tag{A.1.1}$$

where

$$f(E) = \left[1 + \exp\frac{E - E_F}{kT}\right]^{-1} \tag{A.1.2}$$

Now, using the following relationship

$$\frac{\partial f(E)}{\partial E} = -\frac{f(E)[1 - f(E)]}{kT} \tag{A.1.3}$$

σ can be expressed in the following form

$$\sigma = q \int N(E)\,\mu(E)\,kT\left[\frac{\partial f(E)}{\partial E}\right] dE \tag{A.1.4}$$

In the Davis–Mott model, the Fermi level E_F is situated near the middle of the gap and thus sufficiently far away from E_C, the energy which separates the extended states from the localized ones (Fig. A.1.3), so that the Maxwell–Boltzman statistics can be used to describe the occupancy of states. Since, $(E - E_F) \gg kT$ in this case,

$$f(E) = \left[1 + \exp\frac{(E - E_F)}{kT}\right]^{-1} \cong \exp\left[\frac{-(E - E_F)}{kT}\right] \tag{A.1.5}$$

According to Mott, the mobility drops sharply at E_C or E_V, but it is not exactly known how the mobility depends on the energy in both the conduction regimes.

In the non-degenerate case and under assumptions of constant density of states and constant mobility, the conductivity due to electrons excited beyond the mobility edge is given by

$$\begin{aligned}\sigma &= q\, N(E_C)\, \mu_C\, kT \int \left[\frac{\partial f(E)}{\partial E}\right] dE \\ &= q\, N(E_C)\, \mu_C\, kT \exp\left[\frac{-(E_C - E_F)}{kT}\right]\end{aligned} \tag{A.1.6}$$

where μ_C denotes the average mobility at the mobility edge. The electron density at the extended states is then given by

$$n = N(E_C) \int_{E_c}^{\infty} \exp\left[\frac{-(E - E_F)}{kT}\right] dE$$

which upon integration yields

$$n = q\, N(E_C)\, kT \exp\left[\frac{-(E_C - E_F)}{kT}\right] \tag{A.1.7}$$

Let us define $\sigma(E_C) = q\; N(E_C)\; \mu_C\; kT$. Now, if $N(E_C) =< \frac{N(E)}{3} >$ where $< N(E) >$ denotes the average value of the density of states function over the main band. Then

$$\sigma(E_C) = q\; N(E)\; \mu_C \left(\frac{kT}{3}\right)$$

Mott calculated this minimum conductivity before the start of an activated process i.e. just at E_C, which is given by

$$\sigma(E_C) = \text{const.} \left(\frac{q^2}{ha}\right) \tag{A.1.8}$$

where a depends on the lattice constant and lies between 0.026 and 1. $\sigma(E_C)$ is usually in the range of $200 - 300\,(\text{ohm cm})^{-1}$. Taking this constant to be 0.026, one finds

$$\mu_C = 0.078 \left[\frac{\frac{q}{ha}}{N(E_C)\, kT}\right] \tag{A.1.9}$$

In the nearly free electron model

$$N(E) = \frac{mk}{2\pi^2 h^2} \tag{A.1.10}$$

On the other hand, the maximum energy E_{max} of the band, which also yields the width B of the band is given by

$$E_{max} = \frac{\pi^2 h^2}{2ma^2} = B$$

where $k_{max} = (\pi/a)$. Therefore, $N(E)B = [2a^3]^{-1}$. Introducing this result in (A.1.9), we find,

$$\mu_C = 0.078 \left[\frac{2qa^2 B}{hkT}\right] \quad \text{(A.1.11)}$$

Around room temperatures, $\mu_C \sim 10\,\text{cm}^2/\text{Vs}$. This corresponds to the mean free path comparable to or less than the interatomic distance. From (A.1.6), it follows that

$$\sigma = \sigma_0 \exp\left[\frac{-(E_C - E_F)}{kT}\right] \quad \text{(A.1.12)}$$

where

$$\sigma_0 = q\, N(E_C)\, \mu_C\, kT$$

as shown in Fig. A.1.5. There is also an alternative way of arriving at an expression for μ_C. We know that $\mu_C = (qD/kT)$ where $D = (1/6)\,\nu a^2$. Hence, we get

$$\mu_C = \left(\frac{q}{kT}\right)\left(\frac{1}{6}\right)\nu a^2 \quad \text{(A.1.13)}$$

The value of σ_0 then works out to be

$$\sigma_0 = \left(\frac{h\nu}{B}\right)\left(\frac{q^2}{ha}\right)$$

which is identical to (A.1.8).

(b) Conduction in Band-tails If the wave functions are localized, the conduction can take place only by the thermally activated hopping process. Every time an electron moves from one localized state to another, it exchanges energy with a phonon. It is expected that in such a case the mobility will have a thermally activated nature as given below

$$\mu_{hop} = \mu_0 \exp\left[\frac{-W_1(E)}{kT}\right] \quad \text{(A.1.14)}$$

The pre-exponential factor μ_0 has the following form

$$\mu_0 = \left(\frac{1}{6}\right)\nu_{ph}\left(\frac{qR^2}{kT}\right) \quad \text{(A.1.15)}$$

where R is the distance covered in one hop. The density of states function of the band-tail states may be represented as

$$N(E) = \left[\frac{E - E_A}{\Delta E}\right] N(E_C) \quad \text{(A.1.16)}$$

where $\Delta E = (E_C - E_A)$. Substituting (A.1.14) and (A.1.16) in (A.1.4), we find after necessary simplifications

$$\sigma_{\text{hop}} = \sigma_{0,\text{hop}} \left(\frac{kT}{\Delta E}\right) \exp\left[-\frac{E_A - E_F + W_1}{kT}\right] \tag{A.1.17}$$

as shown in Fig. A.1.5.

(c) Conduction in the Localized States at the Fermi Energy If the Fermi energy lies in a band of localized states near the energy gap centre, as predicted by the Davis–Mott model, carriers can move between the states via the phonon-assisted tunnelling process. An estimate of this type of conductivity, and its temperature dependence was given by Mott. Let us consider an electron which is just scattered by a phonon from one localized state to another. The energy difference between the states is denoted by W. The probability p that an electron will jump from one state to another is determined by the following three factors

1. The probability of finding a phonon with an excitation energy W which is given by the Boltzman factor $\exp(-W/kT)$.
2. An attempt frequency ν_{ph} whose upper limit is the Debye frequency ($\sim 10^{12}$ to $10^{13}\ \text{s}^{-1}$).
3. The probability of the electron transfer from one state to another. This factor depends upon the overlapping of the wave functions and should be given by $\exp(-2\alpha R)$. Here, R is the distance which at higher temperatures tends to approach the interatomic spacing and α is a quantity which is the representative of the rate of fall of the wave function at a particular site.

The probability rate p that an electron would jump from one site to another must therefore be expressed as

$$p = \nu_{ph} \exp\left(-2\alpha R - \frac{W}{kT}\right) \tag{A.1.18}$$

Making use of the Einstein's relation $\mu = (qD/kT)$ with $D = (1/6)pR^2$, the conductivity may be expressed as

$$\sigma = \left(\frac{1}{6}\right) q^2 R^2 N(E_F)\, \nu_{ph} \exp(-2\alpha R) \exp\left(\frac{-W}{kT}\right) \tag{A.1.19}$$

where we have made use of (A.1.4) and (A.1.18). As the temperature is lowered, the number of phonons and their energies decrease and the more energetic phonon-assisted hops will become progressively less favourable. Carriers will then tend to hop to larger distances in order to find sites, which lie energetically closer than the nearest neighbours. This mechanism is called "variable range hopping (VRH)". The factor $\exp(-2\alpha R)\exp(-W/kT)$ will have a maximum value for a particular transition. In order to find the most probable hopping distance, Mott used the following optimization procedure: If $N(E_F)$ is the density of states per unit volume per unit energy range, then the number of energy states within an energy range W is given by $(4/3)\pi R^3 N(E_F)W$. The electron can leave its site only if the number of accessible states is at least one. Therefore, the most probable hopping distance may be found by solving the following equation:

$$\left(\frac{4}{3}\right) \pi R^3 N(E_F) W = 1$$

or

$$W = \frac{3}{4\pi R^3 N(E_F)} \tag{A.1.20}$$

Substituting this value in (A.1.18), the jump probability is given by

$$p = \nu_{ph} \exp\left(-2\alpha R - \frac{3}{4\pi R^3 N(E_F) kT}\right) \tag{A.1.21}$$

The most probable jump distance can now be obtained by minimizing the exponent of (A.1.21) as follows

$$Z = -2\alpha R - \frac{3}{4\pi R^3 N(E_F) kT}$$

Therefore, $(\partial Z/\partial R) = -2\alpha - [3/\{4\pi N(E_F)kT\}](-3R^{-4}) = 0$ in order that Z is a maximum. That is,

$$2\alpha = \frac{9}{4\pi N(E_F) kT R^4}$$

or

$$R = \left[\frac{9}{8\pi\alpha N(E_F) kT}\right]^{1/4} \tag{A.1.22}$$

R, in the above equation measures the most probable distance. Substituting for R in the expression for Z above, we find

$$Z = -2.7 \left[\frac{\alpha^3}{kN(E_F)}\right]^{1/4} \left(\frac{1}{T^4}\right)$$

From (A.1.19) we may then write

$$\sigma = \sigma_0(T) \exp\left(\frac{-A}{T^{1/4}}\right) \tag{A.1.23}$$

where

$$A = -2.7 \left[\frac{\alpha^3}{kN(E_F)}\right]^{1/4} \tag{A.1.24}$$

and

$$\sigma_0(T) = \left[\frac{q^2}{2(8\pi)^{1/2}}\right] \nu_{ph} \left[\frac{N(E_F)}{\alpha kT}\right]^{1/2} \tag{A.1.25}$$

In principle, the two parameters viz. α and $N(E_F)$ can be evaluated from the slope of a plot of $\ln(\sigma\sqrt{T})$ vs. $T^{-1/4}$ and from the intercept of $T^{-1/4}$ axis. The slope of the curve would be

$A = -2.7[\alpha^3/kN(E_F)]^{1/4}$ and the intercept is $\ln[\{q^2/2(8\pi)^{1/2}\nu_{ph}\}\{N(E_F)/\alpha kT\}]^{1/2}$. Also, one can derive an idea of the most probable hopping distance R at a given temperature by inserting the values of α and $N(E_F)$ in (A.1.22). Although the $T^{-1/4}$ dependence of $\ln(\sigma\sqrt{T})$ is widely observed (Fig. A.1.5), findings seem to indicate that the above expressions are only qualitative. The theory of energy distribution of the density of states is of major importance in the theory of variable range hopping.

The modified Davis–Mott model is shown in Fig. A.1.6.

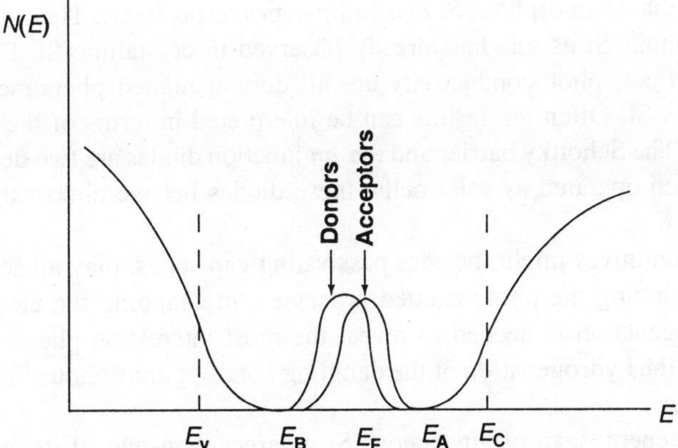

Fig. A.1.6 The modified Davis–Mott model: density of states function $N(E)$ Vs. the energy E plot.

A.1.3 Amorphous silicon defects and passivation

Amorphous Si is a covalently bonded solid with atoms arranged in an open network with correlations in order upto the third or fourth nearest neighbours. The short range order is directly responsible for the observable semiconducting properties such as optical absorption and activated electrical conduction. Amorphous Si when nominally pure is permeated with dangling bonds as evidenced by a detectable ESR signal indicating 5×10^{19} spins/cm^3. The electron energy levels of the dangling bonds lie between the conduction and the valence band states of the fully paired electrons. These states in the gap contribute to optical absorption and electrical conduction processes masking the measurement of the energy gap by both the processes. Furthermore, there is a large density of gap states, which act as fast non-radiative recombination centres with the result that the photoconductivity or photoluminescence is uninterestingly small in pure amorphous Si. Finally, the Fermi level which is essentially pinned by the gap states does not move significantly when the trace impurities of the conventional shallow donors or acceptors are incorporated within the sample. Since normal annealing procedures reduce the ESR signal, it was originally presumed that ideal amorphous Si might be approached by the annealing process. The assumption here was that the annealing was able to reduce the effects due to the dangling bonds by the reconstruction and the rearrangement of the amorphous network. However, it was discovered later that the effects of annealing are minimal. If the dangling Si bonds cannot be paired to each other, the opportunity still exists to pair them with other atomic orbitals. Hydrogen appears to be the most suitable for this purpose. Following the glow discharge of silane, several other procedures have now become available for the incorporation of hydrogen into the amorphous Si network. These include the reactive sputtering with a gas containing hydrogen, proton implantation etc. In all cases, it was presumed that hydrogen passivates dangling bonds thereby revealing the interesting properties of intrinsic amorphous Si.

Many interesting properties of hydrogenated amorphous Si have been studied to date. These include the thermally activated conductivity, the optical absorption edge, photoluminescence, electroluminescence and photoconductivity. In addition, the standard shallow donors and acceptors have also been shown to dope hydrogenated amorphous Si to *n* and *p*-types respectively. Then similar phenomena can be observed in amorphous Si as one has already observed in crystalline Si. Extrinsic conductivity, thermo-power, Hall effect, photoconductivity are all doping related phenomena which have been observed in amorphous Si. Often the results can be interpreted in terms of the processes previously described for crystals. The Schottky barrier and the *pn* junction diodes are two devices which are made of amorphous Si. When operated as solar cells, these diodes behave almost the same way as their crystalline counterparts.

Hydrogen or other additives might, besides passivating gap states, play an active role in enlarging the band gaps, in sensitizing the photo-excited processes, in changing the electron-lattice coupling etc. How much hydrogenation is needed to reveal the most interesting phenomena is still an open question. In summary, the hydrogenation of the dangling bonds of amorphous Si has revealed many of its interesting properties.

Usually the optical energy gap of amorphous Si is larger than that of its crystalline counterpart (1.12 eV). For amorphous Si, the energy gap lies in the range of 1.82–2.23 eV. This reaches its maximum value when the hydrogen content is about 18% and it starts to decrease once again when the hydrogen content is increased to 21%. The increase of the band gap is due to the incorporation of hydrogen that passivates the dangling bonds. The decrease in its value when the hydrogen content increases beyond 18% is probably due to hydrogen related defects being introduced into the specimen.

A.1.4 Optical properties of amorphous semiconductors: Absorption spectrum

Most absorption processes in amorphous semiconductors involve the transition of electrons from the valence to the conduction band. Thus, the incident photon energy must be equal to the energy gap or larger. For optical absorption of photons, their frequency must satisfy the following relation:

$$\nu \geq \frac{E_G}{h} \tag{A.1.26}$$

The fundamental absorption edge is defined by the following equation:

$$\nu = \frac{E_G}{h} \tag{A.1.27}$$

The absorption spectrum of an amorphous material is shown in Fig. A.1.7. The curve can be divided into three distinct regions

i) The region A represents higher absorption ($\alpha > 10^4\ \text{cm}^{-1}$). This type of absorption is associated with electronic transitions from the extended valence states to the extended conduction band states.

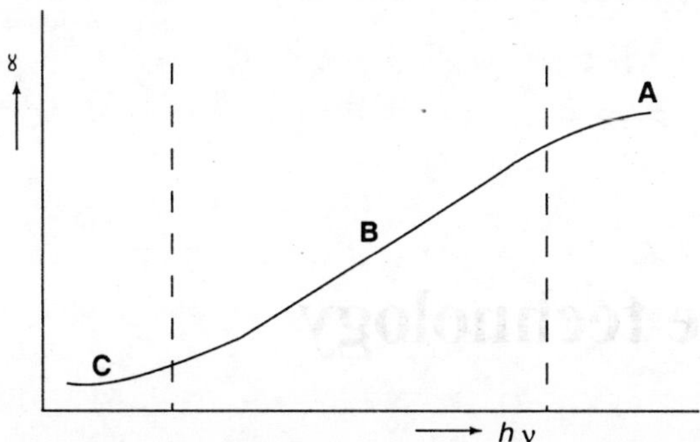

Fig. A.1.7 *A Schematic representation of the absorption spectrum of an amorphous material*

ii) The region B is exponential in nature and is observed frequently with crystalline semiconductors. In this case $\alpha(w)$ lies between 1 and 10^4 and it can be described by the following relation:

$$\alpha(\omega) \sim \exp\left(\frac{h\omega}{E_G}\right) \tag{A.1.28}$$

when E_G lies in the range of 0.05 to 0.08 eV. This is due to the transition between the tail states.

iii) The region C represents the weak absorption tail, which can represent various optical transitions.

Appendix II

Basic device technology

Semiconductor devices can be made only out of ultrapure semiconductor materials. The first consideration is therefore to develop a technology to produce ultrapure semiconductors. Secondly, one has to look for suitable means to grow a single or a number of *pn* junctions within it (depending on the requirements). This has necessitated the development of a number of *pn* junction fabrication technologies. In this chapter we will be presenting a brief review of the aforesaid methods.

A.2.1 Bulk Crystal Growth

Requirements for the growth of device grade semiconductor is really very stringent. Not only must the semiconductors be available in the form of large single crystal ingots but their purity must also be controlled within very close limits. Elemental Germanium and Silicon are obtained by the chemical decomposition of GeO_2, $SiCl_4$(or $SiHCl_3$) respectively. Once the basic semiconductor material has been isolated, it is melted and cast into ingots. The materials in such forms are polycrystalline consisting of many crystalline grains of the diamond structure oriented in different directions. To obtain a crystal having a specific orientation it is necessary to maintain a careful control over the boundary between the molten material and the solid during cooling from the molten state.

(a) Growth from the melt The usual technique of growing single crystals involves selective cooling of the molten material along a particular direction. Fig. A.2.1 shows a silica crucible containing molten Ge which may be pulled through a furnace so that the solidification begins at one end of the bar and then proceeds throughout its entire length. To facilitate the crystal growth, a small seed is placed at the end of the bar which is cooled first. If the rate of cooling is carefully controlled and the position of the interface between the solid and the melt is slowly moved along the length of the crucible, the semiconductor atoms would start growing in a diamond lattice. The shape of the grown crystal is however determined by the crucible dimensions. Ge, GaAs and some other semiconductor crystals are grown in this fashion. This is known as the horizontal Bridgeman method. In a modified version of this procedure, a small portion of the polycrystalline material is melted and the molten zone is moved down the crucible at a convenient rate so that a single crystal gets formed behind the zone as it moves. The major disadvantage of growing a crystal by this method is that the crystal is constantly in touch with the walls of the crucible. As a result, undesirable stresses are applied by the walls of the crucible on the growing crystal producing deviations from the perfect crystal structure. For Si particularly, this is a serious problem.

An alternative procedure which eliminates this problem involves the pulling of the crystal from the melt as it grows (Fig. A.2.2). In this procedure, a seed crystal is lowered into the melt and is then pulled

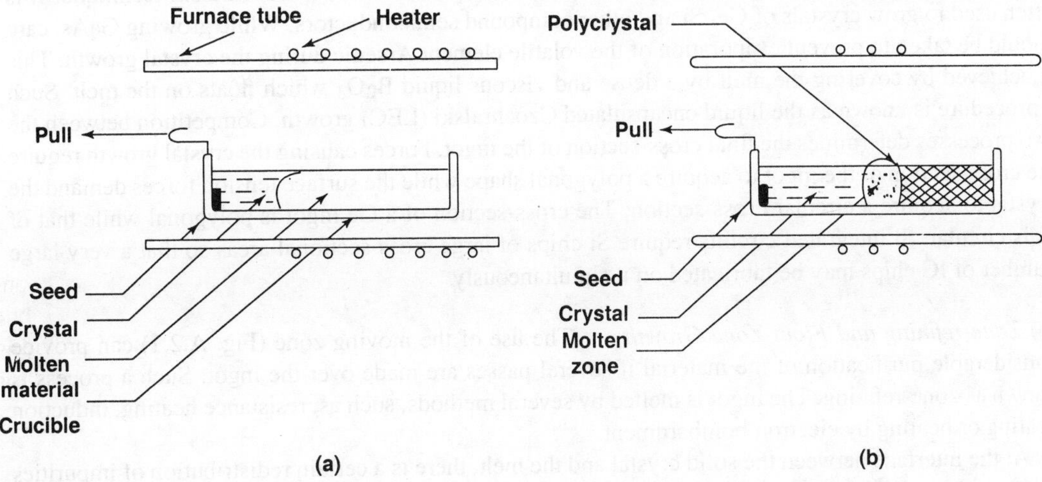

Fig. A.2.1 *Crystal growth from the melt in a crucible: (a) solidification from one end of the melt (horizontal Bridgman method), (b) melting and solidification in a moving zone*

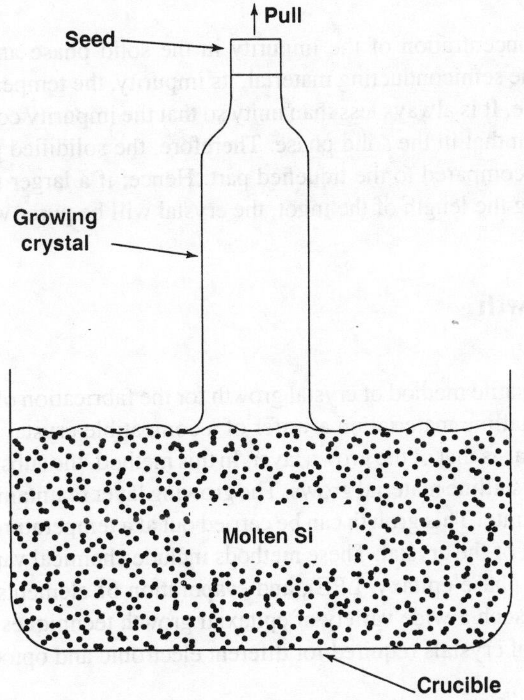

Fig. A.2.2 *Czochralski method*

up slowly allowing the crystal to grow on the seed. The crystal is also rotated gently during the growth to provide the necessary stirring action to even out the effects of temperature variations which may give rise to inhomogeneous solidification. This method is known as the Czochralski technique. It is often used to grow crystals of Ge, Si and other compound semiconductors. While growing GaAs, care should be taken to prevent evaporation of the volatile element Arsenic during the crystal growth. This is achieved by covering the melt by a dense and viscous liquid B_2O_3 which floats on the melt. Such a procedure is known as the liquid encapsulated Czochralski (LEC) growth. Competition between the two processes determines the final cross-section of the ingot. Forces causing the crystal growth require the cross-section of the ingot to acquire a polygonal shape while the surface tension forces demand the crystal to acquire a circular cross-section. The cross-section of a Ge ingot is polygonal while that of Si is circular. Si integrated circuits require Si chips of large cross-sectional areas so that a very large number of IC chips may be fabricated on it simultaneously.

(b) Zone-refining and Float-Zone Growth The use of the moving zone (Fig. A.2.1) can provide considerable purification of the material if several passes are made over the ingot. Such a process is known as zone-refining. The ingot is melted by several methods, such as, resistance heating, induction heating or heating by electron bombardment.

At the interface between the solid crystal and the melt, there is a certain redistribution of impurities between the two phases. The quantity that determines this is called the distribution coefficient and is defined as

$$k_d = \frac{C_s}{C_l} \tag{A.2.1}$$

where C_S measures the concentration of the impurity in the solid phase and C_l, that in the liquid phase. k_d is a function of the semiconducting material, its impurity, the temperature of the solid-liquid interface and the growth rate. It is always less than unity so that the impurity concentration in the liquid phase is always greater than that in the solid phase. Therefore, the solidified portion of the ingot will contain smaller impurities compared to the liquefied part. Hence, if a larger number of passes of the molten zone are made along the length of the ingot, the crystal will be purer with every pass.

A.2.2 Epitaxial Growth

The most important and versatile method of crystal growth for the fabrication of semiconductor devices is the growth of a thin crystalline material on a wafer of a compatible crystal structure. The substrate may also be the same material as that of the grown layer. In this method, the substrate behaves as the seed crystal on which the new crystalline material grows. The growing layer maintains the orientation and the crystal structure of the substrate. This growth can be carried out at a temperature which is usually much lower than the melting point of the crystal. These methods include chemical vapour deposition (CVD), growth from a melt (liquid phase epitaxy, LPE), and evaporation of elements in vacuum (molecular beam epitaxy, MBE). With such a wide variety of epitaxial growth techniques available, it is possible to grow the different types of crystals required for diferent electronic and optoelectronic applications.

(a) Liquid phase epitaxy It is possible to grow crystals of many semiconductors from a liquid solution at temperatures well below their melting points. Since a mixture of a semiconductor with

a second element can melt at a lower temperature than the semiconductor itself, it is advantageous to grow crystals from the solution at the temperature of the mixture. This method is called the liquid phase epitaxy (LPE). In this method, the solid solution can be placed on top of the wafer in a variety of ways. The direct method involves holding the wafer in a graphite slider and moving it into the pocket containing the melt (Fig. A.2.3). After the epitaxial growth, the surface of the wafer is wiped off. In this way, multiple layers of GaAs and AlGaAs layers can be grown.

(b) Vapour phase epitaxy The advantages of high purity and low temperature which characterize LPE growth can also be achieved during the growth from the vapour phase. Crystalline layers can also be grown onto a substrate from a chemical vapour of the semiconducting material or from the mixtures of chemical vapours containing the semiconductor. In one method, a gas of $SiCl_4$ reacts with H_2 to give Si and anhydrous HCl

$$SiCl_4 + 2H_2 = Si + 4HCl \tag{A.2.2}$$

This reaction occurs at the surface of the heated crystal and thus provides the necessary Si atoms for the growth. HCl remains gaseous in the reaction chamber and does not interfere with the growth.

The equipment to carry out the vapour phase epitaxial growth requires a chamber in which gases can be introduced and a method to heat the Si wafer. Hydrogen gas is passed through a heated vessel containing $SiCl_4$. The mixture of the two gases is next introduced into the reaction chamber over the hot Si substrate. The Si slices are placed on a graphite susceptor or some other material that can be heated to the reaction temperature by means of the radio frequency heating coil. The above reaction occurs approximately at 1250° C. There are other reactions which may be employed at somewhat lower

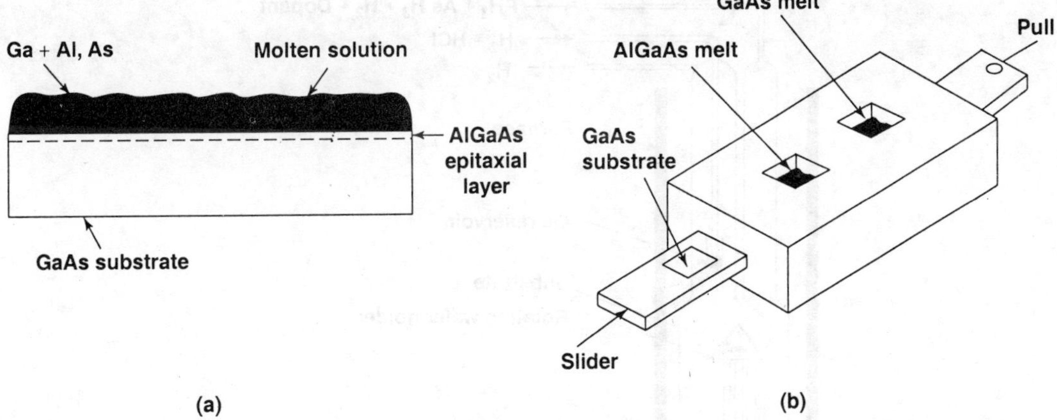

Fig. A.2.3 *The liquid phase epitaxial (LPE) growth of AlGaAs on a GaAs substrate: (a) cross-section of the sample in contact with a Ga rich melt containing Al and As, (b) the carbon slider used to move the GaAs substrate between various melts. In this case, two pockets are provided, containing melts for AlGaAS and GaAs growths. The GaAs substrate on the slider is moved first into the AlGaAs growth chamber; after the growth of this layer, the excess melt is wiped off as the slider moves the substrate to the next growth chamber*

temperatures. The pyrolysis of silane (SiH_4) at 1000° C is an example. At the reaction temperature silane breaks as follows

$$SiH_4 = Si + 2H_2 \tag{A.2.3}$$

The lower reaction temperature reduces the migration of impurities from the substrate to the growing layer and enables one to grow an abrupt junction. In some applications, it may be necessary to grow thin Si layers on insulating substrates.

The vapour phase epitaxial growth technique is also useful for III–V compounds e.g., GaAs, GaP and GaAsP which are widely used for the fabrications of LEDs and semiconductor lasers. Fig. A.2.4 illustrates a vapour phase reactor for the growth of these materials. Substrates are held at about 800° C on a rotating wafer holder while Phosphine (PH_3), Arsine (AsH_3) and Gallium Chloride (GaCl) gases are mixed and passed over the sample. GaCl is obtained by reacting anhydrous HCl with molten Ga in the reactor. The variation of the composition of GaAsP can be controlled by altering the mixture of Arsine and Phosphine gases. Another useful method for the epitaxial growth of compound semiconductors is the metal organic vapour phase epitaxy (MOVPE) or organometallic vapour phase epitaxy (OMVPE). For example, the organometallic compound trimethyl gallium $(CH_3)_3Ga$ can be reacted with Arsine to form GaAs and methane:

$$(CH_3)_3Ga + AsH_3 = GaAs + 3CH_4 \tag{A.2.4}$$

This reaction takes place at about 700° C and high quality GaAs layers can be obtained by it. Other compound semiconductors may also be grown by this method. For example, trymethylaluminium can be added to the gas mixture to grow AlGaAs. Such a method of growth is used widely for the fabrication of solar cells and lasers. The variability of the compositions of gas mixtures allows the growth of multiple thin layers.

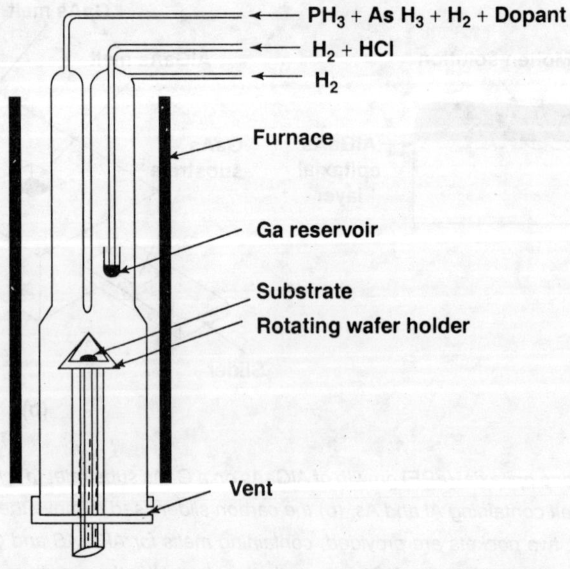

Fig. A.2.4 *Schematic diagram for vapour phase epitaxy (VPE)*

(c) *Molecular beam epitaxy* (MBE) In this method the substrate is held in high vacuum while molecular or atomic beams of the constituents of the solid layer to be grown impinge upon the surface. For example, in the growth of AlGaAs layers on GaAs substrates, the Al, Ga and As components along with dopants are heated in separate cylindrical cells (called Knudsen cells). Collimated beams of these constituents escape into vacuum and are directed onto the surface of the substrate (Fig. A.2.5). The rates at which these atomic beams strike the surface is controlled very closely and the growth of a high quality crystal results. The sample is held at relatively low temperatures ($\sim 580°$ C for GaAs) in this growth procedure. Abrupt changes in the doping or in the composition can be obtained by controlling shutters in front of the individual beams. Using slower growth rates ($< 1\mu$ m/h), it is possible to control the shutters to make compositional changes on the scale of the lattice spacing.

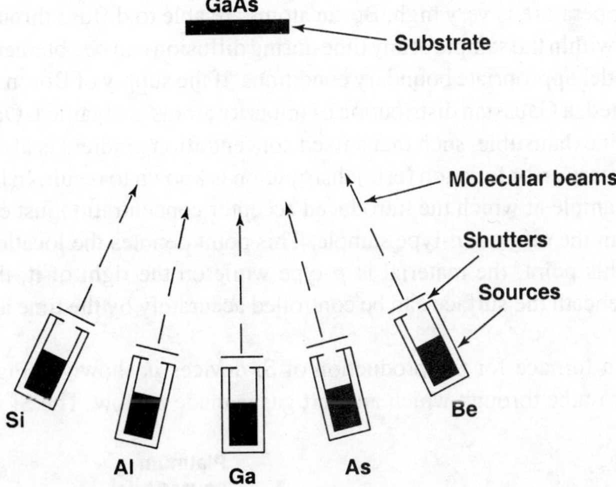

Fig. A.2.5 The crystal growth by molecular beam epitaxy (MBE)

A.2.3 Alloying Technology

A convenient technique of making *pn* junctions is by alloying a metal to a doped semiconductor sample so that it is doped to the opposite conductivity type. This method was used in the early days of fabrication of *pn* junctions. As an example of alloying, a sample of *n*-type Si can be heated with a pellet of Aluminium on it to form a solid solution from which the *pn* junction grows on the parent crystal. As, Al and Si are heated to about 500° C, a molten solution of the two materials is formed. The proportion of Si to Al in this alloy melt is well above its solid solubility limit at lower temperatures. As the temperature is lowered, Si grows out of the alloy mixture because of its reduced solid solubility. The grown Si is also doped *p*-type because Al behaves as an acceptor impurity to Si. The regrown Si crystal has the same lattice structure as the original substrate. Such a growth process is similar to the liquid phase epitaxy (LPE) already described earlier.

A.2.4 Diffusion technology and photolithography

By 1960, the alloying technology was replaced by the impurity diffusion as the most common technique for forming the *pn* junctions. This coupled with selective masking made possible the fabrication of integrated circuits. Selective diffusion is an impressive technique because of its controllability, accuracy and versatality. Diffusion results because of the random motion of impurity atoms and also because they tend to move in the direction of decreasing concentration. Such motions for impurity atoms take place only at higher temperatures (~1000° C). At such high temperatures many of the atoms of the host crystal move out from their original sites, leaving vacancies into which impurity atoms can move in.

If *n*-type Si wafer is placed in a furnace at 1000° C in a gaseous atmosphere containing a high concentration of Boron atoms, a sharp concentration gradient exists at the interface of the sample and the gas. Since the temperature is very high, Boron atoms are able to diffuse through the Si crystal. The impurity distribution within the sample at any time during diffusion can be obtained by solving the Fick's diffusion equation under appropriate boundary conditions. If the supply of Boron atoms to the semiconductor surface is limited, a Gaussian distribution of impurity atoms is obtained. On the other hand, if the supply of B atoms is inexhaustible, such that a fixed concentration gradient is always maintained at the surface, a complementary error function (erfc) distribution is known to result. In both these cases, there is some point in the sample at which the introduced acceptor concentration just equals the background donor concentration in the original *n*-type sample. This point denotes the location of the *pn* junction. Towards the left of this point, the material is *p*-type while on the right of it, the material is *n*-type. The junction depth beneath the surface can be controlled accurately by the time and the temperature of diffusion.

A typical diffusion furnace for the production of Si devices is shown in Fig. A.2.6. The furnace core surrounds a silica tube through which an inert gas is made to flow. The Si wafers are introduced

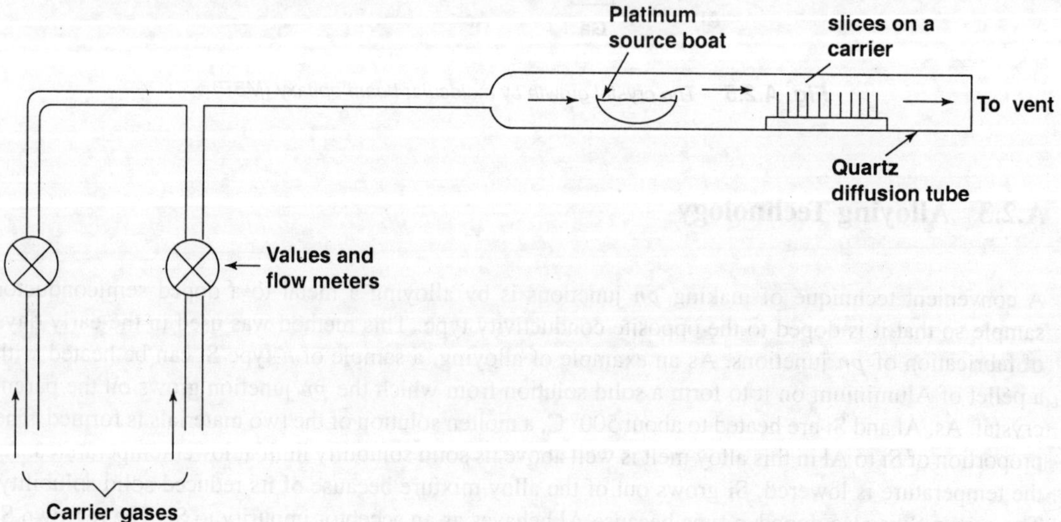

Fig. A.2.6 (a) *An experimental set-up to carry out the diffusion process (solid source system)*

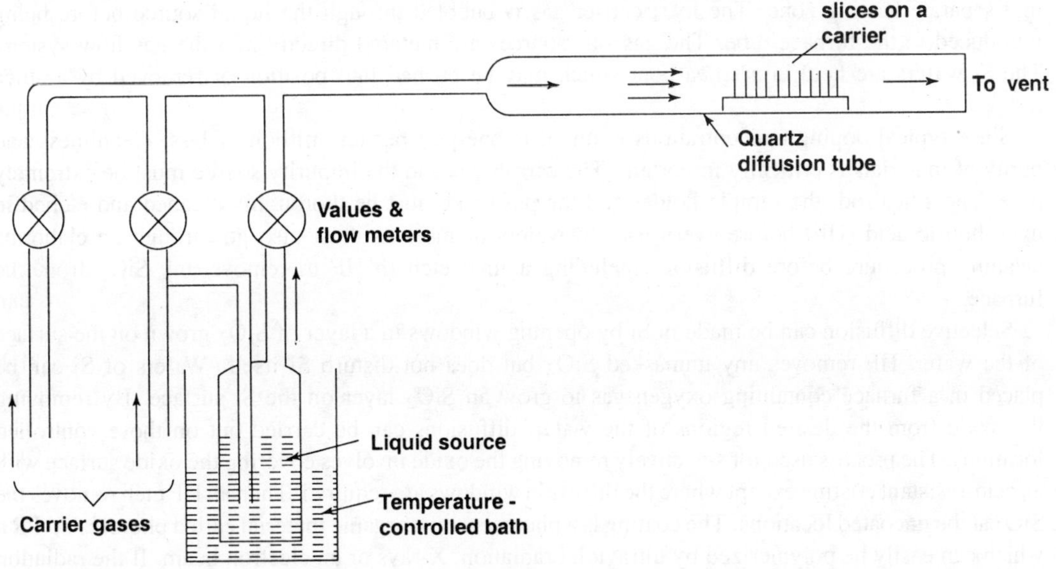

Fig. A.2.6 *continued (b) An experimental set-up to carry out the diffusion process (Liquid source system)*

within the tube for diffusion and impurity atoms are introduced into the gas flow over the samples. Common impurity source materials for diffusion to Si are B_2O_3, BBr_3 and BCl_3 for boron and PH_3, P_2O_5 and $POCl_3$ for phosphorus. Solid sources are placed upstream in the silica tube preferably

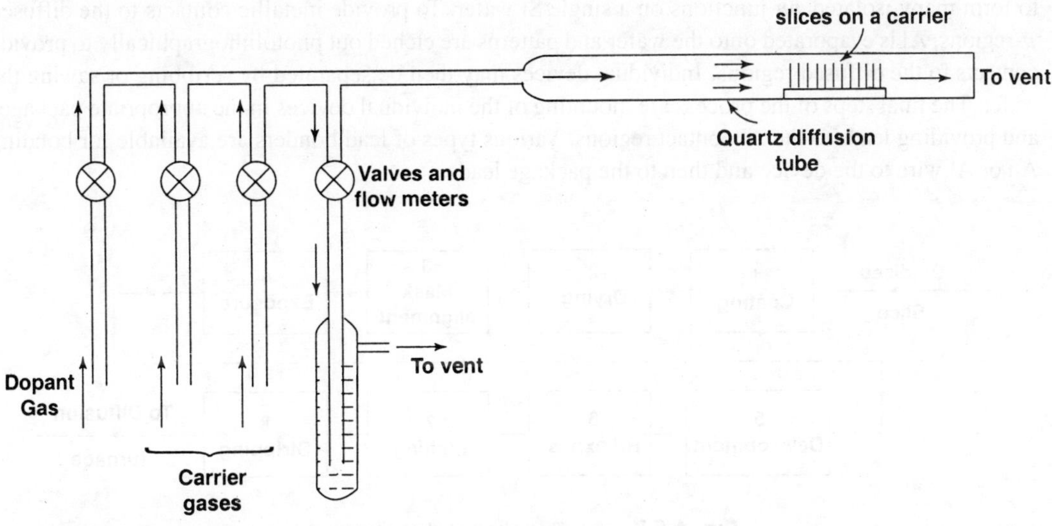

Fig. A.2.6 *continued (c) An experimental set-up to carry out the diffusion process (Gaseous source system)*

in a separate heating zone. The inert carrier gas is bubbled through the liquid source before being introduced to the furnace tube. The gaseous sources are metered directly into the gas flow system. The Si wafers are held in a silica boat which may be pushed into position or removed by a silica rod.

Since typical doping concentrations required is one part per ten million or less, cleanliness and purity of materials is critically important. The carrier gas and the impurity source must be extremely pure. The silica rod, the sample holder and the push rod must be thoroughly cleaned and etched in hydroflouric acid (HF) before every use. Si wafers themselves must also go through an elaborate cleaning procedure before diffusion, including a final etch in HF to remove any SiO_2 from the furnace.

Selective diffusion can be made in Si by opening windows in a layer of SiO_2 grown on the surface of the wafer. HF removes any unmasked SiO_2 but does not disturb Si itself. Wafers of Si can be placed in a furnace containing oxygen gas to grow an SiO_2 layer on the Si surface. By removing the oxide from the desired regions of the wafer, diffusions can be carried out on those controlled locations. The process used for selectively removing the oxide involves covering the oxide surface with an acid-resistant coating except where the diffusion windows are required. Then an HF etch removes the SiO_2 at the uncoated locations. The coating is a photosensitive organic material called photoresist (PR), which can easily be polymerized by ultraviolet radiation, X-rays or an electron beam. If the radiation is passed through a mask containing a desired pattern, the coating can be polymerized everywhere except where the pattern is to appear. The unpolymerized areas may then be removed by a suitable solvent prior to the etching step which removes SiO_2. Later these pockets of SiO_2 may be removed by etching and the polymerized regions formed over the SiO_2 film is also removed by an appropriate treatment. This technique is known as photolithography and is illustrated in Fig. A.2.7. The masks for such processes are generated by a computer and then reduced photographically to appropriate dimensions.

Selective diffusions through the open windows may then be carried out following the usual procedure to form many isolated *pn* junctions on a single Si wafer. To provide metallic contacts to the diffused *p*-regions, Al is evaporated onto the wafer and patterns are etched out photolithographically to provide contacts to the diffused regions. Individual devices may then be separated by scribbing or sawing the wafer. The final steps of the process are mounting of the individual devices in the appropriate packages and providing leads to the Al contact regions. Various types of lead bonders are available for bonding Au or Al wire to the device and then to the package leads.

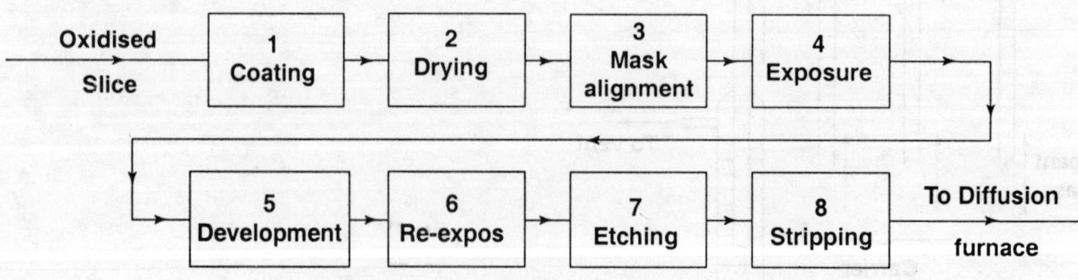

Fig. A.2.7 *(a) Flow-chart of photolithography*

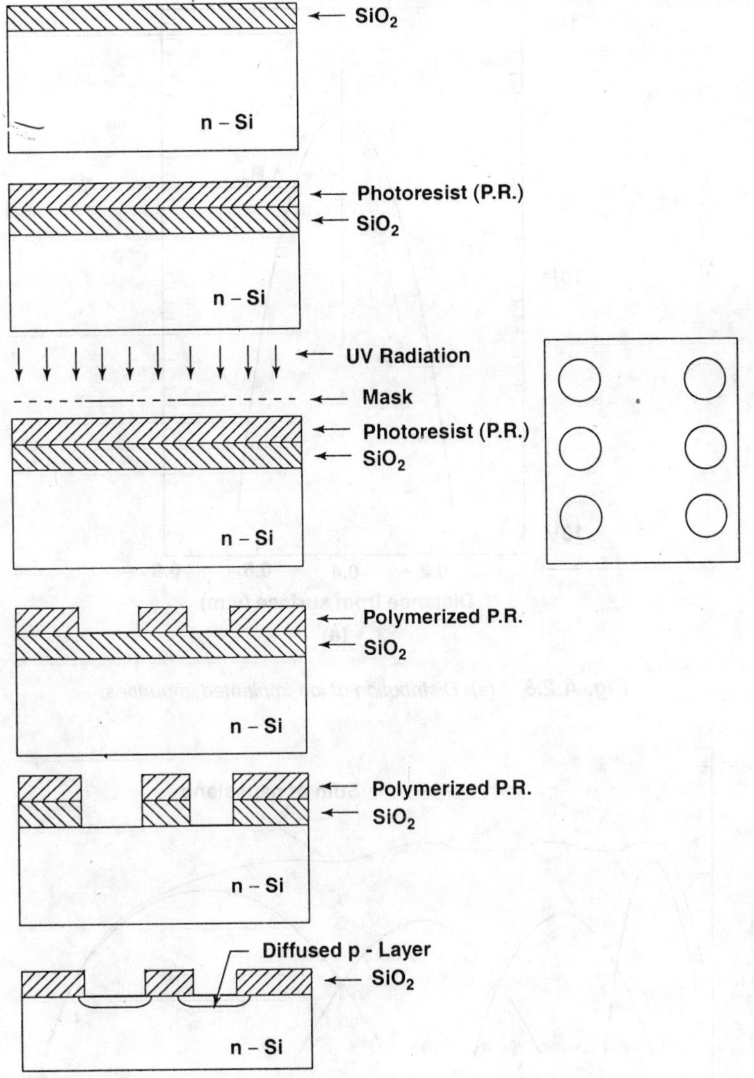

Fig. A.2.7 *continued (b) Fabrication of planar pn junctions by planar technology*

A.2.5 Ion implantation

A useful alternative to the high temperature diffusion is the direct implantation of energetic ions into the semiconductor wafer. In this process, a beam of impurity ions is accelerated to kinetic energies ranging from several keV to several MeV and is directed onto the surface of the semiconductor wafer. As the impurity atoms enter the crystal, they give up their kinetic energies to the lattice in collisions and finally they come to rest at some average penetration depth, called the projected range. Depending on the impurity atoms and their energies, this range in semiconductors may vary from a few hundred

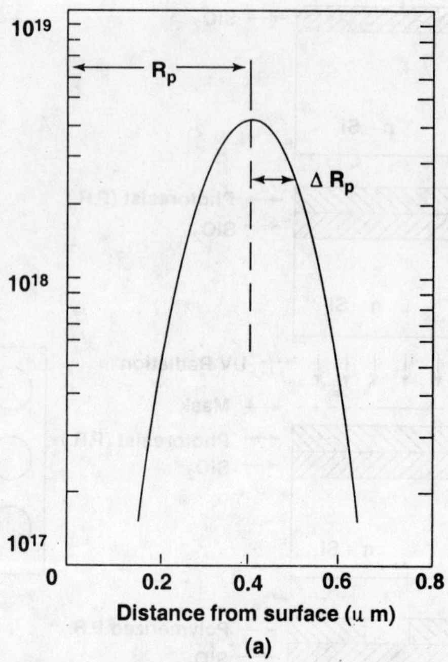

Fig. A.2.8 *(a) Distribution of ion-implanted impurities*

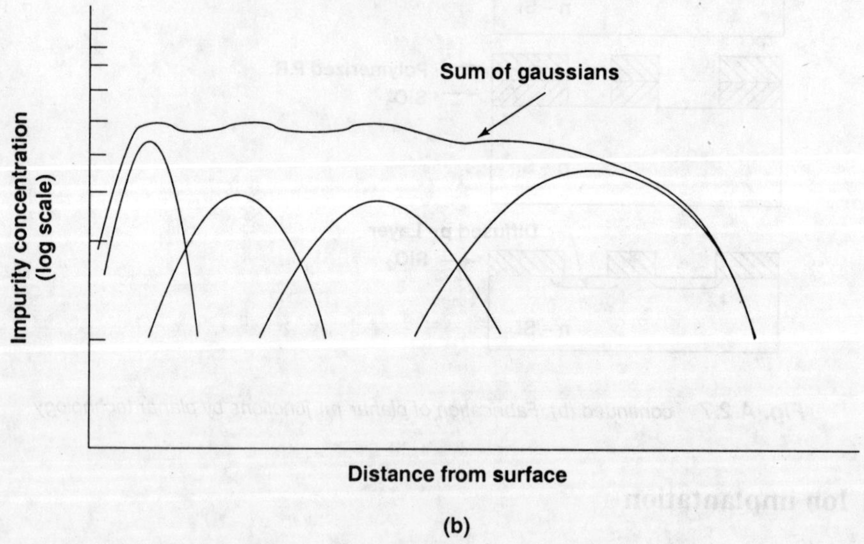

Fig. A.2.8 *continued (b) A relatively flat distribution obtained by summing a number of Gaussians implanted at selected energies and doses.*

angstroms to about 1μ m. For most implantations, the ions come to rest distributed almost evenly about the projected range R_p, as shown in Fig. A.2.8. An implanted dose of ϕ ions/cm^2 is distributed approximately by the following Gaussian formula:

$$N(x) = \left[\frac{\phi}{(2\pi)^{1/2}\Delta R_p}\right] \exp\left[-\frac{1}{2}\left\{\frac{(x - R_p)}{\Delta R_p}\right\}^2\right] \quad \text{(A.2.5)}$$

where ΔR_p, called the straggle measures the half-width of the distribution at $e^{-1/2}$ of the peak. Both R_p and ΔR_p increase with increasing implantation energy. By performing several implantations at different energies, it is possible to synthesize a desired impurity distribution e.g., a uniformly doped region.

In a typical ion implanter, (Fig. A.2.9) a gas containing the desired impurity is ionized. It is next extracted into the acceleration tube. After accelerating them to the desired kinetic energies, ions are next passed through a mass separator to ensure that only the desired ions enter the drift tube. The ion beam is then focussed and scanned electrostatically over the surface of the wafer in the target chamber. Repetitive scanning in a raster pattern provides exceptionally uniform doping of the wafer surface. The target chamber commonly includes automatic wafer-handling facilities to speed up the implantation process. An obvious advantage of this process is that it can be carried out at relatively low temperatures. Consequently, dopings can be carried out without disturbing the previously diffused regions. The ions may be blocked by a metal or a photoresist layer. Very shallow and well-defined doped layers can be generated by this technique. One of the major advantages of this process is the precise control of the doping concentrations. Since the ion beam current can be measured very accurately during the implantation process, a precise amount of impurities can be introduced within the sample. One problem with this doping technique is the lattice damage which results from collisions between the host atoms and the implanted ions. However, most of the damage can be removed in Si by heating the crystal after

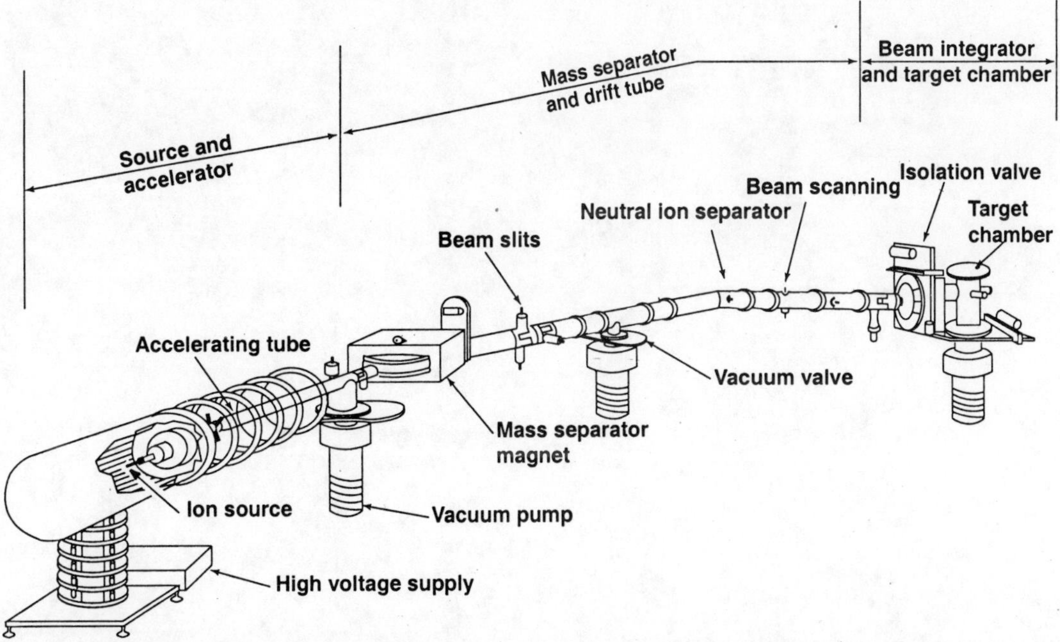

Fig. A.2.9 *Schematic diagram of the 400-keV ion implantation facility at the University of Texas.*

implantation process. This process is called annealing. Although Si can be heated to 1000° C without much difficulty, GaAs and other compounds tend to dissociate at such high temperatures. For example, As evaporation from GaAs during annealing can be prevented by encapsulating GaAs with a thin layer of Silicon nitride during the annealing operation. Another approach to annealing either Si or compound semiconductors is to heat the sample only briefly (~10 s) using a flash lamp rather than a conventional furnace.

Index